TEACHING
An Introduction to the Profession

SJTEC

South Jersey Teacher Education Consortium

Rowan University
Atlantic Cape Community College
Camden County College
Cumberland County College
Gloucester County College
Salem Community College

Edited by
Frank J. Orlando, D. Mark Meyers,
Joseph J. Pizzillo, and Lynne C. Levy

Selected chapters from:
Introduction to Teaching: Becoming a Pr
by Donald Kauchak, Paul Eggen, and Car

D1530735

PEARSON
Custom
Publishing

PEARSON
Prentice
Hall

Selections taken from:

Introduction to Teaching: Becoming a Professional
by Donald Kauchak, Paul Eggen, and Candace Carter
Copyright © 2002 by Pearson Education, Inc.
Published by Merrill Prentice-Hall
Upper Saddle River, New Jersey 07458

Chapters 11-15 copyright © 2004 by Frank J. Orlando and Lynne C. Levy

This special edition published in cooperation with Pearson Custom Publishing.

Printed in the United States of America

10 9 8 7 6 5 4 3

ISBN 0-536-75849-2

BA 998583

LR/DE

Please visit our web site at *www.pearsoncustom.com*

PEARSON CUSTOM PUBLISHING
75 Arlington Street, Suite 300, Boston, MA 02116
A Pearson Education Company

CONTENTS

Chapter 4

Changes in American Society: Influences on Today's Schools   106

PART 3

Foundations

Chapter 5

Educational Philosophy: The Intellectual Foundations of American Education   138

The Profession

CHAPTER

1

Why Become
a Teacher?

Welcome. You're beginning a study of teaching, one of the most interesting, challenging, and noble professions that exists. No one has more potential for touching the personal, social, and intellectual lives of students than do caring and dedicated teachers.

You're probably reading this book for one of two reasons; either you've decided that you want to be a teacher, or you're in the process of deciding. Our purpose in writing this chapter is to provide some information that will shed additional light on that decision, as we try to answer the following questions:

- Why do people decide to teach?

- What are some of the rewards in teaching?

- What are some of the difficulties in teaching?

- Is teaching a profession?

- How will educational reforms affect your life as a teacher?

4

Case STUDY

Before I became a teacher, I majored in Business Administration in college and worked for 10 and a half years in the banking industry. I held jobs as a receptionist, an accounting clerk, a customer support representative, and a staff auditor. My last job in business—staff auditor—was fun because I got to travel, meet new people, and periodically train other workers. Still, even this wasn't rewarding; I was just a number in a crowd trying to get noticed.

I've always wanted to make a difference, and I've always enjoyed working with young people. Then a couple of years ago I read a book in which the author described the difference between a person's "job" and a person's "work." Your job is how you make money; your work is how you contribute to the world. It really crystalized everything for me. Business, for me, was a job, but I didn't really have any "work," and I longed for it.

In some ways, I think I've always wanted to be a teacher. I remember all the way back to my fourth grade teacher, Mrs. May. She was like my second mother because she was always so willing to help, and she seemed to care about me, just like my mother did at home. And I also remember my tenth-grade history teacher, Mr. Fleming, who explained how important school was for us to develop and grow. We would complain that his tests were so hard, and he would laugh and tell us how good they were for us; he thought history was *so* important. You had to like it, because he loved it so much. All the kids talked about Mr. Fleming and his antics, like when he came into class in his coonskin cap and buckskin outfit. And he asked questions that would make us think, like, "Why does a city way out in Iowa have a French name like Des Moines?" I never fell asleep in his class. I still remember it, and it was years ago.

So, to make a long story short, I went back to school, and this time I did what I've always wanted to do. Of course it's tough some days. The kids are sometimes "off the wall," and I periodically feel like I'm drowning in paperwork, but when you see the light bulb go on for someone, it's all worth it. Now, my job and my work are the same thing. (Suzanne, 35, mother of two and a recent entry into teaching.)

▨ ▨ ▨

Many of you reading this book have characteristics similar to Suzanne's. You're intelligent and introspective, and you've had a number of life experiences. Perhaps you're married, have children, and your spouse is employed successfully in some other profession. You've thought a great deal about becoming a teacher, and you're clear about your reasons for wanting to teach.

Others of you are less certain. You're also intelligent, but you're young, single, and still in the process of deciding what you want to do with your life. You've enjoyed your school experiences, and most of your ideas about teaching are based on them. The idea of working with and helping young people is attractive, but your thinking hasn't gone much past that point.

That's okay. This text is designed to provide you with a close-up and in-depth look at teaching. Either way—if you've already made the decision to teach, or if you're still in the process of deciding—this book will help you understand what teaching is all about: the rewards and difficulties involved in it, the kinds of students you're likely to encounter, what your professional and legal responsibilities to them are, how our schools have evolved to their present state, and a number of other issues that will influence your decision and perhaps ultimately your career.

This chapter is intended to help you begin developing that understanding. Let's get started.

■ WHY PEOPLE DECIDE TO TEACH

To begin this section, please respond to the Interest in Teaching Inventory that follows.

Interest in Teaching Inventory

Circle the number for each item that best represents your thinking. Use the following scale as a guide.

1 = Strongly disagree
2 = Disagree
3 = Somewhat disagree
4 = Agree and disagree
5 = Somewhat agree
6 = Agree
7 = Strongly agree

1. A major reason I'm considering becoming a teacher is job security.   1   2   3   4   (5)   6   7

2. My family has strongly influenced my decision to become a teacher.   1   2   3   4   (5)   6   7

3. Long summer vacations are very important to me as I consider teaching as a career.   1   2   (3)   4   5   6   7

4. I've never really considered any other occupation besides teaching.   (1)   2   3   4   5   6   7

5. A major reason I'm considering becoming a teacher is my desire to work with young people.   1   2   3   4   5   6   (7)

6. I'm thinking of becoming a teacher because I'd like to be of some value or significance to society.   1   2   3   4   5   (6)   7

7. A major reason I'm considering becoming a teacher is my own interest in a content or subject matter field.   1   2   3   4   5   (6)   7

8. A major reason I'm considering entering teaching is because of the influence of a former elementary or secondary teacher.   1   2   3   4   5   (6)   7

9. The opportunity for a lifetime of self-growth is a major reason I'm considering becoming a teacher.   1   2   3   4   5   6   (7)

Major: Elementary/Secondary (Circle one)

If secondary, what content area? _____

Gender: Male/Female (Circle one)

Age: _____

We gave this survey to several classes of students taking a course similar to the one you're now in, averaged their responses, and ranked them from most (1) to least (9) important reasons for becoming a teacher. Let's see how your responses compare to our students' answers.

We see from Table 1.1 that the desire to work with young people (Item 5) and to contribute to society (Item 6) were our students' two most important reasons for considering teaching. These reasons are consistent with Suzanne's thinking as she described it in the introduction to the chapter, and they're also consistent with polls conducted by the National Education Association over nearly a 25-year period (National Education Association, 1997).

Item	Item Focus	Average Response of Students	Survey Rank
		Table 1.1 **Responses to Interest in Teaching Inventory**	
1	Job security	4.3	6
2	Family influence	3.9	8
3	Summer vacations	4.0	7
4	Other careers not considered	2.6	9
5	Work with youth	6.4	1
6	Value to society	6.3	2
7	Content interest	5.4	4
8	Influence of teachers	5.0	5
9	Self-growth	5.5	3

Increasing Understanding 1.1

In Table 1.1 we see that the lowest average response on the Interest in Teaching Inventory is for Item 4, and the highest average responses are for Items 5 and 6. Are these consistent results? Explain.

Let's look more closely at these and other reasons that people go into teaching.

To answer the "Increasing Understanding" questions online and receive immediate feedback, go to the *Increasing Understanding* Module in Chapter 1 of the Companion Website at: **http://www.prenhall.com/kauchak,** type in your response, and then study the feedback.

▪ REWARDS AND DIFFICULTIES IN TEACHING

As with any occupation, people choose to teach because they think it will be rewarding. Some of these rewards are intrinsic—they come from within us—while other rewards are more tangible, like money or free time. Let's look at these rewards in more detail.

Intrinsic Rewards

Intrinsic rewards *are personally satisfying for emotional or intellectual reasons.* A number of people, such as Suzanne and the people in our survey, enter teaching searching for intrinsic rewards; they seek the emotional or intellectual satisfaction that goes with believing they are making a contribution to the world.

Emotional Rewards Let's look at some different ways that teachers receive emotional rewards from their teaching. The following are notes shared with us by teachers. The contents of the notes are taken verbatim.

▪ ▪ ▪

Kasia, 23, calls her boyfriend, Jeff. The middle school in which she teaches has "Teacher Appreciation Week" and she has just received a dozen roses from a group of eight of her third-period, seventh-grade science students.

"I was always on them about whispering, too," she excitedly tells Jeff. "I maybe would have expected this from my fifth period class, but never from this bunch."

"Let me read the note I got from them," she continues. " 'Thank you for all that you've done for us and for all the wonderful things that you've teached [sic] us. You are truly an amazing teacher. Thank you again.

Happy Teacher Appreciation Week,

Sincerely,

Alicia, Rosa, Shannon, Tina, Stephanie, Melissa, Jessica, and Becca.' "

"That's wonderful," Jeff laughs. "Good thing you're not their English teacher."

"I know. I showed Isabel [the students' English teacher] the note, and she broke up. 'So much for grammar,' she said."

• • •

Judy, 32, a teacher in the same school, brought home the following note from two parents.

Dear Mrs. Holmquist,

   Thank you very much for working so diligently with Michael this year. I think he now has a better understanding of the world. I hope he told you that he lived in Egypt for nearly two years. We have a large amount of Egyptian souvenirs should your class like to view them. Again, thanks for all of your work day after day.

   Sincerely,

   Shirley and Bob Wood

• • •

Miguel Rodriguez, 29, another middle school teacher, received the following note from one of his students.

Mr. Rodriguez,

   I wanted to think of some creative way to thank you for being the best teacher I ever had. (But I couldn't ☺ .)

   Even though all the geography skills I'll ever use in my life I learned in second grade, I just wanted to say thanks for teaching me how to really prepare for life in the years to come.

   Everyday I looked forward to coming to your class (and not just because of Mike [a boy in the class]). I always enjoyed your class, because there was a hidden message about life in there somewhere.

   Your [sic] my very favorite teacher and you've taught me some of the best lessons in life I could ever learn. Thank you so much.

   A grateful student,

   Erica Jacobs

(P.S. No, I didn't write this to raise my grade ☺ .)

• • •

The notes you've just read and the flowers Kasia received symbolize some of the emotional rewards in teaching. Each teacher had an understandably satisfying emotional reaction to the tokens of appreciation. "They're what keep you going," Judy commented matter-of-factly in a discussion of her enjoyment of her work.

Sharon, a first-grade teacher and another veteran, also looks to emotional rewards in her teaching. "The beginning of the day gets me going," she said, smiling, during an interview in which we asked her about her continued commitment to her career. "I stand at the door, and the children give me a hug, a high-five, or a handshake when they come in the room. Even if the previous day was a bad one, all those little faces are enough to get me started all over again."

Sometimes students show their affection in strange ways.

• • •

Kerry, a first-year teacher, entered her classroom first thing in the morning on her birthday. After entering her room with a custodian's help, Kerry's students had moved *all* the desks to the center of the room and wrapped them together with tape and toilet paper. How would you react?

Kerry was delighted. "I called [the perpetrators] out of class and had them come down and [another teacher] took a picture of them standing out in the middle of it all. I left it here all day. I made them sit on the floor. It was really fun. It was really a fun day" (Bullough, 1989, p. 86).

• • •

It helps to have a sense of humor when you teach.

All teachers reap emotional rewards from their experiences. Sharon's wide-eyed first graders, a middle school student like Erica Jacobs, or juniors and seniors in high school, who are struggling to become adults, are all sources of emotional satisfaction for teachers.

Increasing Understanding 1.2

For which group of teachers—teachers of elementary school students (grades K–5), middle school students (grades 6–8), or secondary school students (grades 9–12)—are emotional rewards likely to be the greatest? Explain.

Teachers' interactions with their students provide a major source of intrinsic rewards.

David Ling, an eighth-grade physical science teacher, enthusiastically says to his students, "Let's think about these questions and try and figure out what they have in common." He then writes the following on the board:

Why do we have seatbelts in our cars?

Why does an automatic washer have holes in the drum?

How does a dog shake the water off itself when it comes out of a pond?

The bemused students look at the list, and after several seconds David continues, "Now, what have we been studying?"

"Inertia," Taneka responds after hesitating briefly.

"Exactly," David smiles. "So, let's review for a minute. What is inertia? . . . Go ahead, Dana."

". . . The tendency . . . of something moving to keep on moving . . . straight."

"Or something not moving to remain still," Jermel adds.

"Excellent, both of you," David nods. "Now, a challenge. Let's answer the questions on the board using the idea of inertia."

With David's guidance, the students conclude that if their cars are suddenly stopped, their bodies have a tendency to keep moving because of their inertia, and the seatbelt stops them, so they don't get hurt. They also conclude that water is separated from clothes in the washer, because the water goes straight out through the holes in the drum, but the clothes are kept in it. Finally, they determine that as the dog shakes one way, and then stops, the water keeps moving, and the same thing happens when it shakes the other way. So, the dog uses the principle of inertia to shake the water from itself.

"Neat," Rebecka says. "Where'd you get that stuff, Mr. Ling?"

"I gradually thought them up," David smiles. "The more I study, the more examples I find. . . . That's what we're here for. We study science, so we can learn how the world around us works."

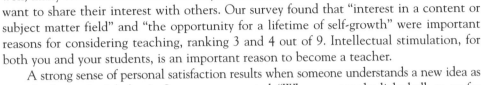

Increasing Understanding 1.3

For which group of teachers—teachers of elementary school students, middle school students, or secondary students—are intellectual rewards likely to be the greatest? Explain.

Intellectual Rewards While some emotional rewards are almost certainly present as well, many teachers teach because they're interested in the content they're teaching and want to share their interest with others. Our survey found that "interest in a content or subject matter field" and "the opportunity for a lifetime of self-growth" were important reasons for considering teaching, ranking 3 and 4 out of 9. Intellectual stimulation, for both you and your students, is an important reason to become a teacher.

A strong sense of personal satisfaction results when someone understands a new idea as a result of a teacher's help. As Suzanne commented, "When you see the light bulb go on for someone, it's all worth it." Sharing with students our love of a content area and seeing students get excited about the same things we do are important intellectual rewards of teaching. Not surprisingly, they are also important reasons veteran teachers remain in the field.

Extrinsic Rewards

In addition to emotional and intellectual rewards, teaching also attracts people for external reasons. **Extrinsic rewards** are *career-linked positive factors such as job security (ranked 6 in our survey) and summer vacations (ranked 7).* The job security found in teaching is greater than that in most other occupations. For example, after acquiring

Interactions with other teachers provide opportunities for intellectual stimulation and growth.

some experience—usually about three years—teachers are typically awarded tenure. Originally designed to attract good people and protect them from political pressures, tenure provides teachers with job security and is a concrete extrinsic reward. (You will study teacher tenure in detail in Chapter 7.)

In addition to job security, teaching has other extrinsic rewards. According to an old joke, a student was asked to identify three reasons for going into teaching. After pondering the question and being unable to think of any better reasons, the student finally wrote, "June, July, and August."

For some, working in a profession with long vacations is rewarding. In addition to the summer, teachers have vacations at precisely the time when vacations are most attractive—the Friday after Thanksgiving, the winter holiday season, and spring break, for example.

In addition to job security and vacations, additional extrinsic rewards include:

- Work schedules. Because teachers' schedules are similar to students' schedules, many teachers are able to be home after school with their own children.

- Autonomy. **Autonomy,** or *being in control of one's own existence*, has been identified as a basic need by researchers who study human motivation (Ryan & Deci, 1998). Teachers have a great deal of autonomy in their work. In spite of growing concerns about increased regulation and external control, teachers largely decide what and how to teach and, at times, make crucial decisions about students' lives. The autonomy and sense of control over their classrooms allow teachers to express themselves personally and creatively.

- Status. Despite perceptions to the contrary, the teaching profession enjoys considerable occupational status; the public views teaching as not only demanding, but also prestigious (National Education Association, 1993; Rowan, 1994). If you have doubts about teachers' status, think about the trepidation with which parents often approach a parent–teacher conference. They want nothing more than to hear that everything is okay in school and that their child is growing socially and intellectually. Into no other profession's hands is so much care of young people placed.

These intrinsic and extrinsic rewards are not mutually exclusive, of course. The decision to teach or to stay in teaching is influenced by a number of factors; most people choose teaching for both intrinsic and extrinsic reasons, such as the intellectual challenge combined with autonomy.

Increasing Understanding 1.4

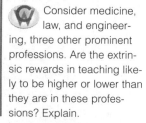

Consider medicine, law, and engineering, three other prominent professions. Are the extrinsic rewards in teaching likely to be higher or lower than they are in these professions? Explain.

Case STUDY

Kevin is having a difficult time in James Washington's class. He has missed several days during the grading period, he's disruptive, and he seldom turns in his homework.

James has tried to contact Kevin's mother, a single parent; he left three messages on her answering machine during the last week alone. She hasn't called back.

James works in a school with a large number of underachieving students. Janet Levy, the school principal, is under heavy pressure from the district leadership to raise student test scores, and she is putting similar pressure on the teachers.

"What does Mrs. Levy expect?" James complains to Manuela Martinez, a colleague, after school one day. "Kevin is gone more than he's here; he never turns in his homework; his mom won't call me back. And I'm supposed to get him to learn like those kids in Orange Park [an affluent suburb]. I'm not making enough money to be this stressed. No wonder everyone is trying to transfer out of here."

■ ■ ■

Difficulties in Teaching

James's lament is more common than we would like it to be. In many parts of the country, and particularly in some rural areas and inner cities, teachers face daunting problems. Two of the most common issues involve working conditions and salaries. Let's look at them.

Working Conditions Working conditions are a concern for teachers. School leaders, like Janet Levy, appear unsympathetic; parents or other caregivers, like Kevin's mother, are unresponsive and don't support teachers' efforts; and students are sometimes disruptive or unmotivated. Situations like this are important sources of teacher stress.

Teacher stress has been linked to reduced job satisfaction, poorer relationships with students, decreased teacher effectiveness, and teacher burnout. It is an important reason teachers choose to leave the profession (Abel & Sewell, 1999).

Other difficulties exist. For example, teachers complain about spending so much time on nonteaching requirements and duties, such as filling out student progress reports and other paperwork, monitoring hallways before and after school, checking restrooms for misbehavior, and taking students to and from lunch, that they don't have the time, or energy, to teach effectively. A common lament is, "If they would only give me the time and resources I need, I could teach these students something!"

Salaries Teacher salaries are another concern. Low salaries frequently are cited as a major reason people either avoid teaching as a career or leave teaching after a few years (Metropolitan Life Insurance Company, 1995). Salaries are improving, however. For instance, the average teacher salary in the United States for the 1997–1998 school year was more than $39,000 per year, ranging from a high of more than $50,000 in New Jersey to a low of just below $28,000 in South Dakota. In the same year, the average beginning salary was slightly less than $26,000 (National Center for Educational Statistics, 1999). Beginning teacher salaries for each state in 1997–1998 are shown in Table 1.2.

Your salary will depend on a number of factors, such as the local cost of living and the location of the school district. As you'll see in Chapter 7, property taxes are the major funding source for schools, so teachers' salaries depend, in part, on property values. Also, urban districts typically have higher salaries than their rural counterparts because of the higher cost of living in urban areas.

Other economic factors also exist. Annual salary increases are virtually guaranteed, and, as we said earlier in the chapter, vacation periods are ideal. Medical, dental, and retirement benefits are provided, and job security is high. In addition, teachers are often paid supplements for extra duties, such as club sponsorships, coaching, chairing departments (such as chairing the English department in a middle school), and mentoring beginning teachers (Darling-Hammond, 1998). In schools with year-round schedules, teachers work eleven months of the year—versus nine or ten months—and are paid accordingly.

You might also consider teaching in a private school; approximately 13 percent of all teaching jobs are in private schools (National Center for Educational Statistics, 1997). Their average starting salaries are about 30 percent lower than in public schools, however (Ingersoll, 1997), and the difference increases to more than 40 percent for maximum salaries. Private schools often waive the licensing requirements that public school teachers are required by law to meet, and they usually don't provide the same insurance benefits that public schools provide. One survey, for example, indicated that nearly half of all public schools provide paid medical, dental, and retirement benefits, whereas only about one-fifth of private schools did (Ingersoll, 1997).

Table 1.2	Beginning Teacher Salaries for Each State			
State	**Salary**		**State**	**Salary**
Alabama	$27,388		Missouri	$24,125
Alaska	33,162		Montana	21,045
Arizona	24,917		Nebraska	21,949
Arkansas	21,000		Nevada	28,641
California	27,852		New Hampshire	23,927
Colorado	24,867		New Jersey	28,319
Connecticut	29,506		New Mexico	23,297
Delaware	25,493		New York	30,204
District of Columbia	27,234		North Carolina	22,150
Florida	25,266		North Dakota	19,146
Georgia	26,706		Ohio	22,535
Hawaii	26,744		Oklahoma	23,676
Idaho	20,248		Oregon	26,098
Illinois	28,183		Pennsylvania	29,581
Indiana	24,716		Rhode Island	26,300
Iowa	22,475		South Carolina	23,427
Kansas	22,445		South Dakota	20,340
Kentucky	23,536		Tennessee	22,140
Louisiana	22,843		Texas	24,736
Maine	21,554		Utah	22,241
Maryland	27,010		Vermont	25,183
Massachusetts	27,238		Virginia	25,272
Michigan	27,064		Washington	23,860
Minnesota	26,266		West Virginia	22,529
Mississippi	20,630		Wisconsin	24,077
			Wyoming	22,230

Source: From National Center for Educational Statistics. (1999). *Digest of educational statistics.* Washington, D.C.: U.S. Department of Education.

Given these disparities, you might ask, "Why would a teacher choose to teach at a private school?" Some answers include:

- Lack of a licensing requirement
- Commitment to an ideal
- Smaller school bureaucracy
- Smaller classes
- Greater parental involvement

Teachers often choose to work in private schools because they aren't required to take the professional education courses needed for licensing, the school is dedicated to religious or intellectual principles consistent with the teacher's beliefs, communication between administrators and teachers is simpler, and parents whose children attend private schools tend to be more involved in school activities than are parents in public schools.

Whether you plan to teach in a public or private school, choosing any career is ultimately an individual decision, and it depends on a person's values and needs. Whether or not the salaries and benefits in teaching are adequate is a matter of personal judgment.

Putting Rewards and Difficulties into Perspective

Your satisfaction with your teaching career will also be influenced by the specific situation in which you work. **Physical conditions of teaching** are *the school facility and the equipment*

Time spent in administration or noninstructional activities can drain teachers' time and energy.

it contains. The **psychological conditions of teaching** are *the behavioral and emotional characteristics of the students, administrators, and other teachers.* Both can strongly influence student learning as well as teacher satisfaction (Lawrence-Lightfoot, 1983; Metz, 1978).

The student–teacher ratio is one of the most important physical conditions. A survey conducted by the National Center for Education Statistics (1998) showed that from state to state the students-per-teacher ratio ranges from 13.7 to 24.1. These figures can be misleading, however. Because school administrators, counselors, and special educators are counted as "teachers" in the statistics, the actual ratios can be considerably higher; 25 to 35 students in K–12 classes are common.

The social and emotional conditions of teaching are also important. Teaching is heavily interpersonal, and the human-to-human interactions you have with your students, school administrators, and colleagues will have a powerful influence on your satisfaction with your career. Most students and parents are cooperative to work with, and most administrators are cooperative and supportive. Others are similar to Kevin, his mother, and Janet Levy. If the emotional and intellectual rewards of teaching—like those Kasia, Judy, Miguel, and David received—outweigh the frustrations James described, and if the salary and benefits are adequate, it may be a good career choice for you. If not, another career may be preferable.

Increasing Understanding 1.5

As you anticipate a teaching career, do you believe that teaching is more or less difficult than it was ten years ago? Explain.

■ THE TEACHING PROFESSION

What does it mean to be a professional? Are teachers professionals? Is professionalism more important now than it has been in the past? We try to answer these questions in this section as we look at teaching as a profession.

Characteristics of Professionalism

Researchers examining the concept of *professionalism,* and professions such as medicine and law, identify the following characteristics of a profession (Ingersoll, 1997; Labaree; 1992):

- ■ A specialized body of knowledge
- ■ Extended training for licensure

■ Autonomy

■ Ethical standards for conduct

A Specialized Body of Knowledge Professionals understand and can utilize a specialized body of knowledge. A physician, for example, can recognize symptoms of diseases and other ailments and is able to prescribe medications, surgical procedures, or other forms of therapy to eliminate the symptoms and their causes. This requires specialized knowledge, and it's a major reason people seek the advice and help of physicians.

Is this true for teaching? Research indicates that effective teachers possess at least four kinds of knowledge (Borko & Putnam, 1996):

■ Knowledge of the content they're teaching, such as a thorough understanding of math, science, geography, or literature.

■ Pedagogical content knowledge, such as the ability to illustrate concepts like *equivalent fractions* in math or *nationalism* in history, in ways that are understandable to students.

■ General pedagogical knowledge, such as the ability to maintain an orderly classroom or guide student learning with questions.

■ Knowledge of learners and learning, such as the understanding that learners, even in high school, tend to be egocentric, seeing the world from their own perspectives and often ignoring the views of others.

A knowledge base allows teachers to make decisions in complex or ill-defined situations, and this decision-making process is one of the differences between a professional and a **technician,** *a person who uses specific skills to complete well-defined tasks,* such as an electrician wiring an outlet. Technical skills are important, of course, but the decision-making process is less complex in technical areas.

Decision making in teaching is incredibly complex. Jackson (1968), in his classic study of elementary classrooms, suggested that teachers make more than 800 decisions a day; Murray (1986) estimated the number at 1,500. Even using the conservative figure, this translates into more than 130 decisions per hour in a 6-hour teaching day!

What kinds of decisions do teachers have to make? Let's look at three examples:

Increasing Understanding 1.6

 Some people believe that teaching isn't a profession because people other than teachers also "teach." For example, young people learn a great deal from their parents, the clergy, and friends. Make an argument both for and against this theory of why teaching isn't a profession. (Use medicine as a point of reference, that is, to what extent do people other than physicians practice medicine?)

Case STUDY

A kindergarten teacher has just distributed materials for an art project and is surveying the room to see if everyone has started. She notices that Jimmy is staring out the window with his thumb in his mouth and tears in his eyes. It is the beginning of the school year, and Jimmy still isn't used to being away from home. Should the teacher wait a minute and see if the art materials will do the trick, or should she intervene?

■   ■   ■

A middle school teacher is getting frustrated. Mary is obviously more interested in her friends than in English, and the teacher can't keep her from talking. He calls on her; she doesn't hear the question. Should he reprimand her, repeat the question, or go on to another student?

■   ■   ■

A high school teacher has just distributed an assignment. She goes over the work in depth, explaining its importance and how it should be done. She concludes by reminding the class that the grade for the assignment counts as one-fourth of the semester grade. An audible "Who cares?" follows. Should the teacher ignore it and go on, or should she respond? (Kauchak & Eggen, 1998, p. 181).

■   ■   ■

Increasing Understanding 1.7

If you were the middle school teacher, would you reprimand Mary, repeat the question, or go on to another student? Explain your reasoning. (The feedback for this question will give you a research-based answer.)

A teacher's ability to make decisions quickly in circumstances such as these is crucial, and the wisdom of these decisions depends on a teacher's knowledge.

An additional aspect of professional knowledge is the ability and inclination to learn. Just as physicians must continually upgrade their knowledge of therapies, medications, and surgical procedures, teachers must stay abreast of progress in their field. For instance, it makes sense intuitively to encourage students who aren't successful to work harder, but research indicates that this suggestion may be counterproductive. Young children generally believe they're already working hard, so they're bewildered by the suggestion, and older students believe the need to work hard is an indicator of low ability (Tollefson, 2000). Effective teachers stay informed of research in their fields, and they adapt their teaching to reflect this research.

Training for Licensure As with physicians, lawyers, and engineers, teachers must earn a license that allows them to practice their profession. The license is intended to certify that the teacher is knowledgeable and competent and, as with other professions, teachers must renew their licenses to confirm that they are staying current in their fields. Teachers need at least a bachelor's degree prior to licensure, and in many states they must complete the degree in a content area, such as math or English, before they begin teacher preparation experiences. Licensure also requires clinical experiences, such as internships, which are designed to ensure that teachers can apply the professional knowledge they've acquired to the real world of schools.

Autonomy Professionals have the authority to make decisions based on their professional knowledge. When a person sees a physician because of stomach pains, for example, no set of standards mandates treatment or medication; physicians are given the authority to treat patients as they see fit. Those suggesting that teaching isn't a profession argue that states and districts, instead of teachers, are prescribing **curriculum**—*what teachers teach*—and **assessment**—*how student understanding is measured.* This lack of autonomy, they assert, makes teachers technicians instead of professionals.

We disagree. States and districts are indeed prescribing **standards**—*what students should know and what skills they should have upon completing an area of study* (such as fourth grade language arts, or Algebra I)—that must be met before students are allowed to move from one grade to another or to graduate from high school. However, in spite of these mandates, teachers have a great deal of control over what is taught, how they will teach it, and how students will be assessed. Also, the enormous number of decisions teachers make each day depends primarily on their own judgment. Teachers have a great deal of autonomy in their professional lives.

Case STUDY

To begin this section, consider the following examples.

You are an ardent advocate of gun control; you believe that access to guns should be strongly regulated and have said so in class. Eric, one of your students, brings a newspaper editorial to school in which a compelling argument *against* gun control is made. You don't allow the student to share the editorial with the class.

■ ■ ■

Greg is a very difficult student in one of your classes. He is continually disruptive and periodically shouts insults at other students and sometimes even at you. You've tried everything you know to control his behavior, but you've been unsuccessful. Finally, in exasperation one day, another student tells him, "Shut up! I can't think!" after one of his outbursts. To your surprise, Greg is embarrassed and sits quietly for the remainder of the period. Now, finding that public embarrassment seems to be the only way to keep Greg from being disruptive, you use it as a technique to manage his behavior.

16

Brittany, a student with a specific learning disability in reading, is on the borderline between failing and passing. When final grades are due, you see that she has a failing average. You pass her, reasoning that since she has a disability, she deserves a break. Perhaps she didn't understand the wording on some assignments or quizzes.

■ ■ ■

Professional Ethics Have you behaved "ethically" in these examples? How do you know? **Ethics** *describes moral standards for good behavior*; all professions have a code of ethics intended to guide professionals as they attempt to answer difficult questions like the ones we just asked. Ethical standards are so important to professionals that they are often written into employment contracts.

The National Education Association, the largest professional organization in education, has prepared a code of ethics that is intended as a guide for the professional behavior of teachers in working with their students. It is outlined in Figure 1.1.

Let's look at your actions based on the information in the NEA Code of Ethics. Item 2 in the Commitment to the Student principle (Principle I) in the Code states that a teacher "shall not unreasonably deny the student access to varying points of view." In our first example, you didn't let Eric share the editorial with the other students, so you have denied them access to varying points of view. Whether or not your denial is "unreasonable" is open to interpretation as is the case with ethical standards in any profession.

In the second example, you were desperately searching for a technique to manage Greg's behavior, and you found that embarrassment was the only thing that seemed to work. However, Item 5 in Principle I states that the teacher "shall not intentionally expose the student to embarrassment or disparagement." This case is clear; in your desperation and frustration, you intentionally are using embarrassment as a technique with Greg, so you are in violation of the ethical code.

In the third example, you have given Brittany a break *because* she has a disability. Item 6 in Principle I says the teacher "shall not on the basis of race, color, creed, sex,

Professional knowledge allows teachers to make the split-second decisions essential for effective teaching.

Preamble

The educator, believing in the worth and dignity of each human being, recognizes the supreme importance of the pursuit of truth, devotion to excellence, and the nurture of democratic principle. Essential to these goals is the protection of freedom to learn and to teach and the guarantee of equal educational opportunity for all. The educator accepts the responsibility to adhere to the highest ethical standards.

The educator recognizes the magnitude of the responsibility inherent in the teaching process. The desire for the respect and confidence of one's colleagues, of students, of parents, and the members of the community provides the incentive to attain and maintain the highest possible degree of ethical conduct. The Code of Ethics of the Education Profession indicates the aspiration of all educators and provides standards by which to judge conduct.

The remedies specified by the NEA and/or its affiliates for the violation of any provision of this Code shall be exclusive and no such provision shall be enforceable in any form other than one specifically designated by the NEA or its affiliates.

Principle I—Commitment to the Student

The educator strives to help each student realize his or her potential as a worthy and effective member of society. The educator therefore works to stimulate the spirit of inquiry, the acquisition of knowledge and understanding, and the thoughtful formulation of worthy goals.

In fulfillment of the obligation to the student, the educator—

1. Shall not unreasonably restrain the student from independent action in the pursuit of learning.
2. Shall not unreasonably deny the student access to varying points of view.
3. Shall not deliberately suppress or distort subject matter relevant to the student's progress.
4. Shall make reasonable effort to protect the student from conditions harmful to learning or to health and safety.
5. Shall not intentionally expose the student to embarrassment or disparagement.
6. Shall not on the basis of race, color, creed, sex, national origin, marital status, political or religious beliefs, family, social or cultural background, or sexual orientation unfairly:
   a. Exclude any student from participation in any program;
   b. Deny benefits to any student;
   c. Grant any advantage to any student.
7. Shall not use professional relationships with students for private advantage.
8. Shall not disclose information about students obtained in the course of professional service, unless disclosure serves a compelling professional purpose or is required by law.

Principle II—Commitment to the Profession

The education profession is vested by the public with a trust and responsibility requiring the highest ideals of professional service.

In the belief that the quality of the services of the education profession directly influences the nation and its citizens, the educator shall exert every effort to raise professional standards, to promote a climate that encourages the exercise of professional judgment, to achieve conditions which attract persons worthy of the trust to careers in education, and to assist in preventing the practice of the profession by unqualified persons.

In fulfillment of the obligation to the profession, the educator—

1. Shall not in an application for a professional position deliberately make a false statement or fail to disclose a material fact related to competency and qualifications.
2. Shall not misrepresent his/her professional qualifications.
3. Shall not assist entry into the profession of a person known to be unqualified in respect to character, education, or other relevant attribute.
4. Shall not knowingly make a false statement concerning the qualifications of a candidate for a profession position.
5. Shall not assist a noneducator in the unauthorized practice of teaching.
6. Shall not disclose information about colleagues obtained in the course of professional service unless disclosure serves a compelling professional purpose or is required by law.
7. Shall not knowingly make a false or malicious statement about a colleague.
8. Shall not accept any gratuity, gift, or favor that might impair or appear to influence professional decisions or actions.

Source: From National Education Association. (1995). Code of Ethics of the Education Profession, NEA Representative Assembly. Reprinted by permission.

AN ETHICAL DILEMMA

As you're sitting in the teachers' lounge one day, Dana, one of your colleagues, says, "Well, you know that Sheri [another teacher in the school] was brought up on charges of plagiarism when she was working on her master's degree. I guess she got away with it, because her advisor had a lot of political clout, or something, and the whole incident was swept under the rug."

Dana shrugs, gets a cup of coffee, and leaves the room.

Several days later, you hear Dana repeat her story to another teacher in the lounge.

1. Is Dana behaving ethically in making her remarks to you, and later, to the other teacher?

2. As a professional, should you intervene? In other words, should you say something to Dana? Should you say something to Sheri? Should you say anything to the school principal or other administrator?

3. Suppose that Dana's accusations are true, that is, Sheri actually was accused of plagiarism. Is Dana then behaving ethically in making her statements?

4. What would you do in this situation?

To answer these questions online and receive immediate feedback, go to the Reflect on This Module in Chapter 1 of the Companion Website.

national origin, marital status, political or religious beliefs, family, social or cultural background, or sexual orientation unfairly grant any advantage to any student." As with our first example, a violation of the code of ethics is a matter of interpretation; it isn't clear whether or not you have "unfairly" granted an advantage to Brittany because she has a disability.

The point in these examples is that standards for ethical behavior exist in teaching—even when situations aren't clear-cut—as they do for any other profession.

Are Teachers Professionals?

The information in the preceding section suggests that teaching is a profession and teachers are professionals. Not all people agree, however. Some arguments against teaching being a profession include:

- Lack of rigorous training
- Lack of a unique function
- Lack of autonomy
- Lack of accountability

Lack of Rigorous Training The academic rigor of teachers' professional training has historically been criticized (Gross, 1999; Kramer, 1991). Entrance into teaching isn't highly competitive, particularly on intellectual grounds, and many proposed reforms suggest that pedagogical content knowledge, general pedagogical knowledge, and knowledge of learners and learning be de-emphasized in favor of knowledge of content (Gross, 1999). The argument is often made, though not supported by research, that the only thing that teachers need is knowledge of the subjects they are teaching.

Lack of a Unique Function Whereas only physicians are allowed to practice medicine and only lawyers can legally practice the law, critics suggest that a great many people—other than licensed teachers—practice education. (We addressed this issue initially in Increasing Understanding 1.6). For instance, some young people are involved in formal religious training provided by their churches, where their instructors are certainly acting as teachers, and some children are "home schooled" by their parents, a practice allowed by law.

Lack of Autonomy In an earlier section we argued that teachers have a great deal of autonomy. While we maintain this position, it is important to note that teachers have less autonomy than other professionals. For example, unlike physicians and lawyers, teachers are supervised and evaluated by their immediate school administrators, and a substantial portion of the curriculum is mandated by states or districts. Teachers have little to say about the standards for licensure, and many teachers even have to sign in at the beginning of the day and sign out at the end.

Lack of Accountability Critics also argue that teachers are not accountable for student learning. If a student is unable to read at the end of the third-grade, for example, little consequence exists for the third-grade teacher. Further, when teachers achieve tenure, they are secure in their jobs. Barring a sexual offense or clear incompetence, removing a tenured teacher is extremely difficult.

Putting Teacher Professionalism into Perspective

The issue of whether or not teaching is a profession is controversial, and it won't be resolved in the near future. Without question, the training required for professions like medicine and law is more rigorous than the training required for teaching, though rigor in teacher education is on the rise (Olson, 2000a). Prospective teachers are expected to know and do more, and, increasingly, their understanding and skills are being assessed with tests.

Also, while children are taught by a number of different sources, such as family and the church, the primary institution responsible for helping children learn to read, write, and do math, for example, is the school. Teachers are seen as the people primarily responsible for student learning and intellectual development.

With respect to autonomy, a battle currently is being fought on both sides of the issue. Some would curtail teachers' autonomy by mandating what and how to teach, as well as specifying how to assess student learning. Others argue that this technical view of teaching is unfeasible and unproductive; teaching requires too many decisions to be reduced to mandates, and attempts to do so discourage creative people from considering teaching as a career.

Also, the accountability issue isn't unique to education. Admittedly, teachers don't lose their jobs if their students perform poorly on standardized tests, but similar examples exist in other professions. For instance, physicians don't lose their right to practice medicine if they prescribe an antibiotic for an ear infection, and the infection doesn't go away, and attorneys don't lose their right to practice law if they lose a case.

The issue of professionalism has important implications for teaching and for you as a prospective teacher. One of the most important is this: *If you expect to be treated as a professional, then you must act like a professional.* Commit yourself to academic excellence. Voice your criticisms of courses and experiences that are light on content and low in standards. Make every effort to thoroughly understand the body of knowledge in your profession.

Professional ethics guide teachers in their interactions with students, parents and caregivers, and colleagues.

Classroom Windows

CLASSROOMS IN ACTION: THE REAL WORLD OF TEACHING

Having looked at the reasons people choose to teach, the rewards and difficulties in teaching, and teacher professionalism, you now have the opportunity to look at three teachers in action. To complete this activity, do the following:

■ View the video episodes titled "Classrooms in Action: The Real World of Teaching."

■ Read the written transcripts of the three episodes and answer the following questions online by going to the *Classroom Windows* Module in Chapter 1 of the Companion Website at: **http://www.prenhall.com/kauchak.** Go to the Website and follow the directions on your screen.

■ Answer the questions that follow:

1. For which of the three teachers are the emotional rewards likely to be the greatest? Explain.

2. For which of the three teachers are the intellectual rewards likely to be the greatest? Explain.

3. Based on what you saw in the episodes, which teacher do you believe has the most difficult job? Explain.

4. For which teacher is knowledge of content most important? Pedagogical content knowledge? General pedagogical knowledge? Knowledge of learners and learning? Explain.

5. How much autonomy do you believe each teacher had in designing and conducting his or her lessons? Explain.

6. To what extent do you believe each teacher demonstrated the characteristics of a professional? Explain.

To answer these questions online and receive immediate feedback, go to the Looking Through Classroom Windows Module in Chapter 1 of the Companion Website.

One way of promoting professionalism is to encourage and endorse high standards for licensure. Professional organizations in education historically have been criticized for fighting high standards, but this is now changing (Blair, 2000). Endorse these changes and encourage others to support them as well.

Take your code of ethics seriously. Anything less detracts from the profession and detracts from you as a person and your status as a professional.

◪ BECOMING A TEACHER IN AN ERA OF REFORM

You're beginning your teacher-preparation experience in one of the most tumultuous periods in the history of American education. Critics, both inside and outside the profession, are calling for **reforms,** which are *suggested changes in teaching and teacher preparation intended to increase the amount students learn*. To implement these reforms, teachers must be well-prepared, and leaders in education are saying that we need to professionalize teaching (Blair, 2000). We examine the implications of these reform efforts in this section.

Reform: What Does it Mean?

Educational reform attempts to improve schools through changes in the way they are organized and run. To place recent reform efforts in perspective, we should point out that the process of change and reform has been a part of education throughout its history. From colonial times to the present, schools and teachers have been fair game for outside critics. The openness and accessibility of teaching makes it a unique profession; everyone has been in school. All people have views about teaching, and most of them have opinions about how to improve education. When you study the history of education in Chapter 5, you will see how different reforms have shaped education.

The modern reform movement is often traced to 1983, when the National Commission on Excellence in Education published *A Nation at Risk: The Imperative for Education Reform*. This widely read document suggested that America was "at risk" of being unable to compete in the world economic marketplace because our system of education was inadequate. The terms "at-risk students" and, more recently, "students placed at risk" can also be traced back to this document; these students were at-risk of not acquiring the knowledge and skills needed for success in our modern society. Since 1983 a great many suggestions have been made for improving our nation's schools and the teachers who work in them.

Because discussions of reform are so prominent in education today, we have made it a theme for this book. To introduce you to this theme and the idea of reform, we briefly examine three of the more prominent reforms here:

- Changes in teacher preparation
- Standards-based education
- Accountability and high-stakes testing

Changes in Teacher Preparation   Earlier in the chapter we noted increased calls for teacher professionalism, and we examined characteristics of professionalism as they relate to teaching. Reforms in teacher education have implications for the move toward greater teacher professionalism. These reforms include:

- Raising standards for acceptance into teacher-training programs.
- Requiring teachers to take more rigorous courses than they have in the past.
- Requiring higher standards for licensure, including teacher tests.

- Expanding teacher-preparation programs from four years to five.
- Requiring experienced teachers to take more rigorous professional development courses (Blair, 2000).

Some of these suggestions are almost certainly going to affect you. We'll describe two as examples. First, you probably will be required to pass a test before you're awarded your teaching license. At the present time:

- Thirty-nine states require prospective teachers to pass a basic skills test.
- Twenty-nine states require high school teachers to pass tests in the subjects they plan to teach.
- Twenty-seven states require principals to evaluate new teachers (Olson, 2000a).

The American Federation of Teachers, the second largest professional organization for teachers in the United States, recently proposed that prospective teachers pass tests aimed at basic content, such as math and English, as well as tests designed to measure teachers' knowledge of teaching principles (Blair, 2000). This proposal signals a change in policy from the past and suggests that teacher testing is not only here to stay, but is likely to increase.

Second, you will likely be required to take more courses in English, math, science, history, and geography than have been required of teachers in the past. In addition, there is a movement to require all teachers, elementary and secondary, to major in a content area for their undergraduate degree. The rationale behind this push is that teachers can't teach what they don't know themselves.

Whether or not these reforms will result in the hoped-for improvements in education remains to be seen and will continue to be debated. One thing is virtually certain, however. Efforts to reform schools, teachers, and the way teachers are prepared will continue, and you will begin your career as a teacher in the middle of these efforts. Joan Baratz-Snowden, spokesperson for the American Federation of Teachers, summarizes this trend, "It is a new day. Standards-based education is significantly different, and we have to prepare teachers to be successful in it." (Blair, 2000).

Standards-Based Education A great deal has been written about Americans' and American students' lack of knowledge about their world. Research suggests, for example, that 60 percent of adult Americans don't know the name of the president that ordered the dropping of the atomic bomb, 42 percent of college seniors can't place the Civil War in the correct half century, most Americans can't find the Persian Gulf on a map, and 43 percent are unable to find England (Bertman, 2000). While these examples focus on history and geography, even greater concerns have been raised about math, science, and writing. The result has been a move toward **standards-based education,** which is *the process of focusing curriculum and instruction on predetermined standards*. The following are examples of standards for middle school math students created by the National Council of Teachers of Mathematics.

■ ■ ■

Number and Operations Standard for Grades 6–8

Instructional programs from prekindergarten through grade 12 should enable all students to compute fluently and make reasonable estimates:

In grades 6–8 all students should:

- Select appropriate methods and tools for computing with fractions and decimals from among mental computation, estimation, calculators or computers, and paper and pencil, depending on the situation, and apply the selected methods;
- Develop and analyze algorithms for computing with fractions, decimals, and integers and develop fluency in their use;
- Develop and use strategies to estimate the results of rational-number computations and judge the reasonableness of the results;
- Develop, analyze, and explain methods for solving problems involving proportions, such as scaling and finding equivalent ratios. (National Council of Teachers of Mathematics, 2000, p. 214)

■ ■ ■

States also publish standards to guide learning in different content areas:

■ ■ ■

Science: "In Science, students in Missouri public schools will acquire a solid foundation, which includes knowledge of . . . properties and principles of force and motion" (Missouri Department of Elementary and Secondary Education, 1995).

Reading: (Grades 6–8) "Demonstrate inferential comprehension of a variety of printed materials." Grade 8 benchmark: "Identify relationships, images, patterns or symbols and draw conclusions about their meaning" (Oregon Department of Education, 1996).

Social Studies: (Grade 5) "The student will describe colonial America, with emphasis on . . . the principal economic and political connections between the colonies and England" (Virginia Board of Education, 1995).

■ ■ ■

As you can see, these standards are often general and vague. Not until they are translated into specific learning activities or test items do teachers or students have a clear idea of what should be learned or how it will be measured.

The standards movement is widespread; virtually all states have specified standards for at least some of the content areas, and students as well as teachers are being held accountable for meeting these standards.

Teaching in an Era of Reform

We said earlier in this section that we have made *reform* a theme for this book, and you've seen "changes in teacher preparation" and "standards-based education" as two examples. To involve you in examining prominent reforms, we are including a feature in each chapter called "Teaching in an Era of Reform." We will introduce the feature in this chapter and illustrate how you will be asked to respond. The feature includes the following elements:

- A reform issue, such as retaining students who don't pass tests in the same grade (discussed in Chapter 6), or *learner-centered* versus *teacher-centered instruction* (discussed in Chapter 9), is presented and discussed.
- The issue is "put into perspective" by the inclusion of arguments for and against the reform.
- You are then asked to take a position with respect to the issue by going to the Website for *Education Week* (a widely read newspaper devoted to education), studying several articles that discuss the issue, and responding to the articles in writing.

We will illustrate the process in the next section, using "accountability and high-stakes testing" as the reform issue.

Teaching in an Era of Reform

ACCOUNTABILITY AND HIGH-STAKES TESTING

In response to concerns about students graduating from high school without the skills needed to succeed either in college or the workplace, reformers have called for greater accountability for both students and teachers. **Accountability** means that *students are required to demonstrate that they have met specified standards or that they demonstrate understanding of the topics they study as measured by standardized tests, and teachers are being held responsible for students' performance.* Calls for accountability resulted from evidence indicating that students were being promoted from grade to grade without having mastered essential content; some students were graduating from high school barely able to read, write, and do mathematics effectively, and even more had limited scientific literacy and a general lack of understanding of our world.

High-stakes tests are *tests used to determine whether or not students will be promoted from one grade to another, graduate from high school, or have access to specific fields of study.* When students aren't allowed to graduate from high school because they fail a test, for example, the "stakes" are very high, thus the term "high-stakes tests."

High-stakes testing is widespread. For example:

- Every state but Iowa has adopted standards in at least some academic subjects.

- Forty-eight states have testing programs designed, in large part, to measure how well students perform on those standards.

- Twenty-one states plan to issue overall ratings of their schools based largely on their students' performance.

- At least eighteen states have the authority to close, take over, or overhaul schools that are identified as failing (Olson, 2000b).

Putting Reform into Perspective

As you might expect, high-stakes testing is very controversial, with critics arguing that it limits what teachers do. Critics assert that teachers spend too much of their time in school helping students practice for the tests and that teacher creativity is eliminated, because they must narrowly focus their teaching on the content of the tests.

Standards and the movement toward accountability may require teachers to work individually with students to ensure that all learn essential knowledge and skills.

Pressure to do well on the tests is so great that some teachers and administrators have been driven to cheat; they help students with the tests or even give them answers (Viadero, 2000b). In Massachusetts, high-stakes testing became so controversial that the state's largest teachers' union, in a highly unusual move, launched a $600,000 television campaign that sharply criticized the *Massachusetts Comprehensive Assessment System* exam, an exam students in the state must pass to graduate (Gehring, 2000).

 Increasing Understanding 1.8

Virtually everyone reading this text has taken either the SAT (Scholastic Aptitude Test) or the ACT (American College Testing) program to determine whether you can get into a particular college or university. Are these "high-stakes" tests? Explain.

Advocates of testing, while conceding that teacher preparation, materials, and the tests themselves need to be improved, argue that the tests are the fairest and most effective means of achieving the aims of democratic schooling. Further, they assert, evidence indicates that educational systems that require content standards and use tests that thoroughly measure the extent to which the standards are met greatly improve the achievement for all students, including those from disadvantaged backgrounds (Bishop, 1995, 1998). Hirsch (2000) summarizes the testing advocates' position: "They [standards and tests that measure achievement of the standards] are the most promising educational development in half a century" (p. 64).

You Take a Position

Now it's your turn to take a position on the issue discussed in this section. Go to the *Education Week* Website at **http://www.edweek.com**, find "search" on the first page, and type in one of the following two search terms: *high-stakes tests* or *accountability*. Locate a minimum of three articles on one of these topics and then do the following:

1. Identify the title, author, and date of each article and write a one-paragraph summary of each.

2. Identify a pattern in the articles. (An example of a pattern would be if each article—or even two of the three—suggests that parents approve of high-stakes tests.)

3. After identifying the pattern, take one of the two following positions:
   - The pattern suggested in the articles, if implemented, *is* likely to improve education.
   - The pattern suggested in the articles *is not* likely to improve education.

State your position in writing and document your position with information taken from the articles. Give your response to your instructor.

To answer these questions online, go to the Take a Position Module in Chapter 1 of the Companion Website.

Now, let's look at a possible response to this feature. The response consists of three parts:

- A summary of three articles found on the *Education Week* Website (**http://www.edweek.com**). (Remember to double click on "search" on the right side of the page and enter *high-stakes testing* in the box under "Enter your search terms.")
- A description of the pattern found in the articles.
- A position on whether the pattern, if generally implemented, would or would not improve education.

The following is a sample response:

The Three Selected Articles

1. *LA Set To Retain 4th, 8th Graders Based on State Exams* by Erik Robelen, in the May 24, 2000, issue

2. *Arizona Poised to Revisit Graduation Exam* by Darcia Bowman, in the November 29, 2000, issue

3. *Standardized Testing and Its Victims* by Alfie Kohn, in the September 27, 2000, issue

Summary of the Articles

In the first article, Erik Robelen reported that nearly one-third of Louisiana's fourth and eighth graders failed the state's high-stakes test in the spring of 2000. Students who failed will have the opportunity to attend summer school and retake the tests in July, and those who fail a second time face the prospect of repeating a grade next fall. An appeals process exists that allows students who failed the tests, but meet certain other criteria, to request permission to continue to the next grade.

In the second article, Darcia Bowman reported that Arizona education officials are considering delaying a requirement that the state's high school students pass the *Arizona Instrument to Measure Standards* test to graduate, because too many students are failing the test, and large differences exist in the performance of minority and White students. State officials emphasize that this move doesn't imply that Arizona is calling an end to the state's efforts to implement standards and accountability.

In the third article, Alfie Kohn sharply criticizes the increased emphasis on testing and points out that our students are being tested to a greater extent than at any time in history. He is most critical of basing important decisions, such as graduation or promotion, on the results of a single test, and points out that most professional organizations, such as the American Educational Research Association, and the National Council for Teachers of Mathematics hold a similar position. Yet, he notes, just such high-stakes testing is currently taking place, or is scheduled to be introduced soon, in more than half the states.

The Pattern Found in the Articles
A clear pattern exists. States are now implementing high-stakes tests, and several states are also requiring—or are at least considering requiring—that students pass high-stakes tests in order to be promoted to the next grade level or to graduate from high school.

A Possible Position Taken with Respect to the Articles
This pattern—requiring students to pass high-stakes tests to be promoted or graduate—will not help education. As Darcia Bowman points out, not all Arizona students are being taught the content in the standards. Retaining students in a particular grade because they are unable to demonstrate understanding of content they haven't been taught obviously is unfair. Erik Robelen quotes Lorrie A. Shepard, an education professor at the University of Colorado at Boulder: "Every leading body has said you shouldn't make those decisions on the basis of a test alone."

What you've just read is an example that you can use for reference when you're asked to respond to the "Teaching in an Era of Reform" feature in Chapters 2–10. It doesn't mean that your responses must mirror this one. Good luck.

Exploring Diversity: Cultural Minorities and High-Stakes Tests As we saw in the previous section, high-stakes tests are very controversial. An important part of the controversy focuses on critics' claims that these tests are destructive for cultural minorities, particularly Hispanic and African American students who consistently score lower on standardized tests than do their White and Asian counterparts (Bowman, 2000; Viadero & Johnston, 2000). An example of the controversy surrounding the issue occurred in 1999 when the *Mexican-American Legal Defense and Educational Fund* (MALDEF) filed a federal lawsuit seeking to end the practice of requiring students to pass a test to graduate from high school in Texas. MALDEF argued that the Texas Assessment of Academic Skills (TAAS) is unfair to thousands of Hispanic and African-American students (Wildavsky, 1999).

The MALDEF lawsuit was just one case in a long line of controversies over race and testing. All raise the same question: As standardized tests are used increasingly to measure and improve student performance—with important consequences for not measuring up—will historically lower-scoring African-American and Hispanic students be treated fairly? MALDEF's answer to the question is, of course, no, but not all educators—includ-

A major element of many current reform efforts is increased emphasis on testing in schools.

ing some in Texas—agree. For example, one school district in Houston made increased scores on the TAAS a high priority, which resulted in dramatic improvement in the performance of the students, who were 86 percent Hispanic and 88 percent economically disadvantaged (Johnston, 2000).

Other educators have suggested comprehensive strategies for decreasing the achievement gap between minority and nonminority students, and testing is an integral part of those strategies. Increasing minority achievement is the goal, and supporters of testing dismiss criticisms by saying that the critics tacitly assume that eliminating tests will somehow increase achievement; test supporters assert that this simply is not true (Viadero & Johnston, 2000).

However, several issues related to high-stakes testing with minority students remain unanswered. One is whether the tests are sufficiently accurate to justify using the test scores to make important decisions about students' academic lives (Kohn, 2000). A second issue relates to technical problems involved in testing minorities in general (Land, 1997) as well as ESL students, who speak English as a second language (Abedi, 1999). High-stakes test designers need to ensure that test scores reflect differences in achievement rather than cultural or language differences. Finally, deciding student grade promotion or graduation solely on the basis of one test score is being increasingly criticized by a number of prestigious educational professional organizations including the American Educational Research Association and the National Council of Teachers of Mathematics.

Unquestionably, testing is necessary to measure the learning progress of all students, both minorities and nonminorities. Whether or not progress from one grade to another or graduation from high school should be linked to performance on the tests remains an open and troubling question.

The Changing Role of Teachers

Increased accountability and testing for students are reforms that are facts of life for teachers. How will these reforms change your role as a teacher? At least four implications are likely.

First, you'll need to know more. Compared to teachers in the past, you'll be expected to know more English, math, science, history, and geography. The general education requirements for teachers almost certainly will increase, and prospective teachers will be expected to demonstrate their understanding of these subjects on tests before they will be allowed to teach.

Second, you will be held responsible for student learning, and allowances for the increasingly diverse backgrounds of your students probably will not be made. In other words, you will be held responsible for your students' performance regardless of their home environments, background experiences, or motivation. To meet these expectations—in addition to your knowledge of English, history, and other forms of content—your pedagogical content knowledge, general pedagogical knowledge, and knowledge of learners and learning will have to be thorough. In addition, you probably will be tested on the material you learn in your teacher preparation classes. Your performance on these tests may determine if you get a license and whether you will be allowed to teach.

Third, in spite of controversies, testing will be an important part of your teaching life. As we said earlier, you will be tested before you're allowed to enter the profession, and the students you teach will be tested regularly. Proposals are being made to provide merit pay for teachers whose students do well on these tests and to review teachers whose students do not (Bradley, 2000; Hoff, 2000).

Fourth, as you begin your career, you will probably have less autonomy than teachers had 10 or even 5 years ago. You'll be expected to help your students meet the standards mandated by your state or district, so the number of decisions you'll be allowed to make on your own will be reduced. This is a dilemma. As we saw earlier in the chapter, educational leaders are advocating an increase in the professionalization of teaching, and professionals have autonomy. At the same time, other leaders are mandating standards that reduce teacher autonomy, which detracts from professionalism.

Finally, you will need to be highly adaptable. Some specific reforms will be abandoned, only to be replaced by new reforms. Your ability to understand and quickly adapt to these changes will strongly influence your success in and satisfaction with a teaching career.

Despite the negative effects of some reform efforts, teachers still have considerable autonomy in their classrooms.

■ SUMMARY

Why People Decide to Teach
Research indicates that the most frequently given reason that people choose to teach is their desire to work with young people and make contributions to society. Other reasons to enter teaching include intellectual growth and interest in a content area.

Rewards and Difficulties in Teaching
Teaching is both rewarding and difficult. Intrinsic rewards include helping young people grow emotionally, socially, and intellectually, and extrinsic rewards include desirable vacation times, autonomy, and status. Difficulties include working with students who aren't motivated and are difficult to manage, as well as unresponsive parents, administrators who aren't supportive, and a great many nonteaching duties that are associated with the job.

The Teaching Profession
Professionals in any field understand a specialized body of knowledge, train for licensure, have a great deal of autonomy, and use ethical standards to guide their professional conduct.

Some people argue that teachers are not professionals, suggesting their training isn't rigorous, they don't provide a unique service, they lack autonomy, and accountability is lacking. Others contend that teaching is a developing profession, evolving over time.

Becoming a Teacher in an Era of Reform
The reform movement in education includes emphasis on higher standards for learners and teachers as well as accountability. Prospective teachers will also encounter a number of reforms calling for higher standards, more rigorous training, and increased testing.

The Changing Role of the Teacher
Emphasis on reform is likely to mean that teachers will need to be more knowledgeable, they will be held more responsible for student learning, and testing will be an increasingly important part of their work. Teachers will probably have less autonomy than they have had in the past, and they will need to be increasingly adaptable.

■ IMPORTANT CONCEPTS

accountability	high-stakes tests	reforms
assessment	intrinsic rewards	standards
autonomy	physical conditions of	standards-based education
curriculum	teaching	technician
extrinsic rewards	psychological conditions of	
ethics	teaching	

■ DISCUSSION QUESTIONS

1. Do the reasons cited in the chapter for becoming a teacher change with the grade level or content area targeted by teachers? Why?
2. Do you believe teaching is more or less rewarding than it was in the past? More or less difficult? Why do you think so?
3. Which of the intrinsic and extrinsic rewards in teaching are likely to become more important in the future? Which are likely to become less important?
4. Is teaching a profession? If not, what would be necessary to make it one?

5. Will the move toward teacher professionalism be beneficial for teachers? Why or why not?

6. Are the different dimensions of reform, such as standards, accountability, and high-stakes testing, good or bad for education? Why do you think so?

■ VIDEO DISCUSSION QUESTIONS

 The following discussion questions refer to video segments found on the Companion Website. To answer these questions online, view the accompanying video, and receive immediate feedback to your answers, go to the Video Discussion Module in Chapter 1 of the Companion Website at **http://www.prenhall.com/kauchak.**

1. Dr. Urie Triesman is a professor of mathematics at the University of Texas at Austin and director of the Charles A. Dana Center for Math and Science Education. His work focuses on school reform and ways that schools can be helped to improve. He is concerned that individual school and teacher autonomy often conflict with central-ized testing programs. What does Dr. Triesman believe is the proper balance between these two forces? Do you think centralized testing jeopardizes school and teacher autonomy? Explain why you believe it does or does not.

2. Theodore Sizer is the director of the Coalition for Effective Schools, which attempts to reform high schools. As we've seen in this chapter, testing is being proposed as a major reform tool. In Dr. Sizer's opinion, what questions should people ask when they consider using standardized tests to assess student learning? Do you think Dr. Sizer's cautions are justified? Explain.

■ GOING INTO SCHOOLS

1. Interview two teachers; if possible, one teacher should be in his or her first year, and the other teacher should have taught for at least five years. Ask them the following questions:

    a. Why did you choose to teach? Please give me all the reasons that apply to your decision.

    b. What are some of the most rewarding aspects of teaching? Please provide some specific examples.

    c. What are some of the most difficult parts of teaching? Please provide some specific examples.

    d. Are you more or less confident in your ability to help kids learn than you were before you started?

    e. How effective was your pre-service teacher-preparation program in helping you learn to teach? What would have made it more effective?

    f. Do you plan to stay in teaching, or do you plan to move to a different job or profession? If you plan to leave teaching, what are your reasons?

    g. In one sentence, please describe the process of teaching.

    h. Do you believe that teaching is a profession? Explain your reasons.

    i. Please rate the importance of each of the following for teachers, using the scale that follows:

    1 = Not at all important

    2 = Not very important

    3 = Somewhat important

4 = Quite important

5 = Extremely important

1. Knowledge of content, such as math, science or language arts.
2. Knowledge of teaching techniques, such as questioning and classroom organization.
3. Knowledge of students, such as how they learn and what motivates them.

Of the three types of knowledge that we see here, which is the most important? Least important? Or are they all equally important?

Compare the two teachers' responses and analyze them in terms of the content in this chapter.

2. Interview a teacher and ask him or her the following questions:
    a. To what extent do standards and testing influence what is taught and how it is taught in your school?
    b. What are some concrete examples of the standards and how the standards are tested?
    c. Has the standards and high-stakes testing movement been good or bad for education? Why do you feel this way?
    d. Will the standards, testing, and accountability movement increase or decrease in importance in the next 5 to 10 years? Why do you think so?
    e. How have the standards and accountability movements affected your satisfaction as a teacher?

Summarize these responses and explain your personal views on standards and testing.

 Virtual Field *Experience* | **If you would like to participate in a Virtual Field Experience, go to the *Field Experience* Module in Chapter 1 of the Companion Website.**

■ ONLINE PORTFOLIO ACTIVITIES

 Portfolios are collections of a professional's work and evidence of accomplishments, such as a series of pictures that a photographer has taken, together with awards that the photographer has received. Just as photographers, artists, and other professionals develop portfolios to document their personal growth, so can teachers. Teaching portfolios can include evidence of changes in your thinking, such as reflections about your reasons for becoming a teacher (which we suggest in the first activity of this chapter), letters of commendation and recommendation, teaching units you've prepared, and videotapes of lessons you've taught. What you choose to include depends on your personal and professional judgment. (A detailed discussion of teaching portfolios is found in Bullock & Hawl, 2001, Campbell et al., 2001, as well as in Chapter 10 of this text.)

The following are suggested activities that will help you begin. As you continue in your program, you will add a great many items to your portfolio, and you may choose to delete some that you had selected initially.

Each of the activities is linked to an INTASC (Interstate New Teacher Assessment and Support Consortium) principle. The INTASC principles describe what you, as a beginning teacher, should know and be able to do when you first walk into a classroom. You will hear much more about the INTASC principles as you move through your teacher-preparation program. (A detailed description of the principles appears in Chapter 10.)

To complete these activities online, go to the *Portfolio Activities* Module in Chapter 1 of the Companion Website to submit your response.

Portfolio Activity 1.1

Why I Want to Become a Teacher

INTASC Principle 9: *Professional Commitment*

Look again at your responses to the Interest in Teaching Inventory that you saw at the beginning of this chapter. For each of the items that you marked either a 6 (Agree) or a 7 (Strongly Agree), write a brief explanation for your choice. For example, if you marked 7 for Item 2, "My family has strongly influenced my decision to become a teacher," a possible response could be the following:

> My dad is a teacher. He didn't directly encourage me to teach, but I remember how excited he would be when he came home and talked about some kid who finally "got it." Also, he was always telling some funny story about kids he worked with. I could see how much fun he had teaching.

Now, look at each of the items that you marked either a 1 (Strongly Disagree) or a 2 (Disagree). Again, write a brief explanation for your choice. What do your responses to these items tell you about your personal reasons for becoming a teacher?

Portfolio Activity 1.2

Professional Standards and Teaching

INTASC Principle 3: *Adapting Instruction*

In the chapter you saw how standards increasingly are being used to guide what teachers do and what students learn. This portfolio activity asks you to visit the text's Companion Website at **http://www.prenhall.com/kauchak**. After accessing the Website, click on *Professional Organizations*. You'll find Website addresses for 13 different professional organizations such as the International Reading Association or the Council for Exceptional Children. Find one that interests you, click on it, and find the organization's professional standards. Summarize the standards in several paragraphs and then explain how they will guide your teaching behavior. Provide a specific, concrete example to illustrate your explanation.

Portfolio Activity 1.3

Exploring Pedagogical Content Knowledge

INTASC Principle 1: *Knowledge of Subject*

In this chapter you saw that professionals have a specialized body of knowledge and that teachers must possess pedagogical content knowledge—the ability to illustrate topics in ways that are understandable to students.

To illustrate your understanding of pedagogical content knowledge, do the following:

1. Select a topic of your choice, such as *inertia* in science, *similar triangles* in math, *rules for forming plural nouns* in language arts, or *longitude* and *latitude* in geography.

2. Identify the grade level at which you believe the topic will be taught.

3. Create two examples that illustrate the topic. Your ability to create the examples is an indicator of your pedagogical content knowledge at this point. (This portfolio activity will be an excellent way to begin thinking about instruction and what teachers need to do to help their students learn. Additional entries will document the growth in your thinking.)

To help you understand how to do complete this assignment, we've provided one example from math, using the topic of *similar triangles*. (Similar triangles are pairs of triangles that have proportional sides and equal angles.) In the example, if we measured the lengths of the sides of the two triangles and their angles, we would find that the sides of DEF are twice as long as the sides of ABC, and the angles for the two triangles are equal. These are the types of examples that you would create for and use with your students if you were a math teacher.

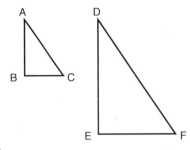

The Teaching Profession

The lives of teachers are complex. In a typical school day, teachers are asked to make a great many decisions and fulfill roles ranging from instructor to children's caretaker to public ambassador. These many roles make teaching simultaneously demanding and satisfying, both intellectually and emotionally.

Compared to teachers in the past, you'll be asked to perform roles that are changing, and you'll work with people who are changing as well. Retirements and demographic changes in the United States will create a different teaching force for tomorrow's schools. We examine these changes in this chapter as we try to answer the following questions:

■ What is it like to be a teacher?

■ What are the different roles that teachers perform?

■ Who will you work with?

■ How will the trend toward professionalism affect your life as a teacher?

Let's see how the answers to these questions influence the lives of real teachers.

Maria Lopez, a 3-year veteran of teaching, pulls into her school's parking lot at 7:30 A.M. As she walks through the main office, she checks her mailbox and greets the school secretary. "Any news on Antonio?" she asks, checking on a student she had referred for testing for special services. When the secretary replies, "Not yet," Maria shrugs with a concerned look on her face and continues down the empty halls to her classroom.

Unlocking the door, she remembers that this is going to be a busy day. It begins with a fourth-grade team meeting and ends with a district in-service workshop. As she glances at the clock, she mutters, "I better scurry. Jana [the team leader] has a fit when we're late."

At 7:46 A.M., she enters Jana Torry's classroom and smiles with relief when she notices that she's not the last one there. Jana begins the meeting at 7:50 A.M., and the team discusses the possibility of grouping all of the fourth graders for reading. After discussing the question at some length, they decide to keep their own students for reading. They then turn to the new statewide assessment test in math. After a number of questions, the group asks Maria to compare the test with their current math textbook to determine the fit; she will report her findings at the next meeting. As the meeting adjourns, Maria glances at her watch and realizes that she has just enough time for a quick visit to the bathroom before the kids arrive.

"Hmm. A school assembly. They're going to be wired today, so I need to keep them busy," she thinks as she shuffles papers on her desk, looking for her plan book.

Maria schedules her day as follows:

8:30 A.M.–10:00 A.M. Language Arts (Spelling, writing, grammar)
10:00 A.M.–11:00 A.M. Math
11:00 A.M.–11:15 A.M. Break (Recess)
11:15 A.M.–11:45 A.M. Science
11:45 A.M.–12:10 P.M. Lunch
12:10 P.M.–1:40 P.M. Reading
1:40 P.M.–1:50 P.M. Break (Bathroom)
1:50 P.M.–2:15 P.M. Social Studies (Safety Assembly)
2:15 P.M.–3:00 P.M. Art/Music/P.E. (Safety Assembly)

After writing the schedule on the board, Maria also writes down the next day's assignments to make sure her students will know what to do when they enter her classroom.

At 8:25 A.M. the playground bell rings and students start trickling into her classroom.

"Good morning, Mrs. Lopez," and "Hi, Mrs. Lopez" greet her as she hurries around the room, making last minute preparations for her math and science lessons. From 8:30 A.M. to 10:00 A.M., she works with small groups of students on language arts, calling four or five students at a time to one corner of the room while the others work quietly at their desks. As she works with the groups, she keeps one eye on them and the other on the rest of the class. Several times she gets up from her small-group lesson to help students or remind them to finish their work. Kevin requires several reminders, and Maria remembers that she is meeting with his mother and the special-education referral team after school today.

Math goes smoothly as she hands back homework from the previous day. After clarifying a few problems in the homework, Maria hands out kits of multicolored blocks and has students work in groups and use the blocks to solve and illustrate problems involving place value.

After break, which Maria supervises because this is her week, her class begins science. The class is studying ecosystems, and Maria has different groups investigating different ecosystems around the world on the Internet and preparing reports, which they'll share with the whole class.

Lunch is a time for Maria to relax for a few minutes with her colleagues. After walking her class to the cafeteria, Maria ducks into the teachers' room, grabs her lunch bag, and collapses in one of the stuffed chairs. Lunch is spent talking about a variety of topics ranging from families, kids, the new math tests, local politics, and the possibility of getting a new principal.

When the students return from lunch, Maria assigns a story from their literature book and asks them to answer questions that she has written on the overhead projector. As the class reads, she works with different groups of students on the book report presentations they'll make to the whole class. There is a nice, busy hum to the class that Maria recognizes as productive work. Abruptly the P.A. system announces the order that classes should get ready to go to the safety assembly. Maria quickly has her class put away their projects and line up for the assembly.

The assembly is a zoo. The policeman and fireman that come, while well intentioned, talk too much, and much is over the heads of the students. The kids get restless. Maria uses eye contact and fingers to the lips to quiet her students. She can't really blame them; she's bored, too. Mercifully, at 2:45 P.M. the program is over, and Maria has 15 minutes to prepare her class for departure. Different teams clean up different parts of the room as Maria writes homework reminders on the board.

As the last straggler leaves her room at 3:15 P.M., Maria sits in her chair and exhales loudly. "Phew, we made it!" she thinks as she hears a knock at the door. Kevin's mother has arrived for the meeting to discuss having him tested for a learning disability. With any kind of luck, the meeting will end by 4:00 P.M., giving her time to hop into her car and drive to her in-service class. Her day is not over yet.

■ ■ ■

Dave Loft, a third-year high school teacher, arrives at Hillcrest High at 6:45 A.M., just as the sky begins to show the first traces of dawn. He has a departmental meeting this morning, where he and his fellow English teachers will analyze the state's new English guidelines and discuss the implications for their high school's curriculum.

After checking his mailbox, Dave unlocks his classroom door and reads his e-mail. He is experimenting with a volunteer parent reading program for his Basic Sophomore English courses and uses e-mail to supplement after-school phone calls to coordinate the system. While having parent volunteers saves Dave a lot of time making comments on papers, he still has to read and grade each one, and the coordination of the project eats up hours during the week.

Dave enjoys the departmental meeting, but keeps looking at his watch, remembering all the organizational tasks he has to complete for the day's classes. In analyzing the new state guidelines, Dave and his colleagues discuss a number of works of recent fiction that could be used to meet the standards. Dave finds the discussion stimulating and thinks to himself, "Ah, this is why I became a teacher."

After the meeting, Dave hurries to his classroom, just beating the bell that announces 5 minutes until Advisory Homeroom, an experiment designed to make the school more humane and person-oriented. Every morning Dave meets with his first period Basic Sophomore English class for 15 minutes before the formal class begins. During this time Dave takes care of administrative duties like attendance and announcements but also uses the time to get to know his students better. It seems to be working, as his first period class, while not the sharpest, is his favorite. He has fewer management problems in this class and, because he knows his students better, class discussions are more lively, personal, and productive.

From 8:00 A.M. until noon, it's a steady stream of students. Dave has four of his six classes in the morning and teaches 50-minute periods with 5-minute intervals in between. Even between-class intervals are crazy, with both incoming and exiting students wanting to talk about assignments, grades, and sometime even ideas.

Dave eats lunch in his room during his prep period, grading papers as he wolfs down a sandwich. He gave up his formal planning period to take on an additional class for extra pay. The extra money helps, but the extra class means not only one more class to teach but also many more papers to grade. "Why did I ever go into English?" he mutters with a smile, and starts on his next pile of student essays. He recalls the exchange he had the other day with Ricardo, another third-year teacher. They were discussing the relative merits of different kinds of assessments; Ricardo was extolling the benefits of short answer and multiple-choice tests that could be graded quickly. "Maybe Ricardo is right," Dave thinks, "but how are they ever going to learn to write if they don't write a lot?"

At 3:15 P.M., the final class bell rings, and Dave has 15 minutes to prepare materials for Debate Club, which he sponsors. He enjoys working with the students and getting to know them better as people, but jokingly reports to his wife that the $800 they pay him for doing this averages out to less than minimum wage. Her reply, "So, you must not be doing it for the money," causes both of them to laugh.

■ ■ ■

■ TEACHING: A TIME PERSPECTIVE

Let's think about Maria and Dave. What were their days like? How did they spend most of their time? How do their days compare to a typical day for you?

In this section we use time as a lens through which we'll view teaching. Time is useful for at least three reasons. First, the way we spend our time defines our lives; we spend more of our waking hours involved in our careers than in any other part of life. Once you become a teacher, how you spend your time will greatly influence your satisfaction with your career. Second, the way we spend our time says a great deal about what is important to us; and third, time is a useful way to analyze different teaching situations.

The School Year

Let's begin by looking at the school year. For students, a typical school year lasts 180 days, beginning a few days before or after Labor Day in September and ending in early June. (Some districts are now starting school in early August, so that the first semester is completed before the winter holiday.) For teachers, the school year is several days longer, with time before the students begin allocated to planning, meetings, and getting classrooms ready (for example, putting up bulletin boards, counting books, and requisitioning everyday supplies like paper and scissors). In addition, teachers spend several days after students are finished finalizing grades, packing up their room, and getting organized for next year.

However, this simple picture of 9-months-on, 3-months-off is becoming increasingly clouded by changes in the school calendar. One is **year-round schooling** in which *students spend 3 months on and 1 month off, rather than the traditional 9–3 pattern.* The 9–3 pattern has its historical roots in our agrarian past, when children were needed during the summer months to plant and harvest crops. One of your authors remembers feeling cheated when he visited his farm-living cousins in May and discovered that they were out of school already so they could help with spring planting. You may encounter year-round

Time provides a useful lens through which to analyze the lives of teachers.

Increasing Understanding 2.1

In what kind of districts or schools are you most likely to encounter year-round schools? Why? What implications might these have for you personally?

To answer the "Increasing Understanding" questions online and receive immediate feedback, go to the *Increasing Understanding* Module in Chapter 2 of the Companion Website at **http://www.prenhall.com/ kauchak,** type in your response, and then study the feedback.

scheduling in your first job; nearly 1.5 million students in more than 20 states attend public schools on a year-round schedule (National Association for Year-Round Education, 1998). Primary reasons for this schedule change are to alleviate crowding by more efficiently using physical facilities and to minimize the inevitable forgetting (sometimes called "summer loss") that occurs over the summer.

Interestingly, there have been obstacles to year-round schooling; these obstacles come from several different sources. One obstacle is parents; summer has become a time for family vacations and summer camps, and parents resist intrusions on this family time. A second obstacle is the large amounts of money sometimes needed to install and run air conditioning in schools built for cool-weather use. A third obstacle is teachers themselves; many use summers as a time to supplement their teaching salaries or to work on recertification, new areas of certification, or a master's degree.

The School Week

In the United States, the 40-hour workweek is the norm. How does teaching compare to this norm? Study after study shows that the average teacher spends between 45 and 50 hours per week in school-related work, with the average being around 46 hours (Cypher & Willower, 1984; *Metropolitan Life Survey*, 1995; National Center for Education Statistics [NCES], 1997). Thirty-three hours of this is time that teachers are required to be at school, with the remainder spent either with students outside the classroom or at home grading papers or planning.

Bear in mind that these are just averages. In one study, 35 percent of teachers reported working more than 55 hours per week (NCES, 1997). Beginning teachers and experienced teachers changing level or assignment (for example, fourth to first grade or middle school math to science) probably spend considerably more time per week than the average.

Table 2.1	How Teachers Spend Their Time	
Activity		**Percentage of Day**
Working with students		
Instruction		27.5
Testing and monitoring		10.1
Supervision		7.8
Total working with students		45.4
Peer interactions		25.6
Desk and routine work		20.0
Travel		5.3
Private time		3.5

Source: From "The Work Behavior of Secondary School Teachers" by T. Cypher and D. Willower, 1984, *Journal of Research & Development, 18,* pp. 19–20. Reprinted by permission.

These work patterns vary slightly for elementary and secondary teachers (NCES, 1997). As a group, secondary teachers work more hours per week than elementary teachers (46.5 hours versus 44 hours); this difference is largely because secondary teachers supervise more extracurricular activities like sports and clubs. We saw this with Dave Loft, who worked with the Debate Club after his formal teaching day.

The average length of a school teacher's workweek compares favorably with other occupations requiring a bachelor's degree. Managerial positions require the most hours per week at 46 hours, followed by salespeople and service workers (for example, social workers) at 44 hours, and administrative support positions (for example, administrative assistant) at 42 hours.

How do these figures compare with the number of hours worked by teachers in other countries? Primary teachers in 20 industrialized countries worked an average of 829 hours per year; primary teachers in the United States averaged 958 hours per year (NCES, 1997). As we'll see shortly, working conditions and the specifics of teaching also vary considerably from country to country as well as from school to school, within a district, between school districts, and between states. These differences can affect your personal satisfaction with a teaching career, so you need to explore these differences when you seek your first teaching position.

Teaching is a career involving hard work and long hours. Unlike many other occupations, teachers don't punch a time clock and leave their jobs behind when they leave school. Teachers will often talk about their students to spouses and friends (if they'll listen), and many teachers even report dreaming about their classes. If you are looking for a neat 9 to 5 job with few emotional entanglements, teaching may not be for you.

A Typical Workday

What is a typical workday for teachers? How do Maria's and Dave's experiences compare with those of other teachers? Let's look at some national statistics. As we can see from Table 2.1, teachers spend the largest part of their day working with students. Though instruction occupies the majority of that time (27.5 percent), other student-related activities, such as monitoring and supervision, also occupy major chunks of teachers' time. We saw this in Maria's day when she was expected to monitor students on the playground, take her class to lunch, and supervise her students during the assembly.

Peer interactions occupy the next largest chunk (25.6 percent) of teachers' time. Maria and Dave both had meetings before their school day, and Maria had one after. More and more, teachers are being asked to provide input into curricular and instructional issues affecting their teaching, a trend connected to the move toward greater teacher professionalism (Rowan, 1994). In addition, teachers spend a large amount of their day (20 percent) planning, preparing for instruction, and grading student papers and work. In all likelihood, both Maria and Dave took batches of papers with them when they finally left the school building. Teachers' days don't end when students leave or even when they go home. Teachers report they often get lesson ideas while they're driving in their cars or shopping (McCutcheon, 1982). You'll find many teachers grading papers as the rest of the family goes about their regular evening activities. Teaching is a full-time job.

Grade-Level Differences

The way teachers spend their day differs dramatically by grade level, and these differences have important implications for you as a teacher. The majority of elementary teachers (62 percent) work in self-contained classrooms, versus only 6 percent of secondary teachers (NCES, 1997). (In all likelihood, this 6 percent is composed of resource or special education teachers.) The remaining elementary teachers not in a self-contained classroom teach in team (9 percent), enrichment (11.2 percent), or pull-out programs (10.5 percent). At the secondary level, over 84 percent of teachers work in departmentalized settings where students rotate to different classes every hour.

The differences in teachers' workdays have implications for you, especially if you are wondering which level is best for you as a teacher. The elementary level, with its emphasis on self-contained classrooms, provides you with greater opportunities to work in-depth with a group of students, getting to know them better than in the departmentalized structure of the secondary level. This is a definite plus; as we saw in Chapter 1, the relationships we form with our students are a major source of satisfaction in teaching.

The secondary level also has advantages. Departmentalization allows you to focus on a specific content area (or areas) and share your interest with your students. Recall from Chapter 1 that interest in a content area and opportunities for self-growth are major intrinsic reasons that people choose teaching as a career. Departmentalization also places you in contact with other people in your school who share your interest in a subject matter area. The 26 percent of the day that secondary teachers spend meeting with others will be more focused on issues related to content in your major or minor. Dave experienced intellectual stimulation during the discussion with his colleagues about the new English curriculum. Recall from Chapter 1 that these intellectual rewards are major factors influencing people to enter and remain in the teaching profession.

Which is better for you? That's a major reason you're taking this course—to decide.

Comparisons with Other Countries

Time comparisons with teachers in other countries are interesting, especially when they come from countries like Japan and China, where students outperform their U.S. counterparts in crucial areas like math and science (Calsyn, Gonzales, & Frase, 1999; Stigler, Gonzales, Kawanaka, Knoll, & Serrano, 1999). The typical Japanese teacher arrives at school around 7:30 A.M., like their U.S. counterparts, but stays there until 6:00 P.M. (Sato & McLaughlin, 1992). Most U.S. teachers are free to leave a half hour after students depart; many teachers leave at that time, preferring to grade papers and plan at home. (This is why you seldom see a teacher leaving school empty-handed—bags, briefcases, and

---

Increasing Understanding 2.3

The time figures in Table 2.1 are averages for all teachers. How might these figures change for teachers working in learning, enrichment, or pull-out programs? How might they change for teachers in self-contained classrooms? What implications might this have for a person considering different types of teaching positions?

Teaching
in an Era *of* Reform

CHANGING THE CLOCK

Among the many reforms suggested for improving schools, one in particular may affect your life as a teacher. It focuses on time and the way it's allocated (National Education Commission on Time and Learning, 1994). Two major reforms with respect to time have been suggested:

1. Lengthen the amount of time students spend in school.

2. Change the way time is scheduled.

Lengthen the Amount of Time Students Spend in School

It makes sense to conclude that the more time students spend in learning activities, the more they will learn; this conclusion is confirmed by research (Karweit, 1989; Nystrand & Gamoran, 1989). In addition, reformers point to other industrialized countries, like Japan and Germany, where the school year is longer (Japan, 240 days, and Germany, 216 days) and test scores on international comparisons are higher (Stigler et al., 1999). As a result, reformers advocate increasing the amount of time students spend in school. This can be accomplished by lengthening the school day, the school year, or both, or by having students attend summer school.

Interestingly, most proposals focus on the school year, leaving the school day relatively unchanged. Most people believe that development places limits on how long students can productively learn and stay in school in one day. Little kids (and big ones, too) tire over the school day, and the last hour of the school day presents special challenges for teachers wanting to motivate their students. However, in many Asian countries, like Japan and Korea, students routinely attend classes all day and then after school go to either enrichment classes in areas like art or music or additional tutoring classes, arriving home hours after school lets out.

A major time reform is the move to additional summer coursework, especially for students who are experiencing problems in school. The prevalence of summer school is expanding rapidly; this expansion is due largely to accountability measures that require students to pass tests before they're promoted to the next grade. "Powerful national movements to end the automatic promotion of students who aren't ready for the next grade and to hold all students to stricter academic standards have converged to swell the ranks of summer school" (Gewertz, 2000, p. 1). Currently 27 percent of school districts have some type of mandatory summer program for failing students, and this number is likely to become larger with the increased emphasis on testing and accountability (Gewertz, 2000). In the summer of 2000, 650,000 students in New York—nearly one-fourth of the district's enrollment—were enrolled in summer school, a sevenfold increase over 1999. Detroit expected a four-fold increase from 1999 to 2000 (Gewertz, 2000). What is not known is what effect programs like this will have on student learning.

Class Scheduling

Schools are also experimenting with different class schedules, particularly in middle schools and high schools. One experiment is **block schedules,** which *increase the length of classes*, often doubling typical periods. The basic purpose behind block scheduling is to minimize disruptions caused by bells and transitions and to provide teachers with not only extended periods of time for teaching but also greater flexibility. Block schedules work especially well in areas like science, home economics, and art, where labs and projects often take longer to complete than the traditional 50-minute period.

Different forms of block schedules exist. For instance, the school year for most high schools is organized into two semesters, and students typically take six classes a day, each of which is about 50–55 minutes in length. A popular variation is called a **four-by-four block schedule,** in which *students take four classes a day, each of which is approximately 90–100 minutes in length*. Courses that took a year in the traditional system are completed in one semester in the four-by-four plan. In an **alternating-day block schedule,** *classes are approximately 90–100 minutes long, students take eight classes a semester, and classes meet* *every other day.* A student's Algebra II class, for example, could meet on Monday, Wednesday, and Friday of one week, Tuesday and Thursday of the next week, Monday, Wednesday, and Friday of the third week, and so on. Like other experiments with school time, the educational benefits of block scheduling are not clear.

 Increasing Understanding 2.4

Is block scheduling likely to be more effective for high-SES (socio-economic status) or for low-SES students? Explain.

Putting Reform into Perspective

Reformers who advocate longer school days, longer school years, or both, commonly point to two sources of information. One is the cross-country comparisons mentioned earlier. Critics argue that one reason students in countries like Japan score higher is because they go to school longer. The second argument for increasing the school day or year is research that shows a link between time studying a subject and the amount learned (Karweit, 1989). When researchers compared elementary teachers who allocated more time to math instruction, for example, they found that their students scored higher on math achievement tests—an intuitively sensible finding. Though the link is not a strong one, there is no denying that more time does provide more opportunities for learning.

However, research indicates that teachers often fail to effectively utilize the time they now have, sometimes spending more than one-third of their class periods on noninstructional activities (Kauchak & Eggen, 1998; Karweit, 1989). If teachers better utilized the time they now have, increasing the length of days and years wouldn't be necessary, experts assert. Further, research on long-term student achievement resulting from programs such as summer school shows mixed results, causing some school leaders to question whether or not the investment in additional time and resources is worth it (Gewertz, 2000).

Block-scheduling advocates argue that time is better utilized with these schedules because students spend less time in transitions, that is, moving from one class to another and getting settled after the move. Also, teachers spend less time in noninstructional activities, such as taking roll and beginning the class. In addition, both students and teachers seem to like block schedules. Students have fewer classes for which they must prepare,

and teachers have fewer students per semester, so they get to know the students better, and they have more time for preparation.

These reforms have the potential to change your life as a teacher. For example, summer school and extended school years may result in greater pay; they'll also mean less time for vacations and alternative summer employment. Scheduling changes within the school day will also influence your planning and teaching. The teachers we've talked to about block scheduling either love it or hate it. It does provide more time for teaching, but the longer class periods can be challenging from a motivational perspective.

If teachers tend to primarily lecture, longer class periods can become mind-numbing. In addition, if teachers aren't helped in changing their instruction to better utilize the time, the end of extended periods often gets taken up by students doing homework for the next day. The key, as always, is the orientation and expertise of the teachers. Time and schedules per se do not directly affect learning; teachers who use time effectively can.

You Take a Position

Now it's your turn to take a position on the issues discussed in this section. Go to the *Education Week* Website at **http://www.edweek.com,** find "search" on the first page, and type in one of the following search terms: *school calendar* or *block schedule.* Locate a minimum of three articles on one of these topics and do the following:

1. Identify the title, author, and date of each article and then write a one-paragraph summary of each.

2. Determine if a pattern exists in the articles. (Each article—or even two of the three—suggesting that altering the school calendar is a good idea would be a pattern, for example.)

3. Take one of the two following positions:
   - The pattern suggested in the articles, if implemented, *is* likely to improve education.
   - The pattern suggested in the articles *is not* likely to improve education.

Document your position with information taken from the articles and your study of the text (including this chapter and any other chapter of the text).

To answer these questions online, go to the Take a Position Module in Chapter 2 of the Companion Website.

Increased teacher input into school deci-
sions may positively influence teacher
autonomy and professionalism, but may
pull teachers away from classrooms and
students.

boxes contain the evening's chores.) As opposed to their U.S. counterparts, Japanese teachers work a 240-day school year, but their annual salaries are only about 95 percent of what U.S. teachers make.

There are also major differences in terms of how teachers from these countries spend their time while in school (Ma, 1999; Sato & McLaughlin, 1992). For example, teachers in Japan spend about half as much time as U.S. teachers in direct classroom instruction. The rest of the time is spent in professional planning, conferring with colleagues, and helping to govern their schools. While some reformers advocate moving toward this Asian model, with its emphasis on teacher autonomy, governance, and professionalism, this takes teachers away from their first love—working with students (Lortie, 1975).

This is a real professional dilemma—not only for the profession, but for you as a teacher. At the personal level, do you want to spend more time working with students, working with other teachers on curriculum projects, or helping run the school you work in? At the professional level, greater teacher involvement in school governance is seen as one way for teachers to have greater power and autonomy, resulting in a positive move toward increased teacher professionalism (Rowan, 1994). However, more time spent in governance and working with other teachers means less time spent with students.

The other side of the coin is that teachers *do* want input into decisions that influence their professional life and resent being told to do things without being consulted. Research shows that teachers' satisfaction and their commitment to their school is dependent on their involvement in school decision making (Sergiovanni, Burlingame, Coombs, & Thurstone, 1999). When you interview for your first teaching position, you may want to ask the principal how teachers in the school are involved in decision making and then weigh the principal's response against your personal professional goals.

One of the most important aspects of taking this class is the opportunity to learn more about yourself and how you would enjoy a teaching career. With an understanding of the benefits and liabilities of the profession, you can confirm or reconsider your decision to prepare for and begin a teaching career. We encourage you to seek all the information you can at this point in your education about the nature of current and future teaching opportunities, especially ones which match your interests in working with students and teaching in content areas you're excited about. We write this chapter with this end in mind—to provide a realistic description of the teaching profession and resources you can use in your search for information as you explore a teaching career.

■ TEACHING: DEALING WITH COMPLEXITIES

What does it feel like to actually teach? What challenges do classrooms and students present? How do teachers deal with these challenges? Let's look at three teachers at different stages of their professional development who also teach at different grade levels.

Case
STUDY

Ken, an elementary teacher in a third/fourth-grade split classroom shared this incident in his teaching journal:

My class is sitting in a circle. I look up and notice that one of the girls, Sylvia, is crying. Joey, she claims, has called her a fat jerk. The rest of the students all look at me to watch my response. I consider the alternatives: send Joey into the hallway and talk to him in a few minutes; have Joey sit next to me; ask Joey to apologize; direct Sylvia to get a thick skin; ask Sylvia, "How can you solve this problem?"; send Joey to the principal; have Joey write an apology letter; ask Joey, "Why did you do this?"; ignore the situation completely; keep Sylvia and Joey in from recess for a conference; put Joey's name on the board; yell at Joey; send Sylvia and Joey into the hallway to work out the problem; tell them to return to their seats and write in their journals about the problem.

It took me about 10 seconds to run through these alternatives, and after each one I thought of reasons why it wasn't a good idea. By the time I looked up at Sylvia after this brief period of thought, she had stopped crying and was chattering away with a friend about something else. On the surface, the problem had gone away (Adapted from Winograd, 1998, p. 296).

■ ■ ■

Kerry, a first-year middle school English teacher, experienced the following management struggles on the first day back to school after a 4-day holiday (Veteran teachers will attest that students typically are wired the day before as well as the day after a long school holiday.) Kerry knew her students would be excited and she was correct—the students were excited, difficult to settle down, wild. Students chatted excitedly about their weekends and showed one another items they had brought from home, as Kerry vainly shushed and urged them to quiet down. She sensed it was going to be a long day. Finally, she got them settled down and began the day's lesson, but it was a continual struggle to keep their attention.

Throughout the day, the struggle continued. She was constantly surrounded by students who needed help or who did not listen carefully to her directions. As the day progressed, her frustration grew. By afternoon she was nearly frazzled; the students were winning. Seventh period finally arrived, and the end of the day was in sight. P.A. announcements from the office were supposed to begin the period, but they often came late, so teachers never quite knew when to begin class. Kerry waited, while the students talked noisily. Finally the announcements began. Once these were over, she gave the students a quiz on a movie they had seen. This quieted them down. However, as they finished the quiz, the noise level began to creep up. The team leader, whose class was also noisy, walked by and commented, "It's so noisy in here today, I'm going crazy myself!" When the buzzer finally sounded, indicating the day's end, Kerry had "had it"; rather than hold them after class as she had threatened earlier, she let them go, just to get rid of them.

It was, in Kerry's words, a day that nearly drove her "crazy." She was angry and frustrated. "Today they were just screwing off! All these little toys they have. Wanting to look at each other's stuff. Combs. Brushes. I should take them and hit them on the head with the stupid things! It drives you nuts." This was not one of her better days teaching (adapted from Bullough, 1989, p. 73).

■ ■ ■

Two high school student teachers are talking about their frustrations in taking attendance on the day of a special school dance held during regular class hours.

Cheryl: One boy comes in, he's dressed up. He says "I have to go to the dance." Comes in early and tells me, good kid. I'm like, "OK, that's fine Aaron." Then Kent comes in 5 minutes late. This is tall Kent, has his own band, and never lets me mark him tardy even though he's always tardy. He says, "I'm, going to the dance!" After I've already started class! "Ahem. Thank you, Kent. Please sit down." So he's wanting to leave but I can't let him go because he just interrupted my class and . . . I was so mad at him. So I say, "Do you have a ticket?" And he's like, "Well, yeah," and pulls out a ticket from the movie he went to on Friday night and I say, "No, that's not the right ticket." He wasn't . . .

Dani: What color was it?

Cheryl: Pink.

Dani: What was the color for the. . . ?

Cheryl: The other guy who was legit had a gray one. But then, then, I don't know. And I mean WHO KNOWS! I said, "You're not on my excused list" but neither was the other guy and I'm like . . .

Dani: I didn't even get an excused list! I didn't even know this dance was happening . . . I kind of heard something over the intercom (Dulude-Lay, 2000, p. 4).

■ ■ ■

What do these cases have in common? They all illustrate the bewildering and sometimes frustrating world of teaching. Why can teaching be so bewildering and frustrating? Researchers who have analyzed the management demands of teaching identified several dimensions of classroom life that make it complex and demanding (Doyle, 1986). They found that classrooms are:

■ **Multidimensional**—*large numbers of events and tasks take place.*
■ **Simultaneous**—*many things happen at once.*
■ **Immediate**—*classroom events occur rapidly.*
■ **Unpredictable**—*classroom events often take unexpected turns.*
■ **Public**—*classrooms are public places where teachers are in "fishbowls."*

Let's examine these dimensions more closely.

Multidimensional

Think about all the different roles you'll perform today. You're a student, but you might also be a parent, friend, and co-worker. Your life is multidimensional. In a similar way, at any one time there are likely to be a number of events occurring in your classroom, requiring you to perform multiple roles. While a teacher works with one group of students, other students are working on various assignments. Pull-out programs, which take students needing special help out of the classroom, cause additional logistical problems. Even when teachers try to simplify their instruction with whole-group instruction, each student has a different agenda and may be on a different page, literally and figuratively. Ken found this out when he tried to begin his lesson.

External events, like announcements, assemblies, and school functions, are the bane of teachers because they add to the complexity and also rob teachers of valuable instructional time. Kerry, Cheryl, and Dani had to rearrange their teaching around P.A. announcements and school dances. Teachers often say, "If I only had time to teach." This complaint will become more important as teachers are held increasingly accountable for their students' learning through standards and increased testing.

Simultaneous

Increasing Understanding 2.5

How are the concepts of "multidimensional" and "simultaneous" similar? Different? Which of the two is more alterable by the teacher?

Not only are classrooms multidimensional, busy places, but events in classrooms often occur at the same time. While Cheryl and Dani are trying to take roll and begin class, students come in needing immediate attention, asking questions, showing hall passes, and presenting admission slips if they were absent yesterday. While Kerry and Ken are trying to teach, management problems arise. Knowing which problem to attend to first can be challenging, if not bewildering.

Immediate

Increasing Understanding 2.6

Re-examine Table 2.1, which describes how teachers spend their time. Which of the time categories are subject to the dimension of immediacy? Explain.

We learned in Chapter 1 that teachers make somewhere between 800 and 1,500 decisions everyday. Beyond the sheer numbers, the fact that the decisions need to be made *right now* adds to the demands on the teacher. Sylvia is crying; Ken needs to do something immediately. Kent comes in with a bogus hall pass; Cheryl needs to decide immediately whether to honor it or not. Unfortunately for new teachers, the immediacy of classroom life requires split-second decision making.

Unpredictable

Every teacher plans—not only for instruction but also for management. The better ones plan extensively in an attempt to anticipate unpredictable events.

■ ■ ■

One first-grade teacher, attempting to involve students in a lesson about a story they read about shoes, brought a shoe into class. Pulling it out of a bag, she began, "What can you tell me about this shoe?" "It's red," Mike responded. The shoe was black—there was no sign of red on it anywhere!

■ ■ ■

The teacher had planned extensively, even bringing in concrete objects to illustrate ideas and themes in a story. But she hadn't planned for this response. In a similar way, neither Ken nor Cheryl and Dani could predict events that would require split-second decision making. In teaching, there is little time for thoughtful analysis and consideration of the pros and cons of alternatives as they occur. It is often easy to see after the fact what we should

Classrooms are complex places requiring split-second decision making by teachers.

have done differently, but in the heat of the moment we have to respond immediately to unanticipated events. Classrooms are exciting, unpredictable places—a major reason that people find teaching both interesting and challenging.

Public

When we teach, we teach in front of people. In a sense, we are on stage. Teachers' triumphs and mistakes occur in the public arena for all to see. And mistakes are inevitable. One of the authors, in his first year of teaching, recalls this incident.

■ ■ ■

I was having a rough time quieting my class as they worked on an assignment. After several futile attempts, I said loudly, "All right, this is it! I don't want to hear one more peep out of this class!" The class was momentarily quiet. From behind the cover of held up textbooks came a squeaky "Peep." The class watched and waited while I quickly (and publicly) sorted out my options. Finally, I smiled and said, "Very funny. Now, let's get down to work." This seemed to break the ice, and the students finally settled down. I had learned an important public lesson on ultimatums.

■ ■ ■

As we work with students, we are bound to make mistakes, and our actions can have far-reaching consequences. A teacher ignores one incident of misbehavior—an alternative that Ken considered. What does this communicate to other students—that the teacher condones calling Sylvia a fat jerk and that it's all right to verbally abuse other students? The student teacher allows one high school student to slip out of her class with a bogus pass. What will other students think (and try next time)? A fishbowl is an apt metaphor for classroom teaching; as we swim through our classroom day, not only students but other professionals watch us, as Kerry discovered when a colleague said the noise was bothering her, too.

Does your first year of teaching have to consist of a series of endless, unpredictable decisions? Yes and no. Learning to teach is an exhausting task filled with unanticipated and unpredictable events. One book about the experiences of first year teachers is aptly named *The Roller Coaster Year* (Ryan, 1992). Learning to teach, with all of its emotional ups and downs, can be like a roller coaster. Because of this, your first year will be both exhausting and overwhelming. Take solace in the fact that millions of other beginning teachers have not only survived but flourished.

The teacher-education program that you're in right now or considering entering can help in two major ways. The first is through a series of courses that will provide you with concepts—concepts like withitness and overlapping—to help you understand how experienced teachers appear to teach so effortlessly. **Withitness** is *a teacher's awareness of the multiple activities students are doing simultaneously in a classroom and the ability to communicate that awareness to them.* **Overlapping** is *being able to attend to more than one of their activities at a time.* Neither withitness nor overlapping are effortless; experienced teachers make it appear so because they are knowledgeable and good at what they're doing (Berliner, 1994).

The second way your teacher-education program can assist you in becoming a teacher is through structured clinical experiences in schools (McIntyre, Byrd, & Foxx, 1996). By observing teachers in action, by talking with them about what they're doing and why, and by interacting with students to gauge their reactions to teachers' actions, teacher-education students not only become more knowledgeable but also more skilled. By accessing the wisdom of experienced teachers and trying ideas out for yourself, you'll be able to create and define yourself as a teacher. Again, we wrote this book to assist you in this process.

■ THE MULTIPLE ROLES OF TEACHING

As we saw in previous sections, teachers perform multiple roles, which take up significant portions of a teacher's day. In this section, we analyze these multiple roles and examine implications these roles have for you, a prospective teacher.

Caring Professionals

Teachers are people who care about their students. Educational researchers have documented the importance of caring for students as a critical, central dimension of teaching (Brint, 1998; Noddings, 1992). **Caring** refers to *teachers' abilities to empathize with and invest in the protection and development of young people* (Chaskin & Rauner, 1995). Caring is more than warm, fuzzy feelings that make people kind. In addition to understanding how students *feel*, caring teachers are committed to their students' growth and development. They attempt to do their very best for the people under their care (Noddings, 1992).The importance of caring is captured in one fourth-grader's comment, "If a teacher doesn't care about you, it affects your mind. You feel like you're a nobody, and it makes you want to drop out of school" (Noblit, Rogers, & McCadden, 1995, p. 683).

To students, a teacher's ability to care is linked closely to how good a teacher he or she is. In one study, students were asked to identify characteristics of a good teacher. "Understanding student problems" and "Being kind and friendly" were rated most important (Boyer, 1995). Knowledge of content and classroom management, dimensions of teaching often cited as essential for learning, were rated as being much less important by students.

Caring is evidenced in the "people orientation" of teachers and is a major reason they go into teaching. For most teachers, a central source of satisfaction is derived from helping students grow socially and emotionally. Teachers enjoy being with students for the majority of their workday and looking after the needs of their students in a variety of ways.

Let's see what Tangia Anderson, an inner-city high school teacher, has to say about the care-giving dimension of teaching:

■ ■ ■

People ask, "Who are teachers? What does it take to be a teacher?" One reply might be, "Teachers are anyone who can put-up with children." But I would disagree!

Increasing Understanding 2.7

How does the caring dimension of teaching relate to how teachers spend their time during the day? (See Table 2.1.) In terms of this table, what are some different ways that teachers show they care? Explain.

Another person might say, "Teachers are people who couldn't survive in the business world." But again, I would disagree! I say that teachers are people who genuinely care about the students they work with (T. Anderson, personal communication, 3/7/99).

■ ■ ■

Can students tell when teachers care? Let's listen to one high school student:

■ ■ ■

Nichole: People here don't have many people to talk to. I don't. The teachers . . . some of them don't care about their students. They say, "They [administrators] want me to teach and I'm going to do it no matter what." I don't like that. I like them to say, "I'm here to teach and help you because I care." That's what I like. But a lot of them are just saying, "I'm here to teach, so I'm gonna teach." I don't think that's right.

Interviewer: Do they actually say that?

Nichole: It's more an attitude, and they do say it. Like Ms. G. She's like . . . she never says it, but you know, she's just there and she just wants to teach, but she doesn't want to explain the whole deal.

Interviewer: How do you know that?

Nichole: I could feel it. The way she acts and the way she does things. She's been here seven years and all the kids I've talked to that have had her before say, "Oooh! You have Ms. G.!" Just like that.

Interviewer: But a teacher who really cares, how do they act?

Nichole: Like Mr. P. He really cares about his students. He's helping me a lot and he tells me, "I'm not angry with you, I just care about you." He's real caring and he does teach me when he cares (Kramer & Colvin, 1991, p. 13).

■ ■ ■

Caring is important for all students; for students on the margins, it often makes the difference between success and failure, between staying in school or dropping out.

What does caring feel like in a fourth-grade classroom? Let's listen to one teacher's perspective.

■ ■ ■

I may not be on the same social studies textbook chapter as the other fourth-grade teachers, and I'll probably be late returning standardized tests to the assistant principal, but I think my kids know they're important to me. I see it in tiny, fleeting moments. I see it when a student says, "Mrs. Carkci, I wish you could come to my house for the weekend. That would be fun." I see it when a boy writes to me to ask if I will take him to the movies, or when a girl gives me a goofy smile after I've led the class down the hall taking giant, silly steps. I'm proud that a girl believes it is okay to ask, "Why in America do people speak lots of languages, while in Vietnam, they only speak one language?" Or that a boy knows I will encourage him to pursue his question, "Who invented the planets?" (Carkci, 1998, p. C3.).

■ ■ ■

Caring not only facilitates learning, it is an integral part of learning.

Caring often involves attending to the physical and emotional needs of our students. Teachers are caretakers who must continually make decisions about the needs and safety of their students. Every age group has risk factors, which the teacher needs to be aware of and closely monitor. A teacher has to be a diagnostician who can recognize the needs of students and find or develop ways to fulfill these needs. To accomplish that, teachers continually have to observe and monitor the physical, emotional, and intellectual well-being of their students. For example, one of the authors took her kindergarten students on frequent walking field trips. She felt these field trips were essential to helping her students see how schoolwork was related to the real world, but she was worried about their physical safety. To keep them together for safety, she used a rope with handle knots that the

Structured clinical experiences during your teacher-education program will provide you with opportunities to experiment with different teaching strategies and ideas.

students had to hold while walking across heavily trafficed streets on their monthly visits to the seashore. Students were told that if anyone let go of the rope, the class had to return to the school (which never happened).

Teachers often have to first take care of the immediate needs of their students in the classroom, and sometimes outside of it, before they can proceed with instruction. Students can't learn when they have pressing problems, such as hunger or safety threats, occupying their minds. Many elementary teachers keep a box of crackers or granola bars in their desks for students who, for whatever reason, didn't have breakfast that morning. Many parents, especially newcomers to the country, are unaware of free breakfast and lunch programs available to low-income families. Caring teachers go the extra mile to make sure their students' families know about and take advantage of these services.

Occasionally, teachers have to be defenders of their students' rights as well as guardians of their safety. Teachers are responsible for the physical and mental safety of their students. Maria Lopez checked on the testing status of one of her students before class and spent time after school working with the parent of another student who needed special services. If teachers don't detect these special student needs, often no one will.

Teachers must also learn the signs of abusive situations that their students might be experiencing at home or school. There are clear guidelines that require teachers to report student abuse in any context and, as we'll see in Chapter 9, teachers are legally required to report this abuse.

Child neglect is an increasing form of abuse that teachers also need to guard against. Several years ago, one of the sixth-grade students in our colleague's class came to school with his pajamas in his backpack. He showed them to his teacher at the end of the school day and asked her not to send him home on the bus, explaining that he wasn't safe at home. Our colleague acted quickly to protect the student by following established procedures. Many abused or neglected students who face emotional or physical abuse at home do not inform their teachers of their personal circumstances, which makes recognition of abuse a difficult, but critical function of a teacher's caretaking role.

Increasing Understanding 2.8

In Chapter 1 we found that knowledge was an essential element of professionalism. How does teacher knowledge affect teachers' ability or capacity to provide care?

The protection of students' rights at school is another dimension of caring that teachers may face when other staff or volunteers make inappropriate decisions. For example, while working in K–12 schools, we have seen staff deny services to students based on their existing placement in one special program. If we had not brought it to the administration's attention that students are entitled to and need *all* the services for which they are qualified, placement in additional, needed programs would not have occurred.

Students with diverse backgrounds, such as English-as-a-Second-Language learners and those with exceptional abilities, are sometimes overlooked or ignored in schools. Teachers are in a unique situation to defend these students' rights to receive the best education a school can provide for them. Teacher caring takes many forms.

Creator of Productive Learning Environments

The design of learning environments that promote student growth and development is the second most important function teachers perform. With the knowledge that students learn best when they enjoy and are involved in learning activities, teachers need to create productive and interesting learning situations.

Motivating students to learn within and outside of their class can be a challenging task. Tangia Anderson, a teacher in a large urban high school, comments,

■ ■ ■

Increasing Understanding 2.9

Identify at least two functions of a teacher that Tangia demonstrated while fostering motivation in her students.

This means we have to dig deep down inside and reach for new strategies and teaching methods that relate to what our students have to face day to day when they are not in a school environment. We often have a student or groups of students who make teaching a challenge. The best thing to remember is to continue to provide a meaningful lesson for the entire class. The student or students who are challenging the teacher may want to use a different strategy. My immediate goal is to get the students participating without making a big issue. For example, in teaching students how to type without looking at their fingers, I always had students that were not motivated to learn the keyboard. So I made the typing assignment like a racing game and told the students to see if they could type without looking at their fingers while racing their classmates. The first three times I participated in the race and then I noticed that my previously idle students started typing to see if they could win. Before I knew it, they were racing with the class and I didn't say a word. Next time we did it, they wanted to start the next race (T. Anderson, personal communication, 3/23/99).

■ ■ ■

In working with students, actions speak louder than words. Tangia comments on the importance of teacher modeling.

■ ■ ■

Increasing Understanding 2.10

Explain how withitness and overlapping relate to the following dimensions of teaching discussed earlier in the chapter: multidimensional, simultaneous, and immediate.

Effective teachers model the expected behaviors or outcomes they want their students to know or learn. Times have long changed from "Do as I say and not as I do," because students will often do the opposite. They will do exactly what they see. When a teacher models for his or her students, students see that the teacher believes in what he or she is doing and the teacher really wants the student to understand the concept or idea. From day one in the classroom, I try to demonstrate the expected behaviors and attitudes I want my students to have. For example, respect for others is an important value I try to teach in my classes. When I teach, I use, as well as visually provide, positive words on the board for my students to use when talking with others and I consciously avoid negative words. Respect for other people's feelings is important and I want my students to know that we can communicate in a positive way to get what we need accomplished without being negative (T. Anderson, personal communication, 5/28/99).

■ ■ ■

Caring teachers attend to the physical and emotional needs of their students.

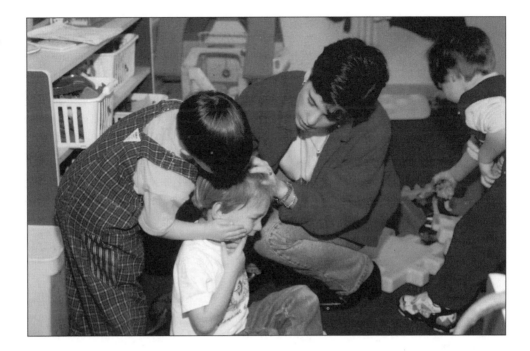

Handling students' different needs in a class can be complex and challenging, similar to juggling. To keep lesson momentum and make the constant transitions required both within and between lessons, teachers need both withitness and overlapping (Kounin, 1970). While we observed Tangia teaching, we saw her use both withitness and overlapping in one of her classes.

Case STUDY

Tangia stood in the hallway just outside her classroom door, monitoring students during the passing period as they moved to their next class. In a warm tone, she greeted each student who entered her class with "Good morning." While greeting students, Tangia also monitored the activities of students who had already entered her classroom. Her students settled into their seats before the next bell rang. Students often asked her questions as they entered the classroom. As Tangia monitored both places and listened to her students, she noticed one student approach her desk, which was at the back of the classroom, away from the lesson area. The student eyed a candy jar that was on Tangia's desk along with other personal items, including a gift that had been placed there the previous period. When the student turned back to see if Tangia was watching, he found her looking right at him as she answered questions in the doorway. The student waited a few seconds until she was done speaking, then pointed at her candy jar and said, "Mrs. Anderson, can I have one of these?" Tangia saw the opportunity to address the student's sloppy attire, which was evident in his slouching pants and untucked shirt. She responded, "Yes, if you tuck in your shirt," which the student did with a smile as he took a piece of candy and went to his seat. When the passing-period bell rang, Tangia proceeded to the front of her class and began her lesson (T. Anderson, personal communication, 1/17/99).

To begin, Tangia pointed to a chart of "Acceptable Business Phrases" at the front of her class and discussed various contexts in which the different expressions should be

Increasing Understanding 2.11

Teachers have to make quick decisions while teaching and doing the many duties they are assigned. Analyze Tangia's response to the student who requested candy at her desk. How does it illustrate caring? How does it illustrate withitness and overlapping?

Increasing Understanding 2.12

How was caring illustrated in this teaching episode?

used. Students had to identify those different contexts on the phone, using voice tone and vocabulary to judge the state of mind and response of the persons they called. Tangia asked students to identify words and tones that indicated receptivity by the call receiver, versus those which might be indicators of nonreceptivity. To illustrate the difference she asked, "How could you tell my receptivity when you entered class? The students' responded, "You greeted us when we came in and said 'Good morning' in a friendly voice."

In response to "How might an unwelcome call receiver sound?" several students raised their hands. Tangia called on one student and patiently waited while he slowly collected his thoughts and then gave a response. Two males and one female started talking over the selected student, interfering with his response. Tangia silently pointed at each of the interrupters to indicate the need for their silence and patience. When the first student had finished his response, Tangia then called on another student who had been waiting silently with a raised hand. The lesson continued with students calling each other on actual business phones in their classroom, using hypothetical scripts to pose simulated problems (T. Anderson, personal communication, 4/28/99).

■ ■ ■

By actively involving students in realistic problem solving, Tangia is ensuring that the students' school world is preparing them for the real world.

Teachers often have to struggle with overcrowded classrooms and inadequate resources. Resourceful teachers find the means for accomplishing challenging teaching tasks, such as finding materials for concrete demonstrations of a concept or volunteers to assist with classroom activities. Tangia Anderson's resourcefulness can be seen in her classroom, where she creates lessons for her business-education students with real business equipment, such as the central telephone system that was donated by a local business. This required numerous calls and visits to corporate offices in her city, but it paid off in increased learning and motivation.

Resourcefulness is an essential quality of teachers, especially now that there is an emphasis on students' learning content by constructing their own ideas through problem solving with concrete objects. One of the authors was told by a principal that he was hired largely because the principal was impressed with his resourcefulness; during his interview, the author had explained how a leftover lobster dinner had become the focal point of a productive language arts lesson during a teaching internship.

Ambassador to the Public

Another important role that teachers perform is "ambassador to the public"; they are representatives of the school in which they teach. To the public, teachers *are* the school; they represent the closest human link to their children's education. When parents gauge the quality of their children's schools, only safety is rated as more important than teacher quality (Olson, 1999). Teachers are constantly scrutinized by the public eye and discussions about their perceived competence are continual. Unfortunately, sometimes this public scrutiny can be not only critical but negative (Allison, 1995; Bullough & Baughman, 1997). To respond to potential criticism, teachers need to know how to demonstrate publicly the positive accomplishments that they and their students are making in schools. This communicates to parents that they are on the same team, with students' learning and well-being foremost in their minds.

Learning is a cooperative venture, and teachers, students, and parents are in it together. In a comprehensive review of factors affecting student learning, researchers concluded the following:

■ ■ ■

Increasing Understanding 2.13

Take each of the positive outcomes from greater home–school cooperation and explain how parents could potentially influence each.

Because of the importance of the home environment to school learning, teachers must also develop strategies to increase parent involvement in their children's academic life. This means teachers should go beyond traditional once-a-year parent/teacher conferences and work with parents to see that learning is valued in the home. Teachers should encourage parents to be involved with their children's academic pursuits on a day-to-day basis, helping them with homework, monitoring television viewing, reading to their young children, and simply expressing the expectation that their children will achieve academic success (Wang & Walberg, 1993, pp. 278–279).

■ ■ ■

Communication with parents or other primary caregivers is not an appendage to the teaching process; it is an integral part of the teacher's job.

Students benefit from home–school cooperation in at least four ways (Cameron & Lee, 1997; Epstein, 1990):

- Higher academic achievement.
- More positive attitudes and behaviors.
- Better attendance rates.
- Greater willingness to do homework.

These positive outcomes result from parents' increased participation in school activities, their more positive attitudes about schooling, and teachers' increased understanding of learners' home environments (Weinstein & Mignano, 1993). Responding to a student's unresponsive behavior is easier, for example, when his teacher knows that his mother or father has just lost a job, his parents are going through a divorce, or there's a serious illness in the family.

Barriers to Parental Involvement   Involving parents in the education of their children is a desired goal, but it doesn't happen automatically. Economic, cultural, and language barriers are often difficult to overcome. Understanding is a first step in resolving these difficulties.

Effective teachers create productive learning environments that motivate students to learn.

Economic barriers. Communication and involvement take time, and economic commitments often come first out of necessity. First among these is employment; holding two and even three jobs often prevents parents from helping their children with homework (Ellis, Dowdy, Graham, & Jones, 1992). Often parents lack economic resources, such as child care, transportation, and telephones, that would allow them to participate in school activities. Parents want to be involved in their children's schooling, but schools need to be flexible and provide help and encouragement.

Cultural barriers. Discontinuities between students' home cultures and the culture of the school can also be barriers to home–school cooperation (Delgado-Gaiton, 1992; Harry, 1992). Students may come from homes where the parents experienced schools that were very different from the ones their children have to cope with. Also, some parents may have only gone through the elementary grades or may have had negative school experiences. One researcher described the problem this way:

■ ■ ■

Underneath most parents is a student—someone who went to school, sometimes happily, sometimes unhappily. What often happens when the parent-as-adult returns to school, or has dealings with teachers, is that the parent as child/student returns. Many parents still enter school buildings flooded with old memories, angers, and disappointments. Their stomachs churn and flutter with butterflies, not because of what is happening today with their own children, but because of outdated memories and past behaviors (Rich, 1987, p. 24).

■ ■ ■

Parents like these may require encouragement and support if they are to become involved.

Language barriers. Language can be another potential barrier to effective home–school cooperation. Parents of bilingual students often do not speak English; this makes home–school communication more difficult. In these situations, the child often has the responsibility of interpreting the message. Homework poses a special problem because parents are unable to interpret assignments or provide help (Delgado-Gaiton, 1992).

Schools often compound the problem by using educational jargon when they send home letters. The problem is especially acute in special education, where legal and procedural safeguards can be bewildering. For example, parents often don't understand Individualized Education Plans or even remember that they've signed one (Harry, 1992). Many parents feel ill-prepared to assist their children with school-related tasks, but suggestions from school describing specific strategies in the home can be effective in bridging the home–school gap (Gorman & Balter, 1997; Hoover-Dempsey, Bassler, & Burow, 1995).

Strategies for Involving Parents The National Parent Teacher Association (PTA) has issued standards for parent/family involvement programs (see Table 2.2). These standards emphasize the central role that parents and caregivers play in their children's education. In addition they suggest broad, comprehensive ways that parents can be involved in their children's schools.

Virtually all schools have formal communication channels; these may include interim progress reports, which tell parents about their children's achievement at the midpoint of each grading period, open houses, during which teachers introduce themselves and describe general guidelines and procedures, parent–teacher conferences, and, of course, report cards. Although these schoolwide processes are valuable, as an individual teacher, you can do more to enhance the communication process in several ways.

■ Send home a letter at the beginning of the school year describing your expectations and how parents can assist in their children's learning. Enlist the aid of students, other teachers, or parents to translate the letter into students' home language.

Increasing Understanding 2.14

In what types of educational settings—urban, rural, suburban—are teachers most likely to encounter barriers to greater parent involvement? What implications might this have for you as a first-year teacher?

Table 2.2	**National Parent Teacher Association Standards for Parent/Family Involvement Programs**
Standard I	Communication between home and school is regular, two-way, and meaningful.
Standard II	Parenting skills are promoted and supported.
Standard III	Parents play an integral role in assisting student learning.
Standard IV	Parents are welcome in the school, and their support and assistance are sought.
Standard V	Parents are full partners in the decisions that affect children and families.
Standard VI	Community resources are used to strengthen schools, families, and student learning.

Source: From National Parent Teacher Association, (2000). *Standards for Parent/Family Involvement Programs.* [Online]. Available: *http://www.pta.org/programs/INVSTAND.* Reprinted by permission.

- Maintain communication by sending students' work home frequently. Short notes describing upcoming topics and projects along with ways that parents can assist their children communicate caring as well as create a learning partnership with the parents or caregivers.

- Invite parents and caregivers to visit your classroom and contact you if they have questions or concerns.

- Involve parents in school activities by inviting them in to talk about their occupations and asking them to participate in activities like band, chorus, sports and booster clubs.

One first year teacher had this experience in calling parents:

■ ■ ■

I started [calling] because I had some kids right off who really had trouble. So, I felt like I needed to call just so they wouldn't get totally lost so soon. I had to deal with them, somehow. I really like parent/teacher conferences a lot, [but] I've discovered that a phone call is just as good. I've been getting [very] positive feedback from . . . parents. Like, "Oh, I'm so glad you called. Not one teacher called me ever last year. He had so much trouble." I just . . . decided I'm going to call a couple of parents every night. It's really [having] a positive [effect on] what's happening in the classroom. I'm also going to call some parents for positive reasons. There are some kids who really deserve to have a teacher call and say [something good] (Bullough, 1989, p. 112).

■ ■ ■

Increasing Understanding 2.15

Refer to Table 2.1. Identify an additional barrier to increased home–school cooperation. What are some things teachers can do to overcome this barrier?

Research shows that parents want to be involved in their children's education (Elam, Rose, & Gallup, 1995). Teachers can capitalize on this by providing opportunities for parents to learn about and participate in their children's education.

Technology provides another channel for improving communication. A voice-mail system, for example, allows teachers and parents to communicate despite their busy schedules (Cameron & Lee, 1997). One voice-mail system, called the Bridge Project, enables teachers to post daily assignments and reminders about things like field trips on a bulletin board that parents can access 24 hours a day, 7 days a week.

Collaborative Colleague

As we saw earlier, a significant portion of a teacher's time (almost 26 percent) is spent working with peers. Teachers need to be team players as well as colleagues with the other teachers in their schools. They work together cooperatively in committees to accomplish many tasks for their students, school, and district in order to make their instruction more effective and their school a better place in which to learn. Collaboration skills are important for educators in all levels of education. Part of the administrative evaluation of teachers, starting at their job interview, focuses on these collaboration skills. In fact, some

58

Reflect *on* This

PARENT–TEACHER CONFERENCES

You are a first-year teacher in an inner-city middle school, it's mid-October, and you just survived your first parent–teacher conferences. For 2 days you sat in the school gym with all the other middle school teachers waiting for parents to come and talk to you about their son or daughter. There are 147 students in the school, yet only 33 parents showed up. Where were the other 114? You sent notes home with all your students but noticed a number of these in the wastebasket. Unfortunately, the majority that did show up were parents of A and B students wanting to know how they could help their children learn better. Only two parents of failing students came, and none of the parents or guardians of your ESL students were there. You're discouraged, especially since other teachers seemed to have a better turnout.

1. What are some possible reasons that more parents didn't come to talk with you?
2. What might you have done differently prior to the conferences?
3. What can you do now to establish better linkages to your students' homes?

Ⓦ *To answer these questions online and receive immediate feedback, go to the Reflect on This Module in Chapter 2 of the Companion Website.*

administrators evaluate teachers by counting the number of committees in which they are productive members!

Students who are considering a career in teaching might want to ask themselves the following question:

■ ■ ■

Am I the kind of person willing and able to enter a profession subject to all kinds of pressures, criticisms, and calls for change, secure as I can be at my stage of the game that besides being responsible for the education of students in my classroom, I have a responsibility to gain a voice in whatever decisions are made that affect the school as a social-education organization (Sarason, 1993, p. 6).

■ ■ ■

To be productive, especially in a group where some teachers disagree with others' recommendations for action, teachers have to be skilled negotiators and collaborators. In their interactions with colleagues, students, and parents, they have to be confident communicators. If you have not had experience in voicing your opinions in small and large meetings, you will need to learn that skill as a teacher. In addition, having accurate and current information is needed to support your claims and position in professional discussions.

Learner and Reflective Practitioner

Teachers need to learn and grow throughout their careers. As professional educators, teachers must continually update current information for the content of their courses, as well as research about improved methods of instruction. "A professional is someone who has something to profess. Your obligation to yourself and your profession is to know what is going on, that is, what others are experiencing, studying and writing" (Sarason, 1993, p. 138). Teachers need to continually update their "knowledge of students, conceptions of learning, pedagogical content knowledge, and knowledge of goals and curriculum" (Hillocks, 1999, p. 109).

All the important teacher functions previously discussed require an accurate and current information base. Tangia Anderson reflects on the learning dimension of teaching:

■ ■ ■

As a teacher, I continually look for new ways of reaching and teaching my students. Learning how to become a more effective teacher is a good feeling. To be a teacher, you

Increasing Understanding 2.16

Ⓦ Would the role of collaborative colleague be greater at the elementary or secondary level? How might the kinds of peer interactions change at each of these levels?

Teachers serve as ambassadors to parents, helping them understand how schools can help their children learn.

want to continue learning new ways to keep lessons interesting, manage your classroom, assist other teachers, and communicate effectively with parents. When teachers learn new ways to make their lessons more meaningful, they enjoy teaching (T. Anderson, personal communication, 5/27/99).

■ ■ ■

Teachers need to reflect continually on their practice and on the information they learn. Asking questions of your practice may be the most significant thing you can do to make yourself a better teacher.

Being a **reflective practitioner** means *constantly evaluating the effectiveness of your practice.* Self-reflection as a teacher is the first step to understanding one's practice, enabling you to see how it might be modified for improvement (Palmer, 1998). Reflective journaling, where we document our successes, challenges, and needs as teachers, is a useful reflection device. Feedback from other educators who have read and written informative responses to your reflections can provide valuable insights about your teaching. That's why we encourage you to keep a journal as you progress through this course. Reflection on practice prepares teachers in advance for their various decision-making functions by making them aware of the different decisions they've made and the outcomes of those decisions.

Increasing Understanding 2.17

How does reflection relate to the different dimensions of professionalism—which include a specialized body of knowledge, extended training for licensure, autonomy, and ethical standards— that were discussed in Chapter 1?

■ WHO WILL YOU WORK WITH?

In this section of the chapter, we examine the teaching workforce. Knowledge of teacher demographics can be helpful to you in several ways. First, it gives you a snapshot of your colleagues—the people you'll be working with. In addition, it can provide insight into possible job opportunities. For example, male and female minority teachers as well as male teachers at the elementary and preschool levels are in short supply. These teachers will be actively recruited when they graduate from college.

In 1996 there were 3.1 million teachers in the United States, with slightly less than 90 percent of these teaching in public schools (NCES, 1997). To place this figure into

60

**Increasing
Understanding 2.18**

The teacher–student
ratio is often cited as
one index of the quality of a
school district and the quality of a teacher's work life.
How does the high percentage of support personnel
affect this? What are the
advantages and disadvan-
tages of reducing the percentage of administrators
and support staff?

perspective, the number of K–12 teachers represents 2.1 percent of the total U.S. workforce, which is slightly lower than in other industrialized countries. Surprisingly, teachers
comprise only 52.1 percent of the total school staff, with the remainder consisting of
administrators and support staff (for example, secretaries, janitors, and other instructional staff like counselors and school psychologists).

In contrast, teachers comprise more than three-fourths of all public-education employees in Japan, Belgium, and Italy and more than 60 percent in most other industrialized countries (Darling-Hammond, 1998). One comparison between Riverside, California, and Zurich,
Switzerland, two districts with approximately the same number of students, revealed that
Zurich had almost twice as many teachers (2,330 versus 1,223). Critics contend that U.S.
schools are top-heavy, with too many resources going to bloated bureaucracies.

The number of new teachers needed is projected to increase by 4 percent each year
until the year 2009 (NCES, 1997). This increase will result from a number of factors,
including increases in the K–12 student population, increased expenditures for education,
attempts to decrease class sizes, and the reform movements you read about in Chapter 1.
You've all experienced the teaching profession from the other side of the teacher's desk.
Let's see how accurate your perceptions are of the "average" teacher.

A Demographic Profile of the Teaching Force

1. Approximately what percentage of the teaching force is male?
    a. 10%
    b. 25%
    c. 35%
    d. 50%

2. How old is the average teacher?
    a. 25
    b. 35
    c. 45
    d. 55

3. Approximately what percentage of the teaching force is minority?
    a. 5%
    b. 10%
    c. 15%
    d. 20%

4. New teachers, directly out of college, differ from the rest of the teaching force. They are:
    a. Younger, more likely to be female, less likely to be minority, and less likely to be
       married.
    b. Younger, less likely to be female, less likely to be a minority, and less likely to be
       married.
    c. Younger, more likely to be female, more likely to be minority, and less likely to
       be married.
    d. Younger, more likely to be female, less likely to be minority, and more likely to
       be married.

Read the following sections to see how accurate your perceptions are.

Gender

Most teachers are female, a historical trend since the 1800s. At one time, the percentage of
female teachers reached 85 percent, but today the figure is closer to 74 percent. This figure is

**Increasing
Understanding 2.19**

How could a begin-
ning teacher use the
information in Table 2.3 to
maximize the possibility of
obtaining a teaching position? What are the advan-
tages and disadvantages of
this strategy?

Table 2.3	Public School Teachers' Gender by Assignment	
Area	Female	Male
Elementary	91	9
Math/Science	52	48
Social Studies	38	62
English/Language Arts	80	20
Special Education	84	16

Source: From *America's Teachers: Profile of a Profession, 1993–1994,* National Center for Education Statistics, 1997, Washington, DC: U.S. Department of Education.

The ability to communicate ideas and work collaboratively with colleagues are essential teacher skills.

higher than in most industrialized countries, where the average is around 65 percent (NCES, 1997). As we can see from Table 2.3, this percentage varies considerably by grade level and content area. The highest percentage of females is found at the elementary level and in English/language arts and special education. The highest percentage of male teachers is found in social studies and in math/science. Interestingly, despite attempts to attract males to the elementary level, the percentage of males there has not changed significantly in the last 10 years. At the preschool level, the percentage of males is even lower; less than 5 percent of early childhood teachers and caregivers are male (Galley, 2000).

Age

The teaching population is aging; this may have major implications for prospective teachers. In 1993, the average age of school teachers was 43, with proportionally more older teachers in high-demand areas like math and science (Darling-Hammond & Sclan, 1996). The average teacher had more than 15 years of teaching experience and more than

Increasing Understanding 2.20

What are some possible reasons for the decline in the percentage of minority teachers? Is the percentage of minority teachers likely to increase or decrease in the future? Why?

MINORITY TEACHERS AND WHAT THEY BRING TO THE PROFESSION

As the number of minority students in U.S. schools continues to grow, attempts to recruit minority teachers have also increased. Nearly one-third of school-age children in the United States are cultural minorities, compared to only 12 percent of the teaching force (Archer, 2000). Efforts to recruit greater numbers of minority teachers include early recruitment programs aimed at high schoolers, specially targeted scholarship programs, and programs designed to attract older, career-changing minorities.

Why all this interest and effort? What do minority teachers bring to classrooms that is so important? Researchers attempting to answer this question have focused on three areas:

- The need for minority role models.
- The need for effective instructors.
- The need for alternative perspectives.

Let's look at these areas.

Minorities as Role Models

Research clearly indicates that effective role models increase motivation and learning for all children (Bruning et al., 1999; Schunk, 2000). This is particularly important for cultural minorities. Minority teachers demonstrate to minority students that success and professional status are attainable for all people—including cultural minorities. Equally important, they demonstrate that being successful doesn't detract in any way from their cultural identity. For example, a study of Yup'ik Eskimo students in rural Alaska found that the tribe was losing its native language because young children either were not interested in the language or were ashamed of speaking it (Lipka, 1998). The presence of a native Yup'ik teacher reversed the pattern.

We lived right next to the school, and my sister lived with us for the year. We spoke only Yup'ik all of the time, so by the end of the year many of the students were no longer ashamed either to speak, or learn to speak, Yupik. My husband and I felt we had really done something good for those students because they began to identify themselves as Yup'ik and acquired their own language (Lipka, 1998, p. 50).

The importance of modeling is also demonstrated by the fact that many minority teachers say that minority teachers in *their* past were powerful influences on their decision to choose teaching as a career (Gordon, 1993; Toppin & Levine, 1992). Minority students begin believing that they too can succeed academically and become teachers when they see successful minority adult role models.

Minorities as Effective Instructors

Researchers also suggest that minority teachers may bring increased understanding of minority students' backgrounds and needs to learning activities (Villegas, 1991). For example, in a study of instructional styles, effective African American teachers used standard English to give directions and regulate behavior, but used "performances," stylized ways of speaking that resembled African American preaching styles, to motivate students during lessons (Foster, 1992).

As another example, in the study of Yupik instruction mentioned earlier, a Yupik teacher used an interdisciplinary unit on smelting, or drying fish for the winter, as a means to teach geography, science, mathematics, sanitation, family traditions, and cultural values (Lipka, 1998). Students took part in smelting in the classroom through observation, practice, and teaching other students. There was a high degree of interest and participation because the unit was relevant to the students' lives and culture.

Minority Teachers Bring Unique Perspectives to the Profession

Minority teachers also bring valuable alternative perspectives to teaching. Many minority teachers view teaching as a "calling" in which they have opportunities to work with and help minority students (Gordon, 1993). For example, one Chicana student teacher reported, "I began my student teaching experience thinking that minority students had to be saved from a harsh and cruel world which was existent in the schools. Consequently, when I saw the faces of many minority students, I set out to make a difference in their lives" (Kauchak & Burbank, 2000, p. 6). This commitment permeated the teacher's work with students, making her an important advocate for her students.

Minority teachers also help other teachers understand minority students and assist them in looking at the world in different ways. Because they come from minority homes and communities, they can become effective spokespersons for these students (Gordon, 1993; Kauchak & Burbank, 2000; Toppin & Levine, 1992).

Unquestionably, minority students need role models with whom they can identify. Further, diversity and the perspectives people from different backgrounds provide have always been one of our country's strengths. However, all teachers can be role models and effective instructors for African American, Hispanic, Native American, Asian students or other minority students. Further, any intelligent and sensitive teacher can design meaningful interdisciplinary units for their students, such as the one on drying fish that was described earlier.

Just as student diversity can enrich learning for every student, diversity among teachers can add perspectives that make every teacher more effective. The key is professionalism, which is also one of the themes of this book. Professionals—minority and nonminority—have a shared vision; they communicate with and learn from each other; and they're committed to providing the best for all students, not just those whose ethnic and cultural backgrounds are similar to their own.

New Teachers

In 1998, 200,545 new teachers graduated from college, a whopping 49 percent increase from 1983. How do new teachers differ from the existing teacher pool? The answer is more complex than at first glance because the pool of "new" teachers includes newly graduated teachers (approximately 34 percent of the total), recently graduated candidates who delayed entry into teaching (19 percent), persons re-entering the teaching force (30 percent),

and transfers from other teaching positions (17 percent)(Darling-Hammond & Sclan, 1996). So, when you go to the orientation meeting at your first school, only 53 percent of the people at the meeting will have never taught; the other 47 percent will be transfers and re-entries into the profession.

Market forces both within and outside of education influence the mix of people entering the teaching profession. For example, during the 1980s teaching positions were harder to find, leading many new teachers to accept positions in business and other occupations. During the 1990s, as the demand for more teachers increased, the profession saw more delayed entrants and re-entrant teachers.

How do newly graduated or "newly minted" teachers compare to the existing teaching force? They are more likely to be female (79 percent versus 74 percent for the total teaching force), white (91 percent versus 87 percent), and younger (28 years old versus 43 years old) (Darling-Hammond & Sclan, 1996). An increasing number of students are entering teacher-education programs after they've graduated from college (Bradley, 1999). These post-baccalaureate students tend to be older—around 30—and are more likely to be male than are students in undergraduate programs. In response to this demand, 65 percent of teacher-education programs have special programs for these post-baccalaureate students; approximately 9 percent admit only students who have already graduated from college.

These characteristics are important because they will help to shape the teaching force for the twenty-first century. This teaching force will be your colleagues, the people whom you'll spend significant portions of your school day working with. When you interview for your first teaching position, make a special effort to meet your potential colleagues. They can provide valuable insights into the school you'll be working in as well as help you decide whether your work with them will be productive and enjoyable.

 Increasing Understanding 2.21

Think about the class you're in now. Does this national profile match your class? What factors might account for differences?

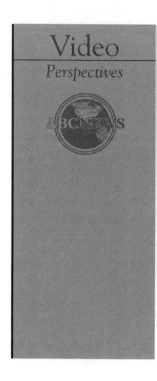

TEACHER SHORTAGE

This ABC News video segment explores the recent teacher shortage from the perspectives of Bob Chase, President of the National Education Association (NEA), and Vicki Rafel of the National Parent Teacher Association (NPTA). Low salaries along with a lack of mentoring and support for beginning teachers are identified as critical reasons for the shortage. Other factors involved, but not discussed, include an aging teacher workforce, a growing student population, and reforms dictating lower student–teacher ratios.

Think about This

1. How might the challenges of the multiple roles of teaching contribute to the teacher shortage?

2. How might the current teacher shortage influence the age, gender, and race–ethnicity of the teaching force?

3. How might the current teacher shortage influence the current profile of "new teachers"?

4. What actions could policy makers take to alleviate the current teacher shortage?

Ⓦ *To answer these questions online and receive immediate feedback, go to the Video Perspectives Module in Chapter 2 of the Companion Website.*

Minority teachers serve as effective role models for minority youth and bring unique and valuable perspectives to teaching.

47 percent held master's degrees or higher (NCES, 1997). Only 13 percent of the teaching force had fewer than 3 years of experience, 65 percent had 10 years or more, and 34 percent had 20 or more years. The aging teaching population, combined with projected increases in the K–12 student population, has resulted in predictions that more than 200,000 new teachers will need to be hired annually for the next decade (Bradley, 1999b).

Race–Ethnicity

The majority (87 percent) of U.S. teachers are White, with the largest numbers of minority teachers being either African American (8 percent) or Hispanic (4 percent). The percentage of minority teachers has declined slightly in recent years, a trend that has many educators concerned because the percentage of minority youth in our schools is steadily increasing. One-third of all public school students in the United States are of African American, Asian, or Hispanic descent. The proportion of students from non-European backgrounds approaches 90 percent in many large urban areas (Darling-Hammond, 1996).

■ SUMMARY

Teaching: A Time Perspective
Teachers work within time frameworks. The school year typically consists of a 180-day period, although this is changing in many areas with year-round schooling and summer school. Teachers' workweeks are slightly longer than the national 40-hour norm; much of this additional time is spent outside of the classroom and school. During the school day, teachers spend the majority of their time working with students, but peer interactions and deskwork also take up significant chunks of teachers' days.

Teaching: Dealing with Complexities
The complexity of teaching is influenced by several characteristics or dimensions of classroom life. Classrooms are multidimensional, with many events occurring immediately and simultaneously. In addition, classroom life is also public and unpredictable. These aspects of the classroom make learning to teach both challenging and rewarding.

The Multiple Roles of Teaching
Teachers assume multiple roles, the most important being caring professionals. Teachers demonstrate caring through promoting student development and protecting their students' welfare. Teachers are also instructors who create productive learning environments.

Three teacher functions occur outside the immediate classroom. As ambassadors to the public, teachers communicate classroom accomplishments and help create effective home–school linkages. As collaborative colleagues, they work with other teachers to make their schools more effective. As a learner and reflective practitioner, they continue their professional growth throughout their careers.

Who Will You Work With?
The currently aging teaching force has implications for beginning teachers. As more teachers retire, a number of teaching-position openings will occur. The typical U.S. teacher is White, female, and 43 years old. These demographics change with teaching level and location and are expected to change over time.

New teachers differ from the existing teaching force in several ways. They are more likely to be White, female, and younger. A surprisingly low number of teachers (61 percent) enter teaching immediately after graduation, and more than one out of five leaves within 5 years. Understanding who your colleagues will be can make your first teaching position more enjoyable and rewarding.

■ IMPORTANT CONCEPTS

alternating-day block schedule	multidimensional dimension of classrooms	simultaneous dimension of classrooms
block schedule	overlapping	unpredictable dimension of classrooms
caring	public dimension of classrooms	year-round schooling
four-by-four block schedule	reflective practitioner	withitness
immediate dimension of classrooms		

■ DISCUSSION QUESTIONS

1. If you could change any dimension of the way teachers spend their time (see Table 2.1), what would it be? Why?

2. Which of the proposed alternatives in terms of time—year-round schools, a longer school year, or block scheduling—have the most potential for increasing student learning? Which are most attractive to you as a prospective teacher? Which are least attractive?

3. Is teaching likely to become more or less complex in the future? Why?

4. Is the dimension of caring more important at some levels (for example, in elementary versus secondary schools) than at others? Why or why not?

5. Is the importance of teachers working with parents likely to increase or decrease in the near future? Why?

6. What are the pros and cons of considering demographic shortages (for example, males in elementary school, females in social studies) when hiring teachers?

■ VIDEO DISCUSSION QUESTIONS

The following discussion questions refer to video segments found on the Companion Website. To answer these questions online, view the accompanying video, and receive immediate feedback to your answers, go to the *Video Discussion* Module in Chapter 2 of the Companion Website at **http://www.prenhall.com/kauchak.**

1. Dr. Urie Triesman is a professor of mathematics at the University of Texas at Austin and director of the Charles A. Dana Center for Math and Science Education. He believes teachers and their professional development are central to school reform. What does Dr. Triesman believe are some concrete things teachers can do within their own schools to further their professional development? Which do you think have the most potential for furthering teachers' professional development?

2. As we saw in this chapter, involving parents is important for school success. How does Dr. Triesman believe that parents can be enlisted as political allies in school reform efforts? Which of these strategies would be most useful to you as a teacher?

3. Dr. John Goodlad is professor emeritus and co-director of the Center for Renewal at the University of Washington and president of the Independent Institute for Educational Inquiry. He believes that caring is essential to effective teaching. What does Dr. Goodlad feel are some concrete ways in which teachers can structure their classrooms to facilitate the development of caring relationships? Which of these strategies will be most useful to you as a teacher?

■ GOING INTO SCHOOLS

1. Interview a teacher concerning local experiments with time and scheduling. Ask about the existence of the following in the teacher's district:
    a. year-round schooling
    b. extended school year
    c. summer school
    d. alternate (for example, block) schedules

    How prevalent are these? How effective are they? How popular are they? Analyze the teacher's response and decide whether these experiments with time are beneficial for education.

2. Interview a teacher to find out if his or her day differs from the one depicted in Table 2.1.
    a. Are these percentages typical? If not, where are they different and why?
    b. To what extent does the teacher's time allocation fluctuate from these averages from day to day? What causes these fluctuations?
    c. If the teacher could change one aspect of the way his or her time is allocated, what would it be?

    Analyze these responses using information from this chapter.

3. Observe a teacher interacting with students and identify instances where the following dimensions of teaching occur:
    a. multidimensional
    b. simultaneous
    c. immediate
    d. unpredictable
    e. public

    Which of these appears to present the greatest challenge to teachers? Least? In a paper describe, how these different dimensions affect the professional lives of teachers.

4. Interview two teachers about the different roles of teachers (caring professional, instructor, etc.). Ask them to rank these roles in terms of importance and to explain why they ranked them the way they did. Compare the two teachers' responses in a paper and describe how their rankings differ from yours.

5. Visit a school district office or a state office of education and ask to see the statistics on the current teaching force in your area. How do they differ from the national averages? Why? Describe these differences and explain what implications these differences might have for employment opportunities for you.

If you would like to participate in a Virtual Field Experience, go to the *Field Experience* Module in Chapter 2 of the Companion Website.

■ ONLINE PORTFOLIO ACTIVITIES

To complete these activities online, go to the *Portfolio Activities* Module in Chapter 2 of the Companion Website, and submit your response.

Portfolio Activity 2.1   **Time and Learning**

INTASC Principle 7: *Planning*
Go to the *Portfolio Activities* Module for Chapter 2 of the Companion Website and click on "Time and Organization." Read the information and then write a one- or two-paragraph summary of the section. Then offer at least two specific, concrete ways in which teachers can maximize their *instructional time* and at least two specific, concrete ways in which teachers can maximize *engaged time*.

Portfolio Activity 2.2   **Caring**

INTASC Principle 2: *Learning*
INTASC Principle 5: *Motivation and Management*
Explain why a caring teacher will have students who learn more than students taught by a teacher who isn't caring. List at least four specific, concrete things teachers can do to demonstrate that they care about their students.

Portfolio Activity 2.3   **Parental Involvement**

INTASC Principle 10: *Partnership*
Write a one-page paper that explains your philosophy with respect to involving parents and caregivers in their children's education. Include in your paper:

- Why you believe parental involvement is important.
- Specific ways in which you will communicate your students' learning progress with parents or other caregivers.
- Specific ways in which you will involve parents or other caregivers.

PART 2

Students

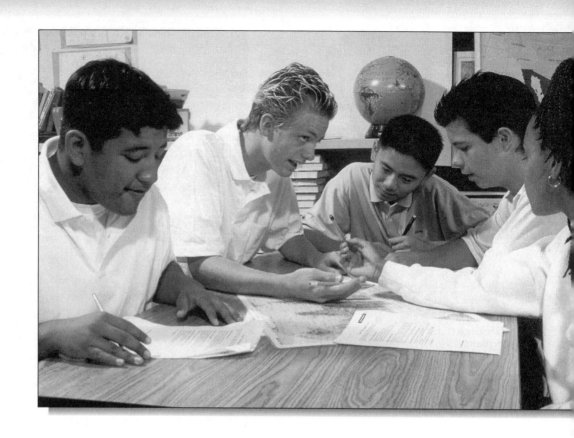

CHAPTER 3

Learner Diversity

Differences in Today's Students

Teachers begin their careers expecting to find classrooms like the ones they experienced when they were students. And in some ways, they are. Students go to school to learn, but they also want to have fun and be with their friends. They expect to work, but they often need encouragement from their teachers. They're typical kids.

However, classrooms and students are changing—the student population of our schools is becoming increasingly diverse. Students come from different cultures and speak many different languages at home; they possess a range of abilities and talents; and issues involving differences between boys and girls are receiving increased attention. In this chapter, we try to answer the following questions:

- What is cultural diversity, and how does it influence student learning?

- How are the educational experiences of boys and girls different?

- How do schools accommodate ability differences in learners?

- What are learning styles, and how should teachers respond to them?

- Who are learners with exceptionalities, and how can schools best meet their needs?

Let's examine how learner diversity influences the lives of today's teachers.

Shannon Wilson, a fifth-grade teacher in a large urban elementary school, walked around her classroom, helping her students with their social studies projects, which they were working on in small groups. A number of hands were raised, and she felt relieved that she had Maria Argalas, her special-education resource teacher, to help her. Shannon had 27 students in her class, seven of whom did not speak English as their first language. Fortunately five of the seven were Hispanic, and Maria was able to assist them in their native language when they became confused or needed help. Shannon paired the other two, Kwan and Abdul, with other students who could help them. Maria also assisted Shannon by working with four of her students who needed special-education help.

Shannon's class was preparing for Parents' Day, an afternoon when parents and other caregivers could join the class in celebrating the different countries that students came from. Student projects, focusing on these different countries, were designed to provide information about each country's history, geography, and culture. The class had been studying these different countries in social studies all year; a large world map with pins and yarn on it included a photo of each student attached to his or her country of origin. While many of the pins were clustered in Mexico and Central and South America, the map showed that there were students from all over the world. Each student had been encouraged to invite someone from his or her family to come and share a part of the family's native culture. Some were sharing food, while others were bringing music or native dress from their different homelands.

■ ■ ■

■ CULTURAL DIVERSITY

What kind of clothes do you wear? What kind of music do you like? What kind of food do you eat? These and other factors, such as religion, family structure, and values, are all part of your culture. **Culture** refers to *the attitudes, values, customs, and behavior patterns that characterize a social group* (Banks, 1997).

Culture's enormous impact is illustrated by its influence on all aspects of our lives. An activity as basic as eating is one example. For instance, culture determines what foods we eat; when we eat (such as the number of meals and at what time of the day); with whom we eat (only with others of the same gender, with children, or with the extended family); how we eat (at a table or on the floor; with chopsticks, silverware, or the fingers); and the rituals of eating (in which hand the fork is held, asking for or being offered seconds, and belching to show appreciation of a good meal). The influence of culture can also be found in people's responses to other basic needs like shelter and clothing.

Culture impacts virtually every aspect of our lives (Gollnick & Chinn, 2002), and it influences school success through the attitudes, values, and ways of viewing the world embedded in it.

An important part of culture is a person's ethnic background. **Ethnicity** refers to *a person's ancestry; the way individuals identify themselves with the nation from which they or their ancestors came* (deMarrais & LeCompte, 1999; Gollnick & Chinn, 2002). Members of an ethnic group have a common history, language (although sometimes not spoken), customs, and traditions.

Over 14 million people immigrated to the United States during the 1970s and 1980s. Between 1980 and 1994, classrooms in the United States underwent the following changes (U.S. Bureau of Census, 1996):

Figure 3.1   **Changes in School-Age Population, 2000–2020**

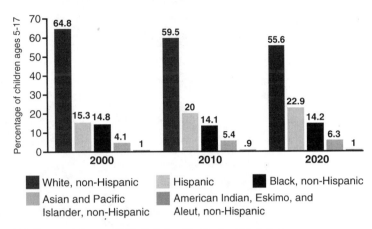

Source: Data from U.S. Bureau of Census, 1998, Statistics, Washington, DC: Author.

■ An increase in Asian American students of almost 100 percent.

■ An increase in Hispanic students of 46 percent.

■ An increase in African American students of 25 percent.

■ An increase in White students of 10 percent.

Experts estimate that by the year 2020 our country will see considerable increases in the number of Hispanic and African American students; a dramatic increase in Asian/Pacific Islander and American Indian/Alaskan Native populations will occur as well. At the same time, the White student population will decrease by 9 percent (U.S. Bureau of the Census, 1998; Young & Smith, 1999). Figure 3.1 shows some of these predicted changes. Each of these groups brings a distinct set of values and traditions that influences student learning.

Cultural Attitudes and Values

Our students come to us with a long learning history. Cultural patterns exist in their dress, family roles, interactions with parents and peers, and attitudes and values. When they enter our classrooms, they bring these attitudes and values with them. Some complement learning; others conflict with it.

Language is an example. Students are sometimes hesitant to drop the use of nonstandard English dialects in favor of "school English" because this might alienate their peers and distance their families. The same problem occurs in second-language learning. Research indicates that programs encouraging students to drop their native language in favor of English cause distancing problems with parents, many of whom cannot speak English (Wong-Fillmore, 1992).

Even school success can be an issue. To succeed in school is interpreted by some as rejecting a native culture; to become a good student is to become "White"—adopting White cultural values and rejecting their own. Students who study and become actively involved in school risk losing the friendship and respect of their peers. John Ogbu, an anthropologist who investigates minority achievement, believes that in many schools, peer values either don't support school learning or actually oppose it; students form what

The increasing cultural diversity of students provides teachers with both opportunities and challenges.

he calls "resistance cultures" (Ogbu & Simons, 1998). Low grades, management and motivation problems, truancy, and high dropout rates are symptoms of this conflict.

Cultural Interaction Patterns

Cultural conflict can occur in the interaction patterns typically found in most classrooms. Let's look at an example:

Case STUDY

A second-grade class in Albuquerque, New Mexico, was reading *The Boxcar Children* and was about to start a new chapter. The teacher said, "Look at the illustration at the beginning of the chapter and tell me what you think is going to happen." A few students raised their hands. The teacher called on a boy in the back row.

He said, "I think the boy is going to meet his grandfather."

The teacher asked, "Based on what you know, how does the boy feel about meeting his grandfather?"

Trying to involve the whole class, the teacher called on another student—one of four Native Americans in the group—even though she had not raised her hand. When she didn't answer, the teacher tried rephrasing the question, but again the student sat in silence.

Feeling exasperated, the teacher wondered if there was something in the way the lesson was being conducted that made it difficult for the student to respond. She sensed that the student she had called on understood the story and was enjoying it. Why, then, wouldn't she answer what appeared to be a simple question?

The teacher recalled that this was not the first time this had happened, and that, in fact, the other Native American students in the class rarely answered questions in class discussions. She wanted to involve them, wanted them to participate in class, but could not think of ways to get them to talk (Villegas, 1991, p. 3).

■ ■ ■

Why did this happen? One explanation suggests that Native American children are not used to the fast-paced, give-and-take patterns that characterize many American classrooms. When involved in a discussion, they were uncomfortable and, as a result, were reluctant to participate.

Another example illustrates differences between White and African American students (Heath, 1989). Teachers made directives to students such as, "Let's put the scissors away now." Accustomed to this indirect way of speaking, White students interpreted this as a command; African American students, used to more direct commands like, "Put your scissors away, now," did not. Failure to comply was then viewed as either a management or motivation problem—a result of the mismatch between home and school cultures.

Similar cultural differences also caused problems during instruction. From their home experience, White children, accustomed to using language to explore abstract relationships, knew how to answer when asked questions requiring specific answers, such as, "Where did the puppy go?" and "What's this story about?" African American children, by contrast, were accustomed to questions that were more "open-ended, story-starter" types that didn't have a single answer. In addition, African American children "were not viewed as information-givers in their interactions with adults, nor were they considered appropriate conversation partners and thus they did not learn to act as such" (Heath, 1982, p. 119). When teachers learned to use more open-ended questions in their instruction, participation of African American students increased. In addition, African American students began to understand that answering teacher questions was part of the educational game, designed to increase their involvement and learning.

Educational Responses to Cultural Diversity

Historically, different metaphors have been used to respond to cultural diversity. The "melting pot" was one of the first. The goal of the melting pot approach was **assimilation,** *a process of socializing people so they fit into the dominant social norms and patterns of behavior.* Assimilation attempted to make members of minority cultural groups "similar" to those belonging to the dominant cultural group in society—typically Whites of European descent.

The melting pot metaphor was especially popular in the early 1900s, when large numbers of immigrants from southern and eastern Europe entered the United States. Society assigned schools the task of teaching these immigrants how "Americans" were supposed to think, talk, and behave. Immigrants, eager to become "American" and share in this country's economic wealth, generally accepted these efforts.

A shift in thinking occurred in the middle of the twentieth century. People realized that the "melting pot" had never totally worked, as indicated by neighborhoods and groups that continued to speak their home languages, celebrate their unique cultural festivals, and maintain their cultural habits (such as the foods they ate). The contributions of different cultural and ethnic groups were increasingly recognized, and leaders began to realize that some educational practices aimed at assimilation were actually counterproductive. For example, in an effort to encourage English proficiency, schools in the Southwest often didn't allow students to use Spanish, even on playgrounds. Schools became hostile places where students had to choose between friends and school. In hindsight, this policy probably did as much to alienate Hispanic youth as it did to encourage English-language development.

To remedy these problems, a new educational approach to dealing with cultural diversity was developed. **Multicultural education** is *a catch-all term for a variety of strategies schools use to accommodate cultural differences and provide educational opportunities for all* *students*. The melting pot metaphor was replaced with others such as "mosaic" or "tossed salad," in which each culture's unique contributions could be recognized and valued. Multicultural education seeks to recognize and celebrate cultural differences and contributions to our American way of life.

Multicultural Controversies Multicultural education has become controversial. Critics contend that multicultural education is divisive, placing too much emphasis on differences between cultural groups rather than commonalities that bind all of us together (Schlessinger, 1992). Textbooks have been scrutinized; recently, a spokesperson for the American Textbook Council criticized modern history textbooks as emphasizing multicultural themes at the expense of basic information about history (Sewall, 2000). Conservative columnists in the popular press, such as *U.S. News and World Report* consistently criticize multiculturalism, identity politics, and political correctness.

Proponents of multicultural education assert that building upon students' culture is nothing more than sound teaching; by recognizing, valuing, and utilizing students' culture and language in their instruction, teachers help students link the topics they're studying to what they already know, a process consistent with effective teaching and learning (Eggen & Kauchak, 2001; Ormrod, 2000).

In addition, proponents of multicultural education point out that the United States has always been a nation of immigrants, and that this diversity has always been recognized in a number of ways, including music, holidays such as St. Patrick's Day, Mardi Gras, and the Chinese New Year, and different ethnic foods. Good multicultural education continues this tradition by recognizing and building upon different students' cultural heritage.

Regardless of the controversies surrounding multicultural education, one promising approach to working with diverse student populations is called *culturally responsive teaching*.

Culturally Responsive Teaching Culturally responsive teaching *acknowledges cultural diversity in classrooms and accommodates this diversity in instruction* (Gay, 1997). It attempts to accomplish this goal in three ways:

- Accepting and valuing differences.
- Accommodating different cultural learning styles.
- Building on students' cultural backgrounds.

Accepting and valuing differences. By recognizing and accepting student diversity, teachers communicate that all students are welcome and valued. This is particularly important for cultural minorities, who sometimes feel alienated from school. In our opening case study, Shannon did this by asking her students to identify their ethnic homelands on the map. This showed an interest in each student as a unique individual and also helped students see commonalities and differences with other students.

Genuine caring is an essential element in this process of accepting and valuing differences. Teachers can communicate caring in several ways, including the following:

- By giving students their time, such as being available before and after school to help with schoolwork as well as to talk about students' questions and interests.
- By demonstrating interest in students' lives, such as asking about Jewish holidays, Muslim holy days, and festivals like Kwanza.
- By involving all students in learning activities, calling on all students as equally as possible.

Increasing Understanding 3.2

Use American's eating habits to explain why the "mosaic" or "tossed salad" metaphors are more accurate than the "melting pot" metaphor.

Increasing Understanding 3.3

What did Shannon do to communicate that she accepts and values cultural differences?

Culturally responsive teaching builds on students' cultural backgrounds, accepting and valuing differences and accommodating different cultural learning styles.

Each of these suggestions communicates that all students are welcome and valued.

Accommodating cultural learning styles. Teachers who are sensitive to possible differences between home and school interaction patterns can adapt their instruction to best meet their students' needs. For example, we saw earlier that the communication patterns of Native Americans may clash with typical classroom practices. Recognizing that these students aren't comfortable in teacher-centered question-and-answer activities, teachers can use different strategies, such as cooperative learning, to complement teacher-centered approaches.

Similarly, knowing that White and African American students have different communication patterns, teachers can incorporate more open-ended questions in their lessons and give word directions more directly, such as "Put your scissors away now."

As another example, when a teacher learned that her Asian American students were overwhelmed by the bustle of American schools, she tried to keep her classroom quiet and orderly and encouraged shy and reluctant students to participate with open-ended questioning, extra time to respond, and gentle reminders to speak a bit louder (Park, 1997).

Accommodating cultural learning styles can result in what Ogbu (1987) calls "accommodation without assimilation," the process of minority students adapting to the dominant culture (including schools) without losing their cultural identity. Others use the term "alternation"—the ability to comfortably function in both cultures (Hamm & Coleman, 1997). The challenge for teachers is to help students learn about the "culture of schooling"—the norms, procedures, and expectations necessary for success in school—while honoring the value and integrity of the students' home cultures.

Increasing Understanding 3.4

To which metaphor—"melting pot" or "tossed salad"—does the concept of accommodation without assimilation most closely relate? Explain.

Reflect on This

HOW CULTURAL DIFFERENCES AFFECT LEARNING

You've been invited to a community awards ceremony at a local church that is to honor Pacific Island students from your school. (This invitation and the events that followed actually happened to one educator.) You gladly accept, arrive a few minutes early, and are ushered to a seat of honor on the stage. After an uncomfortable (to you) wait of over an hour, the ceremony begins, and the students proudly file onto the stage to receive their awards. Each student is acknowledged, given an award, and applauded. After this part of the ceremony, you have an eye-opening experience.

The children all go back and sit down in the audience again, and the meeting continues with several more items on the agenda. The kids are fine for a while, but then they become bored and start to fidget. Fidgeting and whispering turn into poking, prodding, and open chatting. You become a little anxious at the disruption, but none of the other adults appears to even notice, so you ignore it, too. Soon, several of the children are up and out of their seats, strolling around the back and sides of the auditorium. All adult faces continue looking serenely up at the speaker on the stage. Then the kids start playing tag, running circles around the seating area and yelling gleefully. No adult response—you are amazed and struggle to resist the urge to quiet the children. Then some of the kids get up onto the stage, run around the speaker, flick the lights on and off, and open and close the curtain. Still nothing from the Islander parents! You don't know what to do (adapted from Winitzky, 1994).

1. What cultural differences were encountered that could potentially affect the way these students would benefit from American classrooms?

2. What would you do if you were at the awards ceremony?

3. What adaptations could a teacher make to help students such as these learn better in classrooms?

To respond to these questions online and receive immediate feedback, go to the Reflect on This *Module in Chapter 3 of the Companion Website.*

Building on students' backgrounds. Effective teachers also learn about their students' cultures and use this information to promote personal pride and motivation in their students, as the following illustration demonstrates:

▪ ▪ ▪

In one third-grade classroom with a predominately Central American student population, youngsters are greeted most mornings with the sound of salsa music in the background, instruction takes place in both English and Spanish, magazines and games in both languages are available throughout the classroom, maps of both the United States and Latin America line one wall with pins noting each student's origin, and every afternoon there is a Spanish reading lesson to ensure that students learn to read and write in Spanish as well as English. . . . The teacher argues very clearly that a positive instructional environment for these students must be tailored to the home cultures (Shields & Shaver, 1990, p. 9).

▪ ▪ ▪

The benefits of building on students' cultural backgrounds are felt in both the classroom and the home. In addition to increased student achievement, another benefit is that parents become more positive about school, which in turn enhances student motivation (Shumow & Harris, 1998). Shannon recognized this when she invited parents and other caregivers to share their cultural heritage with her class. Students bring to school a wealth

Increasing Understanding 3.5

In this chapter's opening case study, what does Shannon do to build upon her students' cultural backgrounds? Provide at least two specific examples.

of experiences embedded in their home cultures. Sensitive teachers build on these experiences, and all students benefit.

Language Diversity

One of the most prominent parts of any culture is its language; because language diversity and the responses to it are so controversial, we are devoting a major section to it.

As a result of immigration, increasing numbers of students with limited backgrounds in English are entering U.S. classrooms. The number of non-English-speaking and limited-English proficiency (LEP) students in the United States increased by more than 50 percent between 1985 and 1991, and between 1991 and 1993 the language minority population increased 12.6 percent compared to an increase of only 1.02 percent in the general population (Weaver & Padron, 1997).

The diversity in language is staggering. Currently, there are over 3.2 million students in U. S. schools whose first language is not English. California has 1.4 million of these **English-as-a-Second-Language (ESL)** students, comprising nearly 40 percent of the student population in that state (U.S. Department of Education, 1998; Office of Bilingual Education and Minority Language Affairs, 1999; Stoddart, 1999). Nationwide, the number of students whose primary language is not English is expected to triple during the next 30 years. The most common language groups for these students are Spanish (73 percent), Vietnamese (4 percent), Hmong (1.8 percent), Cantonese (1.7 percent), and Cambodian (1.6 percent).

Language Diversity: The Government's Response The federal government, through legislation and court rulings, has attempted to address the needs of ESL students. For example, Congress passed the Bilingual Education Act in 1968, which provided federal funds for non-native English speakers. In 1974 the U.S. Supreme Court ruled unanimously, in a controversial San Francisco case, Lau v. Nichols, that schools must take steps to help students who "are certain to find their classroom experiences wholly incomprehensible" because they don't understand English. The Court held that the San Francisco School District unlawfully discriminated on the basis of students' national origin by failing to address children's language problems. Though federal guidelines specified that language minority students should be taught academic subjects in their native languages, a number of alternative solutions have arisen.

Language Diversity: Schools' Responses Schools across the country have responded to the challenge of language diversity in several ways. Some of them are outlined in Table 3.1. While all of the programs are designed to teach English, they differ in how quickly English is introduced and to what extent the first language is used and maintained. **Maintenance programs** place the greatest emphasis on using and sustaining the first language; ESL and **immersion programs,** with their heavy emphasis on English acquisition, place the least emphasis on a student's first language.

Logistics are often a factor when schools consider which type of program to use. When there are large numbers of ESL students who speak the same language (such as Spanish-speaking students in Los Angeles), maintenance and **transition programs** are feasible because one teacher who speaks the students' native language can be hired. When several different first languages exist in the classroom, however, it isn't feasible to find teachers who speak all of the languages. High schools, with students going from one content classroom to the next, also present logistical challenges, and ESL programs are more likely to exist at this level.

Increasing Understanding 3.6

Which approach to helping ESL students is the most culturally responsive? Which is the least? Explain why in each case.

Teaching

in an Era of Reform

BILINGUAL EDUCATION

Bilingual education has been the focus of a number of controversial reform efforts. As you saw earlier, national reform efforts with respect to this issue first began when Congress passed the Bilingual Education Act in 1968, and the 1974 court case *Lau v. Nichols* (the San Francisco case described in the last section) demonstrated the government's commitment to providing services for non-native English speakers.

The magnitude of the challenges involved in this reform is difficult to overstate. For example, in Arizona an estimated 37 percent of the state's ESL students were enrolled in bilingual programs in 1999, and in California, roughly one third of the state's 1.4 million ESL students were enrolled in bilingual education (Schnaiberg, 1999a, 1999b). The Los Angeles Unified School District alone had over 100,000 of its 310,000 ESL students enrolled in bilingual education programs.

As with all reforms, bilingual education has been attacked and criticized, with critics contending that it is:

- Divisive, encouraging non-native English speaking groups to remain separate from mainstream American culture.
- Ineffective, slowing the process of acquiring English for ESL students.
- Inefficient, requiring expenditures for the training of bilingual teachers and materials that could better be spent on quality monolingual programs.

Proponents counter that bilingual programs make sense because they provide a smooth and humane transition to English by building on a student's first language. In addition, they argue that being able to speak two languages has both practical and learning benefits (Garcia, 1993). From a practical standpoint, a truly bilingual person is able to live and communicate in two worlds, which may open economic and career doors. From a learning perspective, there is growing evidence that being able to speak two languages provides intellectual benefits. For example, because of their knowledge of two languages, bilingual students better understand the role of language in communication and how language works (Diaz, 1990).

Critics views prevailed in California; in a 1998 counter-reform, voters passed Proposition 227, a ballot initiative that sharply reduced bilingual education, replacing it with English-only immersion programs for ESL students. A similar measure passed in Arizona in 2000, and other states, such as Utah and Colorado, are considering similar initiatives (Schnaiberg, 1999a; Zehr, 2000a, 2000b).

Putting Reform into Perspective

What does this reform and counter-reform mean? First, the effectiveness of bilingual education is a complicated issue with few absolute answers. Some research indicates that students in bilingual programs score higher in math and reading and have more positive attitudes toward school and themselves (Arias & Casanova, 1993). In addition, contrary to an argument that newcomers to the United States are learning English more slowly than in previous generations, the opposite appears to be true (Waggoner, 1995). Further research indicates that knowledge and skills acquired in a native language—literacy in particular—are "transferable" to the second language (Krashen, 1996), and while conversational English, such as that spoken on the playground, is learned quite quickly, the cognitively demanding language needed for academic success is learned much less rapidly (Peregoy & Boyle, 1997).

However, other research indicates that immersion programs are working. For instance, one California school district reported that standardized test scores for students in the early grades—those most affected by the move from bilingual to immersion programs—improved from the 35th to the 45th percentile in just one year; additional research found similar positive results across California (Barone, 2000). For a report on "The Initial Impact of Proposition 227 on the Instruction of English Learners," go to the *Web Links* Module in Chapter 3 of the Companion Website at **http://www.prenhall.com/kauchak.**

So, what does all this mean for you as a teacher? First, the issue of bilingual education is likely to be a subject of hot debate for years. Second, while bilingual programs have been reduced, they haven't been eliminated, and job opportunities in bilingual education are widespread. For example, there are currently 50,000 bilingual education vacancies in the United States, with 21,000 vacancies in California alone (Sack, 2000b). This is one of the areas of greatest need in education; prospective candidates who speak two languages, especially Spanish, are in high demand across the country. Third, you will almost certainly have non-native English speakers in your classroom, and your ability to make informed professional decisions will be crucial for their learning success.

In working with diverse students, your professionalism will be tested perhaps more than in any other area of your work.

Research offers the following suggestions:

■ Create a warm and inviting classroom environment by taking a personal interest in all students and involving everyone in learning activities.

■ Mix teacher-centered instruction with cooperative learning groups where students can interact informally, learning English and practicing their language skills as they study content.

■ Provide peer tutoring and assistance in which students more proficient in English help their less proficient counterparts. Peer tutoring is also beneficial to the tutor, illustrating the instructional benefits of helping someone else learn (Miller et al., 1994).

■ Use many examples and illustrations to provide concrete referents for new ideas and vocabulary (Peregoy & Boyle, 1997; Echevarria & Graves, 1998).

These strategies represent good instruction for all students; for ESL students, they are essential.

You Take a Position

Now it's your turn to take a position on the issues discussed in this section. Go to the *Education Week* Website at **http://www.edweek.com,** find "search" on the first page, and type in one of the following two search terms: *bilingual education* or *Proposition 227.* Locate a minimum of three articles on one of these topics and do the following:

1. Identify the title, author, and date of each article, and then write a one-paragraph summary of each.

2. Determine if a pattern exists in the articles. (Each article—or even two of the three—suggesting that bilingual education be abolished would be a pattern, for example.)

3. Take one of the two following positions:

■ The pattern suggested in the articles, if implemented, *is* likely to improve education.

■ The pattern suggested in the articles *is not* likely to improve education.

Document your position with information taken from the articles and your study of the text (including this chapter and any other chapter of the text).

Ⓦ *To answer these questions online, go to the Take a Position Module in Chapter 3 of the Companion Website.*

Bilingual education maintains students' first language, using it as the foundation for learning English.

Table 3.1	Different Programs for ESL Students		
Type of Program	Description	Advantages	Disadvantages
Maintenance	First language maintained through reading and writing activities in first language while English introduced.	Students become literate in two languages.	Requires teachers trained in first language. Acquisition of English may not be as fast.
Transition	Students learn to read in first language and are given supplementary instruction in English as a Second Language. Once English is mastered, students are placed in regular classrooms and first language is discontinued.	Maintains first language. Transition to English is eased by gradual approach.	Requires teachers trained in first language. Acquisition of English may not be as fast.
Immersion	Students learn English by being "immersed" in classrooms where English is the only language spoken.	When effective, quick transition to English. Does not require teachers trained in second language.	Loss of native language. "Sink or swim" approach hard on students.
English-as-a-Second-Language Programs (ESL)	Pull-out programs where students are provided with supplementary English instruction or modified instruction in content areas (also called Sheltered English programs).	Easier to administer when dealing with diverse language backgrounds.	Students may not be ready to benefit from content instruction in English. Pull-out programs segregate students.

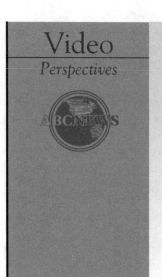

Video Perspectives

ABCNEWS

CALIFORNIA PROPOSITION 227

This ABC News video segment features Ron Unz, a co-author of California Proposition 227 and a financial supporter of the Arizona bilingual initiative, and Teresa Bustillos, an opponent of the bill. They debate the merits of the reform initiative that was passed by the voters of California in 1999. Proponents of the bill argue that bilingual education hinders the learning of English by providing an artificial crutch to ESL learners. Proponents argue that bilingual education provides a more gradual and natural transition to English.

Think about This

1. What arguments and evidence do proponents of Proposition 227 make in its defense?

2. What arguments and evidence do critics of Proposition 227 make in its defense?

3. How would you have voted on this issue? Why?

To answer these questions online and receive immediate feedback, go to the Video Perspectives Module in Chapter 3 of the Companion Website.

■ GENDER

‧ ‧ ‧

What Geri Peterson saw on her first day of teaching advanced-placement calculus was both surprising and disturbing. Of the 26 students watching her, only four were female, and they were sitting quietly in the back of the room. One reason that Geri had gone into teaching was to share her interest in math with other females, but this situation gave her little chance to do so.

‧ ‧ ‧

Lori Anderson, the school counselor at an urban middle school, looked up from the desk where she was working on her annual report to the faculty. From her course work at the university and her internship, she knew that boys traditionally outnumber girls with respect to behavioral problems, but the numbers she was looking at were disturbing. In every category—referrals by teachers, absenteeism, tardies, and fights—boys outnumbered girls by a 2 to 1 margin. In addition, the number of boys referred to her for placement in special-education classes far exceeded those for girls. This was a problem that her faculty needed to think about.

‧ ‧ ‧

Gender and Society

The fact that males and females *are* different is so obvious that we usually don't think about it. However, some important but often unnoticed differences exist between the sexes (Feingold, 1995). For example, women generally are more extroverted, anxious, and trusting; they're less assertive and have slightly lower self-esteem than their male counterparts; and their verbal and motor skills tend to develop faster than boys. The play habits of boys and girls are different; boys are typically more "rough and tumble."

Why do these gender differences exist? Research suggests a combination of genetics and environment (Berk, 2000). Genetics result in physical differences such as size and growth rate and may also influence other differences such as temperament, aggression, and early verbal and exploratory behaviors.

Environment plays a part as well. From the day they are born, boys and girls are treated differently (Eisenberg, Marlin, & Fabes, 1996). Girls are given pink blankets, are described as cute and pretty, and are handled delicately. Boys are dressed in blue, are regarded as handsome, and are seen as tougher, better coordinated, and hardier. Fathers are rougher with their sons and involve them in more physical stimulation and play; they tend to be gentler with their daughters and offer more sex-stereotyped toys, such as dolls and stuffed animals. The results are obvious; boys and girls grow up looking and acting differently.

Gender and Schooling

The differences between boys and girls should generally be celebrated. They're problems only when societal or school forces limit the growth and academic potential of students—either male or female.

Consider these findings which suggest that schools are failing to meet the educational needs of girls:

■ In the early grades, girls are ahead of or equal to boys on almost every standardized measure of achievement and psychological well-being. But by the time they graduate from high school or college, they have fallen behind.

■ In high school, girls score lower than boys on the SAT and ACT, two tests that are critical for college admission. The difference is seen especially at the higher achievement levels, and the greatest gender gaps occur in science and math.

■ Women score lower on all sections of the Graduate Record Exam, which is required to get into most graduate programs, as well as the Medical College Admissions Test and admission tests for law, dental, and optometry schools (Campbell & Clewell, 1999; Sadker, Sadker, & Long, 1997).

Other research suggests that schools also fail to meet the learning needs of boys:

■ Boys outnumber girls in remedial English and math classes, are held back a grade more often, and are two to three times more likely to be placed in special-education classes.

■ Boys consistently receive lower grades than girls, and score lower than girls on both direct and indirect measures of writing skills.

■ Boys are more likely to be involved in serious misbehavior, especially when this misbehavior involves aggressive acts.

■ The proportion of both bachelor's and master's degrees earned favors women by a ratio of 54 to 46 (Riordan, 1999; Willingham & Cole, 1997).

Let's examine some possible explanations for these findings. Again, a combination of genetics and environment is likely. Since little can be done about genetics, more attention has been given to environment, particularly **gender-role identity** differences, *expectations and beliefs about appropriate roles and behaviors of the two sexes.*

Gender issues are controversial. For instance, in 1992 the American Association of University Women published *How Schools Shortchange Girls*, which argues that different treatment of boys and girls by both teachers and society seriously hampers the educational progress, self-esteem, and career choices of girls and women. In 1998 they published *Gender Gaps: Where Schools Still Fail Our Children*, in which many of the earlier claims are reiterated.

Counterclaims are also made. For example, Christina Sommers, author of *The War Against Boys: How Misguided Feminism Is Harming Our Young Men* (Sommers, 2000), points out that—in addition to lower achievement, more frequent misbehavior, and more frequent placement in special-education classes—boys are less likely to do their homework and are more likely to cheat on tests, wind up in detention, and drop out of school. Yet it's the myth of the "fragile girl" that continues to receive the lion's share of attention.

The controversies are likely to continue. So, what are the facts? First, gender-role identity differences aren't a problem unless they perpetuate stereotypes or negatively influence behavior, learning, or expectations for school success. Research indicates that this may be happening, particularly in math, computer science, and engineering.

Gender and Career Choices Look around the classroom you're in for this course. If it's a typical education course, approximately three-fourths of the students in it are women. The same would be true in nursing classes, but you would find the opposite in math, science, and computer-related fields.

Differences in students' views of gender-appropriate careers appear as early as kindergarten (Kochenberger-Stroeher, 1994). In spite of a strong and systematic effort to address the needs of both boys and girls in today's schools, when asked about future potential career options, boys continue to be more likely to choose doctor and engineer and girls are more likely to mention nurse or secretary (Riordan, 1999). Significantly, when kindergarten children choose nontraditional roles for males or females, their choice is based on personal experience (for example, "One of my friend's dad is a nurse").

Where do the stereotypes of "appropriate" careers for boys and girls originate? Ironically, the most powerful source is parents, especially mothers. For instance, one study found that negative gender-stereotyped attitudes toward girls' ability in math adversely

Role models are effective in preventing students from forming gender-stereotypic views about appropriate careers.

influenced daughters' achievement in math and their attitudes toward it (Campbell & Beaudry, 1998). Parents can also have powerful positive influences on their children. Martha, a chemistry software developer, reported,

■ ■ ■

My mother always engendered in me the attitude that I could do absolutely anything I ever want to do. So she really gave me the confidence that is a big part of success in academics and maybe in other things—sometimes you get to a point where you don't have that much either skill or knowledge, and you have to just go on your guts or your confidence. You have to just kind of push your way through something until you have the time to accumulate the knowledge. And I think that that's something she engendered in me just by always being herself so confident of my abilities, rightly or wrongly. And my father certainly never detracted from that. He always portrayed her as being the smarter of the two. So I was raised in an environment where women were not only capable but were even potentially very well and highly regarded (Zelden & Pajares, 2000, p. 229).

■ ■ ■

Gender-stereotypic views can also negatively influence career decisions. Girls are less than half as likely as boys to pursue careers in engineering and physical and computer sciences (American Association of University Women, 1998). At the Massachusetts Institute of Technology, one of the premier science and technology universities in the country, one-third of the total graduates are women; it is interesting to note that 52 percent of the biology majors are women, but only 15 percent of its computer science graduates are women (Hale, 1998). At the high school level, only 17 percent of students taking the College Board Advanced Placement Test in computer science were women (American Association of University Women, 1998). The percentage of female doctors (20 percent), lawyers (21 percent), and engineers (8 percent), as well as professors in science-related fields (36 percent), remains low (U.S. Bureau of the Census, 1996; U.S. Department of Education, 1998). The problem of gender-stereotypic views of math,

Increasing Understanding 3.7

How do the percentages of females in various occupations relate to the concept of gender-role identity?

science, and computer-science-related careers seems to be especially acute for minority females (O'Brien, Kopola, & Martinez-Pons, 1999).

Single-Gender Classrooms and Schools One response to gender-related problems has been the creation of **single-gender classes and schools,** *where boys and girls are segregated for part or all of the day* (Mael, 1998). Researchers have found that girls are more likely to ask and answer questions in girls-only middle school math classes than in other coeducational classes (Streitmatter, 1997). Girls also preferred this type of learning environment, saying that it enhanced their ability to learn math along with their view of themselves as mathematicians.

Research on single-gender schools has also revealed similar positive effects, both for girls and boys. Girls who attend single-gender schools are more apt to assume leadership roles, take more math and science courses, have higher self-esteem, and hold firmer beliefs that they are in control of their destinies (Datnow, Hubbard, & Conchas, 1999). Advocates of all-male schools claim that they promote male character development and are especially effective with males from low-income and minority families.

Although research shows positive effects of single-sex schooling for both general achievement and achievement in gender-stereotyped fields like math and science, this research also raises other issues (American Association of University Women, 1998; Mael, 1998). For example, single-gender schools and classes can increase stereotyped views of the opposite sex (Datnow et al., 1999) and fail to prepare students for the "real world," in which males and females must work together. In addition, some critics question the legality of single-sex classrooms and schools based on Title IX, a federal law that prohibits discrimination on the basis of gender (Zehr, 2000c). More research is needed about the long-term effects of these experiments and the ways that they help (or hinder) students of both genders learn and develop.

Gender and Schooling: Implications for Teachers What does this say to you as a teacher? First, you should be aware that you may have stereotypical attitudes of your own, and, since attitudes influence behavior, you should monitor how you interact with the boys and girls in your classroom. For instance, research indicates that teachers typically call on boys more often than girls, probably because boys are more verbally assertive or aggressive (Altermatt, Jovanovic, & Perry, 1998). Also, boys are more likely to ask questions and make comments about ideas being discussed in class (Sadker et al., 1991); these differences increase as students move through school. In the extreme, these patterns can result in girls becoming less involved in learning activities.

As a teacher, what can you do? At least four possibilities exist:

- Make an effort to present cases of men and women in nonstereotypical roles, such as female engineers and male kindergarten teachers.
- Encourage equal participation in all classes, particularly in math and science classes. One demanding but extremely effective technique is to call on everyone in your classes individually and by name, regardless of whether or not their hands are raised.
- Arrange to have science and computer experiments and demonstrations prepared and conducted by boys and girls equally. Research shows that experiments tend to be dominated by boys (Sadker et al., 1991).
- Encourage girls to go into science-related fields. Significantly, girls who do so reported that the encouragement received from teachers was an important factor in their career decisions (American Association of University Women, 1992).

Increasing Understanding 3.8

In single-gender classrooms and schools, should the teachers be the same gender as the students? Explain alternate positions, using the information given in this section.

Increasing Understanding 3.9

Using the concept of gender-role identity, explain why teachers may experience difficulties in recognizing gender-related differences in their interactions with students.

The powerful influence that teachers can have on students is captured in the following quote from a 42-year-old female mathematics professor.

■ ■ ■

It was the first time I had algebra, and I loved it. And then, all of a sudden, I excelled in it. And the teacher said, "Oh no, you should be in the honors course," or something like that. So, there's somebody who definitely influenced me because I don't think I ever even noticed. I mean, I didn't care one way or the other about mathematics. It was just something you had to do. I remember she used to run up and down the aisle. She was real excited. . . . She said, "Oh, you gotta go in this other class. You gotta." And she kind of pushed a little bit, and I was willing to be pushed (Zelden & Pajares, 2000, p. 232).

■ ■ ■

When teachers believe in their students, students start believing in themselves. Open communication is essential. Simply telling your students that teachers often treat boys and girls differently and that you're going to try to treat them equally is a positive first step. Then make your best effort to be true to your commitment.

No one is suggesting that boys and girls are the same—nor should they be the same. Rather, the goal is to attempt to provide the same academic opportunities and encouragement for all.

Sexual Harassment

Hey, babe. Lookin' good in that sweater!

Hey, sugar. Want to make me happy tonight?

Comments like these are heard in many classrooms and hallways in our nation's schools. Sexual harassment is a problem that affects both males and females and makes classrooms and hallways less conducive to students' learning and development. **Sexual harassment** is *unwanted and unwelcome sexual behavior that interferes with your life* (American Association of University Women, 1993, p. 6). According to a survey of students in grades 8 through 11, four out of five teenagers reported some type of sexual harassment in schools (AAUW, 1993). Sexual comments, gestures, and looks, as well as touching and grabbing were most commonly cited (see Figure 3.2).

Figure 3.2	Sexual Harassment in U.S. Schools

Source: From American Association of University Women (1993). *Hostile hallways: The AAUW survey on sexual harassment in America's schools.* New York: Louis Harris and Associates. Reprinted by permission.

Sexual harassment often occurs in school hallways, and teachers can play a powerful role in preventing it there and in the classrooms.

Several aspects of the study depicted in Figure 3.2 are disturbing. One is the high incidence of sexual harassment that occurs in schools; schools and classrooms should be safe places for learning. Another is a finding that only 7 percent of the harassment cases were reported. In addition, more than half the students surveyed didn't even know if their school had a policy on sexual harassment.

Harassment is a particularly acute problem for homosexual students. One national survey found that 91 percent of gay students had heard anti-gay comments, 69 percent had been verbally abused, and 34 percent reported being verbally abused on a daily basis (Galley, 1999). As the following example shows, sometimes the abuse isn't only verbal.

■ ■ ■

When I was changing classes, I had all the books in my hands. . . . I'd hear someone mutter "faggot" and have my books knocked down. People are walking over me as I'm trying to gather my books. I don't have time to turn around to see who said it (Sears, 1993, p. 129).

■ ■ ■

Students report that harassment such as this makes them feel "sad and worthless," and "powerless" (Shakeshaft et al., 1997). This harassment contributes to higher rates of depression, substance abuse, and suicide for gay students (Berk, 2000).

Schools and teachers need to do a better job of making classrooms and hallways safe. All students—boys and girls, heterosexual and homosexual—have a right to harassment-free schools. Teachers have an important role in ensuring that this happens. Talk with your students about the problem and emphasize that no form of sexual harassment will be tolerated.

■ ABILITY DIFFERENCES

When you look out at your first class, you'll see obvious similarities and differences. Your students will be about the same age, and their dress and hairstyles will often be similar. They'll come from different cultural backgrounds, and you'll have both boys and girls. Less obvious, however, is their ability to learn. In virtually any class, you'll work with students who master the content effortlessly while others struggle just to keep up. In this section we examine these differences and how schools accommodate them.

What Is Intelligence?

We all have intuitive notions about intelligence; it's how "sharp" people are, how much they know, how quickly and easily they learn, and how perceptive and sensitive they are. But how should intelligence really be defined?

Consider the following questions and decide if they would be included on an intelligence test.

1. On what continent is Brazil?
2. A coat priced $45 is marked one-third off. When it still doesn't sell, the sale price is reduced by half. What is the price after the second discount?
3. Who was Albert Einstein?
4. How far is it from Seattle to Atlanta?
5. How are a river and a plateau alike?

The answer may surprise you. *All* of the items are similar to items found on the Wechsler Intelligence Scale for Children (Wechsler, 1991), one of the most widely used intelligence tests.

Experts define **intelligence** as *the capacity to acquire knowledge, the ability to think and reason in the abstract, and the ability to solve problems* (Snyderman & Rothman, 1987; Sternberg, 1986). What do the test questions that we listed have to do with these three dimensions? First, they suggest that background knowledge and experience are crucial in performance (Perkins, 1995), and second, research consistently indicates that these factors are crucial in people's ability to solve problems and think in the abstract (Bruning, et al., 1999).

Changes in Views of Intelligence

Historically, researchers believed that intelligence was a single trait and that we all exist somewhere along a continuum of general intelligence. This thinking has changed; many researchers now believe that intelligence is composed of several distinct dimensions.

Harvard psychologist Howard Gardner (1983, 1995) illustrates this position. He proposed a theory of **multiple intelligences (MI),** the suggestion that *overall intelligence is composed of eight relatively independent dimensions* (see Table 3.2).

Gardner's theory makes intuitive sense. For example, we all know people who don't seem particularly "sharp" analytically but who excel in getting along with others. This ability serves them well, and in some instances they're more successful than their "brighter" counterparts. Other people seem very self-aware and are able to capitalize on their personal strengths and minimize their weaknesses. Gardner explains these examples by saying the people described are high in interpersonal and intrapersonal intelligence, respectively.

Most classrooms focus heavily on the linguistic and logical-mathematical dimensions and virtually ignore the others. If these other dimensions are to develop, students need experiences with them. For example, cooperative learning activities can help students develop interpersonal intelligence; participation in sports or dance can improve bodily kinesthetic abilities; and playing in the band or singing in choral groups can improve musical intelligence.

Increasing Understanding 3.10

If experience is crucial to performance on tests of learning ability, how might performance be affected by growing up in a minority culture?

Increasing Understanding 3.11

If educators were to apply Gardner's theory, what would an elementary-level report card look like? A high school report card?

Table 3.2	Gardner's Eight Intelligences	
Dimension	Description	Individuals Who Might Be High in This Dimension
Linguistic intelligence	Sensitivity to the meaning and order of words and the varied uses of language.	Poet, journalist
Logical-mathematical intelligence	The ability to handle long chains of reasoning and to recognize patterns and order in the world.	Scientist, mathematician
Musical intelligence	Sensitivity to pitch, melody, and tone.	Composer, violinist
Spacial intelligence	The ability to perceive the visual world accurately, and to recreate, transform, or modify aspects of the world on the basis of one's perceptions.	Sculptor, navigator
Bodily kinesthetic intelligence	A fine-tuned ability to use the body and to handle objects.	Dancer, athlete
Interpersonal intelligence	An understanding of interpersonal relations and the ability to make distinctions among others.	Therapist, salesperson
Intrapersonal intelligence	Access to one's own "feeling life."	Self-aware individual
Naturalist intelligence	The ability to recognize similarities and differences in the physical world.	Biologist, anthropologist

Source: Adapted from H. Gardner and Hatch, 1989, Multiple intelligences go to school, *Educational Researcher,* 18(8), 4–10; and Chekles, 1997, The first seven . . . and the eighth, *Educational Leadership,* 55, 8–13.

Ability: Nature versus Nurture

No aspect of intelligence has been more hotly debated than the issue of heredity versus environment. The extreme **nature view of intelligence or ability** *asserts that ability is solely determined by genetics;* the **nurture view of intelligence or ability** *emphasizes the influence of the environment.* Differences between these positions are very controversial when race or ethnicity are considered. For example, research indicates that some cultural minority groups collectively score lower on intelligence tests than White American children (Brody, 1992; McLoyd, 1998). People who emphasize the nurture view explain this finding by arguing that minority children have fewer stimulating experiences while they are developing.

People adhering to the nature view argue that heredity is the more important factor. In their highly controversial book *The Bell Curve,* Hernstein and Murray (1994) concluded that the contribution of heredity outweighed environmental factors in influencing the intelligence-test scores of minority populations, especially African Americans. Methodological problems, such as inferring causation from correlational data, caused other experts to reject this position (Jacoby & Glauberman, 1995; Marks, 1995).

In considering the nature–nurture debate, most experts take a position somewhere in the middle, believing that ability is influenced both by heredity and the environment (Yee, 1995). In this view, a person's genes provide the potential for intelligence, and stimulating environments make the most of the raw material.

The opposite is also true; many learning environments don't provide enough stimulation to help children reach their full potential (Ceci, 1990; Loehlin, 1989). For example, researchers tracked children born of low-income parents but adopted as infants into high-income families. The enriched environments resulted in children who scored an average of 14 points higher on intelligence tests than did their comparable siblings (Schiff, Duyme, Dumaret, & Tomkiewicz, 1982).

Formal experiences can also increase intelligence-test scores (Ceci & Williams, 1997). Attempts to directly teach the skills measured by intelligence tests have been successful with preschool and elementary students (Consortium for Longitudinal Studies, 1983; Sprigle &

Schoefer, 1985), adults (Whimbey, 1980), and students with learning disabilities (Brown & Campione, 1986). A longitudinal study of disadvantaged, inner-city children also indicated that early stimulation can have lasting effects on intelligence (Garber, 1988).

Ability Grouping and Tracking

The most common way schools respond to differences in learner ability is by **ability grouping,** which *places students of similar aptitude and achievement histories together and attempts to match instruction to the needs of different groups.*

Ability grouping is popular in elementary schools, and typically exists in two major forms. **Between-class ability grouping** *divides all students in a given grade into high, medium, and low groups;* **within-class ability grouping** *divides all students in a given classroom into high, medium, and low groups.* Most elementary teachers endorse ability grouping, particularly in reading and math.

In middle, junior high, and high schools, ability grouping goes further, with high-ability students studying advanced and college preparatory courses and their low-ability counterparts receiving vocational or work-related instruction. In some cases, students are grouped only in certain areas, such as English or math; in other cases, it exists across all content areas, a practice called **tracking,** which *places students in different classes or curricula on the basis of ability.* Some form of tracking exists in most middle, junior high, and high schools (Braddock, 1990), and tracking has its most negative effect on minorities in the lower tracks (Davenport et al., 1998; Mickelson & Heath, 1999).

Why is ability grouping so common? Advocates argue that it increases learning by allowing teachers to adjust the pace of instruction, methods, and materials to better meet students' needs. Because pace and assessments are similar for a particular group, instruction is easier for the teacher.

However, research has uncovered the following problems:

- Within-class grouping creates logistical problems for teachers, because different lessons and assignments are required and monitoring students in different tasks is difficult (Good & Brophy, 1997; Oakes, 1992).

- Improper placements occur, and placement tends to become permanent. Cultural minorities are under-represented in high-ability classes and over-represented in lower classes and tracks (Good & Marshall, 1984; Grant & Rothenberg, 1986; Oakes, 1992).

- Low groups are stigmatized; self-esteem and motivation of low groups suffer (Good & Marshall, 1984; Hallinan, 1984).

- Homogeneously grouped low-ability students achieve less than heterogeneously grouped students of similar ability (Good & Brophy, 1997).

Negative effects of grouping are related, in part, to the quality of instruction. Presentations to low groups are more fragmented and vague than those to high groups; they focus more on memorizing than on understanding, problem solving, and "active learning." Students in low-ability classes are often taught by teachers who lack enthusiasm and who stress conformity versus autonomy and the development of self-regulation (Good & Brophy, 1997; Ross, Smith, Loks, & McNelie, 1994).

Grouping also affects the students themselves. In addition to lowered self-esteem and motivation to learn, absentee rates tend to increase. One study found that absenteeism increased from 8 percent to 26 percent after students' transition to a tracked junior high (Slavin & Karweit, 1982), with most of the truants being students in the low-level classes. Tracking can also result in racial or cultural segregation of students, impeding social development and the ability to form friendships across cultural groups (Oakes, 1992).

Increasing Understanding 3.12

Based on his theory of multiple intelligences, would Howard Gardner favor ability grouping? Explain why or why not. How might he modify ability grouping?

Teachers minimize the negative effects of ability grouping by using it only in areas where it is absolutely necessary and by adapting instruction to meet the needs of all students.

Increasing Understanding 3.13

What are some possible explanations for the negative effects of ability grouping on students' self-esteem and motivation?

Efforts to reverse the negative effects of grouping and tracking have been positive, but require instructional adaptations. Some of these adaptations for heterogeneously grouped students include the following (Nyberg et al., 1997; Tomlinson, Callahan, & Moon, 1998):

◼ Giving students who need it more time to complete assignments.

◼ Providing peer tutors for students requiring extra help.

◼ Using small group work.

◼ Providing options on some assignments, such as giving students the choice of presenting a report orally or in writing.

◼ Breaking large assignments into smaller ones and providing additional scaffolding and support for those who need it.

Effective teachers adapt instruction to meet the needs of all students, with the need being especially acute for low-ability students (Tomlinson et al., 1998).

◼ LEARNING STYLES

Case **STUDY**

One thing teacher Chris Burnette remembered from his methods classes was the need for variety. He had been primarily using large-group discussions in his junior high social studies class, and most of the students seemed to respond okay. But others seemed disinterested, and their attention often drifted.

Today, Chris decided to try a small-group activity involving problem solving. They had been studying the growth of big cities in America, and he wanted the class to think about some solutions to big cities' problems.

As he watched the small groups interact, he was amazed at what he saw. Some of the quietest, most withdrawn students were leaders in the groups.

"Great!" he thought. But at the same time, he noted that some of his more active students were sitting back and not getting involved.

■ ■ ■

How do you like to study? Do you learn most effectively in groups or alone? Do you prefer teacher presentations or reading a textbook? Your answers to these questions reflect your unique **learning style,** or *your preferred way of learning and processing information.*

We often see differences in learning styles when we present a problem to students; some jump in and try to solve it through trial and error, whereas others sit back and carefully analyze the problem. **Impulsive students** *work quickly but make errors,* and **reflective students** *analyze and deliberate before answering.* Impulsive students concentrate on speed and take chances; reflective students think more and consider alternatives before they answer. Impulsive students perform better on activities requiring factual information; reflective students have an advantage in problem solving.

Another difference among students is described as **field dependence/independence,** *an individual's ability to identify relevant information in a complex and potentially confusing background* (Kogan, 1994). Field-dependent people see patterns as wholes; field-independent people are able to analyze complex patterns into their constituent parts. In a math word problem, for example, a field-independent student would be better at breaking a complex problem into subcomponents using relevant information in solving the problem.

Increasing Understanding 3.14

Ⓦ Would a field-independent person more likely be impulsive or reflective? Why?

Cultural Learning Styles

Learning styles are also influenced by culture and gender. In typical U.S. classrooms, individual initiative and responsibility are emphasized and reinforced by grades and competition. Competition demands successes and failures, and the success of one student can be linked to the failure of another (Cushner, McClelland, & Safford, 1992).

Contrast this orientation with the learning styles of the Hmong, a mountain tribe from Laos that immigrated to the United States after the Vietnam War. The Hmong culture emphasizes cooperation, and Hmong students constantly monitor the learning progress of their peers, offering help and assistance. Individual achievement is de-emphasized in favor of group success.

Case **STUDY**

When Mee Hang has difficulty with an alphabetization lesson, Pang Lor explains, in Hmong, how to proceed. Chia Ying listens in to Pang's explanation and nods her head. Pang goes back to work on her own paper, keeping an eye on Mee Hang. When she sees Mee looking confused, Pang leaves her seat and leans over Mee's shoulder. She writes the first letter of each word on the line, indicating to Mee that these letters are in alphabetical order and that Mee should fill in the rest of each word. This gives Mee the help she needs and she is able to finish on her own. Mee, in turn, writes the first letter of each word on the line for Chia Ying, passing on Pang Lor's explanation.

Classroom achievement is never personal but always considered to be the result of cooperative effort. Not only is there no competition in the classroom, there is constant denial of individual ability. When individuals are praised by the teacher, they generally shake their heads and appear hesitant to be singled out as being more able than their peers (Hvitfeldt, 1986, p. 70).

■ ■ ■

Think about how well these students would learn if instruction were competitive and teacher-centered, with few opportunities for student help and collaboration.

Native American, Mexican American, Southeast Asian, and Pacific Islander students experience similar difficulties in competitive classrooms (Greenfield, 1994; Triandes, 1995). Cooperation is more important to these groups than competition, which they view as silly, if not distasteful. When they come to school and are asked to compete, they experience cultural conflict. Getting good grades at the expense of their fellow students is both strange and offensive. Raising hands and jousting for the right to give the correct answer isn't congruent with the ways they interact at home. If they're forced to choose between two cultures, they may conclude that schools are not for them.

Instructional Responses to Learning Styles

Unquestionably, individual students come to us with different ways of attacking the tasks of learning and solving problems. The key question is "What should teachers do in response to these differences?" and perhaps a more realistic question might be "What *can* they do about these differences?"

One position would take all instruction and tailor it to the distinctive needs and predispositions of individual students. Field-independent students, for example, would be allowed to work on independent projects, while field-dependent students would be allowed to work in small groups. The opposite position strives for balance; for instance, a teacher may attempt to make impulsive students more reflective and vice versa (for example, "Now think a minute. Don't just blurt out the answer!").

Neither of these positions is realistic; in a class of 30 students, it is virtually impossible to individualize your teaching to meet the distinct learning-style preferences of all students. Further, research evidence doesn't support the practice of tailoring teaching to students' individual learning styles (Curry, 1990).

So where does this leave teachers? Is there any value to considering learning style as one aspect of learner diversity? Probably. We believe the concept of learning styles has two impor-

Increasing Understanding 3.15

Using the nature–nurture perspective, explain how cognitive and cultural learning styles are different.

Teachers can meet students' different learning styles by offering a variety of learning options.

**Increasing
Understanding 3.16**

W How are these two
responses to dealing
with learning styles similar
to culturally responsive
teaching?

tant implications for teachers. The first, and most important, suggests the need to vary our instruction. Evidence supports the suggestion that teachers who vary the way they teach are more effective than those who instruct the same way all the time (Shuell, 1996). Alternatives such as individual projects, small-group discussion, cooperative learning, and learning centers provide flexibility in meeting individual learning styles. The second implication is that the concept of learning styles reminds us that our students are indeed different and helps us become more sensitive to differences in the way they act and learn. In turn, we are less apt to interpret these differences as unimportant or inappropriate, and our classrooms become models of tolerance that provide positive learning environments for all students.

■ STUDENTS WITH EXCEPTIONALITIES

**Increasing
Understanding 3.17**

W A teacher has a stu-
dent in his class who
is hearing impaired. This
teacher purposefully talks
louder, faces the student
when he is talking, and
writes important information
on the board. What excep-
tionality is described here?
Explain how the teacher
adapts instruction to help the
student reach full potential.

As we've seen in this chapter, students differ in several ways, and effective teachers consider these differences when they plan and teach. In some cases, students are said to have **exceptionalities,** *differences that require special help and resources if students are to reach their full potential.* Students' exceptionalities can range from mild learning disabilities and physical impairments to being gifted and talented. Help and resources can include special schools, self-contained classrooms designed especially for these students, resource rooms where students can go to receive special help, and inclusion in regular classrooms with the support of specially trained professionals.

Special education refers to *instruction designed to meet the unique needs of students with exceptionalities.* The terms *children with exceptionalities, special-education students, children with handicaps, students with special needs,* and *individuals with disabilities* have all been used to describe students needing additional help to reach their full potential.

Approximately 6 million students in the United States are enrolled in special-education programs, two-thirds of them for relatively minor problems (Galley, 2000; Heward, 2000). Approximately 11 percent of students in a typical school receives special-education services (U.S. Department of Education, 1997).

Federal legislation has created categories to identify specific learning problems, and educators use these categories in developing programs to meet students' needs. However, the use of categories and the labeling that results is controversial (King-Sears, 1997). Advocates argue that categories provide a common language for professionals and encourage specialized instruction that meets the specific needs of students (Heward, 2000). Opponents claim that categories are arbitrary, that many differences exist within them, and that categorizing encourages educators to treat students as labels rather than as people. Despite the controversy, these categories are widely used, so you should be familiar with the terms and the implications they have for working with students.

Four categories make up over 70 percent of the population of students with exceptionalities. They include:

- ■ Students who are gifted and talented.
- ■ Students who are mentally retarded.
- ■ Students who have specific learning disabilities.
- ■ Students with behavior disorders.

Gifted and Talented Students

While we don't typically think of gifted and talented students as having exceptionalities, they are often unable to reach their full potential in the regular classroom. Students who are **gifted and talented** are *those at the upper end of the ability continuum who need special services to reach their full potential.* At one time the term *gifted* was used to identify these

Table 3.3	Acceleration and Enrichment Options for Students Who Are Gifted and Talented	
	Enrichment Options	**Acceleration Options**
	1. Independent study and independent projects	1. Early admission to kindergarten and first grade
	2. Learning centers	2. Grade skipping
	3. Field trips	3. Subject skipping
	4. Saturday and summer programs	4. Credit by exam
	5. Simulations and games	5. College courses in high school
	6. Small-group inquiry and investigations	6. Correspondence courses
	7. Academic competitions	7. Early admission to college

students, but the category has been enlarged to include both students who do well on intelligence tests and those who demonstrate above-average talents in a variety of areas such as math, creative writing, and music (Davis & Rimm, 1993; Subotnik, 1997).

Meeting the needs of the gifted and talented requires early identification; failure to do so can result in gifted underachievers, with social and emotional problems linked to boredom and lack of motivation (Clinkenbeard, 1992; Dai, Moon, & Feldhusen, 1998). Experts recommend using a variety of methods for identifying gifted and talented students, including standardized test scores, teacher nominations, creativity measures, and peer and parent nominations (Davis & Rimm, 1993; Gallagher, 1998). As a teacher you will have an important role in this process.

Programs for the gifted and talented are typically based on either **acceleration,** which *keeps the curriculum the same but allows students to move through it more quickly,* or **enrichment,** which *provides richer and varied content through strategies that supplement usual grade-level work* (see Table 3.3).

Increasing Understanding 3.18

Using information from previous sections in the chapter, explain why standardized testing might miss many minority students who are gifted and talented.

Mental Retardation

Students who are **mentally retarded** *have limited intellectual functioning, as indicated by difficulties in learning, and problems with adaptive skills, such as communication, self-care, and social ability* (Turnbull et al., 1999). Prior to the 1960s, definitions of mental retardation were based primarily on below-average scores on intelligence tests, but this approach had at least three problems. First, errors in testing sometimes resulted in misdiagnoses, and second, disproportionate numbers of minorities and non-English-speaking students were identified as mentally retarded (Hallahan & Kauffman, 1997; Hardman, Drew, & Egan, 1999). Third, individuals with the same intelligence-test scores varied widely in their ability to cope with the real world, and these differences couldn't be explained based on the tests alone (Heward, 2000). Because of these limitations, adaptive functioning was added to the definition.

Learning Disabilities

Students with **learning disabilities (LDs)** have *difficulties in acquiring and using listening, speaking, reading, writing, reasoning, or mathematical abilities* (National Joint Committee on Learning Disabilities, 1994). Problems with reading, writing, and listening are most common. Learning disabilities are assumed to be due to central nervous-system dysfunction.

Students with learning disabilities make up the largest group of students with exceptionalities—approximately half of the special-education population and 4 percent of all students in U.S. schools (U.S. Department of Education, 1998). The category first became widely used in the early 1960s, and the number of school-age children diagnosed as learning disabled has continually increased.

Students with learning disabilities have the following problems:

- Uneven performance (for example, being capable in one area but extremely weak in others).
- Hyperactivity and difficulty in concentrating.
- Lack of follow-through in completion of assignments.
- Disorganization and tendency toward distraction.

**Increasing
Understanding 3.19**

Identify at least one
similarity and one
difference between learning
disabilities and mental
retardation.

Some of these characteristics are typical of general learning problems or immaturity. Unlike developmental lags, however, problems associated with learning disabilities often increase over time instead of disappearing. Students fall farther behind in achievement, management problems increase, and self-esteem decreases (Hardman et al., 1999; Heward, 2000). Lowered achievement and reduced self-esteem intensify and result in major learning problems.

Behavior Disorders

Students with **behavior disorders (BD)** *display serious and persistent age-inappropriate behaviors that result in social conflict, personal unhappiness, and school failure.* In this definition, the terms *serious* and *persistent* are important. Many children occasionally fight with their peers, and all children go through periods when they want to be alone. When these patterns are chronic and interfere with normal development and school performance, however, a behavior disorder may exist.

**Increasing
Understanding 3.20**

Identify at least one
similarity and one
difference between learning
disabilities and behavior
disorders.

Estimates of the frequency of behavior disorders vary (Hardman et al., 1999). Some suggest that about 1 percent of the total school population and about 9 percent of the special education population have the problem (U.S. Department of Education, 1998), whereas others suggest that it's closer to between 6 percent and 10 percent of the total population (Hallahan & Kauffman, 1997). Identification is a problem because the characteristics are elusive, making diagnosis difficult (Turnbull et al., 1999).

Changes in the Way Schools and Teachers Help Students with Exceptionalities

In the past, students with exceptionalities were separated from their peers and placed in segregated classrooms or schools. However, instruction in these situations was often inferior, achievement was no better than in regular classrooms, and students didn't learn social and life skills needed to live in the real world (Bradley & Switlick, 1997). Educators and lawmakers looked for other ways to help these students.

In 1975, the U.S. Congress passed Public Law 94-142, the *Individuals with Disabilities Education Act (IDEA)*, which is intended to ensure a free and public education for all students with exceptionalities. This law was necessary because prior to that time there was considerable variability from state to state in how schools addressed the needs of students with exceptionalities, with many students being excluded or not served at all. IDEA, combined with recent amendments, provides the following guidelines for working with students having exceptionalities:

- Identify the needs of students with exceptionalities through nondiscriminatory assessment.
- Involve parents in developing each child's educational program.

■ Create an environment that is the least restrictive possible for promoting learning.

■ Develop an individualized education program (IEP) of study for each student.

The tremendous impact of IDEA can be seen in the number of students with exceptionalities that are being served. In 1976–1977, just after the law's passage, the nation educated about 3.3 million children with exceptionalities; presently the schools serve over 6 million, an increase of nearly 82 percent (Sack, 2000a). IDEA has affected every school in the United States and has changed the roles of regular and special educators.

The Evolution toward Inclusion As educators realized that segregated classes and services were not meeting the needs of students with exceptionalities, they searched for alternatives. The first was **mainstreaming,** *the practice of moving students with exceptionalities from segregated settings into regular classrooms.* Popular in the 1970s, mainstreaming began the move away from segregated services. Unfortunately, students with exceptionalities were often placed in regular classrooms without adequate support and services (Hardman et al., 1999).

In attempting to solve these problems, educators developed the concept of the **least restrictive environment (LRE),** *one that places students in as normal an educational setting as possible while still meeting their special academic, social, and physical needs.* The LRE includes mainstreaming, but is broader in scope. For example, the LRE could simply mainstream a child into a regular classroom, or it could place the child in separate facilities. Mainstreaming occurs only if parents and educators decide it best meets the child's needs. During the 1996–1997 school year, 46.2 percent of students with exceptionalities received the bulk of their schooling in regular classrooms (Galley, 2000).

As educators considered mainstreaming and the LRE, they gradually developed the concept of **inclusion,** which is *a comprehensive approach to educating students with exceptionalities.* Inclusion has three components:

■ Including students with special needs in a regular school campus.

■ Placing students with special needs in age- and grade-appropriate classrooms.

■ Providing special-education support within the regular classroom.

Initially, inclusion was thought of as additive; students with exceptionalities received additional services to help them function in regular school settings (Turnbull et al., 1999). Gradually, the concept of coordination replaced addition. Special- and regular-education teachers collaborate closely to ensure that learning experiences are integrated into the regular classroom curriculum. For example, rather than pulling a student with special needs out of the classroom for supplementary instruction in math, in inclusion the special-education teacher would plan with the teacher and offer supplementary help linked to the regular math curriculum right in the classroom.

Effective inclusion makes all educators responsible for creating supportive learning environments by attempting to place students with exceptionalities in regular classrooms and providing support for teachers. When inclusion is properly implemented, regular classroom teachers will have students with special needs in their classrooms, but they will be given help from trained specialists.

Inclusion is controversial. The specialized help that teachers are supposed to receive often isn't provided, so teachers are left to cope with students' special needs on their own. Parents are critical; they worry that their children might get lost in regular classrooms, and special educators don't even agree (Turnbull et al., 1999). Advocates contend that placement

Increasing Understanding 3.21

Draw two circles, one inside the other. Label one *inclusion* and the other *mainstreaming.* Explain your labeling.

Inclusion attempts to integrate students with special needs into the regular classroom through instructional adaptations that meet their special needs.

in a regular classroom is the only way to eliminate the negative effects of segregation, whereas opponents argue that inclusion is not for everyone and that some students are better served in separate special classes for parts of the day (Stainback & Stainback, 1992).

What does all this mean for you as a teacher? At least three implications exist. You are virtually certain to have students with exceptionalities in your classroom, and you will be expected to do the following:

■ Adapt your instruction to meet the needs of these students. Actively seek out the help of special educators in the process.

■ Aid in the process of identifying students with exceptionalities.

■ Maintain communication with parents, school administrators, and special educators about the progress of students in your classroom who have special needs.

For up-to-date national information and statistics on the implementation of IDEA, go to the *Web Links* Module in Chapter 3 of the Companion Website at **http://www.prenhall. com/kauchak.**

The Changing Role *of* Teachers

A quaint but outmoded view of schools depicted them as places where students came to absorb and be filled with knowledge and information. Learning involved transmission, and the roles of teachers, students, and parents were clear. Teachers had the answers, students needed to learn the answers, and parents were to make sure their children attended school and did their homework. What went on within the confines of the school walls was the business of the teacher.

We now know that this simplistic view of teaching does not accurately capture the complexities of teaching and learning. Children are more than empty vessels to be filled up; they bring with them a wealth of background experiences and language capabilities that significantly contribute to learning. Parents are not just passive onlookers in the process of learning; they contribute substantially in many subtle, and not so subtle, ways to their children's success in school. When you enter your first classroom as a teacher, you will be expected to build upon your students' cultural and linguistic backgrounds and actively involve parents in their children's learning.

Building on Students' Strengths

To build upon students' strengths, you must discover what these strengths are. Effective teachers do this in a number of ways, including talking with previous years' teachers, examining students' cumulative folders, and conducting comprehensive pre-assessments at the beginning of the school year. But effective teachers need to go beyond these traditional strategies and establish human communication links with their students. Ways of doing this include the following:

- Have students write about themselves and their families at the beginning of the school year. Ask them to share their hopes (and anxieties) about the new school year as well as information about themselves as people, like their favorite foods and pastimes and information about their families.
- Spend time with them at lunch and on the playground. This provides you with valuable opportunities to learn about how they act and feel outside the classroom.
- Make yourself available before and after school for school help. When teachers do this, they find that students often want to talk about much more than school-related homework problems.

The goal with all of these strategies is to get to know your students as human beings. Not only will this make you a more effective teacher, but it will also help you enjoy teaching more.

Working with Parents

Learning is a cooperative venture, and teachers, students, and parents are in it together. In a comprehensive review of factors affecting student learning, researchers reached the following conclusions:

■ ■ ■

Because of the importance of the home environment to school learning, teachers must also develop strategies to increase parent involvement in their children's academic life. This means teachers should go beyond traditional once-a-year parent/teacher conferences and work with parents to see that learning is valued in the home. Teachers should encourage parents to be involved with their children's academic pursuits on a day-to-day basis, helping them with homework, monitoring television viewing, reading to their young children, and simply expressing the expectation that their children will achieve academic success (Wang et al., 1993, pp. 278–279).

■ ■ ■

Communication with parents or other primary caregivers is not an appendage to the teaching process; it is an integral part of a teacher's job.

■ SUMMARY

Cultural Diversity

Due to demographic trends, our schools are becoming increasingly diverse. In the past, schools responded to diversity with the goal of assimilation, hoping to "Americanize" students as quickly as possible. Multicultural education, by contrast, attempts to recognize the contributions of different cultures and build on students' cultural strengths in the classroom.

This increase in diversity is also seen in the languages that students bring to our classrooms. Different approaches to dealing with this language diversity place different amounts of emphasis on maintaining the first language versus learning English as quickly as possible.

Gender

Evidence suggests that both boys and girls encounter problems in today's schools. For girls these problems focus more on achievement, especially in areas like math, science, and computer science, while for boys the problems are more behavioral and connected to learning problems. Causes for these problems range from societal and parental expectations to differential treatment in classrooms. Teachers can play a major role in ensuring that gender differences don't become gender inequalities. Sexual harassment is a problem for both males and females and occurs most often in environments where teachers and administrators allow it to occur.

Ability Differences

A third dimension of diversity found in today's classrooms focuses on students' different abilities to learn. Earlier perspectives viewed ability as unidimensional; the current perspective views ability as multifaceted.

Ability grouping is one of the most common responses to this dimension of diversity. Despite its popularity, research suggests a number of problems with ability grouping, ranging from inappropriate and rigid placements to substandard instruction in some low-ability classrooms.

Learning Styles

Cognitive learning styles emphasize differences in the ways students process information. Cultural learning styles reflect the variety of ways that different groups learn and interact. The concept of learning styles reminds us that all students learn differently; effective teachers are sensitive to these differences and adapt their teaching accordingly.

Students with Exceptionalities

Students with exceptionalities require extra help to reach their full potential. The majority of students with exceptionalities fall into four major categories: gifted and talented, mental retardation, learning disabilities, and behavior disorders. Inclusion is changing the way schools assist students with exceptionalities, providing them with a supporting network of services.

■ IMPORTANT CONCEPTS

ability grouping	behavior disorder	culturally responsive
acceleration	between-class ability	teaching
assimilation	grouping	culture

English as a Second
  Language (ESL)
enrichment
ethnicity
exceptionality
field dependence/
  independence
gender-role identity
gifted and talented students
immersion programs
impulsive students
inclusion
intelligence

learning disability
learning style
least restrictive environment
mainstreaming
maintenance language
  programs
mentally retarded students
multicultural education
multiple intelligences
nature view of intelligence
  or ability
nurture view of intelligence
  or ability

reflective students
sexual harassment
single-gender classes and
  schools
special education
students who are gifted and
  talented
students who are mentally
  retarded
tracking
transition programs
within-class ability grouping

■ DISCUSSION QUESTIONS

1. Is multicultural education more important at some grade levels than at others? Why? Is multicultural education more important in some content areas than in others? Why?

2. Experts debate whether teachers should adjust instruction to match student learning styles or teach students to broaden their learning repertoires. Which approach is more desirable? Why?

3. Which approach to teaching English to LEP students makes the most sense in the particular teaching setting you will find yourself in your first job? Why?

4. Are single-gender classrooms a good idea? Why?

5. What are the advantages and disadvantages of full inclusion? Should it be used with all students?

6. What implications does Gardner's theory of multiple intelligences have for you as a teacher? (Be sure to relate your answer to the grade level and content area(s) you'll be teaching.)

■ GOING INTO SCHOOLS

1. Interview a teacher about the diversity in his or her classroom. Explain how the students differ in terms of the following:
   a. culture
   b. home language
   c. learning styles
   d. multiple intelligences
   e. learning ability

   What does the teacher do to accommodate these differences? Summarize these responses and analyze them using information from this chapter.

2. Observe a classroom and focus on several cultural minority students.
   a. Where do they sit?
   b. Who do they talk to and make friends with?
   c. Do they attend to the class and are they involved?
   d. Do they participate in classroom interaction?

Ask the teacher how these students perform in class and what he or she does to build upon differences in these students. Analyze this response in terms of the information given in this chapter.

3. Ask the teacher to identify several cultural minority students. Interview these students and ask the following questions:
   a. How long have they been at this school?
   b. What do they like the most about school?
   c. What do they like the least about school?
   d. What can teachers do to help them learn better?

   Summarize their responses and suggest several concrete things that teachers can do to make their classrooms better learning environments for cultural minorities.

4. Observe a class during an interactive questioning session.
   a. Note the number of boys and girls in the class.
   b. Where were the boys and girls seated?
   c. Did boys and girls raise their hands to respond equally?
   d. Record the number of times boys and girls were called on. Were they equal?
   e. Did the number of management interventions vary by gender?

   How gender neutral was the class? What can teachers do to make their classes more gender neutral and a better place for both boys and girls to learn?

5. Observe a class working on an in-class assignment. As you do this, circulate around the room so you can observe the work progress of different students. Note the following:
   a. Beginning times—Do all students get immediately to work or do some take their time starting?
   b. On-task behaviors—What percentage of the class stays on task throughout the assignment?
   c. Completions—Do all students complete the assignment? What do they do if they don't complete the work?
   d. Assistance—What forms of help are there for students who need it?
   e. Options—What options are there for students who complete their assignments early?

   From your observations, how diverse is this class in terms of learning ability? What concrete things can teachers do to address this diversity?

6. Interview a teacher to investigate his or her use of the following strategies to deal with differences in learning ability: flexible time requirements, grouping, strategy instruction, and peer tutoring and cooperative learning. Ask these questions:
   a. Are differences in learning ability a problem for the teacher? Explain.
   b. Does the teacher use any of the strategies mentioned in this book? Which ones work and why? Have any been tried that didn't work?
   c. Does the teacher employ any other strategy for dealing with differences in learning ability?

   What implications do the teacher's responses suggest for you and how you would teach in your future classroom?

7. Interview a teacher about working with students with exceptionalities in the classroom. Ask the following questions:
   a. Which students are classified as exceptional? What behaviors led to this classification? What role did the teacher play in identification?

    b. In working with students with exceptionalities, what assistance does the classroom teacher receive from the following people?
- Special-education teacher
- School psychologist or school counselor
- Principal

    c. What does an Individualized Education Program (IEP) look like ? How helpful is it in working with exceptional students in the classroom?

    d. What is the biggest challenge the teacher faces in working with students with exceptionalities?

Summarize your findings. Describe what your approach will be in working with these students.

 Virtual Field *Experience* | **If you would like to participate in a Virtual Field Experience, go to the *Field Experience* Module in Chapter 1 of the Companion Website.**

■ ONLINE PORTFOLIO ACTIVITIES

 To complete these activities online, go to the Portfolio Activities Module in Chapter 3 of the Companion Website, and submit your response.

Portfolio Activity 3.1

Exploring Cultural Diversity

INTASC Principle 3: *Adapting Instruction*

The purpose of this activity is to introduce you to the cultural diversity in an area where you might teach. Contact the State Office of Education in a state where you're thinking of teaching. Addresses and Websites can be found in the Companion Website to Chapter 13; school district telephone numbers can be found at the back of the White Pages of the telephone directory in the business section under "Schools." Ask for demographic information on cultural minorities and ESL students. Summarize the information briefly, identifying major cultural groups and possible implications for your teaching.

Portfolio Activity 3.2

Learning Styles

INTASC Principle 3: *Adapting Instruction*

The purpose of this activity is to make you more knowledgeable about learning styles. Using the references in this chapter as a starting point, locate and read several articles on learning styles. Write a short paper on the implications of learning styles for your teaching. In your paper include information about the following topics: What are learning styles? Which are most important to teaching and learning? How can teachers adapt their instruction to address students' different learning styles?

Portfolio Activity 3.3

Exploring Careers in Special Education

INTASC Principle 9: *Commitment to the Profession*

This activity is designed to acquaint you with teaching career options in special education. Visit the Website for the Council for Exceptional Children, the national professional organization for special educators (the Website can be found in the *Web Links* Module in Chapter 3 of the Companion Website at **http://www.prenhall.com/kauchak.**) Click on "Student CEC" for information on Tools You Need, Career Info., Goals, Chapter Directory, and Regional Contacts. The *Career Info* Module contains additional information on résumé writing, interviewing, and building a professional portfolio. Write a brief description of career opportunities in special education and how your talents and personality might match these.

CHAPTER 4

Changes in American Society
Influences on Today's Schools

Teaching today is more challenging than at any point in our history. In addition to the increasing diversity we discussed in Chapter 3, challenges also come from changes in our society and our students, who have different characteristics than they had in the past. Consider these statistics describing high school students, taken from the 1997 Youth Risk Behavior Survey:

- 51 percent had consumed alcohol during the 30 days preceding the survey.

- 26 percent had used marijuana during the 30 days preceding the survey.

- 7.7 percent had attempted suicide during the 12 months prior to the survey.

- 12.5 percent of males and 3.7 percent of females reported carrying a weapon on school property on 1 or more days during the 30 days prior to the survey.

Fewer of today's students come from "traditional" homes, where the father is the breadwinner and the mother works in the home as the primary caregiver. More come to school hungry, tired, or emotionally drained because of conditions in their homes and communities. They are more sexually active, and they use alcohol and other drugs more often than students did in the past. This chapter analyzes these and other conditions in attempting to answer the following questions:

- How have societal changes affected the students you'll work with?

- Who are students placed at-risk, and what can teachers and schools do to help them learn?

- What implications do changes in our students have for prospective teachers?

Let's begin by examining how the answers to these questions influence the lives of real teachers.

Case STUDY

It is the end of August. Carla Ramirez, a second-year teacher, is excited about the new school year. Relocating to the Midwest because of her husband's job, she has been assigned a first grade classroom in a large urban city. She spends the summer constructing units in the different content areas and is eager to get started.

Two weeks later Carla shuffles into the faculty lounge on her lunch break.

"You look tired. Been getting enough sleep?" her hallmate, 20-year veteran teacher Rae Anne Johnson, asks.

"No, I'm not tired," Carla responds, collapsing in a chair. "Just a little discouraged."

"Anything you want to talk about?" Rae Anne asks after a moment.

Carla hesitates and then replies, "It's my class. I had such high hopes. I had my room all set up with learning centers and neat stuff. I knew what I was going to teach, and I was really looking forward to it. But these kids . . . I don't know . . . I'm really struggling, and now I'm beginning to wonder if it's me."

Rae Anne shrugs, "Maybe, but you're so conscientious. . . . I doubt it. What's got you so down?"

"I can't quite figure it out. Some of the kids are really squirrelly. It's hard to get them to sit down at all. Others literally fall asleep in the middle of lessons. I've got four thumb-suckers and, frankly, some of them just don't seem ready for first-grade work. I hand out a worksheet, and they look at it like I wrote it in Greek or something."

"You might be right. . . . I know it's tough . . . I have some of the same things. One of my kids was all upset yesterday, so I sat her down at recess, and she told me that her parents had had a big fight the night before. And then there's Johnny . . . he's always so droopy, so I asked him if he'd had breakfast this morning. He said he never eats it, so I called his home and told his mother about the school's free breakfast program. I had to call three times to get her . . . I didn't want to just leave a message on the machine. She was all apologetic about sending him to school without it, but she works weird hours, and she's a single mom, so I know it's tough for her too. It's hard for a lot of kids."

"I guess you're right, but they didn't prepare me for this. I was so eager, and, I guess, idealistic about making a difference. Now, I'm not so sure."

■ ■ ■

■ A CHANGING SOCIETY

Our goal as teachers is to provide the best education possible for all students. We want them to enjoy school and learn as much as they can. This happens for students. They come from stable, supportive families, and they have experiences that prepare them for achievement.

For others, unfortunately, this isn't the case. Problems in their families, neighborhoods, and even communities limit their chances for success. In addition, societal influences, such as changes in the economy, the workplace, and peoples' attitudes have all impacted our students' ability to benefit from schooling. The magnitude of the problems facing teachers is reflected in the following lament from an elementary teacher in Atlanta, Georgia:

■ ■ ■

I just don't know what I'm going to do. Every year, my first-grade class has more and more of these kids. They don't seem to care about right or wrong, they don't care about adult approval, they are disruptive, they can't read and they arrive at school absolutely unprepared to learn. Who are these kids? Where do they come from? Why are there more and more of them? I used to think that I was a good teacher. I really prided myself on doing an

Figure 4.1   **A Changing Society**

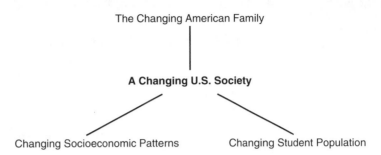

In this section, we examine our changing society and the implications these changes have for teachers and schools. They're illustrated in Figure 4.1 and discussed in the sections that follow.

outstanding job. But I find I'm working harder and harder, and being less and less effective. A good teacher? Today I really don't know. I do know that my classroom is being overwhelmed by society's problems and I don't understand it. What's happening to our schools? What's happening to society? I don't understand all of this and I sure don't know what we're going to do about it (Barr & Parrett, 2001, p. 1).

■ ■ ■

In this section, we examine our changing society and the implications these changes have for teachers and schools. They're illustrated in Figure 4.1 and discussed in the sections that follow.

The Changing American Family

■ ■ ■

With head resting on his hands, Brad looked puzzled when he was asked how many brothers and sisters he had—a seemingly simple question, but not so easy for Brad to answer. He scrunched his face, paused, pushed back in his chair, pursed his lips, rolled his dark eyes, and began counting on his fingers slowly, deliberately, then said, "Let's see, hmmm, six." "Six?" "Wait, seven." "Seven?" "Wait, eight." "That's a hard question." It wasn't meant to be. Brad explained: "I didn't count my sister Mary or my sister Kerrie." "Oh?" "My dad was married to four different ladies and has had quite a few kids." Brad had a hard time remembering when he last saw two of his siblings, who are older and live in other states. Even with his best effort, he was off one child (Bullough, 1999, p. 10).

■ ■ ■

Brad's story, while extreme, illustrates some of the changes occurring in American families. In spite of these changes, the family is still the institution primarily responsible for meeting the needs of young people and helping them adapt to the world. This was true in colonial times and remains true today. But, the ways that families care for and educate their children are shifting.

The "traditional" American family—a husband who is the primary breadwinner, a mother who stays home, and two school-age children—now makes up only 6 percent of the households in the United States. Instead, we see the following patterns (More Families in Poverty, 1993; U.S. Bureau of Census, 1998):

■ Families headed by married couples now make up 55 percent of all households, compared to 71 percent in 1970.

Increasing Understanding 4.1

 Identify at least two things teachers can do to help parents work with their children more effectively on homework and other academic activities.

To respond to the Increasing Understanding questions in this chapter and receive immediate feedback, go to the *Increasing Understanding* Module in Chapter 4 of the Companion Website at **http://www.prenhall.com/ kauchak.**

- Seven out of 10 women with children are in the workforce.
- The divorce rate has quadrupled in the past 20 years; the number of single-parent families is estimated at 25 percent and is expected to increase.
- Sixty-eight percent of all births to teenagers occur out of wedlock.
- The incidence of poverty among single-parent families is between 7 and 8 times higher than in families headed by married couples.
- Sixty percent of teenage families live in poverty, as compared to 14 percent of the total population.

Poverty, divorce, single parents, families where both parents work, and teenage pregnancies pose challenges to parents, their children, and teachers. Work demands for single parents and parents who both work outside the home result in less time being spent with their children in general, as well as less time being spent helping and supervising homework. Research indicates that many parents in today's fast-paced world are spending up to 40 percent less time with their children than parents a generation ago (Kamerman & Kamerman, 1995; Hewlett, 1991). Even when they have time, many parents are uncertain about how to help their children with schoolwork (Gorman, & Balter, 1997).

What does this information imply for teachers? Let's look at an example. One of your authors went to a first volleyball team meeting with his daughter. The team was lined up on the floor and was asked to introduce themselves and their parents/caregivers. The first girl introduced both parents; the second, whose father wasn't there, felt obligated to explain. From that point every girl followed precedent by "explaining" the absence of a parent, and some were embarrassed because their parents were divorced. Teachers can make situations like these easier for students by using words such as, "Would you please introduce your parent, or parents, or caregivers," when asking for introductions. On the surface it may seem like a minor issue, but it is important to students.

Being flexible with meeting times for parent–teacher conferences is another way teachers can accommodate working or single parents. It communicates that you care about your students, you're committed to their education, and you're aware of the pressure of work schedules. In essence, as teachers we should try to be sensitive to these changes in family structure and communicate to our students that we accept and support all types of family patterns.

Child Care When both parents work outside the home or when a single parent leaves the home to make a living, child care becomes an issue. The trend is away from home care; today one-fourth of the children of working parents are cared for in the home compared to 57 percent in 1958 (Leach, 1995).

These trends raise questions about the effects of child care on the emotional and intellectual development of children. Critics contend that young children need the presence of a mother in the home, and child care is not an adequate substitute. Supporters counter that children can adapt to different care patterns and are not jeopardized by alternate child-care arrangements.

Researchers attempting to respond to this issue have focused on the quality of the child care instead of the larger issue of working parents. When children are placed in well-run and supervised child-care facilities, there seem to be few if any adverse effects on the children (Berk, 2000). However, the problem is complicated by the fact that many child-care facilities don't provide high-quality care.

Latchkey Children Latchkey children, *children who go home to empty houses after school and who are left alone until parents arrive home from work,* are another work-related prob-

Latchkey children often face long hours of unsupervised care.

lem. There may be as many as 6 million latchkey kids in our country, and almost 50 percent of working parents acknowledge leaving their children unattended for periods of time after school (Leach, 1995). The problem is complex, ranging from concerns about children's safety to questions of supervision, excessive time spent watching television, and lack of help with homework.

Some schools respond with after-hour programs, but a more common solution is for schools to cooperate with community agencies, such as YMCAs or youth clubs, to offer late afternoon programs. In addition to providing safe, supervised environments, these programs teach children how to respond to home emergencies, use the phone to seek help, make healthy snacks, and spend time wisely.

Changing Socioeconomic Patterns

Researchers have found that parents and caregivers from different backgrounds think about and prepare their children for school in different ways. One of the strongest indicators of these differences is **socioeconomic status (SES),** which is *an indicator that combines parents' incomes, occupations, and levels of education.* Teachers, for example, have relatively high socioeconomic status; they have college degrees, they have professional occupations, and they make middle-class incomes. Plumbers, in comparison, tend to have lower socioeconomic status because they don't work in professional occupations, and they usually don't have college degrees (even though they sometimes make more money than teachers do).

Socioeconomic status is commonly described in terms of three levels—upper, middle, and lower class—with finer distinctions within each. The **upper class** is *the smallest segment of the population (less than 15 percent) and is composed of highly educated (usually a college degree), highly paid (typically above $100,000) professionals.* The upper class comprises

Increasing Understanding 4.2

 Where do you think most new teaching positions will occur, in schools populated by students from upper, middle, or lower SES backgrounds? Why do you think so?

only a small part of the total population but controls a disproportionate amount of the wealth; the gap between the upper and other classes is growing. For example, in 1979 corporate chief executives earned 29 times as much as their employees; by 1988 the figure had grown to 93 times (Phillips, 1990).

The **middle class** *includes managers, administrators, and white-collar workers who perform nonmanual work.* Teachers are included in this category. Middle-class incomes typically range from $30,000 to $70,000, and about 40 percent of the population falls into this category. (Upper-middle-class groups fall between the $70,000 and $100,000 ranges.)

Families in the lower SES class typically make less than $20,000 per year, have a high-school education or less, and work in blue-collar jobs. About 40 percent of the U.S. population is in this category, and the percentage is increasing. The lowest earning segment of this category often depends upon public assistance to supplement their incomes, and members are often the third or fourth generation to live in poverty. The term **underclass** is used to describe *people with low incomes who have difficulty coping with economic problems*; research indicates that escaping this situation is very difficult (Lind, 1995; Reich, 1995).

Poverty

Case STUDY

When Sally gets a spare moment (and there are precious few of them), she loves to draw, mostly fantasy creatures. "What is your favorite thing to draw?" "A mermaid thing, cuz it's not real—there's no such thing as a mermaid—but I like to draw things that aren't real. Fairy tales. Fairies, monsters." She lights up talking about her creations. But Sally's life is not a fairy tale. With her brother she hurries home from school, immediately does her homework, and "I mean *right* after my homework I have to clean up my room and do the dishes for dinner and cook dinner." "You cook dinner? Every day?" Staring straight across the table separating us, and without blinking her blue eyes, Sally responded slightly defensively, "I'm a good cook." For all the talk about food, Sally's greatest fear, she said, was that she will not get enough to eat and will get sick. Who would take care of the family, then? "I worry . . . I [will] end up getting too skinny and die cuz I'm really skinny. I try to keep my health up, but I don't eat that much." I hesitated, not knowing what to say. "Why?" "I try to eat a lot, but I always have to be served last after dinner, but if there's no food left, I can't eat." "What do you do?" "I go to the store and get me a snack, like an orange or an apple." She began [taking care of her brother and cooking] when she was seven years old. Exhausted, she is in bed by 8:30. Sometimes, before falling asleep, her mother reports, she reads, but there are few books in the house, which disappoints Sally who loves books.

Sally's mother works the early morning shift as a waitress in a large and busy café. She has severe diabetes. Watching her at a distance at work, she moves slowly, deliberately, as though her legs are heavy and getting heavier with each step. Her movements are those of a tired, older woman, not of a young woman, tall, thin, and at one time athletic. She seems to will herself from table to table. Once her ten-hour shift is finished, she laboriously walks the four blocks to her apartment, collapses on the old sofa in the front room nearest the door, smokes a cigarette or two, and sleeps. When she gets home from school, this is how Sally finds her mother (Bullough, 1999, pp. 13–14).

■   ■   ■

The lowest end of the SES continuum is characterized by pervasive **poverty,** which the federal government defines as *earning less than $16,000 for a family of four* (U.S. Census Bureau, 1998).

Figure 4.2   **Poverty Levels by Ethnicity**

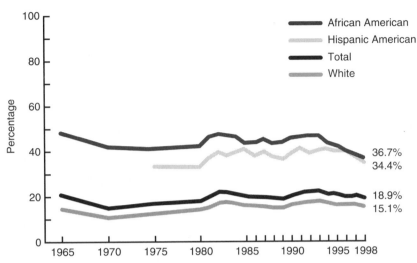

Source: Data from U.S. Census Bureau, 2000, *Historical Poverty Tables, Table 3. Poverty Status of People by Age, Race, and Hispanic Origin: 1959 to 1999.* [Online] Available at http://www.census.gov/hhes/poverty/histpov/hstpov3.html.

Increasing Understanding 4.3

What are some possible ways that poverty can influence learning?

Research on poverty reveals the following patterns:

- Less than 9 percent of America's poor live in inner cities.
- Poverty is most common in small towns and suburban areas (46 percent of all impoverished families live in small towns; 28 percent live in suburban areas).
- Although they comprise only 27 percent of the total population, children constitute 40 percent of the poor.
- Poverty is most common in families headed by single mothers.
- Poverty is more prevalent among minorities than nonminorities (see Figure 4.2).

Some of these results are surprising. For example, many people think that poverty is most prevalent in cities, and most don't realize that 40 percent of our potential leaders for the future are now living in poverty.

The powerful effect that poverty can have on learning is reflected in a recent proposal by Wake County District in North Carolina. This proposal suggests a busing program to ensure that no more than 40 percent of a school's enrollment is composed of students who are eligible for the federal free or reduced-price lunch program (Johnston, 2000b). San Francisco is considering a similar strategy to battle both economic and racial segregation (Kahlenberg, 1999). The programs are based on the belief that high concentrations of students from impoverished backgrounds detract from the students' ability to benefit as much as possible from their school experiences.

Homelessness One of the direct results of poverty is the increase in homelessness. Experts estimate that between one-half and 1 million children are homeless; accurate figures are hard to obtain because of the transient nature of the population (Rafferty, 1995; Gracenin, 1993). Homeless children often come from unstable families, suffer from inadequate diets, and lack medical care (Gracenin, 1993). Because of unstable families, the majority (estimates run as high as 63 percent) of homeless children fail to attend school on a regular basis (Sandham, 2000).

Effective schools attempt to respond to the problem in several ways. Recognizing that the home situation is difficult, they remove barriers by making their admission, attendance, and course requirements flexible (Vissing, Schroepfer, & Bloise, 1994). They also provide outreach services such as counselors, after-school programs, and financial aid for transportation. In addition, school officials coordinate their efforts with other community agencies to ensure that basic needs, such as food and shelter, are met.

One elementary school in Phoenix, Arizona, targets homeless children as its primary clients (Sandham, 2000). It sends school buses around the city to pick up these children and maintains a clothing room that students can visit to pick up fresh underwear and changes of clothes. Volunteer pediatricians staff an on-site clinic that provides free medical care and immunizations. The school even hands out alarm clocks (old-fashioned windups because many of the children don't have access to electricity) to help the children get to school on time in the morning. Teacher dedication and effort make the school work. One teacher commented, "There's something about watching the buses roll out of here, with all the kids' faces pressed against the windows. I get this feeling it's what I should be doing" (Sandham, 2000, p. 29).

As a teacher, what can you do about homeless children? While seemingly simple and insignificant, the most important responses are to be caring and flexible. Demonstrating that you genuinely care about students and their learning is important for all children. For those that are homeless, it's essential.

Socioeconomic Status and School Success Socorro is a fifth grader who is struggling in school. When a researcher went to her house to learn why, here is what he found.

Increasing Understanding 4.4

What is the most effective thing teachers can do to demonstrate that they care about a student?

Case STUDY

During the interview with Socorro's mother, Nick passed through the apartment, apparently returning to work after taking a brief break. The phone rang. Socorro's five-year-old stepbrother curled up in his mother's lap and began talking into her ear. Television was on; there is a television in every room—one is Socorro's. Cable. "I let her do whatever she wants," Socorro's mother exclaims proudly. "She does whatever she wants." Working two jobs, one in housekeeping at a nearby hospital, and another, an evening job as a parking lot attendant to obtain money for a promised trip to Disneyland, leaves her little option: She is not home, often. While at work, her brother, who lives with the family and spends much of his day watching television, tends the children when they are home. Irritated, Socorro says that her uncle expects to be waited on, and she doesn't like it. "I want to support my kids," the mother says, and this requires that she is "never home for them."

Socorro's problem in school, her mother asserts, is that "her mind wanders." Having not read with her daughter nor spoken with her teachers, she is unaware that Socorro cannot read and is struggling; she seems unconcerned that Socorro misses so much school; as her teacher said: "She is out of school more than she is in it." Attending school irregularly, Socorro is slipping further and further behind her classmates. Concerned, teachers made arrangements to place Socorro for part of the day with the special education teacher. They didn't know what else to do, having failed to gain the mother's help getting Socorro to school regularly (Bullough, In press, pp. 48–49).

■ ■ ■

Socioeconomic status is related to school success in several ways. For example, compared to students from low-SES backgrounds, high-SES students score higher on intelligence and achievement tests, get better grades, miss less school, and have fewer suspensions (Macionis, 1997). School dropout rates for students from poor families are twice as high as those for the general population; for students from the poorest families, they exceed 50 percent. The powerful influence of SES on learning can be summarized in one

Poverty can exert a powerful negative influence on school success.

researcher's conclusion, ". . . the relationship between test scores and SES is one of the most widely replicated findings in the social sciences" (Konstantopoulas, 1997, p. 5).

What might cause these differences? At least five factors are likely:

- Basic needs
- Family stability
- School-related experience
- Interaction patterns in the home
- Parental attitudes and values

With respect to basic needs, many low-SES families lack adequate medical care, and an increasing number of children are coming to school without proper nourishment and adequate rest.

SES can also influence the quality of home life. In some low-SES families, unstable work conditions increase economic problems that lead to parental frustration, anger, and depression. These pressures can lead to marital conflicts that result in unstable home environments (Conger et al., 1992). Children then come to school without a sense of safety and security, so they are not as well-equipped to tackle school-related tasks.

SES also influences children's background experiences. For example, high-SES parents are more likely than low-SES parents to provide their children with educational activities outside school (for example, visits to art, science, and history museums; attendance at concerts; books bought or borrowed from the library). They are also more likely to have learning materials at home (including computers, pocket calculators, newspapers, encyclopedias, and dictionaries) and to provide educational experiences outside school (such as, art, music, religious, dance, or computer classes). These activities support school learning by providing an experiential base for school activities (Peng & Lee, 1992).

Increasing Understanding 4.5

What might kindergarten or first-grade teachers do if they discover that important background learning experiences are lacking?

The way parents interact with their children also influences learning (Chance, 1997). Experts estimate that by the age of 3, welfare children have heard 10 million words, compared with 20 million for children from working-class families and 30 million for children from professional homes. In addition, low-SES parents are more likely to "tell" rather than explain and to emphasize conformity and obedience instead of individual responsibility or initiative. Their language is less elaborate, their directions are less clear, and they are less likely to encourage problem solving. High-SES parents talk more with their children, explain ideas and the causes of events, encourage independent thinking, and emphasize individual responsibility (Berk, 2000; Macionis, 1997). These discussions promote language development and prepare children for the kind of verbal interaction found in schools (Heath, 1983). Sometimes called "the curriculum of the home," these rich interaction patterns, together with the enrichment experiences described in the previous paragraph, provide a foundation for reading and vocabulary development (Walberg, 1991).

Finally, the impact of SES is also transmitted through parental attitudes and values. For instance, high-SES parents and caregivers are more likely to read and have books, papers, and magazines around the home. Their children imitate these behaviors, and students who read at home show larger gains in reading achievement than those who don't (Hiebert & Raphael, 1996).

Parents' attitudes are also communicated through their expectations for their children and involvement in their curricular and extracurricular activities. High-SES parents and caregivers expect their children to graduate from high school and attend college and express these expectations in conversations. They communicate the value of a well-rounded education by attending extracurricular activities. One mother commented, "When she sees me at her games, when she sees me going to open house, when I attend her Interscholastic League contests, she knows I am interested in her activities. Plus, we have more to talk about" (Young & Scribner, 1997, p. 12). Unfortunately, research indicates that minority and low-SES students are less likely to participate in extracurricular activities (McNeal, 1997). This is often caused by work demands, transportation problems, or a simple lack of awareness that opportunities to participate exist.

To succeed in schools, low-SES students often need more structure and motivational support than their high-SES peers. In addition, they may need help in seeing connections between learning tasks and the outside world, as well as in understanding that effort leads to accomplishment.

Increasing Understanding 4.6

What do "structure" and "motivational support" mean? Give an example of each to illustrate your explanation.

Changing Student Populations

In the previous sections, we saw how the American family and socioeconomic patterns have changed, and how these changes impact students' chances for success. We now want to look at students themselves, as we examine their sexuality, use of alcohol and other drugs, violence, suicide, and child abuse. These factors are outlined in Figure 4.3 and discussed in the sections that follow.

Changing Sexuality In the past, we tacitly thought of our teenagers as either asexual or restrained. We knew they were going through puberty but assumed that they weren't sexually active (or chose to not think about it).

The facts suggest otherwise. Fifty-three percent of students in grades 9 to 12 have had sexual intercourse (Kann et al., 1993). Everyday in the United States, the following events occur (Children's Defense Fund, 1995):

- 7,742 teenagers become sexually active.
- 2,740 teenagers become pregnant.

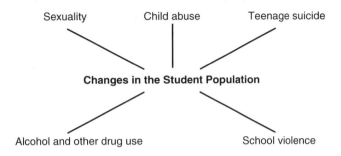

Figure 4.3   **Changes in the Student Population**

■ 1,105 teenagers have abortions.

■ 369 teenagers have miscarriages.

■ 3 children and youths under age 25 die from AIDS.

Today's students are sexually active, and this activity poses a number of risks, including teenage pregnancy and sexually transmitted diseases.

Teenage pregnancy. Adolescence, a time when most teenagers are focusing on their own development, has become a time when many become pregnant and are forced to turn their attention to the welfare of their babies. Each year, U.S. teenagers give birth to more than 500,000 children, giving the United States the highest teenage birthrate among developed countries. In addition, the percentage of teenagers giving birth out of wedlock has increased from 15 percent in 1960 to 84 percent in 1998 (Children's Defense Fund, 1998; U.S. Department of Health and Human Services, 1996). Greater societal acceptance of teenage sexuality, earlier and more frequent sexual activity among teenagers, and a decrease in early marriages are likely reasons for this increase.

Research indicates that the teenage birthrate has recently declined from 62.1 per 1,000 births in 1991 to 52.3 in 1997, a drop of 16 percent (Coles, 1999a). Experts credit the drop to improved contraception use as well as a slight decline in teenage sexual activity.

For a full report on the latest statistics on teenage sexual behavior, consult the *Web Links* Module in Chapter 4 of the Companion Website at **http://www.prenhall.com/ kauchak.**

Teenage pregnancies force students to mature too quickly, diverting energy from their own development to caring for another person. Economics is also a problem; over half of the households headed by teenage mothers live in poverty. Many drop out of school, develop poor work skills, and have limited employment opportunities. They are forced to juggle children with work and, because of inadequate prenatal care, many babies of teenage mothers are born premature or with health problems.

Efforts to deal with the problem of teenage pregnancy focus on programs that encourage mothers to complete their education through home instruction or programs where they bring their babies to school and receive child-care education along with regular classes. Despite these efforts, the majority of teen mothers drop out of school.

Sexually transmitted diseases. Unfortunately, many sexually active teenagers fail to protect themselves from sexually transmitted diseases, such as herpes, genital warts, syphilis, and gonorrhea. AIDS (Acquired Immune Deficiency Syndrome), which can be transmitted through sexual activity, has made the problem more urgent and deadly.

Increasing Understanding 4.7

Identify one advantage and one disadvantage of home instruction for teenage mothers. Do the same for in-school programs.

Teen pregnancies force students to mature too rapidly, diverting attention from their own personal development.

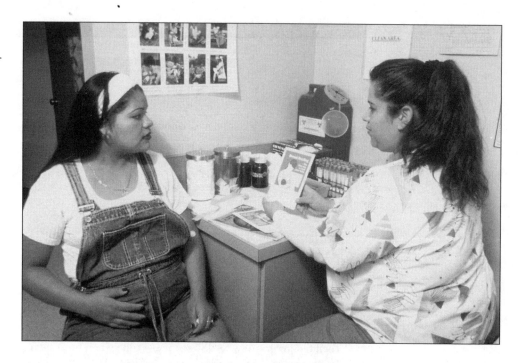

While over 50 percent of teenagers 15 to 19 years old report being sexually active and 19 percent of these teenagers have had four or more sex partners (Kann et al., 1993), only 27 percent of sexually active females and 47% of sexually active males reported using condoms, the only reliable defense, other than abstinence, against sexually transmitted diseases (Stevens-Smith & Remley, 1994). The House Select Committee on Children, Youth and Family estimates that 40,000 teens each year contract HIV, the virus that causes AIDS. While it was first believed that AIDS was confined to homosexual men and intravenous drug users, research indicates that 8 percent of HIV/AIDS cases stem from heterosexual intercourse (Center for Disease Control and Prevention, 1996).

Homosexuality. Experts estimate that between 5 and 10 percent of our students are homosexual. Gay and lesbian students commonly face rejection, which leads to feelings of alienation and depression. As a result, drug use among homosexual youth is much higher than in the heterosexual population (Sears, 1991). Further, while homosexual students account for only 5 to 10 percent of the student population, they commit 30 percent of youth suicides each year (Gibson, 1989).

While the problem has no easy solution, teachers can do much to shape attitudes towards homosexual students (Shakeshaft et al., 1997). They can define appropriate behavior and maintain "zero tolerance" for harassment. Schools and classrooms must be emotionally safe places for *all* students.

Sex education. In response to teenagers' increasing sexuality, many school districts have instituted some form of sex education. The form and content that this takes varies from state to state and community to community. At issue here are two major questions: 1) What is the proper role of the family versus the schools in sex education, and 2) what specific content ought to go into these programs?

Polls show that the majority of parents favor some type of sex education, and courts have upheld school districts' right to offer sex education courses (Fischer, Schimmel, &

Increasing Understanding 4.8

What could teachers do on the first day of class to minimize peer sexual harassment? Throughout the school year?

Figure 4.4   **Student Drug and Alcohol Use**

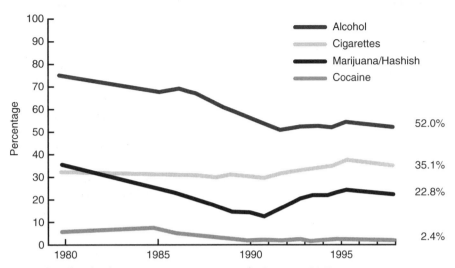

Percentage of High School Seniors Reporting Use in the Previous 30 Days

Source: From Institute for Social Research, (1998). *Monitoring the future.* Ann Arbor, MI: University of Michigan. Reprinted by permission.

Increasing Understanding 4.9

Identify at least two different kinds of background knowledge teachers must have in order to effectively teach about sexuality. (Hint: Recall the different kinds of professional knowledge discussed in Chapter 1.)

Kelly, 1999). Parents who object are free to take their children out of the programs. You'll read more about different curricular approaches to sex education in Chapter 10.

Increasing Use of Alcohol and Other Drugs   After a 20-year period of decline, teenage use of alcohol and other drugs has been on the rise in recent years (see Figure 4.4). In a recent study of high school seniors, 51 percent reported using alcohol, 21 percent reported using marijuana, and 2 percent reported using cocaine in the last 30-day period (U.S. Department of Education, 1996). This pattern of drug use starts early, with 21 percent of 8th graders, 33 percent of 10th graders, and 39 percent of 12th graders reporting drug or alcohol use in the last year (Institute for Social Research, 1998). Research indicates that 10.5 million U.S. youth ages 12 to 20 use alcohol, and 4.1 million youth ages 12 to 17 smoke (Coles, 1999b). Between 1992 and 1996, the daily use of cigarettes increased for 8th, 10th, and 12th graders, and the percentage of students in each grade level who reported illicit drug use increased substantially (Federal Interagency Forum on Child and Family Statistics, 1997). Alcohol and drug use are often associated with other risk factors such as poverty, low SES, family instability, and academic problems at school.

For information on this problem from the federal Substance Abuse and Mental Health Services, go to the Web Links Module in Chapter 4 on the Companion Website at **http://www.prenhall.com/kauchak.**

Despite the stereotyped belief that drug use is primarily an inner-city problem, research reveals that drug-use problems are actually most acute in rural areas (Coles, 2000). Rural teens are more likely to use a variety of drugs, ranging from cocaine to amphetamines to alcohol.

Critics contend that a major reason for teenage use of alcohol and other drugs is the mixed messages society sends about them. The media, and particularly teenage pop culture, often glorify alcohol and other drugs, implying that they are not only acceptable but preferred ways of dealing with problems like stress, loneliness, or depression. Unfortunately, as

**Increasing
Understanding 4.10**

 Identify two specific ways in which alcohol or other drug use interferes with learning.

teenagers become drug dependent they not only place themselves at risk for other problems like suicide, health risks, and automobile accidents, but they also fail to develop healthy coping mechanisms for life's problems (Berk, 1997). Dependence on drugs can also reinforce alienation, encouraging students to drop out of school life.

Efforts to curtail drug use include programs that teach students facts about drugs as well as programs that help them learn how to make their own decisions, understand and avoid peer pressure, and work to develop self-esteem. Probably best known is the Drug Abuse Resistance Education (DARE) program that started in California and spread across the country. Research on these programs is mixed, however, and evidence suggests that concerted, long-term efforts are needed (Portner, 1993).

Similar criticisms have been directed at the U.S. Department of Education's Safe and Drug-Free Schools program, which provides more than $500 million annually to local school districts with virtually no strings attached. A review of the program found that taxpayer dollars paid for a variety of questionable strategies including motivational speakers, puppet shows, dunking booths, magicians, clowns, and tickets to Disneyland. Even though two federal reports were highly critical of the program and the Congressional Budget Office recommended eliminating it, Congress continues to fund it. This is an example of the problems involved in "throwing" money at educational problems. The need is there, the intent is good, but the implementation is lacking.

Other research suggests that intense, coordinated efforts can curtail teenage smoking (Portner, 1999b). The state of Florida combined an aggressive anti-smoking advertising campaign, increased law enforcement efforts aimed at minors, and a 50-cents-per package increase in the price of cigarettes. Cigarette use among middle schoolers dropped 19 percent; smoking declined 8 percent among high schoolers. Despite these results, the Florida legislature, under pressure from tobacco lobbies, cut funding for this program from $70 million to $45 million.

Increasing Crime and Violence

Case
STUDY

For the past few months, Juan and his mother have been in hiding, the entire time he has attended Lafayette Elementary. His 29-year-old mother has been in gangs since she was twelve, and her sons, including Juan, grew up believing that at some point they would gain membership for themselves, and in gaining membership would enjoy status and achieve a measure of safety for themselves and their families. One bloody evening, however, crushed her and Juan's world-view, leaving behind a fearful, small boy and a mother overwhelmed with regret. Looking at his hands, Juan quietly revealed what had happened; it's a story he doesn't like to share: "My uncle was murdered in front of my house with guns." He worries about dying. "They were guys, they were wearing ski masks with beanies on their heads. The [killer], he looked at me and pointed the gun at me and pointed it back to my uncle and shot it. That is when I grabbed both of my cousins, his little kids, and I threw them on the ground and jumped on top of them." "You acted like a hero," I said, more than a little surprised by the tale. Proudly: "I did good for protecting my family." He continued: "It was supposed to be a drive-by [shooting], that is where they are in a car and they just roll down the windows and shoot at people. They were supposed to do a drive-by at some gangsters, and they . . . just shot when [my uncle] was outside with his girlfriend. The girl, his girlfriend, just got shot in the leg. Now she has a metal thingy at her knee and down her leg that connects to her foot." Juan was traumatized, and in the story I found an answer to the principal's question posed before we spoke, "If you can gain any insight into why Juan is so angry, I'd appreciate it" (Bullough, 1999, pp. 22–23).

■ ■ ■

Safety is a basic need for all individuals. Unfortunately, one in four students reports some kind of violence-related problem in their schools (Louis Harris & Associates, 1996), and 40 violent school-related deaths occurred during the 1997–1998 school year (Portner, 1999a). An average of 14 children die each day from gunfire in the United States— approximately one every 100 minutes (Children's Defense Fund, 1999). The problem of school violence came to national attention with the Columbine, Colorado, tragedy where two students went on a rampage, gunning down 13 students before killing themselves.

Parents, taxpayers, and educators rate school safety the highest on a list of concerns about school quality (Olson, 1999). The cost of school crime and vandalism is staggering, more than $200 million a year, according to some estimates (Geiger, 1993).

Theft is most common, constituting 62 percent of all crimes against students, and nearly 5 percent of teachers reported theft crimes (U.S. Department of Education, 1998). In addition, about 4 out of every 1,000 teachers were victims of violent crime at school. Approximately 3 percent of high school seniors reported carrying a gun to school at least once during the previous 4-week period, and during the 1996–1997 school year, more than 5,000 students were expelled for possession or use of a firearm (U.S. Department of Education, 1998).

Up-to-date information on national efforts to curb violence in schools can be found in the *Web Links* Module of Chapter 4 in the Companion Website at **http://www.prenhall. com/kauchak.**

Student concerns about safety and violence are highest at the eighth-grade level and decline as students get older. Urban students (33 percent) are more likely to report serious problems with violence than suburban students (22 percent) or rural students (18 percent), and concerns about violence are greatest in high-poverty areas (Louis Harris & Associates, 1996).

School violence is often associated with gangs, but the proportion of young people actually joining gangs is small. The Justice Department estimates that the number of youth gang members numbers is only 250,000 out of the 47 million U.S. youths ages 12 to 25 (Stepp, 1996).

School Violence and the Teacher   As a teacher, you will be asked to deal with the problems of aggressive students and the possibility of violence. Involving parents is a good first step (Brophy, 1996; Powell et al., 2001). The vast majority of parents (88 percent) want to be notified immediately if school problems occur (Harris, Kagay, & Ross, 1987). In addition, school counselors and psychologists, social workers, and principals are all trained to deal with these problems and can provide advice and assistance. Experienced teachers can also provide a wealth of information about how they've handled similar problems. You won't have to face persistent or serious problems of violence or aggression alone, and as you continue with your teacher-preparation program, you'll be taught specific skills for dealing with classroom discipline.

While violence and aggression may seem frightening, they should be put into perspective. Though they are possibilities, the majority of your day-to-day teaching problems will be issues of student cooperation and motivation. Most problems can be prevented, others can be dealt with quickly, and some require individual attention. We all hear about students carrying guns to school and incidents of assault on teachers in the news. However, considering the huge numbers of students that pass through schools each day, these incidents remain very infrequent.

Increasing Suicide   The suicide rate among adolescents has tripled in the last 30 years and is now the third leading cause of teen death, after accidents and homicide. Each year about 5,000 youths take their own lives, 7 percent of adolescents report attempting

Increasing Understanding 4.11

Why might student concerns about safety and violence peak at the eighth-grade level? What implications does this have for middle schools? For middle school teachers?

Increasing Understanding 4.12

Parents consistently rate discipline and safety among their top concerns about schools (Rose & Gallup, 1998). Given what you've read in this section, are these concerns justified? Defend your position with information taken from this section.

Teaching

in an Era of Reform

EFFORTS TO MAKE OUR SCHOOLS SAFER

Many types of reform exist. Because of the enormous publicity generated by school shooting incidents around the country, some reform efforts focus on making our schools safer places to learn and work. These efforts fall into three general categories: schoolwide security efforts, zero-tolerance programs, and school uniforms.

Schoolwide Security Programs

Schoolwide security programs are designed to make schools safe havens for teaching and learning (Bushweller, 1998). Many schools are adopting comprehensive security measures, such as having visitors sign in (96 percent of schools), closing campuses during lunch (80 percent of schools), and controlling access to school buildings (53 percent of schools). Some schools are adding more rigid policies, such as hallway police, student photo ID badges, transparent book bags, handheld metal detectors, and breath analyzers to check for alcohol. Students are being warned to avoid jokes about violence and are being given hotline numbers to anonymously report any indications that a classmate could turn violent. Many schools are also making discipline more strict, creating peer buddy systems and adult mentorship programs, and teaching conflict-resolution skills (Bender & McLaughlin, 1997; Sauter, 1995).

Zero-Tolerance Programs

Zero-tolerance programs that *punish offenses, such as school disruptions, drugs, and weapons, with automatic suspensions* are becoming increasingly popular across the nation (Skiba & Peterson, 1999).

As a result, the annual U.S. suspension rate went from 3.7 percent to 6.9 percent between 1974 and 1998, an 86 percent increase (Johnston, 2000a). The most common reasons students are expelled include bringing firearms to school (94 percent of schools), other weapons (91 percent), possessing drugs (88 percent), alcohol (87 percent), or tobacco (79 percent), and committing acts of violence (79 percent). During the 1996–1997 school year, 6,093 students were expelled for bringing weapons to school. The majority of the expulsions occurred in high schools (56 percent), though middle schools and junior highs (34 percent) and elementary schools (9 per-

cent) also used expulsion as a disciplinary measure (Bushweller, 1998).

School Uniforms

A growing number of schools are requiring students to wear uniforms. Proponents claim that gang clothing and designer sports clothes contribute to violence, fights, and overall delinquency. In addition, clothes serve as a visual reminder of the economic disparities between students. Long Beach School District in California started the school uniform trend, and about 20 percent of the nation's school districts, including Chicago, Miami, and Phoenix, allow individual schools to require uniforms (Portner, 1999a).

Putting Reform into Perspective

The need for safe schools is obvious, and the premise behind zero-tolerance programs—that students who seriously disrupt the learning environment for the majority of the school population should be removed—is intuitively sensible. Students can't learn when they're worried about either their physical or emotional well-being. Not surprisingly, because of the publicity generated by incidents of school violence, both parents and other taxpayers rank school safety as the most important characteristic of an effective school (Olson, 1999).

In addition, the results of the Long Beach experiment with school uniforms are impressive. After the uniform policy was implemented, school crime dropped by 76 percent, assaults declined by 85 percent, weapons offenses dropped by 83 percent, and attendance figures rose. Proponents argue that these results are due to students being required to wear uniforms.

However, zero-tolerance programs have problems. Because they don't discriminate between major and minor disruptions, they sometimes target trivial and innocent transgressions. For example, one 5-year-old child was suspended for finding a razor blade at his bus stop and showing it to his teacher, and in another case, a 6-year-old child was suspended for kissing one of his classmates (Skiba & Peterson, 1999).

In addition, when expulsion occurs, only 56 percent of students are sent to an alternative placement; the remainder are sent home to fend for themselves, making the likelihood of truancy and crime even greater. One student describes the problem in this way:

Schoolwide security programs attempt to make schools safe places to learn.

• • •

When they suspend you, you get in more trouble, 'cause you're out in the street. . . . And that's what happened to me once. I got into trouble one day 'cause there was a party, and they arrested everybody in that party. . . . I got in trouble more than I get in trouble at school, because I got arrested and everything (Skiba & Peterson, 1999, p. 376).

• • •

Expelled students typically fall farther behind, experience increased social difficulties, and sometimes never return to complete school (Barr & Parrett, 2001).

Other critics point to the disproportionate number of minorities affected by these programs (Johnston, 2000a). African American students made up 17 percent of all U.S. students in the 1998–1999 school year but accounted for 33 percent of all students who were suspended, whereas White students made up 63 percent of enrollments and 50 percent of all suspensions. Explanations for these uneven rates range from higher rates of poverty to inexperienced teachers, crowded classrooms, and academically sterile learning environments.

School leadership is significant in implementing effective zero-tolerance policies (Johnston, 2000a). For instance, one middle school in Dade County, Florida, had an expulsion rate of 34 percent, whereas another school that serves basically the same student population had an expulsion rate of only 2.8 percent. Students at the second school who were involved in a fight, for example, were given alternative punishments such as in-school suspensions or work assignments (such as cleaning the cafeteria) instead of being suspended.

Finally, critics of school uniforms point to research indicating that school uniforms have no direct result on behavioral problems or attendance (Brunsma & Rockquemoro, 1999). Instead, they argue, the positive effects are due to greater parental involvement in the school and a visible and public symbol of commitment to school improvement and reform.

As with all reforms, efforts to increase school safety are neither totally positive or negative. Unquestionably, schools must be safe. How this is accomplished remains controversial. Despite difficulties, zero-tolerance programs are, in all likelihood, here to stay, and experimentation with school uniforms is likely to continue. As a professional, you need to be as knowledgeable as possible about these issues, so you're in a position to make informed contributions to the decision-making process.

You Take a Position

Now it's your turn to take a position on the issues discussed in this section. Go to the *Education Week* Website at **http://www.edweek.com,** find "search" on the first page, and type in one of the following three search terms: *school security*, *zero tolerance*, or *school uniforms*. Locate a minimum of three articles on one of these topics and do the following:

1. Identify the title, author, and date of each article, and then write a one-paragraph summary of each article.

2. Determine if a pattern exists in the articles. (Each article—or even two of the three—suggesting that school uniforms are a good idea would be a pattern, for example.)

3. Take one of the two following positions:
    - The pattern suggested in the articles, if implemented, *is* likely to improve education.
    - The pattern suggested in the articles *is not* likely to improve education.

Document your position with information taken from the articles and your study of the text (this chapter and any other chapter of the text).

To answer these questions online, go to the Take a Position Module in Chapter 4 of the Companion Website.

Reflect *on* This

REPORTING CHILD ABUSE

You're a middle school teacher in a rural district, and you meet with your homeroom students every day. You use homeroom to take care of daily routines and to get to know your students as individuals. Janine has always been a bright, happy student who gets along well with her classmates. Lately she seems withdrawn, and her personal appearance is disheveled. As you periodically look at her, you see that she seems hesitant to make eye contact. You ask her to come in after school to talk. She says she has to go right home to help care for her younger brothers and sisters, so you suggest her lunch break instead. She reluctantly agrees.

When she comes in, she appears nervous, fidgeting with her hands and refusing to look at you. You ask her how she feels, and she replies, "Fine." You mention that she seems to be different lately, preoccupied. She only shrugs. You ask if there is anything bothering her, and she shakes her head no. You reaffirm your availability if she ever wants to talk, and she smiles briefly. As she gathers her book to get up and leave, her sweater slides off her shoulder, revealing bruises.

"Janine, what happened to your arm?"

"Oh, I fell the other day."

"But how did you hurt the inside of your arm?"

Janine's pained and embarrassed expression suggests that a fall wasn't the cause.

"Did someone try to hurt you, Janine? You can tell me."

"Only if you promise not to tell," she blurts out.

Without thinking, you agree. She then proceeds to tell you tearfully about an angry father who has been out of work for months and who becomes violent when he drinks. As she leaves, she makes you promise that you won't tell anyone.

1. You promised that you wouldn't tell anyone about your conversation with Janine. Should you keep or break the promise?

2. Who could you talk to about this problem? How much information should you reveal in the conversation?

3. What would you do in this situation?

W *To answer these questions online and receive immediate feedback, go to the* Reflect on This *Module in Chapter 4 of the Companion Website.*

suicide, and 29 percent report thinking about it (McIntosh, 1996). For every teenager that commits suicide, 100 more will try (Portner, 2000). While girls are 3 times more likely than boys to attempt suicide, boys are 4 times more likely to succeed. Boys tend to employ more lethal means such as firearms, while girls favor more survivable methods such as pills.

Causes of teen suicide vary, but most are related to the stresses adolescent youth face. They include family conflicts, parental unemployment and divorce, drug use, failed peer relationships, and peer harassment of homosexual youth.

Some potential suicide indicators include the following:

- Abrupt change in the quality of schoolwork.
- Withdrawal from friends or classroom and school activities.
- Neglect of personal appearance or radical changes in personality.
- Changes in eating or sleeping habits.
- Depression, as evidenced by persistent boredom or lack of interest in school activities.

Teachers who observe these signs should contact a school counselor or psychologist; early identification is essential.

Increasing Understanding 4.13

W Why is the role of the teacher so important in identifying potential suicide victims?

Teachers play a critical role in identifying child abuse.

Increasing Awareness of Child Abuse Child abuse is another serious problem in today's society. Estimates indicate that as many as 3 million school children suffer from either physical or mental abuse (U.S. Department of Health and Human Services, National Center on Child Abuse and Neglect, 1996). Because abuse and neglect are often hidden, reliable figures are difficult to obtain. Half of all abuse victims suffer from neglect, about one-fourth experience physical abuse, and about 12 percent are sexually abused. When sexual abuse occurs, it most commonly involves a family member or friend. Though child abuse can occur at any level, it tends to be associated with poverty and is often linked to parental substance abuse.

Teachers are in a unique position to identify child abuse because they work with children on a daily basis. Symptoms include:

- Neglected appearance.
- Sudden changes in either academic or social behavior.
- Disruptive or overly compliant behavior.
- Repeated injuries such as bruises, welts, or burns.

Teachers in all 50 states are legally bound to report suspicions of child abuse. Teachers and schools are protected from civil and criminal liability if the report is made honestly using behavioral data such as the symptoms we've just listed.

Increasing Understanding 4.14

Is child abuse easier to detect at the elementary or secondary level? Why?

■ STUDENTS PLACED AT-RISK

The conditions we've been describing in this chapter—changing families, poverty, violence, alcohol and other drugs, suicide, and child abuse—are serious problems for the students we teach. In many instances, two or more of them occur together, placing students at-risk for academic failure.

Students placed at-risk are *those in danger of failing to complete their education with the skills necessary to survive in modern society* (Slavin, Karweit, & Madden, 1989). The term is borrowed from medicine, where it refers to individuals who don't have a specific disease

Table 4.1	Characteristics of Students Placed At-Risk	
	Background Factors	Educational Problems
	Low SES	High dropout rates
	Inner city	Low grades
	Male	Retention in same grade
	Transient	Low achievement
	Minority	Low participation in extracurricular activities
	Non-native English	Low motivation
	speaker	Poor attendance
	Divorced families	High rate of drug use
		Misbehavior in classes
		Low self-esteem
		High criminal-activity rates
		Low standardized-test scores
		Lack of interest in school
		High suspension rates

but are likely to develop it, such as an overweight person with high blood pressure being at-risk for a heart attack. It became widely used after 1983 when the National Commission on Excellence in Education proclaimed the United States a "nation at risk" (National Commission on Excellence in Education, 1983), emphasizing the growing link between education and economic well-being in today's technological society. For example, between 1979 and 1996, the real earnings of 25 to 34-year-old male dropouts fell by 28 percent (Murnon & Tyler, 2000). Compounding the problem is the fact that the percentage of 18 to 24 year olds who left school without a diploma increased from 21.2 percent in 1994 to 25.3 percent in 1998. In recent years, much attention has been focused on problems and issues involving students placed at-risk (Barr & Parett, 1995; Manning & Baruth, 1995). Almost certainly, you will have some of these students in your classes.

Table 4.1 outlines some of the academic, social, and emotional problems students placed at-risk experience. The presence of "male" as a background factor should be clarified, however. Though males are more likely than females to experience difficulties in school and to drop out, female students who do drop out are more likely to end up in poverty than male dropouts (American Association of University Women, 1992). In addition, many girls who drop out are pregnant and are left with the burden of single parenting on a below-the-poverty-level income. Being placed at-risk is a problem facing both male and female students.

Before continuing, we want to offer an additional note of caution. Some critics contend that the term *at-risk* is ill-advised (Franklin, 1997; Benard, 1994), arguing that the label results in low teacher expectations for the students, which contributes to underachievement. As teachers, we need to be sensitive about the possibility of negative stereotyping and continually ask ourselves, "Am I demanding as much as possible from these students, and am I providing every opportunity for their success?" The following sections describe some ways to increase the likelihood of this happening.

It Takes a Village: The Community-Based Approach to Working with Children Placed At-Risk

This chapter has focused on changes in society that can influence student learning and success, such as poverty, violence, and drug use. Responses to these negative influences have varied from denial to making our schools into "fortresses"—safe havens in troubled communities. More recent approaches have focused on actively involving parents and other members of the community in redesigning schools to better meet the needs of children placed at-risk (Comer et al., 1996).

Increasing Understanding 4.15

What does negative stereotyping mean? Give an example of how negative stereotyping might affect student learning.

One example is the School Development Program, created by Yale psychiatrist James Comer (Comer, 1994). It integrates schools and the community by bringing principals, teachers, and parents together in school planning and management teams. School services, such as counseling and support for students with learning problems, are coordinated through teams of psychologists, counselors, and special educators. This coordination is important because services for students are often hit-and-miss and fragmented. For example, one depressed, pregnant, drug-using teenager saw three different counselors each week: a suicide prevention counselor, a parenting counselor, and a drug abuse counselor. None of them talked to each other (Tyson, 1999). Educational programs need to focus on educating the whole child by attending to children's physical, social, emotional, and academic growth through coordinated efforts.

Begun in New Haven, Connecticut, the School Development Program has spread to more than 500 schools across the country. Evaluations indicate that the program works. Achievement has increased significantly, self-concepts have improved, and absences, suspensions, and management problems have declined in the schools where the program is fully implemented (Comer, 1994).

Students Placed At-Risk: Promoting Resilience

In this chapter, we've presented research examining societal factors that place students at-risk for school failure. More recent studies, however, have focused on **resilient students**— *those who have been able to rise above difficult conditions to succeed in school and other aspects of life* (Wang, Haertel, & Walberg, 1995). Researchers have become interested in resilience for both theoretical and practical reasons. Theoretically, studying resilience helps us understand the process of development, especially in youth placed at-risk, and practically, it identifies practices that result in healthy, academically successful learners.

Resilient children have well-developed "self systems," including high self-esteem and feelings that they are in control of their destinies. They set personal goals, possess good interpersonal skills, and have positive expectations for success (Benard, 1993; Wang et al., 1995). These strengths result in higher academic achievement, motivation, and satisfaction with school (Waxman & Huang, 1996).

How do these adaptive skills develop? First, resilient children have relationships with caring adults who hold high moral and academic expectations for them. (Think about the impact you might have on a student; you could be that caring adult.) Second, they come from schools that are both demanding and supportive; in many instances, their schools serve as "homes away from home." Let's look more closely at how schools and teachers help develop resilience in students.

Effective Schools for Students Placed At-Risk Effective schools focus on mutual respect between teachers and students and on personal responsibility and cooperation (Barr & Parrett, 2001; Kim, Solomon, & Roberts, 1995). They emphasize:

- Safe, orderly school climates, including an understanding of the meaning behind and purpose of school and classroom rules.
- Academic objectives focusing on mastery of content.
- Caring and demanding teachers and high expectations for all students.
- Cooperation, a sense of community, and pro-social values.
- Student responsibility and self-regulation; decreased emphasis on external controls.
- Strong parental involvement.

These same strategies seem to work in other countries and cultures; a study done with students placed at-risk in Israel arrived at essentially the same conclusions (Gaziel, 1997).

Increasing Understanding 4.16

Explain how these characteristics of effective schools could contribute to resiliency in students placed at-risk.

Schools and teachers exert a powerful influence on developing resilience in their students.

Effective Teachers for Students Placed At-Risk Well-run and academically focused schools are important, but alone, they aren't sufficient. Professional teachers who are highly skilled and sensitive are critical (Waxman, Huang, Anderson, & Weinstein, 1997). In Chapter 1 we said that professionals are skilled in making decisions in ill-defined situations. This ability is essential in working with students placed at-risk because their needs and personal sensitivities make them particularly vulnerable to failure, personal slights, indicators of favoritism, and questions about the relevance of school.

What makes a teacher effective with students placed at-risk? How can teachers help students develop resilience and make connections between their lives and the classroom? Let's have students tell us. First, a ninth-grader offers this view:

■ ■ ■

Well it's like you're family, you know. Like regular days like at home, we argue sometimes, and then it's like we're all brothers and sisters and the teachers are like our guardians or something.

And the teachers really get on you until they try to make you think of what's in the future and all that. It's good. I mean it makes you think, you know, if every school was like that I don't think there would be a lot of people that would drop out (Greenleaf, 1995, p. 2).

■ ■ ■

An interview with other high school students offers additional perspectives:

■ ■ ■

Melinda: I act differently in his [Appleby's] class—I guess because of the type of teacher he is. He cuts up and stuff. . . . He is himself—he acts natural—not tryin' to be what somebody wants him to be . . . he makes sure that nobody makes fun of anybody if they mess up when they read out loud.

Bernard: [I like him] just by the way he talk, he were good to you . . . he don't be afraid to tell you how he feels—he don't talk mean to you, he just speak right to you . . . some teachers only likes the smart people—and Coach Appleby don't do that.

LaVonne: Appleby's fun, he helps you when you feel bad, he'll talk to you. Appleby's got his own style, he makes his own self . . . he's not a brag . . . he get(s) into it—what

Video
Perspectives

MAKING THE GRADE

This ABC News video segment profiles Kathy Morgan, a guidance counselor at All Hallows School, an all-boys school in the inner-city South Bronx. When Kathy first arrived at the school in 1997, less than 20 percent of the graduates went on to college. Through Kathy's and other teachers' concerted efforts, nearly 100 percent of graduating seniors now go on to college.

Think about This

1. In what ways would the students at All Hallows School be considered at-risk?
2. In what ways did the personnel at All Hallows school attempt to make their students resilient?
3. Based on research examining resilience, in what ways was All Hallows School effective for students placed at-risk?
4. All Hallows School is a private, religiously oriented all-boys school. What successful elements of the school's program could be implemented in co-ed, public schools?

Ⓦ *To answer these questions online and receive immediate feedback, go to the Video Perspectives Module in Chapter 4 of the Companion Website.*

they [the students] like. Appleby always has this funny grin. . . . He's funny, he tells jokes, laughs with the class. He makes me want to work, he makes me want to give and do something. . . . He show me that I can do it (Dillon, 1989, pp. 241–242).

■ ■ ■

Alienation from school is a problem for students placed at-risk (Dillon, 1989; Goodenow, 1992a). Boredom, lack of involvement, and feelings that they are unwelcome keep them on the fringe, prevent them from participating in school experiences, and lower motivation. When bright spots appear, they are usually the result of teachers who care about these students as people and as learners.

How do teachers communicate this caring? First, they make a special effort to know all of their students. One teacher advised,

■ ■ ■

I think with children one of the things you have to do first is to get to know them. Even with those you find a little bit hard to like at first, you have to find something that you really appreciate about that child so that you can really teach [him or her], because if you don't you're not going to get any place (Darling-Hammond, 1998, p. 80).

■ ■ ■

Another teacher noted,

■ ■ ■

Individual kid's needs, awarenesses, and differences are part of understanding the whole teaching process. Whether you have a kid sitting in the front row because he has a visual problem and you have to have an auditory contact, a kid back there who doesn't speak English, a kid who has parents who are breaking up, a kid over here who has just been in a fight with somebody outside the classroom, or a kid who has physical handicaps, it all depends on the situation. . . . There are all types of problems and, of course, the more you know, it puts you in a better situation (Darling-Hammond, 1998, p. 81).

■ ■ ■

Knowing your students will help you relate to them as people as well as help you adapt instruction to their special needs.

A study examining the practices of teachers working with urban junior high students placed at-risk helps us understand differences between teachers who are more and less effective in working with youth placed at-risk. The study used the terms *high impact* and *low impact* to describe these differences (Kramer-Schlosser, 1992). **High-impact teachers** *create caring, personal learning environments and assume responsibility for their students' progress.* They talk with students, find out about their families, and share their own lives. They maintain high expectations, use questioning to involve students in lessons, and emphasize success and mastery of content. They motivate students through personal contacts and attempts to link school to students' lives.

Low-impact teachers, in contrast, *are more authoritarian, distancing themselves from students and placing primary responsibility for learning on them.* They view instructional help as "babying the student" or "holding the student's hand." Instruction is teacher-directed and lecture-oriented, and primary responsibility for motivation is the student's.

Students placed at-risk think of low-impact teachers as adversaries who are to be avoided if possible and tolerated if not. In contrast, these students seek out high-impact teachers, both in class and out. Caring, communication, and ". . . relationships with teachers were related to marginal students' behaviors and attitudes. Marginal students reported losing interest in learning when teachers distanced themselves" (Kramer-Schlosser, 1992, p. 138). Other studies have found effective teachers for students placed at-risk to be approachable, pleasant, easy to relate to, accepting, concerned, caring, and sensitive to the needs of students (Sanders & Jordan, 1997). Caring, personalized learning environments are important for all students; for students placed at-risk, they are essential. But beyond the human element, what else can teachers do?

Increasing Understanding 4.17

What are some concrete things that teachers of at-risk students can do to demonstrate that they care?

Case STUDY

As students entered the classroom after recess, they saw a review assignment on the chalkboard. Teacher Dena Hines took roll, and the students got out their books and started on the assignment. Five minutes later, Dena began teaching with a brief review of the previous day's lesson. Since the students were able to answer her questions quickly and correctly, she felt that the class knew the content and was ready to move on.

As she introduced two-column subtraction, she explained the new idea and gave each student bundles of 10 popsicle sticks bound together with rubber bands. She then guided the students through the steps by having them take the bundles apart to illustrate the process; Dena asked many questions as she went along. She also used questioning to help students link the manipulatives—the popsicle sticks—to the numerals she wrote on the board. Then she had students solve problems on their own mini-chalkboards and hold them up so she could check their solutions. Whenever mistakes occurred, she stopped, explained the errors, and helped students correct them.

When 90 percent of the class was solving the problems correctly, Dena started the students on additional practice problems, which they checked in pairs when they were done. As they worked, she helped those still having difficulty, moving around the room to respond to pairs who disagreed with each other or had questions.

■ ■ ■

How should teachers adapt their instruction to meet the needs of students placed at-risk? The overall suggestion is to offer more structure and support, as Dena did, while still challenging students and emphasizing concrete and real-world applications. In a study involving 140 classrooms, researchers found that achievement in reading and math was enhanced by teachers who emphasized challenge, application, problem solving, and use of student ideas and solutions (Knapp, Shields, & Turnbull, 1995).

Caring teachers with high expectations for success help students placed at-risk succeed in school.

Effective instruction: structure and support. Teachers of students placed at-risk don't need to teach in fundamentally different ways; instead, they need to apply effective strategies more systematically. They should provide enough instructional support to ensure success while at the same time teaching students strategies that allow them to take control of their own learning. Effective practices for students placed at-risk include the following (Gladney & Green, 1997; Wang et al., 1995):

- High expectations.
- Emphasis on student responsibility.
- Frequent feedback and high success rates.
- Interactive teaching with frequent questions.
- Increased structure and support through clear teacher explanations and modeling.

High expectations for student success are a key to the effectiveness of these strategies. But how is this accomplished? One student recalls a former teacher:

■ ■ ■

My sixth-grade teacher was a coach. She could yell, scream, cajole, and nag with the best of them. But we knew that the constant pushing was for our benefit. "You know you can do better," was her favorite phrase. We laughed about her repeating it so often. On the playground and in our neighborhoods we would tease each other when we were not successful at stickball or double Dutch. "You know you can do better," we would sing and quickly dissolve into laughter. Funny, the sound of her voice repeating that phrase haunted me as a college student, as a graduate student, and as a university professional: "You know you can do better!" (Ladson-Billings, 1994, p. 25).

■ ■ ■

Through her daily interactions with students, this teacher was able to instill in them the feeling that they truly could do better.

Increasing Understanding 4.18

Which of these characteristics of effective instruction would be most effective in promoting student resilience? Why?

INVOLVING STUDENTS

You're a first-year English teacher at Roosevelt High School, an urban school in the Midwest. The year hasn't been easy, but you seem to be turning the corner in most classes—except for one. Your first-period class, composed mostly of low achievers, continues to struggle. The course overview describes the class as an introduction to the mechanics of writing: grammar, punctuation, and basic writing skills. At the encouragement of your department chair, you use the text that is assigned, which stresses basic skills through exercises and worksheets. After months of student complaints, you decide to throw out the text and involve your students in writing projects. The first assignment, "Suggestions for a Better Roosevelt High School," is a disaster. Students don't know where to start, and the few assignments that are handed in are discouragingly poor. You regroup and begin by teaching pre-writing skills like brainstorming, note-taking, and outlining. The next assignment is better, but when you try to have students critique each others' work in groups, the class degenerates into chaos. Most students sit back and talk about the upcoming football game and what they are going to do that weekend. The few that focus on the assignment have difficulty hearing each others' comments.

1. What were the advantages and disadvantages of using the textbook originally?
2. Why are you having such difficulties in involving the students in writing? What could you have done differently?
3. Why did you encounter problems in involving students in small-group work?
4. What would you do now?

To answer these questions online and receive immediate feedback, go to the Reflect on This *Module in Chapter 4 of the Companion Website.*

Working with today's students requires redefined roles for teachers. Traditionally, teachers' efforts were limited to their work in classrooms, and their focus was on academics. Today's student population requires teachers to think more broadly and to consider their students' overall emotional and physical development in addition to academic growth.

Increasingly, schools are being asked to safeguard children's well-being. They're required to report suspected cases of child abuse and neglect. Many provide free breakfasts and lunches for the children of poverty. Effective schools are islands of safety and security in an often chaotic and sometimes dangerous world. Teachers often play a crucial role in ensuring that all of children's needs—physical, social, emotional, and intellectual—are being addressed.

Teachers' instructional roles are also changing. In an ideal world, students come to school motivated and prepared to learn. Some students do, while others do not; in those cases, teachers are being asked to promote motivation and student involvement in addition to helping students understand the topics they're teaching. Stagnant teaching strategies, such as lecturing, that place students in passive listening roles won't work. Many students simply stop listening, and some put their heads down on their desks, making no pretense of paying attention.

Teachers are also being asked to make personal contact with students—not as "buddies," but rather as concerned caregivers committed to the total well-being of students. Expert professionals have always taken a personal interest in their students, but this dimension of teaching has become more important as many students come to our schools feeling like they're unwelcome. Teachers play an essential role in creating schools that are student-friendly along with classrooms that are warm and caring.

Tomorrow's teachers are also being asked to move outside the classroom. Effective outreach programs encourage parents to become actively involved in their child's education (Hoover-Dempsey, & Sandler, 1997; Shumow & Harris, 1998), and teachers are an integral part of these programs. Working with parents and other people in the community is now an integral part of teachers' jobs. Working with tomorrow's students will be more difficult and more challenging. It can also be more rewarding.

■ SUMMARY

A Changing Society

Society is changing in a number of ways, and these changes have important implications for schools. Traditional family configurations have evolved into alternative patterns that include single parent and extended families. The majority of mothers now work, raising concerns about child care and latchkey children. Poverty presents a number of challenges, ranging from hunger to homelessness.

Teenagers themselves are also changing. They are becoming sexually active at an earlier age, placing themselves at risk for pregnancy and sexually transmitted diseases. The use of alcohol and other drugs, violence, suicide, and child abuse all present challenges to youth as well as the teachers who work with them.

Students Placed At-Risk

Students placed at-risk face a number of challenges to school success. Community-based approaches to working with students placed at risk actively involve parents in designing and implementing educational programs. Effective schools for students placed at-risk create a safe, orderly learning environment in which academic goals are foremost. Studies of successful or resilient children suggest that caring home and school environments with supportive, understanding adults can help these students withstand societal challenges. Effective teachers for students placed at-risk combine interpersonal contacts with instructional structure and support. In working with at-risk students, teachers are advised to combine challenge with this support.

■ IMPORTANT CONCEPTS

students placed at-risk	middle class	underclass
high-impact teachers	poverty	upper class
latchkey children	resilient students	zero-tolerance programs
low-impact teachers	socioeconomic status (SES)	

■ DISCUSSION QUESTIONS

1. How would your role as a teacher change if you worked in an upper-SES suburb? A lower-SES part of a city?
2. How would your actual instruction change if you worked in an upper-SES suburb? A lower-SES part of a city?
3. What role should schools play in dealing with teenage sexuality?
4. What role should schools play in dealing with drug and alcohol abuse?
5. What strengths do students placed at-risk bring to the classroom? How can teachers take advantage of these strengths?
6. What will be the biggest challenges in working with the parents of students placed at-risk?

■ VIDEO DISCUSSION QUESTIONS

The following discussion question refers to video segments found on the Companion Website. To answer this question online, view the accompanying video, and receive immediate feedback to your answer, go to the Video Discussion Module in Chapter 4 of the Companion Website at **http://www.prenhall.com/kauchak.**

1. Theodore Sizer is the director of the Coalition for Effective Schools, which attempts to reform high schools. A major challenge facing high-school reform is helping students placed at-risk develop resiliency. From Sizer's perspective, what is the most important thing that schools can do to develop resiliency in students? How do these suggestions compare to information given in this chapter?

■ GOING INTO SCHOOLS

1. Ask a teacher to identify a student who is at-risk for school failure. Arrange to interview the student.
   a. Get to know the student as a human being. (What does the student like to do when not in school—hobbies, music, sports, friends, activities, favorite foods, etc.) Does the student work? Does he or she like the job? What does the student want to do after graduating? Does he or she intend to graduate? If not, why not?
   b. What does the student like about school? Dislike? How could schools be changed to make them better?
   c. What does the student like about this class? Dislike? How could the class be changed to make it more pleasant? To make it a better learning environment?
   d. What is the student's favorite subject? Least favorite? Why?
   e. Which kinds of teachers does the student like? Dislike? What advice does the student have for you as a new teacher?
   f. How does the student learn the best? What do teachers do to help him or her learn? Interfere with learning?
   g. What motivates the student in school? Out of school? How important are grades? In which classes does the student work the hardest? Why?

   Summarize these responses into a profile of the student. What do the student's responses suggest about teaching students placed at-risk?

2. Interview a teacher who works with students who are placed at-risk. Ask the following questions:
   a. How are at-risk students similar to and different from other students?
   b. What strengths do at-risk students bring to the classroom?
   c. How do you adapt your teaching to meet the needs of at-risk students?
   d. What successful strategies do you use in working with the parents of at-risk students?
   e. What are the rewards and challenges of working with at-risk students?

   How do the teacher's responses compare with research in this chapter? What do these responses suggest about teaching students placed at-risk?

3. Interview a counselor at a school that has significant numbers of students placed at-risk. Ask the following questions:
   a. What proportion of the students in the school are considered at-risk? How does the school identify them?
   b. What special programs within the school are designed for these students?
   c. What types of outreach activities does the school have for connecting with the community?
   d. What kinds of different roles do teachers play in this school?

   How effective is this school in addressing the needs of students placed at-risk? Based on the information in this chapter, how might this school be changed to better address these needs?

4. Identify a classroom with a high number of students placed at-risk. Observe a lesson in that class and analyze it in terms of the following:

  a. Emotional tone (for example, supportive and warm)
  b. Student–teacher interactions
  c. Teacher expectations
  d. Interactive teaching (for example, questions, groupwork)
  e. Frequency of feedback

Analyze the interaction in terms of the suggestions made in this chapter and make suggestions for changes.

 Virtual Field *Experience* | **If you would like to participate in a Virtual Field Experience, go to the** *Field Experience* **Module in Chapter 4 of the Companion Website.**

■ ONLINE PORTFOLIO ACTIVITIES

 To complete these activities online, go to the *Portfolio Activities* Module in Chapter 4 of the Companion Website to submit your response.

Portfolio Activity 4.1   **Investigating Chapter I Programs and Students**

INTASC Principle 3: *Adapting Instruction*
Locate the Websites for your state's Office of Education or for several local school districts. (Local school districts' phone numbers can be found under "Schools" in the commercial White Pages at the back of a phone book. From there you can get Website addresses.) Click on the module that has information on Title I programs and answer the following questions:

1. Which districts or schools offer the largest number of Chapter I programs?
2. What kinds of students (that is, students from which cultural minority groups) are found in these programs?
3. What is the curriculum in these programs?
4. What is instruction like in these programs?

Based on this information, what are some ways that you can prepare yourself to teach in schools that have high percentages of Title I students?

Portfolio Activity 4.2   **School Safety and Security**

INTASC Principle 5: *Motivation and Management*
This activity is designed to familiarize you with school safety and security procedures in your area. Locate the Websites of several local school districts. Click on "Student Conduct Policies and Procedures" and read how each district handles discipline and safety issues. How are the procedures similar and different? How would they affect your life as a teacher?

Portfolio Activity 4.3   **Managing Difficult Students**

INTASC Principle 5: *Motivation and Management*
This portfolio activity is designed to help you begin developing a coherent philosophy and strategies for dealing with difficult or hard to manage students. Locate a book on classroom management that discusses the problems of dealing with difficult students. We recommend Brophy (1996) and Powell et al. (2001), but there are many other excellent choices. Based on the information that you read, describe effective management practices for difficult students, and how teachers can deal with this problem.

PART 3

Foundations

CHAPTER

5

Educational Philosophy

*The Intellectual Foundations
of American Education*

Philosophy often seems rather remote and disconnected from everyday life, but this isn't at all the case. We each have a "philosophy of life;" for many people, this philosophy is tacit and not clearly defined, but for others it is well-articulated. Our philosophy is the set of principles we have chosen to live by; it's what guides us in our daily actions.

As with individuals, professions and professionals have philosophies that guide their practice. This is the topic for this chapter, as we try to answer the following questions:

- What is philosophy?

- What topics do students of philosophy study?

- How do traditional philosophies influence the process of learning to teach?

- What are the most prominent philosophies of education, and what implications do they have for education?

- How do you begin to form your own philosophy of education?

Let's begin the process by looking in on a conversation between two teachers.

140

Case STUDY

"What's happening?" Brad Norman asked Allie Skinner as he walked into the lounge during the lunch period.

"Working on this quiz," Allie mumbled, glancing up at him.

"You sure do test the heck out of your kids, don't you? Every time I come in here you're either writing a quiz or scoring one, or recording grades, or something."

"Well, it isn't that I love tests so much, but . . . well, you know what I think . . . ."

"Yeah, yeah, I know," Brad replied, waving his hand. "If you don't challenge them, they don't learn. . . . I guess I'm just more interested in trying to motivate them. . . ."

"Wait a minute," Allie interrupted. "I'm as interested in motivation as you are; it's just that I have some different views about how you get there."

"I know you think that *pushing* the kids. . . ." Brad began again.

"High expectations," Allie interrupted with a wry smile.

"Whatever," Brad shrugged. "I know you think that having *high expectations,*" he continued, rolling his eyes at the words, "is important, but I don't see how testing and all that stuff relates to motivation."

"Do you want to hear about it?" Allie nodded. "Might be boring."

"Sure, but keep it brief," Brad smiled.

"Well, this is what I believe . . . and you've got to be true to what you believe, I think, or you just blow back and forth like a leaf in the wind. I've given all this a lot of thought, and this is the best I've been able to come up with so far. I mean, I'll change my mind when I get some evidence that I'm wrong."

"You were going to keep it brief."

"Yeah, yeah, . . . well . . . anyway, I know kids have changed over the last however many years. They don't come to school with the same sort of desire to learn as they once did. Now, I do still believe that kids want to learn, or maybe more specifically, they want to believe they did learn something when they're finished with a topic, or class, or year of school, or whatever. On the other hand, they're not intrinsically motivated, and by that I mean, I don't think they're motivated to study stuff for it's own sake. I think they're often extrinsically motivated, motivated to study as a means to some end, like a good grade, or recognition from their classmates, or compliments from the teacher or something like that.

"Now, I was reading in one of my journals awhile back, and the authors were talking about the link between achievement and self-esteem, and it really made sense. I thought about what they said, and I do believe that kids feel good when they learn something, particularly if it's challenging. I also think that the more they know about a topic, the better they like it. For example, wouldn't you agree that an expert in some area, like a person who really understands literature, or poetry, or physics, is more motivated in that area than a novice, a person who doesn't know much about literature?"

"Look at yourself; you're really into surfing the Internet; you talk about it all the time. The better you've gotten at it, the more you like it, and the more you want to do it."

"Yeah, probably . . . I guess so," Brad shrugged.

"So, my goal is to get them to learn as much as possible about everything, like I mean the topics I'm teaching. The more they learn, the more intrinsically motivated they're going to be, and they're going to be motivated because they're getting good at the topic, and they're acquiring expertise about it."

"Now, there's real, practical stuff out there that they need to know, and there's only one way they're gonna learn it. . . . That's practice and experience. So, I've got to get them to study and practice. One way of doing that is to give them a lot of quizzes. They study for the quizzes, they get lots of feedback, and they tell me they learn a lot. Ultimately they like it, and further, their self-esteem improves, and it improves because they've learned a lot. That's the way it works. It's a win–win all the way around. . . . That's how I think the world works. I'm getting paid to help kids learn. If I don't do my very best to make that happen, I'm not earning my salary."

"Some of what you're saying makes sense," Brad acknowledged. "However, your view is a bit narrow for me. First, I think kids would be intrinsically motivated if school wasn't so boring. How motivated would you be if you had to sit and listen to dry teachers drone on all day, every day?"

"I like the idea of kids knowing stuff too, but school involves more than that. Where in your scheme do kids learn to solve problems, and make choices and wise decisions? A head full of facts may be great if your goal in life is to be good at quiz shows, like "Who Wants to Be a Millionaire?" or "Jeopardy," but the person who really succeeds is the one who continues to learn and is able to adapt to changes in the world by solving the large and small problems they encounter. So, the only way they're going to get good at making decisions is to be put in situations where they're forced to make decisions. They need lots of experience in making decisions and solving problems. That's what life's all about.

"Plus, thinking about doing my job, it would be a heck of a lot easier to just make the kids cram some stuff in their heads, but I would be doing them, their parents, and ultimately our whole society a disservice if I didn't bite the bullet and prepare them for life outside of school."

"And, as long as I'm at it," Brad continued, holding up a hand to prevent Allie from interrupting, "exactly what is real? You said '. . . there's real, practical stuff out there that they need to know.' For instance, let's say that, based on this conversation, you conclude that I'm naive and idealistic. On the other hand, I conclude that I'm actually more practical than you are, because I think schooling should help kids learn to make wise decisions and be adaptable, which requires learning activities where they're forced to make decisions. What is the reality? Am I naive, or am I practical? Who's to say? Reality is in fact this. To you, I'm naive, and you will operate based on that belief. To me I'm not. So, reality is what we perceive it to be, and there's no objective source *out there* to decide which view is the 'right one.'"

"Aw, c'mon," Allie countered. "Sure I acknowledge your point, but look at that oak tree outside the window. You can perceive it to be anything you want, but it's still an oak. And, it doesn't matter what anybody thinks, two plus two is four, not three, not five, not anything in between."

"Plus, I'm not talking about a '. . . head full of facts.' Knowing stuff means that they understand it well enough so they can apply it to whatever situation comes up. For instance, you want them to make wise decisions. They can't make a *wise* decision if they don't know anything."

Just then the bell rang, announcing the end of their planning period and signaling the transition to the next class. Allie and Brad left, agreeing to disagree and promising (or threatening) to continue the discussion later.

■   ■   ■

Let's stop now and consider Brad and Allie's conversation. They were discussing ideas at the heart of learning and teaching, and they obviously disagreed on several of them. However, both had given a good deal of thought to what is important in teaching and why it's important. The result was a philosophy of education that guided their work. This is what our chapter is about.

■ PHILOSOPHY AND PHILOSOPHY OF EDUCATION

What is philosophy, and what does "philosophy of education" mean? At its most basic level, **philosophy** is described as *a search for wisdom* (Ozmon & Craver, 1995), and we see evidence of this search in Allie and Brad's reflections. Allie, for example, said, "I've given all this a lot of thought, and this is the best I've been able to come up with so far. I mean, I'll change my mind when I get some evidence that I'm wrong." She examined her beliefs in an effort to find the wisdom to be the best teacher she was capable of being.

While his beliefs and conclusions were different, Brad was pursuing the same goal. This is why philosophy is important for teachers. A **philosophy of education** *provides a framework for thinking about educational issues and dilemmas, and it guides professional practice.*

All professions have "philosophies" that help guide practitioners in their thinking and actions. For example, the famous architect Frank Lloyd Wright came from the "organic" school of architecture. According to this school, homes and other structures should be a part of the environment; they shouldn't exist apart from their surroundings. The photo on the left reflects this belief. We see that the house blends into its background so well that it almost appears to be a natural part of the setting.

A contrasting architectural philosophy holds that "form follows function." This view suggests that structures must first be functional; the way they're built then depends on that function. The photo on the right reflects this belief.

Other professions have their own philosophies, that is, their systems of beliefs that guide decisions about professional practice. For example, the shift in emphasis from curing illnesses after they occur to lifestyle changes that prevent illness in the first place reflects a philosophical change in medicine. Holistic medicine, where patients' beliefs and

Philosophy exerts a powerful influence on other professions, such as architecture.

emotions, in addition to their physical symptoms, are taken into account in diagnosis and treatment, represents another philosophical shift. Similar competing philosophical systems can be described for law, engineering, and other professions.

Philosophy and Theory: How Are They Different?

Philosophy and theory overlap in many ways, and the distinction between the two is often blurred. In fact, some authors suggest that philosophy is a theory—a theory about knowledge, truth, reality, and good (Hampshire, 1966; Jacobsen, 1999). It is generally more understandable, however, to think of philosophy and theory differently. For example, when we see a student wearing a prominent sports figure's football jersey, we explain it by saying that the boy is imitating a high-status model. Our explanation is based on psychology's social cognitive theory as a basis for explaining the boy's behavior. **Theories** are *sets of related principles, based on observation, that we use to explain additional observations.* We observed the boy wearing the sports figure's jersey, and we explain the observation using the principle that says, "People tend to imitate behavior they observe in others," along with a second principle suggesting that "Individuals are more likely to imitate someone with high status than someone with low status." These principles are based on observations, and they form part of social cognitive theory.

Philosophies are based in part on theories. For example, Allie's emphasis on high expectations is based in part on theories of motivation. Philosophy goes beyond theory, however, not only to explain the way things are, such as why the boy wears the jersey and why students are motivated, but also to suggest the way things *ought to be* and to analyze theories, ideas, and beliefs. For example, Allie suggested that schools ought to emphasize knowledge and understanding, whereas Brad thought they ought to focus on decision making and problem solving. Further, Allie expressed the *belief* that kids basically want to learn but that they're not intrinsically motivated. Brad expressed the opposite belief. In this regard, both Allie and Brad stepped beyond theory into the realm of philosophy.

We see similarities in other professions. For example, in architecture, one school suggests that structures ought to be a part of the environment, whereas another school believes that being functional is the highest priority. In medicine, one school of thinking emphasizes prevention through healthy lifestyles, while another focuses on healing through drugs and antibiotics. *This description of the way education, architecture, medicine, or any other profession ought to practice is called* **normative philosophy.**

Branches of Philosophy

Just as other areas of inquiry, such as biology, geography, or literature, have different areas and topics of study, so does philosophy. In philosophy these include:

- Epistemology
- Metaphysics (Ontology)
- Axiology
- Logic

Let's examine them.

Epistemology Let's look again at Allie and Brad's discussion. Allie stated, "Now, there's real, practical stuff out there that they need to know, and there's only one way they're gonna learn it. . . . That's practice and experience. So, I've got to get them to study and

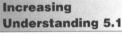

Increasing Understanding 5.1

We said that philosophy guides practice. Does theory also guide practice? Explain.

To answer this question online and receive immediate feedback, go to the *Increasing Understanding* Module in Chapter 6 of the book's Companion Website at **http://www.prenhall. com/kauchak.**

**Increasing
Understanding 5.2**

A woman is shopping for a new car. In making her decision, she places primary emphasis on cars' mileage ratings, their repair records, and evaluations from organizations such as the American Automobile Association. Is her "way of knowing" primarily the scientific method, intuition, or authority? Explain.

**Increasing
Understanding 5.3**

With respect to epistemology, are Allie and Brad's views quite similar or are they quite different? Explain, citing evidence taken directly from the case study to support your position.

**Increasing
Understanding 5.4**

Character educators see learners as unsocialized and in need of moral discipline. In contrast, moral educators see learners as undeveloped, needing stimulation to construct more mature moral views. Are these contrasting positions more closely related to metaphysics or to epistemology? Explain.

practice." She argued that *the way learners come to know* the ideas they learn is through practice and experience.

Allie was making an epistemological argument. **Epistemology** *deals with the question of how we come to know what we know.* A variety of ways of knowing exist. The scientific method, in which principles are tested with observable facts, is one. Intuition, authority, and even divine revelation are others.

Constructivism, a prominent learning theory, raises interesting epistemological questions. Constructivism argues that, instead of behaving like tape recorders, which reproduce words and music in their original form, people "construct" understanding that makes sense to them. For example, many people have "constructed" the idea that we're closer to the sun in summer (in the northern hemisphere) because it's warmer in summer than in winter, when in reality we're actually farther away from the sun in summer. In thinking this way, people draw analogies between proximity to a candle or a bonfire and the sun's distance to the earth (Mayer, 1998). The way we have come to understand why summer is warmer than winter is to construct ideas that make sense to us.

Epistemology is important for teachers because it suggests the teaching methods that they will use. If teachers believe in constructivism, for example, they provide a variety of experiences for learners and lead discussions that will help them construct valid understandings of the way the world works. In contrast, if we believe that authority is the most important way of knowing, we're likely to lecture and expect students to reproduce on tests what we've told them.

Metaphysics While epistemology examines *how* we know, **metaphysics**—or **ontology**—*considers what we know* (Osborne, 1996). Metaphysics considers questions of reality, and ultimately, what is real. With respect to metaphysics, Allie and Brad are far apart. Allie argued, "Now, there's real, practical stuff out there that they need to know . . ." but Brad countered, ". . . reality is what we perceive it to be, and there's no objective source *out there* to decide which view is the 'right one'." Allie believes a reality independent of our perception exists, but Brad believes that perception and reality are inextricably intertwined.

Metaphysics has implications both for the way we teach and for the goals we establish. For instance, since Allie believes in a reality independent of people's perceptions, her goal is for students to understand that reality. In contrast, since Brad believes less strongly in an objective reality, his goals more strongly emphasize students learning to critically examine their own thinking. The teaching methods both Allie and Brad will use will be those that best help students reach these goals.

Axiology Axiology *considers values and ethics;* axiological issues are now prominent in American education. Because of current problems, such as drug abuse, teen pregnancy, and juvenile violence and crime, educators generally agree that some form of moral education is needed in schools, although they disagree on the form it should take (Wynne, 1997). One view, labeled **character education** *argues that values, such as honesty and citizenship, should be emphasized, taught, and rewarded* (Doyle, 1997). A contrasting view, called **moral education,** *emphasizes the development of students' moral reasoning and doesn't establish a preset list of values that learners should acquire* (Kohn, 1997). But regardless of which view they favor, all educators believe that the development of moral thinking and moral behavior are important goals for schools.

Let's look again at Allie and Brad's conversation. Allie argued, "I'm getting paid to help kids learn. If I don't do my very best to make that happen, I'm not earning my salary." Brad retorted, ". . . it would be a heck of a lot easier to just make the kids cram some stuff in their heads, but I would be doing them, their parents, and ultimately our whole society a disservice if I didn't bite the bullet and prepare them for life outside of school." Both teachers argued that they wouldn't be behaving ethically if they weren't true to their beliefs about what is important. Though they were probably unaware of it, this part of their conversation was concerned with axiology.

Logic   Let's look again at some of Allie's thinking. While not in these exact words, it could be described in the following sequence. She suggested that:

> "The more people learn, the more intrinsically motivated they become."
> "You [Brad] have learned a lot about the Internet."
> "You want to surf the Internet more now than ever before. [You're more intrinsically motivated.]"

Logic is *the process of deriving valid conclusions from basic principles*, and Allie was illustrating a form of logic called *deductive reasoning*. Deductive reasoning begins with a proposition, called a major premise, which can be a principle or generalization such as "The more people learn, the more intrinsically motivated they are." The major premise is followed by a fact, called a minor premise, such as "You have learned a lot about the Internet." A deductive reasoning sequence is completed with a conclusion that follows from the two premises. In Allie's case the conclusion was an explanation for why Brad spent time surfing the Internet.

Inductive reasoning is the counterpart to deductive reasoning. For instance, when students see that a rock and paper clip hit the floor at the same time if they're dropped simultaneously, they conclude that objects fall at the same rate regardless of weight (if air resistance is negligible). Based on the specific instances (the rock and the paper clip), the students make a general conclusion about falling objects.

Logic helps both teachers and learners examine the validity of their thinking. For instance, in social studies we try to help students see that if we stereotype a specific cultural group based on the behavior or appearance of a few members of the group, we're using faulty inductive reasoning. Similarly, many controversies in education and other aspects of life exist because proponents and critics disagree on the validity of conclusions, which are the products of deductive reasoning. For instance, critics of character education conclude that it emphasizes indoctrination (Kohn, 1997). This conclusion is based on the premise that a system based on rewards indoctrinates rather than teaches (a major premise), and character education utilizes rewards (a minor premise). Proponents of character education disagree with both the major premise and the conclusion.

■ TRADITIONAL SCHOOLS OF PHILOSOPHY

Throughout history, philosophers worked to systematically describe how the world works, that is, they've tried to answer questions about reality and what is real (metaphysics), how we know (epistemology), what is good and valuable (axiology), and whether or not our thinking is clear and accurate (logic). Many of these efforts have resulted in cohesive philosophies. Four of them are considered by many to be the traditional philosophies that undergird most educational decisions (Jacobsen, 1999). They are:

- ■ Idealism
- ■ Realism
- ■ Pragmatism
- ■ Existentialism

We turn to them now.

Increasing Understanding 5.5

You're being asked to respond to margin questions, such as this one. We have concluded that questions such as these will increase your understanding of this book. Identify a major premise and a minor premise on which this conclusion could be based.

Idealism

Let's look once more at Allie and Brad's conversation. Brad argued, ". . . let's say that, based on this conversation, you conclude that I'm naive and idealistic. On the other hand, I conclude that I'm actually more practical than you are . . . . What is the reality? Am I naive, or am I practical? . . . To you, I'm naive, and you will operate based on that belief. To me I'm not. So, reality is what we perceive it to be, and there's no objective source *out there* to decide which view is the 'right one'."

Brad argued that ideas are the ultimate reality, which is a basic principle of idealism. Idealism is the oldest of the Western philosophies, having originated with the great Greek philosopher, Plato. **Idealism** *is the belief that, since the physical world is constantly changing, ideas are the only reliable form of reality.*

■ ■ ■

Plato was born at the height of Greek civilization into an aristocratic family in Athens (his birth date is estimated to be about 428 B.C.). Along with Socrates (his teacher and mentor) and Aristotle, Plato was one of the three philosophers of ancient Greece that laid the philosophical foundations of Western culture.

Plato wrote in the form of imaginary dialogues between Socrates and his students. Plato's goal in writing the dialogues was to faithfully represent Socrates' thinking; in the dialogues, Socrates questioned his students' beliefs and assumptions about truth, beauty, and other philosophical topics. His questioning, as illustrated in the dialogues, led to the modern concept of the *Socratic Method* or *Socratic Questioning.*

■ ■ ■

Since, for idealists, ultimate reality exists in the world of ideas, teaching and learning should focus on these ideas. A curriculum based on idealism emphasizes mathematics because of its logic, precision, and abstraction. It also emphasizes great works of literature, art, and music because of their enduring contributions. The thinking of great men and women in history would be studied because of the ideas they offered.

Increasing Understanding 5.6

Would idealists support the scientific method, or would they be critical of it? Explain. To which of the four branches of philosophy is this question most closely related? Explain.

Idealism emphasizes great works of literature, music, and art, which contain powerful ideas from important contributors to our culture.

Teachers have a critical role for idealists. Learners are unlikely to understand enduring ideas without support and guidance. Teachers provide this guidance by helping students become more precise and logical thinkers and by helping them understand the ideas that have existed throughout history. For example, an English teacher might have students read Melville's *Moby Dick* because it emphasizes the conflict between good and evil, an enduring idea. Younger children might study White's *Charlotte's Web* because it deals with a moral dilemma, another time-honored concept.

Idealism has been criticized as elitist and overemphasizing cold, rational ideas at the expense of emotions, feelings, and the personal side of people. It is elitist because the ideas chosen for analysis often come from a small, wealthy, and privileged part of the population. It is considered coldly cognitive because it emphasizes the rational and logical over other dimensions of human experience.

Realism

In contrast with idealism, which argues that ideas are the ultimate reality, **realism** *holds that the features of the universe exist whether or not a human being is there to perceive them.* Realism is also an ancient philosophy, Aristotle being one of its original developers. Allie's argument, ". . . look at that oak tree outside the window. You can perceive it to be anything you want, but it's still an oak. And, it doesn't matter what anybody thinks, two plus two is four, not three, not five, not anything in between." This argument is consistent with realism. Realists argue that there are important ideas and facts that must be understood, and they can only be understood by studying the material world. Realists emphasize science and technology and strongly endorse the scientific method. They argue that ignorance of information about diet, disease, and natural disasters, for example, has caused much of the suffering in human history, and the accumulation of knowledge in areas like science and medicine has improved the quality of life for many people.

■ ■ ■

Aristotle was born in 384 B.C. and studied at Plato's Academy. A great thinker and teacher, he is believed to have participated in the education of Alexander the Great, one of the greatest military leaders in history.

Aristotle studied and wrote about an amazing array of topics ranging from logic, philosophy, and ethics to physics, biology, psychology, and politics. Deductive reasoning and the scientific method were both influenced by his thinking.

■ ■ ■

Critics who argue that American education is in decline because the curriculum has been "dumbed down" with too many superfluous courses and too much emphasis on "self-esteem" are expressing views consistent with realism. A curriculum consistent with realism emphasizes essentials, such as math, science, reading, and writing, because they are tools to help us understand our world. The periodic national focus and refocus on basic skills is also consistent with this view.

Teachers working within the philosophy of realism emphasize observation, experimentation, and critical reasoning. Their goals are for learners to think clearly and understand the material world. They tend to de-emphasize formal emphasis on feelings and other personal factors, arguing that positive feelings and the improvement of self-esteem are an outgrowth of knowledge and understanding.

As with idealism, critics of realism argue that it is inappropriately narrow in its failing to take the whole person—the physical, emotional, and social in addition to the intellectual domain—into account in the learning process.

Pragmatists attempt to connect subject-matter content to children's interests.

Pragmatism

Though it has ancient roots, pragmatism is considered a modern—even American—philosophy, with John Dewey being one of its primary proponents. Dewey (1902, 1906, 1923, 1938) wrote extensively on education, and his work has arguably had more impact on American education than has any other body of literature. His ideas continue to be actively debated by educators today (for example, Prawat, 1998; Proefriedt, 1999).

■ ■ ■

John Dewey (1859–1952) is one of the most important American philosophers in history. Educated in his native Vermont and at Johns Hopkins University, Dewey enjoyed a long career as an educator, psychologist, and philosopher. He initiated the progressive laboratory school at the University of Chicago, where his reforms in methods of education were put into practice. As a result, *progressivism,* a prominent educational philosophy, is associated with his work.

■ ■ ■

Pragmatism *shares some views with realism, but is less rigid. It rejects the idea of absolute, unchanging truth. Instead, truth is what works, hence the term* pragmatism. For example, our primitive ancestors needed and ate a diet high in fat because it might be a long time between meals, and they were very active as hunter–gatherers. Now, we have a problem. Our evolved selves still enjoy, even crave, fat, but we no longer need as much because we've become sedentary. Historically, truth was that fat was important and healthy; now truth is that fat is less important and too much is unhealthy. A high-fat diet no longer "works."

For pragmatists, *experience* is a key idea. As we've gathered experiences with respect to diet, for example, we've observed the consequences of those experiences and have adapted (or are trying to adapt) accordingly.

This example illustrates the pragmatists' contention that truth isn't an abstract idea, nor is it simply a material aspect of the world. Rather, it represents the interaction

Increasing Understanding 5.7

Based on the conversation in our opening case study, would Allie or Brad's views be more closely related to pragmatism? Cite evidence from the case to support your contention.

between the individual and the environment. Further, truth is personal and relative. For example, some people need more fat in their diet than do others.

Because truth changes, individuals need methods for dealing with these changes. As a result, teachers adhering to pragmatism place the processes involved in learning on an equal plane with content. Direct experiences and problem solving are emphasized. Information needed to solve problems comes from many sources, so studying content areas in isolation isn't effective or practical; interdisciplinary education that focuses on using various academic disciplines to analyze and solve problems is more "pragmatic."

Critics of pragmatism contend that it undervalues essential knowledge. Pragmatism, with it's educational counterpart, *progressivism*, has been blamed by conservative critics for the decline in performance by American students compared to students in other industrialized countries. Critics further contend that pragmatism too strongly emphasizes student interests at the expense of essential knowledge (Ravitch, 2000).

Defenders of pragmatism, and particularly Dewey's work, argue that the critics are either misrepresenting Dewey or don't understand him. "He saw clearly that to ask, 'Which is more important: the interests of the child or the knowledge of subject-matter?' was to ask a very dumb question indeed. The teacher's task, for Dewey, was to create an interaction between the child's interest and the funded knowledge of the adult world . . ." (Proefriedt, 1999, p. 28). Pragmatism doesn't de-emphasize the importance of knowledge; instead, it attempts to connect it to children's interests.

Existentialism

Compared to idealism, realism, and pragmatism, existentialism is quite radical. **Existentialism** is *a philosophical view suggesting that humanity isn't part of an orderly universe; rather, individuals create their own existence in their own unique way.* Influenced by the horrors of World War II, existentialist writers, such as Jean-Paul Sartre, have a pessimistic view of humanity, seeing it as essentially meaningless on a small, isolated planet in an uncertain universe where nothing is determined. If nothing is determined, people have total freedom, freedom to take advantage of others, promote racial strife, or cause conflicts. However, we're also free to promote peace and harmony. With total freedom comes total responsibility. Unwise choices can't be blamed on God's will, other people, or prior experiences.

■ ■ ■

Jean-Paul Sartre (1905–1980) was educated in Paris and Göttingen, Germany. He participated actively in the French resistance to German occupation in World War II, and the experience of the war, combined with his study of earlier existentialist writers, strongly influenced his thinking. He wrote philosophy, fiction, and political treatises, becoming one of the most respected leaders in post-war French culture.

■ ■ ■

Existentialism makes a contribution to education because it places primary emphasis on the individual, and in doing so, it reminds us that we don't teach math, science, reading, and writing; rather, we teach people, and the people we teach are at the core of learning.

Existentialists would have us change our attitudes about education. Education isn't something a student is filled with and measured; education is an individual's search for personal understanding. Existentialist educators decry tracking, measurement, and standardization, arguing that these practices detract from individuals' opportunities for growth. Schools, they suggest, should be places where students are free to engage in activities because these activities are interesting to them and help students define who they are.

Whereas science and technology are important for realists and pragmatists, an existentialist curriculum would place more emphasis on the humanities, because the humanities

Table 5.1	The Traditional Schools of Philosophy			
	Idealism	Realism	Pragmatism	Existentialism
Metaphysics	Reality is the world of unchanging ideas.	Reality is the physical world.	Reality is the interaction of the individual and the environment.	Reality is the subjective interpretation of the physical world.
Epistemology	Knowing is the personal rethinking of universal ideas.	Knowing is observing and understanding natural laws.	Knowing is the result of experience based on the scientific method.	Knowing is making personal choice.
Axiology	Values are absolute based on enduring ideas.	Values are absolute based on natural law.	Values are relative.	Values are chosen by the individual.
Educational Implications	Curricula focus on content that emphasizes time-honored ideas.	Curricula focus on content that emphasizes natural laws.	Curricula and instruction focus on problem solving and the scientific method.	Instruction emphasizes discussion designed to increase individual self-awareness.

examine human existence, relationships between people, and tragedy as well as triumph. An existentialist teacher, for example, might have students read Albee's *Who's Afraid of Virginia Woolf* to consider why a couple remains together when all they seem to do is develop greater and greater ways of hurting each other.

On a more positive note, existentialism has influenced the thinking of humanistic educators such as Carl Rogers (1967) and Abraham Maslow (1968, 1970), who advocate a learner-centered and non-directive approach to education. Empathy is an important teacher characteristic, and teachers, they argue, should care for their students unconditionally, helping students feel like worthy individuals. Teachers should be students, and students should be teachers. Current emphases on communities of learners, in which teachers and students work together to accomplish learning goals, are consistent with this view.

Critics of existentialism remind us that we all live in a social world, which, whether we like it or not, has rules; total freedom is impossible. However, even critics acknowledge the existentialist position emphasizing that personal freedom carries with it personal responsibility.

Each of the traditional philosophies has implications for teaching. An English teacher whose personal philosophy is grounded in idealism, for example, might have her students read Hugo's *Les Miserables* because it examines the issue of morality, which is a time-honored topic. Class discussions would examine historical considerations of morality. Another teacher, whose philosophical leanings are existentialist, would orient class discussions more strongly toward students' personal conceptions of morality. The topic is the same, but the teachers' goals are different because of the influence of philosophy.

Differences among these traditional philosophies are summarized in Table 5.1.

■ EXPLORING DIVERSITY: PHILOSOPHY AND CULTURAL MINORITIES

To this point in the chapter, the philosophies we've examined have been "Western," meaning their origins are European or American. Two principles undergird this Western orientation. The first is the preeminence of the individual, such as an individual's search for truth in

Alternate philosophies remind teachers of the need to view each child as an individual with unique needs and interests.

both idealism and realism, the interaction of the individual with the environment for pragmatism, and an individual's search for a meaningful life for an existentialist.

The second is rational thought and respect for objectivity, science, and the scientific method. Realism and pragmatism, in particular, emphasize science as a way of knowing.

Some philosophers criticize these emphases, citing examples such as the fact that technology dominates our lives, Americans are working more hours per week than they ever have in the past, and they're chronically sleep deprived.

In contrast to Western emphasis on individuality and rationality, some philosophies, such as those embedded in certain Native American cultures, use the shared folklore of elders and knowledge that comes from the heart as their sources of wisdom (Morton, 1988). Because of Native Americans' long history of living in harmony with the land, their philosophies also place emphasis on ecological as well as interpersonal harmony. The emphasis on harmony and cooperation results in valuing individual achievement primarily as it contributes to a group's overall well-being. Competition and individual displays of achievement are frowned upon. Understanding these differences can help explain why Navajo students, for example, are sometimes reluctant to participate in the competitive verbal give-and-take of fast-paced questioning sessions that require individuals to demonstrate how much they know (Villegas, 1991; Tharp, 1989).

Similarly, for some African cultures, feelings and personal relationships are equally or more important ways of knowing than are science and rational thought (Nieto, 1996). Art and music are important means of expression and seeking knowledge. As we look at the history of African Americans, this helps us understand why music was such a prominent part of their lives during slavery, why African Americans have made such a strong contribution to modern and impressionistic art, and why African influences can be seen in much of contemporary music in Europe and the Americas.

Many Asians also value harmony—harmony with nature, life, family, and society. The emphasis on harmony leads to reverence for elders, respect for authority, and adherence to traditions. Because harmony is so important, being polite is highly valued, and feelings and

HOW ALTERNATIVE PHILOSOPHIES AFFECT TEACHING

You're a teacher in a medium-sized school in South Dakota, and you have a number of Native American students in your classes. You're periodically frustrated by the chronic absences of some of these students. It seems that any event—the birth of a new cousin, a grandfather's birthday, the homecoming of an uncle—is an excuse for missing school. You often wonder how these students will ever acquire the skills to function effectively in society.

Further, your Native American students seem to be very slow in responding to your questions, and they appear visibly uncomfortable when you encourage them to respond more quickly. Their delayed responses slow your class down, and other students drift off as you wait for them to respond. It also appears that several Native American students would prefer to not be called on at all.

1. How can your knowledge of alternate philosophies help you understand your Native American students?
2. To what extent are you responsible for encouraging all students to be in school and to be there on time?
3. Should you continue to call on all the students, even though some of them prefer to not be called on at all?
4. What would you do in this situation?

To answer these questions online and receive immediate feedback, go to the Reflect on This *Module in Chapter 5 of the Companion Website.*

emotions tend to be controlled in order to maintain propriety and proper social relationships (McDermott, 1994). Understanding these perspectives helps us understand characteristics commonly attributed to Asian American students. For instance, they are often described as being shy, reluctant to speak out in class, and their nonverbal behavior tends to be restrained, making reading nonverbal cues sometimes difficult (Park, 1997).

On the other hand, using these perspectives as a basis for making conclusions about minority students has been sharply criticized. Critics argue that the descriptions you've just read are little more than stereotypes that grossly oversimplify the complexities of alternative philosophies. For example, some Americans simplistically think of Africa as a country, not realizing that it is a vast continent, more culturally and linguistically diverse than North or South America. To speak of a singular "African philosophy," or Native American or Asian for that matter, does an injustice to these people and their philosophies. Further, people are people, and categorizing them on the basis of sweeping and uncertain philosophical generalizations is questionable at best and perhaps even potentially damaging (Diamond, 1999).

Rather than viewing students as Hispanic, Native American, African American, or any other cultural or ethnic group, we should see students as individuals. For example, concluding that student Ted Chang doesn't speak out in class because of the influence of his Chinese culture, and leaving it at that, might be educationally dangerous. In addition, it is less effective than getting to know him as a person and using this knowledge to try to involve him in learning activities, just as you would try to involve all the students in your classes (Banks, 1994).

Respecting and valuing cultural differences is important. Making decisions that may detract from learning, based on overgeneralizations about these differences, is not. As a teacher, the realization that not all people hold or believe in the same philosophical orientations will make you more sensitive to the important individual differences in your students.

■ PHILOSOPHIES OF EDUCATION

In reflecting on our discussion of the traditional philosophies, we see that they are comprehensive views of life and thought; they weren't developed as philosophies of education, even though each has implications for teaching and learning. We now turn to an examination of philosophical views that focus specifically on education. As you study these philosophies, look for relationships between them and the traditional philosophies you've studied.

In this section, we'll examine four of these philosophies:

- Perennialism
- Progressivism
- Essentialism
- Postmodernism

Perennialism

Increasing Understanding 5.8

Think about Allie's philosophical position in the case study at the beginning of this chapter. In what way (or ways) are her views consistent with perennialism? In what way (or ways) are they inconsistent with the views of perennialists? Explain.

Let's think about the term *perennial* for a moment. It is an adjective meaning perpetual or long-lasting. **Perennialism** is *the belief that nature, including human nature, is constant.* In this regard, perennialists have roots in both idealism and realism (Jacobsen, 1999). As we recall, both believe in the enduring and constant nature of reality—for idealists, enduring ideas, and for realists, the constancy of the physical universe.

Consistent with the beliefs of idealism and realism, perennialists believe in a rigorous intellectual curriculum for all students. For perennialists, education is preparation for future life, and the extent to which students find their studies relevant isn't crucial in the perennialist view. Math, science, and particularly literature are important in a perennialist curriculum because they expose learners to the rigors of logical thought as well as the great ideas that have endured throughout history. The ideal perennialist curriculum would have students study classic works ranging from Homer's *Iliad* to Darwin's *The Origin of Species* (which introduced the theory of evolution), together with a host of works in between.

Perennialism experienced a mild and brief renaissance in the early 1980s with the publication of Mortimer Adler's (1980) *The Paideia Proposal: An Educational Manifesto.* Adler advocated a general curriculum for all students, including math, science, history, geography, literature, and fine arts. Understanding the content of these subject matter areas was a means to an end, however, and not an end it itself. The goal in studying them was to develop intellectual skills, such as writing, speaking, computing, and problem solving. The content, together with these intellectual skills, would lead to higher-level thinking, reflection, and awareness.

Increasing Understanding 5.9

Would perennialists favor vocational education? Explain.

Although Adler's ideas received considerable attention from the popular press, their application in schools was limited. Critics argued that Adler's proposals were elitist, aimed primarily at the highest ability students in schools (Ozmon & Craver, 1995). They also questioned the value of distant and abstract ideas for poorly motivated and intellectually unprepared students.

Essentialism

We've all heard of "back to the basics" movements, which occur in education on a somewhat cyclical basis. "Back to the basics" means that learning should focus on essential basic skills, such as reading, writing, mathematics, and to a certain extent, science and geography. (Many educational leaders now include the use of technology and technological literacy as a basic skill.)

Critics of education and proponents of essentialism periodically write newspaper editorials sounding the alarm about American students' ignorance of the world around them, their inability to communicate either orally or in writing, and their lack of ability to do rudimentary math (American Council of Trustees and Alumni, 2000; Ravitch, 2000). These views are consistent with **essentialism,** which is *the belief that a critical core of information exists that all people should possess.* For essentialists, schools should emphasize basic skills and academic subjects, and students should be expected to master these subjects. The reasons for these emphases and standards are to ensure a literate and skilled workforce in a technological society. Essentialists are concerned about a general "dumbing down" of the curriculum, they decry social promotion of students, and they are wary of student-centered curriculum and instruction.

Many of the reform efforts over the last 20 or more years can be traced to essentialist views. The widely publicized *A Nation At Risk* (National Commission on Excellence in Education, 1983), which recommended that all high school students master core requirements in five "basics"—English, math, science, social studies, and computer science—is one example.

Essentialist philosophy is also found in teacher-education programs. The popularity of books such as *Knowledge Base for the Beginning Teacher* (Reynolds, 1989) and the fact that aspiring teachers are required to take a specified sequence of courses and to demonstrate mastery of essential teaching skills reflect the belief that a core of knowledge exists that all pre-service teachers should master.

Essentialism and perennialism share the view that knowledge and understanding are preeminent, and both are wary of the emphasis on learner-centered education and the focus on learner self-esteem. Essentialists differ from perennialists, however, in perennialists' emphasis on universal truths through the study of classical literature. Essentialists, instead, emphasize knowledge and skills that are useful in today's world. From an essentialist perspective, the sequence of courses you're required to take and the competencies or skills you are asked to master in your teacher-preparation program exist because educational leaders believe that they will help you become a better teacher in today's world.

The essentialist curriculum is more likely to change than is the perennialist curriculum. For instance, as our society becomes increasingly diverse, teacher-preparation programs place greater and greater emphasis on learning to work effectively with learners from diverse backgrounds. This is in response to the increasing diversity of our students as well as a growing recognition of the influence of diversity on learning. This means you will likely take a course in multicultural education, or topics in multicultural education will be included in several of your courses. This emphasis wouldn't have existed 20 years ago. The same is true for technology; most teacher-education programs now have some type of technology component. Whether arrived at implicitly or consciously, these shifts in emphasis reflect essentialist thinking.

Progressivism

Think for a moment about some of the practices we are seeing emphasized in education today. For instance, we encounter "learner-centered curricula," which emphasizes learners' interests and needs (Lambert & McCombs, 1998). We also see hands-on learning activities, particularly in science, where children work with batteries, bulbs, magnets, plants, soil, and a variety of other materials. Learners are asked to write about their own experiences in language arts, and math emphasizes problem solving and learning concepts

Increasing Understanding 5.10

"High stakes" testing, in which students are required to pass standardized tests before they're allowed to graduate from high school, is being emphasized today. Would essentialists react negatively or positively to this trend? Explain.

through hands-on manipulatives. Learners collaborating as they work with these materials and solving these problems is also emphasized. Teachers don't simply deliver information; they guide learners and facilitate the learning process.

These practices are philosophically rooted in progressivism, an educational philosophy grounded in pragmatism. As we saw earlier, for pragmatists, reality is what works. **Progressivism** *emphasizes curriculum that focuses on real-world problem solving and individual development.* As Brad argued in our beginning case study, ". . . the person who really succeeds is the one who continues to learn and is able to adapt to changes in the world by solving the large and small problems they encounter," and "They need lots of experience in making decisions and solving problems. That's what life's all about." These are views consistent with progressivism.

In our discussion of epistemology, we briefly examined constructivism, a view of learning asserting that students don't record understanding; rather, they construct it based on their experiences and background knowledge. Constructivism is consistent with progressivism and its precursor, pragmatism. All three emphasize concrete experiences, real-world tasks, and the central role of the individual in determining reality and promoting learning. As you analyze learning in educational psychology, you will undoubtedly study constructivism in detail. As you do, remember that it's rooted in pragmatism and progressivism.

Progressivism is controversial. As we saw in our discussion of pragmatism, critics contend that the pendulum has swung too far in the direction of children's interests and self-esteem at the expense of knowledge and understanding (Ravitch, 2000). Some of these criticisms are justified and reflect misapplications of Dewey's ideas. For example, progressives complained that schools organized subject matter in a detached manner, alien to the interests and abilities of young children. But these same progressives made no sustained effort to develop or understand alternate ways of organizing knowledge so that it would be more accessible or useable to the learner. They recognized the shortcomings of assigning the learner to a passive, receptive role, but too often substituted for it a set of educationally purposeless activities (Proefriedt, 1999, p. 28). Both progressivism and its precursor, pragmatism—when properly interpreted—suggest that effective education isn't a matter of process *or* content; it is process *and* content.

Postmodernism

During the 1960s, the United States went through major cultural upheavals. The Vietnam War was a concrete marker, and its unpopularity caused skepticism about authority and leadership. Other movements, such as civil rights for minorities, feminism, and gay and lesbian crusades, encouraged critiques of American culture, society, and education. Postmodern philosophy emerged among these critiques.

Postmodernism contends that *many of the institutions in our society, including schools, are used by those in power to control and marginalize those who lack power.* The powerful are typically White males, and those marginalized (lacking power) are unskilled workers, women, and cultural minorities. Postmodernists argue that K–12 and university curricula are racist, sexist, and imperialist. As an example of this, postmodernists point to the continued curricular emphasis on the study of Shakespeare. Shakespeare, a White European male, figures prominently in most high school literature programs. Emphasis on Shakespeare and other White male authors has resulted in little room left for literature written by women, minorities, or people from other cultures. Since White males make curricular decisions, marginalizing those without power continues unabated.

Increasing Understanding 5.11

Of the traditional philosophies—idealism, realism, pragmatism, and existentialism—which would be most acceptable to postmodernists? Explain.

Reflect *on* This

EDUCATIONAL PHILOSOPHY IN THE CLASSROOM

You're an American history teacher and you want your students to do more than simply memorize their way through the information you're teaching. You want them to develop their critical-thinking skills, learn to solve problems, make informed decisions, and get involved in lessons.

This turns out to be a daunting task, however. The students seem to want you to describe every required detail in assignments, and when you call on students who don't have their hands raised, the most common response is, "I didn't have my hand up," or "I don't know." In other cases, they say, "C'mon, just tell us what you want us to know," and "Why do we have to learn this stuff?"

1. To which educational philosophy are your goals most closely aligned? To which are they least aligned?

2. Using one of these educational philosophies how might you respond to students when they ask, "Why do we have to learn this stuff?"

3. Should you "force" students to be involved if they're reluctant to participate? How might you involve reluctant students in lessons?

4. How would you handle the situation just described?

To answer these questions online and receive immediate feedback, go to the Reflect on This *Module in Chapter 5 of the Companion Website.*

Postmodern philosophy raises questions about culture and gender bias in our schools.

A postmodern curriculum would reverse these trends. Literature written by feminist and minority authors would be elevated to a position as prominent or more prominent than traditional literature. Further, traditional literature would be critically examined to see how it has historically shaped our notions of differences, such as race and gender. Issues such as the use of power, personal and group identities, cultural politics, and social

Table 5.2	**Characteristics of the Educational Philosophies**			
	Perennialism	Essentialism	Progressivism	Postmodernism
Traditional Philosophy Most Closely Related	Idealism, Realism	Idealism, Realism	Pragmatism	Existentialism
Educational Goals	Train the intellect; moral development.	Acquire basic skills; acquire knowledge needed to function in today's world.	Acquire ability to function in the real world; develop problem-solving skills.	Critically examine today's institutions; elevate the status of marginalized people (women and cultural minorities).
Curriculum	Emphasis on enduring ideas.	Emphasis on basic skills.	Emphasis on problem solving and skills needed in today's world.	Emphasis on the works of marginalized people.
Role of the Teacher	Deliver clear lectures; increase student understanding with critical questions.	Deliver clear lectures; increase student understanding with critical questions.	Guide learning with questioning; develop and guide practical problem-solving activities.	Facilitate discussions that involve clarifying issues.
Teaching Methods	Lecture; questioning; coaching in intellectual thinking.	Lecture; practice and feedback; questioning.	Problem-based learning; cooperative learning; guided discovery.	Discussion; role play; simulation; personal research.
Learning Environment	High structure; high levels of time on task.	High structure; high levels of time on task.	Collaborative; self-regulated; democratic.	Community-oriented; self-regulated.
Assessment	Frequent objective and essay tests.	Frequent objective, essay, and performance tests.	Continuous feedback; informal monitoring of student progress.	Collaborative between teacher and student; emphasis on the exposure of hidden assumptions.

Increasing Understanding 5.12

Throughout this text, you've been asked to respond to margin questions such as this one. The fact that these questions exist and the types of questions being asked best reflect which of the educational philosophies? Explain.

criticism would enjoy prominent positions. Historical events would be examined from the perspective of power, status, and marginalized people's struggles in those contexts. For instance, Columbus's discovery of the New World has been presented historically as a critical point in European expansion and colonization, and the beginning of modern history in North and South America. Postmodernism would recognize that fact but would emphasize the brutalization of Native Americans by the Spaniards, the ravaging of the indigenous people by diseases such as smallpox (for which they had no natural immunities), their enslavement, and the fact that conquering and colonization were two major goals for explorers.

Postmodernism has sparked hot debate. As postmodernists have risen to positions of power in some universities, for example, the study of Shakespeare has been eliminated from the curriculum in favor of feminist and minority authors. This has caused outrage among perennialist or essentialist thinkers. They argue that postmodernism has resulted in the abandonment of schools as places for intellectual pursuits, contending instead that schools are being used for political purposes. They contend further that postmodernism is as control-oriented as traditional philosophies and institutions; it merely wants to establish controls more to its followers' liking (Ozmon & Craver, 1995).

Classroom applications of the educational philosophies are summarized in Table 5.2.

Teaching

in an Era of Reform

THE ESSENTIAL-KNOWLEDGE DEBATE

Among the criticisms of American education and American students, lack of knowledge about our country and our world is being increasingly voiced. Editorial headlines such as "Historical illiteracy is plaguing many in high schools and colleges" are appearing with greater frequency. Authors then cite facts such as the following: Only 1 in 3 college seniors randomly chosen from 55 top-rated colleges and universities identified George Washington as the American general at Yorktown, and only 22 percent identified the Gettysburg address as the source of the statement "Government of the people, by the people, for the people" (American Council of Trustees and Alumni, 2000). In another survey, only 42 percent of college seniors placed the Civil War in the correct half century, and most adult Americans couldn't find the Persian Gulf on a map (Bertman, 2000). The situation is no better in math. For example, one study asked U.S. fifth graders to solve the problem $45 \times 26 = ?$; only 54 percent were successful (Stigler and Stevenson, 1990).

In response to these criticisms, reformers argue that American students lack the essential knowledge needed to function effectively in today's world. This has resulted in standards—statements about what students should know and what skills they should have—being written in virtually all content areas. E. D. Hirsch (1987), who wrote the controversial but widely read *Cultural Literacy: What Every American Needs to Know*, further illustrates this essentialist position. Hirsch identified a vast list of facts, concepts, and people that he believed all citizens should know in order to function effectively in American society. Since then, he has produced a series of edited paperbacks for parents and teachers that make up what he calls "The Core Knowledge" curriculum. Hirsch has developed products such as *What Your Third Grader Needs to Know: Fundamentals of a Good Third-grade Education (the Core Knowledge Series)* (1994), and *What Your Sixth Grader Needs to Know: Fundamentals of a Good Sixth-grade Education (the Core Knowledge Series)* (1995). Similar titles exist for each of the grade levels from kindergarten through sixth grade.

The content Hirsch advocates is quite sophisticated. For instance, *What Your Sixth Grader Needs to Know* has a section on American civilization that encourages students to understand the country's affairs within the context of global current events; a selection from Maya Angelou's *I Know Why the Caged Bird Sings;* speeches by John F. Kennedy and Martin Luther King, Jr.; plus sections on genetics and biographical portraits of pioneering scientists. Essentialists, as illustrated by Hirsch's work, argue that learners need to know much more than basic skills like reading, writing, and rudimentary math.

Putting Reform into Perspective

Reformers make a valid point, and our country's leaders are alarmed. In response to the American Council of Trustees and Alumni report (2000), members of Congress were so concerned that a resolution was introduced warning that lack of historical knowledge is dangerous for our country's future.

In addition, research on learning indicates that background knowledge is crucial for developing understanding of new content (Bruning, Schraw, & Ronning, 1999; Eggen & Kauchak, 2001). All new learning depends on and builds on what learners already know. For instance, to understand the relationships among people's growing distrust of authority, the civil rights movement, and the Vietnam War, people must know that each began in the 1960s. Similarly, to understand the problems of sub-Saharan Africa, we must also understand European colonialism as well as the geography and climate of this vast area. Knowledge builds on knowledge, and when knowledge is lacking, learning suffers.

Citizens agree that knowledge is important and that our young people lack it. Hirsch's "Core Knowledge" series is popular with both parents and teachers, and many reviewers have responded positively to it. Criticisms that the series focuses on rote memory rather than understanding have gone largely unnoticed or have been sharply refuted.

However, is teaching an increasing number of facts really the way to make students more culturally aware? Public-school students already take several American history courses during their school years (at least one during middle school and another in high school, plus smatterings during their elementary years). But they apparently retain little of the content, as indicated by the survey results cited earlier. So the issue is more complex than simply requiring more content and courses. Students apparently aren't learning from the courses they do take, so essentialism as normative philosophy doesn't provide a complete answer.

The issue is further complicated by an examination of goals. As we said earlier in this section, essentialists argue

The essential-knowledge debate raises important questions about curriculum— what is taught in schools— as well as instruction.

that American students lack the "essential" knowledge needed to function effectively in today's world. However, research indicates that personal motivation and the ability to use strategies to acquire knowledge are better predictors of later success than is the accumulation of knowledge (McCaslin & Good, 1996). "It is the affective and motivational characteristics of workers that our employers worry most about. They depend on employees to show up on time, to get along with others, to care about doing well on the job. . . . They do not find the technical ability of the workforce to be a problem for them" (Berliner, 1992; pp. 33–34).

In essence, does increased knowledge make people happier and more productive workers? Motivational research suggests that increasing learner readiness and eagerness to learn should be the primary goals of schools, not acquiring a vast storehouse of inert knowledge. This position is more consistent with pragmatism and progressivism than with essentialism.

Finally, the question of what knowledge is "essential" is critical. For example, Hirsch (1987) identifies information such as "Who was Spiro Agnew?" and "What is a carnivore?" as essential. Why is this information more important than knowing, for instance, who Cesar Chavez was or what macrobiotic means? (Marzano, Kendall, & Gaddy, 1999). Further, the sheer amount of knowledge called for by standards is overwhelming. Nearly 14,000 benchmarks in 14 subject-matter areas have been written, resulting in "far too many standards and not enough time in the day or year to teach them all" (Marzano et al., 1999, p. 68).

Unquestionably, a dilemma exists. You will be asked to help students reach standards, but you won't have time to accomplish the goal. This will mean that you will have to make decisions that make your job more complex and demanding, not simpler. As more experts question the effectiveness of the "high-stakes" testing of essential knowledge (for example, Linn, 2000), the pendulum is likely to swing back to some extent. How far it will go is anyone's guess.

You Take a Position

Now it's your turn to take a position on the issues discussed in this section. Go to the *Education Week* Website at **http://www.edweek.com**, find "search" on the first page, and type in one of the following two search terms: *essential knowledge* or *basic skills*. Locate a minimum of three articles on one of these topics and then do the following:

1. Identify the title, author, and date of each article and then write a one-paragraph summary of each.

2. Identify a pattern in the articles. (Each article—or even two of the three—suggesting that school districts are increasing their emphasis on basic skills would be a pattern, for example.)

3. After identifying the pattern, take one of the two following positions:

   ■ The pattern suggested in the articles, if implemented, *is* likely to improve education.

   ■ The pattern suggested in the articles *is not* likely to improve education.

State your position in writing, and document your position with information taken from the articles.

Ⓦ *To answer these questions online, go to the* Take a Position *Module in Chapter 5 of the Companion Website.*

■ DEVELOPING AS A PROFESSIONAL: FORMING A PERSONAL PHILOSOPHY OF EDUCATION

You've now studied the traditional philosophies—idealism, realism, pragmatism, and existentialism—along with the educational philosophies—perennialism, progressivism, essentialism, and postmodernism.

Now what? As a prospective teacher, what do you do with this information? What was the point in studying it? What does it have to do with you as a developing professional? These are questions we try to help you answer as you study this section.

Before we begin, we want to emphasize that we're going to offer one avenue for answering these questions and forming your personal philosophy of education. Other authors might offer different possibilities, or you may find an alternative path that better suits you. Keep this in mind as you read the following paragraphs: What does philosophy have to do with you as a developing professional?

Given this precaution, let's begin by making a direct attempt to answer the last question—what does philosophy have to do with you as a developing teacher? *Philosophy is important because it helps you explain and defend your educational goals—what you try to accomplish in your classroom.* Professional educators are able to articulate what they're doing and why. For instance, if you walked into a classroom, saw students working on basic skills, and asked the teacher why she was involving her students in this activity, she should be able to give you a clear and specific answer. If she were an essentialist, the answer might be that basic skills are part of a core of knowledge that learners need to function effectively in the world. However, some teachers do an activity because it is next in the text or curriculum-guide sequence, or because they did it last year; these teachers may not know why they are involving students in the activity. These are clearly inadequate and unprofessional reasons.

When teachers are clear about their philosophies, they can make systematic changes when they conclude that their teaching practices are in error or inadequate. If their philosophies aren't clear, change is unlikely, or it happens at random. In either case, professional growth doesn't occur. This is one reason professions (and professionals) need philosophies.

As you begin to form your own personal philosophy of teaching, keep at least three ideas in mind. First, any philosophy is evolving and dynamic. This means that it will change as you learn and gather experience. Therefore, don't be concerned if your philosophy is initially uncertain and loosely formed. It will crystalize and become clearer as you think about and use it over time. Second, your personal philosophy is likely to include elements of more than one traditional and educational philosophy. Third, be willing to change your views if you find that they are in error. People have a tendency to cling to ideas, once formed, merely because they have the idea; they somehow tacitly feel that changing their minds is a sign of weakness or fuzzy thinking. Nothing could be farther from the truth. In fact, changing your views is an indicator of the open-mindedness necessary for personal and professional growth.

The Role of Beliefs in a Philosophy of Education

Let's begin. Early in the chapter we said that philosophy *provides a framework for thinking, and it guides professional practice.* To begin establishing this framework for thinking, first try to identify and examine your beliefs. Allie and Brad both did a good job of describing their beliefs. Allie's, in particular, were well thought out. For example, she said:

■ ■ ■

"They [kids] don't come to school with the same . . . desire to learn as they once did."

". . . they want to believe they did learn something when they're finished with a topic, or class. . . . "

". . . they're not intrinsically motivated. . . ."

". . . [kids] feel good when they learned something, particularly if it's challenging."

". . . the more they know about a topic, the better they like it."

". . . there's real, practical stuff out there that they need to know, and there's only one way they're gonna learn it. . . . That's practice and experience."

■ ■ ■

The following questions might help you get started in the process of identifying your own beliefs.

■ What is the purpose of schooling? Should students be focusing on content, or is the development of self-concept, interpersonal skills, and other personal qualities more important?

■ Are students basically good and trustworthy, or do they need constant monitoring?

■ Is motivating students part of my job, or should motivation come from within each student?

■ Is my role as a teacher to pass knowledge on to students, or should I be guiding students as they learn on their own?

■ How do people know things? Is intuition important and valuable? How important are feelings? Is evidence always, or often, necessary?

■ How do students best learn? Should I push them, or should they be left largely on their own?

Examining Your Beliefs

Once identified, beliefs should be examined and analyzed. This is where epistemology becomes important. How does Allie know that her beliefs are valid? Do they "feel" right? Do they make sense intuitively? Is feeling or intuition adequate to justify beliefs, or must she have research evidence to indicate that they're valid? If Allie is an existentialist, intuition and feelings are perfectly acceptable in validating her beliefs. On the other hand, if Allie is a realist or a pragmatist, feelings and intuition are not adequate or trustworthy; she must have evidence.

From this discussion, we can see why understanding the traditional philosophies and philosophies of education is important. For instance, if Allie describes herself as an essentialist but then accepts feelings and intuition as validation for her beliefs, her thinking is inconsistent, and she should reconsider what she really believes about knowing, learning, and teaching.

Forming a Philosophy

■ ■ ■

My job is to help these kids learn as much as they can about the topics I teach, so that's what I try to do every day. Kids basically want to learn. They may not be too crazy about it initially, and some of them might be in it mostly for grades to start with, but the more they learn about the topics, the better they like what they study. Relevance isn't as critical to the kids' motivation as understanding and success are. If the kids understand the stuff, they'll like it, and they'll feel better about themselves.

So, my goal is to get them to learn, really learn, not just memorize information. I want them to know why, how they know, and what would happen when conditions change. If I get them to learn, really learn, motivation and self-esteem take care of themselves.

Increasing Understanding 5.13

Throughout this book, we've provided references for the information we've presented. What does this imply about our epistemological beliefs? What does this imply about our axiological beliefs? Explain in each case.

Table 5.3	An Analysis of Allie's Philosophy of Education	
Belief Statement	**Component of Her Philosophy**	
"They [kids] don't come to school with the same . . . desire to learn as they once did."	"They may not be too crazy about it initially. . . ."	
"They want to believe they did learn something when they're finished with a topic, or class. . . ."	"Kids basically want to learn."	
"They're not intrinsically motivated."	"Some of them might be in it mostly for grades to start with."	
"[Kids] feel good when they learned something, particularly if it's challenging."	"If the kids understand the stuff, they'll like it, and the better they'll feel about themselves." "I want them to know why, how they know, and what would happen when conditions change."	
"The more they know about a topic, the better they like it."	"The more they learn about the topics, the better they like what they study. Relevance isn't as critical to the kids' motivation as understanding and success are."	
"There's real, practical stuff out there that they need to know, and there's only one way they're gonna learn it. . . . That's practice and experience."	"We're going to have class discussions, do homework, go over it, have quizzes, and go over them."	

I know that I can get them to learn. We're going to have class discussions, do homework, go over it, have quizzes, and go over them. If I do my job, they'll learn.

■ ■ ■

What you've just read is a succinct description of Allie's philosophy of education. It is clear, well-articulated, and consistent with her beliefs. The relationships between her beliefs and the components of her philosophy are outlined in Table 5.3.

Because her philosophy is clear and well-articulated, it can effectively guide her thinking as she defines her goals and designs learning activities and assessments. Her philosophy helps her ensure that her goals, learning activities, and assessments are consistent with each other. While you may or may not agree with her goals or the rationale for them, the fact that she's clear in her thinking increases the likelihood that her students will reach the goals, and she will be more likely to make conscious choices to change and improve her teaching when evidence and her thinking indicate that change is needed.

You now have the following information:

Increasing Understanding 5.14

Look again at Brad's thinking, as indicated by his conversation with Allie. Based on this information, describe what you believe is his philosophy of education. Explain how the philosophy is based on his beliefs.

- The description of Allie's philosophy.
- Your own description of Brad's philosophy, based on your response to "Increasing Understanding 5.14."
- Your analysis of your own beliefs.

Using this information, you're now ready to compile your ideas into a normative philosophy that will guide your thinking and actions.

We said earlier that your philosophy will likely incorporate elements of the different philosophies we've discussed. We see this in Allie's thinking. Her view that an objective reality exists, independent of the world of ideas, is consistent with realism; from essentialism, she drew the belief that a body of important information exists that all students need to know in order to function effectively in today's world; and her concerns for her students' personal needs, emotions, and self-esteem most closely relate to existentialism.

Dialoguing with other professionals can help beginning teachers shape their own developing personal philosophy of education.

Looking Through

Classroom Windows

EXAMINING PHILOSOPHIES OF EDUCATION

Having examined both traditional and educational philosophies, as well as considering your own, you now have the opportunity to analyze the philosophies of two different teachers. To complete this activity, do the following:

- View the video episode containing two different classroom lessons titled, "Examining Philosophies of Education."
- Read the written transcripts of the two lessons and answer the following questions online by going to the *Classroom Windows* Module in Chapter 6 of the Companion Website at **http://www.prenhall.com/kauchak**. Go to the Web site and follow the directions on your screen.
- Answer the questions that follow:

1. Which of the traditional philosophies is most nearly reflected in Judy's teaching? Explain.
2. Which of the traditional philosophies is most nearly reflected in Bob's teaching? Explain.
3. Which of the educational philosophies is most nearly reflected in Judy's teaching? Explain.
4. Which of the educational philosophies is most nearly reflected in Bob's teaching? Explain.
5. Which teacher, Judy or Bob, most clearly reflects your own personal philosophy of education? Explain.

To answer these questions online and receive immediate feedback, go to the Looking through Classroom Windows *Module in Chapter 5 of the Companion Website.*

The Changing Role of Teachers

The philosophies presented in this chapter have different implications for teachers. For example, perennialism and essentialism suggest that teachers should be knowledgeable in the topics they teach and able to help students learn this information. Progressivism also implies that teachers should be skilled in guiding learning, but it more strongly emphasizes the process of learning than do the first two. Postmodernism focuses on a critical examination of the traditions that have existed in education and in society at large.

Research on the way people learn continually expands, school environments are becoming increasingly complex, and our student populations are the most diverse in our history. For example, estimates suggest that during the next 20 years, dramatic increases in the percentage of Hispanic, African American, Asian American (including Pacific Islanders), and Native American students will occur in the school population (Young & Smith, 1999). These factors suggest that teaching will become more sophisticated and more demanding in the future than it has ever been in the past. In addition, teachers experience pressure from administrators, standardized tests, and mandated curricula to target their teaching toward basic skills. Everyone agrees that all students should leave school knowing how to read, write, and do math, but views differ about how much emphasis should be placed on these basic skills. Should they be the core of the curriculum? Should we teach basic skills first and then use them to teach other content, or should they be integrated into units where students use them in writing and problem solving? How important are other goals, such as learning to work with others and understanding how the world around us works?

A clear philosophy of teaching and learning provides a basis for answering these and other difficult educational questions. In an increasingly complex world, it is essential that teachers develop coherent philosophies of education to guide them as they attempt to do what is best for the students they teach.

In constructing your personal philosophy, you will combine traditional and educational philosophies in the same way.

Hopefully, this chapter has provided you with the background needed to begin this journey and has caused you to think about teaching in a different way. At this point, you won't have all the answers needed to decide what education should be and how you can help make it that way. But if you are now able to begin asking some important questions, then our goal for the chapter has been fulfilled. Good luck.

■ SUMMARY

Philosophy and Philosophy of Education

Philosophy is a search for wisdom. In forming a philosophy, a professional teacher searches for the wisdom to maximize learning for all students.

Philosophy provides a framework for thinking, and it guides professional practice. Although it overlaps with theory, philosophy differs from theory in that we try to explain events and behavior, as they are, on the basis of theories, whereas philosophies go further to suggest the way events and behaviors ought to be.

Traditional Schools of Philosophy

Idealism, realism, pragmatist, and existentialism are often called the traditional philosophies. Their views of reality, ways of knowing, and what is valuable and good often differ considerably.

Each has implications for teaching and learning. Idealists would create a curriculum focusing on absolute and time-honored ideas. Realists would also emphasize absolutes, but in contrast with the thinking of idealists, these absolutes would focus on natural laws. Pragmatists see the world in relative terms, and they would emphasize experience and practical understanding, validated by the scientific method. Existentialists would take a more extreme position, with the curriculum emphasizing personal awareness, freedom, and responsibility.

Philosophies of Education
The educational philosophies—perennialism, progressivism, essentialism, and post-modernism—are rooted in the traditional philosophies. Perennialism, as with idealism and realism, focuses on time-honored absolutes. Progressivism, rooted in pragmatism, views goals as dynamic and emphasizes that learning should be experience-based and relevant to students' lives. Postmodernism sees schools and other institutions in need of restructuring, with marginalized people and their works elevated to more prominent positions in the content of schooling.

Developing as a Professional: Forming a Personal Philosophy
When professionals form philosophies, they first identify their beliefs and then examine those beliefs to determine if they're valid. Once a coherent system of beliefs is identified, the beliefs are compiled into an internally consistent view of what the goals of the profession ought to be and what they can do to promote those outcomes. In education, this means that professionals consider what kinds of learning should take place, what conditions will best promote that learning, and what they can do to create those conditions.

▨ IMPORTANT CONCEPTS

axiology	metaphysics	philosophy of education
character education	moral education	postmodernism
epistemology	normative philosophy	pragmatism
essentialism	ontology	progressivism
existentialism	perennialism	realism
idealism	philosophy	theory
logic		

▨ DISCUSSION QUESTIONS

1. Philosophy has four basic areas: epistemology, ontology, axiology, and logic. Which of these is most useful for teachers? Least useful?

2. Technology is becoming increasingly important in society as well as in education. Which of the four philosophies of education—perennialism, progressivism, essentialism, or postmodernism—is most compatible with applications of technology in education? Least compatible?

3. Our students are becoming increasingly diverse. How well do the different philosophies of education address issues of student diversity?

4. Which philosophy of education has the most support in the geographic area in which you plan to teach? What evidence do you have for your conclusion?

5. Of the different philosophies discussed in this chapter, which is most valuable in framing issues for preschool children? Middle school students? High school

students? Does one particular philosophy fit with a content area that you will be teaching?

6. Public school teachers rated the following educational goals in the following order of importance (U.S. Department of Education, 1993):

Goal	*Rank*
Building literacy skills	1
Promoting personal growth	2
Promoting good work habits and self-discipline	3
Encouraging academic excellence	4
Promoting occupational or vocational skills	5

What do these rankings tell us about teachers' philosophical positions?

■ GOING INTO SCHOOLS

1. Interview a teacher and ask the following questions:
   a. What are your most important goals for your students?
   b. What do you emphasize the most in your curriculum?
   c. What do you think is your major role as a teacher?
   d. What is the primary teaching method that you use? Why do you use it?
   e. What are your major classroom-management goals? How do you implement them?
   f. How do you assess student learning?

   Based on the teacher's responses, which of the educational philosophies is most nearly reflected in his or her teaching? If possible, share your analysis with the teacher and discuss your conclusions.

2. Observe a lesson at a grade level or in a content area in which you plan to teach. Describe the teacher's classroom and lesson with respect to the following:
   a. Arrangement of desks: How are the desks arranged?
   b. Explaining versus questioning: Does the teacher primarily lecture and explain, or does the teacher ask a large number of questions?
   c. Student motivation: Does the teacher provide a rationale at the beginning of the lesson that explains why the lesson is important?
   d. Use of examples: Does the teacher use examples, or is the information presented primarily in verbal form?
   e. Classroom order: Are the students orderly and attentive during the lesson? How does the teacher attempt to accomplish this?
   f. Assessment: How does the teacher measure student understanding?

   What do these indicators suggest about the teacher's educational philosophy? If possible, share your analysis with the teacher and discuss your conclusions.

3. Locate a social studies or literature text for a level at which you'll be teaching (for example, elementary or high school). Examine how the text treats the relative contributions of males versus females, minorities versus non-minorities. Does the inclusion of topics or literary selections suggest a perennialist or postmodern philosophy? Defend your answer with specific examples from the text.

4. Locate the teacher's edition of a textbook for a subject or grade level that you'll be teaching. (Every book series comes with a teacher's edition that contains suggestions for how to teach the subject.) These can be obtained from a teacher, in a school-district curriculum library, or in the curriculum library at your college or university.

Read the introduction to the text and identify elements of the following education-al philosophies: perennialsm, progressivism, essentialism, and postmodernism. How well does the text match your own developing educational philosophy?

Virtual Field *Experience*

If you would like to participate in a Virtual Field Experience, go to the *Field Experience* **Module in Chapter 5 of the Companion Website.**

■ ONLINE PORTFOLIO ACTIVITIES

To complete these activities online, go to the *Portfolio Activities* Module in Chapter 5 of the Companion Website and submit your response.

Portfolio Activity 5.1   **Describing Your Philosophy of Education**

INTASC Principle 9: *Commitment*
The purpose of this activity is to assist you in developing your philosophy of education. List your beliefs with respect to learning, learners, and teaching. Then, based on the list, write a two-page description of your philosophy of education as it presently exists.

Portfolio Activity 5.2   **Assessing Your Philosophy of Education**

INTASC Principle 9: *Commitment*
The purpose of this activity is to assist you in developing your own philosophy of educa-tion. To assess your developing philosophy of education, respond to the following state-ments and then answer the questions that follow. Use the following scale in making your responses:

> 1 = Strongly disagree
> 2 = Disagree
> 3 = Neither agree nor disagree
> 4 = Agree
> 5 = Strongly agree

1. Schools should emphasize important knowledge more than students' personal interests.   1 2 3 4 5

2. Teachers should emphasize interdisciplinary subject matter that encourages project-oriented, democratic classrooms.   1 2 3 4 5

3. Schools should emphasize the search for personal meaning more than a fixed body of subject matter.   1 2 3 4 5

4. The primary aim of education is to develop a person's intellectual capacity.   1 2 3 4 5

5. Schools should emphasize basic skills more than humanistic ideals.   1 2 3 4 5

6. Teachers should guide student learning rather than lecture and disseminate information.   1 2 3 4 5

7. The best teachers encourage personal responses and develop critical awareness in their students.   1 2 3 4 5

8. The goals of education should be similar for every-one; all students should understand the important literature, mathematics, and science of Western civilization. 1 2 3 4 5

9. The purpose of schools is to ensure practical preparation for life and work more than personal development. 1 2 3 4 5

10. Curriculum should emerge from students' needs and interests; it *should not* be prescribed in advance. 1 2 3 4 5

11. The best education emphasizes the great works in the arts and humanities. 1 2 3 4 5

12. It is more important for teachers to involve students in activities that analyze and criticize society than to accumulate a lot of information. 1 2 3 4 5

13. Education should enhance personal growth through problem solving in the present more than emphasiz-ing preparation for a distant future. 1 2 3 4 5

14. Human nature's most distinctive quality is the ability to reason; therefore, the intellect should be the focus of education. 1 2 3 4 5

15. Schools often perpetuate racism and sexism that is camouflaged as traditional values. 1 2 3 4 5

16. Teachers should help students learn a common core of knowledge, *not* experiment with their own views about curricula. 1 2 3 4 5

Source: Adapted from Leahy (1995).

Now add up your responses in the appropriate boxes (Strongly disagree = 1; Disagree = 2; Neither agree nor disagree = 3; Agree = 4; Strongly agree = 5).

Perennialism:
Item #4 ____ + #8 ____ + #11 ____ + #14 ____ = ____
Progressivism:
Item #2 ____ + #6 ____ + #10 ____ + #13 ____ = ____
Essentialism:
Item #1 ____ + #5 ____ + # 9 ____ + #16 ____ = ____
Postmodernism:
Item #3 ____ + #7 ____ + #12 ____ + #15 ____ = ____

1. Do you think the survey results accurately reflect your philosophy of education? Why?
2. How are the results from this survey similar to and different from your philosophy of education as you described it in Portfolio Activity 5.1?
3. Why do you think the differences exist?
4. Now, using your scores as the basis, summarize what this survey suggests about your developing philosophy of education.

Portfolio Activity 5.3   **Assessing an Instructor's Philosophy of Education**

INTASC Principle 9: *Commitment*

The purpose of this activity is to help you see how educational philosophies influence teaching practices. Think about an instructor in one of your classes. Based on your observations of the instructor and the way he or she teaches, describe in one page what you believe to be the instructor's philosophy of education.

After you've completed the description, share it with the instructor. Ask if he or she believes that the description is accurate, and if not, to explain why it isn't.

CHAPTER

6

The Organization
of American Schools

We've all attended schools and experienced them as students, so we're familiar with the basic ways they are organized. Elementary schools lead to middle or junior high schools followed by high schools. But what do schools look like from another perspective—that of a teacher?

In this chapter, we look at the way American schools are organized from a teacher's perspective as we try to answer the following questions:

■ What is a school?

■ Why are schools divided into elementary, middle or junior high, and high schools?

■ Why is the organization of elementary schools different from the organization of middle, junior high, and high schools?

■ How will the organization of schools influence your life as a teacher?

■ What is an effective school?

To begin answering these questions, let's look at one teacher in a middle school.

Case
STUDY

"Wow, noon. I need to get going," Chris Lucio said to his colleague April Jackson as he jumped up from the couch in the teacher's lounge, finishing the last bite of his lunch. "My kids will be chomping at the bit trying to get into the room."

Chris hurriedly left the lounge, stopped by the main office to take a quick look in his box to check for notes, phone messages, and mail, and then walked across the courtyard to his building.

Chris is a seventh-grade geography teacher at Lakeside Junior High, one of three junior high schools in Orange Park, a suburb of a large eastern city. Originally a middle school, the 30-year-old Lakeside campus is composed of four main buildings surrounding a center courtyard. A gymnasium and fine arts building, built 10 years ago when Lakeside became a junior high school, sit outside the main buildings, and baseball, softball, and soccer fields, together with tennis courts, complete the campus. The administrative building houses the principal's and other administrators' offices, the cafeteria, which—with a stage on one end—doubles as an auditorium, and the media center and computer lab holding 30 computers. Classrooms are in the other three buildings.

Architectural designs for schools vary, and the Lakeside campus is somewhat atypical. Commonly, schools are housed within a single building that has different wings, or they're in squares or rectangles that enclose courtyards.

"Okay everyone, the bell is going to ring in a couple minutes . . . find your seats quickly," Chris calls out, unlocking the door to his room.

"Mr. Lucio, can I go to the bathroom?" Armondo asks as he stands by the open door.

"Hurry, you don't want to be tardy," Chris responds with a smile.

"This split lunch is a pain," Chris thinks, as the last of the students slide into their seats. It takes me 10 minutes to get the kids settled down after lunch, so we're always wasting time.

"On the other hand, I better not complain. I have a great schedule . . . one prep . . . three advanced and two standard classes. . . . It doesn't get much better than that."

"Are you going to come to our track meet this afternoon?" Devon, another of Chris's students, asks as he enters the room. "We're going to kick butt on Ridgeview."

"Wouldn't miss it," Chris smiles back as he thinks, "Yikes, I almost forgot. . . I promised Joe and Karen [the boys' and girls' track coaches] that I'd be a timer for the 100 and 200."

"What time does it start?" Chris asks Devon.

"Right after school; 4 o'clock, I think."

The split lunch that Chris complains about shapes the schedule at Lakeside. It rotates from day to day and can be seen in the schedule below.

Time	Period				
	Monday	Tuesday	Wednesday	Thursday	Friday
9:20–10:05	1	6	5	4	2
10:10–11:00	2	1	6	5	4
11:05–11:30 A	3	3	3	3	3
11:35–12:05 B					
12:10–12:40 C					
12:45–1:35	4	2	1	6	5
1:40–2:30	5	4	2	1	6
2:35–3:25	6	5	4	2	1

The rationale for the rotating schedule is the belief that students are most alert in the morning and least alert late in the day. If sixth period were always from 2:35–3:25, for example, students in that class would be at a learning disadvantage.

Lakeside's schedule has third period split for lunch, giving the students about a half hour to eat and relax. One-third of the students eat during A lunch, another third during B lunch, and the last third during C lunch. Third period doesn't rotate; school officials chose to keep it this way for the sake of simplicity. Chris and his third period class eat during B lunch.

"The schedule is fine . . . other than the split lunch," Chris shrugs when asked about it. "Once the kids got used to it, it was no big deal."

■   ■   ■

■ WHAT IS A SCHOOL?

Increasing Understanding 6.1

Would a *family* be considered a social institution? Why? To answer this question online and receive immediate feedback, go to the *Increasing Understanding* Module in Chapter 6 of the Companion Website at **http://www.prenhall. com/kauchak.**

We've all gone to school; in fact, if you're in your mid-twenties or younger, you've spent more than half of your life in school. But exactly what is a school, and what does it mean to teach and learn in one? We consider these questions in this section.

The notion of *school* has different meanings. At a simple level, it is a physical place—a building or set of buildings. At another level, it is a place students go to learn. For example, churches have vacation Bible *school*, and we've all heard of students being home *schooled.*

At a third level, school is a **social institution,** which is *an organization with established structures and rules designed to promote certain goals.* Schools are social institutions, and promoting both students' growth and development and the well-being of a country and its citizens are its goals.

A number of social institutions exist in all societies. Churches or religions are social institutions, as are governments. They are organizations intended to make society a better place in which to live.

Using the idea of schools as social institutions as a frame of reference, this chapter looks at the way schools are organized. Some ways of organizing them are better than others, and these differences influence how much students learn and how well they develop. These differences will also influence your life as a teacher. That's why you're studying this topic.

A school is intended to operate as a relatively independent unit within a **school district,** which is *an administrative unit within a geographical area given the responsibility for education within its borders.* A school district may encompass an entire county, or large counties may be divided into more than one district.

School districts vary in a number of ways, including size and clientele. For example, Dade County, Florida, is a large district with a student population that is predominantly comprised of cultural minorities (over 83 percent), whereas Minot, North Dakota, is a small district with few minorities (U.S. Department of Education, 1996). In some districts, the majority of students are eligible for free lunch, and in other, wealthier districts, virtually none of the students are.

You will study school districts, how they're organized, and how they're governed in detail in Chapter 8. What is important now is to remember that individual schools are part of a larger organizational framework called a district. To learn more about school districts where you might want to teach, access the *Web Links* Module of the Companion Website at **http://www.prenhall.com/kauchak.**

Let's turn now to the organization of individual schools.

■ THE ORGANIZATION OF SCHOOLS

Think about the schools you attended as a student or schools you've visited as part of your teacher-preparation program. If the organization was typical for American schools, you first went to an elementary school, which began with kindergarten, or even pre-kindergarten,

followed by first grade, second grade, and so on. You then went to a middle school or junior high school, and finally to a high school.

Let's look at the way these schools are organized, and why they're organized this way. In looking at this organization, we'll examine:

- ■ Personnel
- ■ The physical plant
- ■ Curriculum organization

Personnel

No school is any better than the people who work there. This includes all the people—the administrators, the support staff, and the teachers. Each has a role in making a school an effective social institution.

Administrators and Support Staff All schools—elementary, middle, junior high, and high schools—have **administrators,** *individuals who are responsible for the day-to-day operation of the school.* The administrators include a **principal,** *the individual given the ultimate responsibility for the school's operation,* and probably an assistant principal or vice principal (or both) who supports the principal in his or her work. Lakeside, for example, has a vice principal and two assistant principals. The vice principal's responsibilities include scheduling, collecting student records (such as grades) from teachers, keeping master records for the school, and maintaining communication with district-level administrators and parents. One of the assistant principals manages the physical plant; responsibilities may include distributing lockers to students, coordinating the duties of the custodial staff, and overseeing all maintenance and construction. The other assistant principal is in charge of discipline (including referrals as well as in-school and out-of-school suspension of students), ordering and distributing textbooks to department heads, and maintaining in-service records for teachers.

Depending on the size of the school and the organization of the school district, schools may also have school counselors, school psychologists, and health-care providers, such as school nurses. Their roles will be determined by the school's and district's size and organization. Lakeside, for example, has two full-time guidance counselors and a school psychologist that it shares with other schools. The guidance counselors schedule and coordinate the statewide assessment tests and provide a variety of information about course offerings and future options for students. The school psychologist administers individualized intelligence tests, which are used for making decisions about placing students into programs for the gifted and talented or for students with learning disabilities. The school psychologist also provides individual counseling for students having emotional problems and makes recommendations for further mental-health assistance.

The school also has a full-time, licensed practical nurse. She maintains all student health records, is trained in administering CPR, supervises medical evacuations, and disseminates all medications to students. Students at Lakeside are forbidden from taking even an over-the-counter pain killer, such as an Advil, on their own, and teachers may not give students any form of medication.

In addition, all schools have support staff, which may include the following:

- Secretaries and receptionists, who greet visitors when they come to the school.
- Administrative and instructional support staff, who complete paperwork for the principal and other administrators, duplicate tests and handouts for teachers, and maintain payroll records and other functions.
- Media center specialists, who handle books and different forms of technology.
- Physical plant staff, such as janitors who clean the rooms and buildings and cafeteria workers who prepare school lunches.

Curriculum Specialists Many elementary schools have teachers who specialize in a particular area, such as technology, art, or music; these teachers coordinate their efforts with classroom teachers. For example, schedules are coordinated so that all students can visit a computer center, where the technology specialist works with them for a certain amount of time each day or each week.

Why are we presenting this information? In other words, what difference does it make if you know about the other personnel working in your school and what their roles are?

Here's why. A school is a social institution whose organization is complex, and all the people working in it must contribute to making the school run smoothly. As a teacher, your ability to work with the other personnel in the school will influence how effective you and the school can be. For example, if you have a student who is so unruly that you can't work with him or her in your classroom, you need the support of the assistant principal and/or school psychologist to help you deal with the problem. Although you will probably teach in your classroom without any other adult, your effectiveness in the school will depend on your ability to work with a number of different people.

In addition, a common adage suggests that you can tell a great deal about the social and emotional climate in a school by observing the way a school receptionist greets students and visitors when they enter the school or main office. You also help set the tone for a supportive climate in the way you treat support staff and how important you make them feel. Teachers who request—instead of demand—services, such as having a test duplicated, make support staff realize that they're contributing to the overall functioning of the school. All the personnel in a school working together for the benefit of students is the most important factor in making effective schools what they are.

Increasing Understanding 6.2

What is the most likely reason that school policies are so rigid with respect to administering any form of medication?

Increasing Understanding 6.3

School organizations are more complex than they were in the past. Think about your study of Chapters 3 and 4 and explain why this is likely the case.

Teachers' responsibilities extend beyond their classrooms and include ensuring that the total school facility is a safe and productive place to learn.

The Physical Plant

Schools typically have classrooms, hallways that allow students to move from one room to another, a central administrative office, and one or more large rooms, such as auditoriums, gymnasiums, music rooms, and cafeterias. The physical organization of schools has often been criticized for its box-like structure, with hall upon hall of separate "cells." Critics contend that this structure leads to isolation between teachers and fragmentation in the curriculum. When teachers retreat into their classrooms and close their doors, no one else may know what goes on in there.

In elementary schools, space is available for staff parking, playgrounds, and a driveway used for dropping off and picking up students. Junior high and high schools will have playing fields for football, baseball, softball, and soccer, some will have swimming pools, and high schools will have parking spaces available for students who drive their own cars to school. (Some middle schools, because of a philosophical opposition to competition, may not have gymnasiums or other facilities that support competitive activities.)

School enrollments often increase so rapidly that physical plants can't keep up. As a result, many schools have "temporaries," individual buildings on the perimeter of school campuses that provide additional classroom space.

What does the physical arrangement of a school mean for you as a teacher? It means at least two things. First, when you're in your classroom and shut the door (as many teachers do), you're essentially on your own. For example, you may be responsible for 20 to 30 second graders all day, every day. A similar situation exists for middle and secondary teachers. You'll be in the confines of your classroom, where you'll be responsible for the education and safety of five or six different classes of eighth graders or eleventh graders, again, essentially on your own.

However, your responsibility isn't limited to your classroom. If you teach in an elementary school, you'll also be responsible for escorting your students from your room to the cafeteria and back, or from your classroom to the media center and back. If you're a middle or secondary teacher, you'll be expected to monitor students as they move through the hallways and attend assemblies in the auditorium. You may also sell tickets at football games,

---

Increasing Understanding 6.4

Strong efforts are being made in many areas to eliminate the use of portables or temporaries. Identify at least two reasons why this would be the case.

attend track meets, and go to band concerts. Though your primary responsibilities will be to the students in the classroom, you will also be expected to contribute to the governance and running of the school. All these responsibilities result from the ways schools are organized.

Curriculum Organization

We said earlier in the chapter that schools are social institutions, organizations whose purpose is to help young people grow and develop and prepare them to function effectively in today's (and tomorrow's) world. To function effectively in today's technologically oriented and fast-changing world, students' need to acquire essential knowledge and skills. The task for educators is to organize the **curriculum**—*what teachers teach and what students learn*—in a way that maximizes students' opportunities to master the material and to grow and develop.

How do schools organize the curriculum to accomplish this? As an example, let's consider the following goals:

- Students will be able to recognize the letters of the alphabet.
- Students will be able to read and understand sentences such as "Antonio and Carol worked together on their art project."
- Students will be able to simplify the expression $9 + 4(7 - 3)/2$.
- Students will be able to determine how far a ball has traveled after falling freely for 3 seconds (assuming air resistance is negligible).

These goals, which are part of an overall school curriculum, provide direction for teachers as they consider what to teach.

Historically, educators have decided that the most efficient way of helping students reach these goals is to classify what teachers teach according to different grade levels and ages of students. For instance, a child in kindergarten is expected to reach the first goal, third graders the second, seventh graders in pre-algebra the third, and high school juniors taking physics, the fourth.

School Organization and the Curriculum What is the most effective way to group teachers and students in order to help students learn the content of the curriculum? For instance, does it make sense to have 6 year olds in the same building and walking the same hallways as 17 year olds? Safety, as well as seemingly mundane concerns like the height of drinking fountains and toilets, suggests no.

In general, most school systems are organized into three levels—elementary schools for younger children, middle or junior high schools for young adolescents, and high schools for later adolescents. Despite this general agreement about the three levels, as a teacher you may encounter any number of organizational patterns when you teach. Table 6.1 outlines some of these variations. Other forms of organization exist, of course, but the ones you see in Table 6.1 are the most common.

What do educators use as the basis for making decisions about organizing schools? For example, why do middle schools typically include grades 6, 7, and 8, or grades 7 and 8? Two factors are most common: the developmental characteristics of students as well as economics and politics.

Developmental Characteristics of Students Development refers to *the physical changes in children as well as changes in the way they think and relate to their peers that result from maturation and experience.* For example, fifth graders are typically bigger, stronger, and more coordinated than first graders; they are physically more *developed.* Similarly, typical fifth graders think differently than do first graders. When shown the following drawing,

Table 6.1	Common Ways to Organize Schools	
School Level		**Grade Ranges**
Elementary School		K–3
		K–5
		K–6
Middle School		5–8
		6–8
		7–8
Junior High School		7–8
		7–9
		8–9
High School		9–12
		10–12

typical first graders conclude that Block A is heavier than Block B, because their thinking tends to focus on size—the most obvious aspect of the balance and blocks. Fifth graders, on the other hand, are more likely to realize that the blocks have the same weight, because they recognize that the balance is balanced (level). Their thinking is more *developed*.

Increasing Understanding 6.5

In Chapter 5, we learned that organizing elementary schools into grade levels occurred during the common school movement, which began about 1830. What was the rationale at that time for organizing elementary schools this way?

Differences in social development also exist. For example, when faced with a disagreement about who in a group gets to report on which topic, a fifth grader is more likely to step back, recognize the others' perspectives, and compromise. Socially, fifth graders are more capable of considering where a classmate is "coming from," whereas first graders tend to be more self-centered in their thinking. These differences in social development provide teachers with opportunities to use teaching strategies, such as certain forms of cooperative learning, with older children that might be less effective with younger, less socially developed students.

Similar differences can be found between fifth graders and tenth or eleventh graders. Physically, the older students are young men and women, many think quite abstractly, and they are socially skilled. These developmental differences lead to important differences in the ways schools are organized. For example, students in elementary schools are typically assigned to one teacher who looks after the cognitive, social, and emotional growth of the students. As students mature and their abilities to learn on their own and fend for themselves develop, they are assigned to a number of teachers who also serve as subject-matter specialists.

Economics and Politics Economics and politics are also factors that influence decisions about school organization. As an example, let's look again at Chris's school, Lakeside Junior High School.

When Lakeside was planned over 30 years ago, the middle school movement was gathering momentum. (We discuss middle schools in the next section.) Mary Zellner, who was to be Lakeside's first principal, was an outspoken proponent of middle schools, and she was a respected leader in district politics. Because of her influence, Lakeside was built according to middle school philosophy, part of which de-emphasized competition between students. As a result, the school didn't have competitive athletics, which was the reason the school didn't originally have a gymnasium.

Problems then arose. Orange Park High School, the only high school in the district at the time, became overcrowded because of rapid population growth in the city. District officials solved the problem temporarily by moving sixth graders back to the elementary schools. (The elementary schools were able to absorb them because the students could be distributed among the eight elementary schools in the district.) The middle schools were then converted to junior high schools that housed grades 7, 8, and 9.

The move was also hailed by high school coaches, who claimed that Orange Park High was at a disadvantage because potential athletes came to them without the athletic experiences students attending competing schools enjoyed. These pressures occur nationwide; presently 80 percent of middle-level schools in the United States offer organized competitive sports (Swain, McEwin & Irvin, 1998).

The decision to change the organizational structure was based primarily on economics (with some additional political pressure from high school coaches); it had little to do with the developmental needs of students. Unfortunately, decisions like this are quite common in education.

Let's keep these factors in mind as we look at schools in more depth. We begin by looking at early-childhood programs and elementary schools, and then turn to schools for older students, including high schools, junior highs, and middle schools.

Increasing Understanding 6.6

Are organizational decisions based on the developmental characteristics of students more likely to occur in suburban or inner-city schools? Explain why this is likely the case.

■ EARLY-CHILDHOOD PROGRAMS

Most of you reading this book probably attended kindergarten, and some of you may have even gone to pre-kindergarten. However, one of your authors, educated in a small town in a predominantly rural area, attended neither, because they weren't offered there at the time.

Early-childhood education is *a catch-all term encompassing a range of educational programs for young children including infant intervention and enrichment programs, preschools, public and private pre-kindergartens and kindergartens, and federally funded Project Head Start.* Early childhood education is a mid-20th-century development in this country, although its philosophical roots go back 250 years. The French philosopher Rousseau suggested:

> Do not treat the child to discourses which he cannot understand. No descriptions, no eloquence, no figures of speech. . . . In general, let us never substitute the sign for the thing, except when it is impossible for us to show the thing. . . . Things! Things! I shall never tire of saying that we ascribe too much importance to words (Compayre, 1888).

In saying "Things! Things!" Rousseau was arguing that young children need to play and work with concrete objects rather than being taught with abstract words. This idea is consistent with the need for concrete experiences that the famous developmental psychologist Jean Piaget (1952, 1970) emphasized, and it is at the core of developmentally appropriate kindergarten and early-childhood education.

Developmental programs *accommodate children's developmental differences by allowing children to acquire skills and abilities at their own pace through direct experiences.* Visitors in a developmental classroom are likely to see learning centers around the room that have activities for the children. For instance, one might have a tub of water and items that the

Self-contained elementary schools attempt to meet young students' developmental needs.

children test to see if they sink or float. Another might have a series of big books with pictures and large-print words. A third might have a series of blocks that children use to construct towers and other structures. Instead of traditional teacher-centered instruction, the teacher's role is to provide experiences for children and encourage exploration.

For more information about different early childhood education programs, visit the Website of the National Association for the Education of Young Children (NAEYC), the largest professional association for early-children education. This Website can be found in the *Web Links* Module in Chapter 6 of the Companion Website at **http://www.prenhall.com/kauchak.**

The need for learning-related experiences early in life is increasingly recognized (Ball, 1992; Hartnett & Gelman, 1998), and the benefits of early intervention programs are long-lasting. In a follow-up study of a program emphasizing language skills for pre-K and kindergarten children, researchers found that participants in their 20s had higher test scores in reading and math and were far more likely to attend college than peers who had not participated in the program (Jacobson, 2000b).

A more ambitious program in North Carolina provided nutritional help and social services to children from birth, as well as parenting lessons and a language-oriented preschool program (Jacobson, 1999). Follow-up studies revealed that participants scored higher on intelligence and achievement tests, were twice as likely to attend post-secondary education, and delayed having children by 2 years versus non-program counterparts. Early-childhood education programs pay off, not only in terms of immediate school success but also later in life. In recognition of this, a number of states, including New York and Georgia, are moving towards making preschool accessible to all students (Jacobson, 2000c).

By the mid 1990s, fewer than half of all 5 year olds in the United States were attending full-time programs (U.S. Department of Education, 1996), but this is rapidly changing, with much greater emphasis now being placed on early intervention programs. As full-time pre-K programs become increasingly common, job opportunities in these areas will grow. For more information about this and other early intervention programs, go to the *Web Links* Module in Chapter 6 of the Companion Website at **http://www.prenhall.com/kauchak.**

Table 6.2	Schedules for Two Elementary School Teachers		
A First-Grade Schedule		**A Third-Grade Schedule**	
8:30 A.M.	School begins	8:30 A.M.	School begins
8:30–8:45	Morning announcements	8:30–9:15	Independent work (practice previous day's math)
8:45–10:30	Language arts (including reading and writing)	9:15–10:20	Language arts (including reading and writing)
10:30–11:20	Math	10:20–10:45	Snack/independent reading
11:20–11:50	Lunch	10:45–11:15	P.E.
11:50–12:20	Read story	11:15–12:15	Language arts/social studies/science
12:20–1:15	Center time (practice on language arts and math)	12:15–12:45	Lunch
1:15–1:45	P.E.	12:45–2:00	Math
1:45–2:30	Social studies/science	2:00–2:30	Spelling/catch up on material not covered earlier
2:30–2:45	Class meeting	2:30–2:45	Read story
2:45–3:00	Call buses/dismissal	2:45–3:00	Clean up/prepare for dismissal

ELEMENTARY SCHOOLS

To begin our examination of elementary schools, let's look at the schedules of two elementary teachers and see how they relate to the organization of elementary schools. The schedules are outlined in Table 6.2. Examine them and see what you notice.

Some observations might include the following:

- Both teachers are responsible for all the content areas, such as reading, language arts, math, science, and social studies.
- Their schedules are quite different. Although both teach young children, Sharon, the first-grade teacher, begins with language arts, while Susie, the third-grade teacher, begins by having the children practice their previous day's math.
- The amount of time they allocate to each of the content areas is a personal decision. Susie, for example, devotes 50 minutes to math, whereas Sharon teaches math for 75 minutes.

In addition, both teachers noted that these schedules were approximate and often changed depending on their perception of students' needs and the day of the week. For example, if students were having trouble with a math topic, they might devote more time to math on a given day. (S. Mittelstadt, personal communication, January 22, 1999; S. Van Horn, personal communication, January 21, 1999).

If you observe in elementary classrooms, you're likely to see schedules that vary somewhat from the ones in Table 6.2. This individual teacher freedom and autonomy is characteristic of elementary school organization.

Why are elementary schools organized this way? First, recall the history of elementary schools: typically, a single teacher has been responsible for all of the content areas. We also learned that until about the mid-1800s, elementary schools weren't even organized into grade levels; in fact, a single teacher was responsible for all grade levels and content areas in many rural, one-room schools. As you can see, history has influenced the way elementary schools are organized.

Developmental characteristics of the students also influence elementary schools' organization. We saw earlier that young children look, think, and interact with their peers in ways that are different from older students. Educational leaders have historically believed that young children need the stability of one teacher and a single classroom to function most effectively in school. Schools can be frightening places for little children; self-contained classrooms provide emotional security for young learners. Further, simply moving from room to room, as middle and secondary students do, can be difficult for young children. Imagine a first grader going to room 101 for math, room 108 for language arts, and so on. A rotating schedule, such as Lakeside's, would be even more confusing.

This thinking has been questioned by other educators. For example, expecting one teacher to be knowledgeable enough to effectively teach reading, language arts, math, science, and social studies is asking almost the impossible. As a result, some content areas—frequently science, social studies, art, and music—are de-emphasized by teachers who feel uncomfortable teaching in these areas. So educators, teachers, and parents face a dilemma. Is the social and emotional well-being of students more important than content? Historically, the answer has been "Yes."

■ HIGH SCHOOLS, JUNIOR HIGH SCHOOLS, AND MIDDLE SCHOOLS

To see differences between elementary schools and middle, junior high, and high schools, we only need to compare Chris's experiences (in the chapter opening case) to Susie's and Sharon's. We saw that elementary teachers typically teach all the content areas and set their own schedules. Also, they are responsible for monitoring their students outside the classroom, such as walking with them to the cafeteria.

In contrast, Chris taught only geography, and he (along with all the other teachers in his school) followed a specific, predetermined schedule. The lengths of the periods were uniform for all the content areas, and the beginnings and endings were signaled by a bell. Also, Chris was not responsible for monitoring his students as they moved from place to place on the Lakeside campus, but he was involved in extracurricular activities (like the track meet) that are part of middle schools, junior highs, and high schools.

Why are these upper levels organized this way? To answer this question, let's think back to our definition of schools and remember that they're social institutions—organizations whose purpose is to further the development of children and the welfare of society. Recall from Chapter 5 that views about the role of education have changed over time. For instance, in colonial times, people felt that society would most benefit from having students learn to read and understand the Bible. Much later (near the end of the 19th century), educators felt that society would benefit most by having both college-bound and non-college-bound students take the same curriculum, believing that mental discipline was a primary function of education. Also, schools were reorganized to accommodate the large influx of immigrants, with the goal of helping them assimilate into American society.

As educational thinking continued to change, leaders felt that society needed citizens well-schooled in a variety of practical topics. This emphasis on subject-matter mastery resulted in the departmentalization found in the junior high schools and the high schools that you most likely attended. Let's look at the organization of these schools, starting with high schools.

The Comprehensive High School

Most of you probably attended a **comprehensive high school,** *one designed to meet the needs of all students.* In attempting to do this, most high schools are organized into tracks (Oakes, 1992, 1995). College-bound students study in a college-preparatory track, which

Increasing Understanding 6.7

In both Sharon's and Susie's schedules, shown in Table 6.2, reading, language arts, and math are strongly emphasized. On which of the educational philosophies that you studied in Chapter 5 is this emphasis most likely based?

Increasing Understanding 6.8

Think again about your study of Chapter 5. Identify three reasons that educational leaders decided that all students—college-bound and non-college-bound—should take the same curriculum.

Extracurricular activities provide valuable learning opportunities in areas not typically tapped by traditional classrooms.

allows them to take courses designed to get them ready for college-level work. It might include **advanced placement classes** in English, history, chemistry, or biology; *these courses allow students to earn college credit while still in high school, making college less time-consuming and expensive.* A general track composed of "standard" classes is designed for students of average ability who may or may not go on to college. Students in this track may take some vocational courses, such as word processing or woodworking, designed to provide them with practical skills they can use immediately after graduating, either at home or on a job. A vocational track specifically targets students not going to college, preparing them for careers in areas like automobile repair or technology.

Extracurricular activities such as band, chorus, and athletics like basketball, swimming, soccer, and tennis are also available. These options are intended to help all students develop intellectually, socially, and personally. Educational leaders believe that the more fully developed students are when they leave high school, the better equipped they will be to succeed in college or immediately contribute to society.

Criticisms of the Comprehensive High School   Can a comprehensive high school be all things to all students? Critics say no and focus on two factors: tracking and size.

One of the paradoxes of the comprehensive high school is that different tracks, designed to present quality alternatives, often produce exactly the opposite. Research indicates that instead of providing freedom and choice, tracking segregates students, often leaving many with substandard educational experiences (Oakes, 1992, 1995). Lower-ability, minority, and low-SES students are often steered into vocational or lower-level tracks, where the curriculum is less challenging and instruction is often poor. Instead of effectively preparing students for the world of work, lower tracks often segregate students from their college-bound peers and communicate that challenge and deep understanding are not for them.

A second criticism of high schools relates to size and the impersonal nature of life in many large high schools. As schools become larger, they also can become more impersonal and bureaucratic. One study compared large American high schools to shopping malls in which students mill around looking for entertainment and educational bargains (Powell, Farrar, & Cohen, 1985). Like smart shoppers, the brighter students (or their parents) know what they want and quickly find the more challenging, college-preparatory courses. Lower achievers get lost in the shuffle, spending time but not receiving a quality education.

Concrete suggestions to address these problems came from former President Bill Clinton's Secretary of Education, Richard W. Riley (Sack, 1999). He suggested that high schools should do the following:

- Create schools-within-schools to make them smaller and more personal.
- Turn homeroom periods into student-advisory periods where students can get to know teachers and discuss events relevant to their lives.
- Allow students to keep the same counselor for the entire four years.

Interestingly, these suggestions are similar to ones offered to make junior high schools and middle schools more user-friendly.

Junior High Schools

Elsewhere we saw that schools in the early 20th century were organized into eight elementary and four high school grades. This 8–4 organization changed when emphasis shifted away from basic skills, such as reading and math, and moved toward the more intensive study of content, like history, literature, and science. In-depth study of content areas required teachers to be subject-matter experts. In addition, a growing recognition of the unique needs of early adolescents was being realized. The result was the development of the "junior" high school.

Most junior high schools today have a variety of offerings—although not as comprehensive as those in high schools—and they include competitive athletics and other extracurricular activities. Though initially designed to help students make the transition between elementary and high schools, they are in every sense of the word "junior" high schools; this is the environment in which Chris is teaching.

Middle Schools

Think back to the friends you knew when you were in the sixth, seventh, or eighth grades. Some of the girls were young women, fully developed physically and emotionally, while others were still little girls. Some boys needed to shave, whereas others looked like fifth graders. Many of the boys and girls were becoming more and more attracted to each other, and others were kind of attracted to the other sex but didn't know why. This is the transitional period of early adolescence.

Because of the rapid physical, emotional, and intellectual changes that early adolescents experience, it is a unique period in their development. Other than infancy, at no time in a person's life is change so rapid or profound. As a result, many educators believe that schools should be organized to meet the unique needs of students during this time in their lives.

The result of this thinking, and the fact that junior high schools weren't meeting early adolescents' needs, led to the formation of **middle schools,** *schools specifically designed to meet the needs of early adolescents and help them make the transition from elementary to high schools.* What does teaching in a middle school "look" like? Let's look at an example.

Case
STUDY

Robin West is an eighth-grade teacher in an inner-city middle school. She teaches physical science, and she and her team members have a common planning period. They teach the same group of students and often spend their planning period discussing the students and the topics each is teaching. A number of their students are not native English speakers, and the teachers' discussions often center on what can be done to help students with language problems. In addition, Robin has four students with learning disabilities in her classroom. The teachers try to integrate topics across as many of the four areas as often as possible.

"Can you help me out with anything on graphing?" Mary, the math teacher, asked the others one Monday. "The kids just see graphs as some meaningless lines. I explain the heck out of them, but it doesn't seem to help all that much."

"I know what I can do," Robin offered, after thinking for a few seconds. "I'll do some simple demonstrations and then have them link the demonstration to a graph. . . . Here, look," and she dropped her pen. She then drew a sketch (shown below) on a piece of paper.

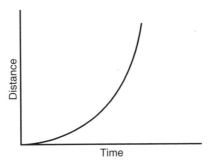

"The graph represents the distance–time relationship when the pen falls," she went on. "Time is on the horizontal axis and distance is on the vertical axis. . . . I'll do this with the kids, and you can refer to what I did when you do your work on graphs," she added, nodding to Mary.

"Great. Thanks. . . . When will you do it?"

"We're between units now, so I can do it tomorrow. . . . Then you and I can talk about it after school for a few minutes, and I'll let you know how it went. . . . By the way, how is Lorraine Williams doing in math?"

"Not good," Mary responded. "In fact, I was going to ask you all about her. She hasn't been turning in her homework, and she seems only 'half there' in class."

"Same thing in history," Keith added. "We'd better see what's going on. . . . I'll call her parents tonight."

■   ■   ■

In this short scenario, we see several middle school adaptations. They include:

■ Organizing teachers and students into interdisciplinary teams. For example, a team could be composed of math, science, English, and social studies teachers who all have the same students and work together to coordinate topics.

■ Creating and maintaining long-term teacher–student relationships with attention to emotional development. Many middle schools implement an "advisor–advisee" period, in which the homeroom teacher meets with students each day to discuss a variety of non-academic topics. Through these advisory periods, teachers get to know students on an individual basis and can more carefully track their academic progress.

■ Interactive teaching strategies. Teachers are encouraged to move away from the lecture-dominated instruction, so common in high schools, and toward instruction based on interactive questioning and student involvement. In addition, greater emphasis is placed on study strategies, such as note-taking and time management.

■ Eliminating activities that emphasize developmental differences, such as competitive sports. Instead, everyone is invited to participate in intramural sports and clubs.

When done well, these characteristics have a very positive influence on students. For instance, interdisciplinary teams allow teachers to efficiently plan for the integration of

Teaching in an Era of Reform

GRADE RETENTION

One basic principle on which the organization of U.S. schools is based is that children progress from grade to grade as they grow older. This makes sense. As children grow and develop, they are exposed to increasingly complex ideas and tasks. However, this natural progression from grade to grade is being challenged by increased interest in **grade retention,** which is *the process of making students repeat a grade if they don't meet certain criteria.*

An important plank in the reform movement is the elimination of "social promotions" through increased use of grade retention for students who fail to achieve at prescribed levels. In a State of the Union address, then President Clinton proclaimed, "No child should graduate from high school with a diploma he or she can't read. We do our children no favors when we allow them to pass from grade to grade without mastering the material" (Quoted in Gordon, 1999, p. 42).

Grade retention is not new, but its popularity as a reform tool is growing. In the past, 5 to 7 percent of public school children (about two children in every classroom) were retained each year (Shepard & Smith, 1990). This figure is likely to grow as a number of states, such as Texas and Louisiana, and several large school districts, including New York, Los Angeles, and Chicago, are either considering or have implemented systems in which students must pass a test to progress to the next grade (Robelen, 2000; White, 1999).

The magnitude of the issue is illustrated in Louisiana, where all fourth and eighth graders must pass a test to progress to the next grade level (Robelen, 2000). In 1999 about 38,000 students, or about one-third of the students taking the test, failed. Those students will be offered summer school and a second chance to pass. Those not passing will repeat fourth or eighth grade.

Putting Reform into Perspective

The concept of grade retention seems logical. For example, allowing students to move from the fourth to the fifth grade when they haven't mastered the content and skills expected of typical fourth graders isn't intuitively sensible. It is also logical to conclude that these students are even less likely to succeed in the fifth grade if they're passed without the necessary understanding and skills. Advocates of grade retention claim that spending a second year in a grade gives learners a second chance to master the content and sends the message that schoolwork is important.

The concepts *social promotion* and *grade retention* are also concrete and easy to understand. As a result politicians, knowing that quality education is important to voters, use the notion of grade retention as a campaign "sound bite" in favor of educational quality to appeal to voters.

 topics across different content areas, as Robin and Mary did with math and science. In addition, when teachers have the same students, they are able to more carefully monitor students' progress, as the team did with Lorraine.

The middle school philosophy also applies to extracurricular activities. One middle school in Plainfield, Indiana, encouraged its students to participate, with the following results. Well over half of the 900 students are involved in some sort of extracurricular activity: 350 in band, 325 in choir, 107 in cheerleading, 100 in basketball, and 85 in cross country (Hill, 1999). How did the school accommodate these numbers? Creatively. For example, they broke the cheerleaders into teams assigned to different sports and made room for basketball players by having two teams and opportunities for within-school sports. The results are encouraging. Students are happy with increased opportunities for participation, and a full trophy case attests to the school's ability to produce excellent athletic and musical programs.

Forming relationships helps students adjust to an atmosphere that is less personal than their elementary schools were, and eliminating competitive sports downplays competition, encourages all to participate in sports, and minimizes the advantages early maturing students have over their later developing classmates.

However, research consistently reveals that grade retention doesn't achieve advocates' claims. Students retained in a grade tend to perform lower on subsequent achievement tests than their nonretained counterparts, and they're also more likely to later drop out of school (Hauser, 1999; Shepard & Smith, 1990). Dropouts are five times more likely to have repeated a grade than are students who complete high school, and the probability of dropping out for students who repeat two grades is nearly 100 percent. Minorities and low-SES children are much more likely to be retained than their White, wealthier counterparts. This fact has sparked a lawsuit challenging the state of Texas' pass-or-don't-graduate policy (Zehr, 1999).

Research also indicates that grade retention causes emotional problems. In one study, children rated the prospect of repeating a grade as more stressful than "wetting in class" or being caught stealing. Going blind or losing a parent were the only two life events that children said would be more stressful than being retained (Shepard & Smith, 1990). The psychological effects of grade retention are especially acute for adolescents, where physical size differences and peer awareness exacerbate the problem.

Finally, alternatives to social promotion exist. Before- and after-school programs, summer-school programs with reduced class sizes, instructional aides who work with target children, and peer tutoring are all possibilities. Each is less expensive than spending thousands of dollars to have children repeat what they have already experienced, and the likelihood of students meeting standards is greater than it is by having them repeat grades (Hauser, 1999; Shepard & Smith, 1990). When grade retention does occur, it is important to provide help targeted at specific areas where problems exist.

 Increasing Understanding 6.10

We see that research consistently indicates that grade retention is harmful to students. Explain why grade retention is so popular in spite of this research. Also explain how this issue is related to teacher professionalism.

You Take a Position
Now it's your turn to take a position on the issue discussed in this section. Go to the *Education Week* Website at **http://www.edweek.com,** find "search" on the first page, and type in one of the following two search terms: *grade retention* or *social promotion*. Locate a minimum of three articles on one of these topics and then do the following:

1. Identify the title, author, and date of each article and then write a one-paragraph summary of each.

2. Identify a pattern in the articles. (Each article—or even two of the three—suggesting that experts believe that social promotion should be eliminated would be a pattern, for example.)

3. After identifying the pattern, take one of the two following positions:

   ■ The pattern suggested in the articles, if implemented, *is likely* to improve education.

   ■ The pattern suggested in the articles *is not likely* to improve education.

State your position in writing, and document your position with information taken from the articles.

 To answer these questions online, go to the Take a Position Module in Chapter 6 of the companion Website.

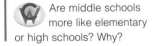

Increasing Understanding 6.9

Are middle schools more like elementary or high schools? Why?

Interactive teaching strategies actively involve students in learning activities that can also develop their thinking and social interaction skills. Research indicates that motivation often drops during the early adolescent years; some researchers believe that this drop is due to increased use of teaching strategies like lectures that place students in passive roles (Pintrich & Schunk, 1996; Stipek, 1998).

The number of middle schools continues to increase compared to junior high schools. For instance, in 1968 about 7,200 schools called themselves junior high schools, but by 1996 the number had dropped to about 1,000 (Viadero, 1996). However, critics suggest that many middle schools, rather than implementing the intended adaptations we saw earlier, still largely resemble the junior high schools they were intended to replace (Bailey, 1997).

■ WHAT IS AN EFFECTIVE SCHOOL?

You're either planning to teach or are thinking about teaching; this is the reason you're taking this course. As you consider job offers from different schools, some important questions you'll want to ask are, How good is this school? Will it be a good school to work in?

Think about the schools you attended, and think about Chris's school. How good were they? What does the term "good" mean? How do you know if a school is good? We try to answer these questions in this section.

While people typically refer to schools as good or not so good, as in "Lakeside is a very *good* junior high school," researchers use the term "effective" instead. An **effective school** is *one in which learning for all students is maximized.* In simple terms, we think of an effective school as one that promotes learning. But what makes a school effective in promoting student learning? Let's see what research has to say.

Research on Effective Schools

Research has identified several characteristics of schools that promote learning. They are outlined in Figure 6.1 and discussed in the sections that follow.

School Organization and Climate This chapter focuses on school organization; the way schools are organized has a significant effect on learning. One important dimension of this organization is size.

School size. Are small schools better than big ones? Is the reverse true? As it turns out, the relationship between size and quality isn't simple or direct. Schools must be large enough to provide the varied curricular offerings needed to help students learn as much as possible, but not so large that students get lost. Research suggests that the ideal size for a high school is between 600 and 900 students. This conclusion is based on research that examined nearly 10,000 students in 789 public, Catholic, and private schools (Lee, 2000).

School size affects low- and high-SES students differently, with size more strongly influencing learning for low-SES students than for high-SES students. In other words, while 600–900 students is the ideal school size for all students (that is, both high- and low-SES students learn more in schools of this size), the reduction in learning in very large or very small high schools is greater for low-SES than it is for high-SES students. The only schools not fitting this pattern are elite private schools that enroll students with similar backgrounds and have the money to provide extensive resources, such as well-equipped science and computer labs.

Unfortunately, a disproportionate number of low-SES students attend either very small or very large high schools. Examples include small rural schools in sparsely populated states, such as Wyoming or Montana, and large, urban schools in major cities like New York or Los Angeles.

How does school size influence student learning? Researchers suggest that school size may affect learning *indirectly.* For example, a very large school doesn't directly *cause* students to learn less than they would in a more ideally sized school; rather, size influences

Increasing Understanding 6.11

Explain why size more strongly influences low-SES students than it does high-SES students. Think about the characteristics of students placed at-risk that were discussed in Chapter 4.

Figure 6.1   **Characteristics of Effective Schools**

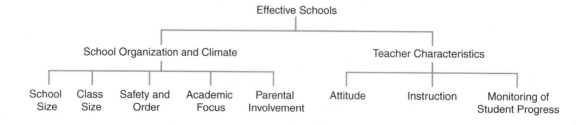

One essential characteristic of an effective school is hallways that are safe and orderly.

other factors (Lee, 2000). As schools becomes larger, it becomes more difficult to create learning communities in which students feel safe to learn and develop. Huge schools tend to depersonalize education, making it harder for teachers and students to know each other and work together.

One solution to the size problem is to create schools within schools, smaller learning communities where both teachers and students feel more comfortable. For example, Creekland Middle School in Georgia has more than 3,100 students, many more than experts recommend for any school, much less a middle school (Jacobson, 2000a). To address this issue, Creekland is divided into five learning communities, each with its own assistant principal, school counselor, and faculty. Students are assigned to one of these communities for the 3 years they attend the middle school, and faculty make a special effort to integrate students into their community.

Class size. In addition to school size, what are some other factors that contribute to an effective school? One of these is class size. Does the number of students in a class influence how much the students learn? This issue is somewhat controversial, with some critics arguing either that class size doesn't matter or that reducing class size isn't worth the cost required to hire extra teachers and provide space and resources.

Research counters these critics' positions. A consistent body of evidence indicates that reducing class size does indeed increase learning for all students; the effects are particularly pronounced in the lower grades and for students in inner-city schools (Robinson, 1990; Rouse, 1997; Wenglinsky, 1997).

Reductions in class size can have both short- and long-term positive effects (Viadero, 1999). In Tennessee, where class sizes were reduced from 25 to 15 students, researchers found immediate gains in reading and math scores. Follow-up studies revealed that the positive effects lasted through twelfth grade. Students in the smaller class dropped out of school less frequently, took more challenging courses, and were more likely to attend college than their counterparts in larger classes. These positive effects were especially strong for African American students.

School safety and order. In a national survey asking students to identify serious problems in their school, 45 percent identified fighting, 54 percent targeted bullying, and 38 percent pointed to stealing. When nine- to eleven-year-old students were asked whether noisy students disrupting class, cheating, and stealing were problems at their school, overwhelming majorities (88 percent, 66 percent, and 51 percent, respectively) said yes (Boyer, 1995). Schools, which should be sheltered communities for learning, often serve as mirrors for the problems of society.

The need for safe and orderly schools is supported by both research and theory. Researchers have described effective schools as places of trust, order, cooperation, and high morale (Rutter, Maughn, Mortimore, Ouston, & Smith, 1979). Students need to feel emotionally safe in schools for learning to occur (Alexander & Murphy, 1998).

Theories of learner development, which we briefly discussed earlier in the chapter, suggest that the need for order is innate (Piaget 1952, 1970). In other words, people are born with a desire to live in an orderly rather than chaotic world. In addition, the psychologist Abraham Maslow (1968), who described a hierarchy of human needs, argued that only the need for survival is more basic in people than the need for safety. Studies of classroom management also confirm the need for order; orderly classrooms promote both learning and student motivation (Purkey & Smith, 1983; Radd, 1998; Wang, Haertel, & Walberg, 1993).

Academic focus. To effective schools, the primary mission of schooling is to promote learning. This mission is clear to the teachers in the school, with the tone being set by the school principal and other administrators. An array of clubs, sports, and other extracurricular offerings exists and is important, but this doesn't take precedence over learning. In effective schools, classes are not canceled so students can attend sporting events, and class time isn't used for club meetings.

One study investigating the effects of academic focus on learning concluded, "Students learn more in schools that set high standards for academic performance, that use their instructional time wisely, and that use student learning as a criterion for making decisions" (Lee & Smith, 1999). Schools with an academic focus are probably more positive places to work because both students and teachers feel that learning is occurring. Look for signs that academic focus is present when you interview for a teaching position at different schools.

Parental involvement. No matter how well they're organized, schools won't be effective if parents aren't involved in their children's education. Learning is a cooperative venture; teachers, students, and parents are in it together.

Research indicates that students benefit from home–school cooperation in a number of ways (Cameron & Lee, 1997; López & Scribner, 1999):

- When parents are involved, students achieve more, regardless of socioeconomic status, ethnic/racial background, or the parents' education level. The more extensive the parent involvement, the higher the student achievement.
- When parents are involved in their children's education, those students have higher grades and test scores, better attendance, and complete homework more consistently.
- When parents are involved, students exhibit more positive attitudes and behavior.
- Educators hold higher expectations for students whose parents collaborate with teachers. They also hold higher opinions of those parents.
- Students' alcohol use, violence, and antisocial behaviors decrease as parent involvement increases.

Effective schools develop mechanisms to allow parents and teachers to work together.

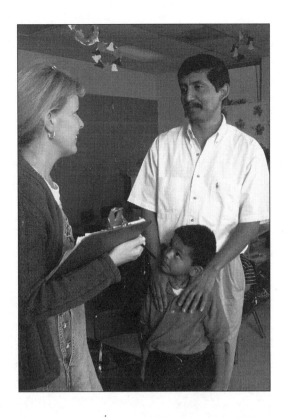

Increasing Understanding 6.12

Earlier we saw that a disproportionate number of low-SES students tends to be enrolled in large schools. Is the involvement of low-SES parents likely to be greater than the involvement of high-SES parents? Explain. (Hint: Think about the influence of SES on learning that was discussed in Chapter 4.)

These outcomes likely result from parents' increased participation in school activities, their more positive attitudes about schooling, and teachers' increased understanding of their students' home environments (Weinstein & Mignano, 1993).

Parental involvement is so important that the National PTA has established *National Standards for Parent/Family Involvement Programs* (National PTA, 1998). These standards are outlined in Table 6.3. To learn more about the *National Standards for Parent/Family Involvement Programs* and suggestions for involving parents in their children's education, go to the *Web Links* Module in Chapter 6 of the Companion Website at **http://www.prenhall.com/kauchak.**

Teacher Characteristics

In the last section, we saw how school size, safety and order, school focus, and parental involvement influence a school's effectiveness and the amount that students learn.

Teachers are also central to a school's effectiveness. Crucial teacher characteristics include:

- Teachers' attitudes.
- The way teachers teach.
- The extent to which student progress is monitored.

Teacher Attitudes. It is difficult to overstate the impact of teachers' attitudes on the way they teach and the amount students learn. One of the most important teacher attitudes is a concept called **personal teaching efficacy,** which is *teachers' beliefs that they can promote learning in all students regardless of their backgrounds* (Bruning, Shraw, & Ronning, 1999). The most significant characteristic of teachers who are high in personal teaching efficacy is that they take responsibility for the success or failure of their own instruction

Table 6.3   **National Standards for Parent/Family Involvement Programs**

Standard	Description
I. Communicating	Communication between home and school is regular, two-way, and meaningful.
II. Parenting	Parenting skills are promoted and supported.
III. Student Learning	Parents play an integral role in assisting student learning.
IV. Volunteering	Parents are welcome in the school, and their support and assistance are sought.
V. School Decision Making and Advocacy	Parents are full partners in the decisions that affect children and families.
VI. Collaborating with Community	Community resources are used to strengthen schools, families, and student learning.

Source: From National Parent Teacher Association (1998). *National standards for Parent/Family Involvement Programs.* Chicago: Author. Reprinted by permission.

Video *Perspectives*

WHAT MAKES A SCHOOL GREAT? PARENTAL INVOLVEMENT

This ABC News video segment focuses on Walton High School in Atlanta, a model school for parental involvement. The benefits of parental involvement are explored from both a parent and school perspective. Reporter Thomas Toch also describes characteristics of an effective school and explains how and why parents should get involved in their children's education.

Think about This

1. What are the major benefits of increased parental involvement in education?
2. What are the essential characteristics of an effective school, and how do they influence learning?
3. Which of these characteristics of an effective school will be most important to you as a first-year teacher?

To answer these questions online and receive immediate feedback, go to the Video Perspectives Module in Chapter 6 of the Companion Website.

(Lee, 2000). In other words, if students aren't learning as much as they should be, rather than blaming students' lack of intelligence, poor home environments, uncooperative administrators, or some other cause, high-efficacy teachers conclude that they could be doing a better job teaching, and they look for ways to increase student learning.

Let's look at an example.

Case STUDY

"What are you doing with those cake pans?" Jim Barton asked his wife, Shirley, a fifth-grade teacher, as he saw her hard at work constructing some cardboard cake pans.

"What do you think?" she grinned at him. "Do they look like cake?" she asked, holding up rectangular cardboard pieces drawn to resemble two cakes cut into pieces, with the pieces intended to be used to illustrate fractions.

"Actually, they almost do," he responded.

"My students didn't score as well as I would have liked on the fractions part of the Stanford Achievement Test last year, and I promised myself that they were going to do better this year."

"But you said the students aren't as sharp this year."

"That doesn't matter. I'm pushing them harder. I think I could have done a better job last year, so I swore I was really going to be ready for them this time."

Jim walked back into the living room with a smile on his face, mumbling something about thinking that teachers who have taught for 11 years were supposed to burn out (Eggen & Kauchak, 2001, p. 463).

■   ■   ■

Shirley is a high-efficacy teacher; she accepts responsibility for the amount her students learn, and she is increasing her efforts to be sure that increased learning occurs.

High-efficacy teachers create high-efficacy schools. Let's look at how learning is influenced in **high-collective-efficacy schools**, *schools in which most of the teachers are high in personal teaching efficacy.* Figure 6.2 provides some insight (Lee, 2000).

Three findings in Figure 6.2 are important. First, all students—high, middle, and low SES—learn more in high-collective-efficacy schools than they do in schools where collective efficacy is lower. This, in itself, isn't surprising; it makes sense that the more teachers strive for student learning, the more students will learn. Second, and more important, low-SES students in high-collective-efficacy schools have achievement gains nearly as high as high-SES students in low-collective-efficacy schools. Third, differences in achievement gains among low-, middle-, and high-SES students in high-collective-efficacy schools are smaller than they are in low-collective-efficacy schools (Lee, 2000). In other words, high-collective-efficacy schools help reduce achievement differences between groups of students who typically benefit quite differently from schooling.

How do high-efficacy teachers and high-collective-efficacy schools accomplish these results? A number of factors contribute, but two are essential: interactive instruction and continuous monitoring of student progress.

Interactive Instruction.   Imagine that you're walking through the hallways of a school and the classroom doors are open. As you walk by each classroom, you glance inside. Can you determine anything about the effectiveness of the school from a simple glance? The answer is yes. If the prevailing pattern is one in which the teachers are asking large numbers of questions, and students are involved in discussions, the likelihood that the school is effective increases. In contrast, if what you see is teachers primarily lecturing, or students spending

Figure 6.2   **Achievement Gains in High-Collective-Efficacy Schools versus Low-Collective-Efficacy Schools**

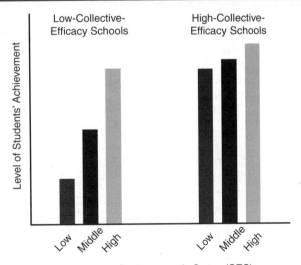

Source: From Lee, V. (2000). Using hierarchical linear modeling to study social contexts: The case of school effects. *Educational Psychologist, 35,* 125–141. Reprinted by permission.

most of their time working alone and doing seatwork, the school is less likely to be effective. This is admittedly simplistic—many additional factors influence how much students learn—but interaction between teacher and students as well as students with each other are essential ingredients for learning (Gladney & Green, 1997; Wang, Haertel, & Walberg, 1995).

Not only is interactive teaching essential for learning, it is also important for motivation (Pintrich & Schunk, 1996). In a study where students were asked to rate different methods of learning, teacher lectures and memorization were rated lowest (Boyer, 1995). In another study, middle school students rated hands-on science and independent research projects as their most memorable schoolwork (Wasserstein, 1995). Effective schools provide opportunities for students to become actively involved in their learning.

Teachers high in personal teaching efficacy—who believe that they can make a difference in student learning—are more likely to promote high levels of teacher–student interaction than their low-efficacy counterparts. "Such teachers view teaching and learning as an interactive process with students cast as active participants, rather than as a one-way flow of information" (Lee, 2000, p. 135).

Continuous Monitoring of Student Progress. A second instructional factor that contributes to schools' effectiveness is the extent to which teachers frequently assess learning and provide students with feedback. Teachers in effective schools collect a great deal of information about students' learning progress. These teachers give frequent quizzes and tests, the assessments measure more than a recall of facts, the teachers return the assessments shortly after they're given, and the test items are thoroughly discussed (Brookhart, 1997; Dochy & McDowell, 1997; Tuckman, 1998). In addition, teachers regularly collect work samples from students and carefully monitor student understanding in class discussions.

Parents' and Other Taxpayers' Perceptions of Effective Schools

How do parents and other taxpayers view effective schools? What is the basis for their perceptions? What do they most commonly look for in judging a school? Let's take a look.

The results of research examining parents' and other taxpayers' perceptions of effective schools are not surprising. As would be expected, they react most strongly to factors that are concrete and observable. For example, as a result of highly publicized incidents of school violence, school safety is a primary concern; in fact, both parents and other taxpayers rank it as the most essential characteristic of an effective school (Olson, 1999).

A second important characteristic is qualified teachers. Again, this isn't surprising, since teachers represent schools and are the people who work most directly with parents' sons and daughters.

A third measure of a schools' effectiveness is standardized test scores. In the absence of other, more concrete indices of school effectiveness, parents look to standardized test scores to tell them how their children are doing as well as how the school is performing. Forty-eight of the 50 states regularly test their students, and 36 states publish annual report cards on individual schools. "In short, parents and taxpayers view school safety and the presence of qualified teachers as two essential ingredients of education. Once those basic conditions are met, they want results" (Olson, 1999, p. 34).

These results are consistent with the characteristics of effective schools discussed earlier. For instance, we saw school safety on both lists. School size has been discussed in the popular press, but it hasn't received the publicity of characteristics like teacher qualifications and test scores. Other factors, such as personal teaching efficacy, interactive instruction, and monitoring of student progress are more complex, making them harder for people outside the profession to understand.

Increasing Understanding 6.13

Do high-SES students need interactive instruction more than low-SES students, or vice versa? Explain, using the information from Figure 6.2 as the basis for your answer.

Increasing Understanding 6.14

Look again at the characteristics of effective schools and effective teachers for students placed at-risk. (See pages 127 and 128 in Chapter 4.) Those characteristics are very similar to the characteristics of effective schools we've discussed here. Explain why this is case.

Reflect *on* This

WORKING TO CHANGE THE SCHOOL ORGANIZATION

You've been offered a job at Henderson Middle School, an inner-city school in a medium-sized city. Henderson boasts some of the most successful basketball and football teams in the city, and it is a primary feeder school for Raines High School, a city football power. The coaches of the two schools closely coordinate the development of the schools' athletes.

Henderson's students typically score quite low on standardized achievement tests, and the school's administrative staff is working to change the school organization. They want to create teams in which a history, English, math, and science teacher all have the same group of students along with a common planning period. They've also gotten a grant to support in-service activities designed to help teachers move away from using lectures as the primary method of teaching and toward more student involvement and integration of topics between different content areas. "We want to see standardized test scores going up, and we want to see more kids on the honor roll. These kids are going to have to compete when they get to high school, and now is the time for them to learn how. These kids—all of them—can learn; all we have to do is believe it, and we can make it happen," urges Adam Argalas, the school principal.

1. To what extent is Henderson consistent with the characteristics of middle schools?

2. In what area (or areas) is Henderson inconsistent with the characteristics of middle schools?

3. Based on the information presented, is Henderson likely to be a relatively effective or ineffective school? How do you know?

4. Would you accept a job at Henderson? Why?

Ⓦ *To respond to these questions online and receive immediate feedback, go to the Reflect on This Module in Chapter 6 of the Companion Website.*

Tracking can result in the segregation of cultural minorities into low-level classes where instruction tends to be less challenging.

Exploring Diversity

Considering Multiple Perspectives

SCHOOL ORGANIZATION AND THE ACHIEVEMENT OF CULTURAL MINORITIES

Emphasis on higher standards and increased accountability is perhaps the most prominent reform that exists in education today. However, all change has unintended outcomes, and one that is important in this case is a widening gap in the achievement of cultural minorities—particularly African American and Hispanic students—compared to their White and Asian counterparts (Hoff, 2000). Between 1970, when the National Assessment of Educational Progress first began systematically measuring American students' achievement, and 1980, African American and Hispanic students made great strides in narrowing the gulf that had separated them from their White peers. However, this progress ground to a halt in the late 1980s, and since then, the gap has either remained constant or widened (Jencks & Phillips, 1998).

A number of explanations have been offered for the differences in achievement, including poverty, peer pressure, and parental values. None seems adequate, however, and research examining these explanations is either lacking or inconsistent (Viadero, 2000).

However, consistent research does exist regarding two aspects of school organization that were discussed earlier in the chapter: tracking and class size. Let's look at them.

Cultural Minorities and Tracking

We saw that comprehensive high schools have been criticized for the practice of tracking, because evidence indicates that educational experiences on lower-level tracks are often substandard (Oakes, 1992, 1995). This evidence is particularly relevant for cultural minorities because they tend to be underrepresented in higher-level tracks, that is, a disproportionate number are found in low-achieving classes. The problem is exacerbated by the fact that minority students tend not to enroll in more demanding classes (Jencks & Phillips, 1998). Table 6.4 outlines some of these differences (Viadero, 2000).

Tracking and minority achievement have a form of negative synergy, that is, student achievement in low-level classes is reduced compared to the achievement of students of comparable ability in high-level classes. And because decisions about tracking are based on students' records of past achievement, the negative relationship between achievement and tracking is magnified. School

Class-size reduction can be an effective tool to increase achievement.

Table 6.4

	Correlation between Taking Advanced High-School Courses and Graduating from College	
Race/Ethnicity	High School Graduates Who Have Completed Algebra 2 and Geometry (%)	Freshmen at Four-Year Colleges Who Graduate within Six Years (%)
Asian American	55.5	65
White	53.1	59
Hispanic American	41.9	46
Native American	35.7	37
African American	35	40

Source: From Viadero, D. (2000). Lags in minority achievement defy traditional explanations. *Education Week, XIX* (28), 1–21. Reprinted by permission.

leaders haven't been able to identify a satisfactory approach to solving this problem.

Cultural Minorities and Class Size

The relationship between class size and minority achievement is more encouraging. Earlier we saw that research supports the contention that student achievement is higher in smaller classes. This research is important, because the effects of reducing class size are greater for cultural minorities than for their White peers (Gewertz, 2000; Robinson, 1990).

Two studies are particularly significant. First, an assessment of a major class-size-reduction project in Tennessee revealed the following (Illig, 1996):

- Children in small classes (about 15 students per class) consistently outperformed children in larger classes.

- Inner-city children (about 97 percent of whom were minorities) closed some of the achievement gap between themselves and nonminority children.

- Children in small classes outperformed children in larger classes, even when teachers in the large classes had support from aides.

In the second study, a four-year experiment with class-size reduction in Wisconsin, researchers found that the achievement gap between minorities and nonminorities shrank by 19 percent in smaller classes, whereas in regular classrooms it grew by 58 percent (Molnar, Percy, Smith, & Zahorik, 1998). The results of the class-size reduction experiment were so compelling that the Wisconsin legislature planned to spend $59 million beginning in 2000 to expand the program to 400 schools (Gewertz, 2000).

However, as with all initiatives, simply reducing class size won't automatically increase achievement. If the other characteristics of an effective school don't exist, reducing the number of students in classes, by itself, won't increase achievement. Narrowing the achievement gap requires the systematic implementation of all the effective school characteristics.

The Changing Role of Teachers

What implications will the patterns described in this chapter have for you as a teacher? At least three are likely.

First, accountability is here to stay. You will be expected to prepare students for high-stakes tests and to balance "teaching to the test" with a well-rounded instructional program. For instance, you will be required to integrate goals and the content in textbooks with the content measured on the tests. Your students will be expected to perform well on the tests, and you'll be held accountable for ensuring that they do. Your salary may even be partially tied to the results, as occurs in some states, such as Texas (Boser, 2000).

Second, you may be expected to spend more time teaching. The school year may start earlier and end later, and you may be asked to teach summer school. You could be involved in a year-round school. As far back as the early 1990s, more than 1.5 million students in over 2,000 schools were on year-round programs (Harp, 1993). This number is likely to increase in the future. In 1999, about half of the nation's big-city systems offered remedial summer programs (White & Johnston, 1999). The New York City School District had over 300,000 students attending summer school in 2000, two-thirds for remedial work and one-third for enrichment programs (Johnston, 2000). For teachers looking for ways to augment their 9-month salary, this is good news. (The New York City program alone required 16,000 teachers.) But teachers who want the freedom of a summer vacation may feel pressured to work during these extra months.

You will need more expertise than has been expected of teachers in the past. For example, you might find yourself teaching in a block schedule, so lecture will be even less effective than it is with traditional schedules. You will need high levels of questioning skills, the ability to organize and facilitate group work, and the aptitude to schedule and monitor individual and small group projects.

These increased demands are consistent with the increased emphasis on professionalism, where teachers are being held more and more accountable for their students' progress. If you want to feel like and be treated as a professional, you must demonstrate the expertise of a professional. This is as it should be.

■ SUMMARY

What Is a School?
A school is a social institution, organized to promote student growth and development as well as the welfare of society. All societies have a number of social institutions in addition to schools, such as churches and governments. Schools are organized within districts, geographical areas that are given the responsibility of education within its borders.

The Organization of Schools
The school organization includes personnel (such as the school principal and other administrators), support staff (such as administrative assistants, maintenance people, and cafeteria workers), and teachers.

The physical plant includes the buildings that house the administration, library, computer labs, cafeteria, and classrooms. In addition, junior high schools and high schools have gymnasiums, playing fields, sometimes swimming pools, and may even have buildings devoted to fine arts.

What is taught—the curriculum—is typically organized into grade levels, and content is intended to be taught to students of different ages.

Early-Childhood Programs
Educators have come to realize the importance of early learning experiences, including early childhood programs such as preschool and kindergarten, for students' long-term school success. Developmentally appropriate programs attempt to match classroom instruction to the learning needs of young children.

Elementary Schools
Elementary schools are organized so that a single teacher is responsible for all, or most, of the instruction in the different content areas. Elementary teachers arrange their own schedules, and the amount of time they allocate to different content areas can vary widely. Typically, elementary teachers emphasize reading, language arts, and math in their instruction, and content areas such as science, social studies, and the arts are de-emphasized.

High Schools, Junior High Schools, and Middle Schools
High schools, junior high schools, and middle schools are organized very differently than elementary schools. Teachers in these schools have content specialties, and they teach—or are supposed to teach—only in these specialty areas.

The comprehensive high school attempts to meet the needs of all students through different tracks. Unfortunately, some research suggests that tracking doesn't work and that large comprehensive high schools may be too large and impersonal.

Junior high schools are aptly named; they are "junior" high schools, with similar curricular offerings and similar extracurricular activities.

Middle schools are intended to meet the developmental needs of early adolescents, who are going through major physical, emotional, and intellectual changes. Middle schools are organized so that teachers can help students more readily make the transition from the cloistered environments of elementary schools to the less personal settings common in high schools.

What Is an Effective School?

Effective schools are those that promote learning for all students. Size is important. Effective elementary schools keep class sizes below 20 students per class, and effective high schools have enrollments in the 600 to 900 range.

In addition, effective schools are safe and orderly, academically focused, and involve parents. Teachers in effective schools take responsibility for student learning, maintain high levels of interaction with students, and continually monitor student progress.

Polls indicate that parents and other taxpayers emphasize school safety and order, highly qualified teachers, and student scores on standardized tests as indicators of an effective school.

The Changing Role of the Teacher

In an era of reform, teachers will be expected to balance accountability with a well-rounded instructional program. They may be asked to spend more time teaching, because reformers are advocating longer school days and school years as well as supplemental programs such as summer school.

■ IMPORTANT CONCEPTS

administrators

advanced placement classes

comprehensive high school

curriculum

development

developmental programs

early-childhood education

effective school

grade retention

high-collective-efficacy
    schools

middle schools

personal teaching efficacy

principal

school district

social institution

■ DISCUSSION QUESTIONS

1. Based on the organization of typical elementary schools, what are the primary advantages and disadvantages of teaching in an elementary school? How could elementary schools be organized differently to improve the education of all students?

2. Based on the organization of typical middle schools, what are the primary advantages and disadvantages of teaching in a middle school? How could middle schools be differently organized to improve the education of all students?

3. Based on the organization of typical high schools, what are the primary advantages and disadvantages of teaching in a high school? How could high schools be differently organized to improve the education of all students?

4. In which kind of school—elementary, middle, junior high, or high school—do teachers have the most autonomy? The least? What implications does this have for you as a prospective teacher?

5. Where are you best suited to teach? Why do you think so? (Your answer should be based on the organization of each type of school—elementary, middle, junior high, or high school—along with your academic and personal characteristics.)

■ VIDEO DISCUSSION QUESTIONS

 The following discussion questions refer to video segments found on the Companion Website. To answer these questions online, view the accompanying video, and receive immediate feedback to your answers, go to the *Video Discussion* Module in Chapter 6 of the Companion Website.

1. Dr. Urie Triesman is a professor of mathematics at the University of Texas at Austin and director of the Charles A. Dana Center for Math and Science Education. His work focuses on school reform and the ways that schools can be helped to improve. He believes principals are essential to effective schools. What does Dr. Triesman believe is the single most important thing that principals can do within a school to promote learning? Do you agree with him?

2. Theodore Sizer is the director of the Coalition for Effective Schools, which attempts to reform high schools. From his perspective, what are some arguments against grouping students together by age? How practical do you think the alternatives are?

3. Dr. John Goodlad is professor emeritus and co-director of the Center for Renewal at the University of Washington and president of the Independent Institute for Educational Inquiry. How does Dr. Goodlad believe that students suffer psychologically from grade retention? What alternatives are there to grade retention? Which of these do you think are most effective?

■ GOING INTO SCHOOLS

1. Go to an elementary school and either a middle, junior high, or high school. Interview a teacher at each school. Ask the teacher to describe the school administration and support staff and to explain the duties of each person. This might include some or all of the following (as well as others):
   - Vice principal
   - Assistant principal
   - Dean
   - School psychologist
   - Guidance counselor
   - School nurse
   - Media-center director
   - Curriculum specialists (such as a technology specialist)

   In addition, ask each teacher how the school is organized and how the organization of the school could be improved so that all students would learn more. Report your results in a paper comparing the two types of schools.

2. Visit the type of school in which you plan to teach. How does the receptionist greet you? Is she pleasant and cordial, or cool and businesslike? As you're standing in the school reception area, watch the receptionist. How does she treat students when they come into the area? Again, is she pleasant and cordial, or cool and businesslike? What does this tell you about the school from a student's perspective? From a teacher's perspective?

3. Visit a school and stand in a hallway as students are moving to or from lunch, or from one class to another. Describe the behavior of the students and the teachers as students are making these transitions. In particular, look for the following:
   - How orderly is the movement? Do students move quickly and with a minimum of apparent confusion?
   - Are teachers monitoring the students' movement? What are the teachers saying? Is the general tone of the teachers' comments and directives pleasant and cordial or harsh and critical?
   - Do students move into classrooms in an orderly way? Are they in their seats and waiting when instruction is scheduled to begin?

   What does this information tell you about this school as a learning environment?

4. Interview a teacher; place special emphasis on questions about the teacher's students. You might include some or all of the following questions:

■ How capable of learning are the teacher's students?
■ What are their lives like at home?
■ Can you overcome home problems if they exist? Why?
■ What could be done to organize the school so that learning could be increased for all students?
■ What is the toughest part of your job?
■ What is the easiest part of your job?
■ What is the most distasteful part of your job?
■ What is the most pleasant or rewarding part of your job?

What do the teacher's responses tell you about teaching in a school like this?

5. Observe the class of the teacher you interviewed. Look for the following:
   ■ The number of questions the teacher asks. Does he or she ask large numbers of questions or is most of the instructional time spent lecturing?
   ■ How much of the teacher's time is spent in instruction (explaining and lecturing or question and answer)?
   ■ How much time do students spend doing seatwork?
   ■ How much time do students spend in nonlearning activities, such as visiting with each other or moving around the room?

On the basis of your observations, decide how well the organization of this classroom promotes learning.

 Virtual Field Experience

If you would like to participate in a Virtual Field Experience, go to the *Field Experience* Module in Chapter 6 of the Companion Website.

■ ONLINE PORTFOLIO ACTIVITIES

 To complete these activities online, go to the *Portfolio Activities* Module in Chapter 6 of the Companion Website to submit your responses.

Portfolio Activity 6.1

Involving Students with Diverse Backgrounds

INTASC Principle 4: *Strategies*
The purpose of this activity is to help you begin thinking about how to adapt your instruction for all students. Suppose about half of your students are cultural minorities. Describe specifically what you would do to be certain that all of your students are as involved in your learning activities as possible.

Portfolio Activity 6.2

Effective Schools

INTASC Principle 5: *Motivation and Management*
The purpose of this activity is to encourage you to think about what an effective school would look like from your personal perspective. Based upon the information in this chapter, write a two-page description of an effective school at the level in which you plan to teach. In the paper, explain how this organization would influence your life as a teacher.

Portfolio Activity 6.3

Involving Parents

INTASC Principle 10: *Partnership*
Write a two-page description of your philosophy regarding parental involvement in their children's education. Include in the description a minimum of four suggestions for involving parents.

CHAPTER

7

School Law

*Ethical and Legal Influences
on Teaching*

At this point in your preparation to become a teacher, legal issues may seem distant, unrelated to your work, and perhaps not very interesting. Imagine, however, that you're an elementary teacher and are called to the main office to talk with a parent. Can you leave your class unsupervised? Or you're a high school teacher and you read a poem that strikes you as a powerful and moving commentary on love. Do you dare share it with your students without the approval of their parents? Perhaps you're a science teacher, and you've discovered a program on the Internet that you would like to use in your classes. Can you legally download and duplicate the information?

The answers to these questions are influenced by legal decisions. Our purpose in writing this chapter is to help you understand how legal issues can influence your life as a teacher. In this chapter, we try to answer the following questions:

■ How do the law and ethics influence teacher professionalism?

■ How is the U.S. legal system organized?

■ What are teachers' legal rights and responsibilities?

■ What legal issues are involved with religion in the schools?

■ What are students' rights and responsibilities?

Let's begin by looking at two teachers struggling with legal and ethical issues.

Case STUDY

Jason Taylor is a science teacher in a suburban school in the Pacific Northwest. The town in which he teaches is considering an open-space initiative that will limit urban growth. Environmentalists support the law because they believe it will help to preserve local farms and wildlife habitat in the area; businesses in the town oppose it because of its potential to curtail economic growth. Jason talks about the initiative in class, explaining how it will help the environment. At the end of his presentation, he mentions that he is the head of a local action committee and that interested students can receive extra credit for passing out fliers after school.

Some parents complain to the principal, claiming that school time shouldn't be devoted to political activity. When the principal calls in Jason to talk about the problem, Jason is adamant about his right to involve students in local politics, claiming that civic awareness and action should be part of every course that is taught. Unconvinced, the principal points out that Jason was hired to teach science, not social studies, and warns that persisting on this path could cause Jason to lose his job. What should Jason do?

■ ■ ■

Sasha Brown looks at the two folders in front of her and frowns. Her job is to recommend one of two students from her school for a prestigious science and math scholarship to the state university. Although the decision will ultimately be made by a committee that she'll be on, she knows that her recommendation will carry a lot of weight because she is chair of the math department.

One of the candidates is Brandon, a bright, conscientious student who always scores at the top of his class. The son of a local engineer, he has a good grasp of mathematical concepts. Sonia, the other candidate, is probably not as strong conceptually, but often solves problems in creative and innovative ways. She's also a female—and a female hasn't won this award in its 6-year history. In addition, Sasha knows that Sonia comes from a single-parent family and really needs the scholarship. Knowing this does not make the selection process any easier.

■ ■ ■

What would you do in these situations? What personal values would you use to resolve these dilemmas? What external guidelines exist to guide you? How does all this relate to teacher professionalism?

■ LAWS, ETHICS, AND TEACHER PROFESSIONAL DECISION MAKING

As you've learned from other chapters, professionalism is a theme of this book. We've said throughout that professionals are responsible for making decisions in ill-defined situations, they have the autonomy to do so, and they base their decisions on a thorough understanding of their professional literature.

There are several important dimensions of this literature. For example, teachers must understand the content they're expected to teach. They must also know how to represent it in ways that make sense to students, and they must understand the intellectual, emotional, and social makeup of their students.

They must also understand the legal and ethical guidelines influencing their profession, what their professional limitations are, and why professional decision making is so important. This chapter examines the law and how it influences teaching. But before we do that, let's put legal aspects of teaching in a larger perspective.

The Law and Its Limitations

You are a teacher in a middle school, and you see a fight between two students on the playground. What must you do? First, you can't ignore the fight, because you're responsible for the safety of the children; in fact, parents have the right to sue a teacher if they can demonstrate that the teacher failed to protect students from injury, a problem called *negligence*. However, should you physically break up the fight, or can you simply report it to the administration? The law is vague on this and other specific legal issues.

Laws regulate the rights and responsibilities of teachers, but they only partially guide our professional decision making. This is true for two reasons. First, laws are purposely general so that they can apply to a variety of specific situations. We saw this illustrated in the example involving a playground altercation; Jason's dilemma at the beginning of the chapter is another case. The law *generally* protects teachers' rights to freedom of speech, but does it protect teachers' rights to campaign politically in their classrooms and deal with issues that may not be part of the assigned curriculum? Unfortunately, the answers to these questions are not explicitly spelled out in laws; therefore, professional decision making is required.

A second limitation of laws is that they've been passed in response to problems in the past, so they aren't necessarily able to provide specific guidelines for future decisions. For example, what are the rights of students and teachers who have AIDS? (We examine this issue later in the chapter.) Technology is another issue. (We devote Chapter 12 to this topic.) It is changing the way we teach, but what kinds of materials can we legally borrow from the Internet? What are the legal limitations to software use in schools? What can be legally copied? Experts are wrestling with these issues, and preliminary guidelines have appeared, but educators must often make decisions based on their knowledge of the law and their professional judgment. We see again why professional knowledge is so important.

**Increasing
Understanding 7.1**

Think back to your study of Chapter 5, which examined philosophical issues and education. How does the section you're reading now relate to your study of that chapter? Explain specifically.

To answer this question online and receive immediate feedback, go to the *Increasing Understanding* Module in Chapter 7 of the Companion Website at **http://www.prenhall.com/ kauchak.**

Ethical Dimensions of Teaching

The law tells teachers what they can do (rights) and what they must do (responsibilities). However, laws don't tell teachers what they *should* do. This is where ethics, which examines values and appropriate conduct, is so important. **Ethics** *provides a set of principles that can be used to decide whether or not acts are right or wrong.*

Professional ethics *are moral principles adopted by a group to provide guidelines for conduct* (Corey, Corey, & Callahan, 1993). For example, the Hippocratic oath, which says that physicians will do their best to benefit their patients (with both curative methods and kindness), to tell the truth, and to maintain patients' confidences, is a code that guides the medical profession. Other professions have similar ethical codes, which are designed to both guide practitioners and protect clients.

We were first introduced to the National Education Association's (NEA) Code of Ethics in Chapter 1 when we discussed teacher professionalism. This code provides teachers with potential guidance in ambiguous professional dilemmas such as we found at the beginning of this chapter. As with the law, however, codes of ethics are limited; they only provide general guidelines for professional behavior. Let's look again at Jason's dilemma to see why this is so. Item 2 within the NEA Code of Ethics states, ". . . the educator shall not unreasonably deny the student access to varying points of view." Has Jason been balanced and fair in presenting both sides of the environmental and political issue? A code of ethics isn't, and never can be, specific enough to provide a definitive answer. Jason must answer the question for himself based on his personal philosophy of education, and within it, his personal code of ethics.

Increasing Understanding 7.2

Earlier we said that laws are limited because they are *general* and *reactive,* that is, written in reaction to problems in the past. Which of these two limitations also applies to professional codes of ethics?

Sasha's dilemma also illustrates the limitations of this code. Item 6 in the NEA Code cautions us not to discriminate on the basis of race, color, creed, or sex, but does it specifically tell us what to do with Sonia? Based strictly on academics, Brandon appears to be the better candidate. However, Sonia's need along with the good that might result from other females seeing a girl receive recognition in math (a traditionally male-dominated area of the curriculum), might influence the decision.

In response to these complexities, teachers are often admonished to "treat all students equally." However, even encouraging teachers to treat all students alike isn't as simple as it appears. Sensitive teachers purposefully call on shy students to involve them in lessons, strategically avoid calling on assertive students who tend to dominate discussions, and give students who have difficulty with English more time to answer questions and finish tests. These teachers treat specific students differently depending on their individual needs; their decisions involve issues of fairness and professional ethics.

These examples illustrate why your personal philosophy of education is important. We saw in Chapter 5 that a philosophy of education provides a framework for thinking about educational issues and guides professional practice. Your personal philosophy will guide you as you make decisions about what is important, what is fair, and why. Since the law and professional codes of ethics can only provide general guidelines, developing a personal philosophy is critical in helping you make the specific decisions that you must make every teaching day.

Having briefly examined the law, ethics, and their limitations, now let's look at the American legal system in more detail.

■ THE U.S. LEGAL SYSTEM

Laws regulating schools and teachers are part of a larger, complex legal system that exists at three interconnected levels: federal, state, and local. This system attempts to use peoples' rights and responsibilities to each other as the basis for defining fairness.

Federal Influences

At the national level, the Constitution is the law of the land. It doesn't provide specific educational guidance, but it has influenced education in two forms: amendments and laws.

Constitutional Amendments Think about the following questions:

■ As a teacher, how much freedom do you have in selecting topics to teach? Are you limited in what books and articles you can ask your students to read?

■ Can you publicly criticize the administrators and school board members for whom you work?

■ How much freedom do students have in running their school newspapers and yearbooks?

The First Amendment to the Constitution guarantees all citizens the right of freedom of speech, but where do you draw the line with respect to the preceding questions? You certainly can't have your students read *Playboy* magazine, but how about *Catcher in the Rye,* a classic American coming-of-age novel with explicit sexual references? Similar uncertainties exist with respect to the second and third questions.

Professional ethics provide broad guidelines for teachers as they make decisions in complex situations.

The Fourth Amendment protects citizens from unreasonable searches and seizures. To what extent does this amendment protect teachers and students? For instance:

■ Can school officials search students' backpacks and purses when they're on school property?

■ Are students' lockers considered to be personal property or can they be searched if school officials suspect they contain drugs or weapons?

The Fourth Amendment provides general guidelines about search and seizure but doesn't specifically answer these two questions.

The Fourteenth Amendment states that ". . . nor shall any State deprive any person of life, liberty, or property without due process of law." What does "due process" mean in the context of schools? For example:

■ Can teachers be fired without a formal hearing?

■ Can students be expelled from class without formal proceedings?

■ How long can a student be suspended from school, and what kinds of deliberations need to precede such a suspension?

Increasing Understanding 7.3

Which amendment is relevant to Jason's situation at the beginning of this chapter? Why?

Again, the Constitution provides general guidelines about due process, but the specifics are left for teachers and other educators to decide. These examples further illustrate why an understanding of legal issues is so important for beginning teachers.

Federal Laws Through the laws it passes, Congress exerts federal influence on education. The Civil Rights Act of 1964 states: "No person in the United States shall on the ground of race, color, or national origin, be excluded from participation in or be denied the benefits of, or be subjected to discrimination under any program or activity receiving federal financial assistance." This law was influential in ending segregation in schools around the country. Similarly, Title IX of the Education Amendment, passed in 1972, prohibits discrimination on the basis of gender. Title IX has played a major role in helping equalize the amount of money spent on boys' and girls' sports. Through both the Constitution and specific laws, the federal government plays a central role in defining the rights and responsibilities of teachers.

State and Local Influences

States also influence education by passing laws regulating teachers' qualifications, working conditions, and legal rights. For example, most states require a bachelor's degree to teach, and many are now requiring a major in an academic area.

States also create departments of education with a variety of responsibilities, such as determining the length of the school year and approving textbooks. They also pass laws creating local school districts that are legally responsible for the day-to-day functioning of schools.

The Overlapping Legal System

The overlapping levels of the legal system have been created to correspond to different levels of responsibility, but conflicts sometimes occur across these different levels. When they do, attempts are made to solve problems and disputes at a lower level before sending them to a higher one. Let's look at two examples.

Case STUDY

Brenda Taylor has been hired to teach American History at a rural high school. Three days before the school year begins, her principal informs her that she will be the debate team sponsor. She objects, saying she knows nothing about debate. When the principal insists, Brenda examines her contract and finds that it includes the phrase ". . . and related extracurricular activities." She complains again to the principal; when he is adamant, she writes a letter to the school board, which then appoints a grievance committee. The grievance committee rules in the district's favor. Not willing to back down, Brenda hires a lawyer, and her case goes to a state court.

■   ■   ■

Henry Ipsinger likes his job in a suburban middle school but disagrees with the school's priorities. In college he had learned that middle schools are supposed to be for all kids, not just the academically and athletically talented. He especially objects to his school's participation in Academic Olympics, an interscholastic academic competition, as well as the school's emphasis on competitive football and basketball.

Henry isn't afraid to express his opinions, and he does so frequently at faculty meetings—to the consternation of his principal. When this doesn't work, he takes his complaints to school board meetings. There his complaints fall on deaf ears, though they raise a number of eyebrows. He then tries politics—openly backing opposition candidates to the school board. Finally he goes too far; at the end of the school year, his contract isn't renewed, with insubordination cited as the cause.

Henry is livid. He hires a lawyer, claiming his First Amendment rights to freedom of speech have been violated. The case works its way through the court system all the way to the U.S. Supreme Court.

■   ■   ■

Can teachers be asked to perform duties in addition to their teaching responsibilities? Can their professional opinions cause them to be fired from their jobs? Both of these questions fall into a gray area called *school law* and are addressed by different court systems.

Since the issues in the two cases we've just described were different, they would be dealt with in different ways and at different levels. Both started at the local level, but the one involving Brenda's conditions of employment moved to the state courts because employment issues are state responsibilities. Henry's case went to the federal courts because freedom of speech is a federal or national right guaranteed by the U.S. Constitution. In a similar court case, *Pickering v. Board of Education* (1968), the·U.S. Supreme Court upheld a teacher's right to publicly criticize school district policies. As we discuss different legal dilemmas and issues, we'll see how their particular legal journeys and outcomes are determined by the particular issue or level concerned.

In the next section, we examine teachers' rights and responsibilities, probably the most important dimensions of school law for teachers.

■ TEACHERS' RIGHTS AND RESPONSIBILITIES

As citizens, teachers enjoy the same legal safeguards as all Americans, including freedom of speech and the right to due process. But because they are entrusted with the care of children, teachers have responsibilities beyond those of other citizens, such as protecting their students from physical and emotional harm. In this section, we examine five areas in which the law influences teachers' rights and responsibilities. They are outlined in Figure 7.1. Let's look at them.

Teacher Employment and the Law

Two of the first things you'll think about when you decide to enter the teaching profession are how to get a teaching job and how to keep it over the years. Legal guidelines will influence your decisions. As you begin this section, think about some ways that the law influences your rights to get and keep a job as a teacher.

Licensure Licensure is designed to ensure that all teachers within a state have achieved satisfactory levels of teaching competence and are morally fit to work with youth. Every state has licensure requirements, which typically include a college degree along with a minimum number of credit hours in specified areas (for example, teaching major or minor).

Figure 7.1   **Teachers' Rights and Responsibilities**

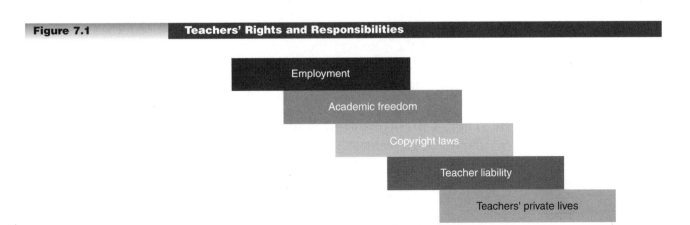

In addition, prospective teachers may be screened for felony arrests or a history of abusing or molesting children. Applicants who fail usually have the right to petition before a state professional-practices board that considers each case individually.

Increasingly, teachers are being asked to pass competency tests that measure their ability to perform basic skills (reading, writing, and mathematics), their background in an academic area (such as biology, history, or English), and an understanding of learning and teaching (Bradley, 2000). These tests are controversial because a disproportionate number of minorities fail them. Despite this problem, when properly developed and validated, these tests have been upheld in courts (Fischer et al., 1999). Individuals who meet these requirements are then licensed, which means they are *eligible* to teach; it doesn't ensure employment.

Contracts A teaching contract is a legal employment agreement between a teacher and a school board. In issuing contracts, school boards must comply with laws that prohibit discrimination on the basis of sex, race, religion, or age. Contracts are legally binding for both parties. School boards can be sued for breaking a contract without due cause, and teachers must honor contracts that they have signed. Many states permit a teacher's certificate to be revoked for breach of contract. The practice of revoking teacher licenses for breach of contract violations is becoming increasingly common as the competition for teachers increases (Archer, 2000).

Teachers should carefully read their contracts and any district policies and procedures manuals covered by the contract. Extracurricular assignments, such as sponsoring school clubs or monitoring sports events, though not specified in an initial contract, may be required later. This is what happened to Brenda Taylor when her contract specified ". . . and related curricular activities." When challenged, courts have generally upheld districts' rights to require these additional responsibilities. However, they have also required a reasonable connection between additional assignments and a teacher's regular classroom duties. So a speech teacher could be asked to sponsor a debate team but might not be legally bound to coach an athletic team if the teacher had no corresponding background experience.

Tenure Teacher **tenure** *provides job security by preventing teacher dismissal without cause.* Tenure is designed to protect teachers from political or personal abuses and to ensure the stability of the teaching force. It is grounded in a principle suggesting that teachers should be hired and fired on their professional merits and not because of who they know or don't support politically. Tenured teachers can be dismissed only for causes such as incompetence, immoral behavior, insubordination, or unprofessional conduct.

When any of these charges are filed, due process must be observed. The teacher must be provided with the following:

- Notification of the list of charges.
- Adequate time to prepare a rebuttal to the charges.
- Access to evidence and the names of witnesses.
- A hearing, which must be conducted before an impartial decision maker.
- The right to representation by legal counsel.
- Opportunities to introduce evidence and cross-examine witnesses.
- A school board decision based on evidence and findings of the hearing.
- A transcript or record of the hearing.
- The right to appeal an adverse decision.

These safeguards, guaranteed by the Fourteenth Amendment, provide teachers with the same Constitutional protections enjoyed by other people in the United States.

Dismissal You'll work hard to obtain a license and perhaps even harder to obtain a teaching position. Obviously, you don't want to lose your job, so it's important to understand your rights when this possibility occurs.

Most districts require a probationary period before tenure is granted (commonly 3 years). During this time, teachers have a yearly contract and can be dismissed for a variety of reasons, such as believed incompetence, overstaffing, or reduced school enrollments. Although some states require districts to provide a formal hearing upon demand when a nontenured teacher is dismissed, this isn't common. Teachers uncertain about their rights during this period should check with their district, state office of education, or professional organization.

Another cause for dismissal of new teachers is lack of honesty or truthfulness on the initial job application. Students who are close to obtaining their degrees are sometimes offered teaching positions during their student teaching. They agree, but due to unforeseen circumstances, are unable to graduate or obtain a teaching license. When districts discover the problem, they can either dismiss the teacher or lower the status to substitute teacher, resulting in lower pay and loss of benefits.

Reduction in force. Because of declining student numbers, budget cuts, or course or program cancellations, districts are sometimes forced to dismiss teachers. In this practice, called **reduction in force** (or "riffing" as it's called in the industry), *teachers with the least seniority—last in, first out—are dismissed from their jobs.* Fortunately, "riffing" occurs infrequently and should be even less common in the near future as increasing numbers of students enter the educational system.

Reduction in force can involve both tenured and nontenured teachers, and it is regulated either by state law or by collective-bargaining agreements between the district and the local professional organization (Fischer et al., 1999). Teachers faced with this possibility should consult representatives from their local professional organization.

Academic Freedom

■ ■ ■

In an attempt to motivate his students, a teacher organizes his classroom around a sports-competition theme called "Learnball." Dividing his students into teams, the teacher institutes a system of rewards that include playing the radio and shooting foam basketballs. His principal objects, and when the teacher refuses to change his methods, he is fired. He sues to get his job back, claiming his freedom of speech had been violated (*Bradley v. Pittsburgh Board of Education,* 1990).

An eleventh-grade teacher is leading a discussion on taboo words. To illustrate his point, he writes the four-letter slang word for sexual intercourse on the board. Parents complain and the teacher is dismissed. He sues to get his job back, claiming his freedom of speech had been curtailed (*Mailloux v. Kiley,* 1971).

■ ■ ■

Academic freedom *refers to teachers' rights to choose both content and teaching methods based on their professional judgment.* Although freedom of speech is protected by the First Amendment, professional academic freedom has limits. What are they?

Teachers are hired to teach a specific curriculum, whether that be first-grade math or high school English. State and district curriculum frameworks exist to guide teachers, and required textbooks are often identified. Within this general framework, teachers are free to teach topics as they see fit. Sometimes these topics and methods are controversial and may result in a teacher being disciplined or dismissed.

In considering issues of academic freedom, the courts consider the following:

- The teacher's goal in discussing a topic or using a method.
- The age of the students involved.
- The relevance of the materials to the course.
- The quality or general acceptance of the questioned material or methods.
- The existence of policies related to the issue.

In applying these principles to the teacher using the "Learnball" format, the courts upheld the district's dismissal. The court based its decision on the fact that this teaching strategy was not widely accepted, and the teacher had been warned repeatedly by the administration to stop using it.

The case of the high school English teacher resulted in the opposite outcome. The teacher's job was reinstated because the court upheld the importance of two kinds of academic freedom: the "substantive" right to use a teaching method that serves a "demonstrated" purpose, and the procedural right not to be discharged for the use of a teaching method not prohibited by clear regulations. The teacher's goal was for his students to understand taboo words and how they influenced literature, a topic that fell under the broad umbrella of the English curriculum. Had this not been the case, the outcome would probably have been different, as it might have been if the teacher had been clearly warned about using this strategy.

When considering controversial topics, teachers should try to decide if they fall within the scope of the assigned curriculum. When discussing controversial topics or using potentially controversial teaching methods, teachers should have a clear educational goal in mind and be able to defend it if objections arise. Academic freedom protects knowledgeable, well-intentioned teachers working within their assigned responsibilities. As a beginning teacher, if you're uncertain about an issue that could involve academic freedom, check with your principal or other school administrator.

Copyright Laws

As teachers, we want to share the most up-to-date information with our students. This can involve copying information from newspapers, magazines, books, and even television programs. Unfortunately, our desire to bring this information into the classroom can violate copyright laws (Murray, 1994).

Copyright laws *are federal laws designed to protect the intellectual property of authors, including printed matter, videos, and computer software*. Just as patents protect the intellectual work of inventors, copyright laws protect the intellectual work of writers, songwriters, and filmmakers. To balance the rights of authors with the legitimate needs of teachers and learners, federal guidelines have been developed.

Fair-use guidelines *specify limitations in the use of print, video, and software materials*. Teachers may do the following:

- Make a single copy of a book chapter, newspaper or magazine article, short story, essay, or poem for planning purposes.
- Copy short works (less than 250 words for poetry; less than 1,000 words for prose) for use in the classroom.

Increasing Understanding 7.4

One of the criteria used by the courts is the age of the students involved. How might this criteria influence the case involving taboo words; that is, would the verdict have been different if the class were in a middle school or an elementary school? Why?

Copyright laws provide guidelines for teachers when they use technology in their teaching.

However, teachers may not create class anthologies by copying material from several sources or charge students more than it cost to make the copies. In addition, pages from workbooks or other consumable materials may not be copied.

Videotapes and software pose unique challenges. They too were created by and belong to someone, and fair-use guidelines also apply to them. For example, teachers may tape a television program, but they must use it within 10 days of taping; they may show it again for reinforcement but must erase the tape after 45 days. One copy, and no more, of computer software may be made for a "backup." Materials on the Internet may not be copied unless specific permission is given or unless the document is published by the federal government.

These guidelines do restrict teachers, but the restrictions are not usually a major handicap. Teachers may want to share the principle of fair use with students to help them understand its purpose and the ways that copyright laws help protect people.

Teacher Liability

∎ ∎ ∎

An elementary teacher on playground duty mingles with students, watching them as they run around. After the teacher passes one group of students, a boy picks up and throws a rock that hits another boy in the eye, causing serious injury. The injured boy's parents sue the teacher for negligence (*Fagen v. Summers*, 1972).

∎ ∎ ∎

A teacher takes a group of first graders on a school-sponsored field trip to the Oregon coast. The teacher has four of the students stand on a log for a photo. A big wave rolls in, causing the log to roll, seriously injuring one of the children. The parents sue the teacher for negligence (*Morris v. Douglas County School District*, 1965).

∎ ∎ ∎

Increasing Understanding 7.5

Would a suit concerning a copyright violation be brought to a state court or a federal court? Why?

Reflect _on_ This

CLASSROOM MANAGEMENT

You're an elementary teacher in a self-contained classroom. You've got a class of 29 lively sixth graders, and you've been struggling all year with classroom management. Damien, a larger than average boy, seems to resist your efforts at every turn.

You like science and have tried to provide concrete, hands-on science activities whenever you can. You've been debating whether or not to do a fun activity on chemical changes where students actually test different "mystery powders" (for example, sugar, salt, and baking soda) with different liquids like water and vinegar. You decide to go ahead with it and strategically place Damien up toward the front of the room where you can watch him. In addition, you pair him with Katie, one of your more responsible female students. Everything is going well until you go to the back of the room to answer a question and hear a student shriek, "Damien." As you rush to the front of the room, you see Katie holding her eye as a mixture of vinegar and baking soda drips down her cheek. Damien is sitting there with a guilty look on his face. As you rush the crying Katie to the office, you wonder if you should have handled the science lab differently.

1. To what extent are you responsible for the actions of students like Damien?

2. If this problem developed into a liability suit, what factors would the courts consider in judging whether you were negligent?

3. In hindsight, were there some things you could have done differently in terms of this science activity?

Ⓦ _To respond to these questions online and receive immediate feedback, go to the Reflect on This Module in Chapter 7 of the Companion Website._

We don't often think of schools as dangerous places, but large numbers of children in small places combined with youthful exuberance and energy can result in falls, scrapes, and accidents. In addition, activities such as field trips, science or woodworking labs, and physical education classes pose special risks.

Teachers are legally responsible for the children under their supervision. The courts employ the idea of _in loco parentis_ in gauging the limits of teacher responsibility. **In loco parentis** _(in place of the parents) means that teachers are required to use the same judgment and care as parents in protecting the children under their supervision._ **Negligence** _occurs when teachers fail to exercise care to protect students from injury._ If negligence occurs, parents may bring a liability suit against a teacher or school district.

In attempting to define the limits of teachers' responsibilities, the courts ask if teachers:

■ Made a reasonable attempt to anticipate dangerous conditions.

■ Took proper precautions and established rules and procedures to prevent injuries.

■ Warned students of possible dangerous situations.

In applying these principles to the rock-throwing incident, the courts found no direct connection between the teacher's actions and the child's injury. The teacher was properly supervising the children, and it happened so quickly that she was unable to prevent the accident. Had she witnessed and failed to stop a similar incident, or had she left the playground for personal reasons, the court's decision would probably have been different.

Field trips pose special safety and legal challenges because of the dangers of transportation and the increased possibility of injury in unfamiliar surroundings. Many school districts ask parents to sign a consent form to inform them of the trip and release school

Field trips and labs pose spe-cial liability challenges to teachers as they work with their students.

Increasing Understanding 7.6

How might these two factors—age and special situations—have influenced the court's deci-sion in the Oregon beach case?

personnel from liability in case of injury. These forms don't do the latter, however; even with signed forms, teachers are still responsible for the safety of the children in their care. The courts ruled in favor of the parents in the Oregon case, because this type of accident is fairly common on beaches along the Oregon coast. The courts ruled that the teacher should have anticipated the accident and acted accordingly.

As they supervise, teachers need to consider the age and developmental level of students, as well as special classroom activities. Young children need more direction and supervision, for example, as do some students with special needs; science labs, cooking classes, some types of technology, and physical education classes pose special safety hazards. In these situations, teachers should plan and carefully teach safety rules and procedures.

In spite of conscientious planning, accidents can and do happen. Beginning teachers should consider the liability insurance offered by different teacher organizations. These organizations also often provide legal assistance to members who are sued. In addition, for around $80 a year, teachers can purchase a personal liability policy good for $1 million in damages (Portner, 2000).

Child Abuse

Case *STUDY*

Anita is a pleasant and attentive middle school student who seems socially well-adjusted. Recently, however, she is unresponsive in class, and she comes to class somewhat disheveled. You watch her, but she will only glance back at you, refusing to maintain eye contact. You ask her to come in after school to talk, and she agrees, although reluctantly.

She comes in nervously, fidgets, and won't look at you. She replies, "Fine," when you ask her how she feels. You continue to chat with her pleasantly, but she is unresponsive, and not wanting to press her, you end the conversation by saying, "Please feel free to come in and talk any time if something is bothering you. . . even if it's just a little thing." As she gets up to leave, you see that she moves rather stiffly.

"Anita, are you sure you're okay?"

"I fell the other day."

"But, how did you hurt your back?"

Anita's expression suggests that a fall wasn't the cause.

"Did someone hurt you, Anita?" you ask firmly.

"Please, please . . . you can't tell anyone," she blurts out.

■ ■ ■

What are your responsibilities in this situation? She begged you to say nothing. Do you honor her request?

The answer is no. All 50 states and the District of Columbia have laws requiring educators to report suspected child abuse (Fischer et al., 1999). In addition, teachers are protected from legal action if they act in "good faith" and "without malice." Teachers suspecting child abuse should report the matter immediately to either school counselors or administrators.

Teachers' Private Lives

Case STUDY

Gary Hansen had lived with the same male roommate for several years. They were often seen shopping together in the local community, and they even went to social events together. Students and other faculty "talked," but Gary ignored the hints that he was homosexual until the principal called him into his office, confronted him with the charge, and threatened dismissal.

■ ■ ■

Mary Evans had been in Chicago for over 8 years and didn't mind the long commute from the suburbs because it gave her an opportunity to "clear her head." She had been living with her boyfriend for several years, and everything seemed fine until one day she discovered she was pregnant. After lengthy discussions with her partner, she decided to keep the baby but not get married. When her pregnancy became noticeable, her principal called her in. She affirmed that she wasn't married and didn't intend to be. He asked for her resignation, suggesting she was a poor role model for her students.

■ ■ ■

An individual's right to "life, liberty, and the pursuit of happiness" is one of our country's founding principles. What happens, however, when teachers' lifestyles conflict with those of the community in which they work? Are teachers' private lives really "private," or can teachers be dismissed for what they do in their free time?

In answering these questions, the courts have relied upon a definition of teaching that is broader than classroom instruction. Teachers do more than help students understand English and history, for example; they also serve as role models for students. This results in greater scrutiny than most citizens receive. Other professionals, such as attorneys or physicians, might be able to lead lifestyles at odds with community values, but teachers might not. What *are* teachers' rights with respect to their private lives?

Teachers have a right to their own private lives but must meet community standards of acceptable conduct.

Unfortunately, clear answers in this area don't exist. Morality and what constitutes a good role model is contextual. For example, in the 1800s, teachers' contracts required them to do the following:

- Abstain from marriage.
- Be home between the hours of 8:00 P.M. and 6:00 A.M. unless attending school functions.
- Wear dresses no more than two inches above the ankle.

More recently, pregnant teachers were required (even if married) to take a leave of absence once their condition became noticeable. Obviously, views of morality change. As one California Supreme Court noted, "Today's morals may be tomorrow's ancient and absurd customs" (Fischer et al., 1999, p. 296).

Moral standards also vary among communities. What is acceptable in large cities may not be acceptable in the suburbs or in rural areas. Cities also provide a measure of anonymity, and notoriety is one of the criteria courts use to decide if a teacher's private activities damage their credibility as role models. For example, many young people are choosing to live together as an alternative to marriage. This lifestyle is less noticeable in a large city than in smaller communities.

Where does this leave teachers? Generalizations such as "Consider the community in which you live and teach" provide some guidance, as do representative court cases. Unfortunately, the law isn't clear with respect to the specifics of teachers' private behavior.

The issue of homosexuality illustrates how schools can become legal battlegrounds for people's differing beliefs. Some people believe that homosexuality is morally wrong, whereas others believe that it is either an inherited condition or a personal choice and has

Teaching
in an Era *of* Reform

EMERGING LEGAL ISSUES

The reform movement is having a profound effect on the educational landscape, requiring both educators and the public to rethink fundamental questions about education. It's not surprising, then, that educational reform is also raising legal issues. They overlap in at least two important areas:

- Teacher licensure.
- Teacher tenure.

Licensure

As you saw earlier in the chapter, tests are increasingly being used to determine who will be eligible for teacher certification. Historically, testing has been limited to entry-level applicants, but this is now changing.

For example, lawmakers from North Carolina passed the ABCs of Public Education Law in 1996, which mandated that teachers in the state's lowest performing schools be required to take a test of general knowledge (Bradley, 1999b). Those who failed the test three times would be dismissed.

The law was highly controversial. In fact, after the North Carolina Association of Educators threatened to sue and other critics argued that the tests would make it difficult to recruit teachers for low-income schools, the state backed off.

A similar reform strategy was proposed in Massachusetts. Governor Paul Cellucci proposed that teachers of low-performing math students be required to take a test measuring their understanding of math content (Bradley, 2000). He further proposed that the results be made public but that no disciplinary actions for teachers be taken. The implementation of this proposed policy is still to be determined by the state's board of education.

Tenure

Reformers are also attacking tenure, suggesting that it protects incompetent teachers and arguing that it is virtually impossible to remove a tenured teacher, regardless of competence. One study of 30 school districts found that only .15 percent of teachers believed to be incompetent were either dismissed or persuaded to resign (Bradley, 1999a). This is only slightly more than one-tenth of 1 percent, and superintendents in these districts estimated that the percentage of tenured teachers who should be dismissed for poor performance is significantly higher.

In 1997 lawmakers in Oregon eliminated tenure for teachers, replacing it with 2-year contracts (Bradley, 1999a). Whether or not other states follow remains to be seen.

Putting Reform into Perspective

Reformers' attempts to improve the performance of students by upgrading the quality of their teachers make

no relevance to schools. When the issue has gone to courts, they have generally ruled in favor of homosexual teachers. In a landmark California case, a teacher named Marc Morrison engaged in a brief homosexual relationship with another teacher. About a year later, the other teacher reported the relationship to Morrison's superintendent, who reported it to the state board of education. The state board revoked his teaching credentials, arguing that state law required teachers to be models of good conduct and that homosexual behavior is inconsistent with the moral standards of the people of California (*Morrison v. State Board of Education*, 1969).

The California Supreme Court disagreed. The court concluded that "immoral" was so broad that it could be interpreted in a number of ways, and no evidence existed indicating that Morrison's behavior adversely affected his teaching effectiveness.

However, in other cases involving criminal or public sexual behavior (for example, soliciting sex in a park), courts have ruled against teachers (Fischer et al., 1999). **Notoriety,** *the extent to which the teacher's behavior becomes known and controversial,* is a key element in these cases.

The case involving the unwed mother further illustrates the murkiness of school law. A case in Nebraska in 1976 resulted in an unwed mother being fired because the school board

---

Increasing Understanding 7.7

A teacher became involved in her city's gay rights movement, passing out leaflets at demonstrations and making speeches. Her school district warned her and then fired her for her activity. What legal issues would be involved here?

intuitive sense. We can't teach what we don't know and, without question, teachers must understand the content they're teaching. Perhaps more than any other professionals, teachers need a broad background of general knowledge that will help them guide and inspire the students they teach.

Similarly, some of the reformers' points with respect to tenure are valid. Dismissal of a tenured teacher is time-consuming and expensive—one California district took 8 years and spent over $300,000 in legal fees to dismiss one tenured teacher (Richardson, 1995). Districts typically respond to the issue by moving incompetent teachers from school to school instead of taking them out of classrooms.

However, while the use of tests to ensure teacher quality has been upheld in courts (Melnick & Pullin, 2000), critics argue that student performance depends on many factors besides teachers' knowledge, the most powerful being the students' own background knowledge and motivation (Kohn, 2000). Critics contend that more effective ways to measure competence exist, direct observation being one. Watching a teacher actually work with students in teaching-learning activities, while admittedly more time-consuming and labor intensive, provides a better indication of teacher competence than a paper and pencil test. However, politicians who pass teacher-testing laws often don't understand this.

The issue of tenure is also complex. It was created to protect teachers from political or personal pressure, and it continues to serve that function. Those who support tenure contend that teachers need protection from the potential abuse of power that can exist if a principal or other district leader has a vendetta against a teacher for unprofessional reasons. But does tenure sometimes protect incompetent teachers? Unfortunately, sometimes the answer is yes.

You Take a Position

Now it's your turn to take a position on the issues discussed in this section. Go to the *Education Week* Website at **http://www.edweek.com,** find "search" on the first page, and type in one of the following two search terms: *teacher licensure* or *teacher tenure*. Locate a minimum of three articles on one of these topics and do the following:

1. Identify the title, author, and date of each article and then write a one-paragraph summary of each.

2. Identify a pattern in the articles. (Each article—or even two of the three—suggesting that teacher tenure be abolished would be a pattern, for example.)

3. After identifying the pattern, take one of the two following positions:

   ■ The pattern suggested in the articles, if implemented, *is* likely to improve education.

   ■ The pattern suggested in the articles *is not* likely to improve education.

State your position in writing and document your position with information taken from the articles and your study of the text. (You may use this chapter and any other chapter of the text.)

Ⓦ *To answer these questions online, go to the Take a Position Module in Chapter 7 of the Companion Website.*

---

claimed there was ". . . a rational connection between the plaintiff's pregnancy out of wedlock and the school board's interest in conserving marital values" (*Brown v. Bathhe*, 1976). In other cases, however, courts have ruled in favor of pregnant unwed teachers, including one in Ohio who became pregnant via artificial insemination (Fischer et al., 1999).

While the law is ambiguous with respect to teachers' private sexual lives, it is clear regarding sexual relations with students. Teachers are in a position of authority and trust, and any breach of this trust will result in dismissal. When teachers take sexual advantage of their students, they violate both legal and ethical standards.

Issues of morality and teachers as role models influence other areas as well. Drug offenses, excessive drinking, driving under the influence of alcohol, felony arrests, and even a misdemeanor, such as shoplifting, can result in dismissal (Fischer et al., 1999). The message is clear: teachers are legally and ethically responsible for being good role models.

Teachers with AIDS AIDS is a special issue with respect to teachers' rights, and the courts have generally used the principle of nondiscrimination towards AIDS-infected people as a legal principle to guide decisions. The legal foundation for this principle was

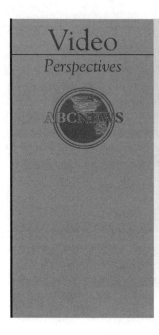

DANGEROUS HALLWAYS

This ABC News video segment describes an incident of school harassment that led to the filing of a lawsuit against a school district. Two seventh-grade girls named Christina and Jessica discuss the harassment they encountered at the hands of four older students. Their parents took the problem to the assistant principal, the superintendent of schools, and finally the school board. Despite death threats and verbal and physical abuse, the older girls were never punished, and Christina and Jessica's parents were advised to homeschool their children.

Think about This

1. Schools are responsible for ensuring the safety of its students. Was the school district negligent with respect to ensuring the girls' safety in this situation? Explain.
2. What other course of action might the school and district have pursued to solve this problem?
3. What would you have done had your child been harassed as these girls were?

W *To answer these questions online and receive immediate feedback, go to the Video Perspectives Module in Chapter 7 of the Companion Website.*

established in 1987 in a case involving an Arkansas teacher with tuberculosis (*School Board of Nassau County v. Arline*, 1987). The courts' dilemma involved weighing the rights of the individual against the public's concern about the possible spread of disease. In ruling in favor of the teacher, the court considered the disease a handicap and protected the teacher from discrimination because of it.

This decision set a precedent for a California case involving a teacher with AIDS who had been removed from the classroom and reassigned to administrative duties (*Chalk v. U.S. District Court Cent. Dist. of California*, 1988). The court ruled in favor of the teacher, using medical opinion to argue that the AIDS-infected teacher's rights to employment outweighed the minor risk of communicating the disease to the children.

■ RELIGION AND THE LAW

Religion provides a fertile ground for helping us understand how conflicting views of education can result in legal challenges. The role of religion in schools is controversial, and teachers and administrators are often caught in the crossfire.

As discussed elsewhere, the Constitution provides for the principle of *separation of church and state*. The **establishment clause** of the First Amendment *prohibits the establishment of a national religion*, and the **free exercise clause** (freedom of speech) of this amendment *prohibits the government from interfering with individuals' rights to hold and freely practice religion*. Given the central role of religion in many people's lives, the issue of religion in schools has become legally contentious. Some of the questions that have arisen include:

■ Can students and teachers pray in schools?
■ Can religion be included in the school curriculum?
■ Can religious clubs have access to public school facilities?

We answer these questions in the sections that follow.

Although the Constitution forbids the establishment of any particular religion in schools, a number of complex issues make this a controversial topic.

Prayer in Schools

In the past, prayer and scripture reading were common in many, if not most, schools. In fact, they were required by law in some states. Pennsylvania passed legislation in 1959 that required daily Bible reading in the schools (but exempted children whose parents did not want them to participate). The law was challenged, and the U. S. Supreme Court ruled that it violated the First Amendment's establishment clause (*Abington School District v. Schempp*, 1963). Nondenominational or generic prayers designed to skirt the issue of promoting a specific religion have also been outlawed. In a New York case, the Supreme Court also held that generic prayers violated the establishment clause of the First Amendment (*Engle v. Vitale*, 1962). Neither schools nor teachers can officially encourage student prayer; it is permissible when student initiated and when it doesn't interfere with other students or the functioning of the school (Walsh, 1999).

The law also forbids the use of religious symbols in schools. For example, the courts ruled that a 2-by-3 foot portrait of Jesus Christ displayed in the hallway next to the principal's office was unconstitutional (Fischer et al., 1999).

In a similar way, the U.S. Supreme Court struck down a Kentucky law requiring that the Ten Commandments be posted in school classrooms (*Stone v. Graham*, 1980). To circumvent the law, some Kentucky educators and legislators are advocating posting the Ten Commandments next to the Bill of Rights and the Magna Carta as important cultural or historical documents (Gehring, 1999a). The constitutionality of this strategy is uncertain at this time.

These cases illustrate a legal trend; prayer and religious symbols are not allowed in public schools because they violate the principle of separation of church and state. In addition to the law, the principle of separation of church and state also acknowledges learner diversity. Our students—Christians, Jews, Muslims, Buddhists, Hindus, and others—belong to many different religions. Imposing a particular form of prayer or religion on all children can be both illegal and unethical, because it can exclude children on the basis of religion.

Increasing Understanding 7.8

Which aspect of the First Amendment—establishment or free exercise—would relate to the case involving the portrait of Jesus Christ? Why?

Although the courts have been clear about denying prayer as a regular part of schools' opening ceremonies, the issue of prayer at graduation and other school activities is less clear. In a landmark case, a high school principal asked a clergyman to provide the graduation invocation and also suggested the content of the prayer. This was ruled a violation of separation of church and state by the U.S. Supreme Court (*Lee v. Weismann*, 1992). The school's involvement in the prayer was the key point; whether or not the court would have banned the prayer if it had been initiated by students or parents is uncertain.

In a recent decision, the Supreme Court voted 6 to 3 against student-led prayers at football games in Texas (Walsh, 2000). Central to the Court's decision was the conclusion that students would perceive the pre-game prayer as "stamped with the school's seal of approval," thus violating the principle of separation of church and state.

Religious Clubs and Organizations

While organized prayer in schools is illegal, extracurricular religious clubs meeting on school grounds may be legal. For example, a student in Omaha, Nebraska requested permission to meet with her Bible study group before school. Officials refused, concerned about the possibility of undesirable groups such as the Ku Klux Klan using the case as precedent. The U.S. Supreme Court ruled in the student's favor, stating that schools must allow religious, philosophical, and political groups to use school facilities on the same basis as other extracurricular organizations (*Board of Education of the Westside Community School v. Mergens*, 1990). The fact that the club was not school sponsored or initiated was central to the court's argument.

In a related case, the Supreme Court recently approved the use of federally funded computers and library books for Catholic schools in Louisiana (Walsh, 2000). The principle of separation of church and state will likely be revisited in future educational court cases.

Religion and the Curriculum

■ ■ ■

A high school biology teacher prefaces his presentation on evolution with a warning, stating that it is only a "theory" and that many theories have been proven wrong in the past. He encourages students to keep an open mind and offers creationism, or the Biblical version of the origin of the world, as an alternate theory. As part of his presentation, he holds up a pamphlet, published by a religious organization, that refutes evolution and argues that creationism provides a more valid explanation. He offers the pamphlets to any interested students.

■ ■ ■

Where does religion fit in the school curriculum? Can a well-intentioned teacher use his classroom to promote religion? Given court decisions on school prayer, simplistic answers might be no or never. But considering the enormous influence that religion has had on human history—art and literature being two important examples—the issue becomes more complex.

Evolution is one point of tension. Concern over this issue dates back to the famous 1925 "Scopes Monkey Trial," where a high school teacher (Scopes) was prosecuted for violating a Tennessee state law that made it illegal to teach "any theory which denies the story of the Divine Creation of man as taught in the Bible and to teach instead that man is descended from a lower order of animals." Scopes argued that the law violated his academic freedom, contending that the theory of evolution had scientific merit and should be shared with his high school biology students. Scopes was found guilty of violating the state law and fined $100, but the decision was later reversed on a technicality.

Since then, several states have attempted to use legislation to resolve the evolution issue. In the 1960s the Arkansas legislature passed a law banning the teaching of evolution in that state. The U.S. Supreme Court declared the law unconstitutional because it violated the establishment clause of the First Amendment. In 1982, the Louisiana legislature, trying to create a middle ground, passed a Balanced Treatment Act, requiring that evolution and creationism be given equal treatment in the curriculum. The U.S. Supreme Court threw out this law, arguing that instead of being balanced, it was designed to promote a particular religious viewpoint.

In a more recent case, the Kansas State Board of Education voted 6 to 4 to remove most references to evolution from state standards (Keller & Coles, 1999). This decision gave local school boards leeway to exclude or downplay the topic because the state standard determines state testing policies. While the decision did not violate any legal statutes, it was highly criticized, not only in the state, but across the country. Bill Nye, public television's "Science Guy," even joined in the criticism.

The broader issue of religion in the curriculum has also surfaced in several court cases. In one, fundamentalist parents objected to the inclusion of several literature stories in the curriculum including *The Wizard of Oz*, *Rumpelstiltskin*, and *Macbeth*, arguing that these materials exposed children to feminism, witchcraft, pacifism, and vegetarianism. A lower court supported the parents, but a higher federal court reversed the decision, asserting that accommodating every parent's religious claims would "leave public education goals in shreds." It supported the right of districts to use religiously controversial materials if they were useful in achieving important educational goals (*Grove v. Mead School District*, 1985). A comparable case in Illinois (*Fleischfresser v. Directors of School District No. 200*, 1994) resulted in a similar outcome. When schools can show that learning materials have a clear purpose, such as exposing students to time-honored literature, parental objections are usually overridden.

Teaching about Religion in Schools

Unfortunately, legal controversies have had a dampening effect on teaching *about* religion in schools. Here we emphasize the difference between teaching *about* different religions and *advocating* a particular one. Religion has had enormous impact on history (for example, the Crusades and New World exploration) as well as on art and literature. Avoiding the study of religion leaves our students in a cultural vacuum that is both inaccurate and potentially dangerous (Nord & Haynes, 1998). But how can we teach about religion without provoking religious controversies?

The U.S. Department of Education wrestled with this problem and developed the following guidelines (U.S. Department of Education, 1995):

- Advocacy of religion by teachers and administrators has no place in public schools.
- Public schools should not interfere with or intrude upon a student's religious beliefs.
- Students may pray in private but cannot do so to a captive audience or compel other students to pray.
- Public schools may teach about the history of religion, comparative religions, the Bible as literature, and the role of religion in the history of the United States and other countries.

In addition, the directive reaffirmed students' rights to distribute religious literature and display religious messages on items of clothing, as protected by the First Amendment.

Critics caution that the Bible should not be used as a history textbook, should not be framed and taught strictly from a Christian perspective, and should not be used to promote Christian faith formation and religious values (Gehring, 2000). The First

Increasing Understanding 7.9

A biology teacher wants his students to know how the Bible is the basis of the theory of creationism. Would this be legally permitted? Why? Under what circumstances wouldn't it?

Figure 7.2

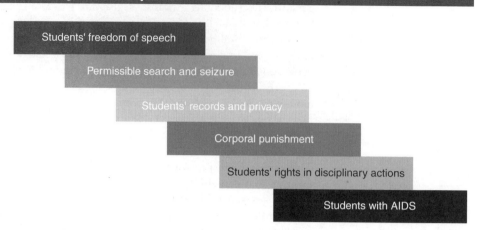

Figure 7.2 Students' Rights and Responsibilities

- Students' freedom of speech
- Permissible search and seizure
- Students' records and privacy
- Corporal punishment
- Students' rights in disciplinary actions
- Students with AIDS

Amendment Center, a national organization promoting free speech, recently published new guidelines "The Bible and Public Schools: A First Amendment Guide" (Gehring, 1999b). The guidelines, endorsed by the National Education Association, the American Federation of Teachers, as well as the National School Boards Association, recommend using secondary sources to provide alternate scholarly perspectives on the Bible as a historical document. These guidelines are available online in the *Web Links* Module of Chapter 7 on the book's Companion Website. These guidelines seem straightforward, but future legal battles over this emotional issue are likely.

STUDENTS' RIGHTS AND RESPONSIBILITIES

As it does for teachers, the law also helps define students' rights and responsibilities. Students' legal rights and responsibilities are important because they provide guidelines for teachers and other educators regarding how students should be treated. They are also important because they provide educational opportunities to teach students about our legal system along with their rights and responsibilities as future adult citizens. These rights and responsibilities are outlined in Figure 7.2 and discussed in the sections that follow.

Students' Freedom of Speech

■ ■ ■

Many parents in an urban middle school are advocating that school uniforms be required. They believe that having students wear uniforms would reduce classroom management problems, discourage gang colors, and minimize social comparisons between wealthy, well-dressed students and less-wealthy students. The school administration has voiced support for the proposal.

The student editors of the school newspaper hear of this proposal and conduct an informal poll of students, which indicates that the majority of students are opposed to uniforms. The editors want to publish these results along with an editorial advocating student choice in what they wear. The principal refuses to let them print the article. What are students' rights in this matter?

■ ■ ■

The law guarantees students' rights to freedom of speech, but students may not disrupt a school's main mission—learning.

As we've repeatedly seen, the First Amendment guarantees American citizens freedom of speech; as teachers, we want our students to understand and appreciate this right as they prepare to be responsible citizens. Do they lose this right when they enter our schools? Yes and no. Yes, they have the right to express themselves in schools, provided doing so doesn't interfere with learning.

The landmark case in this area occurred in the late 1960s during the peak of the controversial Vietnam War. As a protest against the war, three high school students wore black arm bands to school, despite the school's ban on such protests (*Tinker v. Des Moines Community School District*, 1969). The students were suspended and then sued the school district, arguing that the suspensions violated their freedom of speech. The case went all the way to the U.S. Supreme Court, which ruled in favor of the students. The Court ruled that freedom of speech is an essential right for all citizens and that students' freedom of expression should not be curtailed if it isn't disruptive and doesn't interfere with the educational mission of the school.

Students' freedom of speech was tested again in 1986; during a school assembly, a high school student made a student-government nominating speech that contained a graphic and explicit metaphor comparing the candidate to a male sex organ. Not surprisingly, students in the audience hooted, made sexual gestures, and became disruptive. After he was reprimanded, the student sued, claiming his freedom of speech had been curtailed. This case also went to the U.S. Supreme Court, which ruled that "The schools . . . may determine that the essential lessons of civil, mature conduct cannot be conveyed in a school that tolerates lewd, indecent or offensive speech. . . ." (*Bethel School District No. 403 v. Fraser 106*, 1986). The court ruled, in essence, that freedom of speech may be limited if it interferes with learning or with the running of a school.

With respect to freedom of speech, school newspapers pose a special problem. We want students to feel ownership and responsibility for the stories they write and the paper they create. However, school newspapers are an integral part of a school's extracurricular activities

Increasing Understanding 7.10

How are the two cases involving students' freedom of speech similar? Different?

School officials may search students' lockers if they have probable cause to believe they contain something illegal or dangerous.

and should reflect a school's goals. In a pivotal case, students working on a school newspaper wanted to print two articles, one detailing the personal stories of three anonymous, pregnant teenage students, and the other dealing with the effects of divorce on children. The principal objected, arguing that the students in the first story might be identified because of the details in the articles. The newspaper authors sued, with the case reaching the U.S. Supreme Court, which decided that school newspapers could be regulated in cases of "legitimate pedagogical concerns" (*Hazelwood School District v. Kuhlmeier*, 1988).

Where does this leave teachers? We want students to express their views and opinions, both because ownership of ideas promotes learning and because it prepares students to take stands and express personal opinions later in life. However, students also need to learn that individual freedoms have limits; these freedoms may not impinge on the rights of others. By encouraging the open exchange of ideas while reminding students of their responsibilities to each other, teachers can create classrooms that become micro democratic societies. This is an ideal to strive for.

Permissible Search and Seizure

The Fourth Amendment to the Constitution protects American citizens from unlawful searches and seizures, and warrants are normally required before a person or that person's property can be searched. How do these protections apply to students? Again, educators face dilemmas. We don't want to run our schools like prisons or teach students that personal privacy is not a right. However, as drug and alcohol use and violence on school campuses increase, many school leaders feel compelled to search students and use entryway metal detectors to maintain the safety of the schools. Where do the courts draw the line on the issue?

Student freedom from unlawful search and seizure became an issue when a teacher discovered two girls smoking cigarettes in a restroom. When questioned by the vice principal, one student admitted smoking and the other (T.L.O.) denied the charge. The vice principal opened T.L.O.'s purse and found rolling papers in addition to cigarettes, which prompted him to empty the purse. Inside were marijuana, a pipe, empty plastic bags, a number of dollar bills, and a list titled, "People who owe me money" (*New Jersey v. T.L.O.*, 1985). T.L.O. confessed that she had been selling marijuana at school and was sentenced to a year's probation by the juvenile court.

Later, T.L.O. appealed the ruling, claiming that she was the victim of an illegal search. The U.S. Supreme Court reviewed the evidence and upheld both the verdict and the legality of the search, concluding that school searches are legal if they are targeted at a problem. Reasonable suspicion (probable cause) that the student being searched deserves this treatment is required.

In addition to probable cause, the nature of the search is important. Does it involve passing through a metal detector or opening a school bag, or is it more intrusive? The courts have consistently upheld the legality of metal detectors at school entrances, asserting that such searches are nonintrusive (Zirkel, 1999). However, in one case, a high school student was strip-searched for drugs after a police dog mistakenly identified her as carrying drugs. (Authorities later found the false positive occurred because, before school, the young girl had played with her dog, who was in heat.) The school district was required to pay damages to the girl's family (*Doe v. Renfrow*, 1980). While condoning searches for probable cause, the courts remain sensitive to the rights of students. However, school lockers are considered school property and may be searched if reasonable cause (for example, suspicion of possession of drugs or a firearm) exists.

The use of urine tests to detect drug use illustrates how legal issues can become convoluted. In one case, the Supreme Court held that random drug testing for student athletes was legal, arguing that the safety of students and the importance of a drug-free school environment outweighed the privacy rights of student athletes who were participating voluntarily. A later case involved an Indiana youth suspended for fighting (Zirkel, 1999). To be readmitted after a 5-day suspension, the student was required by the school to take a urine test for drugs. In this case, the courts ruled in favor of the student, defending the boy's right to privacy.

Students' Records and Privacy

Students' records—grades, standardized test scores, teacher comments, and letters of recommendation—can determine whether or not they are admitted to special programs or colleges of their choice as well as whether they get jobs they want. What legal safeguards guide the creation and use of these potentially life and career-influencing records?

In 1974, Congress passed the Family Educational Rights and Privacy Act (FERPA), also called the Buckley Amendment. Under this act, schools must:

1. Inform parents of their rights regarding their child's records.
2. Provide parents access to their child's school records.
3. Maintain procedures that allow parents to challenge and possibly amend information if they believe it is inaccurate.
4. Protect parents from disclosure of confidential information to third parties without their consent.

In essence, the **Buckley Amendment** *made school records more open and accessible to parents*.

The law isn't absolute, however. Teachers may jot down notes during a busy school day, such as reminders about a student's behavior, as they try to decide whether or not the child needs special-education services. These notes cannot be made public without the teacher's consent. Also, a teacher's letter of recommendation may remain confidential if students waive their rights to access. To protect teachers in these situations, the Buckley Amendment excludes teachers' private notes, grade books, or correspondence with administrators.

A recent court case involving the Buckley Amendment has implications for classroom practice (Walsh, 2000). A mother in Oklahoma objected to the practice of having her children's papers graded by other students and the results called out in class. She claimed this violated her children's rights to privacy, and a federal circuit court agreed on both counts—student grading and the public disclosure of grades. Consequently, teachers who want to use other parents or students as graders must first seek parental permission. In addition, the court ruling calls into question the practices of publicly displaying graded student work and students passing out corrected or graded assignments and tests.

Because of the extra effort and paperwork required to put these procedural safeguards into place and because of potential encroachments into teachers' private records, administrators and teachers have mixed feelings about this law. However, while not perfect, the Buckley Amendment has improved parents' access to information as they try to make sound decisions about their children, and it has made school officials more sensitive to parents' needs for that information and the importance of confidentiality.

Corporal Punishment

• • •

In one Pennsylvania elementary school, a 36-year-old, 6-foot tall, 210-pound school principal paddled a 45-pound first-grade boy four different times during a school day for a total of 60 to 70 swats. After the incident, the boy needed psychological counseling, cried frequently, and had nightmares and trouble sleeping (*Commonwealth of Pennsylvania v. Douglass*, 1991).

The Fayette County Board of Education in Tennessee specifies that any paddles used to discipline students must be:

■ not less than ⅜ inch or more than ½ inch thick.

■ free of splinters.

■ constructed of quality white ash.

■ 3 inches wide (except handle) and not more than 15 inches long: grades K–5.

■ 3½ inches wide (except handle) and not more than 18 inches long: grades 6–12.

Students can receive a maximum of three swats with this district-approved paddle (Johnston, 1994).

• • •

Corporal punishment is highly controversial, both because of the legal issues involved and because using physical punishment as a disciplinary tool is questionable. As of 1997, it was prohibited in 27 states and the District of Columbia (Fischer et al., 1999), but in a 1977 landmark case the U.S. Supreme Court ruled that corporal punishment in schools is not a violation of the Eighth Amendment to the Constitution (which prohibits cruel and unusual punishment). The court further ruled that states may authorize corporal punishment without prior hearing and without the prior permission of parents (*Ingram v. Wright*, 1977), which left the door open for the use of corporal punishment in the remaining 23 states. So where does that leave prospective teachers?

In the states where corporal punishment is permitted, legal guidelines suggest teachers may use corporal punishment under the following conditions:

Increasing Understanding 7.11

Ⓦ You are a high school teacher and receive a letter from a prospective employer of one of your former students. The letter contains a form that asks you to provide, in addition to a letter of recommendation, information about the student's GPA. What are the legal aspects of this request?

Increasing Understanding 7.12

 How would these guidelines apply to the Pennsylvania principal who paddled a first grader?

■ The punishment is intended to correct misbehavior.

■ Administering the punishment doesn't involve anger or malice.

■ The punishment is neither cruel nor excessive and doesn't result in lasting injury.

Teachers considering this disciplinary option, even though it is legal, should ask themselves several questions:

■ Is this the best way to teach students about inappropriate behavior?

■ Would other options be more effective in encouraging students to consider their behaviors and the effects of those behaviors on others?

■ What does corporal punishment teach children about the use of force to solve problems?

Behavioral psychologists, who regularly use reinforcers and punishers to shape student behavior, have this to say about corporal punishment:

> There should never be a need to use physical punishment with a regular classroom population. If there are severe behavior problems that cannot be treated by other response-weakening techniques in conjunction with positive reinforcement, the classroom structure and the teaching procedures should be carefully examined (Jenson, Sloane, & Young, 1988, pp. 110–111).

Their point is a good one; classroom corporal punishment should be used only as a last resort and under extreme conditions.

Students' Rights in Disciplinary Actions

Case STUDY

Jessie Tynes, a sixth-grade teacher, turned around just in time to see Billy punch Jared. "Billy, what did I tell you about keeping your hands to yourself? This school and my classroom have no room for this kind of nonsense! You're out of this class until I meet with your parents. Come with me to the principal's office where you'll sit until we can solve this problem of keeping your hands to yourself."

■ ■ ■

Sean, a high school junior, was walking to his locker when someone reached in from behind to knock his books on the floor. When he turned around, he saw Dave standing behind him with a smirk on his face. Losing his temper, Sean pushed Dave and a scuffle broke out, which was broken up by Mr. Higgins, the vice principal. Both students received 10-day suspensions from school.

■ ■ ■

Increasing Understanding 7.13

 What amendment to the Constitution guarantees students due process? (Hint: Under what circumstances are teachers guaranteed due process?)

How are these problems similar? How are they different? What legal guidelines assist educators as they try to deal fairly and effectively with school discipline problems?

Both incidents involve infractions of school rules, but they differ in the severity of the problem and resulting actions. These differences are important when the courts consider *due process*, a central issue when students' rights are involved.

Students have a right to an education, and the courts specify that limiting this right can only occur when due process is followed. However, the courts also acknowledge the rights of schools to discipline students in the day-to-day running of schools.

Suspending Billy from class would be considered an internal affair best resolved by his teacher, his parents, and himself. Unless a suspension lasts longer than 10 days or results in expulsion from school, teachers and administrators are generally free to discipline as they see fit, assuming the punishment is fair and is administered equitably.

Actions that lead to out-of-school suspensions, entry on a student's record, or permanent expulsion require more formalized safeguards. These include the following:

1. A written notice specifying charges and the time and place of a hearing.
2. A description of the procedures to be used, including the nature of evidence and names of witnesses.
3. The right of students to cross-examine and present their own evidence.
4. A written or taped record of the proceedings as well as the findings and recommendations.
5. The right of appeal.

As we can see from this list, the procedures involved in long-term suspensions and expulsions are quite detailed and formal. They exist to safeguard students' rights to an education, an economic necessity in today's modern world. They also consume time and energy, so they are generally used only as a last resort.

Students with AIDS

AIDS, or Acquired Immune Deficiency Syndrome, became a major health and legal issue in the schools in the 1980s. Previously thought to be limited to sexually active gay men and drug users who shared hypodermic needles, AIDS entered the school-age population through contaminated blood transfusions.

Battle lines were quickly drawn. Concerned parents worried that the AIDS virus would be spread in school through either casual contact or the sometimes rough-and-tumble world of children on playgrounds. Parents of children with AIDS wanted their children to have access to an education that was as normal as possible. The courts were soon drawn into the fray.

A landmark and precedent-setting case occurred in St. Petersburg, Florida, in 1987 and involved 7-year-old Randy Ray, a hemophiliac who had contracted AIDS through a blood transfusion. Because of his condition and fears about possible spread of the disease, school officials refused to allow Randy and his two brothers, who also had AIDS, to attend school. His parents first reacted by moving elsewhere, but when that failed to open school doors, they moved back to St. Petersburg and sued the school district.

A U.S. district court ruled that the boys should be allowed to attend school with special safeguards including special attention to the potential hazards of blood spills (*Ray v. School District of DeSoto County*, 1987). Subsequent cases involving other students with AIDS have been similarly resolved, with courts holding that these children are protected from discrimination by the Individuals with Disabilities Act of 1991 as well as Section 504 of the Rehabilitation Act of 1973, which protects otherwise-qualified handicapped individuals from discrimination. Central to the courts' decisions has been the potential negative effects of exclusion on the social and emotional well-being of the child. The courts have been clear in rejecting exclusion as the automatic solution to the problem of dealing with AIDS-infected students; instead, they have required schools to address the specific risk factors involved in each case.

Exploring Diversity

Considering Multiple Perspectives

AFFIRMATIVE ACTION

One outcome of the civil rights movement of the 1960s was **affirmative action,** *a collection of policies and procedures designed to overcome past racial, ethnic, gender, and disability discrimination.* The rationale for affirmative action was that merely outlawing discrimination was not enough; society should take steps to correct past discriminatory practices to ensure racial and gender balance in all aspects of society, including schools.

The legal basis for affirmative action comes from at least three sources. The Fourteenth Amendment to the Constitution guarantees equal protection under the law. Titles VI and VII of the Civil Rights Act of 1964 specifically prohibit discrimination in federally assisted educational programs in terms of race, color, religion, sex, or national origin. The Americans with Disability Act of 1991 extends similar protection to persons with disabilities.

Affirmative action affects schools in two important ways: hiring policies for teachers and admission policies for students. In an attempt to remedy past discriminatory hiring practices, a number of school districts are required under affirmative action guidelines to hire more minority teachers. The courts have generally upheld this practice if affirmative action is deemed necessary to reverse past discriminatory practices (Fischer et al., 1999). However, in past instances where discrimination is not seen as a problem, preferential hiring practices for minorities on criteria other than merit or qualifications are discouraged. For example, because of declining enrollments, a school district in New Jersey was forced to reduce the teaching staff in the business department of a high school by one teacher. Two teachers, one White and one African

American, had equal seniority and were considered to be of equal quality. The school board decided to retain the African American teacher, using affirmative action as a rationale. The White teacher sued, claiming she was being discriminated against; federal courts agreed, arguing that minorities had not been underrepresented in the district's teaching force in the past (*Taxman v. Board of Education of Township of Piscataway,* 1996). In essence, for affirmative action to be legal, there must be a logical basis for its use.

Affirmative-action cases such as these have resulted in charges of reverse discrimination, with critics alleging that minorities and women were being given unfair preferential treatment in hiring and admission decisions. One such claim was made in 1974 by Alan Bakke, who was denied admission to medical school, while minority candidates with lower grades and test scores were admitted. The case went all the way to the U.S. Supreme Court, which ruled in a 5 to 4 vote that Bakke should be admitted. However, in making this decision, the Court did not rule out other forms of race-conscious admission procedures (*Regents of the University of California v. Bakke,* 1978).

The issue of affirmative action is likely to remain controversial in the future. Toward the end of the 1990s, voters in California and Washington supported legislation eliminating preferential higher-education admission policies (Dworkin, 1998). In addition, court cases have raised questions about the legality of racial quotas for magnet schools (Dowling-Sendor, 1999). Legal experts in this area conclude, "Whether affirmative action will be mended by government and supported by voters is a question that is likely to continue to challenge schools and colleges during the coming decade" (Fischer et al., 1999, p. 480).

The Changing Role *of* Teachers

Education exists in a complex social environment. The society in which we live is constantly changing; these changes will affect your life as a professional.

One societal trend is the growing tendency to settle problems in court. As one legal expert observed, "Americans are a litigious people" (Fischer et al., 1999, p. vii). We tend to seek lawyers rather than talk, to sue rather than compromise. The United States has more lawyers per capita than any other country on the planet. Teachers, fearful of this trend, are increasingly seeking protection through professional liability insurance (Portner, 2000).

How should the profession respond to all this? A simplistic response would be to embrace this confrontational approach in solving educational disputes. But this "my lawyer's tougher than your lawyer" approach to problem solving is inadequate for at least two reasons. First, it creates adversarial relationships within the profession. Second, and more importantly, it emphasizes standards of professional behavior that are minimal rather than ideal. Instead of looking to courts and lawyers for professional guidance, teachers should try to improve and enforce their professional code of ethics to make it a guiding light in our legally and morally confusing times.

But where does this leave individual teachers, who can be vulnerable to legal challenges? Teachers need to become "legally literate" with respect to their rights and responsibilities as professional educators (Fischer et al., 1999). Knowing their rights provides them with the authority to do what they know is right and just; knowing their responsibilities better enables them to serve their students effectively.

Becoming legally literate has another positive professional consequence. It will improve teaching. Teachers who understand rights guaranteed by the Constitution can help students understand how these rights apply to them and to their lives in and out of classrooms. Teachers can also help students understand their individual responsibilities. Finally, teachers who clearly understand issues involving freedom of speech, freedom of religion, freedom from unreasonable search and seizure, and due process are more likely to behave democratically in their classrooms.

■ SUMMARY

Laws, Ethics, and Professional Decision Making
Laws and professional ethics provide guidelines as teachers make professional decisions. Laws specify what teachers must and can do. Codes of ethics provide guidelines for what teachers should do as conscientious and caring professionals.

The U.S. Legal System
The U.S. legal system is a complex web of interconnected bodies. At the federal level, the U.S. Constitution provides broad guidelines for legal issues, and Congress passes laws that impact education. However, most of the direct legal responsibility for running schools belongs to states and local school districts.

Teachers' Rights and Responsibilities
Teachers have rights and responsibilities as professional educators. Licensure provides them with the right to teach; a teaching contract specifies the legal conditions for employment. Most new teachers are hired on probationary status. Once granted tenure, teachers cannot be dismissed without due process.

Teachers' academic freedom is guaranteed by the First Amendment to the Constitution. However, in deciding upon issues of academic freedom, the courts examine the educational relevance of the content or method involved as well as the age of students.

Copyright laws, designed to protect the property rights of authors, provide restrictions on teachers' use of published materials. New educational copyright issues are being raised by the increased use of videotape, television, and Internet technologies.

Liability poses unique challenges to teachers. The courts hold that teachers act *in loco parentis*, and when they fail to protect the children under their charge, they can be sued for negligence. When deciding on issues of liability, the courts take into account the age and developmental level of the student as well as the kinds of risks involved in an activity.

Teachers' private lives are not as private as some would wish. Because they are expected to be role models to students, what teachers do in the hours away from school is often scrutinized and, if illegal, can result in dismissal.

Religion and the Law
Religion provides a legal battleground in the schools. While banning organized prayer in schools, the courts have approved religious clubs and organizations as well as private

expressions of students' religious beliefs. While the courts disapprove of religious advocacy, teaching *about* religion is legal when it can be justified educationally.

Students' Rights and Responsibilities

Many of the same issues of rights involving freedom of speech and due process that affect teachers also pertain to students. In addition, students are protected from unreasonable search and seizure by the U.S. Constitution, and their education records are protected by federal legislation called the Buckley Amendment.

■ IMPORTANT CONCEPTS

academic freedom	ethics	negligence
affirmative action	fair-use guidelines	notoriety
Buckley Amendment	free exercise clause of the	professional ethics
copyright laws	First Amendment	reduction in force
establishment clause of the	*in loco parentis*	tenure
First Amendment		

■ DISCUSSION QUESTIONS

1. What are the advantages and disadvantages of teacher tenure? What arguments might there be for a longer period of probation before granting a teacher tenure? A shorter period? Should teachers be reviewed periodically after tenure is granted?

2. What is the proper role of religion in the schools? In what areas of the curriculum should religion enter? Should teachers reveal to students their religious beliefs? What should a teacher do if a student shares his or her religious beliefs with the class?

3. Touching can be a powerful way of expressing caring or concern. Should teachers touch their students? In what way and under what circumstances? How might your answer be influenced by the following factors: the age and gender of the students and the age and gender of the teacher?

4. What should be the place of corporal punishment in schools? How might the following factors influence your response: the age of the student, the type of misbehavior, and the age and gender of the teacher?

5. Should teachers' private lives be placed under more public scrutiny than other professionals' lives (such as doctors or lawyers)? Why?

■ GOING INTO SCHOOLS

1. Obtain a teacher's contract from a local school district or teacher. Explain how it deals with the following:
   a. probationary period before tenure
   b. tenure
   c. extra teacher responsibilities
   d. due process
   Compare your findings with information from the text.

2. Obtain a school or district's policy handbook. Explain how it deals with the following:
   a. student records and privacy
   b. student freedom of speech
   c. disciplinary guidelines and due process
   d. student lockers and searches for drugs and alcohol

In a paper, describe what you found and discuss the implications for you as a future teacher.

3. Interview a teacher about professional ethics.
   a. Does the teacher have a copy of either the NEA or AFT Code of Ethics? (If not, share the NEA Code of Ethics from Chapter 1.)
   b. How helpful are these guidelines in professional decision making?
   c. What changes would the teacher like to see made in these codes?

   Re-read the NEA Code of Ethics and using the teacher's comments as a sounding board, decide how helpful this code of ethics would be for a beginning teacher.

4. Interview a teacher about the district's policy in terms of reporting child abuse.
   a. Are the policy and procedures clear?
   b. Does the teacher know what his or her rights and responsibilities are in terms of reporting child abuse?
   c. Has the teacher ever had to report child abuse, and if so, what was the outcome?

   In a paper, describe what your responsibilities would be in reporting child abuse. Also, list any unanswered questions you might have about the process.

5. Interview several middle or high school students to find out about their knowledge of legal issues. Ask them what their rights and responsibilities are in terms of:
   a. freedom of speech
   b. student records and privacy
   c. search and seizure
   d. student rights in disciplinary actions.

   What do their responses tell you about their legal literacy? What could you do as a teacher to increase your level of legal literacy?

Virtual Field Experience

If you would like to participate in a Virtual Field Experience, go to the *Field Experience* Module in Chapter 7 of the Companion Website.

■ ONLINE PORTFOLIO ACTIVITIES

To complete these activities online, go to the *Portfolio Activities* Module in Chapter 7 of the Companion Website to submit your response.

Portfolio Activity 7.1   **School Law and Professional Ethics**

INTASC Principle 10: *Partnership*
Sometimes professional ethics are backed by the law, other times they are not. The purpose of this activity is to acquaint you with connections between the NEA Code of Ethics and legal issues. Reexamine Principle I, Commitment to the Student, in the NEA Code of Ethics in light of the content of this chapter, noting places where the professional ethics overlap with legal issues.

Portfolio Activity 7.2   **Deepening Your Knowledge of Legal Issues**

INTASC Principle 9: *Professional Commitment*
The purpose of this activity is to encourage you to deepen your understanding of one aspect of school law. Choose a topic from this chapter and research it further. (The book *Teachers and the Law*, (1999) by Fischer, et al., is an excellent source.) In a short paper, describe the issue you've chosen and the implications it might have for you as a teacher.

Teaching

CHAPTER

8

The School Curriculum

In your work as a teacher, you'll continually be faced with two questions: "What am I teaching?" and "Why am I teaching that?" These questions are so fundamental that we almost forget that a great deal of thought, decision making, and sometimes even controversy goes into answering them. The answers are critical because they determine the school curriculum—what we expect our students to learn.

Our purpose in writing this chapter is to examine the K–12 curriculum and help you understand your role in influencing what is taught as we try to answer the following questions:

What is curriculum, and how are curriculum and instruction related?

■ How does philosophy influence the curriculum?

■ How do state and local districts attempt to control the curriculum?

■ What is the relationship between textbooks and the curriculum?

■ How do professional organizations influence the curriculum?

■ What kinds of controversies exist in the curriculum?

Case
STUDY

Suzanne Brush, a second-grade teacher at Webster Elementary School, has her students involved in a unit on graphing. After getting her students settled down for math, she began, "I'm planning a party for our class. While I was doing that, a question came to my mind that I thought maybe you could help me solve today. I need to know how I can figure out the class's favorite kind of jelly bean. How could we find out? If you can help me out, raise your hand."

Several students offered suggestions and, after considerable discussion, they finally settled on giving each student several jelly beans and having them indicate which one was their favorite.

"It just so happens," Suzanne smiled, as they decided on the idea, "that I did bring in some jelly beans today, and you'll be able to taste these jelly beans and vote for your favorite flavor."

She then handed out a baggy with seven different-flavored jelly beans in it to each student.

"Okay," she started when everyone was done tasting. "Right now I need your help. . . . Raise your hand, please, if you can tell me what we can do now that we have this information. How can we organize it so that we can look at it as a whole group? Jacinta?"

"See how many people like the same one, and see how many people like other ones," Jacinta responded.

"Okay, can you add to that? . . . Josh?"

"You can write their names down and see how many . . . like black," Josh answered uncertainly.

"That was right in line with what Jacinta said," Suzanne smiled and nodded. "Here's what we're going to do. We have an empty graph up in the front of the room," she continued, moving to the front of the room and displaying the outline of a graph that appeared as follows:

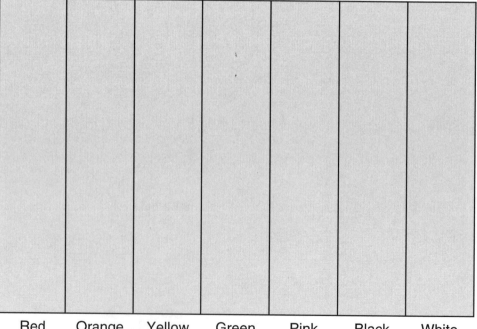

Most Popular Jelly Bean

| Red | Orange | Yellow | Green | Pink | Black | White |

"Yes, Justin," she nodded in response to his raised hand.

"See which ones like red, get the people that like red and write it down; get all the colors like yellow, green, orange, black, yellow, white," he suggested haltingly; Suzanne carefully monitored the attention of the rest of the students while Justin made his suggestion.

"That's a great idea. We're going to do that," Suzanne responded, explaining that she had a series of cut-out cardboard squares that matched the jelly bean colors for the graph. She directed individual students to come to the front of the room and paste the color of square that represented their favorite color on the graph. After all the groups were done, the graph appeared as follows:

Most Popular Jelly Bean

| Red | Orange | Yellow | Green | Pink | Black | White |

"I need your attention back up here, please," she continued. "We collected the information and organized the information up here on the graph. Now we need to study and analyze the information. I need you to tell me what we know by looking at this graph. Candice, what do we know?" she asked, walking toward the middle of the room.

"People like green," Candice answered.

"Candice said most people like the green jelly beans. . . . Candice, how many people like green?"

"Nine."

"Nine people like green. . . . And how did you find that out? Can you go up there and show us how you read the graph?"

Candice went up to the graph and moved her hand up from the bottom, counting the green squares as she went.

"What else do we know by just looking at the graph? . . . Justin?"

"There are three people that like black and three people that like white."

"Three people like black and three people like white," Suzanne repeated, pointing to the black and white columns on the graph. "Let's let Stacey add some more to that."

"No one liked yellow," Stacey answered.

"Nobody picked yellow," Suzanne repeated.

"Okay, what else do we know from looking at the bar graph? . . . Andrew?"

"One took orange."

"Only one person picked orange," Suzanne repeated.

"And one person picked pink. . . . Okay, here we go. . . . How many more people liked green than red?" she asked, changing the direction of the questioning. "How many more people liked the green jelly beans than the red? Look up at the graph. Try to find the information, set up the problem, and then we'll see what you come out with. You have to have a problem set up on your paper."

Suzanne watched as the students looked at the graph and began setting up the problem. She commented, "Quite a few hands, and a few people are still thinking," as she moved across the room. She stopped briefly to offer Carlos some help, continued watching the students as they finished, and then said, "I'm looking for a volunteer to share an answer with us. . . . Dominique? How many more people liked the green jelly beans than the red ones?"

"Nine plus 5 is 14," Dominique answered.

"Dominique says 9 plus 5 is 14. Let's test it out," Suzanne said, asking Dominique to go up to the graph and show the class how she arrived at her answer.

As Dominique went to the front of the room, Suzanne said, "We want to know the difference. . . . How many more people liked green than red, and you say 14 people, . . . 14 more people liked green. Does that work?" Suzanne asked, pointing at the graph.

Dominique looked at the graph for a moment, shrugged her shoulders, grinned sheepishly, and then said, "I mean 9 take away 5."

"She got up here and she changed her mind," Suzanne said with a smile after Dominique responded. "Tell them."

"Nine take away 5 is 4," Dominique said.

"Nine take away 5 is 4," Suzanne continued, "so how many more people liked green than red? . . . Carlos?"

"Four," Carlos responded.

"Four, good, four," Suzanna smiled warmly. "The key was you had to find the difference between the two numbers."

After several more similar problems, she said, "I have one more question, and then we'll switch gears a little bit. How many people participated in this voting? How many people took part or participated in this voting?"

Suzanne watched as the students turned to the graph. "Matt? How many people?" she said as she saw that students were finished and several had their hands raised.

"Twenty-four," Matt answered.

"Twenty-four," Suzanne repeated. "How many people are in the room right now?"

"Uhmm, 24," he answered.

"Is that where you got your answer?" she asked, leaning over him and touching his shoulders. "What was the problem you set up?"

"How many people voted," he answered.

"Matt said 24. Did anyone get a different answer? So we'll compare. . . . I can't call on you if you're jumping up and down," she said as she walked among the students, who were waving their hands energetically.

"Roberto?"

"Twenty-two."

"How many people got 22 for their answer?"

A number of hands went up, and Suzanne asked, "How many people got a different number?" A few students raised their hands.

"How did you solve the problem?" she asked, walking past the table and motioning to Robert. "That's the most important thing."

"Nine plus 5 plus 3 plus 3 plus 1 plus 1 equals 22," he answered quickly.

"Where'd you get all those numbers?"

"There," he said, pointing to the graph.

"He went from the highest to the lowest, added the numbers, and the answer was 22. . . . Matt, why isn't it 24?" Suzanne asked, walking back toward him, smiling.

There's no reply from Matt.

"Raise your hand if you didn't put a square up there," she directed the class, and two students who didn't participate raised their hands. Suzanne explained why the answer wasn't 24.

As time for lunch neared, Suzanne said, "Raise your hand if you can tell me what you learned this morning in math."

"How to bar graph," Jenny responded.

"How to bar graph," Suzanne repeated. "More important, when we set up a problem, what do we have to do to solve the problem. . . . Timmy?"

"Add or subtract."

"Okay, but what do we have to decide *before* we add or subtract?"

"The numbers."

"So, we have to collect the information, and then we have to organize it. We organized it by setting up a bar graph, something that we can look at and talk about and use to decide what we need to do with the information. Then we set up some problems, and we solved them. It's a nice way to look at information and make decisions about certain things," she said as she ended the lesson.

■ ■ ■

■ WHAT IS CURRICULUM?

 To begin this section, let's look back at Suzanne's lesson. She wanted her students to understand that information can be simplified and made more usable by representing it in a graph. She also had her students practice basic arithmetic skills and problem solving by asking questions such as "How many more people liked the green jelly beans than the red?" and then having the students create similar problems.

Suzanne's lesson reflects decisions about both curriculum and instruction. Let's see how they relate to each other.

The Relationship between Curriculum and Instruction

Curriculum has different definitions, ranging from descriptions such as "all the educational experiences students have in school" to "the results of decisions about what content should be taught and what learning experiences students should have." Definitions of curriculum and instruction often overlap, and in some cases curriculum appears to subsume instruction. We will avoid these issues and simply define **curriculum** as *what students learn in school* and **instruction** as *the way they learn the curriculum or the ways in which it is taught.*

Curriculum focuses on learning goals and the reasons the goals have been selected; instruction is the way teachers help students reach the goals. For example, Suzanne wanted her second graders to understand that graphs help us represent information; that goal indicated a curriculum decision. To reach the goal, she had her students sample a variety of jelly beans, pick their favorite flavor, and represent their preferences on a large graph; that method reflected a decision about instruction. Another option would have been for Suzanne simply to explain why graphs are valuable, give her students some information, and then have them graph it. (We examine instruction and learning in detail in Chapter 9.)

The Explicit Curriculum

The school curriculum exists in three parts. The first is the explicit curriculum, which is the curriculum found in textbooks, curriculum guides, courses of study, field trips, and other formal educational experiences (Vallance, 1995); Suzanne's lesson on graphing was part of it. The **explicit curriculum** *includes what teachers are expected to teach, what learners are expected to learn, and what schools are held accountable for.* The explicit curriculum at the elementary level is heavily influenced by language arts and math, as we'll see in the next section.

Curriculum in Elementary Schools To begin this section, let's look again at Sharon and Susie's schedules, which you first saw in Chapter 6. As you may recall from that chapter, Sharon is a first-grade teacher and Susie teaches third grade. Their schedules appear in Table 8.1.

We saw in Chapter 6 that both teachers are responsible for all the content areas, such as language arts, math, and science, and the amount of time each teacher devotes to different content areas is a personal decision.

The way elementary schools are organized has an important influence on the curriculum. To see how, take another look at the schedules. Remembering that we're now focusing on what is taught—the curriculum. What do you notice? Some similarities and differences include the following:

- Both teachers strongly emphasize language arts and math. In a 6-hour instructional day (subtracting the half hour for lunch in each case), Sharon devotes 1 hour and 45 minutes to language arts, and Susie spends a minimum of 1 hour and 5 minutes on this subject.

Table 8.1 **Two Elementary Teachers' Schedules**

Sharon's First-Grade Schedule		Susie's Third-Grade Schedule	
8:30 A.M.	School begins	8:30 A.M.	School begins
8:30–8:45	Morning announcements	8:30–9:15	Independent work (practice previous day's language arts and math)
8:45–10:30	Language arts (including reading and writing)		
10:30–11:20	Math	9:15–10:20	Language arts (including reading and writing)
11:20–11:50	Lunch		
11:50–12:20	Read story	10:20–10:45	Snack/independent reading
12:20–1:15	Center time (practice on language arts and math)	10:45–11:15	P.E.
		11:15–12:15	Language arts/social studies/science
1:15–1:45	P.E.		
1:45–2:30	Social studies/science	12:15–12:45	Lunch
2:30–2:45	Class meeting	12:45–2:00	Math
2:45–3:00	Call buses/dismissal	2:00–2:30	Spelling/catch up on material not covered earlier
		2:30–2:45	Read story
		2:45–3:00	Clean up; prepare for dismissal

The elementary curriculum is heavily influenced by language arts and reading.

Increasing Understanding 8.2

 How much time does each teacher devote to math? What do these allocations suggest about the relative importance of language arts compared to math?

■ Science and social studies receive limited emphasis.

■ Art and music don't appear in the schedules; neither do computers, in spite of today's emphasis on technology.

Both teachers reported that they have computers in their classrooms and that their students take turns working with them. Art and music are handled by resource teachers who come into the classrooms on a rotating basis.

Both teachers also reported that when science and social studies are taught, they are usually integrated with language arts; they are seldom taught independently. This is typical of elementary classrooms (S. Mittelstadt, personal communication, January 22, 1999; S. Van Horn, personal communication, January 21, 1999).

If you observe in elementary classrooms, you're likely to see schedules that vary somewhat from the ones in Table 8.1. However, the emphasis on language arts and math and the de-emphasis on science, social studies, and the arts is likely to be similar.

Increasing Understanding 8.3

Think again about "block" scheduling, which you first studied in Chapter 2. (An example of this would be having classes meet for 90–100 minutes a day for half of the school year.) Identify at least two ways in which block scheduling might influence the curriculum.

Curriculum in Middle and Secondary Schools We also saw in Chapter 6 that middle and secondary schools are organized so that the curriculum is much more structured than it is in the elementary schools. When you were in high school, you passed from class to class based on a bell schedule, and periods were commonly 50 or 55 minutes long. When schoolwide activities were held (such as a pep rally before an athletic event), periods were shortened.

As with elementary schools, the organization of middle and secondary schools has important influences on the curriculum. For example, Chris Lucio, the junior high teacher we featured in Chapter 6, teaches *only* geography. Also, all of his periods are the same length—50 minutes. As a result, in a given year geography receives the same curricular emphasis as does language arts (English), math, and all the other content areas. This would not hold true over the course of several years, as geography has to compete with other social studies subjects such as history, government, and economics.

Integrated Curriculum Think again about a typical school. A middle school seventh grader might have geography from 9:20–10:10, English from 10:15–11:05, and so on through the rest of the day. Critics argue that compartmentalizing the curriculum in this way detracts from learning, because teaching and learning bear little resemblance to the world outside of school. Instead, they argue, schools should consider using an **integrated curriculum** in which *concepts and skills across disciplines are combined and related* (Carter & Mason, 1997). As we saw in Table 8.1, both Sharon and Susie integrated science and social studies topics with language arts; different forms of integration occur informally in many elementary classrooms. For example, teachers might have students read about a science topic and then have them conduct an experiment related to the topic or interview someone who has expertise in the area. As a culminating activity, teachers might have students write about the topic. These activities integrate science with language arts.

In middle and secondary schools, some efforts have been made to formally integrate social studies and English, math and science, or different science content areas. For example, in middle schools, students typically take general science in sixth grade, life science in seventh grade, and physical science in eighth grade. Efforts have been made to integrate these content areas so that students will study related topics from earth, life, and physical science in each of the middle school years. For example, using energy as a focal point, students might study the sun as an energy source in earth science, food as a source of energy in life science, and nuclear power in physical science.

One study at the high school level examined the effects of integrating geometry and art. Teachers integrated these two areas through a unit that culminated in constructing greeting cards that contained elements of both (Schramm, 1997). Comments from students attest to the motivational benefits of interconnected topics: "Geometry has become real to me, not just a subject in school," and "I took geometry but had a hard time understanding. Now I see how the Pythagorean theorem relates to a three-dimensional work of art" (Schramm, 1997, p. 7).

Integrating the curriculum, while intuitively sensible, is controversial. Proponents make the following arguments:

- Integrating curriculum increases the relevance of content by making connections among ideas explicit (Barab & Landa, 1997; Diem, 1996).
- Integrating curriculum improves achievement (Furtado, 1997). Because integrating curriculum is a common feature of block scheduling, it leads to fewer transitions, leaving more time available for instruction (Furtado, 1997).
- Integrating curriculum promotes collaborative planning, which increases communication among teachers (Haschak, 1992).

Opponents of curriculum integration counter with the following arguments:

- Integrating curriculum results in a de-emphasis on some important concepts, since teachers don't have a deep understanding of all the content areas that are to be integrated (Carter, 1997; Roth, 1994).
- Planning and instruction for integrating curriculum are inordinately time consuming (Brophy & Alleman, 1991; Beane, 1997).

Integrated curriculum is most popular at the elementary level, where a single teacher can relate several topics, and at the middle school level, where teams of teachers periodically meet to interconnect content areas. It is least common at the high school level, where a disciplinary approach to curriculum is entrenched. National standards driven by

Curriculum integration, which attempts to connect . separate content areas, is most popular at the elementary level.

subject matter areas, as well as increased emphasis on testing, are likely to encourage this trend at the high school level.

Is there evidence that integrating curriculum increases learning? At present, the answer is mixed, with some research finding positive results. One study found that elementary teachers who integrated reading with science or social studies produced greater reading comprehension in their students (Portner, 2000C). Experts explained the results in terms of students being more motivated to read about interesting topics like pirates and motorboats. However, other research is mixed, finding either no benefits or negative results (Carter & Mason, 1997; Senftleber & Eggen, 1999). Advocates of curriculum integration counter this negative evidence by arguing that the measures presently available are inadequate, unable to assess the "subtle and difficult-to-measure improvements in student learning" (Vars, 1996, p. 151). The debate is likely to continue.

The Implicit Curriculum

A second dimension of the school curriculum, which *represents its unstated and sometimes unintended aspects*, is called the **implicit curriculum** (Eisner, 1985), "hidden curriculum" (Jackson, 1990), or informal curriculum (McCaslin & Good, 1996). It is reflected in the ways teachers present their content, the kinds of routines that are established, the general climate of the classroom, and unstated values and priorities that shape the school day.

A great deal of learning takes place through the implicit curriculum. As an example, let's look at some of the dialogue in Suzanne's lesson.

> *Suzanne:* How many more people liked the green jelly beans than the red? Look up at the graph. Try to find the information, set up the problem, and then we'll see what you come out with. (She stops briefly to offer Carlos some help). . . . I'm looking for a volunteer to share an answer with us. . . . Dominique?"
>
> *Dominique:* Nine plus 5 is 14.

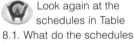

Increasing Understanding 8.4

 Look again at the schedules in Table 8.1. What do the schedules indicate about each teacher's priorities? Explain.

Suzanne: Dominique says 9 plus 5 is 14. Let's test it out. (She asks Dominique to go up to the graph and show the class how she arrived at her answer.). . . We want to know the difference. . . . How many more people liked green than red, and you say 14 people, . . . 14 more people liked green. Does that work?

Dominique: (Looking at the graph) I mean 9 take away 5.

Suzanne: She got up here and she changed her mind (smiling). Tell them.

Dominique: Nine take away 5 is 4.

Suzanne: Nine take away 5 is 4. So how many more people liked green than red? . . . Carlos?

We said earlier that curriculum is what students learn in school. What did Suzanne's students learn in this brief episode? Hopefully, they learned several things. They learned that math is supposed to be more than simply memorizing basic facts; they learned that making a mistake is a normal part of the learning process; and they learned that learning is much more than sitting quietly as a teacher talks. These are powerful messages of the implicit curriculum.

In many ways the implicit curriculum is as important as the explicit curriculum. For instance, expert teachers create orderly classrooms in which learners accept responsibility for their own behavior (DeVries & Zan, 1995; Kohn, 1996), and these teachers invite all students to participate in lessons (Kerman, 1979; McDougall & Granby, 1996). In these classrooms, students learn that the world is an orderly place and that they are responsible for keeping it so. They also learn that all students are welcome and expected to participate and learn. These messages reflect the implicit curriculum and are important parts of students' total learning experience.

Sometimes the implicit and explicit curriculum conflict. For example, research indicates that students who have independent and questioning minds, who are assertive, who challenge authority, and who insist on explanations are sometimes rejected by teachers (Kedar-Voivodas, 1983). This results in a clash between the explicit curriculum, which focuses on learning and mastery of content, and the implicit curriculum, which rewards docile students and conformity (Apple, 1995). What do students learn when they're expected to listen passively as teachers lecture, or if competition for grades is emphasized? They may learn that "playing the game" and "beating the system" are more important than hard work and mastery of content. These are not messages we want schools to send.

Extracurriculum A third component of the curriculum, commonly called the **extracurriculum,** *includes learning experiences that extend beyond the core of students' formal studies.* Virtually everyone has a concept of extracurriculum; it includes clubs, sports, school plays, and other activities that don't earn academic credit.

While outside the explicit curriculum, extracurricular activities are an important part of students' learning experiences. Research indicates that a well-developed extracurricular program is part of an effective school. Students who participate in extracurricular activities tend to be more motivated and get higher grades than those who don't (Coladarcci & Cobb, 1995; Holland & Andre, 1987). Unfortunately, marginal students and students placed at-risk often don't participate in extracurricular activities, which increases feelings of alienation and not belonging in school (Barr & Parrett, 2001; Manning & Baruth, 1995).

Sports exert a powerful positive influence on students, especially minority students. Research shows that participation in sports can reduce behavior problems and increase positive attitudes toward school (Jordon & Brooks, 2000; Sokol-Katz & Braddock, 2000). A comprehensive study of the effects of participation in sports on women found that girls

Increasing Understanding 8.5

Explain why it is important for teachers to be aware that the implicit curriculum exists. Provide an example to illustrate your answer.

Increasing Understanding 8.6

A student participates in a high school jazz band. Under what conditions would this be part of the explicit curriculum? Part of the extracurriculum? Explain your answer.

Extracurricular activities provide valuable learning opportunities for both students and teachers.

who engaged in sports had lower pregnancy rates, were less likely to be sexually active, and had fewer sexual partners (Sabo et al., 1998). Experts explained the results in this way: "Sports might . . . help girls cut loose from the conventional form of femininity that encourage them to establish self-worth mainly in terms of sexuality and heterosexual appeal" (Sabo et al., 1998, p. 22).

Students' desire—or even willingness—to come to school, their need to be part of groups, and their beliefs in their ability to succeed can be strongly influenced by their participation in extracurricular activities like sports. Educators looking for ways to help students develop in healthy ways in this sometimes confusing world might look more closely at extracurricular activities, including athletics, for answers.

Extracurricular activities also offer valuable opportunities for professional growth for the beginning teacher. Sponsoring clubs and coaching teams can provide you with extra pay as well as opportunities to interact with your fellow teachers in different and personal ways. In addition, working with students in these activities can be emotionally rewarding and can provide you with valuable insights into students' personalities and lives. Both of the authors coached sports while teaching in public schools and found the experience time consuming but rewarding. We were able to get to know students in ways not possible in the regular classroom.

■ FORCES THAT INFLUENCE THE CURRICULUM

To this point we've examined the curriculum as it commonly exists. But how does it come to be that way? Why do we see the emphasis on language arts and math that appear in many elementary school schedules? Why are subjects like music and art de-emphasized? Answers to questions such as these can be found in the different forces that influence the curriculum. They are outlined in Figure 8.1 and discussed in this section.

Figure 8.1

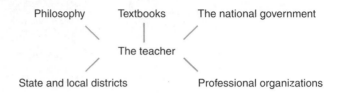

Figure 8.1   Forces Influencing Curriculum

Curriculum and the Professional Teacher

As we've emphasized throughout the book, you're taking this course to introduce you to the world of teaching and to help you understand your crucial role in promoting student learning.

In Chapter 1, we said that professionals are people who use their knowledge and understanding to make decisions in complex and often ill-defined situations. Nowhere will professionalism be more important than in designing the curriculum. While a number of factors influence what is taught and learned, you, the teacher, are at the center of the process (which is why *the teacher* is at the center of Figure 8.1).

We see this illustrated in Suzanne's, Sharon's, and Susie's work. Suzanne emphasized graphing as part of her math curriculum and made a special effort to link the content to students' experiences with a hands-on activity. Because she believes that her students benefit from additional experiences with language, Susie allocates 1 hour and 5 minutes to language arts in the morning, and sometimes teaches additional language arts from 11:15–12:15.

These decisions are the teachers'. No one specifically told Suzanne how much emphasis to place on graphing in her math class. She could have de-emphasized it or even ignored it completely. Also, if Susie chooses to teach science on Monday from 11:15 to 12:15 and additional language arts on Tuesday during the same time, it is her decision—and hers alone—based on her understanding of the content, her students' needs, and her goals. These are professional decisions that only teachers can make.

Middle and secondary teachers have only slightly less autonomy than elementary teachers have. For example, a beginning algebra teacher might choose to spend a great deal of time on basic skills, such as solving problems like $x + 2x + 3x = 24$, or she might choose to emphasize word problems such as:

■ ■ ■

Greg has some coins in his pocket, Sally has twice as many as Greg, and Juanita has three times as many as Greg. They have 24 coins altogether. How many does each student have?

■ ■ ■

Again, these are professional decisions based on knowledge and understanding—understanding of algebra, understanding how to represent it so students can understand it, and understanding what students need and how they learn. One geography teacher might focus on geography and culture, whereas another might emphasize climate and physical features, such as mountains, rivers, and plains. Similar curricular decisions are made in all the content areas every day.

We've said before that teachers are "alone" as professionals when they shut their classroom doors. Closing the door is symbolic, representing teachers' professional control over what is taught in their classrooms and how it is taught. But external forces, some subtle, others not so subtle, creep into classrooms and influence teachers' curricular decisions. Let's examine some of them.

Increasing Understanding 8.7

Teachers who feel strongly that basic skills are a crucial part of the curriculum are basing their decision most nearly on what educational philosophy? Explain.

**Increasing
Understanding 8.8**

Are decisions about curriculum made at the national level, such as by the federal government, or by states and local districts? Why? (Hint: Think about your study of the history of the American educational system in Chapter 5.)

Philosophical Foundations: Sources of Curriculum

We said earlier that curriculum reflects goals and the reasons for teaching them. Because time doesn't allow all possible goals to be taught, decisions have to be made about priorities. For instance, of the following goals, which would you consider to be most important?

- To acquire a thorough understanding of traditional content, such as literature, science, history, and advanced mathematics.
- To develop basic skills such as the ability to read fluently, write effectively, and complete mathematical tasks.
- To develop workplace skills, such as the ability to work with others and solve problems.
- To develop self-esteem and the motivation to be involved in learning for its own sake.

Answers to this question vary and can be controversial. Some educators suggest that the last goal is most important, arguing that intrinsically motivated people will adapt and acquire the skills needed to function effectively in a rapidly changing world. The development of the individual is preeminent in their view. Others favor the third goal, suggesting that society needs people who can solve problems and function well in groups. Still others advocate the first or second goals, asserting that academic skills, knowledge, and understanding are the keys to expertise and the ability to solve today's complex problems.

As we think back to Chapter 5, we see that these arguments come from different philosophical positions, which reflect varying degrees of emphasis on the needs of individuals, our society, or the academic disciplines. In addition, each of these positions also has both strengths and weaknesses, as outlined in Table 8.2.

Many of today's curriculum controversies are rooted in these different philosophical positions. For example, the reform movement has resulted from widespread complaints about young people entering the workforce without the content background, problem-solving abilities, and decision-making skills needed to function effectively in a technological world. Reformers are making an essentialist argument; they're saying that workers lack the basic skills needed to function effectively in today's society.

We see this essentialist position in Sharon and Susie's work with their students. Their schedules reflect their emphasis on language arts, reading, and math, which are all basic skills.

**Increasing
Understanding 8.9**

The emphasis on children's needs is most nearly based on which educational philosophy? Explain.

While essentialism is prominent, the needs of individuals occupy an important place in schools as well. This emphasis is controversial, with critics arguing that the development of self-esteem has lowered standards and decreased achievement (Pintrich & Schunk, 1996). Advocates counter that a major goal of schools should be to give students self-confidence about their ability to learn and that students can't learn if they dislike themselves and the content they're learning.

As a teacher, you will need to think about the students you are teaching, the content, and the time and resources that are available. Based on your understanding of these factors, you then will develop your own philosophy of curriculum. This is not an easy task, but every teacher faces these decisions. Consciously recognizing the task ahead is an important first step in the long professional journey of creating a productive and defensible curriculum for your students.

Having seen how philosophy influences priorities, let's look at some other forces that impact curriculum decisions.

Textbooks

You're a beginning teacher, and you're thinking about what you will teach during the next week. Where will you turn for help? If you're a typical first-year teacher, you will

Table 8.2	**Philosophical Foundations of Curriculum**			
Basis for Curriculum	**Dominant Educational Philosophy**	**Advantages**	**Disadvantages**
Needs of individuals	Progressivism	■ Concern for individuals is placed at the heart of curriculum development. ■ Learner motivation is promoted.	■ Efforts to respond to the special needs of each individual are virtually impossible. ■ Students may not be the best judges of their long-range needs, opting for shallow learning experiences.
Needs of society	Progressivism	■ Students learn to integrate information from a variety of sources. ■ Curriculum is relevant, contributing to learner motivation.	■ Society's needs change rapidly, often making curriculum obsolete. ■ Learners may be steered into career choices too early, limiting long-range opportunities.
Academic disciplines	Essentialism Perennialism	■ Research indicates that expertise and problem-solving ability depend on knowledge.* ■ Schools and teachers are being held accountable, and accountability depends on discipline- based tests.	■ Academic disciplines tend to artificially "compartmentalize" what students learn. ■ Students complain that traditional subjects are irrelevant.

Source: *Bruning, Shraw, & Ronning (1999) *Cognitive Psychology & Instruction* (3rd ed), Upper Saddle River, NJ: Prentice Hall.

Increasing Understanding 8.10

How are educational philosophies reflected in textbooks? For example, what would you expect to see in a math textbook based on essentialism? A math textbook based on progressivism? Explain in each case.

reach for a textbook, the book you'll be using for the content area you're teaching (Bullough, 1989).

For better or worse, textbooks are a fact of teaching life. Research indicates that teachers depend heavily on them; in grades K–8, texts in some form were involved in instruction 95 percent of the time and influenced 90 percent of homework assignments (Venezky, 1992). In some of your university teacher-education classes, you may be encouraged to set textbooks aside or at least not depend heavily on them. If your behavior is consistent with patterns identified by research, you're unlikely to do so (Zahorik, 1991). Some experts believe that textbooks are the most powerful influence on all curriculum decisions (Morrison, 1993).

While textbooks will strongly influence your curriculum decisions, you shouldn't depend on them completely. The following are some reasons why.

■ Needs. The topics presented in textbooks may not be consistent with the specific needs of your students, school, or district. Following a textbook too closely then fails to meet these needs as effectively as possible.

■ Scope. To appeal to a wide market, textbook publishers include a huge number of topics, more than you can possibly teach in the time available. Therefore, you will need

Despite questions about quality, textbooks exert a powerful influence on the curriculum.

to be selective in the topics you teach. Curriculum experts advise, "Schools [and teachers] should pick out the most important concepts and skills to emphasize so that they can concentrate on the quality of understanding rather than on the quantity of information presented" (Rutherford & Algren, 1990, p. 185).

■ Quality. Textbooks are sometimes poorly written, lack adequate examples, or even contain errors of fact. One study of history textbooks found that "Content is thinner and thinner, and what there is, is increasingly deformed by identity politics and group pieties" (Sewall, 2000). One analysis of middle school science texts concluded, "It's a credit to science teachers that their students are learning anything at all" (Bradley, 1999c, p. 5). Similar problems have been found in other areas (Manzo, 2000a). Following a textbook too closely can then lead to shallow understanding or even faulty ideas that detract from learning.

To access up-to-date information about textbook quality, go to the *Web Links* module in Chapter 8 of the Companion Website.

What does this information mean for you as a teacher? As we began this section of the chapter, we said that nowhere in teaching is professionalism more important than in making curriculum decisions. This is particularly true regarding textbooks. It's easy to allow textbooks to make professional decisions for you, such as teaching the next chapter because it's there; unfortunately, this is what many teachers do.

Textbooks can be a valuable resource, and they will certainly influence your curriculum decisions. However, don't be afraid to de-emphasize, or even eliminate, topics and chapters in the text, and include other topics that aren't in it. Curriculum decision making such as this requires understanding, effort, and energy. Teachers report that the process of personal curriculum construction can be one of the most creative and satisfying aspects of teaching (Clandinin & Connelly, 1996).

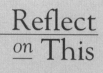

Reflect _on_ This

TEACHING BASIC SKILLS USING PERSONAL EXPERIENCES

You're a first-year, seventh-grade English teacher in an inner-city middle school. Many of the students have difficulty with grammar and standard English in their speech, and spelling is a major problem. Because of this, the school leadership is strongly emphasizing basic skills, such as the ability to spell, punctuate sentences correctly, and use appropriate grammar. The book you're using has a large number of exercises in it, such as the following:

Rewrite the following sentences so that they are capitalized and punctuated correctly.

1. joanne a student in mrs. andersons class said to leroy another of mrs. andersons students would you help me decorate the gym for the dance

Additional exercises focus on using correct grammar.

Your students hate the exercises, and, in some cases, leave entire assignments undone. Frustrated, you decide to abandon the text; instead, you have the students simply write about some of their own personal experiences. They will work on their basic skills by revising and correcting their own writing. Although they are not necessarily enthusiastic, the students are more willing to write, and you're beginning to see some slow improvement.

Your department head overhears a faculty lounge conversation in which you describe what you're doing. "I'm not sure that's a good idea," she comments. "The district is committed to our kids knowing and being able to use basic skills. That's why we're using this book, and it's in our curriculum guides."

"But the kids hate it, and some of them won't try," you protest uneasily.

"Your job is to get them to try," she responds. "That's what we're here for. We're accountable for the kids knowing this stuff."

1. Why do you suppose the students so intensely dislike the book's exercises?
2. Is being able to write using correct grammar and spelling an important goal?
3. In one approach to learning to write, students master basic skills and then use the skills when they write. An alternative is to have students simply write and then develop the basic skills using the writing. Which is the better approach? Why do you think so?
4. What would you do in the situation just described?

To respond to these questions online and receive immediate feedback, go to the Reflect on This Module in Chapter 8 of the Companion Website.

State and Local Districts

We've emphasized that you, the teacher, impact the curriculum more than any other factor, and we've also illustrated how textbooks can affect your decisions. In addition, the state and district in which you teach will influence what is taught.

As we saw in Chapter 8, education is governed at both the state and local level, and the effects of these influences vary from state to state. However, some patterns exist. Let's look at them.

Curriculum Guides Every state publishes curriculum guides to assist teachers in their curricular planning. Often these appear in the form of objectives that students are expected to meet, and these objectives are sequenced by grade level. In addition, districts will sometimes publish their own curriculum guides to augment those published by the state.

**Increasing
Understanding 8.11**

You are required by
your principal to fol-
low state curriculum guides.
You find some factual errors
in one of the sections. As a
professional teacher, what
should you do? Explain.

These curriculum guides are one of the first things that teachers pick up as they plan; teachers are often pressured by their principals to follow them closely (Cuban, 1996). We offer the same recommendations and cautions with these guides as we did with textbooks. Use them thoughtfully and selectively to create a curriculum that makes sense to you and your students. Sometimes, however, it is difficult to resist pressures from curriculum guides because of the powerful influence of testing (Kohn, 2000).

Testing   As you begin this section, you might wonder, What does testing have to do with curriculum? A great deal. An important way that states and districts influence what is taught is through the tests they give. One elementary teacher, reassigned to a different grade level, found out about her new curriculum in this way:

■ ■ ■

When I came up to fifth grade, I really didn't know everything that would be covered in the fifth grade, so one of the teachers said, "Well, this skill will be on the achievement test, and you'll find this on the achievement test, and you'll find this on the test." And I know to teach my children survival skills that I had to teach those. Let's just face it, that's just the way it is. You know, I tell them, "This may be on the achievement test and this is something that I really want to stick" (Brown, 1991, pp. 102–103).

■ ■ ■

Tests provide concrete guidelines about what should be taught, and principals and other teachers often pressure teachers to "cover" all of the knowledge and skills that will be tested sometime during the year.

As we saw earlier in the chapter, reading, writing, and math are strongly emphasized in the elementary curriculum. One reason for this is the fact that they are the content areas for which students are most commonly held accountable; they are the most frequently tested. "What gets tested, gets taught" is a common maxim in education (Cuban, 1996).

As enthusiasm for accountability has increased around the country, all but two states have adopted statewide testing systems (Olson, 1999c). It is extremely likely that the curriculum in your school will be influenced by a standardized test developed or adopted at the state or local level. As a beginning teacher, you need to be aware of the different kinds of tests your students will be required to take. Armed with this information, you can make wise professional decisions about what curriculum is best for your students.

Outcomes-based education.   An additional way that states and districts attempt to influence curriculum is by specifying and testing for specific objectives. **Outcomes-based education (OBE)** *attempts to describe curriculum in terms of objectives or results.* OBE attempts to go beyond the listing of topics to be learned by specifying specific outcomes for a course of study. OBE tries to "put teeth" in these outcomes by testing whether students have attained these goals.

Proponents claim that OBE makes sense; if we want students to attain certain knowledge or skills, we should specify exactly what these are, teach them, and test for them (Manno, 1995). Critics contend that many of the most important skills (like critical thinking or communicating with others) can't be specified in behavioral terms and trying to do so promotes minimal academic standards and "dumbing down" the curriculum.

Graduation Requirements   Another way that states and districts influence curriculum is through graduation requirements. In Chapter 5 we saw that the influential report *A Nation At Risk* (National Commission on Excellence in Education, 1983) attempted to place greater emphasis on academics by calling for more rigorous graduation requirements. Many districts have followed suit by increasing the number of academic courses required for graduation.

Testing, a central component of current reform efforts, exerts a powerful influence on the curriculum, or what is taught.

Increasing Understanding 8.12

A Nation At Risk is most closely related to which educational philosophy: perennialism, progressivism, essentialism, or postmodernism? Explain.

Many states now require 4 years of English and 3 years of math in high school, with similar increases in science and social studies. Critics decry the over-emphasis on certain "basic" subjects at the expense of others like art and music, but the trend is likely to continue.

The National Government

As we saw in Chapter 5, control of education in America was formally removed from the federal government and handed to the states by the Tenth Amendment to the Constitution. However, the federal government has a long and rich history of involvement in education, a role that has increased rather than decreased over time. The federal government's role in curriculum dramatically increased in the 1950s when people began to see education and the curriculum as major vehicles to accomplish national goals. Beginning in the mid-20th century, Table 8.3 outlines some of the major pieces of legislation that are still influencing today's curriculum.

As we can see from Table 8.3, the federal government influences the curriculum in various ways. For example, when you begin your teaching career, you will almost certainly have some students with exceptionalities in your classes; examples include students who have difficulty in reading or children with emotional disabilities. Their presence in your classroom is the result of the Individuals with Disabilities Education Act (IDEA), legislation passed in 1975 requiring that these students have access to the regular curriculum. The National Defense Education Act (passed in 1958) resulted in much greater emphasis on math, science, and foreign languages, particularly in high schools. While varying somewhat over the years, this emphasis still exists today, and well-qualified math, science, and foreign language teachers continue to be in high demand.

Increasing Understanding 8.13

Would you predict that jobs for teachers of students with exceptionalities are more or less plentiful than they were before IDEA was passed? Explain.

Goals 2000: National Educational Goals One of the more prominent federal government initiatives in the 1990s was the Educate America Act, which resulted in Goals

Table 8.3	**The Federal Government's Influence on Curriculum**		
Act	Date	Impact on Curriculum	
National Defense Education Act	1958	Made math, science, and foreign language high curriculum priorities.	
Economic Opportunity Act	1964	Increased emphasis on vocational training and teaching marketable skills.	
Civil Rights Act	1964	Prohibited discrimination on the basis of race, color, or national origin. Intended to provide all students with equal access to the curriculum.	
Elementary and Secondary Education Act	1965	Created Title I, designed to help disadvantaged children acquire basic skills.	
Bilingual Education Act	1968	Provided for teaching the curriculum in students' native languages as they gradually learned English.	
Title IX	1972	Increased girls' participation in physical education and sports.	
Individuals with Disabilities Education Act (IDEA)	1975	Increased participation of learners with exceptionalities in the regular curriculum.	
Environmental Education Act	1991	Stimulated the modern environmental-education movement.	
Goals 2000: Educate America Act	1994	Established a list of goals American education was to reach by the year 2000.	

Table 8.4	**Goals 2000: The National Education Goals**	
Goal	By the Year 2000:	
1	All children in America will start school ready to learn.	
2	The high school graduation rate will increase to at least 90 percent.	
3	All students will leave grades 4, 8, and 12 having demonstrated competency over challenging subject matter including English, mathematics, science, foreign languages, civics and government, economics, arts, history, and geography; and every school in America will ensure that all students learn to use their minds well, so they may be prepared for responsible citizenship, further learning, and productive employment in our nation's modern economy.	
4	The nation's teaching force will have access to programs for the continued improvement of their professional skills and the opportunity to acquire the knowledge and skills needed to instruct and prepare all American students for the next century.	
5	United States students will be first in the world in mathematics and science achievement.	
6	Every adult American will be literate and will possess the knowledge and skills necessary to compete in a global economy and exercise the rights and responsibilities of citizenship.	
7	Every school in the United States will be free of drugs, violence, and the unauthorized presence of firearms and alcohol and will offer a disciplined environment conducive to learning.	
8	Every school will promote partnerships that will increase parental involvement and participation in promoting the social, emotional, and academic growth of children.	

Source: From U.S. Department of Education. (1994). *The national educational goals.* Washington, D.C.: Author.

2000 (U.S. Department of Education, 1994). The act established a list of goals American education was to reach by the year 2000. These goals are outlined in Table 8.4.

The National Education Goals Panel, a bipartisan committee formed to monitor progress toward these goals, met in 2000 and made two major conclusions (Hoff, 1999). The first was that the goals were largely unmet and that significant additional effort would be required to meet them. The second recommendation was that these goals should be retained, giving educators something to aim at and strive for.

Professional Organizations

Educators' professional organizations have also influenced curriculum. Unfortunately, the content areas, such as math, science, and social studies, don't speak with a single voice, so examining the curriculum standards generated by the professional organizations can sometimes be confusing. Science is an example. The National Research Council (1996) published the *National Science Education Standards*, and the American Association for the Advancement of Science (1989) also published a list of recommendations. Both lists of standards are designed to achieve the goal of scientific literacy for all students by the time they leave school, but the lists differ in fundamental ways such as emphasis on scientific literacy for all versus a deep understanding of science by a few. Teachers are often left to sort through these issues by themselves.

Instead of looking at all the standards that the various organizations recommend, we will examine a sampling from three areas (social studies, science, and math), examine patterns that appear in them, and then consider what implications they have for you as a teacher.

Social Studies Standards Let's begin by looking at social studies. The National Council for the Social Studies (1994) presents 10 themes—including culture; people, places, and environments; and civic ideals and practices—that form the framework for their standards. The standards and performance expectations are then attached to these themes.

For example, the standard for the culture theme is: "Social studies programs should include experiences that provide for the study of culture and cultural diversity, so that the learner can. . ."; performance expectations then follow the standard. These expectations (for the early, middle, and high school levels, respectively) ask the learner to:

- Give examples of how experiences may be interpreted differently by people from diverse cultural perspectives and frames of reference.
- Explain how information and experiences may be interpreted by people from diverse cultural perspectives and frames of reference.
- Predict how data and experiences may be interpreted by people from diverse cultural perspectives and frames of reference.

We see how the performance expectations build on each other as students progress through the grades. Additional expectations exist for the culture theme, and each of the other themes has its own set of performance expectations as well. To access the themes presented by the National Council for the Social Studies, go to the *Web Links* Module in Chapter 8 of the Companion Website.

Science Standards Standards from science appear in Table 8.5. Rather than themes and expectations, they are presented in the form of "changes in emphasis" as recommended by the National Research Council (1996).

To access Websites for professional organizations, which in most cases will include the organization's standards, go to the *Web Links* Module in Chapter 8 of the Companion Website.

Increasing Understanding 8.14

 Look again at what is receiving increased emphasis in science. What educational philosophy is best reflected in this increased emphasis? Explain.

■ CONTROVERSIES IN CURRICULUM

In your work as a teacher, you will encounter controversies. Many of them will be related to what is taught (or not taught), that is, the curriculum. We examine some of these curricular controversies in this section when we consider the following:

Table 8.5	**Examples of Changes in Emphasis in Science**	
Area	Increased Emphasis	Decreased Emphasis
Facts and concepts	Understanding concepts.	Knowing facts and information.
Curriculum	Selecting and adapting curriculum.	Rigidly following curriculum.
Content coverage	Studying fewer topics in depth.	Covering many topics superficially.
Communication	Discussion and communication between teacher and students and students with each other.	Answering factual questions presented by the teacher.
Teaching practices	Guiding students in active inquiry.	Presenting knowledge through lecture, books, and demonstrations.

- A national curriculum.
- Societal issues: sex and morals education.
- Diversity: cultural minorities and women in the curriculum.

A National Curriculum

Elsewhere we saw that by the late 1700s, the federal government had removed itself from a central role in operating schools through the passage of the Tenth Amendment. This gave each state major decision-making power concerning what would be taught in that state's schools. The principle of state control of curriculum has been in place since that time.

Today, this principle is being questioned by some prominent voices who advocate a national curriculum. Some of their reasons for wanting a national curriculum include:

- The high achievement of students in countries such as Germany and Japan, which have national standards and national exams.
- The need for stability and coherence in the curriculum. Our population is highly mobile: 20 percent of Americans relocate every year, and some inner-city schools have a 50 percent turnover rate during the school year (Hirsch, 1996). Teachers working with these students often can't tell what they have or haven't already studied.
- Standards vary significantly from state to state; some states have much lower standards and levels of achievement than do others. A national curriculum would create uniform standards for all.

Opponents of a national curriculum also make compelling arguments. Some are wary of a large federal bureaucracy, which would also weaken local accountability. Others believe that a national curriculum would detract from the positive aspects of our cultural diversity; they feel that our disadvantaged students would be even further disadvantaged by a nationalized curricula that would be unresponsive to individual diversity and needs.

A partial response to these opposing views is a federal strategy that recommends, but does not require, exemplary textbooks. For example, the U.S. Department of Education recently published a list of promising and exemplary math texts, most based on recent National Council of Teachers of Mathematics standards (Viadero, 1999a). Even this approach draws criticism. One critic, a conservative math professor, commented, "This is an abomination. It [the math curriculum] has no business being debated by the federal government. . . ." (Viadero, 1999a, p. 14). Defenders of federal leadership in terms of textbooks compare it to *Consumer Reports*, noting that this publication serves an educational function and that not everyone who reads it is forced to buy the same product.

As you begin your career, you will probably see increased federal influence in the form of goals and standards, such as we saw with *Goals 2000*, but state adoption and compliance

Teaching

in an Era of Reform

THE SWINGING MATH PENDULUM

To begin this section, examine Table 8.6. The information in the table is taken from the *Curriculum and Evaluation Standards for School Mathematics*, published by the National Council of Teachers of Mathematics in 1989. As you can see in the table, "memorizing rules and algorithms" and "memorizing procedures" are de-emphasized. Instead, the *Curriculum and Evaluation Standards* strongly emphasized thinking, cooperation, and problem solving, and de-emphasized algorithmic practice, such as practicing the procedure for adding two-digit numbers or practicing long division.

Critics immediately reacted to these changes, raising the following questions:

- Do the standards adequately teach students basic math concepts and facts?

- Can the traditional emphasis on arithmetical and algebraic paper-and-pencil skills be reduced with no detrimental effects on important student learning?

- Can individual students effectively learn mathematics if they often investigate mathematical ideas and problems cooperatively with classmates?

The combination of the critics' concerns together with evidence that instruction based on the 1989 *Standards* was resulting in students with "content light" understandings of mathematics resulted in a pendulum shift back toward more emphasis on skills. The *Principles and Standards for School Mathematics* (National Council of Teachers of Mathematics, 2000), a revision of the 1989 *Standards*, reflects this shift. "Developing fluency requires a balance and connection between conceptual under-standing and computational proficiency. On one hand, computational methods that are over-practiced without understanding are often forgotten or remembered incorrectly. . . . On the other hand, understanding without fluency can inhibit the problem-solving process" (National Council of Teachers of Mathematics, 2000, p. 34). By re-emphasizing that students need to practice some traditional aspects of mathematics, such as long division, the *Principles* developed in 2000 reversed some of the emphasis of the 1989 *Standards*.

Putting Curriculum Reform into Perspective

The changes in thinking of the National Council of Teachers of Mathematics from 1989 to 2000 illustrate a broader trend in curriculum reform. A strong wave of reform appears, criticisms of the reform begin almost immediately, and backlash isn't far behind. Curriculum reform is often like a pendulum, swinging one way, only to return inevitably in the opposite direction (Bradley, 2000c).

A pessimistic view holds that American education is a study in failed curriculum reform (Labaree, 1999; Pogrow, 1996). "It might be said that Americans are always fixing their schools. Each decade another fad emerges. . . . Schools are usually asked to adopt these fads as single ideas laid on top of old structures. Such ideas are poorly assimilated and quickly rejected. . . . This creates a sense within schools that whatever the innovation, 'this too will pass' " (Darling-Hammond, 1998, p. 22). School veterans often simply ignore reforms and go about their business (Ozmon & Craver, 1995), and many teachers believe that the reforms that do occur often

Table 8.6	Examples of Changes in Emphasis in Mathematics	
Area	**Increased Emphasis**	**Decreased Emphasis**
Problem solving	■ Pursuing open-ended problems.	■ Practicing routine problems.
Communication	■ Discussing mathematical ideas.	■ Doing worksheets.
Operations and computation	■ Developing operation sense.	■ Memorizing rules and algorithms.
	■ Using estimation in problem solving and emphasizing sensibility of answers.	■ Memorizing procedures.
Algebra	■ Using a variety of methods to solve equations.	■ Memorizing procedures and drilling on equation solving.
Teaching practices	■ Actively involving students.	■ Having students passively listen to explanations.
	■ Facilitating learning.	■ Dispensing information.

Recent standards reforms in all content areas emphasize student understanding through students' active involvement in learning activities.

aren't actually needed or beneficial (Hirsch, 1996; Public Agenda, 1994).

However, some long-term patterns exist in suggested reforms for virtually all the content areas. These include:

- *Emphasis on understanding.* Each of the content areas is attempting to move away from a focus on memorizing information and toward deeper understanding, as evidenced by student's ability to interpret, predict, communicate, and generate examples.

- *Learners in active roles.* Rather than listening passively to teacher lectures, students are expected to actively participate in the learning process, talking and writing about the ideas they're learning.

- *Teachers guiding learning.* Rather than lecturing, teachers are expected to guide students' involvement in learning activities through skilled questioning that requires thought and understanding.

These trends are hardly controversial and are likely to persist. A great deal of research evidence indicates that emphasis on deeper understanding, active learners, the use of language to express understanding, and interactive teacher questioning promote learning (Bruning et al., 1999). In fact, if these four patterns were consistently observed in classrooms, many of the suggested reforms wouldn't be necessary.

The key element in this process is you, the professional teacher. Never in the history of education has the need for professional decision making, especially in the area of curriculum, been greater.

Increasing Understanding 8.15

What evidence do you see in Table 8.6 that supports the contention that teachers ultimately control the curriculum? Explain.

You Take a Position

Now it's your turn to take a position on the issue discussed in this section. Go to the *Education Week* Website at **http://www.edweek.com**, find "search" on the first page, and type in one of the following two search terms: *curriculum reform* or *curriculum change*. Locate a minimum of three articles on one of these topics and then do the following:

1. Identify the title, author, and date of each article and then write a one-paragraph summary of each.

2. Identify a pattern in the articles. (Each article—or even two of the three—suggesting that basic skills are receiving more emphasis in the curriculum would be a pattern, for example.)

3. After identifying the pattern, take one of the two following positions:

   - The pattern suggested in the articles, if implemented, *is* likely to improve education.

   - The pattern suggested in the articles *is not* likely to improve education.

State your position in writing and document your position with information taken from the articles.

To answer these questions online, go to the Take a Position Module in Chapter 8 of the Companion Website.

THE MATH CURRICULUM IN ELEMENTARY SCHOOLS

Having examined the relationship between curriculum and instruction, the explicit and implicit curriculum, and the forces that influence curriculum, you now have the chance to examine Suzanne Brush's teaching on videotape. To complete this activity, you should do the following:

■ View the video episode titled "The Math Curriculum in Elementary Schools."

■ You may want to review the written transcript of the lesson, which is the introductory case study for this chapter.

■ Answer the questions that follow (feedback for the questions is available at **http://www.prenhall.com/kauchak** in the *Looking through Classroom Windows* Module for Chapter 8):

1. You considered the implicit curriculum in Suzanne's classroom earlier in the chapter. Based on what you see in the video, describe the implicit curriculum in her classroom in more detail.

2. Which of the educational philosophies is most nearly reflected in Suzanne's teaching? Explain why you think so.

3. Consider the forces that influence the curriculum: philosophy, textbooks, her local district, the national government, and professional organizations. Then rate the influence you believe each had on Suzanne's curriculum. Use the following scale for your rating: 4 = Very strong influence, 3 = Strong influence, 2 = Weak influence, 4 = No influence.

Philosophy	1	2	3	4
Textbooks	1	2	3	4
Local district	1	2	3	4
National government	1	2	3	4
Professional organizations	1	2	3	4

Explain your rating in each case.

4. To what extent did Suzanne display professionalism in the episode you saw? Explain your analysis.

ⓦ *To answer these questions online and receive immediate feedback, go to the Looking Through Classroom Windows Module in Chapter 8 of the Companion Website.*

with them will be voluntary rather than mandated. National testing of students, a natural by-product of a national curriculum, is probably unlikely in the near future.

Social Issues in the Curriculum

Think back to your experiences in high school. Did you take a course entitled "Family Life," "Life Management," "Health Education," or something similar? Many students do. These courses often deal with controversial topics, including sex education and moral development.

Sex Education Sex education is controversial for at least two reasons. First, conservatives insist that it shouldn't be part of the school curriculum, believing that it is the sole or primary responsibility of families or churches. They contend that sex is inextricably connected with personal, moral, and religious values, and the proper place for sex education is the home, where parents can embed it in a larger moral framework.

Proponents of sex education counter with the statistics you first encountered in Chapter 4, which include the following (U.S. Department of Health and Human Services, 1996):

Sex education, while controversial, has become a common curriculum component in many school districts.

- Over half of students in grades 9–12 have had sexual intercourse.
- Nearly 8,000 students become sexually active every day.
- Nearly 3,000 girls become pregnant every day.
- Ninety-three percent of teenage girls giving birth are unmarried.

If parents and churches are responsible for sex education, they're doing a poor job, proponents contend. They further argue that sex education is an essential part of every student's education and that schools have both a right and a responsibility to ensure that all students have access to information about their bodies and their developing sexuality. Courts have upheld school districts' rights to offer sex education courses (Fischer, Schimmel, & Kelly, 1999). Parents who object are free to remove their children from attendance.

The second controversial issue is the content of the courses. Some argue that the content should focus strictly on the biology of sex and reproduction, what some call a "plumbing approach." Others suggest that this is ineffective, and personal responsibility and moral development should be included.

Regardless of the controversies, a national study found that 69 percent of public school districts have district-wide policies in place to teach sex education. The study also learned the following about the districts that have sex education policies (Landry, Kaeser, & Richards, 1999):

- Fourteen percent have a comprehensive policy that treats abstinence as one option for adolescents in a broader sex education program.
- Fifty-one percent teach abstinence as the preferred option for adolescents, but also permit discussion about contraception as an effective means of protecting against unintended pregnancy and disease (an abstinence-plus policy).
- Thirty-five percent (or 23 percent of all U.S. school districts) teach abstinence as the only option outside of marriage, with discussion of contraception either prohibited entirely or permitted only to emphasize its shortcomings (an abstinence-only policy). In other words, one school district in three (who have sex education policies in

place) forbids dissemination of any positive information about contraception, regardless of whether their students are sexually active or at risk of pregnancy or disease.

How does the public feel? Overwhelmingly, 93 percent of Americans favor sex education and believe that young people should be given information to protect themselves from unplanned pregnancies and sexually transmitted diseases (Sexuality Information and Education Council of the United States and Advocates for Youth, 1999). It appears that conservatives' positions are at odds with the views of most Americans. David Landry, a nationally recognized expert in this area, observed, "Students aren't receiving accurate, balanced information about how to protect themselves from unplanned pregnancy or disease" (Coles, 1999b, p. 13). This in unfortunate, as the statistics regarding teen pregnancy at the beginning of this section reveal a real student need.

Moral and Character Education The proper place of values and moral education in the curriculum is also controversial. The controversy is less about whether or not it should be taught—most educators agree that it is needed—and more about the form that it should take (Wynne, 1997).

One position, called **character education,** *emphasizes the transmission of moral values, such as honesty and citizenship, and the translation of these values into behavior.* For example, the state of Georgia recently passed a law requiring character education programs to focus on 27 character traits including patriotism, respect for others, courtesy, and compassion (Jacobson, 1999). Instruction in character education emphasizes the study of values, practicing these values both in school and elsewhere, and rewarding displays of these values.

Moral education, by contrast, *is more value-free, emphasizing instead the development of students' moral reasoning.* Moral education uses moral dilemmas and classroom discussions to teach problem solving and to bring about changes in the way learners think with respect to moral issues.

Critics of character education argue that it emphasizes indoctrination instead of education (Kohn, 1997); critics of moral education assert that it has a relativistic view of morals, with no right or wrong answers (Wynne, 1997).

The strength of character education is its willingness to identify and promote core values, such as honesty, caring, and respect for others. Few would argue that these values are inappropriate. However, emphasizing student thinking and decision making is important as well, and this is the focus of the moral education perspective.

For either moral or character education to work, there must be some public consensus about the values included in them. Does such consensus exist? A recent poll suggests that it does (Rose & Gallup, 1999). When asked whether the following values should be taught in public schools, the following percentages of a national sample replied affirmatively: honesty (97 percent), democracy (93 percent), acceptance of people of different races and ethnic backgrounds (93 percent), and caring for friends and family members (90 percent). At the other end of the continuum were acceptance of people with different sexual orientations, that is, homosexuals or bisexuals (55 percent) and acceptance of the right of a woman to choose an abortion (48 percent). In considering which values to promote in their classrooms, teachers should be aware of public attitudes towards these values. This doesn't mean that teachers should avoid discussing controversial topics or values; instead, it suggests being aware of students' current values and beliefs and building upon them. This makes sense both pedagogically as well as politically (Eggen & Kauchak, 2001; Ormrod, 2000).

Service learning. An innovative approach to character education, called **service learning,** *involves students in voluntary social-service projects.* The idea behind service learning is to make students more socially responsible by combining character education with an action component. Service-learning programs can be divided into two main categories:

Increasing Understanding 8.16

Identify at least two different kinds of background knowledge teachers must have in order to effectively teach about sexuality.

Service learning attempts to teach values by actively involving students in helping projects.

those that encourage the goal of social change and those that foster the goal of charity (Kahne & Westheimer, 1996). Examples of service-learning programs that focus on social change include environmental-education projects designed to encourage people to recycle and voter-education projects aimed at getting people out to vote. Charity-oriented projects include delivering food to shut-ins and doing volunteer work in hospitals.

The popularity of service-learning programs is growing. In 1984, only 2 percent of high school students were involved; by 1997, nearly one-quarter participated (Blair, 1999). In addition, 83 percent of high schools currently offer community-service opportunities (Westheimer & Kahne, 2000).

A major policy question is whether to make service learning voluntary or required. The state of Maryland requires 75 hours of service before high school graduation; a number of districts in California, Washington, Pennsylvania, and North Carolina have similar requirements (Fischer et al., 1999). However, not all parents agree with the value of service learning; some have legally challenged the requirement. Courts have upheld the legality of these courses, noting that they promote habits of good citizenship and introduce students to the idea of social responsibility.

Unfortunately, some educational leaders believe teacher preparation programs are not doing an adequate job of preparing future teachers for the issues involved in moral and character education (Jacobson, 1999; Ryan & Bohlin, 2000). If this is true, even greater demands will be placed on your professionalism when you take your first job.

Censorship What do the following books have in common?

Of Mice and Men by John Steinbeck
Diary of a Young Girl by Anne Frank
The Adventures of Huckleberry Finn by Mark Twain
To Kill a Mockingbird by Harper Lee
Leaves of Grass by Walt Whitman

Exploring Diversity

Considering Multiple Perspectives

MINORITIES AND WOMEN IN THE CURRICULUM

A considerable amount of criticism has been directed at the curriculum in American schools because, according to critics, it has failed to adequately represent the contributions of women and cultural minorities. For example, until as recently as the 1960s and 1970s, the majority of the works included in junior high and high school literature books were written by White males, with a few additional contributions by White females. When these books examined authors in depth, the authors chosen were generally White men, such as William Shakespeare, Mark Twain, and Robert Frost.

Recognition of the historical contributions of minorities was similarly lacking. For example, Dr. Charles Drew (1904–1950), an African American, developed the procedure for separating plasma from whole blood. This was an enormous contribution that unquestionably saved many soldiers' lives in World War II. Dr. Charles Norman, (b. 1930), another African American, was the first person to implant an artificial heart in a human. Until recently, most history books ignored contributions such as these.

Increasing Understanding 8.17

On which educational philosophy are the critics' arguments most likely based? Explain.

In response to critics and because of shifts in our society, this has changed. A postage stamp was issued in Drew's honor in 1981, and science fiction writer Isaac Asimov, a friend of Norman's, based his novel *Fantastic Voyage* on work done in Norman's laboratory. History texts have been expanded to include the contributions of women and minorities. Literature books, too, have changed. Many now include works written by minority writers, such as Maya Angelou, Sandra Cisneros, Gary Soto, and Toni Cade Bambara (Probst, Anderson, Brinnin, Leggett, & Irvin, 1997).

The issue is highly controversial, with some critics charging that cultural minorities remain underrepresented in the curriculum (Wong-Fillmore & Meyer, 1996). Content focusing on the contributions of men of northern European descent—often derisively described as a "Eurocentric" curriculum—is perceived as out of balance and irrelevant to minorities. Critics argue that because minorities make up more than one-third of our school chil-

All of these works have, at various times, been targeted for banning in the public school curriculum (People for the American Way, 1991). The language arts area has often served as a battleground for curriculum controversy due to the issue of censorship. **Censorship** occurs in the schools when *the use of certain books in the library or in literature classes is prohibited*.

The controversial and divisive nature of censorship can be seen in a censorship battle that took place in Kanawha County in West Virginia. In the mid-1970s, parents objected to certain language arts books including *The Diary of Anne Frank* as well as works by John Steinbeck and Mark Twain (Manzo, 2000b). Emotions reached crisis level quickly, resulting in death threats to teachers, pipe bombs, and a school boycott. The Ku Klux Klan and John Birch Society got involved, and several local minsters were convicted for their roles in school bombings. Censorship scars are evident even today; recently, district officials who felt censorship pressures ordered health teachers to avoid teaching about the excretory and reproductive systems of the human body. Can you imagine a student asking his health teacher about how the kidneys work and the teacher replying, "We can't talk about that in this class"?

Censorship can also occur with content-area textbooks. For example, a fourth-grade history text used in Utah contained the following passage:

■ ■ ■

People often hurt the land. Automobiles and factories pollute the air. People and factories sometimes dump trash and harmful chemicals into lakes and rivers. These kill birds and

dren (a percentage that is increasing), the curriculum should be further broadened to better reflect their contributions and presence in our society. In addition, critics assert that some time-honored literature, such as Mark Twain's *The Adventures of Huckleberry Finn*, portrays characters in ways that promote racial stereotypes and prejudice.

Some critics argue further that entire curricula should be oriented to specific ethnic groups. For instance, to help African American students understand and appreciate their cultural heritage, proponents of an "Afrocentric" curriculum advocate focusing on the achievements of African cultures, particularly ancient Egypt. Studying the contributions of people with similar ethnicity will increase self-esteem, motivation, and learning, they contend. Afrocentric curricula are currently being experimented with in a number of inner-city school districts (Toch, 1998).

However, these positions have critics of their own. The counter critics question the accuracy and balance of the content and whether the emphasis on differences leads to racial and ethnic separatism (Coughlin, 1996; Ravitch, 1990). They also argue that we've already gone too far in emphasizing cultural differences, resulting in the reduction or elimination of some of the great contributions of literature, such as the study of Shakespeare. Further, they maintain, we are all Americans, and this increased emphasis on diversity has resulted in the failure of students to develop a common cultural heritage and shared national identity (Hirsch, 1987; Schlessinger, 1992).

 Increasing Understanding 8.18

Adler (1982) argues for a "core" curriculum that would be composed of great literary works that have endured over the years. Hirsch (1987) argues for studying the great works, but then going beyond them to include the central ideas and knowledge of a culture, resulting in what he calls "cultural literacy." Which of the educational philosophies that we studied in Chapter 6 is most consistent with Adler's argument? Hirsch's argument? Explain in each case.

The role of women in the curriculum is also controversial. Many feminist groups contend that women continue to be both underrepresented and misrepresented in the curriculum; they argue that students read too many books and materials that portray men as doctors, lawyers, and engineers, and women as nurses, teachers, and secretaries. When this occurs, they assert, girls are sent messages about which careers are and are not appropriate for them (American Association of University Women, 1992).

However, a strong and systematic national effort has been made to address the needs of girls and women in today's schools (Riordan, 1996). In fact, some counter critics argue that the emphasis on girls' needs has gone too far. This is the argument made in *The War Against Boys*, the provocative and controversial book written by Christine Hoff Sommers (2000) that we discussed in Chapter 3.

The debate continues, and the controversy is likely to remain in the future.

fish and make the water unsafe for people. Companies cut down forests. They build roads, dams, and cities. They put oil wells and telephone lines on the land. We need these things, but sometimes they look ugly and destroy nature (Egan, 1997, p. B1).

■ ■ ■

This seems pretty innocuous, but one critic contended,

> This book is a blatant attempt by the federal government and environmentalists to try to 'brainwash' our young students into believing their ancestors were petty opportunists having no conscience about the lands for which they had stewardship (Egan, 1997, B3).

Unfortunately, as textbooks become political footballs, their quality diminishes, as text writers aim for blandness and "the middle of the road" at the expense of accuracy or making a point. This is a problem you'll encounter as you attempt to use textbooks to help students learn.

Censorship is interesting because it raises questions with conflicting answers about other important issues in education. One is parental choice and control over their children's education. Shouldn't parents have a say in the books their children read? A second question involves professional autonomy. Shouldn't teachers be free to select books that they feel are important, if not essential, to student development and learning? In considering these opposing views, the courts have usually decided against censorship of books, ruling that schools and teachers have a right to expose students to different ideas and points of view through literature (Fischer et al., 1999). To get additional information about censorship and banned books, go to the *Web Links* Module in Chapter 8 of the Companion Website.

The Changing Role of Teachers

As you've studied this book, you've seen that several of the chapters end with a section titled "The Changing Role of Teachers." What might be less obvious, however, is the theme that runs through these sections, which is, *the teacher's role is now more complex and demanding than it has ever been in the past*. We also stress that the need for teachers to be professional has never been greater. The kinds and amount of professional knowledge teachers must possess are greater than they've ever been. As an example, think about this chapter. Not only must teachers understand the content they are expected to teach, but they're also expected to make decisions about what topics to include, how extensively textbooks should be used, and to what extent district guidelines should be followed. State and district curriculum guides provide support, but they don't substitute for teachers' professional decisions.

The importance of knowledgeable and highly skilled teachers is supported by research linking teacher quality and student achievement (Bradley, 1999d; Darling-Hammond, 1998). Students in high achieving states, like North Dakota, Minnesota, and Iowa, do as well as students in foreign countries with reputations for high achievement, such as Korea and Japan. Those states have rigorous requirements for teacher education and don't allow districts to hire unlicensed teachers. The opposite is true for the lowest achieving states (National Commission on Teaching and America's Future, 1996). You are ultimately the person who controls the curriculum, and you will ultimately determine, to a large extent, how much your students learn.

In addition, teachers will be required to respond to federal and state mandates that influence the curriculum. The trend is toward increased testing and accountability. Taxpayers want to know if their education dollars are being well spent, students will be expected to learn more, and teachers will be expected to ensure that the learning occurs. These mandates create increased curriculum pressures for teachers.

Despite these pressures, this is an exciting time to be a teacher. The level of professionalism in teaching is increasing, teachers are better prepared than they have ever been in the past, and the challenges in the profession have never been greater. Further, a significant percentage of the teaching force will retire within the next 10 years, so opportunities for leadership roles will also increase. Your future as a teacher has never been more challenging, but at the same time it has never been filled with so many opportunities.

■ SUMMARY

What Is Curriculum?

While defined in a variety of ways, curriculum can be thought of as *what* students learn in schools, and instruction is the way the curriculum is taught. The explicit curriculum is the curriculum found in textbooks and other formal educational experiences, whereas the implicit curriculum is reflected in the climate of the classroom together with its unstated values and priorities.

The formal curriculum is sometimes integrated so that concepts and skills from different disciplines are combined. Integrated curriculum, while somewhat controversial, is common in elementary schools.

Extracurriculum includes learning experiences that extend beyond the core of students' formal studies. Participation in extracurricular activities is correlated with a number of positive outcomes, including achievement and attitudes toward school.

Forces That Influence the Curriculum

The teacher is the most powerful force influencing the curriculum. Ultimately it is the teacher who must decide what is taught and how it will be taught.

A teacher's philosophical orientation, available textbooks, federal mandates, state and local district guidelines, and reform movements sponsored by national committees and professional organizations all influence a teacher's curriculum decisions.

Controversies in Curriculum

Whether or not our country should have a national curriculum is one of the most controversial issues facing American education. Proponents cite the mobility of our population and the achievement of students in other countries with national curricula; opponents fear a large federal bureaucracy, reduction of local accountability, and a decrease in the positive aspects of our cultural diversity.

Sex education, education in morals and values, censorship, and the underrepresentation of women and minorities in the curriculum remain controversial curriculum issues. These issues are likely to remain unresolved in the near future.

The Changing Role of the Teacher

The teacher's role is becoming more complex and demanding, and nowhere is this more true than in the area of curriculum. The decisions teachers will be expected to make in the future include those about curriculum, instruction, and the interpersonal aspects of working with students from diverse backgrounds. Making these decisions requires a knowledgeable and highly skilled professional, one who is comfortable making decisions in ill-defined situations.

■ IMPORTANT CONCEPTS

censorship	extracurriculum	moral education
character education	implicit curriculum	outcomes-based education
curriculum	instruction	(OBE)
explicit curriculum	integrated curriculum	service learning

■ DISCUSSION QUESTIONS

1. Which has the greater influence on students' learning, curriculum or instruction? Why do you think so?

2. Think back to your own experience in schools and then consider what you've read in this chapter. Which has changed more over time, curriculum or instruction? Why do you think so?

3. Some critics argue that the implicit curriculum has more impact on students' overall education than does the explicit curriculum. Do you agree or disagree with this argument? Defend your position with a concrete example.

4. In periods of financial crises, some schools have reduced their extracurricular offerings. To what extent does this detract from students' overall education? Defend your position with a concrete example.

5. Which of the factors that influence the curriculum do you believe will most influence your teaching? Why do you think so?

■ VIDEO DISCUSSION QUESTIONS

The following discussion questions refer to video segments found on the Companion Website. To answer these questions online, view the accompanying video, and receive immediate feedback to your answers, go to the *Video Discussion* Module in Chapter 8 of the Companion Website.

1. Theodore Sizer is the director of the Coalition for Effective Schools, which attempts to reform high schools. In his view, what is the most important thing that schools can do to prepare students for college? Where in the curriculum would we find this emphasis, and how could teachers integrate it into their teaching?

2. Theodore Sizer, the director of the Coalition for Effective Schools, recommends a standard, focused curriculum for all students. How could a standard, focused curriculum be used to encourage student critical thinking? What are the advantages and disadvantages of this approach to curriculum?

■ GOING INTO SCHOOLS

1. Obtain a copy of a teacher's lesson plans for a week. Based on the teacher's plans, what is being emphasized? What is being de-emphasized? What do these lesson plans tell you about the teacher's explicit and implicit curriculum?

2. Examine the teacher's textbook (or textbooks). To what extent do the teacher's lesson plans appear to depend on the textbook(s)? What other resources are the basis for the teacher's plans?

3. Interview a teacher about different forces that shape her curriculum.
    a. Ask her why she emphasizes what she does, and why she de-emphasizes other aspects of her teaching.
    b. How much does she depend on textbooks to determine what she teaches? How much do curriculum guides influence what she teaches? How much does testing influence what she teaches?
    c. Ask her to describe the school's extracurricular program. Find out who participates and why. (For example, Do low-SES students and minorities participate as much as other students?) How important is the extracurricular program, and why does she feel that way?
    d. Ask the teacher to describe her impression of current curriculum reforms. Do they influence what and how she teaches? If so, describe specifically how they are influenced. If not, why not?

    Compare the forces that shape this teacher's curriculum to forces described in this chapter.

4. Interview a teacher about controversial topics in the curriculum. What is her position with respect to the following controversial curricular issues:
    a. Sex education. Should the schools teach sex education, or should it be the responsibility of parents and churches? Why does she feel the way she does?
    b. Morals and values education. Should schools teach morals and values? Is so, how should they be taught?
    c. The underrepresentation of minorities and women in the curriculum. Does she believe minorities and women are underrepresented? If so, how can the problem be solved?

    How does she find out about whether and how these topics should be taught? How much of these decisions are personal ones, and how much guidance or restrictions come from external sources? What implications does all this have for you as a teacher when faced with similar curricular decisions?

5. Observe in a classroom (for an extended period of time if possible).
    a. What rules and procedures guide student behavior? How are they explained or defended?
    b. When the teacher corrects or reprimands a student, what explanation or rationale is given?

c. How does the teacher motivate students? What reasons are given for learning different things?

d. How does the teacher treat students? How do students treat each other?

Based on your observations, what implicit curriculum is being promoted in the classroom? Defend your conclusions with examples taken directly from your observations.

 Virtual Field Experience | **If you would like to participate in a Virtual Field Experience, go to the _Field Experience_ Module in Chapter 8 of the Companion Website.**

■ ONLINE PORTFOLIO ACTIVITIES

 To complete these activities online, go to the _Portfolio Activities_ Module in Chapter 8 of the Companion Website to submit your response.

Portfolio Activity 8.1

Planning for Instruction

INTASC Principle 9: *Commitment*

The purpose of this activity is encourage you to think about the topics you will plan to teach.

Write a two-page description of your philosophy of curriculum, or what is important for students to learn in your class. In it, explain specifically how it is consistent with the description of your overall philosophy of education (which you described in Portfolio Activity 5.1).

Portfolio Activity 8.2

Making Decisions about Curriculum

INTASC Principle 7: *Planning*

The purpose of this activity is to acquaint you with resources, such as textbooks, that will influence your curricular decisions. Locate a textbook for an area in which you will teach. (If you're a middle school science major, for example, you might select a seventh-grade life science book. If you're an elementary major, you can select from a variety of books.)

Photocopy the table of contents from the book. Then identify several topics that you would delete if you were using the book. Also, identify several topics you might add. Defend your additions and deletions and explain how your changes are consistent with your curriculum philosophy.

Portfolio Activity 8.3

Using Curriculum Guides for Planning Decisions

INTASC Principle 8: *Assessment*

The purpose of this activity is to acquaint you with curriculum guides as a planning resource. Analyze either a state or district curriculum guide in one area of the curriculum (or compare two levels).

a. How recent is it?

b. Who constructed it?

c. How is it organized (for example, chronologically, developmentally, topically, and so on)?

d. How do the topics covered compare with a text for this area?

e. How many objectives are listed for a particular course of study?

f. How many objectives per week are implicitly suggested? Is it a realistic number?

g. What types of learning (for example, memory versus higher levels) are targeted?

How helpful would this curriculum guide be for you as a first-year teacher?

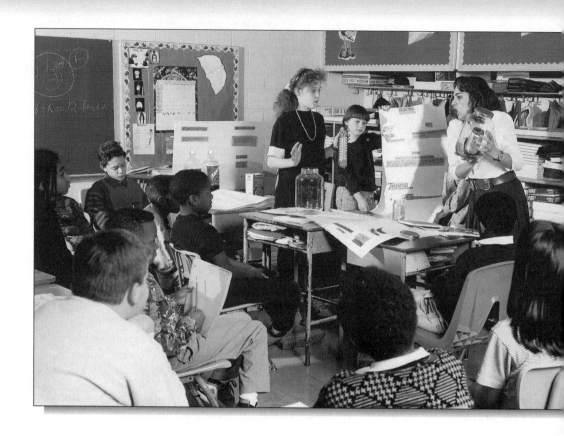

Instruction in
American Classrooms

The reason you're taking this and other courses in your teacher-preparation program is to help you understand American schools, how they attempt to promote student learning, and what teachers can do to contribute to that process. Over the past 25 years, a continually expanding body of research has provided educators with a great deal of information about relationships between what teachers do and what students learn. Our purpose in writing this chapter is to describe some of these relationships as we try to answer the following questions:

■ What kinds of personal characteristics do effective teachers possess?

■ How do effective teachers organize their classrooms so students can learn?

■ What kinds of instructional strategies do effective teachers use?

■ How do effective teachers assess their students?

■ On what theories of learning do effective teachers base their instruction?

Let's begin the process by looking at one teacher's classroom and seeing how she works with her students.

Case STUDY

Martina Hernandez is a fifth-grade teacher at Oneida Elementary School, an inner-city school with a largely low-SES student body. Martina is working with her students on the addition of fractions, and begins today's class with a brief review.

"Look at this fraction," she says, writing 3/4 on the board. "What do we call the number on the bottom? . . . Celena?"

"Uh, denominator."

"Good, Celena. And what do we call the number on the top, Carl?"

There's no reply from Carl.

"Ooh, ooh, I know," Tad interjected.

"Tad, I'm glad you know, but let's give Carl a chance. Remember, we agreed that it's important for everyone to participate, and we're going to work hard to avoid blurting out answers."

"Carl, think about this for a second. Remember, it tells us the number of parts in the fraction. It comes from the term *number*."

". . . Oh yeah, numerator."

"And why do we want to know these terms? . . . Andrea?"

"You said it was . . . so we could talk about the numbers. When we talk about the bottom number, we have something to call it."

"Yes, good Andrea," Martina smiles. "Sure. In this case it's simply for communication. It's much easier for us to call this the 'denominator' than to constantly refer to it as 'the number on the bottom.' Remember, it's very important to understand *why* we want to understand the ideas we study."

"Now, let's look closely at this problem," Martina continues, pointing to the overhead. "It says, 'I drank half a cup of milk with my sandwich, and now I need to add a third of a cup to this recipe. I had one cup of milk in the refrigerator. Do I have enough milk for the recipe?' What should we do first? . . . I want everyone to think real hard now, because you all can do this, and it's important to know how to do problems like this . . . Tanya?"

There's no reply from Tanya.

"First, what does 1/3 mean? Remember when we folded the papers to illustrate fractions?" Martina prompts. She reaches over to her desk, picks up a piece of paper, and folds it so it appears as follows:

"Oh, yes, we had three parts altogether, and we're . . . I'm not sure, like *working* with one of the parts," Tanya responds.

"Excellent, Tanya."

The lesson continues with Martina encouraging her students to see the relationship between the numbers in fractions and different configurations of folded paper.

■ ■ ■

Is Martina a "good teacher?" What specifically did she do to promote learning in her classroom? What could she have done differently to improve her instruction? We try to answer these questions in the next section.

■ LOOKING IN CLASSROOMS TO DEFINE EFFECTIVE TEACHING

Classrooms are logical places to look for answers to questions about good teaching; a line of inquiry focusing on classroom teaching began when researchers found that students in some teachers' classrooms were learning more than in others. In trying to find reasons for these differences, the researchers analyzed literally thousands of hours of teaching, focusing on teachers in both high- and low-achieving classes. After ensuring that students and resources, such as the availability of technology and textbooks, were comparable, they found that the thinking of the teachers as well as the way the teachers taught were different for the two groups (the high achievers and the lower achievers) (Good & Brophy, 1986, 1997). *A description of these differences resulted in a body of knowledge called the* **teacher effectiveness research.** This research found that the personal characteristics of the teachers were different, their planning was different, and their teaching strategies, classroom management techniques, and assessment strategies were also different. This research is important because it established links between teacher actions and student learning in real-world classroom settings.

The dimensions on which effective and less effective teachers differ are outlined in Figure 9.1.

Personal Characteristics

Think about some of the best teachers you've had. When you do, what is the first thing that comes to mind? If you're typical, you believe that they cared about you as a person, they were committed to your learning, and they were enthusiastic about the topics they taught.

These factors describe effective teachers' personal characteristics, and they provide a foundation that guides their work. In this section we examine four of these attributes:

- Personal teaching efficacy
- Caring
- Modeling and enthusiasm
- Teacher expectations

Personal Teaching Efficacy   To what extent can teachers overcome the problems that students bring with them to school? If students lack supportive home environments, can teachers still promote high achievement, or do students' backgrounds overwhelm teachers' efforts? To gain some insight into your beliefs regarding these questions, respond to

Figure 9.1   **Dimensions on Which Effective and Less Effective Teachers Differ**

Personal characteristics

Planning

Teaching strategies

Classroom management

Assessment

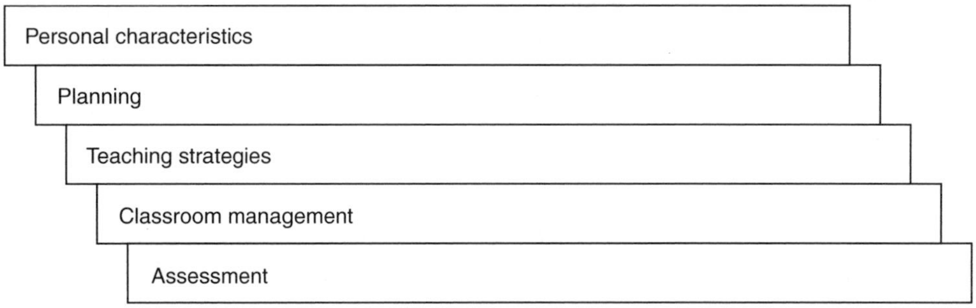

the following statements by circling SA (Strongly agree), A (Agree), U (Undecided), D (Disagree), or SD (Strongly disagree).

1. Students' home environments have a stronger influence on their learning than do teachers.	SA	A	U	D	SD
2. If teachers try hard enough, they will be able to get through to even the most difficult students.	SA	A	U	D	SD
3. If parents' values don't support teaching and learning, teachers can do little to increase student achievement.	SA	A	U	D	SD
4. If students don't remember information from a previous lesson, teachers should know how to increase their retention in the next lesson.	SA	A	U	D	SD

Source: Adapted from "Teacher efficacy: A construct validation," by S. Gibson and M. Dembo, 1984, *Journal of Educational Psychology, 76.*

Researchers asked teachers to respond to statements similar to these, and based on their responses, assessed the teachers' **personal teaching efficacy,** a concept we introduced in our discussion of effective schools in Chapter 6 and defined as *a teacher's belief that he or she can promote learning in all students regardless of their backgrounds* (Bruning, Shraw, & Ronning, 1999). Teachers who are high in personal teaching efficacy take responsibility for the success or failure of their own instruction (Lee, 2000).

When students aren't learning as much as they could, high-efficacy teachers don't blame it on lack of intelligence, poor home environments, uncooperative administrators, or some other external cause. Instead, they redouble their efforts, convinced they can increase student learning. They create classroom climates in which students feel safe and free to express their thinking without fear of embarrassment or ridicule. They emphasize praise rather than criticism, persevere with low achievers, and maximize the time available for instruction. Low-efficacy teachers, in contrast, are less student-centered, spend less time on learning activities, "give up" on low achievers, and are more critical when students fail (Kagan, 1992). High-efficacy teachers also adopt new curriculum materials and change strategies more readily than do low-efficacy teachers (Poole, Okeafor, & Sloan, 1989). Not surprisingly, students taught by high-efficacy teachers learn more than those taught by low-efficacy teachers (Tschannen-Moran, Woolfolk-Hoy, & Hoy, 1998).

Martina displayed several characteristics of a high-efficacy teacher. She had a positive attitude about learning and communicated this attitude to her students. She kept them involved in the lesson through her questioning, encouraged them to think about the reasons for studying the topic, and praised their efforts.

Caring You've made an appointment to meet an instructor about some problems you're having in his class and he shows up 15 minutes late with a mumbled, "I've been so terribly busy lately." As he talks with you, he keeps glancing at his watch, giving you the impression he wants to be somewhere else. In contrast, when you make an appointment and meet with another instructor, he is there at the designated time, and he spends as much time with you as you need. How do you feel in each case?

These simple incidents relate to caring. We all want to be cared about, and advertisers capitalize on that fact with slogans such as, "We care about you after the sale," and "Shop with the people who care."

We saw in Chapter 2 that "caring professional" is one of the many roles of a teacher, and caring is essential for effective teaching. Students can tell when teachers care, all parents want their children to be with caring teachers, and even older university students

Increasing Understanding 9.1

Explain why low-efficacy teachers are likely to spend less time on learning activities than high-efficacy teachers.

To answer this question online and receive immediate feedback, go to the *Increasing Understanding* Module in Chapter 9 of the Companion Website at **http://www.prenhall.com/kauchak.**

Caring, an essential component of effective teaching, connects teachers with students on a human level.

Identify the single most important indicator of caring that exists. Use this indicator to explain why you are likely to react badly when an instructor arrives 15 minutes late to an appointment.

value instructors who genuinely care about them and their learning. **Caring** refers to *teachers' willingness to invest time in the protection and development of young people* (Chaskin & Rauner, 1995). A growing body of research documents the importance of caring for both student achievement and motivation (Bosworth, 1995; Stipek, 1996). Caring teachers are committed to their students' learning and developing competence. They attempt to do their very best for the people under their charge (Noddings, 1995).

Modeling and Enthusiasm   We often hear that "actions speak louder than words," and this statement is especially true for teachers. Teachers are powerful role models for students, and the way they act influences both learning and motivation (Bandura, 1989). **Modeling** simply means *behaving in ways you would like your students to imitate.* For instance, since you want your students to be courteous and respectful to you and each other, you treat them with courtesy and respect. You want them to be diligent and conscientious in their studies, so you demonstrate that you also prepare thoroughly and work hard at your teaching.

Martina modeled patience and understanding with her students in her interactions with them. When Tad attempted to blurt out an answer, Martina patiently reminded him that everyone in the class needs an opportunity to participate. Messages like this, delivered through modeled behaviors, are much more effective than lectures or admonitions.

Your approach to the content you're teaching has similar effects on students. Student interest in a topic is virtually impossible if you make statements such as, "I know this stuff is boring, but we have to learn it," or "This isn't my favorite topic either." In contrast, even the most mundane topic is more palatable to students if you're genuinely interested in it. Teachers who present information enthusiastically increase both student achievement and learners' beliefs about their ability to understand the topics they're studying (Perry, 1985; Perry, Magnusson, Parsonson, & Dickens, 1986). Modeling can make enthusiasm contagious.

Teacher Expectations To begin this section, let's analyze two short interactions between a teacher and her students.

> *Mrs. Vaughn:* What kind of triangle is this? . . . Lisa?
>
> *Lisa:* I . . . don't know.
>
> *Mrs. Vaughn:* Sure you do. What do you notice about the lengths of these three sides?
>
> *Lisa:* They're . . . equal. It's an equilateral triangle.

Now compare what you've just read with the following:

> *Mrs. Vaughn:* What kind of triangle is this? . . . Jessica?
>
> *Jessica:* I . . . I don't know.
>
> *Mrs. Vaughn:* Can you help her out, Gena?

The difference in the way Mrs. Vaughn communicated with Lisa and Jessica may not seem particularly important, but it is. It suggests that she *expected* Lisa to be able to answer the question, but she didn't have the same expectations for Jessica. While a single incident may not be significant, if Mrs. Vaughn's interactions with the two girls represent a pattern, differences in achievement can result (Good & Brophy, 1997).

Research indicates that teachers who have high expectations for students treat them differently than they treat the students for whom they have low expectations. Some differences favoring high-expectation students include:

- Emotional Support. Teachers interact with them more, and the interactions are more positive.
- Teacher Effort. Teachers give them clearer and more thorough explanations and require more complete and accurate answers.
- Questioning. Teachers call on them more often, give them more time to answer, and prompt them more.
- Feedback. Teachers give them more praise and less criticism, and they provide more complete and thorough feedback.

Students are sensitive to these differences, and children as young as first grade are aware of differential treatment (Stipek, 1996). In one study, researchers concluded, "After ten seconds of seeing and/or hearing a teacher, even very young students (third grade) could detect whether the teacher talked about or to an excellent or a weak student and could determine the extent to which that student was loved by the teacher" (Babad, Bernieri, & Rosenthal, 1991, p. 230). This is both amazing and frightening; it places a heavy burden on teachers to communicate caring and high expectations to all students.

Expectations can be self-fulfilling. When we treat students as if they can't learn, they don't try as hard. The reduced effort results in less learning, and a downward spiral begins (Weinstein, 1998). Unfortunately, expectations are often out of teachers' conscious control; they often don't realize that they hold different expectations for their students. As they become aware of these possibilities, however, and with effort, they can learn to treat all students as equally as possible. We examine specific strategies to promote equitable treatment later in the chapter.

 Martina expressed positive expectations for her class when she said, "I want everyone to think real hard now, because you all can do this, and it's important to know how to do problems like this." Learning is maximized when positive expectations are followed up with effective planning and teaching strategies, topics we discuss in the following sections.

Table 9.1	Matrix Used to Compare Northern and Southern Colonies		
	People	**Land and Climate**	**Economy**
Northern Colonies	Small towns Religious Valued education Cooperative	Timber covered Glacial remains Poor soil Short growing season Cold winters	Syrup Rum Lumber Shipbuilding Fishing Small farms
Southern Colonies	Aristocratic Isolated Social class distinction	Fertile soil Hot weather Long growing season	Large farms Tobacco Cotton Unskilled workers Servants and slaves

Teacher Planning

■ ■ ■

Judith Thompson, a fifth-grade teacher, involves her students in a discussion of the events leading up to the American Civil War. She begins the lesson by saying that she wants the students to understand the geography and dynamics of the war. During the 45 minute lesson, she discusses what it might have been like to be a slave, the respective advantages and disadvantages of the North and the South, what Abraham Lincoln was like, and some features of Reconstruction.

As homework, she has the students write a paragraph about the meaning of the term "indivisible."

■ ■ ■

Kathy Johnson, another fifth-grade teacher, is working with her students on the same topic. She uses a map that shows the topography of the North and the South, and she prepares the matrix shown in Table 9.1, which illustrates differences in the people, geography and climate, and economy of the two regions.

She displays the matrix and guides the students as they try to find relationships in the information in the chart and answer questions such as:

▓   Why were the northern colonists more cooperative than the colonists in the South?

▓   Why were the farms so much smaller in the North?

▓   Why was lumbering part of the economy in the North, but not in the South?

▓   Why did shipbuilding occur in the North, but to a lesser extent in the South?

Kathy has the students use the map and the matrix as references as they try to answer the questions. As a homework assignment, she has her students write a paragraph in which they offer reasons why the economy of the North would have been an advantage for the North when the Civil War began.

■ ■ ■

In addition to differences in teachers' personal characteristics, research indicates that effective teachers *think* differently than less effective teachers (Borko & Putnam, 1996; Eggen, 1998). These differences are commonly revealed in the way teachers plan. While planning depends on several factors (such as teachers' beliefs about students' needs, how capable teachers believe students are, what experiences students have already had, and teachers' past experiences with the same topic), differences in the thinking of effective

Careful planning helps teachers define their goals and make sure that instructional activities are aligned with these goals.

and less effective teachers most commonly occur in two areas: the way they think about goals, and the way they align their instruction.

Let's look at them.

Goals and Teachers' Thinking When effective teachers plan, they think carefully about their **goals**—*what they want students to understand or be able to do when they complete the lesson.* As an example, let's look again at Judith and Kathy's work with their students. Judith's lesson wasn't clear or focused. In one 45 minute lesson, she discussed slavery, military advantages of the North and the South, Lincoln, and Reconstruction. The lesson lacked focus because Judith wasn't clear about her goals. She said that she wanted the students to understand the geography and dynamics of the war, but she wasn't able to translate these ideas into the lesson. Her thinking wasn't clear, and as a result, students' learning suffered.

In contrast, Kathy's thinking was very clear, so her goals were precise and focused. She wanted the students to understand how the geography of the North and South affected the economies and lifestyles in the two areas, and in turn, how the economies and lifestyles affected the outcome of the Civil War. Clear goals led to increased learning.

While effective teachers' thinking about goals is clear and precise, they're able to adapt if they see that their students have misconceptions that interfere with learning. For instance, a teacher involving her students in a lesson on *heat* found that her students believed that coats and sweaters *caused* heat, which explained for them the reason we stay warmer in a coat than in a light sweater. Because of these misconceptions, she rethought her goals, changed the direction of the lesson, and had her students put thermometers in coats and sweaters to see which one "caused" more heat. When they found no differences, they were more prepared to accept the idea that clothing traps rather than causes or generates heat (Watson & Konicek, 1990).

Increasing Understanding 9.3

Research indicates that when they plan, beginning teachers write much more on paper than do veterans (Neale, Pace & Case, 1983). Does this suggest that beginning teachers plan more effectively than veteran teachers? Explain.

Instructional Alignment and Teacher Thinking Instructional alignment refers to *the congruence between goals, learning activities, practice in the form of assignments and homework, and assessment.* Effective teachers think about the relationships between their goals and learning activities, and they carefully design the learning activities to be consistent with the goals. Let's look at Kathy's lesson again. She used her map and matrix as a framework to guide the students as they tried to answer questions about the relationships between the geography, people, and economies of the two regions. Her learning activity pointed directly toward her goal, and her homework assignment was an extension of her learning activity.

Instead of helping the students understand the geography and dynamics of the war, Judith discussed what it felt like to be a slave. She then looked at Abraham Lincoln and Reconstruction, neither of which related to either the geography or the "dynamics" of the war. Further, her homework assignment didn't relate to either her goal or learning activity. Her lesson was "out of alignment."

The examples we've just discussed focus on a single lesson. Effective teachers are also clear about their long-range plans, such as units of a week or more, complete grading periods (such as a 9-week period), and even complete semesters and years.

Let's look now at how teachers use teaching strategies to help students learn.

Teaching Strategies

In addition to differences in the personal characteristics of effective and less-effective teachers as well as differences in how they think as they plan, research has also identified important differences in the way they teach. They include differences in:

■ Questioning
■ Presentation of subject matter
■ Feedback

Teacher Questioning In the last 20 years, a major shift in classrooms has occurred. In the past, students were expected to listen quietly as teachers explained the topics they were studying and then work independently at their desks. However, expert teachers knew that kids are naturally active and that the best way to increase learning is to design learning activities in which students are as involved as possible. One of the most effective ways of involving students is through *questioning*. Let's look at an example (Eggen & Kauchak, 2001):

Case STUDY

Diane Smith, another fifth-grade teacher at Oneida Elementary School, is beginning a language arts lesson on comparative and superlative adjectives. She begins by having two of her students hold their pencils up, so everyone can see.

Diane: Condoleza and Daniel, hold your pencils up high, so everyone can see. What do you notice about the pencils? . . . Mary?

Mary: Condoleza's is red and Daniel's is blue.

Diane: OK, what else? . . . Sheila?

Sheila: You write with them.

Diane: Indeed you do! What else, Kevin?

Kevin: Condoleza's is longer.

Diane: That's true. Does everyone see that? Hold them up again.

Condoleza and Daniel hold their pencils up again, and Diane moves to the chalk-board and writes:

Condoleza has a long pencil.   *Condoleza has a longer pencil than does Daniel.*

Diane: Now, let's look at Matt and Aaron. What do you notice about their hair? . . . Maddie?

Maddie: Matt's is longer than Aaron's.

Diane: Good, Maddie. What else? What about the color? Nicholas?

Nicholas: Aaron's is brown and Matt's is blond.

Diane: OK, good, Nicholas. So which one has darker hair?

The Class: Aaron!!

Diane: OK, everyone. I understand your eagerness, and I think it's good. . . . Just as a reminder, what is one of our most important rules in here? . . . Todd?

Todd: We wait until you call on us before we answer.

Diane: OK, excellent everyone. You've all done very well with this. We just need a lit-tle reminder now and then. . . . Now, let's see where we are. What did we say about Aaron's and Matt's hair? . . . Vicki?

Vicki: Aaron's was darker.

Diane: Good!

Diane then writes three more sentences on the board, so they appear as follows:

Condoleza has a long pencil.   *Condoleza has a longer pencil than does Daniel.*
Aaron has brown hair.   *Aaron has darker hair than does Matt.*
Matt has blond hair.

Diane: Now let's look at the adjectives in the sentences on the left compared to the adjectives in the sentences on the right. How do they compare? Heather?

Heather: The adjectives in the sentences on the right have an "er" on the end of them.

Diane guides students to the conclusion that comparative adjectives have an "er" on the end of them, and then repeats the process for superlative adjectives.

■ ■ ■

When done right, questioning can be an exhilarating intellectual experience for both you and your students. The ability to ask effective questions is the most important ability teachers have for guiding student learning (Wang, Haertel, & Walberg, 1993). A teacher skilled in questioning can determine how much students already know about a topic, encourage learners to rethink their ideas, help them form relationships, involve shy or ret-icent students, recapture students' attention, promote success, and enhance self-esteem. Becoming skilled in questioning is difficult, but with effort and experience, teachers can and do become expert at it (Kerman, 1979; Rowe, 1986).

Effective and less effective teachers differ in four areas:

■ Frequency
■ Wait-time
■ Appropriate level of difficulty
■ Equitable distribution

Questioning provides opportunities for the teacher to assess learning and motivate students by actively involving them in learning activities.

Frequency. **Questioning frequency** simply refers to *the number of questions teachers ask;* effective teachers ask many more questions than do less effective teachers. Instead of relying on explaining and telling as their primary teaching strategies, effective teachers develop entire lessons around questioning. We saw this in Martina's lesson, where she used questioning to help students' understand fractions, and we saw it again in Diane's lesson on adjectives. Students involved in question and answer sessions are more attentive than those who listen passively to teacher explanations; as a result, achievement increases (Morine-Dershimer, 1985; Pratton & Hales, 1986).

Wait-time. When students are asked questions, they need time to think. *This period of silence after a question is asked is called* **wait-time.** Giving students a few seconds to think about their answers makes sense, yet in most classrooms—regardless of the students' grade or ability levels—wait-times are very short, often 1 second or less (Rowe, 1986). Increasing wait-time to about 3 to 5 seconds positively influences learning in at least three ways (Rowe, 1986; Tobin, 1987):

- ■ The length and quality of student responses improve.
- ■ Failures to respond are reduced, and voluntary participation increases.
- ■ Student participation in general, as well as participation from minority students, improves.

Appropriate level of difficulty. The kinds of questions teachers ask also influence learning. Teachers often assume that questions demanding higher level thinking are more effective than those requiring mere recall, but this isn't always the case. Both can increase achievement, depending on the teaching situation (Good & Brophy, 1997).

The appropriate level of questions depends on the teacher's goal. For example, if the goal is to practice basic math facts to the point where students can use them without thinking, low-level questions are effective. On the other hand, if the goal is to understand the interplay of factors leading up to the Civil War, as was the case in Kathy's lesson, high-level questions are more effective. Teachers' first concerns should be what they are trying to accomplish—their goals—not the level of questions they ask. When goals are clear, appropriate questions follow.

Equitable distribution. Teachers' questioning patterns send powerful messages to students. For example, if girls or minority students are called on less often, are prompted less, or are given less time to answer than boys or nonminorities, they become less involved in lessons, and gradually they stop paying attention to what is going on. In time, they begin to feel less welcome in the class, and may even come to believe that they're not as bright as those who are called on more frequently or given more time to think.

One solution to this dilemma is to *interact with all students—girls, boys, minorities and nonminorities—as equally as possible.* One way of communicating to students that they all are welcome and expected to learn is through **equitable distribution,** *the practice of calling on all students—both volunteers and nonvolunteers—as equally as possible.*

To understand the process of equitable distribution, let's think about Martina's lesson again. In this brief vignette, we see that Martina asked five questions, she directed them to four different students (Celena, Carl, Andrea, and Tanya), and in each case she called on the student by name. The practice of equitable distribution sends a clear message to students that all are expected to participate and all are expected to learn. Students rarely misinterpret the messages, and it doesn't matter what the teachers' or students' cultural backgrounds are.

Think about what this communicates. By treating students equally, the teacher is saying, "I don't care whether you're a boy or girl, minority or nonminority, high-achiever or low achiever—I want you in my classroom. I believe you're capable of learning, and I will do whatever it takes to ensure that you're successful." When this happens, students come to believe that the teacher expects them to participate and learn. Perhaps even more importantly, because the teacher is making this effort, they believe the teacher is genuinely committed to their learning. No message is more positive.

Equitable distribution is a powerful tool for promoting both achievement and student motivation. Research indicates that teachers who treat their students as equally as possible have higher achieving students, fewer classroom management problems, and higher attendance rates (Kerman, 1979). Equitable distribution also works at the college level; expectation of being called on results in increased student preparation for class, greater retention of information, and greater confidence in what is learned (McDougall & Granby, 1996).

Presentation of Subject Matter Students study a variety of topics in their classes, such as the rules for forming plural nouns in language arts, equivalent fractions in math, density in science, and culture in social studies. Describing and explaining the topics is the most common method teachers use to help learners understand them (Cuban, 1984; Goodlad, 1984). However, research indicates that simply explaining or telling isn't the most effective way of helping students learn (Brenner et al., 1997; Spiro, Feltovich, Jacobson, & Coulson, 1992; Shulman, 1986). Instead, learners need concrete examples that they can use to develop their understanding. For instance, a science teacher might teach the concept *density* by having students compress cotton balls in a drink cup so they see that the compressed cotton is more compact (dense). She might also drop an ice cube into a cup of water and another into a cup of alcohol. The ice floats on the water but sinks in the alcohol, demonstrating that the ice is less dense than the water but more dense

Increasing Understanding 9.4

In this section, we said that effective teachers call on all students as equally as possible, and call on them by name. Predict what less effective teachers do in their classrooms. To what two personal characteristics do these patterns relate? Explain.

than the alcohol. In language arts, teachers can use actual student writing samples to illustrate principles of good organization, grammar, and punctuation. In social studies, the teacher might prepare descriptions such as the following to illustrate the concept *culture:*

∎ ∎ ∎

Pedro is a boy living in a small Mexican village. Every day he rises early, for he must walk the two miles to his school. He has breakfast of beans and bread made from ground corn, leaves the house, and begins his trek. He likes the walk, for he can wave to his papa toiling daily in the cornfields that provide food and income for the family.

When Pedro comes home from school, he often plays soccer with his friends in the village. After dinner, his mother usually plays songs on a guitar while his papa sings, but this evening she must go to a meeting of the town council, where they are trying to raise money for a new addition to the school. No decisions can be made without the approval of the council.

∎ ∎ ∎

Chu is a young girl living in a fishing village in Japan. She is up early and helps her mother with breakfast for her younger brothers and sisters. Chu loves the rice smothered in a sauce made from raw fish that she often eats in the morning.

Chu skips out the door, bowing to her father as she goes. He is preparing tools to go to the docks, where he will meet his partner for their daily fishing expedition. He has been a fisherman for 30 years. Chu comes home from school, finishes her work, and then goes down the street to play ping pong with the rest of the neighborhood boys and girls. She is the best one in the area. Before bed, Chu listens to stories of the old days told by her grandfather, who lives with them.

∎ ∎ ∎

Increasing Understanding 9.5

Describe the differences in the ways that Judith Thompson and Kathy Johnson represented their subject matter. Explain why Kathy's approach was more effective.

Each example includes a description of foods, recreation, the way the people make a living, and aspects of their home life. These are all characteristics of the concept *culture*. Instead of abstract descriptions, the examples provide students with concrete information about what culture is and how it influences our lives.

The importance of high-quality examples in teaching can't be overstated; effective teachers are able to illustrate topics in ways that are understandable to students, whereas less-effective teachers tend to rely on verbal explanations (Shulman, 1986).

Effective Feedback Have you ever been in a class where you had to wait until the midterm exam to find out how you were doing? Have you handed in assignments and had to wait weeks before they were scored and returned? In both instances, you were left uncertain about your learning progress because of the absence of feedback. **Feedback** *is information about current performance that can be used to increase future learning.* The most effective feedback is immediate, specific, and provides corrective information about how well we're doing.

One of the most effective ways of providing feedback is through our interactions with learners. For instance, let's consider the concept *density* again. Students commonly equate density with weight, concluding that heavy objects are more dense than light objects. When they do, they must be provided with feedback that helps them eliminate this misconception. As an example, let's look at a class where the teacher had students compress cotton in a cup to illustrate density.

Teacher: What can we conclude about the cotton now? (after being compressed)

Student: It's heavier.

Teacher: How does the total amount of cotton we have now compare to the amount before we compressed it?

Student: It's . . . the same.

Teacher: So, if the amount is the same, how does the weight now compare to the weight before?

Student: It must be . . . the same.

Teacher: What is different?

Student: The . . . amount of space it takes up. It's "squished" down.

Teacher: Yes, good. The volume is less, but the weight is the same. Only the density has changed.

This kind of interactive feedback is essential for learning. Merely explaining that the weight is the same is much less effective, because students passively listen to the explanation instead of actively wrestling with their own understanding.

Classroom Management

Case **STUDY**

The teacher says, "We have a little filmstrip on weather." And she quickly overviews the content of the filmstrip, which is called "The Weather is Poetry." As the teacher arranges the filmstrip in the machine, she says, "Before we start this, we're going to turn out the light, but you can finish your work anyway. We're going to pick it up afterwards." Greg says, "Miss, I can't see to finish." The teacher says, "Yes, you can. Your eyes will adjust." Andrew is yelling, "Lights off, lights off," four times. Finally, the teacher starts the filmstrip, which is a sound filmstrip. Someone turns the lights off. Everyone starts yelling, "I can't see. It's dark in here." The teacher assures everyone that their eyes will adjust. As the film is running, the students talk, move around. Apparently, two of them go outside to work, although the observer did not notice until later. Some move desks. Observer notes that no one can hear the movie. Joe comes in from the hall and stands at the front of the room to watch. The class finally settles a little. About half are watching the film, and half are working on the assignment in the dark. The teacher walks out of the room. And then she walks about the room. She says, "In a few minutes, you're going to see the part about the mud. That's my favorite part. They describe the sound of people walking in the mud." Greg says, "Turn on the lights." The teacher ignores him. During the filmstrip there is a steady exchange of students with restroom passes. Susan comes in, Joe goes out. The teacher goes out. Robert calls after her sarcastically, "You missed the mud" (From Evertson, C., (1982) *Teacher behavior, student achievement and student attitudes: A multi-classroom study.* Presentation at the annual meeting of the American Educational Research Association, Boston. Reprinted by permission.)

■ ■ ■

Classroom management is the number-one concern of beginning teachers (Rose & Gallup, 1999), and this episode helps us understand why. Students learn less in classrooms that are disorderly, and research indicates that disruptive students are an important source of teacher stress (Abel & Sewell, 1999).

Classroom management refers to *teachers' abilities to create and maintain orderly classrooms.* The importance of classroom management in effectively run classrooms is clear. One group of researchers concluded, "Effective classroom management has been shown to increase student engagement, decrease disruptive behaviors, and enhance use of instructional time, all of which results in improved student achievement" (Wang et al., 1993, p. 262). Effective management is one of the key characteristics of an effective school (Purkey & Smith, 1983), and an orderly classroom increases students' motivation to learn (Radd, 1998).

Commonly overlooked in discussions of management and discipline is the role of effective instruction. Effective teaching and classroom management are interdependent.

Classroom management, when done right, not only maintains an orderly learning environment, but also teaches students about their rights and responsibilities in relation to others.

**Increasing
Understanding 9.6**

Based on what you saw in the beginning episode with Martina Hernandez, does she base her management on an obedience model or on a responsibility model? Cite specific evidence from the episode to support your answer.

It's virtually impossible to maintain an orderly classroom in the absence of effective teaching, and effective teaching is impossible when students are disruptive (Doyle, 1986).

We have two goals when we plan for and implement classroom management. The first is to create environments that promote the most learning possible (Morine-Dershimer & Reeve, 1994), and the second is to help students learn to manage and direct their own learning (McCaslin & Good, 1992).

In attempting to accomplish the second goal, the difference between an obedience orientation and a responsibility orientation is important (Curwin & Mendler, 1988). An **obedience model of management** *teaches students to follow rules and obey authority using reward and punishment.* A **responsibility model of management,** by contrast, *teaches students to be responsible for their actions by explaining reasons for rules and applying logical consequences for behavior.* Differences between these orientations are outlined in Table 9.2.

Let's see how one kindergarten teacher, faced with a handful of wet, dripping students, applied logical consequences in her classroom.

Case
STUDY

The kindergarten boys found a lovely mud puddle in the playground during recess. They had much fun running and splashing and then came back into the room wet and dripping, and they left muddy footprints all over the room.

Their teacher called them aside for a conference. "Boys, we have two problems here. One is that the classroom is all dirty and it needs to be fixed so that the other children don't get wet and dirty. What can you do to fix it?"

One little boy suggested that they could mop the floor.

"Good idea," said the teacher. "Let's find our custodian, Mrs. Smith, and you can get a mop from her and mop the floor. Now what about our other problem, your dirty clothes?"

"We could call our mothers and ask them to bring us clean clothes!" suggested one boy.

Table 9.2	The Obedience and Responsibility Models of Management	
	Obedience Model	**Responsibility Model**
Goal	Teach students to follow orders.	Teach students to make responsible choices.
Organizing Principle	Obey authority.	Learn from actions and decisions.
Teacher Actions	Punish and reward.	Explain and apply logical consequences.
Student Outcomes	Students learn obedience and conformity.	Students internalize the reasons for rules and learn to self-regulate.

Source: From Curwin, R., & Mendler, A. (1998). *Discipline with dignity.* Alexandria, VA: Association for Supervision and Curriculum Development. Adapted by permission.

"Another good idea," said the teacher. "But what if your mothers are not home?"

This was a tougher problem. Finally, one boy said, "I know, we could borrow some clean clothes from the lost and found box!"

"Good thinking," said the teacher. "And what can we do so that you don't lose so much time from class again?"

"Stay out of mud puddles!" was the reply in unison (McCarthy, 1991, p. 19).

■ ■ ■

By involving students in problem solving about their own behavior, the teacher creatively turned the possibility of discipline into an opportunity for learning.

Effective Assessment

■ ■ ■

A middle school science teacher notices that her students have difficulty applying scientific principles to everyday events. In an attempt to improve this ability, she focuses on everyday problems (for example, why different cubes of wood that are the same size float differently in water), which students have to solve in groups and then discuss as a class. On Fridays, she presents another problem (for example, why two clear liquids of the same volume, when put on a balance, don't have the same mass), and the students have to solve it in groups. As they work, she circulates among them, taking notes that will be used for assessment and feedback.

■ ■ ■

A health teacher reads in a professional journal that the biggest problem people have in applying first aid is not the mechanics per se, but knowing what to do and when. In an attempt to address this problem, the teacher periodically has unannounced "catastrophe" days. Students entering the classroom encounter a catastrophe victim with an unspecified injury. With each victim they must first diagnose the problem and then apply first-aid interventions.

■ ■ ■

As we better understand how people learn and how effective teachers contribute to the process, we see that teaching is much more complex than it appears on the surface. Promoting learning requires much more than simply explaining topics to learners. Students interpret what they hear in an effort to make sense of it, and these interpretations may result in distortions and misunderstandings. As teachers, our goal is to prevent these misconceptions, if possible, and to help learners eliminate them if they occur.

Reflect *on* This

MAINTAINING ORDER IN THE CLASSROOM

You're a first-year, sixth-grade world history teacher in an urban middle school, and you're having a difficult time maintaining order in your classroom. Some of your students talk and whisper while you're lecturing and explaining the information in the text. For example, you're beginning the study of factors leading up to World War I, and you explain that one of the factors was increased nationalism—loyalty to a country's language and culture. As you're explaining, some of the students talk openly to each other; a few even get out of their seats and sharpen pencils in the middle of your presentation. You threaten them with referrals and other punishments, which work briefly, but the disruptions soon recur.

Other students seem listless and make no effort to pay attention; several even put their heads down on the desk during the lesson. You try walking around the room as you talk, and you stand near the inattentive students, but neither strategy works well.

1. Why do you suppose some of the students are disruptive?
2. Why do you believe many of the students are inattentive?
3. Are teachers responsible for making sure that students pay attention in class, or should paying attention be the responsibility of students?
4. What would you do in this situation?

To answer these questions online and receive immediate feedback, go to the Reflect on This Module in Chapter 9 of the Companion Website.

But how will we know if learners have distorted or inaccurate understandings of the topics they're studying? The only way we can find out is through **assessment,** which is *the process of gathering information and making conclusions about student learning.* As we better understand learning, we realize that assessment is much more than simply giving a test after a unit. In fact, to promote clear and deep understanding of the topics students study, assessment must be an integral part of teaching. For instance, Martina was continually assessing her students' understanding of fractions during her lesson. Her efforts to help students understand fractions and her assessment of their understanding were inseparable; she was doing both simultaneously.

Assessment, and the grading that accompanies it, can be challenging for first-year teachers. As one first-year teacher commented:

■ ■ ■

Of all the paperwork, grading is the nitty-gritty of teaching for me. Students take their grade as the bottom line of your class. It is the end-all and be-all of the class. To me, a grade for a class is, or at least should be, a combination of ability, attitude, and effort. Put bluntly: How do you nail a kid who really tried with an F? Or how do you reward a lazy, snotty punk with an A? (Ryan, 1992, p. 4).

■ ■ ■

Another teacher explained:

■ ■ ■

Grading is still kind of a problem with me. . . . I try not to play favorites (even though I have them)—I don't like S's personality . . . I do like J's, isn't it unfair? You want to be easier on someone you like. Or harder on someone you don't. . . . I wouldn't mind taking a class on grading. I think grading could be hit much harder in college . . . I just don't know what to do. . . (Bullough, 1989, p. 66).

■ ■ ■

As you progress through your teacher-education program, you'll learn how to assess students in different ways, including alternative assessments.

Changing Views of Assessment: Alternative Assessments Think about your experiences as a student, and think further about some of the tests you've taken. If your experiences are typical, many were multiple-choice, true-false, or fill-in-the-blank tests. These traditional formats—particularly multiple-choice—have been the mainstay of both classroom assessments and standardized intelligence and achievement tests. In recent years, they've been increasingly criticized (Paris, 1998; Reckase, 1997). In response to these criticisms, the use of **alternative assessments,** or *assessments that directly measure student performance through "real life" tasks* (Wiggins, 1996/97; Worthen, 1993) are being emphasized.

Some examples of alternative assessments include:

- Writing an essay or letter to the editor of the school newspaper.
- Comparing the amounts and percentages saved from different newspaper advertisements.
- Designing menus for a week's worth of balanced meals.
- Designing and conducting an experiment to see which brand of aspirin is likely to be most effective.
- Creating an original piece of watercolor art.
- Giving a speech in support of one side of a controversial topic.

In addition to products, such as the essay, menu, or piece of art, teachers using alternative assessments examine the thinking students do as they create the products. For example, the teacher might interview students to examine their thinking as they design the experiment, organize the essay, or create the art.

The idea of alternative assessment isn't new. Oral exams, exhibits of art work, proficiency testing in language, and hands-on assessments in vocational areas, such as word processing, have been used for years. In recent years, however, concerns about traditional testing, primarily in multiple-choice formats, and the perception that our students aren't performing as well as they should be, has caused more widespread interest in alternative assessment.

Alternative assessments commonly occur in two forms. **Performance assessments** *ask learners to demonstrate their competence in a lifelike situation.* Applying first aid, writing an essay, or giving a speech are all examples of performance assessments because they ask students to demonstrate their knowledge in realistic, lifelike situations.

In a second form of alternative assessment, teachers evaluate **portfolios,** which are *collections of student work that are judged against preset criteria.* Research suggests that over half the teachers in the United States currently use portfolios to assess student learning in some area of learning (Viadero,1999a). You were introduced to portfolios in Chapter 1, you are creating portfolio products related to the content of each chapter, and a detailed discussion of teaching portfolios appears in Chapter 10.

One unique feature of portfolios is that students are actively involved in selecting and evaluating portfolio content. For example, in a language arts class, students might select different pieces that they have written over the course of a year. These writing samples then provide concrete evidence of writing progress for parents, the teacher, and the students themselves. (As you develop your teaching portfolio during your teacher-preparation experience, you'll see similar evidence of growth in your teaching expertise.)

Increasing Understanding 9.7

A geography teacher assesses her students' understanding of longitude and latitude by having them identify the longitudes and latitudes of several cities around the world. Is this a traditional or an alternative assessment? Explain.

Alternative assessments provide opportunities for students to demonstrate their knowledge in active, realistic ways.

■ USING OUR UNDERSTANDING OF LEARNING TO DEFINE EFFECTIVE TEACHING

In the first section of the chapter, we looked at research focusing on teachers: their personal characteristics as well as how they involved students, presented topics, and assessed their students' understanding. We saw that some teachers apply these variables more effectively than do others, and as a result, their students' achievement is higher.

We now turn to important questions such as, How do students learn? and How can we use our understanding of learning to teach more effectively? We saw in Chapter 1 that professional teachers have a great deal of knowledge about learners and learning. The answers to these questions provide some of this knowledge.

Psychology, and particularly educational psychology, attempts to explain how we learn and develop. We examine this body of knowledge in this section.

Increasing Understanding 9.8

What were Martina Hernandez's goals? Describe specifically what she did to help her students reach these goals.

Behaviorism

You probably recognize the names Pavlov and Skinner. These learning theorists were major figures in **behaviorism,** *a view of learning that—as the name implies—focuses on specific and observable behaviors.*

Behaviorism dominated learning theory and education for the first half of the 20th century. From a behaviorist perspective, **learning** is *a change in observable behavior occurring as the result of experience.* In a behaviorist classroom, learning occurs when students consistently give specific, observable, desired responses to questions. The way they learn to give these responses is determined by reinforcement and punishment. For example, if a teacher asks, "How do you spell *Tennessee?*" and the student responds "T-e-n-n-e-s-s-e-e," the teacher nods and says, "Right!" Spelling *Tennessee* is specific, the teacher can observe (hear) the correct spelling, and the teacher's smile and comment reinforce the student; consequently, the response is strengthened. However, if the student responds, "T-e-n-e-s-s-e-e," the teacher would correct him or her by saying, "Not quite" or "You'd better check your list," decreasing the likelihood that the student will use the incorrect spelling a second time.

According to behaviorism, the goal of instruction is to increase the number, or strength, of correct student responses. Learning is measured by observing changes in behavior, such as seeing that students correctly spell 12 of 20 words on a list on Monday but correctly spell 16 on Wednesday.

When using behaviorism as a guide for planning and conducting instruction, the teacher designs learning activities that require students to produce specific, observable responses to questions and exercises. Then, during lessons, the teacher reinforces desired responses (as we saw when the student spelled *Tennessee* correctly) and punishes undesired ones.

Let's look now at a teacher using behaviorism to structure his instruction.

Case STUDY

Kevin Lageman, an eighth-grade English teacher at Longview Middle school, is working with his students on pronoun cases.

"All right, listen everyone," Kevin begins. "Today, we're going to begin a study of pronoun cases. . . . Everybody turn to page 484 in your text.

"This is important," he continues, "because we want to be able to use good English when we write, and this is one area where people get mixed up. . . . So, when we're finished with our study here, you'll all be able to use pronouns correctly in your writing."

He then displays the following on the overhead:

- Pronouns use the nominative case when they're subjects and predicate nominatives.

- Pronouns use the objective case when they're direct objects, indirect objects, or objects of prepositions.

"Let's review briefly," Kevin continues. "Give me a sentence that has both a direct and indirect object in it. . . . Anyone?"

"Mr. Lageman gives too much homework," Leon offers, to the laughter of the class.

Kevin smiles and writes the sentence on the chalkboard; he then continues, "Okay, Leon. Good sentence, even though it's incorrect. I don't give you *enough* work. . . . What's the subject in the sentence?"

There's no reply from Leon.

"Go ahead, Leon."

"Ahh, . . . *Mr. Lageman.*"

"Yes, good. *Mr. Lageman* is the subject," Kevin replies, as he underlines *Mr. Lageman* in the sentence and writes "Subject" above it.

"Now, what's the direct object? . . . Joanne?"

". . . *Homework.*"

"All right, good. And what's the indirect object? . . . Anya?"

". . . *Us.*"

"Excellent, everybody."

Kevin continues by reviewing predicate nominatives and objects of prepositions.

He then continues, "Now, let's look at a few examples of pronouns up here on the overhead."

He then displays 10 sentences. The following are the first four.

1. Did you get the card from Kelly and (I, me)?

2. Will Antonio and (she, her) run the concession stand?

3. They treat (whoever, whomever) they hire very well.

4. I looked for someone (who, whom) could give me directions to the theater.

"Okay, look at the first one. Which is correct? . . . Omar?"

". . . *Me.*"

"Good, Omar. How about the second one? . . . Lonnie?"

". . . *Her.*"

"Not quite, Lonnie. This one is a little tricky, but it's the nominative case."

Kevin then points up at the overhead and says, "How about the third one. . . . Cheny?"

". . . I don't know. . . . *whomever,* I guess."

"Excellent, Cheny. Indeed, that's correct."

Kevin continues with the rest of the sentences and assigns a page of similar exercises from the students' books as homework.

On Tuesday, Wednesday, and Thursday, Kevin covers the rules for pronoun-antecedent agreement (pronouns must agree with their antecedents in gender and number) and using indefinite pronouns as antecedents for personal pronouns (*anybody, either, each, one, someone*). He then has the students work on examples as he had done before.

On Friday, Kevin gives a test that is composed of 30 sentences: 10 of the sentences deal with case, 10 more with antecedents, and the final 10 with indefinite pronouns.

The following are some items from the test:

For each of the items below, mark A on your answer sheet if the pronoun case is correct in the sentence, and mark B if it is incorrect. If it is incorrect, supply the correct pronoun.

1. Be careful *who* you tell.

2. Will Renee and *I* be in the outfield?

3. My brother and *me* like water skiing.

Increasing Understanding 9.9

Give an example of the use of punishment in Kevin's interaction with his students. Explain why it is an example of punishment.

■ ■ ■

Now let's look at Kevin's lesson and see how it is based on behaviorism. To elicit observable responses, he displayed exercises such as:

1. Did you get the card from Kelly and (I, me)? and then asked, "Okay, look at the first one. Which is correct? . . . Omar?" Omar responded by saying "Me," and Kevin reinforced him by saying, "Good, Omar." Kevin designed the learning activity so that students could give specific, observable responses, which he could reinforce if correct, as he did with Omar.

Learning to provide specific, observable responses is desirable for some forms of fact learning, such as a learner being able to respond, "54" quickly and effortlessly when asked, "What is six times nine?" Behaviorists often view memorization of facts as a foundation or prerequisite for more complex behaviors. For example, knowing multiplication tables helps in solving word problems, and being able to pronounce words quickly and efficiently helps students comprehend when they read (Mayer, 1998; Bruning et al., 1999).

For many other learning goals, however, behaviorism isn't a satisfactory basis for guiding instruction. For instance, being able to write effectively was Kevin's goal for his students, as indicated by his comment, "This [using pronoun cases correctly] is important, because we want to be able to use good English when we write. . . . So, when we're finished with our study here, you'll all be able to use pronouns correctly in your writing."

Behaviorism emphasizes the learning of discrete items of information through practice and reinforcement.

However, writing is a complex process that includes planning, putting ideas on paper, and revising the ideas until they clearly communicate (Hayes, 1996). Being able to provide specific, observable responses to exercises involving grammar rules is unlikely to result in improved writing ability (Mayer, 1999; Kellogg, 1994). Instead, students learn to write by planning, translating their plans into drafts, and revising. The more they practice and think about their writing, the better their writing becomes.

A primary problem with behaviorism is that it treats learners as if they're passive, that is, they change their behavior in response to reinforcers and punishers. However, anyone who has taught knows that students can be dynamos of energy who want to move and talk and share their opinions. A second problem with behaviorism is that it reduces the teacher's role to simply dispensing rewards and punishers. Teaching is much more than that.

How do cognitive views of learning address these limitations? We try to answer this question in the next section.

Cognitive Views of Learning

To begin this section, let's look at some ideas that students have about a variety of topics.

■ Large objects are more dense than small objects.
■ The larger the number in the denominator, the larger the fraction.
■ The phases of the moon are caused by clouds.

Obviously, teachers didn't teach these ideas, and students certainly weren't reinforced for expressing them. Instead, students created, or "constructed," them on their own. As researchers began to systematically examine students' thinking in cases like these, they arrived at an inescapable conclusion: *learners don't passively respond to the*

Table 9.3	Comparison of Behaviorist and Cognitive Views of Learning and Teaching		
	View of Learning	**View of Learners**	**Role of the Teacher**
Behaviorist	Increase in number of desirable responses resulting from reinforcement.	Passive recipients of stimuli (reinforcers and punishers) from the environment.	Present reinforcers to increase desirable behaviors, and present punishers to decrease undesirable behaviors.
Cognitive	Developing understanding by searching for patterns in the world.	Constructors of knowledge through actively processing information from the environment.	Guide learners in their efforts to make sense of the world.

environment; they actively seek to make sense of it. Researchers' efforts led to what is called the "cognitive revolution," which began about the middle of the 20th century and continues to this day.

The cognitive revolution led to a view of learning dramatically different from behaviorists' perspectives. From a cognitive perspective, **learning** *is a change in a person's mental representations of the world that may or may not result in an immediate change in behavior.* The idea that learners are mentally active is at the core of cognitive learning theory, and it has important implications for teaching. For example, teachers can clearly explain an idea to students, but students don't mentally "record" the idea as presented; rather, they try to make sense of it and link it to what they already know. If the teacher's presentation doesn't make sense, students are likely to retain their existing ideas, such as clinging to the belief that bigger objects are denser. Many teachers incorrectly think that a clear explanation automatically results in student understanding, but this often isn't the case.

Table 9.3 summarizes differences between behaviorist and cognitive views of learning. Let's see what these differences look like in classrooms.

Case STUDY

Leslie Nelson, another English teacher at Longview Middle School, is also working on pronoun cases with her students.

She begins by saying, "We're making progress on the editorial section of the school newspaper we've been working on. I've read the essays you turned in on Friday, and your writing is getting better and better, but we have some things to work on today that will improve your essays even more. She then turns on two overheads; a paragraph is displayed on each. On the left, one paragraph appears as follows:

■ ■ ■

Katrina and Simone were talking. "Did you get that information *from Kelly and me*?" Simone asked.

"No, I didn't," Katrina responded. "What was it about?"

"Kelly wanted to know if it's okay *that Molly and she* run the concession stand on Friday night at the game."

"Sure, that's fine with me," Katrina responded. "The teachers treat *whoever work* there very well, so everything will be fine. By the way, *to whom* do I give the list of people *who are working* that night?"

■ ■ ■

On the right overhead, the second paragraph looks like this:

■ ■ ■

Katrina and Simone were talking. "Did you get that information *from Kelly and I?*" Simone asked.

"No, I didn't," Katrina responded. "What was it about?"

"Kelly wanted to know if it's okay *that Molly and her* run the concession stand on Friday night at the game."

"Sure, that's fine with me," Katrina responded. "The teachers treat *whomever work* there very well, so everything will be fine. By the way, *to who* do I give the list of people *whom are working* that night?"

■ ■ ■

Leslie gives the students a moment to read the paragraphs, and then says, "Get together with your partner and see if you can figure out how these passages are similar and different. You've got two minutes." After two minutes, she calls the class back together and continues, "Look at the parts of the paragraphs that are italicized. . . . Let's start with the first one. What do you notice about them? . . . Devon?"

After a couple seconds, Devon offers, "*Me* over there [pointing at the left screen] and *I* over there [pointing at the right screen]."

"Okay," Leslie nods. "What else? . . . Tonya?"

"Both . . . have *Kelly.*"

"Okay, good. What else? . . . Carlos?"

"*From.*"

"What do you mean, *from?*"

"Both have *from* in the . . . different kind of letters."

"All right, good observations everyone. . . . Now, look at the one on the left again. What part of speech is the word *from*? . . . Andrew?"

" . . . A preposition, I think."

"Yes, excellent, Andrew. It is a preposition. . . . So, let's take a look at this," Leslie continues. She then takes the paragraph off the right overhead and displays the following:

■ Pronouns use the nominative case when they're subjects and predicate nominatives.

■ Pronouns use the objective case when they're direct objects, indirect objects, or objects of prepositions.

She gives the students a few seconds to read the rules, and she then continues, "I'd like you to work with your partner again and decide, based on these rules, which of the two versions up here is correct. Again, I'll give you 2 minutes." When the 2 minutes are up, she continues, "So, which do you believe is correct, . . . 'from Kelly and me' or 'from Kelly and I' . . . Jon?"

"I . . . think it should be 'from Kelly and I.' "

"And why do you think so?"

" . . . It sounds better, I think."

"Listen to this and tell us which one sounds better: 'Kelly and me got some soft drinks,' or 'Kelly and I got some soft drinks.' "

" . . . 'Kelly and I.' "

"Must be, 'from Kelly and me,' " Calvin volunteers.

"Why do you think so?"

"Well, they're . . . not the subject, and *I* was used when it was the subject, . . . so it must be *me.*"

"Hmm, class, think about this. . . . 'Kelly and I' are what part of the sentence?" . . . April?"

"The . . . subject."

"Yes, good. Indeed they are. So, . . . let's go back to the other example. Which is correct?"

Looking Through

Classroom Windows

LEARNING ABOUT BALANCE BEAMS IN FOURTH GRADE

Having examined the personal characteristics, strategies, and classroom management of effective teachers, as well as differences between behaviorism and cognitive views of learning, you now have the chance to examine an actual classroom lesson on videotape. To complete this activity, you need to do the following:

■ View the video episode titled, "Learning About Balance Beams in Fourth Grade."

■ To read the written transcripts of the two lessons and answer the following questions online, go to the *Classroom Windows* Module in Chapter 9 of the Companion Website at: **http://www.prenhall.com/kauchak.** Go to the Website and follow the directions on your screen.

■ Answer the questions that follow:

1. Is Jenny's instruction based primarily on behaviorism or primarily on cognitive views of learning? Explain your reasoning.

2. To what extent did Jenny display the personal characteristics of effective teachers, the strategies of effective teachers, and effective classroom management? Cite specific evidence from the lesson to support your conclusions.

3. Which of the educational philosophies (described in Chapter 5) is most nearly reflected in Jenny's teaching? Explain why you think so.

4. We examined explicit and implicit curricula in Chapter 8. Describe both the explicit and implicit curriculum implied in Jenny's lesson. Cite specific evidence from the lesson to support your conclusions.

5. To what extent did Jenny display professionalism in the episode you saw? Explain your analysis.

Ⓦ *To answer these questions online and receive immediate feedback, go to the Looking Through Classroom Windows Module in Chapter 9 of the Companion Website.*

Leslie continues the discussion until 20 minutes are left in the period. Students then begin revising their paragraphs in light of the information they have learned that day; they turn them in the next day. On Tuesday and Wednesday, Leslie continues the discussion with two additional paragraphs, and on Thursday, she returns the students' writing assignments and completes the discussion of pronouns, their antecedents, and indefinite pronouns.

On Friday, Leslie assigns an additional paragraph to be written as a quiz. The students have to embed at least two examples each of pronoun cases, pronouns and antecedents, and indefinite pronouns in the paragraphs. In addition, she has students read each others' essays, checking for the content they've just been studying.

■ ■ ■

Let's compare Leslie's lesson to Kevin's. Their goals were the same; they wanted their students to correctly apply the rules for nominative and objective cases in their writing. Their approaches were very different, however. Whereas Kevin focused on isolated items of information, such as a sentence like, "Did you get the card from Kelly and (I, me)?" Leslie made her examples more realistic by embedding them in the context of paragraphs—that is, they were like information we find in books, newspapers, and magazines. Second, instead of reinforcing and punishing specific responses, Leslie led a discussion of the rules, why they made sense, and how they were used. Her

Teaching

in an Era of Reform

TEACHER-CENTERED VERSUS LEARNER-CENTERED INSTRUCTION

In Chapter 8, we saw that over-emphasis on memorization and drill-and-practice activities resulted in the math reforms emphasized in the 1989 *Curriculum and Evaluation Standards for School Mathematics*. Critics suggested that this changing emphasis left students with inadequate basic skills, so they called for a new wave of reform, reflected in the *Principles and Standards for School Mathematics* (2000). This is a specific example of broad trends in curriculum reform; reforms occur, criticisms of the reform begin, and counter reforms are then offered. Similar issues exist in instruction. We examine these issues in this section.

Historically, teachers have extensively utilized **teacher-centered instruction,** meaning *teachers carefully specify objectives, present the content to be learned, and actively direct learning activities* (Shuell, 1996). For example, a teacher might want her students to solve algebraic equations for the values of *a* and *b*, such as:

$$4a + 6b = 24$$
$$5a - 6b = 3$$

Using a teacher-centered approach, teachers model and explain the solution to the problem and then have students practice, first with their guidance, and then independently. A lecture, in which teachers systematically present carefully organized information, is another example.

Teacher-centered instruction has been criticized as being based on behaviorist views of learning, focusing primarily on low-level objectives at the expense of deep understanding (Marshall, 1992; Stoddart, Connell, Stofflett, & Peck, 1993). The following lesson segment involving a third-grade teacher who is attempting to help her third graders understand place value illustrates these criticisms:

The teacher, based on the directions given in the teacher's manual, begins by putting 45 tally marks on the chalkboard and circles four groups of 10.

Teacher: How many groups of 10 do we have there, boys and girls?

Children: 4.

Teacher: We have 4 groups of 10, and how many left over?

Children: 5.

Teacher: We had 4 tens and how many left over?

Beth: 4 tens.

Sarah: 5.

Teacher: 5. Now, can anybody tell me what number that could be? We have 4 tens and 5 ones. What is that number? Ann?

Ann: (Remains silent)

Teacher: If we have 4 tens and 5 ones, what is that number?

Ann: 9.

Teacher: Look at how many we have there (points to the 4 groups of ten) and 5 ones. If we have 4 tens and 5 ones we have? (slight pause) 45.

Children: 45.

Teacher: Very good (Wood, Cobb, & Yackel, 1992, p. 180).

Unfortunately, getting the students to say "45" didn't really change the way they understood place value in numbers.

Criticisms of teacher-centered instruction led to a wave of reform; this resulted in the development of **learner-centered instruction,** *which encourages teachers to guide learners toward a thorough understanding of the topics they study,* rather than simply explaining content to them. Prominent professional publications that illustrate this emphasis include *How Students Learn: Reforming our Schools Through Learner-Centered Education,* which was published by the American Psychological Association in 1998, and *The Right to Learn,* which was written by Linda Darling-Hammond (a well-known Columbia University educator) and published in 1998.

Discovery learning, where *the teacher identifies a content goal, arranges information so that patterns can be found, and guides students to the goal,* and **cooperative learning,** which *consists of students working together in groups small enough so that everyone can participate in a clearly assigned task* (Cohen, 1994), are prominent examples of learner-centered approaches to instruction. Leslie Nelson used aspects of both in her lesson. First, she displayed the paragraphs on the overhead and then said, "Get together with your partner and see if you can figure out how these passages are similar and different. . . ." Working together capitalizes on cooperative learning, and looking for similarities and differences is characteristic of discovery learning.

Putting Instructional Reform into Perspective

Teacher-centered instruction is criticized because it emphasizes teacher actions rather than student understanding. As the dialogue on place value suggests, Ann, and probably many others, didn't understand place value, and the teacher did little to increase their understanding. Once students' gave the desired response, they were reinforced with "Very good," and the lesson moved on.

Cognitive views of learning emphasize social interaction and the active involvement of learners in hands-on activities.

This pattern of focusing on student verbalization or overt performance at the expense of understanding occurs in many classrooms (Goodlad, 1984; Stodolsky, 1988); seeing that the instruction is teacher-centered, critics place the blame on the approach, suggesting that—in addition to being based on behaviorism—content is delivered primarily through lecture and explanation. Student thinking is minimized, critics assert; they contend "that the most effective learning takes place when students are able to make choices about what they're doing [and] when they're able to play an active role in making sense of ideas" (Kohn, 1999, p. 43).

Defenders of teacher-centered instruction argue that the problem is not with instructional approach; rather, it is with the teacher's inability to implement it effectively. When teacher-centered instruction is done *effectively*, they argue, none of these criticisms is true (Rosenshine, 1997). Expert teacher-centered instruction keeps learners involved, and understanding and thinking are strongly emphasized. Those who defend teacher-centered instruction further argue that some criticisms of teacher-centered instruction are made on political grounds, teacher-centered instruction not being "politically correct or romantically correct" (Rosenshine, 1997, p. 2).

Similar issues exist with learner-centered instruction. Critics suggest that this approach is one more example of widespread "dumbing down" of the curriculum, that learning basic skills is abandoned in favor of fuzzy thinking, and self-esteem is emphasized instead of understanding (Battista, 1999; Schoen, Fey, Hirsch, & Coxford, 1999). As a result, counter reforms have resulted in a pendulum shift back in the direction of teacher-centered instruction (Stein & Carnine, 1999).

However, emphasizing real-world applications, involving students in learning activities, using high-quality examples and representations, and focusing on deep understanding—all principles of learner-centered instruction—are inarguable.

As with most issues involving reform, teacher decision making and professionalism are keys. No strategy—teacher-centered or learner-centered—is more or less effective than the ability of the teacher implementing it. Teacher-centered approaches are more effective for some topics, whereas learner-centered approaches are better for others. Research suggests that most teachers are eclectic, using both teacher-centered and learner-centered strategies to promote student learning (Viadero, 1999a). Your ability to make decisions about which strategy to use in different situations, and your ability to use both strategies effectively, will determine how much your students learn.

You Take a Position

Now it's your turn to take a position on the issue discussed in this section. Go to the *Education Week* Website at **http://www.edweek.com,** find "search" on the first page, and type in one of the following two search terms: *effective teaching* or *effective teachers*. Locate a minimum of three articles on one of these topics and then do the following:

1. Identify the title, author, and date of each article and then write a one-paragraph summary of each.

2. Identify a pattern in the articles. (Each article—or even two of the three—suggesting that students in high-poverty schools have the greatest need for expert teachers, would be a pattern, for example.)

3. After identifying the pattern, take one of the two following positions:
   - The pattern suggested in the articles, if implemented, *is* likely to improve education.
   - The pattern suggested in the articles *is not* likely to improve education.

State your position in writing, and document your position with information taken from the articles.

To answer these questions online, go to the Take a Position Module in Chapter 9 of the Companion Website.

Exploring Diversity

Considering Multiple Perspectives

THE ACHIEVEMENT GAP AND EFFECTIVE TEACHING

In Chapter 6 we saw that a widening gap exists in the achievement of cultural minorities, particularly African American and Hispanic students, and their White and Asian counterparts (Hoff, 2000). We also saw in Chapter 6 that reducing class size is one promising aspect of school organization that can help close the gap. The effective-teaching research has much more to say about narrowing the achievement gap, particularly in the area of effective instruction. For example, in schools where the achievement gap is narrowing, the following exist (Barth et al., 1999; Haycock, 1998; Viadero, 2000b):

- A vision established by the school leadership that all students can and will learn.
- Specific and demanding goals.
- Teaching that actively involves students.
- Regular and thorough assessment of student progress.

These characteristics are consistent with both the research on effective schools that you studied in Chapter 7 and the effective-teaching research and cognitive views of learning discussed earlier in the chapter. A vision that all students can learn relates to *teaching efficacy*; specific and demanding goals are consistent with effective planning and high expectations; and the active involvement of learners is supported by cognitive learning theory.

Finally, regular and thorough assessment provides both teachers and learners with feedback about learning progress.

Sound instruction isn't enough, however. One study of inner-city minority high school students found that many effective practices were being implemented (Miller, Leinhardt, & Zigmond, 1988). The schools were adapting at every level, from school policies to classroom instruction, and this adaptation kept students in school. However, researchers also found:

- Lowered expectations for students.
- Lack of emphasis on higher level thinking and problem solving, with an increase in low-level worksheets.
- Student apathy and boredom.

In essence, increased efforts to provide instructional structure and support had resulted in a remedial program that lacked intellectual rigor and excitement.

Several programs have been developed to provide challenge for students. The Accelerated Schools Program builds on student strengths by combining high expectations with an enriched curriculum focusing on a language-based approach in all academic areas (Levin, 1988; Rothman, 1991). The Higher Order Thinking Skills Program (HOTS) focuses on teaching students skills such as inferencing and generalizing to help them realize the importance of critical thinking in learning (Pogrow, 1990).

---

approach emphasized a deep and thorough understanding of the rules. Not only was her approach more sophisticated and demanding than Kevin's, but it was also likely to result in more student learning. Her instruction was guided by cognitive views of learning; his was based on behaviorism.

The Changing Role *of* Teachers

Think back to your experiences as a student. If they were typical, you probably spent most of the day listening to your teacher lecture or explain topics to you and then completed a written assignment related to the topic (Goodlad, 1984; Cuban, 1984). At times, you may have spent entire class periods working on a seatwork assignment. Most of the questions the teacher asked, when she asked questions at all, required recall of memorized information. You were expected to work quietly and alone at your desk.

Teaching under these conditions was simpler than it is today (Darling-Hammond, 1998). The teacher's role was more manager of paperwork rather than instructor. Because students spent most of their time listening to the teacher, maintaining an orderly class-

Effective programs for minority students combine challenge with high expectations for success.

Results from both programs have been encouraging. One Accelerated Schools site in San Francisco registered the highest achievement gains on standardized test scores in the city, and spring-to-spring comparisons of achievement gains in one HOTS program showed students were 67 percent above the national average in reading and 123 percent higher in math (Rothman, 1991).

Common to both programs are high expectations, emphasis on enrichment versus remediation, and the teaching of higher-order thinking and learning strategies. These strategies are integrated into the regular curriculum so that students can see their usefulness in different content areas (Means & Knapp, 1991).

This research is encouraging. It suggests that teachers and schools can and do make a difference in student learning. Narrowing the achievement gap obviously isn't easy, and daunting problems remain. The task isn't impossible, however. With sustained effort, that gap can be narrowed.

room was reasonably easy. Teachers' biggest tasks were organizing and explaining the content they were teaching.

What you experienced was essentially *the teacher as technician.* As you recall from Chapter 1, we defined a technician as a person who can apply specific skills in completing a well-defined task, such as an electrician wiring an outlet. Teachers as technicians needed to understand the content they were teaching, and they needed to be skilled lecturers.

As you go out and observe in classrooms, you will likely see many examples of the teacher as a technician. However, this is no longer the ideal. The environment you will enter will be much more demanding; it will require you to be a professional, which means you must be able to apply a broad background of knowledge to make instructional decisions in complex situations. For instance, in addition to organizing the content you plan to teach, you will have to prepare examples and other representations that illustrate the topic in ways that students can understand. Then, instead of lecturing and explaining, you will ask questions that guide your students to their own understanding of the topics.

Preparing meaningful examples is difficult, and asking questions is a very complex process. You must decide, on the spot, what question to ask and whom to call on, while at the same time watching other students to be sure they're paying attention. You prompt students if they're unable to answer, but don't spend so much time with a single student that other students "drift off." These tasks require more than a skilled technician; they require an expert professional.

The diversity of your students will make your teaching even more complex. They will come from a variety of socioeconomic, cultural, and ethnic backgrounds. You'll need to adapt your instruction to students' unique backgrounds and learning styles. The expert professional is able to accommodate these differences to help all the students learn as much as possible.

To join the ranks of these experts, you must be intelligent, hard-working, sensitive, and caring. It is very challenging, but at the same time, one of the most rewarding experiences that exists.

■ SUMMARY

Looking in Classrooms to Define Effective Teaching
Effective teachers teach differently than their less effective counterparts. They believe they are capable of helping all students learn, they are caring, enthusiastic, and they have high expectations for their students. They actively involve students in learning through questioning; they provide detailed feedback about learning progress; they create orderly and learning focused environments; and they use assessment as a mechanism to further increase learning.

Using Our Understanding of Learning to Define Effective Teaching
Historically, learning was viewed as an increase in specific, observable student behaviors, and learners were seen as passively responding to their environments. This was teaching based on a behaviorist view of learning.

Near the middle of the 20th century, views of learning began to change, and learners were viewed as actively attempting to make sense of their experiences. Learners' background knowledge, interaction between the teacher and students, and the quality of examples and representations that teachers use are all essential in helping learners construct their own understanding of the topics they study.

The Changing Role of the Teacher
In the past, a teacher-as-technician perspective was quite common. Teachers simply organized and delivered content to students who listened passively. Now, the teacher-as-professional is expected to provide meaningful examples and representations, accommodate learner diversity, and maintain classroom order while at the same time actively involving students in learning activities. The teacher-as-professional requires work that is much more complex and demanding than it has ever been in the past.

■ IMPORTANT CONCEPTS

alternative assessment	behaviorism	classroom management
assessment	caring	cooperative learning

discovery learning
equitable distribution
feedback
goals
instructional alignment
learner-centered instruction
learning (behaviorist)

learning (cognitive)
modeling
obedience model of
   management
performance assessment
personal teaching efficacy
portfolios

questioning frequency
responsibility model of
   management
teacher-centered instruction
teacher effectiveness
   research
wait-time

■ DISCUSSION QUESTIONS

1. Why is the practice of calling on volunteers to answer a question so prevalent? What are its advantages? What are its disadvantages?

2. Virtually no teacher would suggest that it isn't important to be a good model. Given that belief, why do you suppose some teachers don't model the behaviors they expect their students to imitate?

3. Many teachers lecture instead of guiding their students to their goals using questioning. Why do you think this is the case?

4. Why is the obedience model of management so popular in many schools? What advantages and disadvantages does this perspective hold?

5. What will be the future of alternative assessment? Will it continue to be emphasized, or will emphasis decline in favor or more traditional testing? Why do you think so?

■ GOING INTO SCHOOLS

1. Interview a teacher about the use of questioning strategies to promote learning. Specifically ask the following:
    a. Why and how does the teacher use questions in class?
    b. How does the teacher decide who to call on?
    c. What does the teacher do if a student is unable to respond?
    d. What is the biggest challenge in using questions to promote learning?
    Compare the teacher's responses to the content of this chapter.

2. Observe a teacher in her classroom before she begins her instruction for the day. As you observe, attempt to answer the following questions:
    a. Before she begins her instruction, how much time does she spend on non-instructional activities, such as taking roll, passing out papers, and gathering materials to be used in the lesson?
    b. How does she conduct her instruction? Does she primarily lecture and explain, or does she ask a number of questions and guide her students to the goal with questioning?
    c. How much time does she spend in instruction, and how much time is spent having the students do seatwork?
    d. How often does she reprimand students for misbehavior? How does she reprimand?

e. How often does she praise students for desirable behavior or good answers to questions? Count the number of times she praises students.

On the basis of these observations, decide whether the instruction is based more on behaviorist or cognitive views of learning and teaching.

3. Obtain a copy of a test a teacher has used in reading, language arts, math, science, and social studies (if you're in an elementary school), or get a copy of a test for one of the courses the teacher teaches (if you're in a middle or secondary school). After examining the test, answer the following questions:

    a. What format is used (for example, multiple-choice, true-false, matching, etc.)?
    b. At what level are the items written? (That is, do they require mere recall of information, or do they require the students to apply understanding to new situations?)
    c. Talk with the teacher about his or her goals for the content being assessed. Were the goals and the assessment aligned? (That is, did the assessment measure important goals of instruction?)

4. Interview the teacher about her assessment practices. The following questions can be used to guide the interview.

    a. What does "alternative" or "performance" assessment mean to the teacher?
    b. Does she use alternative assessments in her teaching? If so, how does she use them?
    c. Does she use portfolios? If so, how does she use them?
    d. Examine the contents of a portfolio. What does the teacher include? Ask her how she decides what will be included and what will be left out.

On the basis of the interview, determine one advantage and one disadvantage of alternative assessment formats.

 Virtual Field Experience

If you would like to participate in a Virtual Field Experience, go to the *Field Experience* Module in Chapter 9 of the Companion Website.

■ ONLINE PORTFOLIO ACTIVITIES

 To complete these activities online, go to the *Portfolio Activities* Module in Chapter 9 of the Companion Website and submit your response.

Portfolio Activity 9.1   **Planning for Instruction**

INTASC Principle 7: *Planning*
The purpose of this activity is to help you think about the role of planning in effective instruction. Identify a topic and then write two specific goals related to the topic. Explain why the goals are important.

Portfolio Activity 9.2   **Designing Instruction**

INTASC Principle 1: *Knowledge of Subject*
The purpose of this activity is to assist you in thinking about alignment and ways that teachers can link goals to teaching strategies. Describe how you would help students from

a variety of backgrounds reach the goals you specified in Portfolio Activity 9.1. Be very specific in your description, and explain how you would accommodate background differences in your students.

Portfolio Activity 9.3

Assessing Student Understanding

INTASC Principle 8: *Assessment*

The purpose of this activity is to help you begin thinking about connections between assessment and instruction. Explain specifically how you would measure the extent to which your students reached the goals you described in Portfolio Activity 9.1.

PART 5

Careers

CHAPTER 10

Joining the Profession

10 Joining the Profession

Your path to teaching expertise is long and difficult, but worthwhile accomplishments are rarely easy.

In this chapter, we hope to take some of the surprises out of your first year of teaching and help you begin the transition from thinking like a student, who wants to do well in a course, to thinking like a teacher, who can make professional decisions in complex situations. To help you in this process, we try to answer the following questions:

- Who are beginning teachers, and what happens to them?

- What do beginning teachers believe, and how do these beliefs influence their behavior?

- What kinds of knowledge must teachers possess, and how does this knowledge influence their teaching?

- How are teachers licensed, and what efforts are being made to increase teacher professionalism?

- What can preservice teachers do to make themselves marketable, and how can they secure their first job?

- How can preservice teachers prepare for their first year of teaching?

Case STUDY

My first faculty meeting. Very interesting. Mrs. Zellner [the principal] seems like a really nice person. She went on and on about what a great job the teachers did last year and how test scores were way up compared to the year before. She also extended a special welcome to those of us who are new.

Speaking of new, there sure are a lot of us. I wonder if they're all as scared as I am. I'm not sure what I would have done if Mrs. Landsdorp [the teacher in the room next door] hadn't taken me under her wing. She made me feel a lot better about starting in an inner-city school. So many of the kids come from low-income homes, and English isn't the first language for a lot of them. She said that some of the teachers tend to "write them off" and assume that they can't learn, but that isn't true at all. In fact, a lot of them are quite bright. They just need help and support. She's wonderful. She's sort of gruff, but Andrea [a new friend and second-year teacher] say's she's a softy underneath, and she really loves the kids.

I can't believe how much there is to do—IEPs, progress reports, CPR training, responsibility to look for signs of abuse. When do I teach? I hope I can cut it. (Shelley, a new third-grade teacher, reflecting on her first faculty meeting.)

■ ■ ■

If you choose to teach when you finish your program—and statistics indicate that approximately 60 percent of you will begin teaching immediately after graduating (U.S. Department of Education, 1998e)—you'll join the growing ranks of beginning teachers. Let's take a look at this beginning-teacher population.

■ CHARACTERISTICS OF BEGINNING TEACHERS

You're a beginning teacher. Who are your colleagues? What does the future hold for you? How do you feel about teaching and the people who are now in the profession? We consider these questions in this section as we examine the following:

■ The beginning-teacher population.
■ What happens to beginning teachers.
■ The beliefs of preservice and beginning teachers.

The Beginning-Teacher Population

As the 20th century came to a close, nearly 2.7 million people taught in K–12 education in this country, with about 400,000 teaching in private schools (Snyder, 1999). However, many of these people will be retiring within the next few years. This, combined with increased immigration into our country, growing school populations, and the demand for smaller classes, leads researchers and policymakers to believe that school districts will need to hire about 200,000 teachers a year over the next decade, for a total of more than 2 million new teachers (Fideler & Haselkorn, 1999).

As we've moved into the new millennium, concerns about the looming teacher shortage have been so prominent that the October 2, 2000, issue of *Newsweek* asked "Who Will Teach Our Kids?" on its front cover and made "Teachers Wanted" its feature article. In the next few years, the teaching profession is going to see many more people like Shelley—that is, new teachers.

What do the Shelley's of the profession look like in comparison to the existing teaching force? They are more likely to be female (79 percent versus 74 percent for the total teaching force), White (91 percent compared to 87 percent), and younger (28 years old

Increasing Understanding 10.1

 The minority population of students in this country is increasing significantly. Considering this trend, why do you suppose the teaching population is becoming increasingly White? Also, as opportunities for women have increased in other professions, why is the teaching population becoming increasingly female? Explain in both cases.

To answer this question online and receive immediate feedback, go to the *Increasing Understanding* Module in Chapter 10 of the book's Companion Website at **http://www.prenhall.com/kauchak.**

as opposed to 43) (Darling-Hammond & Sclan, 1996). An increasing number of students have made the decision to enter teaching after they've graduated (as opposed to people like you, who are probably in an undergraduate teacher-preparation program) (Bradley, 1999b). These post-baccalaureate students tend to be older—about 30 years old—and are more likely to be male than are students in undergraduate programs.

What Happens to Beginning Teachers?

What happens to beginning teachers after they graduate from a college or university? As we saw earlier, about 60 percent immediately enter teaching, but a significant number drop out in the first few years (U.S. Department of Education, 1998e). The overall attrition rate for teachers—the percentage who leave the profession—is about 6 percent for public schools and about twice that rate for private schools, with low salaries in private schools being a commonly cited reason (Croasmun, Hampton, & Herrmann, 1999).

The number of *new* teachers who leave during their first year is much higher (about 15 percent). In addition, another 15 percent will leave after their second year, and still another 10 percent after their third year (Croasmun, Hampton, & Herrmann, 1999). Shelley's comment—"I'm not sure what I would have done if Mrs. Landsdorp hadn't taken me under her wing"—helps us understand why. Beginning teachers without mentors and support are nearly twice as likely to leave as those who have structured programs designed to help them make the transition from the university environment to the K–12 classroom.

Other reasons for this attrition also exist.

• • •

Wow! Was I naive. I was tired of sitting in classes, and I wanted so badly to be finished and get out into the "real world." What I never realized was just how cushy being a student was. If I was a little tired, or didn't study enough, I would just coast through class. Now, no coasting. You have to be ready every minute of every day. I've never been so tired in my life. You're in front of kids all day, and then you go home and work all night to get ready for the next day. They have us filling out reports, doing surveys, and everything other than teaching, so I don't get a chance to plan during the day. I can't even make a phone call unless it's during my lunch break or planning period.

And then there's my fourth period. They come in from lunch just wired. It takes me half the period to get them settled down, and that's on a good day.

Sometimes I just need someone to talk to, but we're all so busy. Everybody thinks they're an expert on teaching, because they've been a student. They don't have a clue. Let them try it for two days, and they'd be singing a different tune. (Antonio, a first-year high school English teacher.)

• • •

Antonio's lament helps us further understand why beginning teachers drop out. The paperwork, his fourth period class, and even a seemingly minor inconvenience like not having access to a phone illustrate negative factors such as (Shoho & Martin, 1999):

- Working conditions, in which teachers spend too much time on nonteaching duties, have too little time for planning, and don't have a moment to themselves.
- Dissatisfaction with student behavior and a disorderly teaching environment.
- Loneliness and alienation.

It probably is difficult to believe now, but separation from the support of your professors and other students can be very stressful in the first year of teaching (Bullough, 1989).

Increasing Understanding 10.2

 Of the factors listed here, which can teachers best control? What might they do to improve the situation with respect to the other factors?

Not all is gloom and doom, however.

■ ■ ■

My first lesson with the kids. Chris [her supervising teacher] said I was on my own, sink or swim. I hardly slept last night, but today I feel like celebrating. The kids were so into it. I brought my Styrofoam ball, and I had the kids compare the latitude and longitude lines I had drawn on it and then look at the globe. I thought the first period was supposed to be Chris's lowest, but they did the best. He was impressed.

Now I understand the stuff Dr. Martinez [one of her professors] stressed so much when he was always after us to use concrete examples and question, question, question. I know I have a lot to learn. I thought I could just explain everything to them, but they got confused and drifted off so fast I couldn't believe it. As soon as I started asking questions about the lines on the Styrofoam ball, though, they perked right up. I think I can do this. It was actually a heady experience. (Suzanne, an intern in a seventh-grade geography class.)

■ ■ ■

In Chapter 1, we talked about the rewards in teaching; Suzanne experienced some of those rewards. It is, indeed, a heady experience to see kids understand something new and know that you're the cause of that understanding.

Suzanne's comments also illustrate beliefs typical of preservice and beginning teachers. These beliefs often affect beginning teachers' professional growth. Let's take a look at them.

Beliefs of Beginning Teachers

The course for which this book is used is likely one of the first you'll take in your teacher-preparation program. One of the goals of the course is to help you begin the process of learning to teach.

Research indicates that teachers' beliefs have a strong influence on their teaching and learning to teach (Borko & Putnam, 1996). Our goal in this section is to help you become aware of your beliefs and perhaps dispel some that aren't helpful in your professional growth as a teacher.

To begin, we're asking you to complete a short survey. Using the following scale to guide your responses, circle the number that best represents your beliefs.

5 = Strongly agree

4 = Agree

3 = Agree and disagree

2 = Disagree

1 = Strongly disagree

1. When I begin teaching, I will be a better teacher than most of the teachers now in the field.   1 2 3 4 5

2. As I gain experience in teaching, I expect to become more confident in my ability to help children learn.   1 2 3 4 5

3. The most effective teachers are those able to most clearly explain the content they teach to their students.   1 2 3 4 5

4. I will learn about most of the important aspects of teaching when I get into a classroom.   1 2 3 4 5

5. If I thoroughly understand the content I'm teaching, I'll be able to figure out a way of getting it across to students.   1 2 3 4 5

Beginning teachers face many challenges, which can lead to many personal and professional rewards.

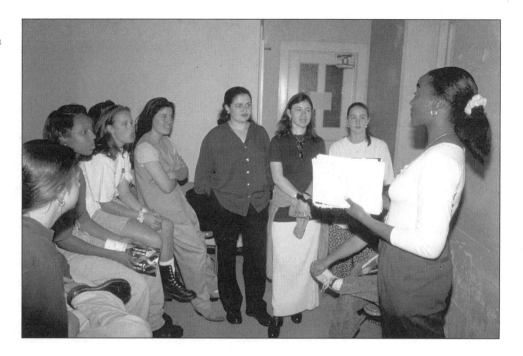

Let's see how you did. If you either agreed or strongly agreed with each of the statements, your beliefs are consistent with those generally held by other students in teacher-preparation programs. Let's see what research tells us about these beliefs.

Item 1: When I begin teaching, I will be a better teacher than most of the teachers now in the field. Preservice teachers are optimistic and idealistic, both of which are very positive characteristics. "Prospective teachers report being confident and self-assured in their teaching ability," but unfortunately, "preservice teachers may be unrealistically optimistic about their future teaching performance" (Borko & Putnam, 1996, p. 678). The danger in this perspective occurs when the realities of classrooms shock beginning teachers, who then feel as though "nobody prepared me for this" (Veenman, 1984). Optimism can turn into pessimism or even cynicism; teachers question their career choice; and, as we saw earlier, about one of six beginning teachers quit within the first year.

Item 2: As I gain experience in teaching, I expect to become more confident in my ability to help children learn. As with Item 1, most preservice teachers expect to become increasingly confident in their ability to help children learn. Unfortunately, the opposite often occurs. As teachers gain experience, they tend to become more controlling and less democratic in their work with students, becoming less confident that teachers in general can overcome the limitations of home environments and family background (Woolfolk & Hoy, 1990).

As we saw in both Chapters 6 and 9, confidence in their ability to influence learning is essential for teachers, because those that believe they make a difference actually teach differently, taking responsibility for the success or failure of their own instruction (Lee, 2000); they don't blame lack of intelligence, poor home environments, uncooperative administrators, or some other external cause. We are emphasizing this point here in the hope that you won't fall into the same trap that snares many beginning teachers.

Item 3: The most effective teachers are those able to most clearly explain the content they teach to their students. People in general, and preservice teachers in particular, believe that teaching is essentially a process of "telling" or explaining content to students (Holt-

Increasing Understanding 10.3

What concept is being illustrated by teachers believing they are capable of helping all students to learn and achieve? What do teachers who take responsibility for the success or failure of their instruction do differently than teachers who blame failure on students' lack of intelligence or home environments?

Current views of learning replace telling as an instructional strategy with interactive dialogue between teachers and students.

Reynolds, 1992). This is likely the result of their own personal histories; in most of their school experiences, their teachers lectured.

Teaching is much more complex than simply telling, however, which Suzanne discovered in her first teaching experience. She was lucky; she quickly recognized the problems with talking too much, but many interns and beginning teachers cling to the belief that explaining is the essence of teaching.

Research corroborates Suzanne's experience and the emphasis Dr. Martinez put on questioning. This research consistently indicates that explaining, by itself, is often ineffective for helping students understand topics in depth (Bransford, 1993; Greeno, Collins, & Resnick, 1996). The video episode you saw in Chapter 9 further illustrates this fact. (If you didn't see the video episode, click onto **www.prenhall.com/kauchak,** go to the *Classroom Windows* Module for Chapter 9, and read the written transcript of the lesson.)

For instance, in that lesson we saw that Suzie (one of the students) was provided with at least three clear and accurate solutions to the problem of making the beam balance: Molly's in the group, Marvin's at the board, and the teacher's. In spite of these explanations, she retained the belief that the beam would balance if the number of tiles on each side of the fulcrum was the same. Explaining did little to change Suzie's understanding. She began to understand only when she was directly involved in an interactive question-and-answer session in an interview after the lesson.

The belief that teaching is "telling" is one of the most difficult to dispel, however, and you may not be convinced in spite of what we're saying here and what you saw in the video episode. Please keep this point in mind when you actually begin teaching.

Item 4: I will learn about most of the important aspects of teaching when I get into a classroom. This is another commonly held belief of preservice teachers. Researchers have found that "Beyond a desire for concrete teaching ideas . . . many preservice teachers believe their teacher education classes are little more than hoops they must jump through before getting into their own classrooms, where they will learn the real 'nuts and bolts' about teaching the only way they can learn them, through experience" (Grant, Richard, & Parkay, 1996). This belief in the central importance of experience in learning to teach is also shared by others both inside and outside the profession (Gross, 1999; Neisler, 2000).

Increasing Understanding 10.4

Offer two reasons why students who go through traditional teacher-preparation programs are more successful and more satisfied in their work than those who experience less formal preservice education.

Like most misconceptions, this has more than a grain of truth to it. Experience *is* crucial to learning, as constructivist psychologists continually remind us. While experience in classrooms is essential in learning to teach, it isn't sufficient by itself. In many cases, experience results in repeating the same procedures and techniques year after year, even when they're ineffective (Putnam, Heaton, Prawat, & Remillard, 1992). Needed are research findings describing ways that teachers can help students learn, as well as supportive learning environments where teachers can try these ideas. Research also consistently indicates that students who go through traditional teacher-preparation programs (such as the one you're in) that combine these kinds of experiences are more successful and more satisfied in their work than those who experience less formal preservice education (Darling-Hammond, 2000a). This is one of the reasons you're studying this book.

Item 5: If I thoroughly understand the content I'm teaching, I'll be able to figure out a way of getting it across to students. One of the most pervasive myths in teaching is that knowledge of subject matter is all that is necessary to teach it effectively. Knowledge of content is essential, of course, but learning to teach effectively requires a great deal of additional knowledge—knowledge you will acquire in your teacher-preparation program. Let's look at the different kinds of knowledge you'll learn as you become a professional.

■ KNOWLEDGE AND LEARNING TO TEACH

■ ■ ■

My kids were off the wall. They wouldn't pay attention, some were disruptive, and those that weren't had their heads down on the desk. I tried enforcing the rules and communicating that I meant business, but it wasn't working.

Linda [a veteran and colleague] saved me. I'm not sure I would have made it through this year if it hadn't been for her. She changed my thinking completely. I was so scared to get the kids involved in lessons, because I was afraid I wouldn't be able to control them, but she said it's just the opposite—kids want to be involved and they want to answer questions, and, if the lesson is any good, they're actually less likely to misbehave. When they act like they don't want to answer questions, it's because they're afraid they won't be able to. "Everyone wants to feel smart," she would say with a laugh. "Plus," she continued, "the more active they are in trying to learn the topic, the more likely they are to truly understand it."

Now, I mostly think about what examples I can use to best illustrate the topics I'm teaching and what I can do to get the kids involved. Wow, what a difference. (Paula, a first-year eighth-grade science teacher.)

■ ■ ■

Let's look again at Paula's comments. She said, "She [Linda] changed my *thinking* completely," and "Now, what I mostly *think* about. . . ." Paula's growth as a teacher is reflected in the differences in the way she *thinks*.

During approximately the last quarter of the 20th century, researchers began to examine differences in the *thinking* of **experts**, *people who are highly knowledgeable and skilled in a field*, compared to **novices**, *people who are inexperienced*, in the same fields. Although the fields varied widely, including areas as diverse as chess, physics, anesthesiology, and teaching, a clear pattern was found. In all cases, the thinking of experts was guided by a great deal of well-organized knowledge, whereas the knowledge of novices either didn't exist or wasn't well-organized (Borko & Putnam, 1996; Bruning, Shraw, & Ronning, 1999). "The accumulation of richly structured and accessible bodies of knowledge allows individuals to engage in expert thinking and action. In studies of teaching, this understanding of expertise has led researchers to devote increased attention to teachers' knowledge and how it is organized" (Borko & Putnam, 1996, p. 674). In essence what teachers know and how their knowledge is organized powerfully affects how teachers view and understand their classrooms and what they do to promote learning.

Research indicates that expert teachers possess at least four different kinds of knowledge (Peterson, 1988; Shulman, 1987):

- Knowledge of content.
- Pedagogical content knowledge.
- General pedagogical knowledge.
- Knowledge of learners and learning.

Let's look at these different kinds of knowledge and see how they can affect your growth as a teacher.

Knowledge of Content

We can't teach what we don't understand. This simple statement is self-evident, and it is well-documented by research examining the relationships between what teachers know and how they teach (Shulman, 1986; Wilson, Shulman, & Richert, 1987). To effectively teach about the American Revolutionary War, for example, a social studies teacher must know not only basic facts about the war but also how it relates to other aspects of history, such as the French and Indian War, our relationship with England prior to the Revolution, and the characteristics of the colonies. The same is true for any topic in any content area.

Pedagogical Content Knowledge

Pedagogical content knowledge is *an understanding of "ways of representing . . . the subject that make it comprehensible to others," and "an understanding of what makes the learning of specific topics easy or difficult . . ."* (Shulman, 1986, p. 9). Pedagogical content knowledge depends on an understanding of a particular topic, such as understanding the factors leading to the American Revolution, but it goes beyond this understanding in that it also includes knowing how to illustrate and explain these factors so they make sense to students.

Teachers who possess pedagogical content knowledge also recognize when topics are hard to understand and illustrate these difficult-to-teach ideas with concrete experiences that make them meaningful. The following are some examples:

- In Chapter 1, David Jackson taught the principle of *inertia* for his eighth-grade science students by using seatbelts in cars, the spin cycle of a clothes washer, and a dog shaking itself off when it came out of a pond.
- In Chapter 8, Suzanne Brush helped her second graders understand graphing by using bar graphs to represent their favorite flavor of jelly bean.
- In Chapter 9, Leslie Nelson used written paragraphs displayed on an overhead to illustrate pronoun cases for her students.

We see the influence of pedagogical content knowledge on Paula's thinking when she commented, "Now, I mostly think about what examples I can use to best illustrate the topics I'm teaching . . . ," and we also see why a thorough understanding of content is important, but not sufficient in itself, in helping learners understand the topics they're studying. Majoring in math doesn't ensure that a teacher will be able to create examples that

Pedagogical content knowledge allows teachers to illustrate difficult-to-learn concepts with concrete examples.

Increasing Understanding 10.5

Describe the pedagogical content knowledge that Suzanne demonstrated in her lesson on longitude and latitude. Be specific in your response.

will help students understand why multiplying two numbers results in a smaller number ($\frac{1}{4} \times \frac{1}{3} = \frac{1}{12}$, for instance), nor does majoring in history ensure that a teacher will think of using a student "crusade" to have extracurricular activities governed by a student council as a metaphor for the real crusades. The ability to do so requires both a clear understanding of content together with pedagogical content knowledge. If either is lacking, teachers often will paraphrase information in learners' textbooks or students will memorize steps that don't make sense to them (such as procedures for graphing equations).

Developing pedagogical content knowledge is one of the most challenging aspects of learning to teach. But throughout your teacher-preparation program, if you are constantly looking for ways of illustrating topics you might teach, then gradually your thinking will develop, and you'll acquire the pedagogical content knowledge that can help you become an expert teacher.

General Pedagogical Knowledge

Knowledge of content and pedagogical content knowledge are "domain specific"; that is, they focus on knowledge of a particular topic or content area, such as multiplying fractions, density, the Crusades, or our judicial system. In comparison, **general pedagogical knowledge** *involves a general understanding of instruction and management that transcends individual topics or subject matter areas* (Borko & Putnam, 1996). Let's look at these two components.

Instructional Strategies Instruction is at the heart of teaching. Expert teachers understand different ways of involving students in learning activities, techniques for checking their understanding, and strategies for keeping lessons running smoothly (Leinhardt & Greeno, 1986). Questioning is perhaps the most important example that exists. Regardless of the content or topic, expert teachers ask questions that get students to think, engage all students as equally as possible (McDougall & Granby, 1996), give them time to think about their responses (Rowe, 1986), and provide prompts and cues when they're unable to answer

**Increasing
Understanding 10.6**

Explain why questioning is such an essential teaching skill. Explain specifically how questioning and *knowledge of learners and learning* are related.

(Shuell, 1996). Expert teachers are also able to provide students with feedback about their understanding of a topic, identifying areas that need additional work.

Classroom Management Regardless of the content area or topic being taught, expert teachers also know how to create classroom environments that are orderly and focused on learning (Doyle, 1986). Understanding how to keep 20 to 35 or more students actively engaged and working together in learning activities requires that teachers know how to plan, implement, and monitor rules and procedures, organize groups, deliver meaningful lessons, and respond to misbehavior.

Classroom management is one of the greatest concerns of beginning teachers (Kellough, 1999), and we address this issue again later in the chapter.

Knowledge of Learners and Learning

In addition to the other forms of professional knowledge, expert teachers also understand the students they work with and how they learn. Knowledge of learners and learning is critical, ". . . arguably the most important knowledge a teacher can have" (Borko & Putnam, 1996, p. 675). We saw this illustrated as Paula reflected on Linda's comments earlier in this chapter. Linda pointed out that kids *want* to be involved, and they *want* to answer questions; if they act like they don't want to answer, it's because they're afraid they won't be able to. In these remarks, Linda demonstrated an understanding of learners, and in saying, "the more active they are in trying to learn the topic, the more likely they are to truly understand it," she demonstrated an understanding of the way students learn.

By sharing this knowledge with Paula, Linda helped her understand what she could concretely do to help her students learn; as Paula explained, "Now, I mostly think about . . . what I can do to get the kids involved. Wow, what a difference."

Each type of knowledge—knowledge of content, pedagogical content knowledge, general pedagogical knowledge, and knowledge of learners and learning—is essential in becoming an expert teacher, and each will influence your thinking as you develop as a professional. As you plan, you will *think* about ways to actively involve your students, because you realize that they will be less motivated (knowledge of learners) and less likely to understand (knowledge of learning) if you lecture and allow them to sit passively through your lessons. You will also *think* about ways to illustrate your topics (pedagogical content knowledge), because you know that the illustrations are the basis for the students' developing understanding (again, knowledge of learning).

From our discussion, we can now see why teachers are unlikely to acquire all the knowledge needed to be effective from experience alone. This is the reason you're in a teacher-preparation program. The knowledge you acquire from it, combined with your experiences in schools, will start you on your way to becoming an expert teacher.

■ JOINING THE PROFESSION

You've seen the different kinds of knowledge and thinking that are needed to become an expert, but, in addition to this knowledge, some formal processes are required to allow you to work in the real world. This is the case for all professionals. For example, physicians, lawyers, and engineers, as well as teachers must be "licensed" in order to work in their professions. In this section, we examine this process as we consider:

- ■ Traditional Licensure.
- ■ Alternative Licensure.
- ■ The Interstate New Teacher Assessment and Support Consortium (INTASC).
- ■ National Board Certification.

During licensure teachers are increasingly being asked to demonstrate their competence through tests and on-the-job performance.

Increasing Understanding 10.7

We see that teacher licensure is a process by which a state evaluates the credentials of prospective teachers. But if teacher quality is so important, then why is the federal government not involved in the certification of teachers? Hint: Think about your study of the history of education in Chapter 5.

Traditional Licensure

In Chapter 7, we saw that in order to teach, public K–12 teachers are required by law (in all 50 states plus the District of Columbia) to be licensed by the department of education in their state. **Licensure** is *the process by which a state evaluates the credentials of prospective teachers to ensure that they meet the professional standards set by the state education agency.* A license means that the state certifies the quality of a teacher's competence in subject area content, educational methodology, teaching skills, and the ability to manage classrooms.

It is likely that you're taking this course in a traditional licensure program. In it you will earn a bachelor's degree with a general education component that includes courses in history, English, math, and science, as well as courses in professional education that are designed to help you develop your professional knowledge—the pedagogical content knowledge, general pedagogical knowledge, and knowledge of learners and learning that we discussed earlier. If you're a secondary major, it is likely that a major, minor, or the equivalent number of hours will be required in the subject area (or areas) that you plan to teach (39 states have this requirement) (Olson, 2000b).

Increasingly, teachers are also being asked to pass competency tests that measure their ability to perform basic skills, such as reading, writing, and math; their background in an academic area, such as chemistry, history, or English; and an understanding of learning and teaching (39 states also have this requirement) (Olson, 2000b). The *National Teachers Examination (NTE)*, also called the *Core Battery of the Praxis II* (Educational Testing Service, 1999), is the most common.

The Praxis Series (praxis means putting theory into practice) is currently being used in 35 states and consists of three components (Educational Testing Service, 1999):

■ Praxis I: Academic Skills Assessments—designed to measure basic or "enabling" skills in reading, writing, and math that all teachers need.

■ Praxis II: Subject Assessments—designed to measure teachers' knowledge of the subjects they will teach. In addition to 70 content-specific tests, Praxis II also

Teaching

in an Era of Reform

THE ALTERNATIVE LICENSURE DEBATE

To meet the demand for more teachers and also recruit more minorities into teaching, many programs have begun to develop alternative routes to licensure. Wide variation in these routes exists from state to state; some states permit alternative licensure only when a shortage of traditionally licensed teachers exists, whereas others create programs specifically designed to prepare people for teaching who don't want to go through a traditional program. Forty states now have alternative licensure programs, and an estimated 80,000 teachers have been licensed in this way (Olson, 2000a).

People seeking alternative licensure must hold bachelor's degrees in the subjects to be taught, such as math, chemistry, or English, and they must pass a licensure test, complete brief, intensive teacher-training experiences, and complete a supervised teaching internship.

The most widely publicized alternative program is called *Teach for America*, which recruits motivated and high-achieving arts and sciences graduates from selected colleges and universities and prepares them for work in rural and urban areas that have difficulty recruiting teachers. *Teach for America* recruits typically attend intensive 3-to-8-week summer training sessions and then sign 2-year contracts (Darling-Hammond, 2000a).

Putting Alternative Licensure into Perspective

Proponents of alternative licensure make several arguments supporting their positions. For instance, most alternative licensure candidates are older than their traditional counterparts, so they've had more life experiences. Because they already have bachelor's degrees, they are more focused on learning to teach than are traditional undergraduates, who must combine their courses in content areas, such as math or English, with their courses in professional education. Also, because these programs are shorter, they can attract minorities and talented and experienced people to the profession in areas of critical need, such as math and science (Shulman, 1992). Proponents also argue that students in these programs are more academically talented than students in traditional programs (Croasmun et al., 1999).

However, graduates of alternative licensure programs receive limited training in pedagogy (such as training that involves the pedagogical content knowledge, general pedagogical knowledge, and knowledge of learners and learning, that we discussed earlier) (Bliss, 1992; Zumwalt, 1990). Intensive mentoring and supervision during the first few months of full-time teaching is supposed to compensate for the lack of formal coursework in these programs, but this support rarely exists (Darling-Hammond, 1992). Teaching is a demanding job in itself, and mentoring a new teacher significantly compounds the demands. Teachers, and even those with the most expertise, often don't have the time to help new teachers "learn the ropes."

 Increasing Understanding 10.8

How can experienced mentors help new teachers acquire pedagogical content knowledge, general pedagogical knowledge, and knowledge of learners and learning? What obstacles exist to the greater use of teacher mentors in the schools?

includes the Principles of Learning and Teaching (PLT) test and the Professional Knowledge test.

■ Praxis III: Classroom Performance Assessments—use classroom observations and work samples to assess teachers' ability to plan, instruct, manage, and understand professional responsibilities. In addition, Praxis III assesses the teacher's sensitivity to learners' developmental and cultural differences.

You are most likely to encounter Praxis I during your teacher preparation, Praxis II after its completion, and Praxis III during your first year of teaching.

The specific requirements for licensure vary from state to state, and the student-advising office in your college or university can describe the specific requirements for your state. If you're planning on moving to another state, your education library may have

Alternative licensure graduates encounter two other problems. First, they're disproportionately assigned to the most demanding teaching situations, such as inner-city schools with high numbers of cultural minorities from low-income households (National Commission on Teaching and America's Future, 1996). This can be a serious problem from their students' perspective, because research indicates that teachers' expertise is a more significant factor in student achievement than even powerful variables such as socioeconomic status (Darling-Hammond, 2000b; Ferguson, 1991). Good teachers can overcome obstacles to learning. The paradox is that students who need competent, experienced teachers the most are often the least likely to have them.

Second, alternative licensure graduates often become frustrated and disillusioned and drop out of the profession. To illustrate this problem, some experts turn again to *Teach for America.* "If anyone could prove the claim that teachers are born and not made, these bright eager students might have been the ones to do it" (Darling-Hammond, 2000a, p. 168). However, one of their graduates describes his experience this way:

• • •

I—perhaps like most TFAers—harbored dreams of liberating my students from public school mediocrity and offering them as good an education as I had received. But I was not ready. . . . As bad as it was for me, it was worse for the students. Many of mine. . . took long steps on the path toward dropping out. . . . I was not a successful teacher and the loss to the students was real and large (Schorr, 1993, pp. 317–318).

• • •

This is only a single testimonial, but it helps explain why the attrition rate for alternative licensure programs is so high. Teaching in a challenging setting with only minimal preparation and support can be disastrous for both beginning teachers and their students. Statistics indicate that the 2-year dropout rate for *Teach for America* graduates is more than three times greater than the national average for new teachers (Darling-Hammond, 2000a).

Conclusive assessments of alternative licensure are difficult to make because there is so much variation between different states' programs. High-quality alternative licensure programs are both time-consuming and costly (Olson, 2000a), and high-quality is essential in an era of increased standards and accountability. Research examining the performance of students taught by teachers from alternative licensure programs is also mixed. Some data suggests students fare as well as those taught by traditionally prepared teachers; other data do not (Olson, 2000a).

You Take a Position

Now it's your turn to take a position on the issue discussed in this section. Go to the *Education Week* Website at **http://www.edweek.com**, find "search" on the first page, and type in one of the following two search terms: *alternative licensure* or *alternative certification.* Locate a minimum of three articles on one of these topics and then do the following:

1. Write a one-paragraph summary of each article.

2. Identify a pattern in the articles. (Each article—or even two of the three—suggesting that an increasing number of people are being licensed through alternative routes would be a pattern, for example.)

3. After identifying the pattern, take one of the two following positions:

   ■ The pattern suggested in the articles, if implemented, *is* likely to improve education.

   ■ The pattern suggested in the articles *is not* likely to improve education.

State your position in writing, and document your position with information taken from the articles and your study of the text. (This chapter and any other chapter of the text can be used.)

Ⓦ *To answer these questions online, go to the Take a Position Module in Chapter 10 of the Companion Website.*

books that describe the licensure requirements for all the states. If it doesn't, you can write or call the state certification office directly. The addresses and phone numbers of the U.S. State Certification Offices are available in the end-of-text Appendix and on the Website that accompanies your book. Go to **http://www.prenhall.com/kauchak**, click on the Appendix, and look up the state in which you're interested.

Beginning Professionalism: The INTASC Standards

• • •

Yikes!! I think I had the wrong impression. I always wanted to be a teacher, and I was told that it was an easy major. I heard that some of the courses were "easy" and I could take a bunch of them at the same time and get them out of the way, while I took the "real" stuff. Now, what's this? They expect me to be able to do all this when I first go into a classroom. I have to know what I'm teaching and then all this about learner development, "variety of instructional strategies," motivation, assessment, and I might get tested on all this stuff. Where'd they get this idea that learning to teach was so easy? (Diedra, a preservice education major told she will be accountable for meeting INTASC standards.)

■ ■ ■

Diedra's reaction is understandable. In the past, learning to teach was easier and the demands on beginning teachers were not as great. This has changed (Berliner, 2000). A rapidly expanding body of literature consistently demonstrates that teaching now requires professionals who are highly knowledgeable and skilled.

The profession is responding. Created in 1987, the Interstate New Teacher Assessment and Support Consortium (INTASC) was designed to help states develop better teachers through coordinated efforts of support and assessment. INTASC has raised the bar by setting rigorous standards for new teachers in important areas such as planning, instruction, and motivation. These standards describe what you should know and be able to do when you first walk into a classroom.

At this point, general standards organized around 10 principles have been prepared, and subject area standards and a Test for Teaching Knowledge (TTK) are being developed. These principles are outlined in Table 10.1. To learn more about INTASC, go to the *Web Links* Module of the Companion Website at **http://www.prenhall.com/ kauchak.**

The principles are expanded by describing the knowledge, dispositions, and performances teachers are expected to demonstrate. For instance, with respect to the first principle, teachers should understand how students' misconceptions in an area—such as believing that the earth is closer to the sun in the summer (in the northern hemisphere)—can influence their learning (knowledge); teachers should be committed to continuous learning (disposition); and they should use a variety of ways of illustrating ideas to make them understandable to students (performance), such as using demonstrations, pictures, technology, and classroom discussion to illustrate the seasons. Similar knowledge, dispositions, and performances are described for each principle.

The INTASC standards are demanding, but this is as it should be. As we've said throughout this book, if you expect to be treated as a professional, you should have the knowledge and skills that allow you to make the decisions expected of a professional. Being able to meet the INTASC standards is a good beginning.

Advanced Professionalism: National Board Certification

Earlier we saw that licensure is the process that states use to ensure that teachers meet professional standards. In comparison, **certification** is *special recognition by a professional organization indicating that an individual has met certain requirements specified by the organization.*

One important form of certification has been created by the National Board for Professional Teaching Standards (NBPTS). Created in 1987 as an outgrowth of the *Carnegie Forum Report, A Nation Prepared: Teachers for the 21st Century*, the board is composed mostly of K–12 teachers, but it also includes union and business leaders and university faculty. NBPTS seeks to strengthen teaching as a profession and raise the quality of education by recognizing the contibutions of exemplary teachers, compensate them financially, give them increased responsibility, and increase their role in decision making. To learn more about NBPTS, go to the *Web Links* Module of the Companion Website at **http://www.prenhall. com/kauchak.**

Table 10.1	The INTASC Principles	
Principle	**Description**	
1. Knowledge of subject	The teacher understands the central concepts, tools of inquiry, and structures of the discipline(s) he or she teaches and can create learning experiences that make these aspects of subject matter meaningful for students.	
2. Learning and human development	The teacher understands how children learn and develop and can provide learning opportunities that support their intellectual, social and personal development.	
3. Adapting instruction	The teacher understands how students differ in their approaches to learning and creates instructional opportunities that are adapted to diverse learners	
4. Strategies	The teacher understands and uses a variety of instructional strategies to encourage students' development of critical thinking, problem solving, and performance skills.	
5. Motivation and management	The teacher uses an understanding of individual and group motivation and behavior to create a learning environment that encourages positive social interaction, active engagement in learning, and self-motivation.	
6. Communication skills	The teacher uses knowledge of effective verbal, nonverbal, and media communication techniques to foster active inquiry, collaboration, and supportive interaction in the classroom.	
7. Planning	The teacher plans instruction based upon knowledge of subject matter, students, the community, and curriculum goals.	
8. Assessment	The teacher understands and uses formal and informal assessment strategies to evaluate and ensure the continuous intellectual, social, and physical development of the learner.	
9. Commitment	The teacher is a reflective practitioner who continually evaluates the effects of his/her choices and actions on others (students, parents, and other professionals in the learning community) and who actively seeks out opportunities to grow professionally.	
10. Partnership	The teacher fosters relationships with school colleagues, parents, and agencies in the larger community to support students' learning and well-being.	

Source: From Interstate New Teacher Assessment and Support Consortium. (1993). *Model standards for beginning teacher licensing and development: A resource for state dialogues.* Washington, D.C.: Council of Chief State School Officers. Reprinted by permission.

The standards, which grew out of the report *What Teachers Should Know and Be Able to Do,* are directed by five core propositions. The propositions and descriptions are outlined in Table 10.2.

National Board certification has five important characteristics:

- It is designed for experienced teachers. Applicants must have graduated from an accredited college or university and must have taught for at least 3 years.

- Applying for National Board certification is strictly voluntary and independent of any state's licensure. It is intended to indicate a high level of achievement and professionalism.

- Acquiring National Board certification requires that teachers pass a set of exams in their area of specialty, such as math, science, early childhood, or physical education and health.

- Additional evidence, such as videotapes of teaching and a personal portfolio, are used in the assessment process.

| Table 10.2 | Propositions of the National Board for Professional Teaching Standards |

Proposition	Description
1. Teachers are committed to students and their learning.	■ Accomplished teachers believe that all students can learn, and they treat students equitably. ■ Accomplished teachers understand how students develop, and they use accepted learning theory as the basis for their teaching. ■ Accomplished teachers are aware of the influence of context and culture on behavior, and they foster students' self-esteem, motivation, and character.
2. Teachers know the subjects they teach and how to teach those subjects to students.	■ Accomplished teachers have a rich understanding of the subject(s) they teach, and they appreciate how knowledge in their subject is linked to other disciplines and applied to real-world settings. ■ Accomplished teachers know how to make subject matter understandable to students, and they are able to modify their instruction when difficulties arise. ■ Accomplished teachers demonstrate critical and analytic capacities in their teaching, and they develop those capacities in their students.
3. Teachers are responsible for managing and monitoring student learning.	■ Accomplished teachers capture and sustain the interest of their students and use their time effectively. ■ Accomplished teachers are able to use a variety of effective instructional techniques, and they use the techniques appropriately. ■ Accomplished teachers can use multiple methods to assess the progress of students, and they effectively communicate this progress to parents.
4. Teachers think systematically about their practice and learn from experience.	■ Accomplished teachers are models for intellectual curiosity, and they display virtues—honesty, fairness, and respect for diversity—that they seek to inspire in their students. ■ Accomplished teachers use their understanding of students, learning, and instruction to make principled judgments about sound practice, and they are lifelong learners. ■ Accomplished teachers critically examine their practice, and they seek continual professional growth.
5. Teachers are members of learning communities.	■ Accomplished teachers contribute to the effectiveness of the school, and they work collaboratively with their colleagues. ■ Accomplished teachers evaluate school progress, and they utilize community resources. ■ Accomplished teachers work collaboratively with parents, and they involve parents in school activities.

■ The primary control of the NBPTS is in the hands of practicing teachers, which increases the professionalism of teaching.

Considering that the NBPTS is for veterans, why are we providing this information in this book—one studied by preservice teachers early in their programs? There are four reasons. First, one of the themes of this book has been professionalism, and the NBPTS is a national effort to professionalize teaching. Second, National Board certification can provide a long-term career goal combined with financial incentives for you as a new teacher. Nearly 200 school districts in 39 states have spent millions of dollars to reward teachers who successfully complete the process, and by late 2000, nearly 5,000 teachers had done so, with nearly 10,000 others awaiting word on whether or not they had passed (Blair, 2000b).

National Board certification requires teachers to demonstrate their expertise through exams and classroom performance.

Third, the descriptions in Table 10.2 emphasize the pedagogical content knowledge, general pedagogical knowledge, and knowledge of learners and learning that we discussed earlier in the chapter. The NBPTS recognizes that increasing professionalism requires teachers to be both highly knowledgeable and skilled in their areas of specialization.

Finally, evidence indicates that National Board certification makes a difference. A study comparing teachers who had successfully completed the process to those who had attempted but failed to achieve National Board certification found that the nationally certified teachers scored higher on nearly all measures of teaching expertise. The study involved at least 75 hours of observation of each teacher, together with interviews and samples of student work (Blair, 2000b). National Board certification is a long-term goal that is well worth pursuing and one we're encouraging you to keep in mind as you begin your career.

Getting Started in the Profession

You now understand the characteristics of people like you—other preservice and beginning teachers, the different kinds of knowledge you need to think and act like a professional, and what it takes to be licensed in any state in the nation. You've also seen what professional organizations expect of you as a beginning teacher and as an expert.

So, when and how do you get started? The answer to when is *now*, and we'll try to answer the question of how in this section as we consider:

- Developing a professional portfolio.
- Becoming marketable.
- Searching for and securing a job.

Portfolios provide a concrete way for beginning teachers to display their developing knowledge and skills.

Beginning Your Professional Portfolio

· · ·

The interview was going okay, but I was uneasy. The principal I was interviewing with was cordial, but she certainly wasn't enthusiastic. "I've had it," I thought to myself. She even quit asking me questions after about 20 minutes. I really wanted the job too.

As I was about to leave, I happened to mention, "Would you like to see my portfolio?" She looked at it for a couple minutes, and then she started asking some probing questions. When she stuck my CD-ROM in her computer and saw me teaching, she really lit up. I got the job! (Greg, a recent graduate and new teacher.)

· · ·

As you begin this section, you might wonder, Why are they talking about a portfolio now when I'm taking my first (or one of my first) courses in education? The answer is simple. The sooner you start on your professional portfolio, the better. A **professional portfolio** is *a collection of work produced by a prospective teacher*. Just as artists use portfolios of produced work to illustrate their talents and accomplishments, teachers use portfolios to document their knowledge and skills. The reason you should start now in thinking about your portfolio is that you may want to include products that you complete early in your program. For instance, suppose you write a particularly good paper for a beginning composition class. You may want to include the paper and the instructor's comments in your portfolio as evidence of your developing ability to communicate in writing. Although this experience will have occurred long before you actively seek a job, it can be a valuable entry nevertheless. The sooner you start thinking about what to include in your portfolio, the less likely you are to omit valuable or important entries.

Portfolios also provide tangible benchmarks that you can use for reflection, and reflection, or thinking about your actions and beliefs, can accelerate your growth as a professional. For instance, suppose you have yourself videotaped teaching a lesson for one of your teaching methods courses. The videotape is a concrete indicator of your skills at that point and provides a tangible basis for your reflection. Later, you may complete another videotaped lesson during an internship experience or student teaching. A comparison of your performance in the two lessons provides a measure of your progress.

Preparing a portfolio typically involves five steps (Martin, 1999):

1. Specify a goal. For example, you're probably taking this course because you've either decided that you want to teach, or you're at least considering teaching. Finding a satisfying job would be a likely goal.

2. Determine how both past and future experiences relate to the goal. For example, you might choose to tutor a student with a reading problem to get professional experience that will make you more marketable.

3. Strategically collect items that provide evidence of your developing knowledge and skill. A video clip of you working with the student would be an excellent entry, for instance.

4. Decide which items in your collection best illustrate your knowledge and skills. For example, since a prospective employer is unlikely to view a bulky collection or series of videotapes, a videotaped lesson is likely to be a better entry than is a clip from a tutoring session.

5. Determine how to best present the items to the person or people connected to your goal, such as the personnel director of a school district in which you want to teach.

As we said earlier, the sooner you start making these decisions, the more complete and effective your portfolio will be.

As you begin, we offer three suggestions:

■ Initially, err on the side of including too much in the portfolio. If you think you might use it, include it now. You can always remove an item, but including an item you've discarded is difficult if not impossible.

■ Always date the entry. If you want to organize your portfolio chronologically, the dated items will make organizing the information simpler.

■ Make all entries and supporting information with clear communication in mind. You're trying to convince a potential employer that you're knowledgeable and skilled, and you want to make his or her decision as easy as possible. A well-organized portfolio creates a positive impression; the opposite occurs with a disorganized one.

Electronic portfolios. As we move farther into the information age, the development of electronic portfolios is becoming more commonplace. They include everything a paper-based product includes, but they do it more efficiently. For example, one CD-ROM disk can hold the equivalent of 300,000 text pages (Lankes, 1995). Typed documents can be scanned into word processing files and stored on floppy disks or CD-ROMs, and video can be digitized and also stored on CD-ROMs. This saves both time and energy. People who want to view a video episode in a paper-based portfolio must find a VCR, review the tape, and put it back into the correct portfolio container. In contrast, video footage in an electronic portfolio can be augmented with text and graphics and accessed with the click of a mouse. This is what got Greg his job. The principal was impressed with both his teaching and the fact that the information in his portfolio was so easy to access.

Electronic portfolios require sophisticated computer equipment, software, and skilled users. In spite of these obstacles, however, it is likely that the expansion of technology will eventually make paper-based portfolios obsolete, so the sooner you develop your technology skills in these areas, the more effective your portfolio will be.

Figure 10.1   A Sample Résumé

Your name
Your address
Your phone number
Your e-mail address

Education (Most recent first)
Year: Degree (For example, B.S. in Education)
             College or University
             Major
             Minor(s)
Year: Previous college or university coursework
Year: High School

Teaching Experience (Most recent first)
Dates: Substitute teaching
             Name of school
Dates: Internship
             Name of school
Dates: Field experience
             Name of school

Work Experience: (Most recent first)
Dates: Employer, job title
             Responsibilities

Extracurricular Activities and Interests
             Organizations to which you belong (Highlight leadership positions)
             Volunteer work (dates)
             Hobbies

Honors and Awards
             Scholarships, grants, honor societies

References
             You might write "available on request" or you may include names and
             addresses. (If names and addresses are included, be sure that you have
             first obtained permission to use the person as a reference.)

Organizing your portfolio. You will want to organize your portfolio to make it accessible to an evaluator. As an organizational guide, put yourself in evaluators' shoes. Remember, they don't know much about you, and you want to make it as easy for them to learn about you as possible. Let communication and ease of access be your guide for organizing the information in your portfolio.

Regardless of whether your portfolio is paper-based or electronic, you will want to start with a title page followed by a table of contents. Then you'll want to include the most impressive entries followed by those that are less significant. Work samples and evidence of performance, such as video clips, are always treated more significantly than testimonial letters, which are often essentially disregarded.

Preparing a résumé. The first item you will want to include in your portfolio is a **résumé,** which is *a document that provides an overview of your background and experience.*

Table 10.3	Making Yourself Marketable	
Suggestion	**Example**	
Develop a minor area of study	If you're a Spanish major, consider a minor in French. If you're a chemistry major, consider a minor in biology.	
Join professional organizations	Most universities have student chapters of the National Education Association as well as student chapters of several other professional organizations. (A directory of professional organizations is on the Website for this book.)	
Tutor a child	Parents often seek tutoring help for their children, and it's a way of earning some extra money.	
Seek leadership positions	People assessing résumés look for leadership roles, because they suggest effective human-relations skills and the desire to be a life-long learner.	
Do volunteer work	Volunteer work can be enriching, and it indicates a desire to contribute to society.	
Become an aide	Schools often hire part-time aides, which can provide valuable experience and a way to earn money.	

Increasing Understanding 10.11

Explain how a portfolio and a résumé are different. Be specific in your explanation. What is the purpose of each?

The organization and contents of a résumé can vary, but clarity and simplicity should again be guiding principles. People reading your résumé want to be able to easily access personal information, such as your address and phone number, and they also want to be able to simply summarize your education, work experience, interests, and references. Some people suggest including a description of the type of position you seek and your educational philosophy, whereas others feel that this information detracts from the simplicity and clarity of the résumé. The office of career planning and placement at your college or university will be able to help you in preparing a résumé; a sample résumé is shown in Figure 10.1

Making Yourself Marketable Along with beginning your portfolio, now is also the time to start making yourself marketable. Your portfolio and résumé can be a guide. It makes sense that the more teaching-related experience you can acquire, the more impressive both your portfolio and résumé will be. You can make yourself marketable in several ways. Some examples are included in Table 10.3.

The suggestions in Table 10.3 can become potential portfolio entries, and descriptions of each can be included in your résumé. If you begin now, by the time you complete your teacher-preparation program, you can build both an impressive portfolio and résumé.

Finding a Job

• • •

I really wish someone had reminded me of these things sooner. When I started, like a lot of others, I didn't take it all too seriously. I'd blow class off now and then, and I didn't always get there on time. I actually did study, but I guess not as hard as I should have.

When I asked Dr. Laslow for a letter of recommendation, he refused. Actually, he said he didn't know me well enough to write a good one. I couldn't believe it. He was nice about it, but he wouldn't write one, advising me to find someone who knew me better and was more familiar with my work. And, a couple others were sort of lukewarm. Now, it's too late. My record is a little spotty and I feel bad about it now, but I can't go back. I used to wonder why Brad and Kelly always seemed to get all the breaks. Now I get it. They just worked at it harder and were more organized. I don't know what I was thinking back then. (Jeremy, a recent graduate without a job.)

. . .

As with preparing your portfolio and résumé, the time to think about getting a job and developing your professional reputation is *now*. Even though you may be 2 or more years away from graduation, you should keep this long-range goal in mind.

If you are conscientious and professional in your approach to your classwork, and if you systematically develop your portfolio and résumé, finding a job will take care of itself. You will be prepared, and you will have established a professional reputation as a student. Let's look at this issue a bit further.

Developing a Professional Reputation Do you know people who seem to get a lot of breaks? Do you get your share? Do your instructors know you and value the work you do for them? There is usually a reason that certain students are known and valued by their instructors and seem to "get all the breaks." The reason is that they take their schoolwork seriously, they're conscientious, and they're reliable. In other words, as students, they behave professionally. Just as teachers out in the field demonstrate professional behaviors, students do as well. Professors like and value conscientious students, and students like Jeremy bother them—because they just don't seem serious about becoming a first-class teacher. The effort and enthusiasm just aren't there. It's easy to understand why Brad and Kelly got breaks while Jeremy didn't. They probably deserved them.

Your professional relationships with your professors are important. Instructors quickly see through artificial attempts to demonstrate conscientious behavior, to "suck up" or to "beat the system." Students can beat the system if they want to, but professors know it, and ultimately the student is the one who loses. Instructors also understand the difference between students who sincerely ask for explanations of scoring criteria and those who wheedle for points. You obviously have the right to speak your mind, and professors want you to do so—as long as it's done in a spirit of learning.

So what can you do to develop your professional behavior? The following are some suggestions:

- Attend all classes, and be on time. If you must miss, see your professor in advance or explain afterwards.
- Work hard, study diligently, and try to learn as much as possible in your classes.
- Extend your classroom behavior to your life. If the opportunity to learn something exists, take it. For example, travel, especially to other countries, provides opportunities to learn about other cultures and the ways they approach education. Trips like this also make valuable entries on your résumé.
- Turn in required assignments on time and follow the established guidelines or criteria. Even if you disagree with the worth of the assignment, complete it and try to learn from it.
- Take tests when they're scheduled. They can then be scored and returned in a timely way, and you'll receive valuable feedback. Students who continually ask to take tests at special times are perceived as not being committed to their schoolwork.
- Participate in class. Offer comments and ask questions. This is a win–win situation. Your reputation as a student will be enhanced, and you will both enjoy your classes more and learn more from them.

If you sincerely and conscientiously attempt to learn and grow—as with finding a job in general—your professional reputation will take care of itself. Set as your goal being the best student you can be, and your professional development will be improved as well.

Table 10.4	Projected Changes in Public School Student Enrollment by Grade Level and Geographic Area (1998–2008)	
	Grades K–8	Grades 9–12
Northeast	−3.8%	+11.9%
Midwest	−4.1%	+1.5%
South	+3.2%	+16.3%
West	+10.8%	+28.6%

Source: From *Projection of Education Statistics to 2008* (p. 17), National Center for Education Statistics, 1998, Washington, DC: Author.

Where the Jobs Are   Since your ultimate goal is to locate a teaching position that will allow you to utilize your skills and develop as a professional, you need to consider factors such as supply and demand. Job opportunities are greater in some areas than others, and you will want to consider these factors as you begin your professional program.

Geography is one example. As you can see from Table 10.4, student growth patterns vary by geographic area and grade level. In general, the greatest student enrollment increases will occur in the western parts of the country and in secondary education, so this is where the greatest demand for teachers will be.

Increasing Understanding 10.12

Explain the job patterns that have just been described. Why, for example, are more jobs available in the inner city than in the suburbs? Why are more jobs available in math than in English?

Within geographic areas, specific locations also influence teacher supply and demand; job opportunities are much greater in rural and inner-city schools than they are in the suburbs, for example. The specific teaching position you seek will also affect your chances for finding a job. Areas such as audiology, speech pathology, bilingual education, English as a second language, foreign languages (especially Spanish), special education, math, physics, and chemistry need teachers more than areas like English or history (Darling-Hammond, Berry, Haselkorn, & Fideler, 1999). In the chapter-opening vignette, Shelley experienced these patterns. She initially looked for jobs at two suburban schools, but there were no openings. However, she had offers in three different inner-city schools.

What implications do these patterns have for you? First, if you haven't already decided on a major, you shouldn't select one based on job availability alone. To be effective, you must want to teach in the area you select. Don't major in chemistry, for example, if you dislike chemistry. However, if you sincerely like chemistry, you now know that there is a high probability of getting a job in this area.

Second, try to become knowledgeable about where teaching jobs exist. The career placement center at your college or university can help you. Then be flexible about where you'll teach. Your first teaching position may not be exactly where you want, but you can use it to gain experience and as a stepping stone to other positions.

Creating a Credentials File   Your college or university will have a placement center designed to help graduates find jobs. An essential service of this center, in addition to providing information about job openings, is to serve as a repository for your credentials file. A **credentials file** is *a collection of important documents you'll need to submit when you apply for a teaching position.* It typically includes background information about you, your résumé, the type of position you're seeking, courses taken, performance evaluations by your cooperating teacher and college or university supervisor, and letters of recommendation (usually three or more). When you apply for a job, you notify the placement center, which will then send your credentials file to the prospective employer. If the district feels there is a potential match after reviewing this file, you'll be contacted for an interview.

Interviews provide opportunities for you to explain your qualifications as well as find out about the position you're applying for.

Interviewing Effectively We've emphasized professional behavior throughout this book and particularly in this chapter. One area in which professional behavior is essential is the interview. This is the setting that almost certainly will determine whether or not you get a job. Some guidelines for interviewing effectively are outlined in Table 10.5.

If you're *genuinely* interested in working with young people, and if you've been conscientious in your teacher-preparation program, the interview will largely take care of itself. Nothing communicates more effectively than a sincere desire to do the job for which you're interviewing.

However, additional preparation can increase the positive impression you make. For example, how would you respond to the following questions, all of which are frequently asked in an interview?

- Why do you want to teach?
- Why do you want to work in this school?
- What is your philosophy of education?
- How would you motivate unmotivated learners?
- How would you handle a classroom management issue?
- How would you organize a unit on (a topic in your area)?
- How would you involve parents or caregivers to help your students learn?

The more specific and concrete you can be in responding to each of the questions, the more positive your impression will be. For instance, in response to the question about your teaching philosophy, the following statement is a specific response that communicates that you're clear about what you would try to do: "I believe that all children can learn, regardless of their backgrounds. I would try my best to make that happen by ensuring that all students are involved in the lessons I teach. I would get them involved by designing interactive learning strategies, using groupwork, and by regularly calling on all of them as often as possible." In contrast, a vague response, such as "I am a humanistic and

Table 10.5   **Guidelines for Interviewing Effectively**

Guideline	Rationale
Be on time.	Nothing creates a worse impression than being late for an interview.
Dress appropriately.	Wear an outfit appropriate for an interview, and be well-groomed. Shorts, jeans, and t-shirts are inappropriate, as is an eyebrow ring. You have the right to dress and groom yourself in any way you choose, but if you are serious about getting a job, you won't demonstrate your freedom of expression during a job interview.
Speak clearly, and use standard English and grammar.	Clear language is correlated with effective teaching, and your verbal ability creates an impression of professional ability.
Sit comfortably and calmly.	Fidgeting, or worse—glancing at your watch—suggests that you'd rather be somewhere else.
Communicate empathy for children and a desire to work with them.	Communicating an understanding of learning, learner development, and instruction demonstrates that you have a professional knowledge base.

Increasing Understanding 10.13

What will determine how able you are to provide a clear and concrete response to an interviewer's question? Hint: Think back to the second major topic of the chapter.

learner-centered teacher" is much less impressive. It's general and vague, and leaves the interviewer with the impression that you're saying some words that you learned in a class.

The more you think about questions such as our earlier examples, the better prepared for the interview you'll be, and the more at ease you'll be during the interview.

Assessing the School   The interview process is a two-way street. Not only are you being interviewed, but you are also interviewing the school to determine whether it will be a good place to work and grow as a professional. You want a job, but you also want to find out if the school is the kind of place in which you want to work. When you interview, you also have the right to ask questions of the principal or other people interviewing you. This not only helps answer questions you may have about the position but also communicates that you are thoughtful and are considering the position seriously.

Some factors to look for include the following:

- Commitment and leadership of the principal. The school leadership sets the tone for the school. Does the principal demonstrate caring for students and support for teachers? The answers to these questions are highly inferential, but you can look for evidence in the principal's manner and comments.

- School mission. Does the principal communicate a clear mission for the school? If you have a chance to talk to other teachers, ask them if the teachers feel like they're a team, all working for the benefit of students.

- School climate. Does the emotional climate of the school seem positive? How do office personnel treat students? Do members of the support staff, such as custodians and cafeteria workers, feel like they're part of the team? Is there a positive and upbeat orientation in the school?

- The physical plant. Are there student work products like art and woodshop projects in display cases and on the walls? Do signs and notices on hallway walls communicate that this is a healthy place to learn? Are the classrooms, halls, and restrooms generally clean and free of debris and graffiti?

- The behavior of the students. Are the students generally orderly and polite to each other and to the teachers? Do they seem happy to be there?

Minority teachers bring unique perspectives and valuable cultural insights into their classrooms.

■ A mentoring program for teachers. Does the school have a beginning support system, such as a mentoring program for first-year teachers? First-year teachers who participate in formal mentoring programs are more likely to succeed and stay in teaching than those who don't (Edwards & Chronister, 2000; Shoho & Martin, 1999).

These questions are difficult to answer in one visit to the school, but they are important. The working conditions in schools vary dramatically, and they can be the difference between a positive and rewarding first year of teaching compared to a year that makes you reconsider your decision to be a teacher. Poor working conditions are one of the most commonly cited reasons that beginning teachers leave the profession (Edwards & Chronister, 2000).

■ SURVIVING YOUR FIRST YEAR OF TEACHING

Although your first teaching job is probably 2 or more years away, now is the time to start learning to think like a teacher. This doesn't mean that you should stop thinking like a student; rather, it merely suggests that you expand your thinking while you have time for learning and growth.

At least three areas of concern will likely emerge during your first year of teaching, and beginning to think about them now can help you get a running start in your first job. These areas of concern include:

■ Time
■ Classroom management
■ Uncertainty

Let's look at them.

Reflect _on_ This

INTERVIEWING FOR A POSITION

You're interviewing for a position in a large, inner-city middle school. The leadership team of the school is composed of the school principal, a vice principal, and two assistant principals. Both the principal and vice principal are involved in the interview, which is scheduled for 1 hour.

You've been asked a number of probing questions, such as, "What was the biggest problem you faced in your internship?" "How would you motivate a class of unmotivated learners?" and "How would you enforce rules with students who are disruptive in your class?"

As you respond, the vice principal appears to listen attentively, but the principal appears distracted. He nods and responds in general terms to your answers, but doesn't follow up on any of the questions.

After 45 minutes have passed, the interview seems to be winding down, so you attempt to ask some questions about the school. The principal cuts you off, saying she has a meeting she must attend. She cordially thanks you for coming and quickly leaves the office, 10 minutes before the scheduled end of the interview. The vice principal, on the other hand, asks you to come into his office and says he is willing to try and answer any questions you have. You spend another half hour with him, and he takes you on a tour of the school, during which the discussion of the school and students continues. The principal's name doesn't come up in the discussion, but the physical plant is clean and attractive, the students are orderly as they move between classes, and one who accidently bumps you says, "Oh, excuse me."

1. Based on your total experience—the interview with the administrators and the tour—what is your impression of the school?

2. What might explain the principal's behavior? Offer at least two possibilities.

3. Suppose you had another interview for a job in a second inner-city school. In this case, the principal's behavior was warm and inviting in the interview, but the students appeared to be less well-behaved in the hallways. Which job would you take if you were offered both? Provide a basis for your decision. (Assume that other factors, such as pay and the distance from your home, are similar.)

4. What else might you do to help yourself decide which job to take?

To answer these questions online and receive immediate feedback, go to the Reflect on This Module in Chapter 10 of the Companion Website.

Time

One of the first crunches you'll experience as a beginning teacher is lack of time. You'll feel like you don't have a second to yourself. As Antonio said in one of the excerpts earlier in the chapter, "I've never been so tired in my life. You're in front of kids all day, and then you go home and work all night to get ready for the next day." In the chapter-opening case, Shelley said, "I can't believe how much there is to do—IEPs, progress reports, CPR training, responsibility to look for signs of abuse. When do I teach?"

Is there a solution to this dilemma? If so, what is it? While a perfect solution doesn't exist, one key is *organization.* A great deal of research, dating back to the 1970s, indicates that effective teachers are very well-organized (Bennett, 1978; Rutter, Maughan, Mortimore, Ouston, & Smith, 1979). The students in one of our classes described a first-year teacher that they had visited: "His desk is a mess. Books and papers piled everywhere.

THE COMPETITION FOR MINORITY TEACHERS

In Chapter 2, we saw that nearly one-third of school-age children in the United States are cultural minorities, compared to only 12 percent of the teaching force (Archer, 2000). The proportion of African American teachers has declined, and the proportion of Latino teachers has increased only slightly; at the same time, the percentage of K–12 students who are members of minority groups is in the midst of a steep incline. Projections indicate that somewhere between 2030 and 2040, cultural minorities will make up more than half of the nation's students.

These trends have resulted in significantly greater efforts to recruit minority teachers. These efforts have been made more difficult by the fact that many African Americans are opting for more lucrative careers in other areas because teaching is no longer viewed as one of their only entrées to the middle class. Because recruiting minority teachers is a challenge, scholarships, loan-forgiveness programs, specific recruitment aimed at bright minority high school and college students, and recruitment of career changers have all been tried in various states.

Because programs for career changers are often successful in recruiting minority teachers, alternative licensure has proven to be another promising avenue for bringing minority teachers into the profession.

These trends and efforts raise at least three issues. The first is need. Educators worry about the implications that a rapidly increasing minority-student population—without a similar increase in the minority teaching force—has for schooling, both for minorities and nonminorities. Many educators believe that minority students need role models that come from their same cultural backgrounds, and they further suggest that minority teachers bring unique perspectives to learning experiences (Archer, 2000a). This position is also supported by theories suggesting that models are most effective when observers perceive the models to be similar to themselves (Pintrich & Schunk, 1996).

He can't find anything there." If he can't find anything there, you can bet that he wastes precious time looking for lesson plans and student papers. If you frequently or even occasionally lament that "I must get organized," now is a good time to start changing your habits. Organization is one of the most essential skills that exist in teaching; it can make the difference between a relatively smooth year and one in which you're continually exhausted.

Classroom Management

Classroom management is consistently identified as one of the most important problems teachers face (Rose & Gallup, 1999); it is one of the primary concerns of beginning teachers (Kellough, 1999); and new teachers often feel ill-equipped to deal with management (Kher-Durlabhji, Lacina-Gifford, Jackson, Guillory, & Yandell, 1997).

Classroom management is never easy, but some guidelines can help. As you move through your program, we're encouraging you to keep the following three ideas in mind:

- Plan for effective management.
- Know your students.
- Use effective instructional strategies.

Let's consider these ideas.

Planning for Effective Management We have emphasized teacher thinking in this book, and nowhere is it more important than in the area of classroom management. Think about and plan for simple procedures, including the following: how students will

However, neither research nor theory suggests that nonminority teachers cannot be effective teachers for minority students; knowledgeable, dedicated, and caring teachers can make a difference for all types of students. Further, research provides few answers to the question of what ratio of nonminority to minority teachers is necessary or sufficient, and no evidence suggests that the percentage of minority teachers must be the same as the percentage of minority students in schools.

The tension between recruitment and standards is a second issue. In the face of increased efforts to recruit minority teachers is a simultaneous effort to raise teaching standards. Associated with raised standards is greater use of standardized tests to screen potential educators, a practice that has a history of negatively and disproportionately affecting minorities.

A third issue involves alternative certification. For example, nearly half of the candidates who have gone through California's alternative program are members of minority groups, as are 41 percent of those who went through the Texas program (National Center for Education Information, 2000). While these statistics are good news with respect to recruiting, alternative certification programs, as we saw in our "Teaching in an Era of Reform" section earlier in the chapter, can be problematic. For instance, first-year *Teach for America* graduates drop out of teaching at a rate three times greater than that for beginning-teacher graduates of traditional programs. If these statistics are representative of alternative licensure programs in general, they're unlikely to solve the lack-of-minority-teachers problem. Further, as we saw earlier, the quality of some alternative licensure programs is low.

However, there is some room for optimism in this area. Trends indicate that the enrollment of African American students in colleges of education increased from 6 percent to 9 percent in the 1990s, suggesting that the downward trend in the African American teaching force might be reversing (Archer, 2000a). However, this increase only slows the diversity gap, and it doesn't address a larger issue that exists in K–12 education: the ability of K–12 schools to produce enough minority graduates who can then go on to become teachers. Surveys indicate that African American, Native American, and Hispanic college graduates are more likely to become teachers than are White graduates. Unfortunately, students in these minority groups are less likely to succeed in and ultimately graduate from high school (Archer, 2000a). Leaders suggest that a nation wanting the teaching force to more nearly reflect the composition of society must first focus its educational efforts on today's elementary and secondary students.

The topic is likely to remain an issue for the foreseeable future.

Increasing Understanding 10.14

Planning for effective management closely relates to what other important idea discussed in the previous section? Explain how the two are related.

hand in papers and how you will return them; if and when students will be allowed to get out of their seats to sharpen pencils; how students will get into and out of groups if they do groupwork in your class; and how materials will be distributed and re-stored. In essence, anticipate potential problems and plan accordingly. Making decisions about these issues in advance will simplify the decisions you must make later in cases that can't be anticipated. A number of valuable books are available to help both elementary teachers (for example, Evertson, Emmer, Clements, & Worsham, 2000) as well as secondary teachers (for example, Emmer, Evertson, Clements, & Worsham, 2000) plan for classroom management.

As you move through your program, keep the issue of management in mind; ask your professors questions, and talk to teachers when you're out in the field. Be a sponge, and take notes on what you see and what the professors and teachers say. As we discussed in the last section, note taking is part of being organized. Because you won't remember everything you hear, taking notes and storing them in a file will give you a leg up on your planning when you begin your first year.

Get to Know Your Students Getting to know your students is important on several levels. It communicates true caring and establishes a human link between you and your students. Knowing your students' names is essential. It communicates that you care about them as people, and you can't teach effectively without knowing them. Commit yourself to knowing all your students by their first name by the end of the first week of school.

Again, watch your professors and teachers out in the field. See how they use students' names in their instruction. You will notice a striking difference in both the instruction

Many of the problems encountered by beginning teachers can be avoided through thorough professional preparation and careful planning.

and the classroom climate when teachers know students' names and address them by name compared to teachers who don't.

Use Effective Instructional Strategies   You might wonder why we're discussing "effective instructional strategies" when the issue is classroom management. The answer is simple. Research consistently demonstrates that it is virtually impossible to maintain classroom order in the absence of effective instruction. In other words, if you're not teaching effectively, the likelihood of having classroom management problems increases dramatically.

The active involvement of students in learning activities is one of the most important aspects of effective instruction. Students who are actively involved in learning are much less likely to misbehave than those who are sitting passively or who don't understand the topic. A guiding principle for your instruction should be, *All students want to learn, and they want to participate*. It may not seem like it at times, but students who act like they don't care or don't want to learn are more nearly demonstrating fear that they *can't* learn.

We saw evidence of this in both Paula and Suzanne's comments in vignettes earlier in the chapter. Paula said, "Now, I mostly think about what examples I can best use to illustrate the topics I'm teaching and what I can do to get the kids involved. Wow, what a difference," and Suzanne commented, "Now I understand the stuff Dr. Martinez stressed so much when he was always after us to use concrete examples and to question, question, question. . . . I thought I could just explain everything to them, but they got confused and drifted off so fast I couldn't believe it. As soon as I started asking questions about the lines on the Styrofoam ball, though, they perked right up."

Look for models of effective instruction in the schools you visit, and seize the opportunity to practice getting students involved in learning activities; particularly practice your questioning. Again, these experiences will give you a leg up when you begin your first job.

Planning for management, knowing your students, and teaching effectively won't solve all of your management problems, but they will make a big difference, so big a difference, in fact, that they can largely determine how successful both your internship and your first year of teaching will be.

Video
Perspectives

ABC NEWS

MENTORING NEW TEACHERS

This ABC News video segment describes a mentoring program for new teachers at Malden Catholic High School in Massachusets. First-year teacher Joe Laferlito explains how mentoring helped him deal with instructional and management issues. Veteran teacher Rich Mazzei describes his role in the process and the benefits of mentoring to him.

Think About This

1. How is mentoring more like teaching? How is it different from traditional classroom teaching?
2. What qualities would you look for in a mentor?
3. In what areas of teaching would a mentor be most helpful? Least helpful?

Ⓦ *To answer these questions online and receive immediate feedback, go to the Video Perspectives Module in Chapter 10 of the Companion Website.*

Uncertainty

Uncertainty is, without question, one of the most disconcerting experiences in life. Being in a situation and not being quite sure of what you're doing or how you're supposed to act is very unsettling. You will experience many uncertainties during your first year.

Can you anticipate and prepare for them? To a certain extent, yes. One way is to be as well-informed as possible. Learn as much as you can about as many aspects of teaching as possible. A second way to prepare is to ask questions. In general, teachers are very cooperative, and veteran teachers in your school will be willing to answer your questions and give advice.

At this point you're preparing for one of the most challenging and rewarding professions in the world—teaching—and when you complete your program, you'll begin some of the most important work that exists. We hope that your study of this book has helped launch you on your way.

■ SUMMARY

Characteristics of Beginning Teachers

The teaching population is aging, and the number of beginning teachers is likely to increase significantly in the next 10 years. The population will become increasingly White, female, and younger than the existing population. A greater number of people are entering teaching after they've earned bachelor's degrees than has occurred in the past.

Beginning teachers drop out during their first year at over twice the attrition rate for teachers in general, and significant numbers also leave after their second and third years.

Preservice and beginning teachers tend to be optimistic about their abilities, but their optimism wanes as they get more experience. They tend to believe that the essence of teaching is "explaining" and that most of what they learn about teaching will occur once they get into classrooms.

Knowledge and Learning to Teach

As the professionalism of teaching increases, more emphasis is placed on what teachers know and how they think. Expert teachers know the content of the subjects they teach; they are able to represent the content in ways that are understandable to learners, which is called pedagogical content knowledge; they have general pedagogical knowledge, such as knowing how to manage classrooms and ask questions effectively; and they know how students learn and develop as well as what motivates learners.

Joining the Profession

The majority of teachers are licensed in traditional programs, which are designed and implemented by each state. Alternative licensure is the process of licensing people to teach who have bachelor's degrees in some academic area by having them complete short, intensive training programs combined with a licensing exam.

In an attempt to professionalize teaching, the National Board for Professional Teaching Standards (NBPTS) has established rigorous standards and assessments for teachers who have completed at least 3 years of successful service. Substantive financial rewards exist in most states for teachers who have successfully completed national certification. The Interstate New Teacher Assessment and Support Consortium (INTASC) is conducting a similar effort for beginning teachers.

The more quickly students in preservice programs begin developing a professional portfolio, gathering experiences that make them marketable, and developing their professional reputation, the better equipped they will be to find a job when they graduate.

Surviving Your First Year of Teaching

Lack of time, classroom management, and the uncertainties of a new job are the three most common problems beginning teachers face. Getting organized, becoming well-informed, and developing their teaching skills are the most effective ways teachers have of preparing for both their internship and their first year of teaching. The time to begin this preparation is now.

■ IMPORTANT CONCEPTS

certification	licensure	professional portfolio
credentials file	novice	résumé
expert	pedagogical content	
general pedagogical knowledge	knowledge	

■ DISCUSSION QUESTIONS

1. What can preservice teachers do to decrease the likelihood that they will leave the profession? What can school leaders do?

2. The National Board for Professional Teaching Standards and The Interstate New Teacher Assessment and Support Consortium are attempting to increase the professionalism of teaching. How successful are they likely to be? Explain why you believe as you do.

3. Some critics suggest that teaching isn't a profession because it doesn't have a body of knowledge on which to base its decisions. How do you respond to these critics?

4. It was suggested in the chapter that you attempt to establish a professional reputation by being conscientious in your classes and attempting to get along with your professors. Is this reasonable? Is it important? Explain.

5. Several suggestions for making yourself marketable were offered in the chapter. Is it reasonable to expect that preservice teachers involve themselves in these activities? Explain.

6. What are the advantages and disadvantages of developing a professional portfolio? To constructing one using technology?

■ GOING INTO SCHOOLS

1. Interview a teacher about developing as a professional. Ask him or her the following questions:
   a. Which do you believe is more important in teaching: understanding content, or understanding how to communicate content to students?
   b. Do you believe that if you understand the content you're teaching well enough that you'll be able to get it across to students? Please explain why you do or do not think so.
   c. Are you more or less confident in your ability to get students to learn than you were as a beginning teacher?
   d. Which do you believe is more effective for getting students to understand the topics you're teaching: explaining the topics clearly, or asking good questions?
   e. What were the most important problems you faced during your first year of teaching?
   f. What suggestions would you offer prospective teachers to help them best prepare for their first year of teaching?

2. Interview a new teacher about his or her job-seeking experiences.
   a. Ask to see the teacher's résumé. How does it compare to the one in Figure 10.1?
   b. Did the teacher use a portfolio? If so, what was included in it? How well did it work? What would he or she have done differently?
   c. How valuable are the guidelines found in Table 10.3 for making yourself marketable?
   d. How well did the teacher's interview(s) go? What questions were asked? What advice would he or she give you regarding the guidelines for interviewing found in Table 10.5?

3. Interview a teacher about NBPTS certification. Explain the process and ask the following questions:
   a. Does the basic idea behind NBPTS certification have value? What are its basic strengths and weaknesses?
   b. Share the propositions behind NBPTS certification found in Table 10.2. Which are more valuable? Should any be added?
   c. Describe the evaluation procedures for selecting teachers. Are these adequate? Should any additional be added?

4. Interview a school administrator. Ask him or her how many teachers in the school are licensed through traditional means and through an alternative licensure process. Ask which process—traditional or alternative—seems to be more effective.

5. Interview a school administrator who is involved in hiring new teachers. Ask the following questions:
   a. What kinds of personal characteristics—such as attitudes and personality traits—do you look for in a new teacher?
   b. What kinds of knowledge—such as content, learning, learner development—do you look for in beginning teachers?
   c. How do you react to dress and manner in an interview? What suggestions do you have in this regard?
   d. How important is a prospective teacher's use of standard English and grammar in an interview?
   e. Do you want to see a prospective teacher's portfolio when you interview him or her? If so, what do you look for?

 Virtual Field
Experience

> If you would like to participate in a Virtual Field Experience, go to the *Field Experience* Module in Chapter 10 of the Companion Website.

■ ONLINE PORTFOLIO ACTIVITIES

 To complete these activities online, go to the *Portfolio Activities* Module in Chapter 10 of the Companion Website to submit your response.

Portfolio Activity 10.1   **Knowledge and Learning to Teach**

INTASC Principle 1: *Knowledge of Subject*

The purpose of this activity is to help you think about the types of knowledge involved in learning to teach. Suppose, for the sake of the activity, that you want to teach the concept *adverbs*. You know that adverbs are parts of speech that modify verbs, adjectives, and other adverbs.

To illustrate the topic, you prepare the following vignette, with the adverbs in italics:

■ ■ ■

Kathy is a middle school student. She enjoys the courses she's studying, but she *openly* admits that when she started middle school last year, it was *much* harder than she had anticipated. In fact she *very often* states that she *quite quickly* decided that her middle school wasn't for her, and she wanted her parents to send her to a private school. Sometimes she could *not* make it through a day without thinking about switching schools. However, she now is doing *very* well academically, so her uneasiness has been put aside. The fact that one *rather* balmy evening she met Jeremy, who now occupies an important part of her school life, has also helped the situation.

■ ■ ■

You prepare the vignette because you know that students understand concepts and rules better when they're put in context. You prepare the vignette and have it displayed on an overhead when the students enter the room.

Describe the knowledge of content, pedagogical content knowledge, knowledge of learners and learning, and general pedagogical knowledge you've demonstrated in preparing for your lesson on adverbs.

Portfolio Activity 10.2   **Motivating Learners**

INTASC Principle 5: *Motivation and Management*

The purpose of this activity is to encourage you to begin thinking about learner motivation. Describe a simple way that you could introduce your lesson on adverbs that would capture the students' attention and bring them into the lesson. Which of the four kinds of knowledge discussed in the chapter are you demonstrating when you develop this motivational strategy?

Portfolio Activity 10.3   **Preparing a Résumé**

INTASC Principle 9: *Commitment*

The purpose of this activity is to establish a beginning point in your development as a teacher. Using Figure 10.1 as a model, prepare a résumé describing your education, experience, interests, and honors at this point in your life. Identify areas in which you should acquire additional education and experiences to make yourself marketable as a teacher.

PART 6

Technology

CHAPTER

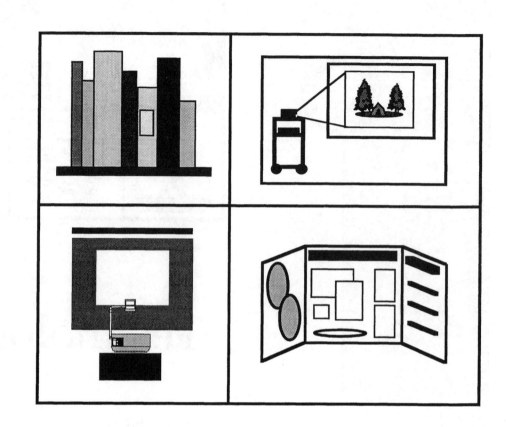

11

Technology:
An Instructional Tool

Lynne C. Levy

I f you were to plot the changing views and concepts regarding the processes of teaching and learning, you would find that there is a significant correlation to the development of technology throughout history. Your students will study, learn, work, and live in the evolving technological society. It is essential that our schools provide the necessary experiences and skills in order to assure their ability to function as productive and self-fulfilling citizens.

In order for this to occur, teachers must have an understanding of the role of technology in their teacher preparation programs as well as in their classrooms. In this chapter we provide an overview of the major traditional types of Instructional Technology. More specifically, it will address the following questions:

- What is Instructional Technology?

- What is the major type of Print Technology?

- What are the traditional types of Audiovisual Technology?

- What are the most common types of Display and Support Technology?

• UNDERSTANDING TECHNOLOGY

Most definitions of "technology" incorporate words such as tools, machines, processes, and inventions as they relate to the betterment of life and society. One area of technology addresses the tools and processes of instruction. This area is called Instructional Technology.

Instructional Technology

The definition and content of Instructional Technology is ever evolving. A seminal model for the field during the 1950s and 1960s was developed by Edgar Dale and called the "Cone of Experience." Building on the work done by Dale in audiovisual communications and learning theory, James Finn was instrumental in bringing the field of audiovisual communications into a new realm in education. He not only helped to further define the content of the field, he introduced a new name for the field. In the mid-1960s he began advocating the use of the words "Instructional Technology." Since that time the definition of the field of Instructional Technology has gone through a number of revisions.

In 1994 the Association for Educational Communications and Technology published *Instructional Technology: The Definition and Domains of the Field* by Barbara B. Seels and Rita C. Richey. The AECT revised definition (1994) states:

> *Instructional Technology is the theory and practice*
> *of design, utilization, management and evaluation*
> *of processes and resources for learning.*

The authors also identify and define the subcategories of the "Development Domain" for this definition. They are:

1. **Print Technologies**
   Print technologies are ways to produce or deliver materials, such as books and static visual materials, primarily through mechanical or photographic printing processes.
2. **Audiovisual Technologies**
   Audiovisual technologies are ways to produce or deliver materials by using mechanical or electronic machines to present auditory and visual messages.
3. **Computer-based Technologies**
   Computer-based technologies are ways to produce or deliver materials using microprocessor-based resources.
4. **Integrated Technologies**
   Integrated technologies are ways to produce and deliver materials which encompass several forms of media under the control of a computer.

While these four areas are generally considered to be the accepted realm of contemporary Instructional Technology, the author of this part of the text has chosen to add one additional area that is of particular importance to educators:

5. **Display and Support Technologies**
   Display and support technologies are ways to supplement the delivery of instruction that do not find easy placement into the others categories. These could include instructional boards, bulletin boards, learning centers, poster making machines, laminating machines, binding devices, etc.

• TRADITIONAL TYPES OF INSTRUCTIONAL TECHNOLOGY

Three of the five identified categories of instructional technology will be discussed in this chapter: Print Technologies, Audiovisual Technologies, and Display and Support Technologies. These technologies are labeled "traditional" because they not only have a history of use in classrooms in the recent past, many are current tools in the classroom. Only the most common technologies in each category will be addressed; however, many others could be identified.

• PRINT TECHNOLOGIES

Print technologies have the most extensive history as an educational tool. Despite the impact of the new and emerging technologies on education, the printed word will continue to play an important role in the learning process and in the classroom. Three main categories of print technology make up the majority of the printed resources that are found in classrooms: textbooks, periodicals (journals, newspapers, newsletters, etc.), and resource or reference books. Textbooks are the most common.

Textbooks

Textbooks have been, and continue to be, one of the primary instructional tools in the process of education. Classrooms may have an extensive array of other and newer technological resources to support the learning process; but there must be a resource to which the student can return, whether at home or in school, in the quest for learning and understanding. Textbooks are the resource that help bring structure to the subject being studied. They are the connecting link between the content, the student, and the teacher.

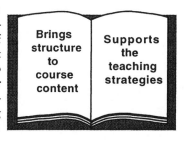

Advantages of Textbooks. As an educational tool, textbooks have many advantages that have made them effective in the educational arena.

1. Textbooks can be used at a pace that is determined by the student.
2. They can be consulted repeatedly by the student for content clarification and review purposes.
3. A well designed textbook will give structure to the content area.
4. Textbooks can be made available to all students at a nominal cost when compared to other media.
5. They are easy to use and do not require support technology in order to be used effectively.

Selecting a Textbook. The selection of a textbook begins with an examination of the course curriculum. This will identify the course content and the instructional strategies for teaching the content. Using this data as the initial criteria, information can be secured from publishers regarding appropriate materials. Once a copy of the text (or the teaching package that includes the text) has been obtained, you can begin to evaluate the materials. This is a two step process. First, a preliminary evaluation of the material is done. If the materials successfully pass this test, then a detailed evaluation is done. The procedure may be terminated at any point.

Preliminary Evaluation. Every textbook evaluation should begin with a preliminary evaluation. This twenty to thirty minute procedure will allow the teacher to eliminate any text that is not appropriate for the identified situation. If the text successfully passes the preliminary evaluation, it should then be examined using detailed evaluation criteria and a related form. Steps for doing a preliminary evaluation include:

1. Identify the copyright date - currentness of material.
2. Read the Preface - underlying philosophy and audience.
3. Read the Introduction - mini-review of book.
4. Review the Table of Contents - match to course outline.
5. Visually examine every page - appeal to the reader.
6. Read three to five pages - readability.
7. Select a topic and read three pages - content and presentation.
8. Proceed to the next evaluation level.

Detailed Evaluation. This step usually involves the use of a textbook evaluation form. Each item is assessed and given a rating of 1, 2, 3, 4, or 5 points. The totals for the books being considered are compared. Criteria from a representative form are shown below.

Author Qualifications
Relevance to Course Curriculum
Scope of Coverage
Depth of Coverage
Objective Presentation of Content
Currentness of Content
Logical Organization
Clear Writing
Appropriate Reading Level
Identified Measurable Objectives
Identified Vocabulary Terms
Identified Review Questions
Identified References/Resources
Illustrations - Black & White
Illustrations - Color
Diagrams, Charts, Drawings - Black & White
Diagrams, Charts, Drawings - Color
Overall Layout
Text/Illustrations - Multicultural
Text/Illustrations - Disabled Individuals
Appropriate Binding
Appropriate Cost
Support Materials - Teacher's Edition of Text
Support Materials - Teacher's Guide/Manual
Support Materials - Workbooks
Support Materials - Assessment Materials
Support Materials - Media/Technology

• AUDIOVISUAL TECHNOLOGIES

The word "audiovisual," or the letters "AV," elicit different images for people. Adults raised during the latter half of the 20th century may envision opaque projectors, filmstrip projectors, 16 mm film projectors, etc. Today's students would probably identify some very different technologies. Five of the most common audiovisual technologies used in the contemporary classroom are discussed in this chapter: Overhead Projectors, Transparencies, Visual Presenters (Document Cameras), Camcorders, and Video Projectors.

Overhead Projectors

The overhead projector is not only very easy to use, it is the most common type of projection technology available in schools. Unlike other projection technologies that are "dated" and have limited current resources available (16 mm films and filmstrips) or are costly (video projectors or visual presenters), overhead projectors are available in many models and at affordable prices.

The Design.   An overhead projector consists of a box with a glass platen (the stage) on the top surface. A powerful lamp is mounted above a reflector on the floor of the box. When the overhead projector is turned on, the light is reflected off the reflector, through a fresnel lens (causing the light to be evenly distributed across the stage), and through the stage. The light continues through the transparency on the stage and the image is transferred to a projection lens and mirror mounted above the box. This mechanism turns the image 90 degrees and projects it onto the screen.

Types of Overhead Projectors.   There are two types of overhead projectors: the standard table-top models and collapsible portable models.

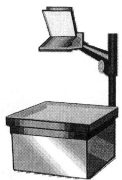

Standard Table-Top Projectors. These projectors are generally larger than the collapsible/ portable models. Although these models do not "foldup," many do have a handle to allow for easy transportation from one location to another.

Collapsible/Portable Projectors.   This group of projectors is less cumbersome than the standard table top models and they are specifically intended to be portable.

Advantages of the Overhead Projector.   The appeal of the overhead projector in both the educational community and the business sector is largely tied to its unique advantages as a tool for instruction/presentation. Normal classroom lighting can be maintained while using the overhead projector; thus the instructor can have better control of the class. Moreover, because the projector is placed in the front of the classroom, with projection taking place over the shoulders of the presenter, the instructor is always facing the class. The variety of uses and the control afforded the instructor over the presentation of materials when using the overhead projector is enhanced by its light weight, ease of operation, and reasonable cost.

Transparencies

Overhead transparencies are usually used with an overhead projector; however, they can also be used with a visual presenter (document camera). They are one of the most common and popular forms of instructional technology employed by teachers. In addition to being easy to make and use, overhead transparencies offer a number of other advantages to the teacher. They can be interspersed with other forms of technology, they can be customized and manipulated in a number of ways, and the pace for use is fully controlled by the teacher.

Materials For Making Transparencies. Instructional transparencies consist of images that are printed on a piece of film. For handmade transparencies, the image is drawn using special markers. In most cases, however, the image is printed using another form of technology. This could be done using a laser printer, a xerographic copy machine, an ink jet printer, or an infrared transparency maker.

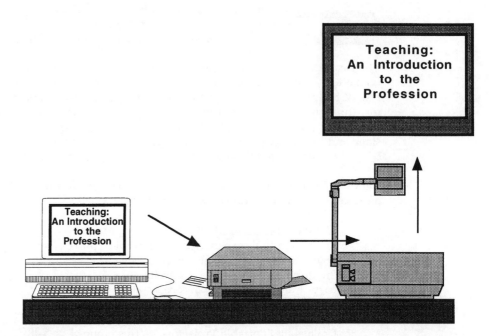

Transparency Film. When selecting transparency film, you must choose a film that is specifically designated for use on the type of machine you are going to use. All transparency films are not interchangeable. You can cause damage to a machine if it is the incorrect type of film. If you are uncertain regarding the type of film, it should only be used for handmade transparencies. The most common types of film include:

- Write-On Transparency Film
- Transparency Film for Plain Paper Copiers
- Transparency Film for Laser Printers
- Transparency Film for Ink Jet Printers
- Film for Infrared (Thermal) Transparency Makers

Visual Presenters (Document Cameras)

Visual presenters are also called document cameras, presentation cameras, and visualizers. They are used in traditional instructional settings as well as in conjunction with video conferencing systems. Their wide appeal is due to the variety of materials that can be shown with this technology. These include all paper documents (books, periodicals, written assignments, newspaper clippings, etc.), transparencies, photographs, 35 mm slides and realia (3-dimensional objects ranging from small tools and coins to plants or a live worm).

The visual presenter is an input technology, and therefore must be coupled with an output technology such as a television monitor or a video projector. Due to the variety of models, the operator's manual for the specific model being used should be consulted.

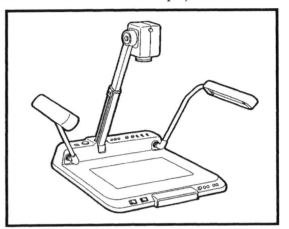

Parts of a Visual Presenter. A typical visual presenter consists of a stage on which the object is placed, a video camera mounted above the stage, directional lights that illuminate the stage from above, and a light built into the stage that allows it to function as an overhead projector for transparencies and slides.

Camcorders

A camcorder is a video camera, a microphone, and a video recorder combined into a single, compact, piece of equipment. In addition to being an audio and video recording unit, the camcorder can also serve as a playback device. When used for this purpose, the unit can either be connected directly to a television monitor or the presen-

tation can be viewed on the camcorder itself. Because they are compact and light weight, camcorders can be easily handled and used even by young children. Consequently, they are a popular tool in many classrooms. In some cases, they are a standard technology tool for teachers and a common reporting and record keeping tool for students.

The camcorder can be held or mounted in various shooting positions. Heavier VHS models are usually placed on the user's shoulder if movement is going to be required, while lighter palmcorders can be hand-held. If a lesson is going to be taped and the camcorder can be placed in a stationary position, it is mounted on a tripod.

Camcorder Formats. Although a number of different manufacturers produce camcorders in various formats and models, they all have the same basic parts and operate in a similar manner.

VHS is the traditional large camcorder that has been available since the early 1980s. This records on full-size VHS tapes, which can be inserted into a VCR for playback.

VHS-C (Video Home System-Compact) is a smaller VHS model than the original unit. This records on smaller cassettes which must be placed in an adapter cassette before playing in a VCR. Often called palmcorders, these are lighter and much easier to handle. Many have an LCD screen for viewing while recording, or for playback.

8 mm is smaller than the VHS-C. Playback is through a cable from the camcorder to a TV or VCR.

High Resolution formats for the VHS, VHS-C, and 8 mm camcorders are also available. These are SVHS, SVHS-C and Hi8. These are more expensive and are usually used by professionals.

DV is the smallest camcorder on the market, but offers the highest resolution. The signal is stored in a digital form, while the picture is recorded on videotape.

Camcorder Features. Standard camcorder features include the following:
- Viewfinder: shows the image that is seen through the lens.
- LCD Screen: functions as a viewfinder, provides instant playback.
- Image Stabilization: keeps the camera steady, even when moving.
- Automatic/Manual Focus: adjusts to the object shown within the frame.
- Zoom Lens: change of image size without moving the camera.
- Backlight: evens out the light.
- Special Effects: fade in/out, color fade effects, titles, and date/time.
- Battery Packs: can provide up to two hours of continuous recording time.

Digital Video Camcorders. Digital Video (DV) camcorders are the result of a merger of digital cameras and video cameras. They allow teachers and students to make their own movies to use on their computer, put on web pages to share with others, or merely edit and save for school or family use. DV camcorders also take still images. Video and still images are saved as DV formats, making pictures sharper than those taken with VHS camcorders.

DV camcorders are not totally digital; they store the signal in a digital form, while still recording on videotape. The tape used, the "mini-DV," is the smallest videotape. The camcorder is also smaller than any of the other types, but the quality is higher than other video formats. Tapes can be copied many times without losing quality; they can also be re-recorded many times.

Video Projectors

Research has shown that large screen projection is more appealing to students than viewing images on either a monitor or a small screen. The video projector makes large screen projection an option for the teacher. Used in classrooms, lecture halls, and auditoriums, this technology works best in a darkened room unless the projector has high lumens. In addition to their use with computers, video projectors can be used with VCRs, visual presenters, DVDs, and any other technology that has a video output jack.

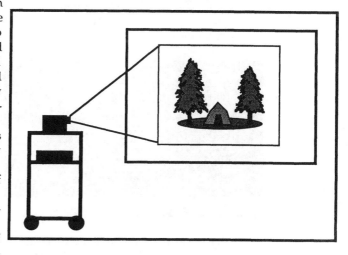

Video projectors can be portable or they can be mounted in the classroom. Because of their small size, they can easily be transported within the school or taken out of the school for presentations at other locations. Most video projectors weigh in the vicinity of ten to fifteen pounds; however, newer portable models weigh between three to five pounds. The newest video projectors use Digital Light Processing (DLP), a space-saving alternative. When selecting a video projector the teacher should investigate the lumens of brightness; the resolution quality compatibility of your computer; the size and weight of the projector; and the overall operational compatibility with your computer.

• DISPLAY AND SUPPORT TECHNOLOGIES

As discussed at the beginning of this chapter, Seels and Richey have identified four areas in the domain of Instructional Technology: Print Technologies, Audiovisual Technologies, Computer-based Technologies, and Integrated Technologies. Display and Support Technologies has been added to incorporate those technologies that are not easily placed within the realm of these headings. Four of the most common technologies from this area are discussed in this chapter: Instructional Boards, Bulletin Boards, Learning Centers, and Cognitive Maps. Additional technologies that would fit into this area include laminating technology, wire coil binding, poster making technology, etc.

Instructional Boards

Instructional boards is the name given to the broad array of boards or surfaces that are used to provide information during the process of instruction. All of these boards provide the user with a means of providing immediate, on-the-spot input to the class. They also afford the opportunity to change the information at any time. Because they are easy to use and cost effective, they are a key instructional tool in the classroom.

Chalkboards (nonmagnetic). Historically, white chalk was used to write on slate boards called blackboards. Today, chalk and chalkboards are both available in a variety of colors. Despite the fact that this technology has changed little over the years, the chalkboard is still a valuable instructional tool for the teacher. Contemporary nonmagnetic chalkboards consist of a writing surface (painted, laminate, etc.) on a backing of a material that is not magnetic (Masonite, composition board, etc.). These boards are the least costly to purchase. Special "blackboard paint" is also available that allows any surface that can be painted to be converted into a chalkboard.

A a B b C c D d E e F f G g H h I i J j K k L l M m N n O o P p Q q R r S s T t U u V v W w X x Y y Z z

White chalk is the primary color of chalk used on a black chalkboard.
Yellow chalk is the primary color of chalk used on a green chalkboard.

Chalkboards (Magnetic). Many educational settings have chalkboards that are a combination chalk/magnetic board. Unlike the less costly chalkboards, these boards are designed to withstand extensive and long term use. Since they have a base surface of metal (usually porcelain-on-steel) they will accept magnetic accessories. This allows the teacher to display posters, charts, maps, student work, etc. on the board without the worry of damaging the writing surface. The materials used in this situation can also be easily and quickly displayed, used, and removed.

Felt/Flannel Boards. This instructional board consists of a rigid backing covered with either felt or flannel. The instructional pieces that are used in combination with the felt/flannel board are either (1) made from the same material or (2) backed with the same felt or flannel. Because these materials have a fuzzy texture, they easily stick together. Felt/flannel boards are especially popular at the preschool and elementary level and are used by the teacher and the students. Consequently, many commercially produced materials and teaching kits are available for this age group.

Multipurpose Boards. Multipurpose boards are also known as "white boards" or "marker boards." The name white board is based on the fact that the writing surface is white. The marker board name emerged from the use of dry erase markers as the writing instrument used on the board surface. The name "multipurpose board" is a more accurate name because the board can be used for a variety of purposes. It can be written on using dry erase markers (no other type should be used); it can serve as a projection screen for any projection technology (overhead, slide, film, etc.); shapes cut from thin plastic sheets will adhere to the surface if rubbed in place; and multipurpose boards that have a steel back can be used as a magnetic display board for posters, student work, etc.

Combination Boards. Combination boards consist of two different types of boards in the same unit. They are available as wall mount or permanent units; as movable units with a board that can be turned to use either of the two different sides; and in an easel format. The two surfaces can be of any combination.

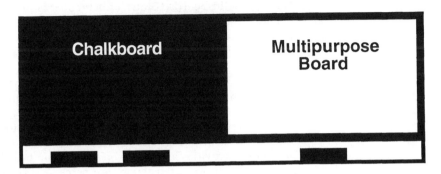

Bulletin Boards

Bulletin boards are the most common form of display technology used in the classroom. Although they are intended to provide information or an opportunity for interaction to a large number of students or a class, they can also serve as a link and point of unification for special-interest groups. All bulletin boards can be grouped into one of four categories:

Announcement Bulletin Boards. This type of board is used to post announcements, schedules, and other types information of interest to individuals who use the room.

Decorative Bulletin Boards. As the name implies, decorative bulletin boards are used to help create a visually appealing and stimulating environment.

Instructional Bulletin Boards. Instructional bulletin boards are tied to specific and identified curricular objectives and provide instruction regarding the objectives.

Motivational Bulletin Boards. These boards are intended to inspire students to reach in their quest for learning or to take action regarding an issue.

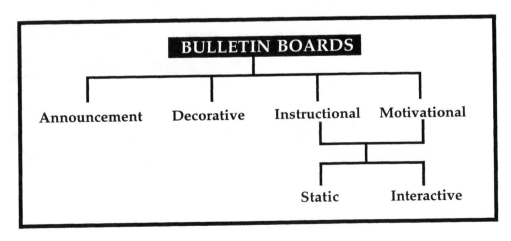

Instructional Bulletin Boards and **Motivational Bulletin Boards** are the two main categories that all teachers should become proficient at creating and using in their teaching. Bulletin boards in these categories can be either <u>static</u> or <u>interactive</u>.

<u>Static Bulletin Boards.</u> Static bulletin boards present information without requiring the student to directly respond to the information. They can be used as an introduction to a topic, a review of the content covered, enrichment regarding a class topic, a means to elicit action from the reader, etc.

<u>Interactive Bulletin Boards.</u> Interactive bulletin boards require the student to engage in some type of activity that is tied to the content and materials on the bulletin board. Interactive bulletin boards also have another unique component: a activity sheet. This identifies questions the student must answer and activities that may or must be undertaken. Answers to complete some of the activities are found on the bulletin board. Others must be found elsewhere. The expected actions are necessary in order to fully benefit from the design of the bulletin board. Like a static bulletin board, the focus could be to introduce a topic, to summarize a topic, provide enrichment, etc.

Learning Centers

The constructivist classroom has received considerable attention in recent years. Far removed from the rote memorization approach to learning, constructivism is concerned with students learning "how to learn." Constructivists believe that knowledge acquisition and learning result from hands-on experiences. The student "constructs" an understanding of concepts and a knowledge base as a result of his/her interactions in the real world. Classrooms that support a constructivist approach to learning are places where individual, collaborative, and competitive activities are commonplace. One of the major questions for constructivists is "How can I provide meaningful educational experiences for a variety of interests, in many areas, on different levels?" The use of learning centers is a viable answer to this question.

Learning Centers are self-contained learning environments where one student, or a small group of students, can independently investigate an area of study in order to meet a predetermined objective. The center includes all the materials, supplies, equipment, and directions needed to undertake a series of activities.

Elements of learning centers include: a clear label or title, identified objectives, sequenced activities, basic/required activities, optional activities, all needed materials, all needed supplies, all needed equipment, information resources, and directions for activities.

Characteristics of learning centers are: a structure for individual or small group participation - determined by the teacher; self-instructing - the teacher is not needed for successful center use; self-correcting - the student has immediate feedback regarding success in undertaking or completing an activity; pacing by the student - starting and stopping is at the discretion of the student; a design for different purposes - they can introduce, develop, or reinforce a concept, foster enrichment, develop awareness, create interest, etc.

Materials at learning centers may include anything and everything that could support the intent of the center: textbooks and resource books; teaching kits; a concept map; manipulatives to engage in the activities; support materials-- paper, scissors, tape, card stock, etc.; photographs of other students engaged in the activity; directions in multiple formats-- task cards and/or videotapes; technology to instruct/guide-- VCR, audio cassette player, videodiscs/player, slide viewer; technology to record the results-- camera, camcorder, tapes, a computer; Internet connection; individual logs or record sheets/ folders; and more.

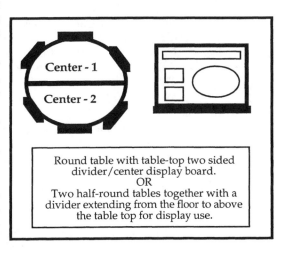

Round table with table-top two sided divider/center display board.
OR
Two half-round tables together with a divider extending from the floor to above the table top for display use.

Assessment of student progress at a learning center takes place on two fronts. It is done by the student and by the teacher.

<u>Self-assessment by the student</u> should be completed at the end of each and every work period at the center. The student could keep a journal of his/her center activity, record activity in individual logs or folders at the center, keep an audio record of the activity, keep a photographic record of results, maintain a portfolio, etc.

<u>Assessment by the teacher</u> is a scheduled, on-going process. This can be done by reviewing student logs or journals, listening to audiotape reports, viewing photographic or video tape records, meeting with students individually and on a regular basis to review progress, reviewing individual portfolios, keep an ongoing photographic record of student activity, etc.

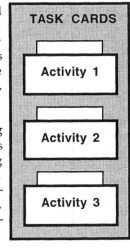

Cognitive Maps (Semantic Maps)

Cognitive mapping is a display technology that is used to give a visual presence to ideas, concepts, facts, and other content areas. Cognitive maps exist in a variety of types (highly structured to very loosely structured) and are known under a number of different names (semantic maps, idea maps, hierarchical diagrams, concept maps, star bursts, and webs to name just a few). They are a planning/organization/ presentation tool used in the business community, by government, by industry, in think tanks, and by various members of the educational community.

Cognitive maps can be modified, and made especially appealing as a teaching aid for the intended audience, if illustrations or photographs are incorporated into the presentation. The illustrations could be cut out of magazines, downloaded and printed from the web, drawn by students, etc. This approach is often found in learning centers.

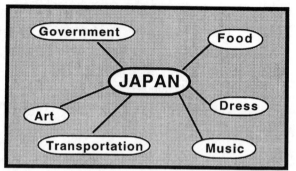

Inspiration® by Inspiration Software is a software program that is designed to assist in the creation of cognitive maps. This program combines the planning and the drawing aspects into one process. *Inspiration* is identified as *"The premier tool to develop ideas and organize thinking. It uses brainstorming, planning, organizing, outlining, diagraming, concept mapping, and webbing."*

Cognitive Map Formats. All cognitive maps are variations of, and can be grouped under, two basic formats: unstructured maps and structured maps.

Unstructured Cognitive Maps begin with a concept, idea, or topic and then branch out into the many related sub-topics or ideas.

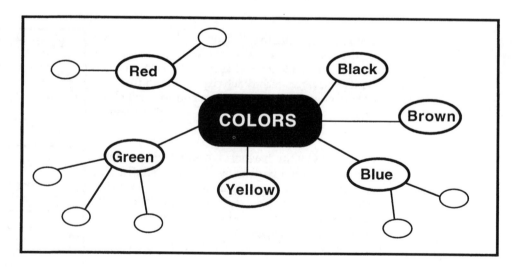

Structured Cognitive Maps also begin with a concept, idea, or topic and then branch out into related sub-topics or ideas. However, there is a discernible structure to the display. It exhibits "levels of consistency." All of the material identified in the map is organized into levels, and each level contains elements of equal weight, meaning, or value. Maps of this type are usually used to present or display information that is already known or to identify voids in the organization or knowledge structure. Hierarchical diagrams, under various names and in various formats, are the most common type of structured cognitive map.

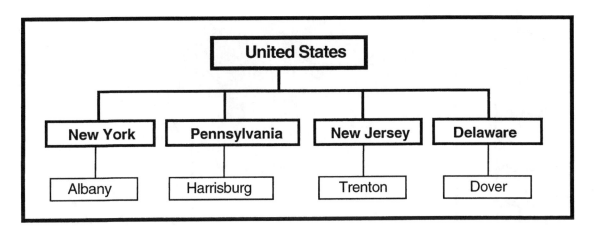

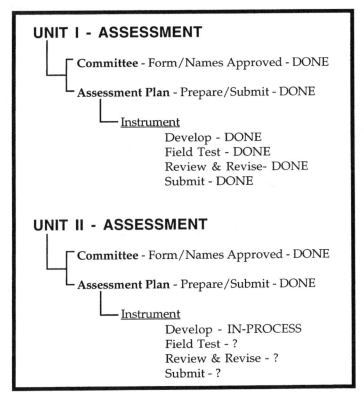

CHAPTER

12

Contemporary Educational Technology

Lynne C. Levy

The computer is the most frequently identified example when contemporary educational technology is discussed. It has not only changed how we teach and learn, it has changed how we think. Whereas sociologists and economists refer to the global village, educators must think in terms of the global classroom. As a future teacher in this classroom, you must have an understanding of the types of contemporary technology tools and how they are used in the teaching/learning process. In this chapter we provide an overview of these tools. More specifically, the following questions will be addressed:

- What is the relationship between education, technology and standards?

- What decisions must be made regarding computers in schools?

- What are the main types of computer hardware?

- What are the main types of computer software?

- How can computer software be used in the classroom?

- How is the Internet used in schools?

- How can the World Wide Web be used as an educational tool?

• EDUCATION, TECHNOLOGY AND STANDARDS

Technology plans have emerged on the national, state, and local levels in recent years. Educators entering the teaching profession should not only have knowledge of the technology plan for the district in which they are employed, they should be familiar with their state technology plan and the national technology plan. The need for planning is especially critical in the area of technology and education. The exponential growth of technology requires that questions and issues be revisited and readdressed on an ongoing basis. Simply purchasing technology and placing it in schools is not an answer. Long-term, short-term, and ongoing planning will be a standard practice in the 21st century. Schools are required to address this on a local level with a district and/or school technology plan; usually these plans are for a three or five year period.

National Educational Technology Standards

The International Society for Technology in Education (ISTE) is the largest international, nonprofit organization in the area of educational technology. ISTE has provided leadership and guidance in the area of technology and teacher education with the creation of the National Educational Technology Standards (NETS) Project. Along with a consortium of distinguished partners and cosponsors they developed NETS for Students, NETS for Teachers, and NETS for Administrators. For students and teachers, the NETS propose a plan for integrating technology into the curriculum, providing technology support, and implementing standards for student assessment and evaluation of technology use. All of the standards can be accessed at the ISTE web site.

Visit ISTE at www.iste.org

Technology in New Jersey

School districts use the NETS standards as they develop their individual technology plan; however they must also follow the State Technology Plan. New Jersey has a commitment to educational technology as evidenced by plans implemented in 1993 and 1997. Educational Technology is embedded in New Jersey's Core Curriculum Content Standards, and is addressed in the state's strategic plan. In New Jersey, the most recent plan, *Working Toward the Future with Our Children: The Education Technology Plan for New Jersey*, went into effect in January, 2003. The Belief Statement reads:

The N.J. Technology Plan can be found at: www.state.nj.us/njded/techno/state_plan.htm

The N.J. Core Curriculum Content Standards can be found at: www.state.nj.us/njded/cccs/

> *All Students, no matter which district or school they attend, will be able to achieve the Core Curriculum Content Standards because they will have unlimited access to people, to a vast array of curriculum and instruction, and to information and ideas -- no matter where they exist.*

The four goals of the plan, which also includes what actions the New Jersey Department of Education has taken to include technology throughout the curriculum in daily activities for students, teachers and administrators, are:

Goal 1: *Students will attain the educational technology and information literacy skills that will assist them in achieving Core Curriculum Content Standards and to succeed in the workplace in the 21st Century;*

Goal 2: *Educators will attain the skills and knowledge necessary to effectively use educational technology to assist students to achieve the Core Curriculum Content Standards;*

Goal 3: *Students, teachers and administrators will have access to educational technology in all learning environments, including classrooms, media centers, schools, and other educational settings, such as community centers; and*

Goal 4: *New Jersey school districts will establish and maintain the technology infrastructure necessary for students and educators to access electronic information and to communicate freely via technology.*

[*The Education Technology Plan for New Jersey*, January, 8, 2003, p. 5]

Through this plan, as well as other endeavors, including grants and financial aid, the New Jersey Department of Education assists districts in planning for educational technology, and making their plans a reality.

A clearer image of the impact of technology infusion in the schools of Southern New Jersey can be obtained by examining some current data. In the *NJ School Technology Survey 2002 Report* [www.state.nj.us/njded/techno/survey/index.html], the survey results indicate that New Jersey's student to multimedia computer ratio is 4.4 to 1. The national ratio is 3.8 to 1 [www.edweek.com/context/topics/issuespage.cfm?id=96], which is closer to the ratio in the counties in Southern New Jersey. The percentage of classrooms with Internet connections statewide was 89.7 in 2002. The Southern county area is much higher.

Southern New Jersey Schools Student to Multimedia Computer Ratio		Southern New Jersey Schools Classrooms with Internet Connections	
Atlantic	3.8 to 1	Atlantic	96.3%
Camden	3.9 to 1	Camden	97.0%
Cape May	3.6 to 1	Cape May	93.7%
Cumberland	3.4 to 1	Cumberland	98.2%
Gloucester	3.9 to 1	Gloucester	97.5%
Salem	3.2 to 1	Salem	97.1%

In addition, statewide, 93% of the public schools have technology coordinators, 95% of the public schools have Web sites, and 94% of the public schools are using Internet filtering software/monitoring software.

• Working Toward the Future with Our Children •
The Education Technology Plan for New Jersey

GOAL 1: **Students will attain the educational technology and information literacy skills that will assist them in achieving the Core Curriculum Content Standards and to succeed in the workplace of the 21st century.**

1.1 Educational technology will be infused into every school district's curriculum and instructional activities.
1.2 All school districts will adopt curricula that include information literacy and educational technology standards aligned with the Core Curriculum Content Standards and accepted national standards.
1.3 All students will demonstrate proficiency in using educational technology and information literacy skills to enhance learning, increase productivity and promote creativity.
1.4 All students will have equitable and easy access to effective and engaging software, CD ROMs and online resources for content delivery as an integral part of every school curriculum. Content materials will meet universal design standards to assure access for students with disabilities.
1.5 All students will have equitable and easy access to the Internet and other distance learning technology to obtain information and resources from remote locations to collaborate, publish and interact with peers, experts and other audiences.
1.6 All students will use technology tools and applications for solving problems, making informed decisions, and participating in authentic, project-based learning.
1.7 All students will act responsibly and ethically when obtaining and using onsite and online information resources.

GOAL 2: **Educators will attain the skills and knowledge necessary to effectively use educational technology to assist students to achieve the Core Curriculum Content Standards.**

2.1 All educators will participate in high-quality professional development activities and attain, at a minimum, intermediate proficiency levels in utilizing educational technology to enhance student achievement.
2.2 All supervision and evaluation practices will address the effective use of educational technology for student achievement of the Core Curriculum Content Standards.
2.3 All educators will use technology tools and applications that provide opportunities for authentic, student-centered, project-based learning.
2.4 All educators will have access to e-mail and other interactive tools to communicate with parents, students and other educators.
2.5 All educators will act responsibly and ethically when obtaining and using onsite and online information resources.
2.6 All schools will have technology coordinators for educators that offer timely, onsite guidance and modeling to enhance teacher and administrator proficiency in using and managing technology-based resources.

GOAL 3: **Students, teachers and administrators will have access to educational technology in all learning environments, including classrooms, media centers, schools, and other educational settings such as community centers.**

3.1 All students and educators will have regular and equitable access to technology equipment (both desktop and portable) when needed in all learning environments. This includes access to technologies with universal design features or other design modifications that assure access for students with educational disabilities.
3.2 All school districts will provide a ratio of five students or less to one multimedia computer in all instructional classrooms, with each of these classroom computers connected to the Internet.
3.3 All districts, schools and classrooms will be connected to broadband, high-speed voice, video and data networks in all learning environments.
3.4 All schools will have Local Area Networks (a system or network of interconnected computers within a school building), and all districts, where appropriate, will have Wide Area Networks (a network that electronically interconnects multiple school networks -- usually within a school district).
3.5 All districts and schools will have high-quality, highly informative, user-friendly Web sites.
3.6 All educators will have easy access to technical support via a technician and/or electronic assistance that is necessary to maintain operating technology equipment (e.g., help desks, hot lines, electronic monitoring, and troubleshooters).
3.7 All school districts will establish relationships with appropriate partners, including, but not limited to, other public agencies and entities, education institutions, community-based organizations and private corporations to increase opportunities for sustained technology access and broad, collaborative learning environments.
3.8 All districts and schools will identify and support the needs of students who do not have access to technology in their homes to enable them to continue their learning through technology when school is not in session.
3.9 All school districts will adopt an Acceptable Use Policy and other means to ensure that all students, teachers and administrators are able to use technology systems, online resources and software in a safe, ethical and secure manner.

GOAL 4: **New Jersey school districts will establish and maintain the technology infrastructure necessary for students and educators to access electronic information and to communicate freely via technology.**

4.1 All school districts will obtain and maintain broadband, high-speed networks and reliable Internet access that enables students and educators to support their curricula activities.
4.2 All school buildings will have the equipment necessary to provide distance learning opportunities when and where it is needed in the school.
4.3 All schools will maintain quality hardware/software with adequate capacity and capability to support successful learning in classrooms, media centers and throughout the learning environment.

• COMPUTERS IN SCHOOLS

Most educators agree that the best use of technology is achieved when it is infused, on an ongoing basis, into the curriculum. When computers are viewed as a "tool" they are used whenever, wherever, and however appropriate. Initially, teachers were elated to have one computer in the classroom. The new technology was usually placed on the teacher's desk. There it could be used for teacher tasks, instruction to small groups, and as a tool for student use. As their uses became more evident, and additional money became available, computers were placed in the classroom in **clusters** of from two to six computers. They could now be arranged in various configurations to serve differing needs.

When a classroom primarily consists of computers and their related support technology, the classroom is referred to as a **computer lab**. This arrangement has many advantages; however, there is one major disadvantage: lab configurations do not lend themselves to group work or any type of activity that requires open table space. When instruction is provided to a large group of students and it concentrates on how to use the technology, the facility is being used as an instructional lab. Open labs are available for teachers and students to use for whatever educational purposes they choose.

The above configurations all have one element in common--the computers are "set in place." During the late 1990s, portable computer configurations began to emerge. Computer technology in schools advanced to another level with **computers on wheels**: laptops in a cart to take to a classroom rather than have labs that take valuable space many schools do not have.

Wireless Technology

The latest development in the infusion of computers into the classroom involves the use of **wireless technology**. With this technology, an AirPort card (Mac) or PC card, along with a transmitting device, is used to create a wireless connection between the computer and the school network connection. The user has all the options of someone using a direct connection. With the wireless connection, a student can use the Internet, correspond via e-mail, or print to a nearby printer without any wires interfering. Wireless routers are connected to the school's network, sending signals for communication within a 100 foot range.

Operating Systems

There is always the debate of which type of computer to have in the classroom: PC (Windows Operating System) or Apple Macintosh. Both are now operating with a graphic user interface, providing users with windows, icons, and text, to make the computer easy to use. The two systems are getting closer to being compatible. *Microsoft Office*, along with other software applications, is compatible between the two systems. Operating systems for both change often: Windows has several variations, and Macintosh has recently changed to a new OSX, making the environment look very much like a PC. New users are finding it easy to go from one system to another; therefore, the type of computer is not really an issue; the greater issue is what is being done with the computer in the classroom.

Technology Fluency

Today's students pick up technology fluency at an early age. When they learn to use a word processor, they can transfer that knowledge over to another word processor. The same holds true for spreadsheets, presentation software, drawing programs, etc. What is important in the classroom is for teachers to focus on the content they want their students to receive. Technology can be the tool to reach the intended goal. This, then, carries over into the workplace--employers expect their employees to know which tool is best for a task, and how to use it effectively.

• COMPUTER HARDWARE

While it is not necessary for the teacher or students to know a lot about how computers work, it is necessary to know enough about the hardware and software in order to use the technology effectively.

The interconnected mechanical and electronic components of a computer system are termed hardware. To have hardware fulfill its potential it must be directed to perform specific tasks. This is the purpose of software, also called a computer program.

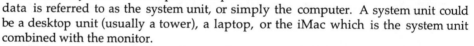

The case that houses the electronic components necessary to run the computer and process data is referred to as the system unit, or simply the computer. A system unit could be a desktop unit (usually a tower), a laptop, or the iMac which is the system unit combined with the monitor.

Each computer has ports--places where external devices such as storage devices, printers, keyboards, etc. are attached. Although there were once serial and parallel ports, the USB (Universal Serial Bus) is quickly becoming the norm for all computers. These cables are "Plug and Play"--they can be changed while the computer is running. Most computers come with two ports, but can be expanded to 127. Many USB peripheral devices are compatible with both PC and Macintosh computers.

Input Devices for the Classroom

Any device which allows the user to enter data, commands, and responses to the computer is termed an input device. Common to every computer is the **keyboard** and the **mouse** (laptops, however, have a built-in keyboard and a **trackpad** in place of a mouse). **Touch screens** are an alternative to the keyboard and mouse, with the monitor responding to a human touch. However, these screens require specialized software. They are most commonly used for young children, or those with physical impairments. Other input devices can be added for specific applications.

Electronic whiteboards are often found in classrooms. Text, drawings, etc. created on the board can be transferred to the computer and saved or printed out. Another type of electric whiteboard is the SMART board. With this technology, a computer image is projected onto the board. Touching the board (instead of using a mouse) operates the computer and manipulates the software.

Scanners are light-sensing devices that read documents, photos, and more; images are then sent to the computer and saved in a file format such as TIFF, JPEG, GIF, PICT, according to their end use. Text can also be scanned; however, the end product is still a graphic image. The image can be digitized by OCR (Optical Character Recognition) software for editing in a word processing program.

A **digital camera** takes photographic images which are stored digitally; then imports them to the computer to be stored and used in a newsletter, portfolio, or other document. They are saved with the file format JPEG, which can also be sent via e-mail or used on a web page. Photos taken with a 35 mm camera can be processed and placed on a CD-ROM to be used in the same way.

Sound and Video can be input into the computer through a **microphone**, while video can be imported from camcorders and video cameras. A **digital video camcorder** is also available. Video, as well as still pictures, is sent to the computer via a firewire cable for editing using video-editing software. Clips can be arranged in any order; visual effects added; and audio in the form of musical soundtracks, voice-overs, or sound effects can be included. Edited movies can be put on a CD or DVD, sent to friends and relatives via e-mail, used on web pages, or used as components of presentations.

Voice (speech) recognition software recognizes the user's speech and imports the user's words into the computer.

Graphics tablets allow students to create artwork on the tablet, and then import the work into the computer. Text can also be recognized by the computer and imported into a word processing document.

Hand-held Computing Devices

Personal Digital Assistants (PDAs), Palms, Pocket/Personal PCs, Hand-held Computers, and Hand-held Devices all fall into the category of Hand-held Computing Devices. Small like a cellular phone or pocket gaming device, these are new tools found in today's classrooms. They might contain a personal organizer, a word processor, a digital camera, Internet and e-mail connectivity, along with several types of calculators, all in one device; for the price of a graphing calculator. In addition to these capabilities, free and inexpensive software can be obtained for use in the K-12 classroom.
Probes are available for science classes, concept mapping is available for language arts, databases of historical facts can be downloaded for research, and eBooks can be downloaded for reading. Built-in features include an on-screen keyboard (a larger, external, keyboard can be added), character recognition (data written with a stylus is interpreted and recognized), synchronization (to communicate with a computer), and an infrared port (to transfer programs and data between units). Advantages are low cost, size, ease of use, and mobility. Concerns expressed by school administrators include cheating (beam information to others), compatibility, distraction (students do not pay attention to other things), screen size, and security.

Output Devices for the Classroom

After data has been input into the computer, it is processed to become output. This can be seen on a monitor, printed on a printer, or listened to through speakers or headsets. Output to be viewed by a large audience can be transmitted through a video projector and shown on a large screen. These can be mounted in the classroom, or serve a portable units to move from one room to another.

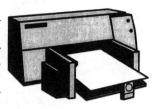

Computer Storage Devices

Storage devices permit the user to store and access documents and programs. The 5.25 inch floppy disk drive was the original storage device, followed by 3.5 inch drives, Zip and Jazz drives, CDs, and DVDs. While many of these drives are internal, or built-in, external drives can be added to the computer system. CD drives are the standard internal drive for computers today.

The **hard disk drive** is where all programs and data are stored; completely enclosed in the computer itself. Currently sized in terms of gigabytes (GB), the larger the drive, the greater the amount of information that can be stored. If you are working between computers, data from the hard drive must be made portable, using one of the following storage devices.

Floppy disks, 3.5" in diameter, contain a magnetic media which has read/write capabilities (read from it, or write to it). A high density disk holds 1.4 MB of data, or approximately 720 pages of text.

Zip disks are thicker than floppy disks, holding from 100 MB to 750 MB of data. The 100 MB disk is equivalent to 70 floppy disks.

Compact Disks (CDs) are built-in to most computers. It is necessary to have a CD drive in the computer to install most programs onto the computer. CD-ROM is Read Only Memory; these cannot be written to. CD-R are recordable, and CD-RW are rewritable. Currently, the main way to save files for portability (away from the home computer) is to "burn" a CD. One CD can hold 650 MB of data, or 250,000 pages of text. CD-RW are the most economical to use, as you can reuse them; while CD-R can only be written on once.

Digital Versatile Discs (DVDs) are the newest high capacity CD-size discs used for storage of movies, games, audio and multimedia. DVD drives are becoming common in computers, with the same drive also playing CDs. Similar to CDs, there is also a recordable format available for storage of large amounts of data, such as classroom-produced movies, music, etc. Storage is from 4.7 GB to 17 GB; 2-8 hours of high-quality video.

USB Flash Drives and **Card Readers** are small portable storage units. Flash drives are available in 16 MB - 1G sizes, while card readers utilize memory cards of various sizes for storage. Data can be stored on these for use in any computer with a USB port.

Media Equivalencies

3.5 " Floppy Disk =
720 pages of text =
1.4 MB memory

100 MB Zip Disk =
70 Floppy Disks =
50,000 pages of text

CD =
250,000 pages of text =
400 3.5" disks =
6-100 MB Zip disks =
650 MB memory

DVD=
2-8 hours
high quality video=
4.7 GB - 17 GB memory

• COMPUTER SOFTWARE

In order for hardware to fulfill its potential it must be directed to perform specific tasks. This is the purpose of software, also known as computer programs. Software is specific to the operating system of the computer. Some, however, is hybrid--it can be used by either Macintosh or Windows operating systems. Most software comes on a CD-ROM and must be installed prior to use. Copyright laws exist for computer software, as they do for books, music, etc. Purchasing a program on a CD means it can only legally be used on one computer. Schools can receive discounts by purchasing lab, site, or network licenses for multiple computers. **Public Domain Software** consists of software that is not copyrighted. It is legal to copy it and distribute it to others. Some children's programs can be found in this format. **Shareware** is software distributed free for a trial period, after which time the user pays a small fee to the author. Games are common in this category.

The software discussed in this chapter is that commonly found in schools for use by teachers, students, and administrators.

Productivity Software

Software that assists educators in completing tasks--writing memos, constructing exams, calculating grades, making presentations, effectively organizing information, and more, is known as productivity software. This same software can be used in and out of the classroom by students for tasks such assignments, class presentations, reports, graphs, etc.

The productivity programs most commonly found in schools are *Microsoft Office* and *AppleWorks*. *Microsoft Office* includes *Word* for word processing, *Excel* for spreadsheets, *Access* for databases, and *PowerPoint* for presentations. *AppleWorks* (formerly *ClarisWorks*) is an easy-to-use integrated program consisting of word processing, database, spreadsheet, presentation, drawing and painting components. Both programs have cross-platform compatibility (data transfers between Windows and Macintosh operating systems).

Word Processing. Using a word processor makes teacher tasks, from memos and reports to worksheets with graphics and tables, much easier. Documents can be formatted quickly and easily, editing can be done with a few keystrokes, text can be moved anywhere (even between documents), type sizes/fonts/styles can be quickly changed, and graphics can be added to produce a more visually appealing document. These same features transfer over to use by students, as they can take advantage of spell and grammar check, ease of editing, and graphics in their documents.

Spreadsheets. Teachers commonly use spreadsheets to calculate grades. Using simple formulas, averages and weighted grades are quickly calculated. This is, of course, only one use. Although it is frequently assumed that the data in a spreadsheet must be numerical, it can be any combination of characters (numbers and/or text). In this context, a spreadsheet can be much more than a calculator to a teacher. It can also house any information normally placed in grids or boxes. A teacher can make tables and charts, produce lesson plan formats, design checklists, or make grids for student worksheets. Any of the numerical data can be transformed into charts and graphs. Students can also produce charts and graphs, tabulate data they collect, calculate budgets, make tables and checklists, and much more.

Databases. A database is a collection of information--often termed an *electronic filing cabinet*. It is a file where information can be stored, sorted and retrieved in various ways; and then viewed and printed in different formats. Information storage is similar to a telephone book, an address book, or a recipe collection; however, fast retrieval of information can only be done with a computer. Data can also be merged into word processing documents for customized correspondence (mail merge), or used to print out labels.

Most schools have all of their student information in a database. This can easily be sent to each teacher, providing demographic and academic information on each student. If this is not available, the teacher can collect data, input it into a database, and access it in various ways. In addition to using a database for administrative purposes, teachers and students can collect data for units being studied; manipulating the data in various ways to analyze the data and produce reports.

Presentations. Teachers and students can easily put together presentations to organize and enhance classroom topics. Programs such as *PowerPoint, Keynote, HyperStudio*, or the presentation component in *AppleWorks*, provide digital support for oral presentations.

These presentations consist of a series of slides displayed on the screen. The presentation can be self-running or controlled by the speaker. A multimedia lecture

or classroom presentation can include text, clip art or digital pictures, video and/or sound, along with animation. Slides can be presented in linear, as well as nonlinear formats. The screens (referred to as slides), are usually configured for an on-screen or large screen presentation. They can also be printed out to be used as color overhead transparencies, and set up to print as presenter's outlines, audience handouts with a place for notes, or handouts depicting the screens in various sizes.

Graphics. Graphics programs fall into two main categories: Paint programs, which are used to create bit-mapped images, and Drawing programs, which are used to create object-oriented images.

Painting environments are typically for the artist creating artwork and doing illustrations. They employ computer-based paint brushes, air brushes, pencils, and other tools. Using these paint tools, colors and shapes are "painted" in the painting document, as they would be painted onto a canvas.

Drawing environments include object-oriented tools such as lines, rectangles, and circles, along with colors, patterns, and textures. Objects can be rearranged on the screen, grouped together, or deleted. Drawing tools can be used for designing classrooms, producing concept webs, adding lines, squares, or circles to documents, and much more. Most word processing programs include tools for drawing.

Clip art includes all ready-made graphics which can be added to documents, signs, flyers, newsletters, cards, web pages, etc. for interest and creativity. Clip art is available either free of charge or commercially, with many sites providing free clip art on the WWW.

Instructional Software

Programs which deliver instruction or support learning activities are categorized as instructional software. **Educational software**, often termed courseware, is a type of instructional software that is specific to a subject(s) (e.g. *Sammy's Science House* or *Math Monsters*); **software tools** fulfill a purpose in any subject (e.g. *HyperStudio* for classroom presentations, or *Inspiration* to draw a concept map).

Educational Software. Educational software in the past has been a model for what is now in use and what is being developed for the future. Educational software was originally grouped into five categories: tutorial, drill and practice, games, simulations, and problem solving. This software, at first simplistic, but enjoyable to children, was often used as a fill-in or stand-alone resource; not part of the set curriculum. With the complexity of many programs, and advancements in technology, most programs are combinations of the above, with an emphasis on multimedia.

Educational software today is software for learning: it is changing the way teachers teach. Curriculum changes are being made to incorporate this software, and what students can do with it, in a specific content area as well as cross-curricular. Much of the software is still on CDs; however, more and more is becoming available on the World Wide Web (for free or a fee).

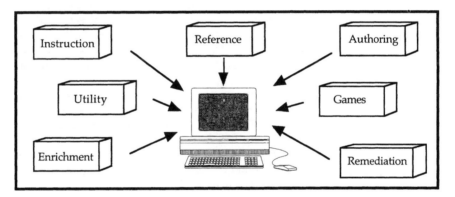

Software Tools. Software tools--e.g. reference, authoring, creativity-- have evolved to support learning activities in any subject area.

> **Reference:** many resources traditionally found in libraries are also available on CD-ROM, as well as the World Wide Web. They include encyclopedias, dictionaries, atlases, almanacs, and references for specific areas. These can address various learning styles, as the text is supplemented with photos, drawings, audio and video.

> **Authoring:** multimedia projects can be produced incorporating text, sounds, graphics, photos, and video using this software. Interdisciplinary projects can be researched, with the final product presented on the computer. [*HyperStudio*® and *PowerPoint* are two examples]

> **Creativity:** writing and graphics are combined to produce illustrated stories, newsletters, and reports. Greeting cards, signs and banners can be made using other creativity programs. [*Kid Pix*® and *The Print Shop*® are two examples]

Recommended Software for the Classroom

The programs discussed below are recommended for both teacher and student use. There are many others in the same and other areas; these are the most popular for the task they accomplish.

HyperStudio: known as a multimedia authoring tool that allows the student or the teacher to easily produce cross-curricular lessons, write term papers, create multimedia resumes, assemble lab reports, or fill a variety of other needs. Text, graphics, animation, sound recording and playback, are a few of the easy-to-use features; these can be combined with access to CDs, laserdiscs, and digitized photos and movies. *HyperStudio* is especially beneficial to the visual learner. It not only supports the integration of technology, critical thinking, and the creative problem solving process; it can be the key to realizing the constructivist classroom. Visit www.hyperstudio.com for additional information and a free preview copy available to download and try for yourself.

Kid Pix: a drawing and painting program for kids of all ages. Any kind of picture can be made using the powerful and diverse tools in this program. Backgrounds, graphic objects, and stamps are provided as starting points. Pictures can be further enhanced with *the wacky brush, talking alphabet stamps, typewriter, moving van* and more. Visit www.kidpix.com for demos and further information.

Photoshop Elements: image-editing software to create high quality images to print, e-mail, put on the web, or use in documents. Similar to *Photoshop, Photoshop Elements* is easier for the teacher or the student to use. It provides all the features needed for everyday editing of photos. Additional information and links to tutorials can be found on Adobe's web site at www.adobe.com (search for *Photoshop Elements*).

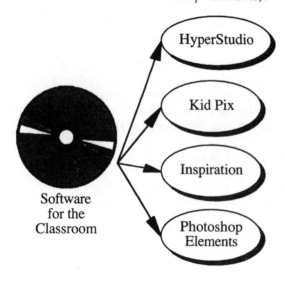

Software for the Classroom

Inspiration: a visual learning tool to help students and teachers develop ideas and organize thinking. It encourages visual learning through the use of diagrams in the form of webs, idea maps, concept maps, outlines, and storyboards. Through these diagrams, students understand how ideas are connected and how they can be grouped together. The visual diagrams help in the retention of information, along with comprehension of concepts and information. *Kidspiration*, for K-5 students, helps young readers and writers organize information, understand concepts and express their thoughts. Visit www.inspiration.com for teaching ideas and a 30-day free trial.

Sample web created with *Inspiration*

Teacher Utility Software

Every teacher can use help in the classroom with daily tasks such as grading; making out tests; and producing worksheets, puzzles, certificates, and other handouts. The computer, along with software known as teacher utility programs, can be of assistance with these tasks. These programs are intended to increase the teacher's effectiveness, making the tasks much easier and decreasing the amount of time involved. Every teacher has different needs; therefore, software must be evaluated prior to purchase to ensure that the program fits the needs of the teacher, and does, indeed, save time and result in enhanced productivity for the teacher.

The majority of teacher utility software is available for purchase; however, some programs are available free, or as shareware, on the Internet. As an added bonus, many of the commercial companies provide demos or samples of their software on the Internet. The teacher can use, evaluate, and compare the various programs prior to purchase.

Administrative Software

Many schools use administrative software programs, some identified as student information systems, to simplify their office tasks. Scheduling, record keeping, grading, class attendance, and progress reports are a few of the tasks these programs feature. Teachers submit lesson plans, take attendance, process lunch orders, and upload their grades to a central computer for processing; all through their desktop computer. Many of the programs are now web-based. Teachers save time, parents can gain access to the children's grades online, and students can track their progress.

• INTERNET COMMUNICATION

There is always a need to communicate with others--colleagues, parents, students, or friends--and exchange information. Frequently, however, problems arise: you do not have time, the other party is not home, now is not a good time to talk, etc. This can be solved by asynchronous communication--sending messages, reading them, and replying to them when the time is available (and you are ready). On the Internet, e-mail, newsgroups, and mailing lists are a few of the tools for asynchronous communication. Other tools, such as chat rooms and instant messaging, are synchronous, as messages are sent and received at the same time.

E-Mail (Electronic Mail)

Of the various tools for communication via the Internet, e-mail is the most common. Through e-mail, messages and files are transmitted via a computer network, allowing you to send, receive and store messages on your computer. E-mail messages not only contain text; graphics, photos, audio, video, computer files, and electronic cards can also be a part of a message.

For anyone with an Internet connection, e-mail is free. You can communicate with friends and colleagues in any state, or another country. In addition to correspondence with those you know, students can have key pals (pen pals using e-mail), while teachers can share ideas and discuss problems with others in their field. **Attachments**, such as photos or computer files, can be sent along with the message.

Mailing Lists and Newsgroups

Along with e-mail for personal correspondence, you can sign up to join **mailing lists (listservs)**. **Mailing lists** are composed of groups of people who share common interests. The mailing list uses e-mail to deliver messages related to a specific topic to your e-mail address. The user subscribes to a mailing list, then receives copies of all mail sent to the list. You can participate by sending messages and/or replying to messages, or by merely observing and reading messages/replies from others.

There are thousands of mailing lists in operation, with many available to teachers as well as to students. Using them, you can communicate with others in your field. Current listings of listservs are available from Internet sites. Two of the most comprehensive sources are Liszt, the mailing list directory, and L-Soft International's CataList site, the front end for the LISTSERV® *LISTS* database .

Newsgroups are like bulletin boards for specific topics, similar to school bulletin boards. They are not e-mail messages like mailing lists, but an online area where you can participate in written discussions about a topic. These discussions and topics change frequently, with each containing the original article and replies in what is called a "threaded discussion." You can join in at any time to post information or messages on the news server, or to read the ongoing dialogue messages.

Chat Rooms and Electronic Messaging

Chatting and Instant Messaging take place in real-time, when users are online.

Chat rooms are virtual areas where people meet and communicate. Areas are topic specific with two or more people communicating at any one time. Real names are not exchanged and caution must be used to be sure real identities, especially of children, are not revealed. While many chat rooms have poor reputations, others, such as Kidlink [www.kidlink.org], are designed for communication among children.

Instant Messaging , such as that provided by *America Online* (free to anyone, not only AOL subscribers), allows you to write messages back and forth to friends whenever you (and the friend) are online at the same time.

• THE WORLD WIDE WEB

The part of the Internet most commonly accessed by educators and students is the World Wide Web (WWW). While technology tools have always played an important role in the process of education, in recent years the World Wide Web has surfaced as the preeminent resource tool for teachers. With an initial investment of time and effort to "surf the web," teachers can access and infuse a virtually unlimited number and variety of materials to use in their teaching. Lesson plans, up-to-the minute news, maps, graphics and photos, curriculum ideas, webquests, puzzles, worksheets, awards, virtual field trips, and much more are available in a matter of seconds. Students can develop sophisticated research and retrieval skills by searching and using the Library of Congress or other databases, take virtual field trips to museums and zoos, or participate in a simulated space shuttle program.

Searching the WWW

When you know the address for a web site, getting there is simple--enter the address in the space provided on your browser (*Netscape, Internet Explorer*, or others), then click on Go or press the Return or Enter key. When you do not have an address, but only know the topic you are seeking information on, you need to use a search tool.

Search engines search the Web for documents that contain the word(s) you have identified. They then provide a list of links to the sites where these documents are located. This entire process is done electronically using computer programs (called robots, crawlers or spiders) that gather words and place them in a database. Two common search engines today are *Google* and *AltaVista*; there are, however, thousands. No two search engines search in the same way. Therefore, it is best to try several to obtain the results desired. While searches provide pages of results, usually looking at the first two pages is sufficient.

Search Directories (e.g. *Yahoo* and *Ask Jeeves*) search using categories and subcategories. They take you through a series of topics that eventually narrow down to a list of site links. Many search engines also have Directories to easily navigate to specific topics.

Metasearch Engines (e.g. *Metacrawler and Dogpile*) search other search engines and report the results, indicating which search engine provided the results. Like regular search engines, individual metasearch engines have their advantages and disadvantages. You must try each search tool to see if it fits your needs.

There are also specific search engines for children (e.g. *Yahooligans* and *Ask Jeeves Kids*), with searches yielding only "safe" sites. Some of these sites are educational portals, or web guides, providing much more than the search engine. Often included are sites for specific interests, safe chat rooms, games, activities, sports, news, clubs, and more.

Educational Portals

A portal is a web site that offers a variety of services from one location, such as a search engine, news, weather, sports, stocks, maps, e-mail, chat rooms, yellow pages, shopping, and more. Home pages of browsers and search engines are common portals. A portal can be chosen as your home page that comes up each time the browser begins. Portals can also be educational sites, providing various services for teachers, parents, and/or students. Many provide tools for online school communities. Depending upon the type of resources provided, there is sometimes a fee associated with these portals.

Educational portals often include: safe web resources for students, online projects, web resources for teachers, current events, safe searching, monthly topics, E-mail, message boards, lesson plans, school or class web pages, online gradebooks, places to post assignments, and/or online calendars.

Examples of Free Educational Portals

AOL	www.AOLatSchool.com
Education World	www.educationworld.com
Scholastic	www.scholastic.com
Teach-nology	www.teach-nology.com

Lesson Plans

Imagine having a file cabinet containing hundreds of lesson plans. This vision is now a reality. Thousands of teachers have freely shared their lesson plans and teaching ideas by making them available on the WWW as a part of various databases and web sites. You may not want to use the lesson plan in its entirety; however, online lesson plans can provide ideas as well as innovative approaches to teaching.

A good starting point is the **ERIC** web site which contains AskERIC Lesson Plans [askeric.org/Virtual/Lessons]. Here you can browse lesson plans by subject or search the Lesson Plan Collection. Another searchable site is **The Gateway to Educational Materials** [www.thegateway.org]. This is a Consortium effort to provide educators with quick and easy access to thousands of educational resources found on various federal, state, university, nonprofit, and commercial Internet sites.

There are many other sources of lesson plans on the Web. Unfortunately, there is no easy way to search all of the databases and instantly find just what you need. Look through some of the choices and bookmark those that have possibilities for your subject/grade level.

Browse AskERIC Lesson Plans by Subject

Arts	Interdisciplinary	Science
Computer Science	Language Arts	Social Studies
Foreign Language	Mathematics	Vocational Education
Health	Philosophy	
Information Literacy	Physical Education	

Online Projects and Field Trips

The World Wide Web is also a place for students of all ages to engage in **collaborative learning projects**. Projects are placed on the Web at nationally acclaimed sites housing online projects, or by individual schools. These projects are for students to collaborate not just with their classmates, but with students around the world. Through these experiences, students learn to use the Web to engage in data exchanges with students from other schools, collaborate on writing projects, and participate in world expeditions and explorations. Most sites and experiences are free; however, some require a registration fee. The **Global Schoolhouse** [www.gsn.org] hosts a variety of collaborative projects each year.

WebQuests are another form of online projects. These are inquiry-oriented activities in which students in your classroom interact with resources on the Web. The activities and web sites to investigate are specified by the teacher or author of the WebQuest. They can be short, lasting for only one or two periods; or longer, where the student searches for, and analyzes, larger bodies of information. WebQuests are often group activities that assign a different role to each member of the group. They can also be interdisciplinary, covering several subjects. WebQuests have proven to be a safe and educationally sound way for teachers to take full advantage of the multitude of resources available on the WWW. To find out more about them, visit **The WebQuest Page** at webquest.sdsu.edu.

Virtual Field trips can be taken to places impossible to visit without the Web. Real-life pictures and movies can bring the sites to life. These electronic trips are a way to integrate the Internet into the curriculum, by allowing students to "visit" places being studied. Visits can be made to the Smithsonian Institute, the Whitehouse, or the Louvre in Paris, along with thousands of other places, by entering a web address.

Student Resource, Reference, and Homework Sites

The WWW is a powerful tool to help in locating reference material and resources for projects, and helping with daily homework. Some sites are specifically for reference, while others are divided into subject areas for homework and project resources.

One outstanding place to start is **B.J. Pinchbeck's Homework Helper** [school. discovery.com/homeworkhelp/bjpinchbeck]. Now hosted by Discovery School, this site has links for doing homework in any area, along with a Reference section featuring over 100 reference books available on the Internet. **Kid Info** [www. kidinfo.com], calling itself "The Web's Best Homework and Teacher/Parent Reference Resource," contains sections for Students, Young Children, Teachers, and Parents. Homework Help, Reference, Fun Sites, Online Books and Reading Activities, and Educational Games are among their categories of resources. **Homework Spot** [www.homeworkspot.com] has subject listings for Elementary, Middle School, and High School. Also included are menus with links to reference and current events sites. Areas include Must See Sites, Field Trips, Exhibits, Reference, etc. Reference sites and books are readily available. B.J. Pinchbeck's page contains a listing of many reference books available on the Web, or try **RefDesk** at www.refdesk.com for links to hundreds of reference sites available.

Filtering Web Sites

It is difficult to supervise every student on the Internet while at school. A question for all schools is whether or not to block access to certain web sites. Parents are concerned that their children might get into sites where they can view inappropriate or dangerous images. Filters are available, most commonly as software programs, to block undesirable key works, phrases, categories, or sites. Most can be customized by the school for age groups, or block specific words and categories. A disadvantage of some of the software is that when some words/categories are blocked, students cannot access educational information that might contain one of these words, used in a different context.

Filters are not foolproof; students often find ways around them. An alternative is to give students specific web addresses to go to (as in a WebQuest), or to provide them with bookmarks to use in class, rather than allowing them to "surf the web." Even if a filter is used, students always need supervision when using the Internet. In addition to filters, Acceptable Use Policies are used by many schools.

Acceptable Use Policies

Many schools, or districts, already have an Acceptable Use Policy (AUP) in place. This is a legal document, for the specific school, adopted to keep inappropriate material out of the classroom. To protect the school, and reassure parents, AUPs outline ethical use of the Internet, including e-mail and chat rooms. Expectations of how students, and faculty, will use school technology resources are detailed, along with procedures and consequences for specific violations. When the AUP is in place, a form must be signed by both the student and their parent(s) before the student is permitted to use the school's Internet connection.

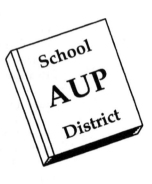

Web Citations

When writing a research paper, it is necessary to cite your sources. Today, it is very possible some resources are from the Internet. Each manual of style has its own format for Internet citations.

An example for an MLA citation from a WWW site would be:

Author (last name, first name). *Title of site or page.* Name of agency or institution. Date of document or visit. <URL address>

For a short-cut, go to **www.noodletools.com/quickcite**. After entering the required information, a MLA citation will be composed, ready to copy into your document. This is not just for web sites, but for e-mail articles, online discussions, online magazine or newspaper articles, CD-ROMs, interviews, books, encyclopedia articles, magazine articles, and scholarly projects.

Distance Learning and Web-Based Courses

There are various types of distance learning programs. One extends the main campus, or classroom, to another location. Using telecommunications technology, the class is sent to one or more additional classrooms. As a form of synchronous learning, students at the remote site(s) can participate in the same way as those at the original site by interactive audio and video transmission. This method is often used in high schools when specialized courses need to be taught to only a small number of students. The schools combine, with the course being taught at one school and transmitted to others. Special rooms for live telecourses (or teleconferencing) are expensive. Each classroom--the one where the course is being taught and the one(s) receiving the class--need sophisticated equipment, in addition to way a means for transmitting the class. Another type of distance learning is for the class to be taped and aired on cable television at various times. In this method of asynchronous learning, students watch the class when convenient, then communicate with the professor, and submit assignments, through e-mail.

Web-based courses and degree programs are becoming more commonplace. Students can take an entire course or program online at some colleges and universities. Effective courses are difficult to plan and execute. Instructors must be trained to design courses to be taken online; and, it has been found that administrative and technical support requires a great deal of time and infrastructure. An alternative is for instructors to deliver part of the course online, or supplement their campus course with materials on the Web. This can be done by using a professor-developed web page, or a web-based course management system such as *WebCT* or *Blackboard*. Through these systems, professors can post lecture notes and presentations, give quizzes, communicate with classes synchronously or asynchronously, post grades, and more. Students have the opportunity to visit a chat room to hold group meetings or study together.

Building Your Own Web Page

You (or your students) can design a web site for your class, your school, your organization, or your family. Having a web site establishes YOU on the World Wide Web. It is not a difficult task, but in the beginning it will be a bit time-consuming. The end result will be worth the effort.

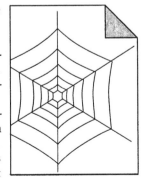

A web site is composed of one or many pages, with the first page called the home page. Each page is supported with links to other places on the Internet, images, sounds, and sometimes even movies! It is no longer necessary to be a programmer, or know HTML (Hypertext Markup Language), to construct a web site. Web authoring programs allow the user to place text and graphics on the page, format and reposition the text and graphics, and make links to other sites on the Internet and places within the site being created. This can be done without knowing how to use HTML. The user manipulates the objects, while the program inserts the code as needed.

A component of the Internet browser, *Netscape*, is *Composer*, a free web authoring program. This will allow you to make a basic web page for yourself, or develop an electronic portfolio to place on your university's network for others to see. Other software programs, such as *Frontpage®* by Microsoft and *Dreamweaver* by Macromedia, can be purchased for more complex pages. *Microsoft Word* includes a wizard for constructing simple pages. In addition, some educational sites offer free and easy tools to construct a site and will even post the site for your classroom. One site offering free pages is **Scholastic** [www.scholastic.com].

Electronic Portfolios

Traditionally, college students have kept examples of work produced in all of their classes to place in a portfolio prior to graduation. Teachers, as well as K-12 students, have also kept their work in portfolios.

One of the newest developments in the area of portfolio creation is the electronic portfolio. Using electronic portfolios, work can be stored digitally; thus eliminating the need to retain the original item. When creating an electronic portfolio, the individual learns to use technology as a communication tool and can take pride in seeing the resulting work as a multimedia production. Text, as well as pictures, video, voice, and music can be part of the portfolio. Along with these multimedia aspects, there is an interactive capability--artifacts can be viewed in a linear or nonlinear format.

Collections and artifacts for portfolios can be stored in a variety of formats and on different types of media. Files can be saved on a CD-ROM, or transferred to a web page for easy accessibility by future employers, parents, teachers, etc.

Many teacher education programs now require their education majors to develop and maintain a professional portfolio. The final result of this ongoing activity is presented as a requirement for program completion. This same portfolio can also be used when interviewing for a teaching position. An electronic portfolio also demonstrates computer and multimedia competencies.

Portfolio items could include:

- Resume
- Teaching philosophy
- Bulletin board examples
- Classroom management plan
- Photos of sporting activities
- Multimedia presentations
- Video of musical productions
- Scanned certificates, letters
- Research papers
- Lesson and unit plans
- Learning center examples
- Photos of artwork, projects
- Newspaper articles
- Video of plays
- Video of classroom activities
- Scanned awards

Need more information and resources?

Visit Kathy Schrock's Guide for Educators to find a library containing over 2000 sites for educators

school.discovery.com/schrockguide

PART 7

New Jersey

CHAPTER

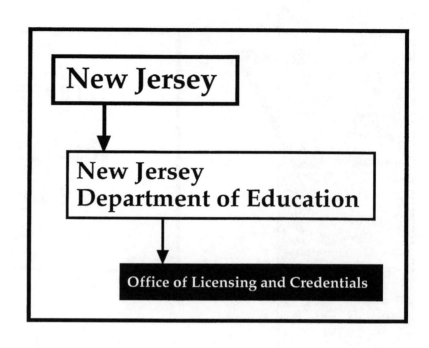

New Jersey

New Jersey
Department of Education

Office of Licensing and Credentials

13 Teaching in
New Jersey

E ducation in the United States is the responsibility of the State. The Federal government may provide direction (legislation) and funding (allocations and grants), but the design of the structure, management of the process, and enforcement of the regulations is a charge to the State.

As a student enrolled in <u>Teaching: An Introduction to the Profession</u>, you have demonstrated an interest in teaching. In most cases you will pursue a career teaching in the public or private schools in New Jersey. This chapter provides an overview of what you need to know to become a teacher in this State. More specifically, we will address the following questions regarding teaching in New Jersey:

- Where and how can I obtain information regarding the requirements for teaching?

- What types of teaching licenses and certificates are available?

- What are the requirements for a Standard Instructional License?

- What are the test requirements for licensure?

- How do I apply for licensure?

- Where are the County Offices of Education located?

- What are The Boyer Topics?

- What is the status of the proposed program restructuring for teacher education?

- What are the proposed New Jersey Professional Standards for Teachers?

TEACHER EDUCATION in NEW JERSEY

This chapter is based on the current NJ Administrative Code. The NJDOE is in the process of rewriting this section of the Code. Consult the NJDOE web site for recent decisions and changes.

• **NEW JERSEY DEPARTMENT OF EDUCATION**
  OFFICE OF LICENSING AND CREDENTIALS
  (Selected material from: New Jersey Department of Education Web Site)

Introduction

The Office of Licensing and Credentials receives many requests for information. Most requests are for the following: information on how to apply for educational licenses; and general information on requirements for specific licenses.

The four major sections to follow contain information about our most frequently asked questions. The first section, "General Information," gives basic information on how to apply for licenses. The next three sections give general information on requirements for specific licenses which are meant as a guide to allow you to determine your current qualifications for licensure. It must be noted that only an examiner from the Office of Licensing and Academic Credentials can make the final decision as to qualifications for licensure in any particular case.

If you feel that you meet the qualifications for a license, or if you would like to know specifically what you need to qualify for a license, you should submit an Application for Licensure with the appropriate fee to the Office of Licensing and Academic Credentials. The same Application for Licensure is used for both licensure application and credential review. The application can be obtained from any county office of education or from the Office of Licensing and Credentials telephone system. To order from the telephone system: Call 609-292-2070. When the telephone is answered, press the numbers 1 and then 3 to reach to the Information Request Line. Press one to order the document entitled "How to Apply for Licensure." This document contains the application. Give your name and address when requested.

All of the following bulleted items may be accessed directly at the NJDOE web site:

www.nj.gov/njded/educators/license

Document List

General Information:

	Document Number Used for Ordering by Mail
• How to Apply for Licensure	1111
• Test Requirements for Licensure in New Jersey	1112
• Licenses Available	1143
• NJ Colleges Offering Teacher Education Programs	1133
• Directory of NJ County Offices of Education	1134
• The Provisional Teacher Program	1113
• The Troops-to-Teachers Program	1115
• Non-Citizen Oath and Affidavit of Intent to Become a Citizen	1114
• Determination of the Equivalent of Studies Completed in Other Countries	1145
• Application for Certification (only available via mail)	1146
• Professional Librarian Licensure	1147

[Updates and changes in requirements will be posted on the NJDOE web site.]

• NEW JERSEY DEPARTMENT OF EDUCATION
NEW JERSEY LICENSES/CERTIFICATES

(Selected material from: New Jersey Department of Education Web Site)

NEW JERSEY LICENSES/CERTIFICATES

- **CERTIFICATE OF ELIGIBILITY (CE):**

  A CE is an initial license issued to persons who meet the academic study, degree and test requirements for licensure. The CE authorizes the holder the opportunity to SEEK employment. This is NOT a license which allows employment. When offered employment, an applicant must be issued a provisional license to legalize employment.

- **CERTIFICATE OF ELIGIBILITY WITH ADVANCED STANDING (CEAS):**

  A CEAS is an initial license issued to candidates for standard licensure who have completed academic, degree and test requirements, and a state approved college teacher education program. The CEAS authorizes the holder the opportunity to SEEK employment. This is NOT a license which allows employment. When offered employment, an applicant must be issued a provisional license to legalize employment.

  NOTE:
  - A candidate is issued a School Business Administrator CE if the degree and/or study requirements are met.
  - A candidate is issued a Substance Awareness Coordinator CE if the degree requirement is met. A candidate is issued a Substance Awareness Coordinator CEAS if the degree and study requirements are met.
  - A candidate is issued an instructional vocational education CE if he/she presents either a baccalaureate degree in the appropriate occupation or four (4) years of full-time work experience in the appropriate trade of occupation.

- **PROVISIONAL LICENSE:**

  A Provisional License is a temporary one-year license issued to a candidate who holds the appropriate CE or CEAS and has been offered employment by a public school district or an approved private school. This license requires the candidate to complete a State-approved district training program or residency leading to a standard license.

- **EMERGENCY LICENSE:**

  An Emergency License is a substandard one-year license issued only in the fields of educational services, Teacher of the Handicapped, Teacher of the Blind and Partially Sighted, Teacher of the Deaf and Hard of Hearing, Teacher of English as a Second Language, Teacher of Bilingual/Bicultural Education and Teacher of Military Science.

  An emergency license is issued only upon application of a public school district, with the approval of the county superintendent. The district board of education must substantiate its inability to locate a suitable, certified teacher due to unforeseen shortages or other extenuating circumstances.

- **STANDARD LICENSE:**

  A Standard License is a permanent license issued to candidates who have met all requirements including experience requirements for State licensure. No novice teacher is issued a standard license (exception is special education) without the completion of one year of mentored teaching under a New Jersey provisional license. If a candidate has less than one year of full time teaching experience under a valid out of state license, the candidate should apply for the appropriate CE or CEAS.

- **COUNTY SUBSTITUTE LICENSE:**

  A County Substitute License allows the holder to temporarily perform the duties of a fully licensed and regularly employed teacher. The substitute teacher may serve for no more than twenty consecutive days in the same position. The license is issued through the county office of education.

• NEW JERSEY DEPARTMENT OF EDUCATION REQUIREMENTS FOR A STANDARD INSTRUCTIONAL LICENSE

(Selected material from: New Jersey Department of Education Web Site)

I. REQUIREMENTS FOR A STANDARD INSTRUCTIONAL LICENSE

1. Bachelor's degree from an accredited college or university.

2. A baccalaureate degree, post-baccalaureate program or advanced degree cumulative grade point average of at least 2.75 when a 4.0 equals an A grade.

3. Passing score in Praxis II/NTE Programs Specialty Area test(s) for secondary teaching, the Elementary Education: Content Knowledge for elementary teachers. See information on test requirements for details and for exceptions.

4. Completion of a major in the liberal arts or sciences for elementary education. Completion of a major in the subject teaching field for an initial endorsement in a subject teaching field. For additional endorsements, completion of at least 30 semester hours in a coherent major in the subject teaching field.

5. Successful completion of one of the following:
   - the provisional teacher program (alternate route to licensure)
   OR
   - a state approved college teacher preparation program and one year of full time mentored teaching under a New Jersey provisional license
   OR
   - a state approved college teacher preparation program and one year of full time teaching under a valid state license.

II. EXCEPTIONS

1. No standard instructional license will be issued unless the applicant has completed requirements in A.1, 2, 3 and 4 above. Exceptions are as follows:

a. <u>Bilingual/Bicultural, ESL and Special Education Licenses</u> -
Currently these fields are not available through the Provisional Teacher Program (Alternate Route) and no Praxis II/NTE test is currently required. Regulations for these endorsements are available upon request.

b. <u>Vocational Instructional Licenses or Certificates</u> -
Applicants must complete the Provisional Teacher Program - Alternate Route. Requirements for admission to the program are a high school diploma/GED and four years of approved occupational experience in the trade to be taught. There is currently no test required. Regulations are available upon request.

2. No emergency instructional licenses will be issued except in the following fields: bilingual/ESL education, military science and special education. Emergency certificates are issued only upon application of a public school district with the approval of the county superintendent of schools.

III. RECIPROCITY

1. Out-of-state applicants qualifying under any form of reciprocity in accordance with the Interstate Certification Compact will have met the content area and professional education requirements but must pass the required test for issuance of an instructional license in a specific field. Transcripts, copies of state licenses, and original documentation of teaching experience will be reviewed to determine eligibility for reciprocity.

2. Out-of-state applicants not entitled to reciprocity shall meet requirements in A.1, 2, 3 and 4 above.

IV. NEW JERSEY LICENSED TEACHERS SEEKING ADDITIONAL SUBJECT TEACHING FIELD ENDORSEMENTS

Holders of a standard N.J. instructional license (except teachers of Military Science and non-degree teachers of Vocational Education) will be issued additional standard instructional licenses when the following is completed:

- Thirty (30) semester hour credits in the subject teaching field on the official transcript of an accredited four (4) year college or university. The courses must be in a coherent sequence covering introductory through advanced level study.

- A passing score on the required licensure test.

V. NEW JERSEY LICENSED TEACHERS SEEKING THE ELEMENTARY SCHOOL TEACHER ENDORSEMENT

Holders of a standard, N.J. instructional license (except teachers of military science and non-degree teachers of Vocational Education) will be issued a standard New Jersey Elementary School Teacher license upon successful completion of the General Knowledge Test of the Core Battery.

• NEW JERSEY DEPARTMENT OF EDUCATION
TEST REQUIREMENTS FOR LICENSURE IN NEW JERSEY
(Selected material from: New Jersey Department of Education Web Site)

INTRODUCTION

Applicants for New Jersey licensure in subject teaching fields and elementary education must pass the appropriate PRAXIS II Subject Assessment test(s) or NTE Programs Specialty Area test. The tests are required for all applicants including those applicants who are licensed in other states.

Certain teaching fields are exempt as noted on the next page.

Applicants for the Speech-language Specialist license must pass the Speech-language Pathology NTE Specialty Area test.

It is your responsibility to register for the correct test(s). Carefully check test requirements and test code number listed on the next page to assure registration for the correct test.

PASSING SCORE

Applicants must achieve the current required passing score(s) for license/certificate issuance. Passing scores are subject to change. A test score must meet the current passing score to satisfy the test requirement. Undergraduates must take Praxis/NTE test(s) in the senior year.

TEST SCORE SERVICE FEE

There is a test score service fee of $10.00 per endorsement that requires a test. The test score service fee must be submitted with your Application for Licensure using a money order or certified check payable to "Commissioner of Education". Do not submit this fee to Educational Testing Service with your test registration form.

INSTRUCTIONS FOR TEST REGISTRATION

Register for Praxis II: Subject Assessment/NTE tests directly through The Praxis Series. Test registration procedures, registration form and other information are included in The Praxis Series Registration Bulletin. The Bulletin is available on the Internet through the Praxis Web Site at:

<u>www.ets.org/praxis</u>

Online registration is also available.

Bulletins are available from Educational Testing Service as follows:

> The Praxis Series
> Educational Testing Service
> P.O. Box 6051
> Princeton, NJ 08541-6051
> (609) 771-7395

Scores on Praxis II: Subject Assessments/NTE tests taken in the State of New Jersey will automatically be sent to the New Jersey Department of Education. If you are tested in another state you must request to have your score sent to New Jersey by coding R7666 on your registration form. You must also include your Social Security number when completing your registration form and answer sheet. Only official score reports from Educational Testing Service are accepted for licensure. Coding the Department of Education (R7666) and your Social Security number precludes delay in license/certificate issuance.

PRAXIS II: SUBJECT ASSESSMENTS/NTE TESTS REQUIRED FOR LICENSURE

Instructional Endorsement	Required Praxis II: Subject Assessment/Tests
Agriculture	Exempt
Art	Art: Content Knowledge (10133)
Bilingual/Bicultural Education*	To Be Announced

Business Education
    Comprehensive
    Bookkeeping and Accounting
    General Business
    Secretarial Studies
	Business Education (10100)

Elementary School Teacher	Elementary Education: Content Knowledge (10014)
English	English Language, Literature, and Composition: Content Knowledge (10041)
English as a Second Language*	To Be Announced
Foreign Languages	
French	French: Content Knowledge (20173)
German	German: Content Knowledge (20181)
Spanish	Spanish: Content Knowledge (10191)
Other Languages	Exempt
Health Education	Exempt
Health and Physical Education	Health and Physical Education: Content Knowledge (20856)
Home Economics	Family and Consumer Sciences (10120)
Industrial Arts	Technology Education (10050)
Marketing Education	Marketing Education (10560)
Mathematics	Mathematics: Content Knowledge (10061)
Military Science	Exempt
Music	Music: Content Knowledge (10113)
Physical Education	Physical Education: Content Knowledge (10091)
Preschool through Grade 3*	To Be Announced
Psychology	Exempt
Reading	Introduction to the Teaching of Reading (10200)
Science	
Biological Science	Biology: Content Knowledge, Part 2 (20232), General Science: Content Knowledge, Part 1 (10431), and General Science: Content Knowledge, Part 2 (10432)
Earth Science	Earth Science: Content Knowledge (20571), and General Science: Content Knowledge, Part I (10431)
Physical Science	Chemistry: Content Knowledge (20241), Physics: Content Knowledge (10261), and General Science: Content Knowledge, Part I (10431)
Social Studies	Social Studies: Content Knowledge (10081)
Special Education	Exempt
Speech Arts and Dramatics	Speech Communication (10220)
Vocational Education*	To be Announced

*No test required for the 2002-2003 academic year

PRAXIS II: SUBJECT ASSESSMENTS/NTE SPECIALTY AREA TESTS

Passing Scores Required for Licensure

CODE	TEST	PASSING SCORE
10014	Elementary Education: Content Knowledge	133
10041	English Language, Literature, and Composition; Content Knowledge	155
10050	Technology Education	560
10061	Mathematics: Content Knowledge	130
10081	Social Studies: Content Knowledge	153
10091	Physical Education: Content Knowledge	139
20856	Health & Physical Ed: Content Knowledge	143
10100	Business Education	580
10113	Music: Content Knowledge	143
10120	Family & Consumer Sciences	550
10133	Art: Content Knowledge	136
20173	French: Content Knowledge	146
10191	Spanish: Content Knowledge	149
10200	Introduction to the Teaching of Reading	560
10220	Speech Communication	560
10261	Physics: Content Knowledge	113
20330	Speech-Language Pathology	500
10410	Educational Leadership: Administration and Supervision	540
10431	General Science: Content Knowledge, Part 1	148
10432	General Science: Content Knowledge, Part 2	133
10560	Marketing Education	580
20181	German: Content Knowledge	146
20232	Biology: Content Knowledge, Part 2	142
20241	Chemistry: Content Knowledge	119
20571	Earth Science: Content Knowledge	134

PASSING SCORES ARE SUBJECT TO CHANGE

- CURRENT TEST DATES, DEADLINES AND TEST FEES FOR EXAMINATIONS REQUIRED FOR LICENSURE IN NEW JERSEY ARE AVAILABLE ON-LINE AT THE NJDOE WEB SITE

- IT IS IMPORTANT TO REVIEW THE INFORMATION REGARDING THE TEST REQUIRED FOR THE SPECIFIC LICENSE/CERTIFICATE FOR WHICH YOU ARE APPLYING, AND TO REGISTER FOR THE APPROPRIATE TEST

- INFORMATION ABOUT REGISTRATION, TEST CENTERS AND SCORE REPORTING IS INCLUDED IN THE REGISTRATION BULLETIN. BULLETINS MAY BE OBTAINED FROM THE ADDRESS IDENTIFIED ABOVE. THE BULLETIN IS ALSO AVAILABLE ON LINE AT THE PRAXIS WEB SITE:

www.ets.org/praxis

- CODE R7666 AND YOUR SOCIAL SECURITY NUMBER ACCURATELY TO PRECLUDE DELAY IN LICENSE ISSUANCE

• NEW JERSEY DEPARTMENT OF EDUCATION
HOW TO APPLY FOR LICENSURE

(Selected material from: New Jersey Department of Education Web Site)

1. NEW JERSEY RESIDENTS

a. Applicants in Approved Teacher Education Programs

Applicants enrolled in teacher education programs in New Jersey colleges must submit applications through the colleges. Applications are available from the college certification officer.

b. Applicants for the Alternate Route to Licensure (Provisional Teacher Program)

The alternate route to licensure provides an opportunity for applicants who have not completed teacher preparation in a traditional college program to participate in district training programs for licensure. Interested applicants should apply through the county office of education of the county in which they live or work.

c. Applicants not in (a) or (b) above should apply through the county office of education of the county in which they live or work.

2. OUT OF STATE RESIDENTS

Out of State residents should apply through the Office of Licensing and Academic Credentials at the address above, attn.: Office of Licensing and Academic Credentials.

3. DOCUMENTS AND FEES REQUIRED FOR LICENSURE

a. Application for Licensure: Complete Part A, #1-17 and Part B, #1-16.

Note Part A, #16 Oath of Allegiance must be notarized. Out of state residents may have the Oath of Allegiance notarized in their respective states. In Part A, #5A, list the license title(s) for which you are applying (see enclosed list of available endorsements). Complete Part A, #5B if you are applying for evaluations only. Complete Part A, #5C and/or #5D if you are applying for duplicate license(s) and/or name change(s).

b. Appropriate fee in money order or certified check payable to the: "Commissioner of Education."

PERSONAL CHECKS ARE NOT ACCEPTED

See the enclosed descriptions of licenses and certificates. Please write your Social Security Number on the front of the money order/ certified check. Fees are as follows:

- Certificate of Eligibility with Advanced Standing OR Certificate of Eligibility in endorsement area requiring a test - $60*
- Certificate of Eligibility with Advanced Standing OR Certificate of Eligibility in endorsement area NOT requiring a test - $50
- Provisional License - $10
- Standard License in endorsement area requiring a test - $60*
- Standard License in endorsement area NOT requiring a test - $50
- County Substitute License - $50
- Emergency License - $50
- Renewal of Emergency or Provisional License - $30
- Duplicate License or Name Change - $25
- Credential Evaluation only (per endorsement) - $30

[*This includes the $10 test score service fee.]

   c. **Applicant's official transcript(s) of all college credits.** A transcript is official if it contains the signature of the registrar or designated official, the seal of the college or university and degree conferral (if applicable).

   d. **Applicants for initial New Jersey instructional (teaching) license(s)/ certificate(s) who have a minimum of one year of full-time teaching experience in another state under a valid out of state license/certificate,** must submit an original letter verifying the teaching experience and a copy of the valid out of state license/certificate under which the experience was completed.

4. TEST REQUIREMENT FOR LICENSURE

Applicants must satisfy the test requirement for licensure in designated license areas. Licensed out of state applicants must also satisfy the test requirement. Applicants in college approved programs must seek advisement from their respective colleges. The Praxis Series code for the Office of Licensing and Academic Credentials is R7666. Passing scores are subject to change. Only official and unopened score reports are accepted. The applicant's Social Security number must appear on the score report. See page 5 for additional information on the test requirement.

5. ISSUANCE

Licenses are issued to the applicant and the original should be kept in his/her possession. Teachers are not entitled to salary without appropriate certification for teaching assignment(s).

6. CITIZENSHIP

License(s)/certificate(s) are issued only to applicants who are citizens or who have declared their intention to become citizens. A notarized affidavit of intent to become a citizen and a notarized non-citizen oath must be submitted with the application of a non-citizen. Please request document number 1114 for these forms.

7. RECIPROCITY

New Jersey is a party to the Interstate Certification Compact for reciprocity with member states in designated instructional areas. Licenses/certificates from other states and transcripts are reviewed to determine if applicants are eligible for reciprocity. Applicants from other states must complete the test requirement.

8. DUPLICATE LICENSURE AND NAME CHANGES

Applicants who seek a duplicate license or name change must complete the Application for Licensure PART A, #1-7 and 17 and PART B, #1-16. A notarized statement of loss must be submitted for lost licenses. The required fee for each duplicate license is $25.00. The fee for each name change is $25.00.

9. TWO-YEAR COLLEGE CREDITS

Courses taken at accredited two-year colleges are accepted toward meeting requirements for licensure only if such courses appear on an official transcript of an accredited four-year college.

10. PHYSIOLOGY AND HYGIENE REQUIREMENT

Applicants must pass an examination in physiology and hygiene, including the effects of narcotics and alcohol. The examination is administered in county offices of education. In lieu of this exam the applicant may present basic military training or college level study in areas such as biology, health or nutrition.

11. **FOREIGN CREDENTIALS**

Foreign credentials must be translated and an equivalence of study in an accredited United States collegiate institution must be established by a credentials evaluation service. Information is available by requesting document number 1145.

NOTE: Licensure regulations and fees are subject to change.

• NEW JERSEY COUNTY OFFICE OF EDUCATION DIRECTORY

COUNTY	ADDRESS	PHONE NUMBER
ATLANTIC	6260 Old Harding Highway Mays Landing, NJ 08330	609-625-0004
BERGEN	One Bergen County Plaza Room 350 Hackensack NJ 07601	201-336-6875
BURLINGTON	3 Union Street, PO Box 6000 Mount Holly, NJ 08060-6000	609-265-5060
CAMDEN	509 Lakeland Road, Forrest Hall Blackwood, NJ 08012	856-401-2400
CAPE MAY	Crest Haven Complex, 4 Moore Road Cape May Court House, NJ 08210	609-465-1283
CUMBERLAND	19 Landis Avenue Bridgeton, NJ 08302	856-451-0211
ESSEX	155 Fairview Avenue Cedar Grove, NJ 07009	973-857-5700
GLOUCESTER	Office: Tanyard & Salina Road Sewell, NJ 08080 Mailing: 1492 Tanyard Road Sewell, NJ 08080-4222	856-468-6500 x34
HUDSON	Office: 595 County Avenue, Bldg. 3 Secaucus, NJ 07094 Mailing: 595 Newark Avenue Jersey City, NJ 07306	201-319-3850

HUNTERDON	10 Court St. Flemington, NJ 08822	908-788-1414
MERCER	1075 Old Trenton Road Trenton, NJ 08690	609-588-5876
MIDDLESEX	1501 Livingston Avenue North Brunswick, NJ 08902	732-249-2900 x112
MONMOUTH	3435 Highway 9 P.O. Box 1264 Freehold, NJ 07728	732-431-7816
MORRIS	<u>Office</u>: 300 Mendham Rd. Morris Twp., NJ 07960 <u>Mailing</u>: Court House, PO Box 900 Morristown, NJ 07963-0900	973-285-8320
OCEAN	212 Washington Street Toms River, NJ 08753	732-929-2078
PASSAIC	501 River St. Paterson, NJ 07524	973-569-2110
SALEM	94 Market Street Salem, NJ 08079	856-935-7510 x8441
SOMERSET	<u>Office</u>: 40 N. Bridge St. Somerville, NJ <u>Mailing</u>: County Administration Building P.O. Box 3000 Somerville, NJ 08876	908-231-7171
SUSSEX	262 White Lake Road Sparta, NJ 07871	973-579-6996
UNION	300 North Avenue East Westfield, NJ 07090	908-654-9860
WARREN	537 Oxford Street Belvidere, NJ 07823	908-475-6329

• THE BOYER TOPICS

Teacher education in New Jersey uses topics identified by Dr. Ernest L. Boyer as a framework to provide instruction that is essential for all beginning teachers. These "Boyer Topics" consist of the following eighteen topics:

I.   **Curriculum and Evaluation**
   A. Organization of subject matter and presentation of subject matter
   B. Development and use of tests and other forms of assessment
   C. Use and interpretation of standardized tests and teacher developed instruments
   D. Appropriate use of textbooks and teachers' guides
   E. Reading process and other language arts skill development
   F. Techniques and materials for fostering the development of reading an other language arts skills

II. **Student Learning and Development**
   A. Student interest, motivation
   B. Preventing classroom disruption and creating a healthy learning climate
   C. Individual and group learning
   D. Language development
   E. Individual differences
   F. Role of technology in early learning

III. **Classroom and School**
   A. Bureaucratic/social structure of public education
   B. The making of teaching decisions
   C. Allocation of instructional time
   D. Setting priorities
   E. Questioning techniques
   F. Student practice and independent work

• THE PROPOSED PROGRAM RESTRUCTURING OF TEACHER EDUCATION N.J.A.C. 6A:9

The existing program structure for teacher education in New Jersey is based on "The Boyer Topics." This is listed under N.J.A.C. 6:11.

The Department of Education has proposed the repeal of N.J.A.C. 6:11, Professional Licensure and Standards and the adoption of a new chapter, N.J.A.C. 6A:9, also entitled Professional Licensure and Standards. The new rules are part of a comprehensive review of all chapters of the New Jersey State Administrative Code.

The State Board of Education intends to consider the proposed new chapter at the third discussion level in June 2003. The code is slated for proposal level in September 2003, with adoption currently scheduled for January 2004. Interested individuals should consult the New Jersey Department of Education web site for decisions and developments regarding this proposal. The most current version of the proposed NJAC 6A:9-3, as of the writing of this text, appears in the next section.

• NEW JERSEY PROFESSIONAL STANDARDS FOR TEACHERS (Proposed)

(Selected material from: Proposed New Jersey Administrative Code 6A:9-3)

6A:9-3.1 Purpose

(a) The Professional Standards for Teachers identify the knowledge, skills and dispositions that teachers need to practice responsibly.

(c) The Professional Standards for Teachers...set forth in N.J.A.C. 6A:9-3.3...belowshall be used in the accreditation of preparation programs, recommendation of candidates for certification and the approval of professional development.

6A:9-3.2 Scope

(a) The Professional Standards for Teachers shall apply to all educators who hold an instructional certificate.

6A:9-3.3 Professional Standards for Teachers

(a) Teacher preparation, district induction, and professional development programs shall align their learning opportunities with the following standards:

1. **STANDARD ONE: SUBJECT MATTER KNOWLEDGE**

   Teachers shall understand the central concepts, tools of inquiry, structures of the discipline, especially as they relate to the New Jersey Core Curriculum Content Standards (CCCS), and design developmentally appropriate learning experiences making the subject matter accessible and meaningful to all students.

   i. Teachers know and understand:

   (1) In-depth the subject matter they plan to teach and the relationship of that discipline to other content areas;

   (2) The evolving nature of the discipline or subject matter knowledge and the need for keeping abreast of new ideas and understanding of the discipline;

   (3) That literacy skills and processes are applicable in all content areas and help students to develop the knowledge, skills and dispositions that enable them to construct meaning and make sense of the world through reading, writing, listening, speaking, and viewing; and

   (4) Concepts inherent in numeracy to enable students to represent physical events, work with data, reason, communicate mathematically, and make connections within their respective content areas in order to solve problems.

ii. Teachers value and are committed to:

  (1) Appreciating multiple perspectives and conveying to learners how knowledge is developed from the vantage point of the knower; and

  (2) Enthusiasm for the discipline(s) they teach and see connections to everyday life.

iii. Teachers engage in activities to:

  (1) Promote the development of critical and creative thinking, problem solving and decision making skills by engaging students in formulating and testing hypotheses according to the methods of inquiry and standards of evidence within the discipline;

  (2) Make effective use of multiple representations and explanations of disciplinary concepts that capture key ideas and link them to students' prior understanding; and

  (3) Evaluate teaching resources and curriculum materials for their completeness, accuracy, and usefulness for representing particular ideas and concepts.

2. **STANDARD TWO: HUMAN GROWTH AND DEVELOPMENT**

Teachers shall understand how children and adolescents develop and learn in a variety of school, family and community contexts and provide opportunities that support their intellectual, social, emotional, and physical development.

i. Teachers know and understand:

  (1) How students construct knowledge, acquire skills, and develop habits of mind and how to use instructional strategies that promote student learning;

  (2) How student learning is influenced by individual experiences, talents, and prior learning, as well as language, culture, family, and community values; and

  (3) How to identify and teach to the developmental abilities of students, which may include learning differences, visual and perceptual differences, cultural and socio-emotional differences, special physical or emotional challenges, and gifted and talented exceptionalities.

ii. Teachers value and are committed to:

  (1) The educability of all children and adolescents;

  (2) The belief that all children and adolescents bring talents and strengths to learning;

(3) Appreciation for multiple ways of knowing;

(4) The diverse talents of all students and to helping them develop self-confidence and subject matter competence; and

(5) The belief that all children and adolescents can learn at high levels and in helping all students achieve success.

iii. Teachers engage in activities to apply learning theory to accommodate differences in how students learn, including accommodating differences in student intelligence, perception, cognitive style, and achievement levels.

3. **STANDARD THREE: DIVERSE LEARNERS**

Teachers shall understand the practice of culturally responsive teaching.

i. Teachers know and understand:

(1) How a person's worldview is profoundly shaped by his or her life experiences, as mediated by factors such as race/ethnicity, social class, gender and special needs;

(2) The supports for and barriers to culturally responsive teaching in school environments; and

(3) The process of second language acquisition and strategies to support the learning of students whose first language is not English.

ii. Teachers value and are committed to:

(1) Respect for individual and cultural differences, and appreciation of the basic worth of each individual and cultural group; and

(2) The diversity of learning that takes place in the classroom, respect for the talents and perspectives of each student and sensitivity to community and cultural norms.

iii. Teachers engage in activities to:

(1) Create a learning community in which individual differences are respected;

(2) Learn about the diverse students they teach, and the students' families and communities;

(3) Use strategies to support the learning of students whose first language is not English; and

(4) Use knowledge of students and their lives to design and carry out instruction that builds on students' strengths while meeting their needs, taking into account issues of class, gender, race, ethnicity, language, sexual orientation, age, and special needs.

4. **STANDARD FOUR: INSTRUCTIONAL PLANNING AND STRATEGIES**

Teachers shall understand instructional planning, design long and short term plans based upon knowledge of subject matter, students, community, and curriculum goals, and shall employ a variety of developmentally appropriate strategies in order to promote critical thinking, problem solving, and the performance skills of all learners.

i. Teachers know and understand:

    (1) How to plan instruction based on students' needs, developmental progress, and prior knowledge;

    (2) Available resources and materials for instructional planning;

    (3) Techniques for modifying instructional methods, materials, and the environment to help all students learn; and

    (4) A variety of instructional approaches and the use of various technologies, along with their advantages and limitations, and use them to promote thinking, understanding, and application of knowledge to address the needs of all students.

ii. Teachers value and are committed to the development of students' critical thinking, independent problem solving, and performance capabilities.

iii. Teachers engage in activities to:

    (1) Identify and design instruction appropriate to students' stage of development, learning styles, strengths and needs;

    (2) Plan instruction based on knowledge of classroom, school and community culture;

    (3) Evaluate teaching resources and curriculum materials for their comprehensiveness, accuracy, and usefulness for representing particular ideas and concepts;

    (4) Identify strategies to create learning experiences that make subject matter meaningful for students, address a variety of learning styles, encourage students to pursue their own interests and inquiries, and help students connect their learning to personal goals;

    (5) Plan and develop effective lessons by organizing instructional activities and materials, incorporating a wide range of community and technology resources, to promote achievement of lesson objectives;

    (6) Use formal and informal forms of assessment, information about students, pedagogical knowledge, and research as sources for active reflection, evaluation, and revision of practice; and

(7) Create interdisciplinary learning experiences that allow students to integrate knowledge, skills, and methods of inquiry from several subject areas.

5. **STANDARD FIVE: ASSESSMENT**

Teachers shall understand and use multiple assessment strategies and interpret results to evaluate and promote student learning and to modify instruction in order to foster the continuous development of students.

i. Teachers know and understand:

(1) The characteristics, uses, advantages, and limitations of different types of assessments (e.g. criterion-referenced and norm-referenced instruments, traditional standardized and performance-based tests, observation systems, and assessments of student work) for evaluating how students learn, what they know and are able to do, and what kinds of experiences will support their further growth and development; and

(2) Measurement theory and assessment-related issues, such as validity, reliability, bias, and scoring concerns.

ii. Teachers value and are committed to the attitude that students' strengths are the basis for growth and their errors are opportunities for learning.

iii. Teachers engage in activities to:

(1) Use multiple sources of data to analyze student performance and to modify future plans and instructional techniques that promote desired student learning outcomes;

(2) Provide students with constructive feedback on their learning and encourage their use of data and self-assessment strategies to monitor their progress toward personal goals;

(3) Accurately document and report assessment data and ongoing student data to parents and professional staff; and

(4) Use a variety of formal and informal assessment techniques to enhance their knowledge of learners, evaluate students' progress and performance and modify teaching and learning strategies.

6. **STANDARD SIX: LEARNING ENVIRONMENT**

Teachers shall understand individual and group motivation and behavior and shall create a supportive, safe, and respectful learning environment that encourages positive social interaction, active engagement in learning, and self-motivation.

i. Teachers know and understand:

(1) The principles and strategies of effective classroom management that promote positive relationships, cooperation and purposeful learning activities in the classroom;

(2) How the classroom environment influences learning and promotes positive behavior for all students; and

(3) How participation supports commitment.

ii. Teachers value and are committed to:

(1) The role of students in promoting each other's learning and recognize the importance of peer relationships in creating a climate of learning;

(2) Taking responsibility for establishing a positive climate in the classroom and participation in maintaining such a climate in the school as a whole; and

(3) The expression and use of democratic values in the classroom.

iii. Teachers engage in activities to:

(1) Maintain a learning community in which students assume responsibility for themselves and one another, participate in decision making, and work collaboratively and independently;

(2) Create a safe and secure classroom climate for all students, by practicing effective listening and group facilitation skills;

(3) Create a positive classroom climate which is socially, emotionally, and physically safe;

(4) Establish and maintain appropriate standards of behavior;

(5) Use instructional time effectively; and

(6) Organize, prepare students for and monitor independent and group work that allows for full and varied participation for all individuals.

7. **STANDARD SEVEN: SPECIAL NEEDS**

Teachers shall adapt and modify instruction to accommodate the special learning needs of all students.

i. Teachers know and understand:

(1) How to access information regarding applicable laws, rules regulations, and procedural safeguards regarding planning and implementing the individual education program; and

(2) Available resources related to educational strategies to accommodate individual differences and to employ positive behavioral intervention techniques to students with special needs.

ii. Teachers value and are committed to the belief that children and adolescents with special needs can learn at high levels and helping all students achieve success.

iii. Teachers engage in activities to:

(1) Apply knowledge of students' abilities/disabilities, experiences, talents, and prior learning as well as language, culture, economics, family and community values to positively affect student learning;

(2) Employ appropriate diagnostic measures and interpret the results to implement strategies that influence patterns of learning and impact the processes of inquiry;

(3) Participate in the design and implementation of the Individualized Education Program (IEP), where appropriate;

(4) Utilize a wide range of teaching techniques to accommodate and modify strategies, services, and resources, including technology, to meet the needs of all learners, including those with exceptionalities; and

(5) Make appropriate provisions (in terms of time and circumstances for work, task assigned, communication and response modes) for individual students who have particular learning differences or needs.

8. **STANDARD EIGHT: COMMUNICATION**

Teachers shall use knowledge of effective verbal, nonverbal and written communication techniques and the tools of information literacy to foster the use of inquiry, collaboration, and supportive interactions.

i. Teachers know and understand the power of communication in the teaching and learning process.

ii. Teachers value and are committed to:

(1) Appreciating the cultural dimension of communication, responding appropriately, and seeking to foster culturally sensitive communication by and among all students in the class; and

(2) Being a thoughtful and responsive listener.

iii. Teachers engage in activities to:

(1) Communicate clearly in English, using precise language and acceptable oral and written expressions;

(2) Assist students individually or as a member of a group to access, evaluate, synthesize and use information effectively to accomplish a specific purpose;

(3) Use effective verbal and nonverbal techniques which foster individual and collective inquiry;

(4) Model effective communication strategies and questioning techniques in conveying ideas and stimulating critical thinking; and

(5) Communicate in a variety of ways that demonstrate a sensitivity to cultures, linguistic, gender and social differences and that may affect communication in the classroom.

9. **STANDARD NINE: COLLABORATION AND PARTNERSHIPS**

Teachers shall build relationships with school colleagues, families, and agencies in the larger community to support students' learning and well-being.

 i. Teachers know and understand:

  (1) The importance of school-family-community interaction and of the unique needs and perspectives of the community;

  (2) The role of the school within the community and how to utilize diverse partnerships to contribute to student learning and development; and

  (3) How to collaborate with other stakeholders regarding the education and well being of students while respecting student privacy and confidentiality.

 ii. Teachers value and are committed to:

  (1) The role of parents and other family members as a child's primary teachers;

  (2) Being concerned about all aspects of the student's well-being and work with school partners to provide opportunities for student success; and

  (3) Being willing to work with other professionals to improve the overall learning environment for students.

 iii. Teachers engage in activities to:

  (1) Identify and utilize family and community resources to foster student learning and provide opportunities for parents to share skills and talents that enrich learning experiences; and

(2) Establish respectful and productive relationships and to develop cooperative partnerships with diverse families, educators and others in the community in support of student learning and well-being.

10. STANDARD TEN: PROFESSIONAL DEVELOPMENT

Teachers shall participate as active, responsible members of the professional community, engaging in a wide range of reflective practices, pursuing opportunities to grow professionally, and establishing collegial relationships to enhance the teaching and learning process.

i.   Teachers know and understand how education research can be used as a means for continuous learning and development.

ii. Teachers value and are committed to:

(1) Refining practices that address the needs of all students and the school community;

(2) Professional reflection, assessment, and learning as an ongoing process; and

(3) Being willing to collaborate with colleagues to give and receive help.

iii. Teachers engage in activities to:

(1) Use reflective practice and the Professional Development Standards to set goals for their professional development plans;

(2) Learn through professional education organizations; and

(3) Make the entire school a productive learning climate through participation in collegial activities.

CHAPTER

- **Rowan University**

- **Atlantic Cape Community College**
- **Camden County College**
- **Cumberland County College**
- **Gloucester County College**
- **Salem Community College**

14

South Jersey
Teacher Education
Consortium

As a student enrolled in <u>Teaching: An Introduction to the Profession</u>, you will undertake a series of activities that are designed to provide you with an overview of the teaching profession. These activities will take place in your classroom, after class, on the web, and in the public schools of New Jersey.

This course is unique in a number of ways. It is a required course for all teacher education majors at Rowan University. However, this course is offered by all of the schools that are members of the South Jersey Teacher Education Consortium. Therefore, you may take this course at Rowan University or at any of the S.J.T.E.C. schools and transfer the course to Rowan University without any loss of credit or content coverage. In this chapter we provide information on the South Jersey Teacher Education Consortium and the course <u>Teaching: An Introduction to the Profession</u>. More specifically, we will address the following questions:

- What is the South Jersey Teacher Education Consortium (S.J.T.E.C.)?

- Which schools are members of the S.J.T.E.C.?

- What is the history and present status of these schools?

- What is the content of the course <u>Teaching: An Introduction to the Profession</u>?

- What materials/resources are used in this course?

• SOUTH JERSEY TEACHER EDUCATION CONSORTIUM (S.J.T.E.C.)

The South Jersey Teacher Education Consortium is a unique collaboration between a four-year institution of higher education with programs in teacher education (Rowan University) and five regional two-year colleges. The consortium was established to facilitate the option of students taking an introductory course on teaching at a two-year institution and being able to transfer the course into a four-year program of teacher education.

Because the teacher education programs at Rowan University are accredited by the National Council for Accreditation of Teacher Education (NCATE), course components for the required introductory course must meet specific criteria. Consequently, not every introduction to teaching course would be acceptable. Beginning in 2002, College of Education administration and faculty from Rowan University and representatives from five regional two-year colleges (Atlantic Cape Community College, Camden County College, Cumberland County College, Gloucester County College, and Salem Community College) held a series of meetings to design a new course that could be successfully offered by all of the member institutions and would meet the requirements of Rowan's teacher education programs. The successful execution of this undertaking required all of the member institutions to agree on the course name, credits, description, objectives, requirements, instructional materials, and support resources.

All of the major introduction-to-teaching texts were examined and one (*Introduction to Teaching: Becoming a Professional* by Kauchak, Eggen, and Carter) was selected for customization for the proposed course. A subsequent series of meetings with representatives from Merrill/Prentice-Hall [Pearson Education] led to the creation of *Teaching: An Introduction to the Profession* by Orlando, Meyers, Pizzillo, and Levy, a book that includes material from the Kauchak text in addition to five chapters written expressly for this publication.

The results of this collaboration between a four-year institution of higher education, five two-year colleges, and a major publisher of education texts include: (1) the creation of the course Teaching: An Introduction to the Profession, (2) the development of a customized course package that includes the customized text *Teaching: An Introduction to the Profession* and three additional publications, (3) the creation of a customized web site, and (4) the development of an extensive variety of resources for the course instructor.

It is anticipated that future endeavors of the South Jersey Teacher Education Consortium will see greater collaboration and increased membership.

• SCHOOLS THAT ARE MEMBERS OF S.J.T.E.C.

The founding members of the South Jersey Teacher Education Consortium are:
- **Rowan University**
- **Atlantic Cape Community College**
- **Camden County College**
- **Cumberland County College**
- **Gloucester County College**
- **Salem Community College**

• ROWAN UNIVERSITY

Rowan University
201 Mullica Hill Road
Glassboro, NJ 08028
856-256-4000

Information about Rowan University and the College of Education is provided in Chapter 15: Rowan University - College of Education.

• ATLANTIC CAPE COMMUNITY COLLEGE

Atlantic Cape Community College
5100 Black Horse Pike
Mays Landing, NJ 08330-2699
609-343-4900

Branch Locations

Atlantic City Center
1535 Bacharach Blvd.
Atlantic City, NJ 08401-4800
609-343-4800

Cape May County Extension
412 Rio Grande Blvd.
Rio Grande, NJ 08242-2018
609-886-7189

About Atlantic Cape Community College

ACCC is a comprehensive two-year public institution serving the residents of Atlantic and Cape May counties, enrolling nearly 6,000 students. Located on 537 acres in the picturesque New Jersey Pinelands, ACCC is 15 miles west of Atlantic City's boardwalk, 45 miles from Philadelphia, and 115 miles from New York City. The college offers more than 40 transfer and career degree programs as well as continuing education professional development and training services. It awards Associate in Arts, Associate in Science and Associate in Applied Science degrees. The college operates nationally recognized casino career and culinary arts programs. The college operates extension centers in Atlantic City and Cape May County. Originally named Atlantic Community College, ACC was the second community college organized in the state of New Jersey in 1964. On January 1, 1999, Atlantic Community College officially became a joint college with Cape May County and in February, 1999, was renamed Atlantic Cape Community College.

Plans are being developed for a comprehensive Cape May County Campus, which will be built on Dennisville Road in Cape May Court House, Middle Township. The facility is expected to be ready for occupancy in Fall 2005.
(Source: www.atlantic.edu)

Website: www.atlantic.edu

Information Available On-Line

Admissions/Registration

- Admission to ACCC
- Ways to Register
- Class Schedules

- Tuition and Fees
- Academic Calendar
- Course Descriptions

• CAMDEN COUNTY COLLEGE

Camden County College
P.O. Box 200
College Drive
Blackwood, NJ 08012-0200
856-227-7200

Branch Locations

Camden City Campus
200 North Broadway
Camden, NJ 08102-1185
856-338-1817

William G. Rohrer Center
1889 Rt. 70 East
Cherry Hill, NJ 08003-2013
856-874-6000

About Camden County College

Camden County College is three distinct campuses with a common mission.

In the years since its opening, the Blackwood Campus has grown to comprise 26 buildings. These structures allow Camden County College to offer more than 100 degree and certificate programs in a traditional collegiate setting.

Camden County College's presence in downtown Camden began in the spring of 1969, when an evening diploma-completion program was offered to 20 students who had completed 10th grade but not graduated from high school. This program helped the students prepare to pass their general education development (GED) test so that they could begin full-time college courses on the Blackwood Campus that September.

A five-story campus building was opened at Camden's Broadway and Cooper Street in 1991, providing the college's first permanent home in the city. The structure features 40 classrooms, a bookstore, a community meeting room, a student lounge, a child care center and laboratories for computer and science instruction. Portions house junior-level and senior-level programs for Rowan University, allowing Camden County College's urban students to continue their studies for a baccalaureate degree at the same campus.

A second Camden City Campus building is being constructed across the street on the block bordered by Broadway and Cooper, Sixth and Penn Streets. The eight-story academic, retail and parking center will allow the college to supplement its current offerings with new technology-driven programs in health, business and computers.

Camden County College's newest site opened in the spring of 2000 as the result of a unique public/private partnership between the college, Cherry Hill Township and the William G. Rohrer Charitable Foundation. The new two-story William G. Rohrer Center, located at Route 70 and Springdale Road in Cherry Hill and named to reflect the generosity of the late banker's endowment, offers undergraduate academic courses as well as credit and non-credit business and industry training in 31,600 square feet of technology-rich space.

Through these physical resources, Camden County College serves an enrollment of more than 13,000 credit students and roughly the same number of non-credit students. Programs cover technical fields like automotive technology and mechanical engineering; health professions like nursing and medical coding; and liberal arts and sciences like English and chemistry. There also is a multitude of recreational offerings, ranging from social dancing to computer studies.

Camden County College is recognized nationally as a leader in technology programs such as robotics, computer-integrated manufacturing and photonics. The college also is recognized regionally as a vital resource for transfer education, customized training and community cultural arts programming.

Most importantly, perhaps, Camden County College is recognized as an institution of higher education that ably completes its mission to offer affordable, high-quality education to the people of Camden County.
(Source: www.camdencc.edu)

Website: www.camdencc.edu

Information Available On-Line
<u>Prospective Students</u>
- How to Enroll   - Tuition and Fees
- College Catalog   - Registration
<u>Programs and Courses</u>
- Academic Programs   - Academic Calendar
- Course Descriptions

• CUMBERLAND COUNTY COLLEGE

Cumberland County College
P.O. Box 1500
College Drive
Vineland, NJ 08362-1500
856-691-8600

About Cumberland County College
Cumberland County College was the first community college in New Jersey to open its own campus in October 1966. Today, the college is dedicated to preparing students and community members for success in the ever-changing global environment.

Cumberland County College is a comprehensive community college that is accessible, learning-centered, and dedicated to serving a diverse community of learners and employers through quality innovative programs, services and the appropriate use of technology for life-long learning.

The college's 100-acre campus provides an outstanding educational and social atmosphere. The Frank Guaracini Jr. Fine and Performing Arts Center, dedicated in 1995, is the cultural center of the region.

Other buildings include the administration building, the academic building, the computer technology center, the library-Internet learning center, the Frank H. Wheaton Jr. Technologies Building, the Dr. Charles Cunningham Student Center, which is being renovated into a "one-stop" enrollment services student center, and the Phillip Alampi Agriculture Building, which features the only aquaculture demonstration/training facility in New Jersey.

There are also plans for constructing the $4.5 million George P. Luciano Family Center for Public Service and Leadership, which will provide world-class meeting and conference facilities for the community.

Cumberland County College enrolls more than 2,800 full-time students during the academic year. Students also attend summer college classes. The college also conducts continuing education courses and customized career education for area businesses.

CCC offers 90 career and transfer programs of study. The college's graduates have successfully transferred to every college in New Jersey and scores of colleges and universities throughout America. In addition to transfer programs, Cumberland offers 28 career education associate degree programs, 38 one-year certificates and seven short-term training programs, which can be completed in 14 weeks.

Career education programs are offered in the fields of business, aquaculture, computer technology, criminal justice, education, engineering technologies, horticulture, tourism, allied health and social services.
(Source: www.cccnj.edu)

Website: www.cccnj.edu

Information Available On-Line
Academics
- Course Schedule   - Student Calendars
- Transferring to a Four-Year College

Admission
- Registration Information

Financial
- Tuition and Fees

• GLOUCESTER COUNTY COLLEGE

Gloucester County College
1400 Tanyard Road
Sewell, NJ 08080
856-468-5000

About Gloucester County College
Gloucester County College is a comprehensive, co-educational, two-year college sponsored by the residents of Gloucester County through the Board of Chosen Freeholders. The College is an accredited member of the Middle States Association of Colleges and Schools. GCC's mission is to be a center for learning that strives for academic excellence, supports the economic development of the community and seeks to enhance the community's quality of life. Through affordable, accessible programs and services, the College promotes intellectual and cultural enrichment, individual achievement, and professional development. The College is committed to being responsible and proactive to the needs of students, staff, and community.

The concept of a community college in Gloucester County dates back to 1965 when the Board of Chosen Freeholders established a citizens' committee to determine the need for such an institution. At a November 1965 non-binding public referendum, the county electorate approved a community college by an overwhelming vote. The New Jersey State Department of Education granted permission for the Freeholders to proceed with plans for the College in April 1966, and by that September, the first Board of Trustees was appointed.

Some 600 charter students were enrolled in September 1968, attending classes at Deptford High School and Monongahela Junior High School. In February 1970, ground was broken for the first buildings on the new campus. That May, GCC held its first graduation for 180 men and women. Thirty-two years later, enrollment for 2002 included over 5400 full-time and part-time day and evening students.

GCC maintains an important physical and cultural presence in the community. Its main campus today occupies 270 acres with five major instructional buildings including nursing/allied health, classroom and laboratory buildings, a new science and technology center, and a police academy. The College also maintains a business center off-site that houses customized training programs for local industry. The College currently employs over 470 full- and part-time personnel.

The College also functions as a cultural center for the county by offering a rich blend of co-curricular activities in art, literature, drama, poetry and music. An active Foundation Board provides strong links to the total community and is a major source of scholarships and grants for both students and College programs.

Gloucester County College is committed to serving the residents of Gloucester County by providing an educational opportunity to any high school graduate or holder of a high school equivalency diploma, and to any individual whose age, military service, or experience makes probable the successful completion of study leading to an academic degree or certificate. The College offers programs, courses, and services in transfer, career, developmental, lifelong learning, and community service areas, with or without formal matriculation for a degree as well as customized training and educational programs for business, industry, and public sector organizations. Through small classes and a dedicated faculty, GCC students develop a sense of responsibility, the ability to communicate effectively, and a greater facility to think clearly and critically.

In addition to its Middle States accreditation, the College has a number of specialty accreditations for its programs. The Nursing program is accredited by the National League for Nursing Accrediting Commission; the Diagnostic Medical Sonography AAS is approved by JRC-DMS; and the Nuclear Medicine Technology program is accredited by the Joint Review Committee on Educational Programs in Nuclear Technology. In addition, the Diagnostic Medical Sonography and Nuclear Medicine Technology Programs are accredited by the Committee on Accreditation of Allied Health Educational Programs (CAAHEP). The Paralegal degree and certificate programs were approved in August 1998 by the American Bar Association (ABA) – ABA Standing Committee on Legal Assistants.

GCC is a member of the New Jersey Association of Colleges and Universities and the American Association of Community Colleges.
(Source: GCC-Office of Institutional Advancement)

Website: www.gccnj.edu

Information Available On-Line

<u>General Information</u>
  - Tuition and Fees   - Academic Calendar
<u>Admission, Registration</u>
  - Admission/Advisement   - Registration Dates
<u>Course Offerings</u>
  - Catalog (request)   - Viewbook (request)

• SALEM COMMUNITY COLLEGE

Salem Community College
460 Hollywood Avenue
Carneys Point, NJ 08069
856-299-2100

About Salem Community College

Salem Community College traces its origins to 1957 when Salem County leaders called for the establishment of career education. Conferences between the Salem County superintendent of schools and the New Jersey assistant commissioner of education led to the foundation in 1958 of Salem County Technical Institute. The institute quickly established a reputation for excellence in postsecondary career education, particularly in the technical and health fields. In January 1971, Salem County Technical Institute became affiliated with Wilmington College. The affiliation enabled institute graduates to receive associate's degrees and to transfer credits towards bachelor's degrees in technology.

Recognizing the college-level caliber of the institute's programs, the Salem County Board of Chosen Freeholders requested approval to grant degree-awarding authority to the institute. The New Jersey Board of Higher Education evaluated the institute's programs and granted the approval. On September 3, 1972, Salem Community College was established by the Board of Chosen Freeholders.

Another milestone occurred in 1979 when the College was awarded regional accreditation by the Middle States Association of Colleges and Schools. This accreditation was reaffirmed in 1984, 1990 and again in 1995.

In April 1997, the Salem Community College Board of Trustees appointed President Peter B. Contini, Ed.D.

Since its founding, SCC has grown significantly in enrollment, programs and facilities. The College now offers a comprehensive list of courses, certificates and degrees. In 1998, SCC opened the Salem Center's permanent home at 174 E. Broadway, Salem, and the Distance Learning Center in Donaghay Hall. The 5,000-square-foot Glass Center, featuring the Paul J. Stankard Gallery, opened in 1999.

Salem Community College offers three degrees: the Associate in Applied Science, the Associate in Science, and the Associate in Arts. SCC also offers one-year certificate programs and the Specialist Series that offer content and skill acquisition in preparation for employment in career specialty areas.

Many programs are designed to prepare students for entry into specialized careers. Others have been developed to parallel the first two years of a four-year college or university program, and are designed to assist students in continuing their education after SCC graduation.

The Carneys Point Campus: SCC's 11-acre campus, in Carneys Point, NJ, is just five minutes from Exit 1 of the New Jersey Turnpike and Exit 4 of Interstate 295. SCC enjoys the advantages of being in a small suburban community while being near Philadelphia and other metropolitan areas.

(Source: www.salemcc.org)

Website: www.salemcc.org

Information Available On-Line

Programs of Study

- General Information
- Course Schedules
- Course Descriptions
- Registration

• TEACHING: AN INTRODUCTION TO THE PROFESSION

This section will provide (1) an overview of the course Teaching: An Introduction to the Profession and (2) information about the instructional resources that will be used in this course. Consult the course outline provided by the instructor for specific details.

Course Name & Credits

Teaching: An Introduction to the Profession (3 credits)

Course Description

This case-based introductory course is designed for students considering a career in teaching. It guides students through the profession, its foundations, realities, challenges, and rewards. Students will evaluate classroom practices using case studies, video methodology, and online resources. They will participate in ten (10) hours of field-based observations.

Course Objectives

Upon completion of this course, students will be able to identify and describe:

- Why individuals choose teaching as a profession.
- The multiple roles of teachers.
- The characteristics of the teaching profession.
- Today's students in a diverse society.
- Societal influences on schools.
- Philosophical foundations of education.
- A personal philosophy of education.
- The organization of schools.
- The ethical and legal issues facing teachers.
- Typical structures of curriculum in schools.
- Processes of teaching and learning.
- Career paths in education.
- Types and uses of technology in schools.
- Professional requirements for teaching in New Jersey.

Field Experience Objectives

During the field experience portion of this course, students will:

- Transition their frame of mind from student to teacher both affectively and intellectually.
- Become familiar with classroom management.
- Develop a reality-based understanding of life in the classroom.
- Develop observational skills:
    - Kinds of active participation,
    - Student-to-student interaction,
    - Focus on learning, not solely on teaching.
- Identify checks for understanding and levels of engagement.
- Identify teaching strategies.
- Practice self-assessment/reflection on individual disposition to teach.

Textbook

- *Teaching: An Introduction to the Profession* (2003)
  Orlando, Frank J.; Meyers, D. Mark; Pizzillo, Joseph J. and Levy, Lynne C.

  (<u>Note</u>: The text for this course is sold as part of a package that
  includes the required supplemental course resources.)

Required Supplemental Course Resources

- *Developing a Teaching Portfolio: A Guide for Preservice and Practicing Teachers*
  Bullock, Ann Adams and Hawk, Parmalee P.
- *Pass the Praxis: The Principles of Learning and Teaching*
  Shorall, Christina Paparozzi
- *Explanations and Implications of the 1997 Amendments to IDEA*
  Turnbull, Rud and Cilley, Melissa

<u>QUESTION</u>: Do I need to keep these books after I have taken, and passed, the course Teaching: An Introduction to the Profession?

<u>ANSWER</u>: Yes. If you take this course at Rowan University, or transfer this course to Rowan University or another teacher education institution, you will complete a prescribed sequence of professional coursework. Teacher Education Programs will require you to pass the appropriate Praxis exams, develop a teaching portfolio, and show an understanding of the Individuals with Disabilities Education Act (IDEA) and the implications for you as a teacher. These topics, and many other topics and issues that will be covered in other courses, are addressed in these four books.

Web Site

A customized web site is also available for the text, *Teaching: An Introduction to the Profession*. In addition to accessing materials related to the text you are able to access the ASCD/Research Navigator web site. The instructor will provide the necessary access information.

Contents of the Supplemental Course Resources

Developing a Teaching Portfolio: A Guide for Preservice and Practicing Teachers
by Ann Adams Bullock and Parmalee P. Hawk

Pass the Praxis: The Principles of Learning and Teaching
by Christina Paparozzi Shorall

Explanations and Implications of the 1997 Amendments to IDEA
by Rud Turnbull and Melissa Cilley

CHAPTER

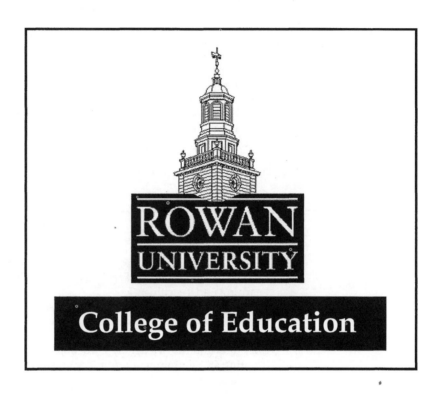

15 Rowan University
College of Education

Rowan University's College of Education is one of the leading teacher education institutions in the United States. The College has consistently earned national accreditation from the National Association of State Directors of Teacher Education and Certification (NASDTEC), the National Council for Accreditation of Teacher Education (NCATE), and is a member of The Holmes Partnership. All of the undergraduate programs are rooted in the evolving knowledge base of teacher education and the related disciplines.

As a student seeking a college degree from a teacher education program (Rowan University) and teaching certification (issued by the State of New Jersey), you should have a full understanding of the requirements for each of these goals. This chapter provides information that will facilitate the process. More specifically, we will address the following questions:

- What is the history and present status of Rowan University?

- What is the history and present status of the College of Education?

- What undergraduate degree/certification programs are offered?

- What are the admission requirements for teacher certification programs in the College of Education ?

- What is the Office of Field Experiences and where is it located?

- What is the John J. Schaub Instructional Technology Center and where is it located?

• ROWAN UNIVERSITY

Rowan University
201 Mullica Hill Road
Glassboro, NJ 08028
856-256-4000

Branch Locations
Camden Campus
200 North Broadway
Camden, NJ 08102
856-756-5400

Website: www.rowan.edu

About Rowan University

This section provides an overview of Rowan University: past and present. It includes a brief history of the University, the Rowan University Mission and Vision, commentary on the Rowan experience, and the current 2003-2004 Rowan University Fact Sheet. Additional information can be obtained at the University's web site and in the current undergraduate catalog.

History of the University

In the short span of 80 years, Rowan University has evolved from its humble beginning as a normal school, with a mission to train teachers for South Jersey classrooms, to a comprehensive university with a strong regional reputation.

In the early 1900s, many New Jersey teachers lacked proper training because of a shortage of schools in the state that provided training. To increase access and opportunity, the state decided to build a two-year training school for teachers, known then as a "normal school," in Southern New Jersey.

Several towns in South Jersey competed to be the site of the new normal school because of the economic benefit and prestige that such an institution would bring. The town of Glassboro was an early favorite because of its excellent rail system, harmonious blend of industry and agriculture, natural beauty and its location in the heart of South Jersey.

To sway the decision, 107 Glassboro residents raised $7,066 and purchased 25 acres, which they offered to the state for the site of the new institution in 1917. The land tract included a mansion and carriage house owned by the Whitney family, prominent owners of the Whitney Glass Works during the 1800s. This show of support, along with the site's natural beauty, convinced the selection committee that Glassboro was the perfect location. A few years later, construction began on the school's first building, now called Bunce Hall.

In September 1923, Glassboro Normal School opened with 236 young women arriving by train to convene in Bunce Hall. Dr. Jerohn Savitz, the University's first president, expanded the curriculum as the training of teachers became more sophisticated. Despite the rigors of the depression, the program was expanded to four years in 1934, and in 1937 the school changed its name to New Jersey State Teachers College at Glassboro.

The college gained a national reputation as a leader in the field of reading education and physical therapy when it opened a clinic for children with reading disabilities in 1935, and added physical therapy for the handicapped in 1944. The college was one of the first in the country to recognize these needs and was in the forefront of the special education movement.

Rowan's second president, Dr. Edgar Bunce, created a junior college program in 1946 to serve World War II veterans taking advantage of the GI Bill.

In the 1950s, Dr. Thomas Robinson, the University's third president, realized the school needed to do more than educate teachers and he expanded the curriculum. During this period, the school experienced rapid growth in curricular offerings, enrollment and building construction. In 1958, the school's name was changed to Glassboro State College to better reflect its mission.

The University received world-wide attention when it hosted a historic summit conference between President Lyndon Johnson and Soviet Premier Aleksei Kosygin. The conference was held in Hollybush, the former Whitney Mansion. The University was chosen because of its strategic location midway between Washington, D.C. and New York. The meetings between the two leaders on June 23 and 25, 1967 led to a thaw in the Cold War and eased world tensions.

Rowan's fourth president, Dr. Mark Chamberlain, guided the college through its next phase of growth as enrollment doubled and it became a multi-purpose institution. As new majors and a Business Administration Division were added, the four divisions grew into schools and a board of trustees was formed.

The fifth president, Dr. Herman James, assumed the leadership of the University in 1984. Under his direction, Rowan created the colleges of engineering and communication and started a doctoral program in Educational Leadership, the first terminal degree offered by any of the schools in the state college system. Dr. James was also responsible for the construction of a new $16.8 million library, an $8.6 million student recreation center, and the $30 million, state-of-the-art engineering school facility.

In July 1992, industrialist Henry Rowan and his wife, Betty, donated $100 million to the institution, then the largest gift ever given to a public college or university in the history of higher education. Later that year, the school changed its name to Rowan College of New Jersey. The college achieved university status in 1997 and changed its name to Rowan University.

To lead Rowan University into the 21st century, the Board of Trustees named Dr. Donald J. Farish as the sixth president in July 1998.

Today, Rowan University is divided into a Graduate School and six academic colleges: Business, Communication, Education, Engineering, Fine & Performing Arts, and Liberal Arts & Sciences. Rowan's nearly 10,000 students can select from among 35 undergraduate majors, seven teacher certification programs, 26 master's degree programs and a doctoral program. The 200-acre campus contains 33 buildings, including six residence halls and four apartment complexes.

Rowan is in the midst of an aggressive 10-year plan that will give the university a national reputation for excellence and innovation and will make it the public university of choice in the region. The plan calls for a greater campus-wide focus on academic and student support initiatives as well as more that $270 million being spent on campus construction and renovation projects.

From the modest normal school begun 80 years ago, Rowan University has become an extraordinary comprehensive institution that has improved the quality of life for the citizens of New Jersey and the surrounding states.

The Rowan University Mission

Rowan provides an exceptional environment for achievement and fulfillment in a dynamic society through rigorous intellectual effort and vigorous personal interaction among all members of its diverse learning community. As a regional public university committed to teaching, Rowan combines liberal education with professional preparation and offers undergraduate through doctoral programs. The Rowan ambition: knowledge through study; responsibility through service; and character through challenge.

The Rowan Vision

Rowan University, at the next level, will continue to focus on its commitment to learning and teaching, combining liberal education with professional preparation. Rowan will advance through the rankings of regional universities on the strength of its excellent undergraduate programs and its noteworthy development of a learning-centered environment. At the same time and without compromising the primacy of its focus on residential, undergraduate education, Rowan University will continue to build on its growing leadership in graduate and continuing professional education.

The Rowan Experience

The Rowan experience focuses on the development of students as whole persons while they are engaged in rigorous academic pursuits. In a context of emphasis on the complete intellectual, physical, emotional, social, and cultural well being of all members of the University community, we emphasize residential learning communities, mentoring programs, a commitment to service learning and volunteerism, and the opportunity for students to work closely with faculty and professional staff in research and professional activities.

Rowan University - Camden Campus

Rowan University's branch campus, the Camden Campus, offers programs and services for residents of the city of Camden and surrounding areas. Students attending the branch campus can take general education courses and complete a full degree program in sociology, elementary education and law and justice studies. The branch campus in Camden further offers a limited number of cross-registration and other support service opportunities in collaboration with Rutgers University-Camden and Camden County College-Camden.

Courses are offered in the day and in the evening for a diverse student body. Computer-assisted instruction, tutoring and course work in the basic skills and in English as a second language undergird the general university curriculum. Day care and flexible course scheduling are available at the Camden Campus for those students who work and also have family responsibilities.

Contact an Admissions counselor to arrange a visit or appointment for more information about attending the University's Camden Campus. Camden Campus offices are open Monday-Thursday, 9 a.m.-10:30 p.m. and Friday, 9 a.m.-5 p.m. The Camden Campus telephone number is (856) 756-5400.

ROWAN UNIVERSITY

A Unique Public Offering

Rowan University (formerly Glassboro State College) is a selective, medium-sized state university located in southern New Jersey between Philadelphia and Atlantic City.

In 1992, Rowan University received a $100 million gift from Henry and Betty Rowan, one of the largest gifts ever bestowed on a public university. The gift has been a catalyst for the University's transformation into a university of regional prominence.

U.S. News & World Report ranks Rowan University as one of the top public universities in the North and Kiplinger's named the University one of the "100 Best Buys in Public Colleges and Universities." Rowan University is listed in Kaplan's "Guide to the 320 Most Interesting Colleges" and Princeton Review's "The Best Northeastern Colleges."

The tree-lined campus contains 42 buildings, including eight residence halls, three apartment complexes, a Student Recreation Center and 21 computer labs.

Academics

Students have access to the resources of a large university without sacrificing the personal attention and small class size of a college. All classes are taught by professors, not teaching assistants. The average class size is 23 students and the student/faculty ratio is 16 to 1.

The University offers 36 undergraduate majors among six academic colleges (Business, Communication, Education, Engineering, Fine & Performing Arts, and Liberal Arts & Sciences).

There are currently more than 26 graduate programs leading to master's and doctoral degrees.

Athletics

Rowan athletic teams dominate their conference and division and have won 11 national championships.

The Student Recreation Center offers an extensive intramural program with 2,500 students participating in 14 sports.

Student Body

The University enrolls more than 9,500 students who represent the Mid-Atlantic States and 30 foreign countries.

More than 150 clubs and organizations offer students professional, cultural and service activities. Students and faculty regularly win national recognition, usually competing with larger universities.

Rowan University graduates are in demand. A total of 95 percent of the class of 2002 was employed or in graduate school within one year of graduation.

Admission

Students entering the University in 2003 had a mean SAT I range between 1,080 and 1,280 and were ranked in the top quarter of their high school classes.

The deadline for freshman and transfer applications for the fall semester is March 15. The deadline for transfer elementary education majors is Feb. 15. Graduate program applicants should contact The Graduate School for application deadline information.

Students who apply to the College of Fine & Performing Arts must arrange a music audition, theater audition or portfolio review.

Open House Dates

The Admissions Office hosts five Open House programs beginning at 1 p.m. Dates for the 2003-2004 academic year are:
- Sunday, October 19, 2003
- Sunday, November 2, 2003
- Sunday, December 7, 2003
- Sunday, March 7, 2004
- Sunday, April 4, 2004

Campus Tours

Campus tours are given most Fridays at 11 a.m. and Mondays at 3 p.m. Check the Admissions Website for specific dates or call the Admissions Office.

The Admissions Office is open on selected Saturdays for tours and interviews. Please call the office to schedule a Saturday appointment.

Scholarships and Financial Aid

Last year, Rowan University awarded students $3.7 million in merit-based scholarships and $46.7 million in need-based awards and loans.

Average Yearly Costs 2003-2004

	In-state	Out-of-state
Tuition and fees	$7,258	$12,654
Room and board	$7,248	$7,248
Total	$14,506	$19,902

All costs are estimates based on full-time undergraduate double-room occupancy and are subject to change.

Important Phone Numbers

Admissions	856-256-4200
	or 800-447-1165
Athletics	856-256-4676
Bursar	856-256-4150
Financial Aid	856-256-4250
The Graduate School	856-256-4050
Public Safety	856-256-4922
Residence Life	856-256-4266
University Switchboard	856-256-4000

**201 Mullica Hill Rd.
Glassboro, NJ 08028
www.rowan.edu**

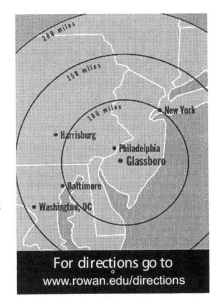

For directions go to
www.rowan.edu/directions

• THE COLLEGE OF EDUCATION

This section provides basic information about the College of Education. Consult the following sources for additional details.
- *Rowan University Undergraduate Catalog 2002-2004*
- College of Education web site at: www.rowan.edu/coe

History of The College of Education

The history of the College of Education mirrors the history of Rowan University as it has undergone a transformation from a normal school to a comprehensive institution, and a Department of Education to a College of Education. The Rowan University teacher education program is the largest and most comprehensive in New Jersey and has consistently earned national accreditation and distinction.

Currently, the College of Education offers B.A., M.A., M.S.T., Ed.S., and Ed.D. degrees through six departments: Educational Leadership, Elementary/Early Childhood Education, Health and Exercise Science, Reading, Secondary Education/ Foundations of Education, and Special Educational Services/Instruction. The College also offers programs that lead to post-baccalaureate certification, advanced certificates, and certificates of graduate study (COGS). The programs in the College of Education are approved through the New Jersey State Department of Education and are consistent with New Jersey Administrative Code requirements. The College of Education has been certified through NCATE (National Council for the Accreditation of Teacher Education) since 1956.

The programs in the College of Education are supported by the Office of Field Experiences which oversees the placement of students for practica, student teaching, and clinical internships. The Schaub Instructional Technology Center provides media and technology services and instruction specifically to the College of Education, and consists of a computer lab, curriculum materials laboratory, and media services. The College also houses several outreach programs to service the surrounding community. These include (1) the Education Institute which provides contract onsite courses, consultants, workshops, and collaborative grant services, (2) the nationally recognized Thomas E. Robinson Beginning Teacher Induction Center which provides workshops/training for new teachers as they enter the workforce, (3) a Reading Clinic which provides diagnostic and remedial reading instruction to area youngsters, and (4) an Assessment and Learning Center which provides special educational diagnostic services.

Dr. Carol A. Sharp is the Dean of the College of Education. A life-long resident of South Jersey, Dr. Sharp has a B.A. from Glassboro State College, an M.A. from William Patterson College, and a Ph.D. from The Pennsylvania State University. She has served as the Director of Rowan University's Faculty Center for Excellence in Teaching and Learning and is a proponent and participant in activities related to Professional Development Schools and teacher certification.

Dr. D. Mark Meyers is the Associate Dean of the College of Education. The former Chair of the Department of Secondary Education/Foundations of Education, he has a B.A., M.A., and Ph.D. from the University of Florida. He is a strong advocate for the infusion of technology in the teaching/learning process.

The College of Education's Shared Vision:

Educators as creators of learning communities.

Mission of the College of Education:

The College of Education at Rowan University provides an intellectually rigorous and challenging environment for the professional preparation of leaders in education and selected health-related services. Built upon a liberal education, the College's programs combine the study of research, theory, and wisdom of practice in diverse settings with a variety of opportunities to apply knowledge and dispositions to practice thus promoting professional achievement and personal fulfillment.

Educational Outcomes:

The following outcomes identify the general knowledge, skills, and dispositions that all graduates of the College of Education at Rowan University are expected to possess. The educator who is a graduate of our initial teacher preparation programs will demonstrate the following:

A. Planning: Acquisition of Knowledge, Skills, and Dispositions relative to:
1. Organizing and Managing Learning Communities
2. Designing Coherent Instruction
3. Advocating for Cultural and Learning Diversity

B. Instruction: Acquisition of Knowledge, Skills, and Dispositions relative to:
4. Engaging Students in Learning
5. Assessing Student Learning
6. Integrating Technology into Learning Communities

C. Partnering: Acquisition of Knowledge, Skills, and Dispositions relative to:
7. Demonstrating Professional Attributes
8. Effective Communication with Diverse Constituents
9. Fostering Relationships through Collaboration

• COLLEGE OF EDUCATION ACCREDITATION

The College of Education is accredited at the basic and advanced levels by the National Council for Accreditation of Teacher Education (NCATE). Our programs have met the national guidelines of the following professional organizations:

- AAHPERD - Am. Alliance for Health, Phys. Ed., Recreation, and Dance
- ACEI - Association for Childhood Education International
- ACTFL - American Council on the Teaching of Foreign Languages
- ASBO - Association of School Business Officials
- CEC - Council for Exceptional Children
- IRA - International Reading Association
- NAESP - National Association of Elementary School Principals
- NAEYC - National Association for the Education of Young Children
- NASP - National Association of School Psychologists
- NCSS - National Council for the Social Studies
- NCTE - National Council of Teachers of English
- NCTM - National Council of Teachers of Mathematics
- NSTA - National Science Teachers Association

• COLLEGE OF EDUCATION
UNDERGRADUATE DEGREE / CERTIFICATION PROGRAMS

The College of Education has Undergraduate Degree/Certification Programs in:
- Early Childhood Education
- Elementary Education
- Collaborative Education (Co-Teach)
- Health and Exercise Science
- Reading Education
- School Nurse
- Secondary Education
    (Business, English, Foreign Language, Math, Science, Social Studies)
    (Art, Music: College of Fine and Performing Arts))
- Teacher of the Handicapped

Contact information and web site addresses are provided below:

• Early Childhood Education

Department:	Elementary/Early Childhood
Dept. Office Location:	Robinson Hall, Second Floor
Dept. Office Phone No.:	(856) 256-4735
Program Coordinator:	Dr. Lorraine Wylie
Program Advisor:	Ms. Gloria Spinella
Advisor Phone No.:	(856) 256-4500 x3087
Advisor e-mail:	spinella@rowan.edu

• Elementary Education

Department:	Elementary/Early Childhood
Dept. Office Location:	Robinson Hall, Second Floor
Dept. Office Phone No.:	(856) 256-4735
Department Chair:	Dr. Susan Taber (on-leave)
Academic Advisor:	Ms. Kathleen L. Small
Advisor Phone No.:	(856) 256-4737
Advisor e-mail:	small@rowan.edu

• Collaborative Education (Co-Teach)

Department:	Elementary/Early Childhood
Dept. Office Location:	Robinson Hall, Second Floor
Program Coordinator:	Dr. Janet Moss
Program Advisor:	Ms. Gloria Spinella
Advisor Phone No.:	(856) 256-4500 x3087
Advisor e-mail:	spinella@rowan.edu

• Health & Exercise Science

Department:	Health & Exercise Science
Dept. Office Location:	Esby Gym, Room 102
Dept. Office Phone No.:	(856) 256-4784
Department Chair:	Dr. Richard Fopeano
Academic Advisor:	Mr. Melvin Pinckney
Advisor Phone No.:	(856) 256-4576
Advisor e-mail:	pinckney@rowan.edu

• Reading Education (Teacher of Reading, Certification Program)

Department:	Reading
Dept. Office Location:	Robinson Hall, First Floor
Dept. Office Phone No.:	(856) 256-4770
Department Chair:	Dr. Cindi Hasit
Academic Advisor:	Dr. Kathy Ganske
Advisor Phone No.:	(856) 256-4500 x3831
Advisor e-mail:	ganske@rowan.edu

• School Nurse

Department:	Special Educational Services/Instruction
Dept. Office Location:	Robinson Hall, First Floor
Dept. Office Phone No.:	(856) 256-4746
Program Advisor:	Dr. Marie Cammarota
Advisor Phone No.:	(856) 256-4705
Advisor e-mail:	cammarota@rowan.edu

• Secondary Education
(Business, English, Foreign Language, Math, Science, Social Studies)
(Art, Music: College of Fine and Performing Arts)

Department:	Secondary Education/Foundations of Education
Dept. Office Location:	Robinson Hall, Second Floor
Dept. Office Phone No.:	(856) 256-4755
Department Chair:	Dr. Holly G. Willett
Academic Advisor:	Dr. William J. Clarke
Advisor Phone No.:	(856) 256-4761
Advisor e-mail:	clarkew@rowan.edu

• Teacher of the Handicapped

Department:	Special Educational Services/Instruction
Dept. Office Location:	Robinson Hall, First Floor
Dept. Office Phone No.:	(856) 256-4746
Department Chair:	Dr. Joy Xin
Academic Advisor:	Mr. Nicholas Schmelz
Advisor Phone No.:	(856) 256-4734
Advisor e-mail:	schmelz@rowan.edu

• Transfer Students

Transfer Student Advisor:	Mr. Jeffrey Margolis
Office Location:	Office of the Dean, Robinson Hall, Second Floor
Advisor Phone No.:	(856) 256-4500 x3089
Advisor e-mail:	margolis@rowan.edu

• Department Web Sites

Elem./Early Childhood:	www.rowan.edu/mars/depts/elemed/majors.html
Collab. Ed. (Co-Teach):	www.rowan.edu/mars/depts/speced/coteach.htm
Health & Exer. Sci.:	www.rowan.edu/mars/exersci/
Reading:	www.rowan.edu/mars/depts/reading/reading.htm
Spec. Ed. Serv. & Inst.:	www.rowan.edu/mars/depts/speced/underpr.html
Sec. Ed. / Found. Ed.:	www.rowan.edu/mars/depts/seced/seced1.htm

- **COLLEGE OF EDUCATION**
  ADMISSION REQUIREMENTS: TEACHER CERTIFICATION PROGRAMS
  (Material from: Rowan University, College of Education Web Site)

I. Requirements for Admission to Teacher Certification Programs

Application procedures initiated in the required sophomore field experience course. Application filed during sophomore year for four year RU students; approval granted at the beginning of the junior year. Application filed during first semester of junior year for transfer students; approval granted at the end of the semester.

1. Attainment of minimum score on the Rowan University placements, as determined by the College of Education.
2. Demonstration of proficiency in oral and written communication through completion of appropriate general education course work.
3. Successful completion of the course, Teaching as a Profession [Teaching: An Introduction to the Profession].
4. A minimum of 30 semester hours in General Education.
5. A minimum overall GPA of 2.5.
6. Completion of minimum number of credits in/for the major; number determined by the certifying department.
7. Satisfactory performance and evidence of interest in teaching as demonstrated in the sophomore field experience.
8. Departmental interview / narrative statement prepared by instructor of sophomore field experience course.
9. Qualifying score on Praxis I: Pre-Professional Skills Test or Comp.-Based Test.
10. For additional information regarding licensure and specific requirements, visit the New Jersey State Department of Education.

II. Requirements for Admission to Pre-Student Teaching Experience (Junior Practicum)

Application filed during first semester of junior year; approval granted same semester.

1. A minimum overall GPA of 2.5, with a grade of "C" or better in all course work.
2. Admission to certification program.
3. Completion of minimum number of courses in major; determined by certifying department.
4. Completion of 60 semester hours applicable to student's program.

III. Requirements for Admission to Student Teaching

Application for student teaching filed during junior year; approval granted after completion of junior year; Application filed for New Jersey Teacher Certification Testing Program -- Praxis II* / NTE Examination.

1. A minimum overall GPA of 2.75, with a grade of "C" or better in all course work.
2. A minimum GPA of 2.5 in coordinate or technical major (Individual departments/majors may require higher GPA).
3. A minimum GPA of 3.0 in subject matter specialization for secondary education students.
4. A minimum GPA of 3.0 in professional course work.

5. Completion of minimum number of courses in major; determined by certifying department.
6. Completion of 90 semester hours applicable to student's program.
7. Recommendation of junior field experience supervisor.
8. Recommendation from Liberal Arts/Fine Arts/Business chairperson or adviser for secondary education students.
9. Approval by College of Education certifying department.

IV. Requirements for Institutional Recommendation for Certification (Certificate of Eligibility with Advanced Standing)

Application filed with the Office of the Registrar at the beginning of the final semester of the program, preliminary approval occurs during final semester; departmental/institutional recommendation occurs after completion of senior year.

1. A minimum overall GPA of 2.75, with a grade of "C" or better in all course work.
2. A minimum GPA of 2.5 in coordinate or technical major.
3. A minimum GPA of 3.0 in subject matter specialization for secondary education students.
4. A minimum GPA of 3.0 in professional course work (for certification candidates).
5. Successful completion of student teaching.
6. Recommendation of public school personnel.
7. Attainment of baccalaureate degree.
8. Approval of department recommending certification.

V. Requirements for New Jersey Instructional Certificate

Application is filed with the Dean's Office, College of Education, Robinson Hall, according to the schedule announced by the College on their web site. Applications can be also be down-loaded from this web site, obtained from department advisors, or from the Office of the Registrar, Savitz Hall.

1. Institutional recommendation.
2. Attainment of appropriate score on New Jersey Teacher Certification Test -- Praxis II*/ National Teachers Exam (NTE).
3. State Department of Education verification of transcripts and related documents.
4. Enters teaching with a "Certificate of Eligibility with Advanced Standing" (signifying completion of collegiate preparation program with an academic major; recommendation by dean/director; and a passing score on appropriate praxis II/NTE).
5. Receives offer of employment to teach in field of qualification with Provisional Instructional Certificate.
6. Receives Provisional Certificate upon offer of employment.
7. Successful completion of provisional year under mentorship program. (Presently, candidates for the Teacher of the Handicapped certification are exempt from the Praxis II and induction year process.)
8. Recommendation by public/private school for permanent instructional certificate.
9. For additional information regarding licensure and specific requirements, visit the New Jersey State Department of Education.

• COLLEGE OF EDUCATION
OFFICE OF FIELD EXPERIENCES

(Material From: Office of Field Experiences Web Site)

The major focus of the Office of Field Experiences is the placement of students requiring field experience in a school or clinical setting.

Location: College of Education, Robinson Hall, 2nd floor across from the elevator.

Personnel: Robert W. Kern, Ed.D., Director
Philip F. Sidotti, Assistant Director
Carol DeBoard, Secretary
Dottie Comer, Secretary

Hours: 7:30 a.m. to 5:00 p.m., Monday through Friday.
(During the summer Monday through Thursday).

Phone: 856-256-4725

Web Site: www.rowan.edu/ofe

Web Site Information: Mantoux Test Information
Praxis I & II Information
Information on Placements
Clinical Practice Applications
Policy Manual and Handbook for Clinical Practice

• COLLEGE OF EDUCATION
JOHN J. SCHAUB INSTRUCTIONAL TECHNOLOGY CENTER

The John J. Schaub Instructional Technology Center is a service branch of the College of Education at Rowan University and includes a Computer Laboratory and a Instructional Materials Laboratory.

The Center provides facilities, technology, materials, and training in the four areas of Instructional Technology: print technology, audio-visual technology, computer technology, and integrated technology. It is the primary Instructional Technology resource and training facility for students in the College of Education.

Schaub Instructional Technology Center

Director: Lynne C. Levy, Ed.D

Web Site: www.rowan.edu/coe/schaub

Site Links: Computer Lab Information
Instructional Materials Lab Information
Weekly Lab Schedules
Workshops for Education Majors
Selected Educational Links

Schaub Computer Laboratory

Location: Robinson Hall, Room 207

Director: Lynne C. Levy, Ed.D

Hours: Hours vary due to instructional sessions that are scheduled throughout the year. The hours for the current week and the following week are posted on the door and on the Schaub web site. The schedule is updated every Friday.

Phone: 856-256-4711

About the Schaub Computer Lab:

The Schaub Computer Laboratory contains 26 Macintosh G4 computers with operating system OSX and an instructor's teaching station with large screen projection. When the facility is not being used for class instruction or College of Education in-service workshops, it serves as an open laboratory for the University's student body.

Alomg with the software options that are available in labs throughout the campus, the computers in the Schaub Computer Laboratory have a variety of specialized educational packages installed for faculty and student use. Software available in the lab includes:
- AppleWorks 6
- Microsoft Office (including Word, PowerPoint and Excel)
- Inspiration 7
- Photoshop Elements 2
- HyperStudio
- Kid Pix Studio Deluxe
- Netscape and Internet Explorer for Internet access

A portion of the Computer Laboratory also serves as the storage and dissemination point for the College of Education's "instructional technology on wheels." These are instructional technology carts/stations that can be borrowed by College of Education faculty for use in classes that are held in Robinson Hall. Representative options include a visual presenter and monitor, large screen projection systems for use with either a Macintosh or a PC computer, laserdisc players, and iBooks (laptop computers with wireless technology).

Schaub Instructional Materials Laboratory

Location: Robinson Hall, Room 212

Director: Frank J. Orlando, Ed.D

Hours: Hours vary due to instructional sessions that are scheduled throughout the year. The hours for the current week and the following week are posted on the door and on the Schaub web site. The schedule is updated every Friday.

Phone: 856-256-4710

About the Schaub Instructional Materials Lab:

The Schaub Instructional Materials Laboratory is a specialized collection of selected curriculum materials and resources that support and augment the various professional education courses in the College of Education.

College of Education students and faculty are welcome to use and review textbooks, teaching kits, professional literature, journals, and a variety of multimedia materials. The print materials do not circulate.

The resources in this specialized facility assist faculty and students in the various technology related student instructional modules that are a part of all teacher education programs in the College of Education.

In addition to housing curriculum materials, educational journals, videos, laserdiscs, etc., the Instructional Materials Laboratory provides the following services and technology for College of Education students and faculty:

- Transparency Making
- Laminating
- Xerographic Copying
- Plastic Comb Binding
- Ellison Lettering Machine